The Insatiable Earl

The
Insatiable Earl

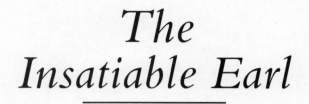

A LIFE OF JOHN MONTAGU,
FOURTH EARL OF SANDWICH
1718–1792

N. A. M. Rodger

W·W·NORTON & COMPANY
New York   London

Copyright © 1993 N. A. M. Rodger
First American Edition, 1994

All Rights Reserved.

ISBN 0-393-03587-5

W. W. Norton & Company, Inc.
500 Fifth Avenue, New York, NY 10110
W. W. Norton & Company, Ltd.
10 Coptic Street, London WC1A 1PU

Printed in Great Britain

1 2 3 4 5 6 7 8 9 0

Table of Contents

for Susan

Illustrations

Preface

In history as in every branch of learning we are dwarfs standing on the shoulders of giants. Every book draws largely on the work of those who have gone before, and much of this one will be recognizable to experts in the eighteenth century. My debt to the published work of other scholars will I hope be obvious from the notes and bibliography. What is original in the book derives chiefly from what I have read in manuscript, and my first thanks are owing to the owners and custodians of documents who allowed me to read and quote them. Above all I must thank John Montagu for allowing me complete access to the papers of the fourth earl, all of which were still at Mapperton when I worked on them. I can only hope that the book does justice to his generosity, and to the merit of his ancestor.

In addition I acknowledge the gracious permission of Her Majesty the Queen to quote documents from the Royal Archives; and the permission of his Grace the Duke of Grafton, his Lordship the Marquess of Tavistock and the Trustees of the Bedford Estates, their Lordships the Marquess of Normanby, the Earl of Mansfield, and the Earl of Rosse; Mr Peter de Sausmarez and Mr Peter Rowley, to consult and quote their manuscripts. Like all historians, I have numberless obligations to the staff of libraries and record offices, in particular those of the National Maritime Museum, the British Library, the London Library, the Bodleian Library, Nottingham University Library, and my former colleagues of the Public Record Office. In person or by correspondence I was helped by the County Record Offices of Essex, Huntingdonshire, Staffordshire, Suffolk and Warwickshire, the Kent Archives Office, the Public Record Office of Northern Ireland, and the Rowe Music Library of King's College, Cambridge. Dr B. Woelderlink, Director of the Dutch Royal Archives, Mrs Marie Draper, archivist of the Bedford Estates, Mr John Dann, Director of the William L. Clements Library of the University of Michigan, and Dr Mary L. Robertson of the Henry

E. Huntington Library, San Marino, California, went well beyond the line of duty in searching for things on my behalf. For diverse offices of friendship and pieces of advice I thank Mr Andrew Best, Dr C. J. Kitching, Dr Michael Duffy, Mr G. Stevens Cox, and Mr Rodney Williams. I am grateful to Professor Daniel A. Baugh, Professor Ian Christie, Dr Roger Knight, Mr Richard Ollard and Dr H. M. Scott who read this book in draft and whose suggestions have greatly improved it. Indeed in many different ways Dr Knight and Mr Ollard have sustained the book and its author over many years and vicissitudes. Professor William Weber generously allowed me to read in proof parts of his book *The Rise of the Musical Classics*. I am indebted for many kindnesses to Mr and Mrs George Brown, in whose farm I stayed while working at Mapperton. Finally I acknowledge the generosity of the Society of Authors, which made possible much of the research for this book by a grant from the K. Blundell Fund.

For help with the illustrations for the book I must again thank John Montagu, and likewise the British Library, the Department of Prints and Drawings of the British Museum, the National Maritime Museum, the National Portrait Gallery, the Courtauld Institute, the Ministry of Defence Art Collection, the Royal Marines Museum, the Royal Naval Museum, The Portsmouth Naval Base Property Trust, Prudence Cuming Associates, Dr Lindsay Stainton, Mr James Taylor, Mr J. G. Coad, and Dr Ulrich Schneider, Director of the City Museums of Aachen.

In the end, however, I and the book owe most of all to my wife, who bore and forbore throughout the long years of research, and the longer months of writing.

N.A.M.R.
Acton, Michaelmas 1992

Introduction

Readers of *1066 and All That* will remember the list of Victorian discoveries ending with the mackintosh, 'invented by another Scottish nobleman whose name is now forgotten'.[1] Much the same might be said of the inventor of the sandwich. Familiar in our mouths as a household word, he has suffered the indignity of being forgotten as a man and remembered as a thing. When he is remembered, the ideas associated with his name are few and wrong. The 1974 edition of *Chambers Biographical Dictionary*[2] allows him a single sentence: 'corrupt politician, remembered as the inventor of *sandwiches*, to eat at the gaming table'. No man is so obscure that there is not one true and interesting thing to say about him, and certainly not one who pursued a varying career in high politics, public office, diplomacy and war over half a century. A man who could remember the start of the elder Pitt's career, and lived to oppose the younger Pitt; who carried into the period when modern political parties were beginning to form the habits and attitudes shaped when Sir Robert Walpole was in power; who served in Cabinet with Newcastle, Pelham and Chesterfield, George Grenville and Lord North; who played a significant rôle in the strategy and diplomacy of the War of the Austrian Succession in the 1740s, and the War of American Independence thirty years later; connected at one time with Frederick Prince of Wales, and forty years later with his grandson the future Prince Regent; twice Secretary of State and three times First Lord of the Admiralty; Sandwich is not without interest to the student of public affairs. For the naval historian, Sandwich's nearly twenty years at the Admiralty, spread from 1744 to 1782, cover some of the most important administrative, social and political developments in the history of the Royal Navy, in all of which he was intimately involved, and in many of which he was himself the prime mover. The friend of Anson and Garrick, the opponent of Wilkes and Charles James Fox, the patron of Cook and the champion of Handel,

Sandwich connected many diverse lives. He was passionately fond of the theatre and the opera, an innovatory patron whose influence on English musical life can still be discerned today. He cultivated enthusiasms for cricket, skittles, tennis, yachting and fishing. He was a linguist, classicist and orientalist of more than common achievements and considerable influence, a bold traveller in his youth and later a patron of explorers, an amateur of history, astronomy and numismatics.[3] Wit, rake, poet and musician, he was also a man whose private life was wounded by tragedy. He suffered the madness of his wife and the murder of his mistress, the deaths in turn of four sons, both his daughters-in-law and all but one of his grandchildren.

This is not an obscure or colourless life, and it is certainly not a life without evidence. Sandwich left to his descendants a collection estimated to include about nineteen thousand letters and papers,[4] much of which has never been systematically explored. On the more restrictive definition of letters written to or by Sandwich in person, there are at least twenty-five thousand surviving among the family papers and in other archives.[5] A cynic would suggest that this alone explains why no scholarly biography of him has ever been attempted. His life has only twice been written in the two hundred years since he died. In 1799 the Reverend John Cooke, chaplain of Greenwich Hospital, published his late patron's *Voyage Round the Mediterranean* prefaced with a forty-page memoir; and in 1962 George Martelli issued his *Jemmy Twitcher*. No well-written book which quotes original documents is to be despised, but it could not be said to have floated its subject into the flood-tide of historical knowledge.

The absence of the usual 'Life and Letters' with which the Victorians dignified the lives of many men far less important than he, left him the victim of glancing treatment in works devoted to other subjects and other people. Although during his career he had passed through some controversial episodes and periods of violently partisan politics, by the time of his old age and death his merits were widely recognized. Even when he was least popular it is not difficult to find unprejudiced admirers, both in private correspondence and public print.[6] 'Lord Sandwich is not a popular man', wrote George Selwyn in 1782, 'but I have lived long enough to have remembered other Ministers less popular, if possible, and who have been since reverenced, and by the most respectable among those who traduced them'.[7] The obituaries were respectful if not fulsome,[8] and histories written up to the 1830s, when there were still many people alive who had known him, are generally laudatory.[9] The treatment changed with the mid-Victorian and later 'Whig historians'.

Macaulay, Trevelyan and their disciples were active both as historians and politicians, and they believed that the political parties of their own day had their origin in the period of the American rebellion. Rockingham, Charles James Fox and even Wilkes were seen as the ancestors of their own party, while Lord North, Sandwich and their colleagues were thought to have given birth to the Conservative party which they knew and disliked. Moreover they argued that George III's ministers had abetted him in a conscious attempt to subvert the British constitution and overthrow its liberties, an attempt which had aroused rebellion in America and agitation in Britain. In the resulting campaigns their supposed political ancestors had been on the side of the angels, while North, Sandwich and the rest were cast as the corrupt tools of a would-be despot.

These ideas were long ago abandoned by serious historians, and even in America (where the word came to mean something quite different) Sandwich would hardly now be called a 'Tory'. He himself would have thought the label absurd and disgusting. A devoted Whig all his life, a defender of 'Revolution principles' who had abandoned his ancestors' Jacobitism, taken arms against the Pretender and defied the Tories at the Lichfield Races riot of 1747, he had no difficulty in establishing his true allegiance, and no contemporary thought to doubt it. In fact his whole career was passed in an age of weak or non-existent party structure. By the 1730s the Tories, though still strong, were effectively excluded from national political office. By the 1780s the old structures had broken down completely, but only with powerful hindsight is it possible to discern new political parties forming in embryo.

The belief that the Whigs and Tories of Queen Victoria's later years could be observed in action as far back as the 1770s or even further involved the Whig historians in a number of difficulties. It was not an age in which every historian indulged in original research, but on the basis of a limited range of printed sources, mostly representing violent partisans of the opposition of those years, they had little difficulty in painting a simple and highly-coloured view of the period. But if Rockingham and Fox were secular saints, Sandwich and North the willing instruments of royal despotism, what was to be said about the Sandwich and North who had been Fox's colleagues in government in 1783, and in opposition for the rest of the 1780s? The answer in practice was, nothing.

A further difficulty presented itself in relating the private (in many cases, distressingly public) lives of the politicians of the day to their actions as ministers. The Victorian and Edwardian historians wrote in an age when religion had invaded the sphere of public life; a minister's private character was highly relevant to the performance of his official duties. But acquaintance with even a limited range of evidence from the time made it clear that Fox, and even more Wilkes, had been men of the grossest depravity, with gifts of charm and friendship unsupported by loyalty or principle. The contrast with George III's unshakeable rectitude and North's happy marriage was by no means what these historians wished or expected to find. Sandwich, it may be suggested, was a heaven-sent escape from this dilemma. It can hardly be complete coincidence that the crimes with which they charged him – corruption, treachery, womanizing, gambling – were mostly not typical of him, but were exactly those which marked Fox and Wilkes. Only in his dealings with women was he an unremarkable and fairly discreet representative of the morals of his day. The spectacular crimes and follies of Fox were entirely foreign to him, but they were loaded upon him by the Victorian historians and he was driven out as a scapegoat into the wilderness.

This view of Sandwich as immoral in private, and consequently corrupt in public life, survived the appearance of increasing quantities of evidence, but was seriously undermined by the publication by the Navy Records Society in the 1930s of four volumes of his papers dealing with the American War.[10] Although a fifth volume intended to cover administration and patronage was overtaken by the Second World War,[11] the published papers dealing with the strategy and operations of the American War revealed beyond doubt an energetic and conscientious minister. Taken with other evidence now available, and with a much more sophisticated understanding of the nature of politics, they have ruined for ever the old simplicities which for so long served in place of a realistic and impartial assessment of the man and his work. What the new evidence has not done is to construct such an assessment. We now know who he was not, but we hardly know who he was. What evidence we have, and what attention has been paid him, is heavily concentrated on the period of the American War, when he was already a minister of thirty years' experience passing middle age, and on the subject of the conduct of the war, which was even then only one of his responsibilities. Much of the scholarly work which has been done even on this period remains unpublished, including not less than six university theses on naval administration during the war,[12] and two on naval operations.[13] In addition there are at least four unpublished theses which bear on other aspects of his service at the Admiralty,[14] and others which illuminate his political and diplomatic career.[15] These alone provide an abundance of material with which to paint a new picture of him, and the mass of his correspondence provides a great deal more.

The difficulty which faces the biographer of Lord Sandwich is not only the quantity of evidence, but the length and diversity of a life which presents so many points of interest, and could be written from so many points of view. Sandwich the politician and diplomat, Sandwich the war minister and strategist, Sandwich the naval administrator and reformer, Sandwich the patron of music and scholarship, Sandwich the rake, even Sandwich the cricketer might form the subject of a life in themselves. My approach has been to try to integrate all these aspects, both in order to build up a picture of the whole man, and in order to illustrate the age in which he lived, which cannot be done by fragmenting it. No biography can present the complete picture of any subject, even one in which its hero was heavily involved, but it can draw attention to the multiplicity of links between apparently diverse people and subjects which compose a real society, and are easily overlooked by thematic history. I hope this is a picture of the complete Lord Sandwich, but it is deliberately not a balanced picture, in the sense of giving in the book the same weight to each aspect of his career as it bore in his actual life. In particular I have not used Sandwich's life to retell the high politics of half the eighteenth century. Sandwich was as near a professional politician as it was possible for a peer to be, but for reasons which are themselves interesting, and which I have tried to discuss, he was only intermittently a politician of the first rank. As a statesman, administrator and diplomat his achievements were as much in spite as because of his political weight. Only a few political episodes in which he was a prime mover are not already well known, and high politics is the only subject for which his unpublished papers have been much exploited. I have therefore not attempted to use this book to cover thoroughly ground which has been so often and so well tilled by scholars whose abilities and knowledge I cannot hope to match. The reader will find here, I hope, an account of political developments sufficient to provide the context of Sandwich's career. I have concentrated on other areas of national life to which he made an original and important contribution.

First among these is undoubtedly the Navy, which was his first love and in many ways his life's work. His work at the Admiralty can only be understood by going back to his beginnings in public office as a young man, when he served with the Duke of Bedford and Lord Anson in the 1740s. He brought to the American War a mind formed by the experiences of the War of the Austrian

Succession, and an education in naval affairs which had begun with Anson. What he achieved, and what he was trying to achieve, have to be seen in that long perspective. In his case as in others much is distorted by looking at the American War in isolation. So much has been written about that war, yet so much remains to write, that it would be easy to allow it to take over a biography of Sandwich. Sandwich's naval administration before and during it has been often studied but seldom published. His handling of patronage remains largely unknown. His part in the grand strategy of the war can hardly be treated until we have more and more sophisticated knowledge; as it is we have no modern general history of the war at sea.[16] A large book could and perhaps should be written solely about Sandwich's part in it, to balance the numerous studies devoted to Lord George Germain and the land war in America. This book is not it; a comprehensive study of the American War at sea would have doubled its length and completely overbalanced its treatment. Instead I have isolated a number of key incidents and issues, and used them as examples of the way Sandwich handled his wartime responsibilities, and the part he played in the decisions of the ministry as a whole. There is a great deal more which could be said, much of it very interesting, but it cannot all be said here without distorting the life of Sandwich as a whole, and overtaxing the patience of the most indulgent readers. Those whose primary interest is in this war may be disappointed, as may those who specialize in any one of the many other subjects and periods on which this book touches, but much of the interest in Sandwich's life derives from its range and diversity, and would be lost if it did not express them.

CHAPTER I

A Traveller from an Antique Land
1718–1744

There can have been few situations in history more privileged than an eighteenth-century English earldom, and few young men inherited an earldom in such disadvantageous circumstances as John Montagu, the fourth Earl of Sandwich. He was born on 13th November 1718, four years after the death of Queen Anne, the last monarch of the house of Stuart to which his family owed its rise and its title. Before he was four his father Lord Hinchingbrooke was dead. When he was nine his mother remarried, but she seems to have effectively abandoned him some time before that.[1] At about seven he was sent to board at Eton, though still too young to be officially entered at the school[2] – a not unusual practice at the time.[3] His grandfather the third earl seems to have been feeble-minded, and had managed to dissipate almost the whole of the family's never large fortune before he was finally confined for insanity. His countess, the formidable daughter of Lord Rochester, the wit, poet and courtier of Charles II, managed his career and for as long as she could passed off his condition as 'a melancholy which amounted to vapours and no more', but by 1704, when he lost his post as Gentleman of the Horse to Queen Anne's husband Prince George of Denmark, it could be concealed no longer.[4] When he died shortly before his grandson's eleventh birthday he was living under restraint in the Yorkshire home of his uncle Wortley Montagu to whom he had mortgaged his estates, while Montagu himself inhabited the family home at Hinchingbrooke, outside Huntingdon.[5] His widow the countess, loyal to the dynasty to which her family and her husband's owed their fortunes, had already gone to live in Paris, taking with her most of what remained of the family's income. There she shone as a wit and luminary in Parisian society, and a devotee of the exiled Stuart court at St Germain.[6]

So John Montagu became at the age of ten the fourth Earl of Sandwich, and the head of a family in unfortunate circumstances.

The Sandwiches had never been extraordinarily wealthy or powerful. His great-great grandfather, Admiral Montagu, commander of
the principal fleet of the English republic in 1659, had won his earldom by his cautious support for the restoration of Charles II. He
enjoyed it less than twelve years before being killed in action when
his flagship the *Royal James* was burnt by Dutch fireships at the battle
of Solebay. The Montagus were originally substantial Northamptonshire gentry. Sir Sidney Montagu, a younger son, bought the ram-
bling old house at Hinchingbrooke, a medieval nunnery with Tudor
additions, from the Cromwells in 1627.[7] His son the admiral received
enough from Charles II to support the dignity of an earl, but by the
time the fourth earl succeeded much of that was gone, and what was
left was largely controlled by his grandmother in Paris.

   This was doubly unlucky because the young man's parents had
thrown in their lot with the new Hanoverian regime. Eton was then
in an indifferent educational condition, but politically it was strongly
identified with the new monarchs. Westminster was much the more
distinguished school, but evidently Lady Hinchingbrooke preferred
to avoid its somewhat Tory atmosphere.[8] This naturally created a
rift between Lord Sandwich (as we must now call him) and his
grandmother, which threatened to lose him most of his slender
inheritance. She let it be known that she would leave her property
to her Parisian friends rather than to 'a person she always abhorred,
and heartily detested'.[9] At the same time his Jacobite connections
rendered the young man suspect to the governments of George I
and George II.[10] It is difficult to know whether the suspicion
of disloyalty or the certainty of poverty were more disabling to a
young man with a public career to make in early eighteenth-
century England.

   It is probably significant that in Sandwich's copious surviving correspondence there is no letter to or from his mother and virtually
no mention of her, though she did not die until 1761. He left home
at about the age of seven. His younger brother was sent to sea at
eleven.[11] In 1730, effectively orphans, they became wards of the
Court of Chancery, which established a scheme of trusteeship for
them.[12] This was a legal arrangement consequent on Lady Hinchingbrooke remarrying, and does not imply that she no longer cared for
her sons, but it does nothing to correct the impression that she (and
perhaps also her new husband Francis Seymour) were not sorry to
be rid of the boys. Though Sandwich was proud of his family and
interested in its history, he never mentions his parents in his letters.
His school, by contrast, occupied that prominent share in his affec-

tions which the modern reader expects to find in the memories of late nineteenth-century public schoolboys, but which was by no means so common a century before. It may be suggested that in any age those who look back on their schooldays as the happiest in their lives, found there a security and affection which their home life had not provided. Eton, his masters, and his schoolfellows seem for Sandwich to have provided some sort of substitute for the family life he had never enjoyed.

An eighteenth-century public school was not the obvious place to find security. Anarchic, often violent, the schools were attacked by many moralists as nurseries of vice at which the boys learnt dissipation if they learnt anything at all.[13] For this reason many young gentlemen were educated by tutors at home.[14] Those who went to school might have the opportunity to acquire a substantial, if narrow, education, but how often they actually did so is unclear. Accustomed as we are to the achievements of the nineteenth-century public schools, applying the spirit of the industrial age to the mass-production of capable classicists, we are apt to over-estimate the capabilities of the unreformed public schools of the eighteenth century. Swift said that Lord Carteret carried away from college more learning than became his rank and fortune;[15] few of his contemporaries laid themselves open to such a charge. It was an age in which every gentleman was expected to have at least a veneer of classical learning, sufficient to lard his speeches with suitable quotations – but it is noteworthy how often the same quotations recur, and how many of them come from Virgil, most accessible of the Latin poets. The widespread practice of learning set books by heart provided a ready store of quotations without generating any profound understanding of the language.[16] As for Greek, the young Lord Belgrave caused a sensation by quoting Demosthenes in the original in his maiden speech in 1788.[17] The virtues of the schools were social rather than educational; they obliged the young nobleman to mix with boys of very varied origins. A regime of violence and neglect, hardly supervised by the masters (of whom there were very few), taught the young gentleman to fend for himself if it taught him nothing else. For the future leaders of society, who as men would have to manage others in local and national politics, the boisterous austerity of public school was a valuable preparation for public life.[18] This was far more useful to a young nobleman like Sandwich than sound learning, and most young noblemen drew the appropriate conclusion.

Sandwich, however, was not a typical young nobleman. He said himself that his tutor Dr Sumner 'took me under his care at a time when I was in [a] track of idleness which without his assistance would probably have led me to my ruin'.[19] If so it was the last time in his life when he voluntarily chose a track of idleness. The first-class mind and the ferocious energy which marked his adult life were already evident in the schoolboy who stood head of the Fifth Form in 1732,[20] and who emerged from Eton with a thorough knowledge of the Latin classics and a working command of Greek. He later told the Austrian statesman Count Kaunitz that he was at ease with the classical tongue, but he preferred to avoid the treaty-Latin of the Austrian chancery.[21] His classical learning was certainly not unique, and it would not have stood comparison with that of the best professional scholars of the day, but in a man of his station it was unusual enough to draw admiring comments throughout his life. At Trinity College Cambridge, where he went in 1735, he and his cousin and contemporary Lord Halifax were the first noblemen ever to take part in the public declamation of classical authors in the College chapel.[22] There seems to have been only one part of the literature of the ancient world with which he was unacquainted, if we may judge from his unwisely betting a neighbour that the name 'Bartimeus' was not to be found in the New Testament.[23] Amongst the many gentlemen who could remember a handful of classical tags, there were very few who could claim to have read Silius Italicus for pleasure.[24]

The reason why Sandwich was interested in the longest, and arguably the dullest, surviving poem in classical Latin was the information it gives about the Near East in ancient times. On leaving Cambridge in 1737 he went to Europe on a grand tour. This was a conventional way for a young man of good family to finish his education, perfect his French and visit some of the more accessible classical sites in Italy. France and Italy were the limit of most such tours, though Germany and the Low Countries might be included. Visiting the Turkish empire was certainly not part of the conventional curriculum, but Sandwich was anxious to see for himself the noblest and best-preserved remains of the ancient world, so in July 1738 he and a small group of friends sailed from Leghorn in the chartered merchantman *Anne Galley* bound for the East.[25] With them they took the Swiss painter Liotard to record their travels and discoveries. Calling at Elba, Corsica, Sardinia, Capri and several ports in Sicily they sailed to Greece – still at this date an obscure province of the Turkish empire and known to Western travellers only from Pausanias and other classical guide-books. Having thoroughly explored the Parthenon and the ruins of Athens, Sandwich sailed in the ship's longboat to visit Salamis and Delos. On the island of Antiparos he and his companions climbed six hundred feet into a huge cave, never before explored so deep. From the Aegean islands they sailed to Constantinople, where they stayed some months. Here Sandwich adopted Turkish dress and engaged a tutor to teach him as much about the people (including their language) as he had time to learn.

> During our stay in this vast metropolis I applied my whole thoughts towards informing myself of the maxims and customs of a people so different from those, which I had till then been conversant with.[26]

The result is a long and learned essay on Turkish society, history and manners. It includes a striking tribute to the cleanliness of Turkish women: 'a person who had ever experienced an intrigue with a Turkish woman, would have no further taste for the ladies of any other country.'[27]

From Constantinople they sailed via Cyprus to Alexandria and began to explore Egypt. A local sailing vessel carried them up the Nile to Cairo, where Sandwich described the Whirling Dervishes. Here they stayed six weeks, exploring the monuments in the surrounding country. Sandwich climbed into the Great Pyramid to the inner burial chamber. On the return voyage from Egypt the ship was becalmed in the Gulf of Sirte. They were almost starving when they made Lampedusa where they were assisted by a hermit, the only inhabitant of the island. A visit to Malta allowed Sandwich to write a substantial description of the place and its history. Thence they sailed to Lisbon, Cadiz, Gibraltar, Malaga, and Minorca, finally concluding the voyage at Genoa.

In an age coarsened by mass tourism, it is hard to convey the astonishment contemporaries felt at this remarkable and dangerous voyage.[28] Merely to travel so far by sea was unusual enough, while the learned narrative Sandwich brought home of his observations and discoveries in Greece, Turkey and Egypt was sufficient to place him at once in the forefront of the tiny group of scholar-travellers who could speak about the Orient with authority. Had his narrative been published at the time, rather than sixty years later after his death, it would certainly have made his public reputation for learning; as it was it was cited with respect by those orientalists who had read it in manuscript.[29] It can still be read today with interest, and with respect for the author's achievement. The numerous Greek

and Latin inscriptions copied into it (at least fifty of them hitherto
unknown),[30] the monuments accurately sketched, the acute historical
observations, all bear witness to a well-educated and powerful mind.
Since the author of the extremely hostile article on Sandwich in
the *Dictionary of National Biography* attributes the authorship to an
unknown tutor, apparently on the grounds that so bad a man could
not possibly have written so learned a book, it should be said that
two drafts of the manuscript in Sandwich's hand survive, from which
it is clear that he wrote it himself, initially in stages on the course
of the voyage, the final version apparently soon after his return. His
posthumous editor, the Reverend John Cooke, confined himself to
adding *Memoirs of the Noble Author's Life*, and making numerous
stylistic alterations, every one of which tends to burden Sandwich's
plain, sinewy prose with pompous superfluities.[31]

Besides the manuscript of his *Voyage Round the Mediterranean*,
Sandwich brought back a considerable collection of antiquities,
including,

> two mummies and eight embalmed ibis's from the catacombs of Mem-
> phis; a large quantity of the famous Egyptian papyrus; 50 intaglios;
> 500 medals . . . a marble vase from Athens, with two figures in *basso
> relievo*; and a very long inscription, as yet undecyphred, on both sides
> of a piece of marble about two feet in height.[32]

This last he found under some rubbish in the wood-yard of the local
merchant who served as British consul in Athens. 'He set no sort of
value on it; and wondered much that his Lordship would be at the
trouble of carrying it away', but his Lordship had seen enough to
realize the value of the piece. It proved to be an account of the
expenses of the Athenian magistrates sent to celebrate the feast of
Apollo at Delphi on the 101st Olympiad, 374 BC. It was the oldest
dated inscription then discovered. Sandwich presented it to his old
college, and three years later one of the fellows published a learned
work reproducing and explaining the inscriptions (a speed of publication which could well be imitated by modern archaeologists).[33]

Sandwich's voyage to the East did more than simply make his reputation as an intrepid traveller and a serious scholar; it had a significant
effect in encouraging Western interest in the Orient, and in the sys-
tematic study of the physical (as opposed to the literary) remains of
classical antiquity. The paintings of Liotard (who stayed five years
in Constantinople) helped to generate not only a fashion for Turkish

dress, but an interest in things Turkish.[34] Soon after his return, Sandwich himself was involved in founding a series of influential societies. In February 1742 he became the first president of the Egyptian Society, formed by a small group of travellers and scholars, including all those in England then known for their travels in the East, to encourage the study of ancient Egypt. In the fashion of the times, the study was not exclusively serious; meetings were always held over dinner, and were social as much or more than scholarly occasions. The officers of the society were dignified with Turkish or Arabic titles: Sandwich was 'Sheik' (President), the secretary was the 'Reis Effendi', the Treasurer, 'Hasnedar', and there was also a 'Mohausil' (collector of reckonings) and a 'Gumrocjee' (inspector of medals). Sandwich, and probably the others, sometimes attended in Arab or Turkish dress. All this may give the modern reader the impression of a purely frivolous body, but it nevertheless represents a significant step on the long road to truly scholarly investigation of the ancient world, and in its short life the society heard four learned papers, besides examining antiquities produced by the members, Sandwich's mummified ibis among them.[35]

The Egyptian Society seems to have been defunct by the time Sandwich founded the Turkish Society or Divan Club in 1744, its membership drawn exclusively from those who had visited some part of the Ottoman Empire. This time Sandwich's title was the 'Vizir'. Several of the Egyptian Society's members were involved in this too, and it had several points of similarity, but to judge from its surviving minute book, entitled 'Al Koran', it was more social and less scholarly than its predecessor.[36]

This society too lasted only a couple of years, but while he was participating in these short-lived bodies, Sandwich was becoming involved in another which was destined to have a longer life and a greater influence. The Society of Dilettanti, to which he was elected in 1740 soon after it was founded, combined the scholarly and the convivial in the usual eighteenth-century style, but it came to have a more serious and a more durable engagement with the ancient world. The example of Sandwich, Lord Charlemont and other travellers to the East inspired the society in 1763 to send an expedition to Asia Minor to record the ruins of the Greek cities of Lycia. Sandwich was one of the organizers of this, arguably the first archaeological expedition ever launched from Britain. He was also chairman of the committee of the Dilettanti which had much to do with the foundation of the Royal Academy.[37] All these activities show Sandwich as a young man with a deep knowledge of the ancient world and a serious interest in it, one who by his travels and his subsequent activities had a measurable effect in expanding the eighteenth century's understanding of the ancient world, and the modern Near East.

While he was in Florence in 1737 Sandwich met the Hon. Charles Fane, the British minister at the court of the Grand Duke of Tuscany.[38] At the same time he probably met Fane's sister Dorothy, who stayed part of that year with him.[39] They were married on 3rd March 1741 in St Margaret's Westminster.[40] We know nothing of the circumstances of their courtship, but it may fairly be inferred that calculation of the fortunes and interests of the respective families played much less of a part than it would normally have done in a noble marriage of the day. Sandwich of course was his own master, and must have chosen Dorothy Fane for herself. His motive was certainly not money. Her father Viscount Fane was a minor Irish peer in modestly comfortable circumstances – certainly no worse than Sandwich's – but he had four daughters to provide for, and a son who could be expected to marry and provide an heir to the family estates. Miss Fane's marriage portion was £3,000,[41] an inconsiderable sum measured against the legitimate expectations of an English earl, and she had no likely hope of inheriting anything more. From the point of view of the Fanes, Sandwich was a social prize, but his income would barely suffice to keep their daughter in the state to which she was accustomed.

We can catch only glimpses of the young couple early in their married life. Very few letters survive between them, no doubt because they were usually together; we shall see that they went to unusual lengths to avoid being apart more than necessary. Those contemporaries who do notice them speak without exception of a respectable, indeed admirable pair, living modestly on a modest income, avoiding the temptations of the fashionable world:

> I honour Lord Sandwich for his wise and generous contempt for money in a point in which there are other things superior to it; he bears an excellent character, there is much prudence in knowing how to separate one's particular happiness from that which is reckoned so in the world's opinion: if Lord Sandwich takes greater pleasure in the conversation of a fine woman than in viewing a collection of medals and pictures, he is right to prefer Miss Dolly Fane with £5000 to Miss Spinckes with £50,000 . . . He has a good estate sufficient for the becoming state of a nobleman . . . Miss Fane is a happy woman to have a lover so great, so generous and so good.[42]

In the same year, 1741, one of Sandwich's old schoolfellows visited them at Hinchingbrooke and left a description of their way of life:

> I can defer no longer giving you an account of Lord Sandwich. He is very strong in the country interest, and takes all his measures to continue it. He is married to the sister of Mr Fane who was resident at Florence – a very agreeable and sensible lady. His lordship keeps only a pair of horses and drinks nothing but port wine. His whole way of living turns upon this principle, to keep himself out of necessity. He is regular in all respects, and what is a very good and Christian thing, Johnny, he never swears an oath.[43]

In 1747 an Irish clergyman visited the couple in the Hague, and wrote a long description of them to his former pupil Lord Charlemont, full of pointed contrasts between the temperate virtue of the Sandwiches' life and the idle frivolity of Charlemont's.

> Ken you not my lord Sandwich playing tennis, playing his harpsichord, and steering the navies, the councils, and the senates of Great Britain at 29 years of age? Could he do this without great acquisitions of knowledge?[44]

The one letter which survives from Lady Sandwich to her husband, written in 1748 when he was on the Continent, deals with politics.[45] It gives the impression of an intelligent woman fully involved in her husband's career. The tone is businesslike rather than emotional, but the subject was business, it was an age when husbands and wives were usually formal rather than intimate on paper, and she suspected that their letters were being intercepted by political opponents, which must have imposed some restraint. Nevertheless she signs herself 'my dearest Lord most unalterably yours', a strong demonstration of affection within the conventions of the day. Happily married to a woman of 'good sense and infinite merit',[46] newly come of age and installed in his seat in the House of Lords, Sandwich was ready to begin the career in public life which was the birthright of every peer who desired it, and the burden of every one who did not.

Young as he was, Sandwich the traveller had already demonstrated courage and independence. He was soon to acquire a reputation for hard work and mastery of the subject in hand which was by no means universal among public men. Confident and extrovert, he had many friends in society – but he was too good a politician not to make enemies as well. To be alert and watchful was indispensable for success in an age when politics partook so much of intrigue, but it was not a lovable quality. Moreover he never sufficiently concealed his ambitions, and many contemporaries were repelled or alarmed by them. He looks out of Northcote's portrait with an uncomfortable, piercing gaze; a Young Turk about to be let loose on an old empire.

In 1740 Britain was at war with Spain, and in the process of being drawn into the complex of European wars collectively known as the War of the Austrian Succession. Britain's ally Austria was engaged with both France and France's allies Prussia and Bavaria, while the French were giving assistance little short of war to Spain, and Spain in turn was fighting Austria in northern Italy. Though Britain and France were not yet fighting one another directly, the pressures in that direction were growing daily. This was of all situations in contemporary politics the one likely to arouse the most violent controversy. The accession of George I to the throne in 1714 had completely altered the map of British domestic politics.[47] The Tory party from which Queen Anne had drawn her governments was relegated, not simply to opposition in the modern sense, but to a position outside respectable politics. For George I, George II and Sir Robert Walpole their chief minister, only the Whigs who had secured the Protestant Succession by engineering the 'Revolution' of 1688, and safeguarded it when Queen Anne died, were loyal and reliable enough to participate in the political process. The Tories, tainted with Jacobitism, were excluded from power. Though there remained many members of Parliament and peers who could be identified as Tories, the struggle for power by legitimate means was effectively confined to rival groups of Whigs. Even this struggle was muted by the career of Sir Robert Walpole, whose long dominance of the House of Commons from the 1720s to 1742 has led to him being identified (somewhat anachronistically) as the first British prime minister.

The result by the time Sandwich entered politics was a situation in which formal political parties, though by no means extinct, had come to be a less useful way of explaining the realities of Parliamentary and national politics than the manoeuvrings of various factions, interest groups and small parties within the Whig fold.[48] Ignoring the distinction of Whig and Tory, the House of Commons in the 1740s might be very broadly divided into three groups. The 'Court' consisted of ministers, courtiers and others personally or professionally attached to the Crown, who were reliable supporters of the ministry. The 'Country' encompassed all those MPs, notably but not only those who represented county constituencies, who prided themselves on their independence and viewed all government, or at least all government power, with suspicion. Though in no sense a formed opposition, these men could be relied upon to treat the proposals of ministers with reserve, and the large fraction of them who were Tories if not concealed Jacobites did not balance this sentiment with loyalty to the king in person. Between these two classes lay smaller groups, composed of Whigs who shared the ideology of the administration, and differed only because they were out and wanted to be in. It was among these groups that allies had to be sought to make up a working majority, which gave them and their leaders a consequence out of proportion to their numbers. When Court and Country very roughly balanced one another, even a small group available for recruitment to the administration might command considerable influence. Since all these men were in principle committed to the same ideology, politics tended to resolve itself into a struggle for power between men divided by ambition rather than principle. It was, as one of Sandwich's colleagues put it, 'those capital occasions of strife called *places*, which, next to that which produced the Trojan war, are, of all others, the most apt to set mortal men at variance'.[49]

This struggle was conducted, at least in wartime, in terms of principles, or rather propositions, which were deeply traditional in English politics, and which had been given new force and form by the accession of monarchs who were both kings of Great Britain and Electors of Hanover. The 1689 Act of Settlement established in principle a division between the king and the elector, forbidding English ministers to be swayed by Hanoverian considerations, but in practice the distinction was unworkable. Foreign affairs and war were in constitutional theory and actual practice the personal responsibility of the monarch, into which it was highly improper for Parliament to pry, further than it had to to vote the necessary money. This of course was an infinitely wide exception, especially in wartime, and above all in an age when government was so little involved in the domestic life or economic affairs of the country that foreign affairs and warfare constituted a great part of the national business of Parliament (as distinct from the local and private legislation which occupied much of its time). Parliament had acquired certain rights to deal in foreign policy, including the approval of treaties passed while Parliament was in session. But however passionately the Houses of Parliament debated foreign affairs, there were limits on the extent to which it was either possible or decent to interfere in the king's right to be in charge, and in practice the English king and the German prince could not be separated. British policy was made from a

Continental standpoint which recognized that the country was and always had been involved in European politics, that she had hopes to fulfil and dangers to avoid which could only be achieved by participation. But the nation as a whole was deeply distrustful of any participation in the affairs of foreigners. Xenophobic by tradition, ignorant of foreign affairs which had always been conducted as the private concern of the monarch, bred up to regard themselves as a free people defended by a great navy from the threat of foreign invasion, and by the lack of a standing army from the threat of domestic tyranny, the English regarded Continental entanglements with deep suspicion. In particular they were easily and often persuaded that their own national interests were sacrificed to preserve those of Hanover, the strategic advantages of their own insular position thrown away because the electorate was militarily indefensible. Moreover alliances with European powers, even if they did not involve operations for the defence of Hanover, invariably involved military operations somewhere on the Continent, and called for British troops, or troops in British pay. It remained an article of faith in British political rhetoric that the only use of a standing army was the use to which Oliver Cromwell had put it and James II was supposed to have intended to put it, the use to which contemporary monarchs like Louis XIV of France or Frederick II of Prussia were putting it – to establish and sustain a despotic government. It was true that Britain in the 1740s had in fact had a standing army for nearly a century, but at least it was as small, dispersed and inefficient an army as possible, and it was common ground among politicians of all sorts that that was the way it had to remain if Britain's unique and perfect constitution were not to be threatened by the spectre of arbitrary government.[50]

Naval power, on the other hand was, as Wellington put it at the end of the century, the 'characteristic and constitutional defence'[51] of the country. All politicians agreed that it was the principal and essential means of national defence, and all opposition politicians agreed, whatever the circumstances of the moment, that the Navy and naval policy were being shamefully neglected in favour of truckling to Continental, above all Hanoverian interests. In the language of the time, these were the arguments of the 'Patriots' (meaning the anti-Hanoverians), the first resort of the politician, and for those like Dr Johnson who disliked Whig politicians, the last resort of the scoundrel. Nothing was more universally and reliably popular than the cry that the nation's true interest was being sacrificed to 'this execrable, detestable, ruinous, ill advis'd, ill concerted, romantick, quixote, senceless, all consumeing land war' (as Lord Tyrconnel called it in 1748).[52] Naval war, on the other hand, was still regarded by many, in spite of three centuries of experience to the contrary, as potentially profitable as well as glorious. The country had gone to war in 1739, against the judgement of Walpole's government, with a widespread expectation that there would be nothing to do but usher fleets of Spanish galleons laden with silver into English ports.[53] Moreover public interest in colonies and their economic benefits was growing, and there were serious arguments that money spent on the Navy paid dividends in colonial conquests and their economic benefits which merely defensive alliances on the Continent could never do.[54]

When Sandwich took his seat in the House of Lords in February 1740 he was therefore entering a political arena in which the battles were passionate, but in many respects unreal. In foreign affairs there was a large gap between the rhetoric which convinced even intelligent and otherwise well-informed men, and the realities encountered by the few who were called upon to assume responsibility as the King's ministers. If rhetoric alone had swayed Parliament it would have been impossible to have supported the King's government with voting majorities for money bills, which would have exposed the fundamental weakness of the British constitution as established in 1689. It clearly provided that the sovereign retained within his prerogative power the control of war and foreign affairs, and equally clearly stated that the House of Commons had ultimate control of the national finances, but it provided no means of settling disputes between them. In practice successive monarchs could rely on the loyal, though not automatic support of a majority of MPs. That the king's government must be carried on, that he had the right to call on the services of every loyal subject, and that opposition was disreputable if not treacherous were conventional truths which were universally accepted until late in the century. Independent MPs were always suspicious of ministers, and those of Jacobite sympathies might be thinking of a different king, but not until the 1780s, under the stimulus of novel circumstances, did theorists like Edmund Burke begin to work out a justification for the idea of opposition as a normal and respectable constitutional mechanism. In the political world in which Sandwich grew up and passed most of his active life, opposition was identified as 'faction', the manoeuvring of unscrupulous men determined to gain power for their own ends. Nor was the identification altogether unfair, for within the mass of Whigs the differences of principle were so narrow that gaining and losing power was the essential issue, and party was really a matter of self-interest. Of course political parties still help ambitious men to gain power, but this ambition has become relatively respectable in an age when formed parties are also the vehicles of alternative policies and approaches to government. Ambition was not respectable in Sandwich's day: the disinterested service of the king and the pursuit of personal honour, not personal advancement or bureaucratic drudgery, were the proper activities for a gentleman in public life.[55]

This was doubly true for a peer. His earldom gave Sandwich an assured and eminent position in public life and an automatic seat in Parliament, but it placed him in a position which did not perfectly fit his circumstances and temperament. By his time even the most archaic constitutional theorists had long ceased to justify the position of the House of Lords by reference to the inherited virtue of noble blood. Its rôle was understood to be one of maintaining the balance between the two centres of real power, the Crown and the House of Commons.[56] The king was exposed to the temptations of arbitrary power, the Commons to the pressures of 'democracy', a word which still carried the pejorative sense of the original Greek, meaning 'mob-rule'. With no necessity to seek either the favours of the people to gain election, or the favours of the king to gain office, the peers were immune to both, placed by Providence on a happy pinnacle of independent authority from which they could survey the political battle and intervene only when the national interest, in which they had so large a stake, demanded it. The young George III, always a reliable barometer of conventional wisdom, wrote in 1760 that 'if the power of the Lords should be annihilated, Despotism would instantly follow the loss of liberty'.[57] In Lord Suffolk's words, the House of Lords was 'the hereditary Council of this kingdom, not subject to the caprice of interested electors'. Sandwich fully shared the conventional view of 'that Democratic Interest which this House was constituted to restrain'.[58]

This position, however, carried several implications which were uncomfortable for Sandwich. The justification for the peers' position now rested explicitly on their inherited property, not their inherited virtue. It was because they were wealthy beyond any risk of pressure or temptation that they could deal with Crown and Commons on equal terms. The legal mechanism of the strict settlement, by this time almost universal in propertied families, had the effect of tying up a family's capital, which meant in practice its landed estates, and passing them intact to future generations.[59] However spendthrift or incompetent any one head of the family might be, however large the debts he might accumulate, strict settlement made it very difficult to sell off the core of the family estates. Families might still be ruined, especially by a lack of sons to inherit, or a profusion of daughters to endow, but by the mid-eighteenth century inherited wealth was as stable as it could well be. Consequently it was not unreasonable to treat the Lords collectively as a great weight of inherited property ballasting the ship of state and preventing it from heeling either to tyranny or democracy. But for a poor peer all this was uncomfortable; the established idea of the constitution implied that a peer needed some minimum level of wealth in order to function. In 1701 a bill had been proposed which would have established such limits; £4,000 a year for a viscount, for example, and more for an earl.[60] The same was implied in a rough-and-ready way by the exclusion from the Lords of all Irish peers and all but sixteen elected representatives of the Scottish peerage, for as a body the Irish and Scots peers were significantly poorer than the English. It could therefore be objected that a peer with a very modest fortune like Lord Sandwich was in a political sense illegitimate. This would be even more so if he displayed ambition to hold public office. Ambition in itself was suspect; ambition fuelled by the need of money was doubly suspect in one who was supposed to be above either, which was why some ministers thought it dishonourable to draw their salaries.[61] A pamphlet of 1742 put it that aristocrats, 'must be strangers to those vicious falsehoods and corruptions which necessity first, and then habit, puts men upon practising, whose lives are spent in the pursuit of their fortunes'.[62] What would have been perfectly acceptable and even laudable in a man of humble birth making his way in public service by his ability and diligence – the 'man of business' who is so distinctive a feature of eighteenth-century life – was damaging in a peer.

In a different way the lack of money was equally a disadvantage to anyone, peer or commoner, who intended to play a prominent part in public life, or needed to play a prominent part to satisfy his ambitions. The constitutional rôle of the House of Lords was essentially a passive one. It was a safeguard, to be called into action if either the king or the House of Commons got out of hand, but in ordinary circumstances playing a relatively subordinate part in political life. Though its political weight was certainly greater in the eighteenth century than it is in the twentieth, it was already clear to all that real Parliamentary power rested in the Commons. It was there that anyone had to operate who sought to build up any sort of following. Peers of course had to do so indirectly, but they had the obligations and opportunities which flowed automatically from the possession of great estates, they were looked up to as the natural leaders of the towns and districts where their estates lay, and those who had the inclination and the time could convert that influence into political power by getting members of Parliament elected in their interests. In the days before the eighteenth-century electoral system had been studied in detail, it used to be thought that such relationships were essentially corrupt, and that a large number of seats were 'rotten boroughs' under the entire control of their proprietors. We know now that among the wide variety of seats with electorates large and small, franchises open or restricted, there were virtually none which could be controlled by a proprietor without effort.[63] Eighteenth-century electors were swayed more by local than national considerations, and contests when they occurred were usually about local issues and local personalities, but this did not mean that the electors were indifferent to politics. On the contrary, whoever they were they expected their representatives, or would-be representatives, to pay close attention to their welfare, to visit them often and deal with them personally, to bestow repeated favours and attentions on them, their friends and relatives as well as on the community as a whole. All this demanded great expenditure of time and effort, and in most constituencies several hundred pounds a year in money. Though there were some corrupt constituencies, it was not usually a question of bribery, even indirect, but of the constant expense of cherishing and patronising the community. This community was not only the electorate, which might be quite small, but the electors' families, friends and dependents – usually a considerable fraction of the whole population.[64] Moreover MPs and peers were thought of as representing not only the constituencies which elected them but also the regions in which their property lay, so that substantial towns like Birmingham which elected no MPs were held to be 'virtually represented' by the local landowners.[65] All this was not at all a democratic system in the modern sense of giving an equal weight to the opinion of every adult, but it was a demotic system in the sense that the great were obliged to deal personally even with humble men and women in order to gain their favour and conciliate their interests.

Such a system presented a further obstacle to the poor peer. The smaller his estates, the smaller the area in which he had natural claims to influence and the more numerous his rivals round about. The less money he had to dispose of, the more difficult he would find it to pay for the favours which every self-respecting constituency demanded, to stand at the head of every subscription list, to provide civic feasts and municipal improvements, to employ the poor and advance the suppliant, to let tenancies at low rents to favoured supporters, and buy goods at high prices from local tradesmen. Above all the poor landowner needed to avoid that horror of every eighteenth-century politician, a contested election. Most often local interests would agree on candidates – the fact that there were two members for each seat facilitated compromise – but if the election went to a poll the candidates were involved in huge expense. The Northampton election of 1768 ruined two noble houses, Halifax and Northampton, and 'seriously embarrassed' Lord Spencer.[66] There was usually only one polling station, to which the electors had to be transported sometimes from hundreds of miles away, and lodged and fed during their stay.[67] In a county election with an electorate of thousands very deep pockets were needed. The author of *An Earnest Address to the Freeholders of the County of Huntingdon*, published in 1768, described contested elections as productive of 'discord, confusion, rancour, hatred, drunkenness, sedition, tumult, rapine, diseases and death';[68] another commentator claimed them as 'a remaining proof of the Existence of Original Sin';[69] but the politicians could have borne all these evils had it not been for the expense.

So Sandwich's modest fortune, though sufficient for his private needs, was quite inadequate for a career in politics. His assets were a first-class mind and a capacity for hard work which were unusual in a peer of the day. Neither of these could be deployed, however, unless he could gain office, which he could not hope to do by himself. He therefore joined the political group headed by the Duke of Bedford, the great magnate of the neighbouring county. This connection was cemented, and may even have been originated, by his marriage, for Charles Fane was MP for Tavistock in Bedford's interest, and one of the duke's closest friends and political colleagues.[70] Bedford was an example of the peer in politics which both contrasts with and illustrates Sandwich's position. On the death of his elder brother, 'cut off suddenly in the prime of a profligate youth' in 1732,[71] Bedford became head of the Russells, the family who had the strongest claim to have made the Glorious Revolution of 1688, and a plausible claim to be the richest house in the three kingdoms. His annual income was about £56,000 and rising rapidly as his Bloomsbury estate was built upon.[72] His name, his rank and his money made him a great politician automatically, though the number of MPs who followed him was only three, and he had few talents as a politician or as a minister. Haughty, opinionated, irascible, obstinate and erratic, he deployed an original mind and a good education without the restraints of experience or common sense.[73] Though a good speaker and not incapable of work when the mood took him, he had no interest in business and was to ignore many of the responsibilities of a minister. Such a man was ill-fitted to conciliate others, and carried weight in politics in spite rather than because of his personal qualities. But for Sandwich, setting out in public life with no such advantages as the duke enjoyed, a patron and leader was essential.

He therefore appeared in the House of Lords in 1740 as a member of Bedford's party, and a part of the wider Whig opposition striving for the fall of Sir Robert Walpole. When Walpole was driven from office in February 1742 he was replaced by a coalition led by his erstwhile colleagues, the brothers Henry Pelham and the Duke of Newcastle (the 'Old Whigs'), combined with former opposition leaders such as Lord Carteret (the 'New Whigs'). Most of the opposition, including the Bedfords, remained in the cold. They therefore redoubled their attacks on the reconstructed ministry, couching them in the traditional style of opposition, and with the more enthusiasm as Carteret was that rare thing in British politics, a knowledgeable and enthusiastic 'Continental', and his policy of engagement with Hanover was deeply unpopular in Parliament, however attractive to the king. Sandwich first appeared before the public eye as a fiery opposition speaker denouncing the administration's Continental commitment, especially its decision to hire a large contingent from the Hanoverian army, supposedly to support British policy.

> Suspicion is now heightened into certainty; we no longer *believe*, but we *know* the public is to be betrayed. Our countrymen are insulted by those who take our pay, who, perhaps, owe to our protection, their continuance as a distinct and unconquered people, and who are certainly indebted to our liberality, for their exemption from the misery and poverty, under which their ancestors languished.[74]

Sandwich was producing speeches like this in the Lords at the same time as young William Pitt and his Grenville cousins were saying the same things in the Commons. This was what the public wanted to hear, and it rapidly brought the young peer into public notice.[75] It also earned him (and Pitt) the dislike of George II, who was not pleased by insults to his native country.[76] Sandwich's contemporaries were agreed that he did not speak with much natural eloquence, but unlike many of his Parliamentary contemporaries he frequently mastered his subject before he spoke to it, and his solid facts and lucid argument commanded attention and respect.[77] We have, indeed, one speech reported from him at this time which might stand as evidence of real powers of oratory, lamenting that,

> We are entangled in a labyrinth of which no end is to be seen, and in which no certain path has been discovered; that we are pursuing schemes which are in no degree necessary to the prosperity of our country, by means which are apparently contrary to law, to policy, and to justice; and that we are employed in a foreign quarrel only to waste that blood, and exhaust that treasure, which might be employed in recovering the rights of commerce, and regaining the dominion of the sea.[78]

But in an age when Parliamentary reporting was illegal and precarious, when speeches were printed which were not just inaccurate but wholly imaginary,[79] much depended on the reporter, who in this case was Samuel Johnson. Sandwich's own style, in speech as in writing, was plain and clear without rhetorical flourishes. By these means he made his reputation, and contributed to the triumph of the opposition. In December 1744, four years after he had taken his seat in the Lords, and a few months after war had finally broken out with France, the ministry was reconstructed again by the ejection of Carteret and the addition of opposition groups (the 'New Allies') including the Bedfords. At the age of twenty-six Sandwich was about to begin his ministerial career.

CHAPTER II

At the Board of Admiralty
1744–1748

Bedford and Sandwich took office together, the duke as First Lord of the Admiralty, and Sandwich as his colleague. They had insisted on choosing the Admiralty in spite of resistance from the outgoing ministry, and it was very probably Sandwich's enthusiasm for naval affairs which inspired them.[1] He had always been interested in his ancestor the admiral, whose manuscript journal he read with interest,[2] and he already had much more experience of seafaring than most young men of his station. With them Bedford and Sandwich brought the naval hero of the hour, Rear-Admiral George Anson, just returned from his epic four-year voyage round the world. Though from the military point of view Anson's voyage had been something of a disaster, in which most of the men and all but one of the ships of the squadron had been lost, for Anson himself it was a triumph of skill and fortitude, and he had captured a Spanish galleon and returned with enormous wealth in the authentic style of Sir Francis Drake. The achievement was perfectly calculated to recommend him to politicians who had identified themselves with the 'Patriot' argument that sea power was the natural, glorious and profitable way for Britain to make war. Anson, moreover, though still only forty-seven, was clearly identified as the rising man in the Navy, whose appointment carried weight within the Service as well as with the political nation at large.

The Board of Admiralty which they joined had become an accepted part of the structure of British government, without completely solving the many political and administrative problems involved in running the largest, most complex and easily the most expensive activity of the state. The members of the Board were, in full, the 'Lords Commissioners for executing the Office of Lord High Admiral', and the office had last been filled by an individual thirty-five years before. In theory the commissioners were more or less equal, ranking in their patent in order of social rank. Bedford came first, as a duke, followed by Sandwich, Captain Lord Archibald Hamilton and Captain Lord Vere Beauclerk (dukes' younger sons), Lord Baltimore (an Irish baron), and finally two commoners, Anson and the young MP George Grenville. In reality the First Lord was always the minister, and almost always sat in Cabinet,[3] while the responsibilities of his colleagues varied according to circumstances and personalities from the advisory to the purely nominal. Although it was usual for at least one or two members of the Board to be officers of the Navy, there was no convention of any one of them acting in the modern style as 'First Sea Lord'. For most of the preceding thirty years the First Lords had themselves been eminent admirals who combined both the professional and the political rôles, and the junior members of their boards had been essentially political placemen, drawing a salary and signing their names as necessary. This last was not a sinecure in wartime, for hundreds of orders issued from the Admiralty every day, each of which had to be signed by three members of the Board. Junior naval Lords of the Admiralty, as a rule, divided into those too elderly to go to sea, who served on much the same basis as other placemen, and those young enough to have ambitions, who in wartime expected to have the chance to fulfil them at sea. For these officers a seat at the Board was an important step on their road to the top of their profession, and when there were squadrons to command they would not wish to damage their chances of glory, promotion and prize money by toiling at a desk. This meant that in wartime the naval lords with recent sea experience were not present to give their professional advice for much of the year.[4]

This consideration was relevant to the situation of Bedford's new Board, for with a French war and the prospect of fleet action, Rear-Admiral Anson could be expected to go to sea. Lord Archibald, on the other hand, was in his seventies and had been at the Board for most of the past fifteen years; he was a minor politician and experienced administrator rather than an active sea officer. Beauclerk was younger and still cherished naval ambitions, but his weight in the political world was greater than his reputation in the Navy. In real terms Anson was the dominant sea officer at the Board, even though he was nearly the most junior member of it, because of his professional standing and his close relations with Bedford and Sandwich.[5]

Anson is a famous, and yet an obscure figure in naval history. Notoriously taciturn in his own day, reluctant to put anything on paper for the benefit of future historians, he is a difficult man to evaluate, and it has generally been easier to say how important he was than why. Naval historians have been inclined to treat him as the real head of the Admiralty Board from 1744 when he first joined it, virtually until his death in 1762, although he did not become First Lord until 1751. Unfortunately it is always difficult to assess the internal dynamics of a Board, theoretically composed of equals and in practice transacting all its business collectively around a table, because only its collective decisions are recorded. The Board of 1744–48 is almost unique in that circumstances kept its members apart for much of the time and obliged them to transact affairs in writing. Furthermore most of the more important Board members, including Bedford, Sandwich and even Anson himself, have providentially left collections of papers reflecting their activities. It is therefore possible to know a great deal of what was going on, and to judge the opinions and influence of the members of the Board during a period of great importance for the Navy and the country.

Bedford and his colleagues took office in a mood of disquiet and even anger at the condition of the Navy. As politicians they were committed to the view that it was supremely important, and had been mismanaged by the previous administration. Since the naval war had opened with a bungled battle in the Mediterranean, followed immediately by a violent quarrel between the commander-in-chief and his second, Admirals Mathew and Lestock, Lord Winchelsea's Board certainly did appear in a poor light, and it had probably been a mistake to appoint the first civilian First Lord for thirty-eight years to preside over an unpopular 'Hanoverian' grand strategy.[6] More generally, there was an impression of drift, complacency and inertia in both the internal discipline and the civil administration of the Navy, which the new Admiralty were determined to do something about. In considering exactly what they were trying to do, and what responsibility they bore as individuals for the various measures, it is helpful to distinguish the military and civil side of the Admiralty's authority.

For the seagoing Navy, the Sea Service as the eighteenth century called it, the Admiralty was primarily concerned with discipline and personnel. It appointed all commissioned and some warrant officers, and it issued all routine orders for the movement of ships. It had very little to do with grand strategy and the employment of fleets in wartime, for that was the province of the king in theory, but in practice the Cabinet, since there had not been a king familiar with naval affairs since James II fled the country in 1688. Orders for all major naval movements were issued in the king's name by one of the two Secretaries of State, and sent either directly to the admiral concerned with a copy for the Admiralty's information, or to the Admiralty which would then issue orders to the same effect. The Board as a whole controlled convoy escorts, local patrols and movements in port, but it had very little to do with major naval operations. The First Lord, as the Navy's Cabinet minister, was expected to provide the professional advice on which the government could base its decisions, and invariably played a large part in drafting the orders which were then sent to his Board. This convention had grown up under a succession of First Lords who were also senior officers, and presented some difficulties with a civilian like Bedford who had no experience of public office of any kind, let alone of naval operations or grand strategy.

The Admiralty had even less to do with the civil administration of the Navy. The management of the dockyards, which were by far the largest and most complex industrial enterprises in the world, was the responsibility of the Navy Board, a body quite distinct from the Admiralty but in principle subordinate to it.[7] It was responsible for all aspects of shipbuilding, design and maintenance and for the purchase and issue of all naval stores other than food. It also warranted many of the subordinate officers and ran the reserve in which most of the Navy's ships spent their peacetime years. This was a huge task, calling for a staff of over a hundred in the Navy Office alone (four times the size of the Admiralty secretariat), besides the Board's thousands of employees in the yards. The Admiralty Office in Whitehall was sufficient to accommodate not only the Board's entire staff, but official residences for all the Board members. Those like Sandwich who had no town houses lived as well as worked there.

In addition the Admiralty was also responsible for the Victualling Board, which purchased, manufactured, packed, stored and issued the enormous quantities of food and drink required by fleets at sea, and for the Sick and Hurt Board which cared for the Navy's sick and wounded, and for prisoners of war of all services. Finally the Admiralty enjoyed a working relationship (not always a good one) with an independent department, the Ordnance Board, which was responsible for issuing guns and warlike stores to both fighting services and was subordinate to neither.

The control of the naval boards, above all of the Navy Board, presented the Admiralty with many of the difficulties which in every age have presented themselves to the political head of a department trying to enforce change on reluctant subordinates with a monopoly of technical knowledge. The Navy Board consisted largely of civilian administrators, but its most important members were the Controller of the Navy, who was always a sea officer on half-pay, and the Surveyor of the Navy, who was always a former dockyard Master Shipwright. The Controller presided at the Board and undertook a disproportionately large share of its business, including most of what called for sea experience. The Surveyor designed the Navy's ships, with the help of a couple of senior draughtsmen. A long-serving Controller soon acquired a knowledge of naval administration of a range and complexity which Admiralty Boards never encountered and seldom appreciated, while the Surveyor stood at the head of an essential and exceedingly technical profession which neither sea officers nor civilians understood, but about which officers usually held strong opinions.

Such men were in an excellent position to resist proposals which they did not like, but for many years before 1744 they had had no occasion to do so. Sir Charles Wager, First Lord from 1733 to 1742, was an admiral and administrator of great experience and a politician high in the favour of Sir Robert Walpole. He seems to have run the peacetime Navy efficiently, and as 'a man who inspired loyalty and promoted harmony',[8] he was well calculated to preside over a turbulent and quarrelsome profession. What he did not attempt was any serious disturbance of the long-settled routines of naval administration. By 1744 the Navy Board was two hundred years old, and its members between them had a weight of seniority and experience which no Admiralty could match. Richard Haddock the Controller was a captain of forty-nine years' seniority, and the son of a previous Controller. Sir Jacob Acworth, the Surveyor of the Navy since 1715, had entered the Navy under Charles II and was serving his seventh sovereign.[9] Haddock was old and feeble; Acworth was old and formidable.[10] By contrast Bedford was thirty-five and Sandwich twenty-six when they took office. In order to force reform on a reluctant Navy Board they had to impose their authority on men deeply versed in highly technical business of which they knew nothing, men who had held high office before the young peers had been born. What was more the members of the Navy Board – 'the Principal Officers and Commissioners of the Navy', to give them their full title – were by convention permanent office-holders, with 'a provision for my life', as one of them put it.[11] They might be persuaded to retire, but could not be dismissed except for gross misconduct. Though the Admiralty's right to appoint the members of the

Navy Board was undisputed, they had to take their vacancies as they happened in the course of nature.

The young would-be reformers at the Admiralty had many things in mind to change, but probably the most urgent and difficult was the design of warships. Here Anson, with his recent sea experience and wide range of contacts in the Navy, took the lead in articulating officers' unhappiness. British ships of the line were generally believed to be too small to bear the weight of armament they were given, to carry their lower tier of guns sufficiently high out of the water for the ports to be opened in a seaway, and to sail well. Experience of war with Spain and now France brought British officers into contact with ships which they judged to be larger and much better than their own, and aroused vocal discontent.[12] With frigates it was the same story; French ships were often much faster and better adapted to their purpose than their British counterparts.

It used to be said that these problems arose from the well-meant imposition of 'establishments' in 1719 and 1733 which laid down the dimensions and armament of each class of ship. The object had been to simplify the administrators' task in supplying stores, especially spars and rigging, and the admirals' task in handling their fleets in formation, which was nearly impossible with ships of widely differing design and performance. It was said, however, that these laudable objectives had been bought at the expense of rigidity and ossification. Modern studies have shown that the establishments were not in practice regarded as compulsory, and that they rather reflected than enforced a conservative approach to design in a long period of peace.[13] Furthermore the differences between British and foreign designs were not simply between bad and good, but between different approaches reflecting different traditions and requirements. British ships were heavily built for long working lives in all weathers, small and relatively cheap in proportion to their armament. French designs, by contrast, were large and fast in good weather, but lightly built and lightly armed for their size, with a high initial cost and shorter working lives.[14] British officers were not interested in costs, and tended to compare gun for gun rather than size for size. Moreover it was prizes taken from the enemy which they had the chance to compare in detail, and as captors they were in the position of vendors selling their property to the Navy; naturally they did not undervalue the prizes' good qualities, and when the Master Shipwrights were critical or the Navy Board offered too low a price, they attributed it to their 'secret reluctance & jealousy of admitting French Men of War into our Service, whereby so visible an advantage in sailing is discover'd on their side as probably may not be agreable'.[15] But the sea officers' discontent was in some respects really justified.

The Admiralty's first moves were to order a halt to the construction of ships building to existing designs, the alteration of some not yet too far advanced, and the preparation of new designs more nearly resembling foreign types. At the same time a weighty committee of flag officers was summoned to recommend a new establishment, and a committee of master shipwrights met in the mould loft at Deptford Dockyard to prepare standard designs for future construction.[16]

The success of these measures was mixed. They gave the Navy its first specimens of what was to become the standard two-decker ship of the line, the '74' (meaning a ship of seventy-four guns), and it resulted in a number of significant improvements, but no real revolution in ship design was achieved, and the new ships proved when they went to sea to share many of the disadvantages of the old. The admirals' committee moved cautiously a short way in the direction Anson wanted, but its recommendations proved to be as much a curb as a spur to progress.[17] The greatest obstacle was Sir Jacob Acworth, who did not take kindly to being taught his business by a collection of amateurs half his age, could not be shifted, and would not retire. Anson and Sandwich agreed,

> in wishing that Sir Jacob should retire with every Circumstance that can make his old age easy & happy, but retain no influence in Naval Architecture. For it is high time Ships began to have bottoms to them, & more Expedition as well as better Oeconomy prevail'd in the Dock Yards. This cannot happen whilst he has any Influence, for whilst he has any he will have all. We know Sir Jacob to have so much of the Nature of Pompey the great in him that he cannot bear an equal, & if Mr Allen should have so much of the temper of Julius Caesar about him that he cannot brook a Superior – What must ensue but civil war added to the many Indecorum's & distresses the Dock Yards at present labour under. Things will go on worse than ever, the same laziness, the same want of Oeconomy, the same aversion & discouragement to Ingenuity, nothing will be sufferd to continue in the yards but Cousins, & Flatterers, & nothing turn'd out but bad Ships & able Shipwrights.[18]

The best that could be achieved was the appointment of Joseph Allin as joint Surveyor in July 1746, and he proved to be much less adventurous a designer than Anson had hoped. When Sir Jacob finally died in 1749 after sixty-four years' unbroken service, only limited progress had been made in improving the design of British battleships.

With frigates the new Board had more success. Relatively small, cheap and rapidly built, they were often designed by the master shipwrights of the yards or by private shipbuilders, rather than by the Surveyor, so that new influences could be more easily and swiftly assimilated. Unlike line-of-battle ships, frigates had more or less direct competitors in privateers with which they could be compared, and enemy prizes of rival design were relatively common.[19] An important part in developing better frigate designs was played by Benjamin Slade, Master Shipwright of Plymouth Yard, who seems to have been the favourite designer of Anson and his naval followers, and the one they came most often into contact with in these years when the main squadrons were operating from Plymouth. The French privateer *Tigre*, taken in 1747, was entrusted to his hands. 'As all our Frigates sail wretchedly', Anson wrote to Bedford from his flagship off Ushant,

> I intreat your Grace that an order may be immediately sent from your Board to the Navy Board to direct Mr Slade the Builder at Plymouth to take off the Body of the French *Tyger* with the utmost exactness, and that two Frigates may be order'd to be built with all possible dispatch; of her dimensions and as similar to her as the Builders Art will allow; let Slade have the building of one of them.[20]

Slade investigated the designs of other French prizes, sending Anson plans, models and proposals.[21] None of the prizes was copied exactly, for the French ships with all their speed were cramped, unseaworthy and weakly built, but the British designers, including Slade, Allin and others, worked with considerable success to adapt the best aspects of foreign designs to their own requirements. They also investigated older British designs, notably the very fast royal yacht *Royal Caroline*, as a source of frigate types. The result was that by the end of the war in 1749 a number of promising new frigates were at sea.

The Admiralty's attempts to persuade or force the Navy Board to adopt new warship designs was an example of the general problem of asserting its authority which presented itself almost as soon as the new Admiralty took office. In its first few months a rapid succession of orders were issued to provide all sorts of statistics and returns for the information of the new Board. They asked for a statement of the cost of raising men since 1739, and another of money unpaid from the time of the last five Treasurers of the Navy. They demanded lists of the Navy in 1710 (at the height of Queen Anne's war) and 1745, lists of ships built and rebuilt from 1702 to 1710 and from 1739 to 1744, detailed returns of the Navy from 1738 and of the tonnage of each rate of ship. They called for a comparison of the Navy Estimates for the first five years of Queen Anne's war with the five years of war just passed, and for the reasons for the increase in the Navy's debt. They ordered returns of the numbers of men employed in the dockyards from 1702, and the amount of overtime they had worked. They enquired about the Crown's rights to mast trees growing in the forests of New England, and about the suitability of prahms (a type of sailing barge) for naval service. The Navy Board was ordered to investigate, and soon after to adopt, the heavier rigging and recut sails proposed by Anson; to begin the new naval hospital at Haslar near Portsmouth which had been proposed to the previous Admiralty; to lay transporter buoys in the Cremyll passage so that ships could warp up to Plymouth Dockyard when the wind was foul; and to make trial of 'Mr Sutton's Machines' for ventilating ships' holds.[22] The records of the Admiralty show nothing like this activity from previous Boards – and nothing like the response from the Navy Board that Bedford and his colleagues were looking for.[23] Early in their career they clashed violently over the Navy Board's refusal to alter its established mode of letting contracts merely because a new firm offered to dredge the Medway much more cheaply than the existing contractors.[24]

In this case the Navy Board were defending a weak position and had to retreat, but in the broader issue of the management of the dockyards the Admiralty ran into frustrating obstacles. Delays to ships refitting frequently occurred because of poor co-ordination between the senior officials of the yards, and between the yards and the ships' officers. Each side blamed the other, and the Admiralty tended to take the sea officers' side. But the management of the yards was extremely complex, and neither Board had a good hold on its subordinates. The senior officer of each dockyard was the Commissioner, invariably a captain on half-pay, and technically a member of the Navy Board on detached service. He was not, however, the actual manager of the yard, because each of the senior officers of the yard took his orders directly from the Navy Board in London. In dealing with the Master Shipwright, the Master Attendant, the Clerk of the Cheque and the Storekeeper, who ran the main departments of each yard, the Commissioner could supervise, advise, warn and report, but he could not give direct orders. Being on half-pay he had no authority over sea officers either. The port admiral or senior officer, who did, was not supposed to deal directly with the yard officers but had to go through the commissioner. The system had the effect of diffusing responsibility and authority, and making it extremely difficult to impose change. Frustrated by the Navy Board's failure to tackle repeated complaints of delay to ships coming out of dock whose stores were not ready when needed, the new Admiralty ordered Admiral Steuart at Portsmouth to interfere directly with the management of the yard. The result was a violent controversy which achieved nothing but much ill-will.[25] The fact was that the Admiralty and the Navy knew very little of the detailed workings of the yards, and were obliged to rely on the co-operation of the Navy Board and its subordinates. Indeed the Navy Board itself was in a similar position in relation to the yard officers. It was easy to express dissatisfaction when things went wrong, more difficult to diagnose the problem, very difficult indeed to enforce a solution on reluctant subordinates whom it was impossible to dismiss and difficult to replace. In the management of the yards, the experience of Bedford's Admiralty showed only that reform was much harder than they had supposed.

The Sea Service, on the other hand, was the Admiralty's own proper sphere of authority, and Anson at least knew what needed to be done there. Moreover his following of officers, the core of which was the little band who had survived the *Centurion*'s voyage round the world, were distributed among the most active and favoured positions in the fleet, and acted as an informal advisory committee. One part of Anson's work concerned the efficiency of the ships at sea, in signalling, tactics, gunnery and manoeuvres.[26] Here he acted on his own authority as commander-in-chief of the main fleet for much of the time between 1746 and 1748, and indirectly through his pupils and followers as they rose to commands. His colleagues at the Admiralty watched these developments with admiration, but they fell largely outside the authority of the Admiralty as it was understood, which could do no more than issue exhortations.[27] When Anson and then his junior colleague Edward Hawke won two victories in quick succession in 1747, it was the admirals not the Admiralty who won the credit. By 1748 Anson's brother could assure him that he had no more glory left to win at sea, and could remain at the Admiralty with a clear conscience:

Nothing surely remains to be added to your Fame in commanding
Squadrons: a Discipline unknown before, a new Manner of Cruizing,
and a decisive way of Engaging the Enemy (which by the by I am
glad to hear Howe has imitated) have already secur'd you all merit of
that kind in its largest extent: Then to frame and direct the Whole
Plan is much more glorious to yourself as well as more beneficial to
the Public, than to execute with all the Ability and Success imaginable
only a part of it.[28]

What the Admiralty was keenly interested in was the discipline of
the Navy, 'too much relaxed' and urgently in need of restoration.[29]
Its immediate inheritance from its predecessors was the failed battle
of Toulon, leading to a Parliamentary investigation, a court martial
ordered on openly political grounds and conducted under heavy political pressure, the condemnation of the commander-in-chief who
had led bravely into battle, and the acquittal of the subordinate who
had hung back.[30] Accompanying this were several eminently justified
courts martial on captains for cowardice. The admiral who had presided at the court martial and condemnation of one junior officer was
sued by him in the civil courts and condemned to pay heavy damages.
The other members in turn were then sued, one of whom was at the
time presiding over one of the courts martial following the battle of
Toulon. The court immediately refused to act further, and passed a
resolution intended for the king reflecting on the Chief Justice of
Common Pleas in terms which nearly got them imprisoned.[31] 'Unless
effectual measures be taken to discourage this Attempt', the Admiralty
complained, 'and to prevent the like hereafter, it will be impossible to
carry on any Government or Order in the Navy'.[32]

The effect on discipline of all these proceedings was thoroughly
destructive, but there was relatively little the Admiralty could do
about them. Much of its work was really Anson's in disseminating
by precept and example a new spirit of devotion to duty among the
officers. Sandwich did what he could to the same effect, for example
by undertaking to have a painting done at his expense of every
successful sea action.[33] The Board soon found itself embroiled in a
series of test cases which sharply illustrated the gap between the
professional standards they were trying to spread, and the traditions
of the Navy on the one hand, and the conventions of civil, more
particularly of political society on the other. The first arose in the
crisis year of 1745, with a French invasion expected and a Highland
rebellion in progress. A strong squadron was assembled in the
Downs to counter invasion, and the command was given to Admiral

Edward Vernon. He was both a senior officer of ability, and a politician violent in the opposition, 'Patriot' interest, consequently a recent colleague of Bedford and his friends. In spite of this he had been chosen by Wager to command the 1740 Caribbean expedition, which had achieved spectacular initial success but very little more.[34] In his new command he proceeded to bombard the Admiralty with suggestions and requests. His strategic ideas were in many respects profound and prescient, but he had never been an easy man to work with, and his relations with the Admiralty began to deteriorate as he addressed them more and more in the tones of a very senior officer dismissing contemptible amateurs. No Admiralty Board could have put up with that, least of all one headed by the Duke of Bedford, and after a final row over Vernon's claim to appoint officers without reference to the Board he was ordered to haul down his flag. He then pursued his grievance in a series of pamphlets in which he published most of his correspondence with the Admiralty, as a result of which he was dismissed from the Navy.[35]

Vernon's troubles can be seen as the victory of an ungovernable temper over a first-class mind, but they were equally the consequence of the temper of the times in which an officer's primary allegiance was not to the impersonal concept of duty or to the Service as a whole, but to the king as an individual and to his own personal honour, which in practice meant his reputation and whatever he felt it necessary to do to uphold it.[36] An officer's honour might be offended, in his own eyes, by any order which threatened to lower his consequence, to limit his power and influence, to direct his career or operations in some direction less advantageous than he felt he deserved. Honour required that a captain should have every opportunity to vindicate his courage and conduct, that is to say, that he should have the best possible ship on the best possible station. A man of nice honour had the right to demand it, and he expected his demand to be met. Tedious, unspectacular duty in obscure and unprofitable situations was inherently dishonourable, to be rejected by a gentleman as a matter of principle. All this was the common coin of polite society from which most commissioned officers were drawn, and to which all belonged by virtue of their commissions as officers in the king's sea service. The notion of duty which Anson and the Admiralty were working towards was radically different both from the traditions of the Navy and the conventions of civil society. More than one generation was to pass, and society was to change in many ways before it could be said to have been thoroughly implanted in the conscience of the average sea officer.

The Vernon case was hardly settled before another contest arose between new and old principles. Two members of the Board, Sandwich and George Grenville, had brothers in the Navy, and in the spring of 1747 both William Montagu and Thomas Grenville were commanding ships in the main fleet under Vice-Admiral Anson. Like captains throughout the Navy, they were anxious for a 'cruise' – the chance, that is, to cruise individually or in a small group in a suitable area to pick up enemy merchantmen inward bound with rich cargoes; in short the chance that every sea officer longed for, to make their fortunes. Having brothers on the Admiralty Board gave them unequalled influence, and George Grenville intended to use it. Sandwich, on the other hand, was determined that neither brother should enjoy any improper favour, which in practice meant that they would get their cruise only when Anson judged that it was safe to release them. At a time when the main French fleet was expected to put to sea and Anson needed all his ships with him, George Grenville grew impatient, demanded the release of the two ships, and when he was refused tried to get the order issued by a trick without Bedford and Sandwich discovering. He failed, and the result was a sharp quarrel between him and his Admiralty colleagues, and between Sandwich and his younger brother.[37] Captain Montagu, 'Mad Montagu' as he was known in the Navy, was a violent and unstable character, combining professional talents with a talent for getting himself into trouble, and a constant source of vexation to admirals under whom he served, as well as to his elder brother.[38] 'My brothers general behaviour', Sandwich wrote to Anson,

> and his particular conduct to me; affects me so much, that I cannot write upon it with any degree of connection; I find mild treatment will not save him, & indeed I think at the same time nothing will.[39]

Sandwich consistently supported the admirals, as he supported Anson, but it needs to be emphasized that in doing so he was flying in the face of orthodoxy, adopting standards which were a novelty even in the Navy, and flouting the universal convention by which men of influence like himself and George Grenville had a perfect right if not an obligation to use that influence to advance their families. It was not the last time he was to get into trouble by upholding the alien concept of duty.

In dealing with the officer corps as a whole, the Board concentrated initially on trying to reinforce and define the 'military' character of the sea officers as persons under discipline. At this date the officers' ranks were not completely distinct from jobs they performed: a lieutenant held that rank not because he had been commissioned to the rank as such in the Navy as a service, but from the date he had first been commissioned as First, Second, Third or Fourth Lieutenant of a named ship, and he received a fresh commission for each successive appointment. A Post Captain took rank from the date he had first been commissioned to command a 'post ship', one of the major warships which were ranked in descending order of size from First to Sixth Rates; there was no other way of reaching the rank. Likewise the quasi-rank of Master and Commander, a step between lieutenant and post captain which it was possible to leap over, came only from a commission to command a sloop or other warship too small to have a post captain. These ranks had never been legally defined, so that it was difficult to know, for example, whether a lieutenant who had been promoted to master and commander outranked one who had not but stood senior on the lieutenants' list. Foreigners found it impossible to equate British naval ranks with their own, so that captains abroad found themselves being treated as army subalterns. The new Admiralty obtained an Order in Council defining sea officers' ranks in relation to army ranks, and to emphasize the disciplined nature of the Service it established the first uniform for commissioned officers.[40] Orders were issued allowing officers to draw their pay annually, instead of having to wait for their ships to pay off at the end of a commission (as the rest of the ship's company still did).[41] This was not only a practical help to the officers, but also emphasized their character as permanent members of a disciplined service. The Admiralty began a revision both of the 'General Printed Instructions' (the forerunner of the later Queen's Regulations and Admiralty Instructions) which defined officers' duties, and of the Articles of War which established the disciplinary system of the Navy.[42]

A particular problem had to be tackled over the appointment of admirals. Although promotion up to post captain was in principle on merit, admirals had always been chosen from the top of the captains' list by strict seniority. There was no mechanism for retirement, rank was for life, promotion to admiral was regarded by many as the right of every captain who reached the top of the list, and consequently longevity was a major criterion for the choice of flag officers. Though captains were passed over for promotion, it was regarded by them as a major grievance, and invariably generated trouble within and without the Service.[43] Furthermore the number and rank of admirals were still affected by the organization of the fleet as it had been in Charles II's time seventy years before. Then a single, very large, main fleet, commanded by the Admiral of the Fleet if not by the Lord High Admiral in person, had been divided into three grand divisions, the centre with red ensigns, the van with white, and the rear with blue. Each of these in turn was divided into three, the centre and the whole division commanded by the full admiral, the van by the vice-admiral, and the rear by the rear-admiral. The whole fleet therefore called for nine flag officers: the admiral of the fleet commanding the whole, and the centre of the centre division; the admiral of the white commanding the van as a whole, and the centre division of it; and so on down to the rear-admiral of the blue commanding the rear of the rear division. By the 1740s this had long ceased to bear any relation to the actual organization of the fleet, but until December 1743 there were still only nine admirals, chosen by seniority, and George II had just rebuffed an attempt by the previous Admiralty to increase the number formally established.[44]

Bedford's Board tackled this problem with a series of interlinked measures. The king was persuaded to allow more than one flag officer of each rank, so that it was in principle possible to promote as many admirals as were actually needed. The hallowed principle of seniority was not directly attacked, but a new rank of 'rear-admiral without distinction of squadron' was created, to which senior captains could be promoted on the clear understanding that their sea careers were at an end. In effect, though not in form, this was a retirement scheme for elderly captains, who were compensated with the dignity and the half-pay of a rear-admiral. It was now possible to reach down the captains' list as far as necessary, choosing the able officers for active flag rank, and pushing aside the unsuitable and worn-out as 'yellow admirals'.[45] It is hardly possible to exaggerate the importance of this step, which made it possible for British fleets to be commanded by officers chosen on merit, still vigorous enough in mind and body to bear the strains of high command. It only required to complete it a similar scheme for the compulsory retirement of elderly admirals, which it seems Anson wanted but could not obtain.[46]

Another serious problem affecting the discipline and efficiency of the sea service was the position of the Marine regiments. From Charles II's time it had been customary to raise extra infantry regiments in wartime to serve as marines in the fleet, but they remained in all respects part of the army. This presented continual problems of divided control and indiscipline at sea, and an administrative nightmare ashore. The army structure of proprietary regiments managed as private businesses by their colonels was quite unsuitable for forces which seldom served together as regiments, but went to sea in small detachments borne on the books of ships. The result was that by 1746 the financial affairs of the Marine regiments were in chaos. A committee of the House of Commons investigated and recommended that they be transferred to naval control, and in February 1747 the Admiralty took control. The Marines retained their unsuitable regimental structure, and they remained an impermanent force which was to be disbanded at the peace, but a significant step had been taken in improving their efficiency.[47]

While all these reforms were in agitation, the Admiralty was also fighting a naval war. It is not necessary here to describe the course of the war in detail, but it is important to discuss its major strategic development, the rise of the Western Squadron. The idea of guarding the English Channel by keeping the main fleet not in the Channel but out to windward in the Western Approaches was not a new one – something like it had been adopted in 1588 on the advice of Sir Francis Drake – but it was first articulated and thoroughly developed during this war. The principle was simple. The prevailing winds blow from the South-West, up the Channel. Neither France nor Spain had a naval base in the Channel, so any enemy fleet had to come from the westward. An invasion force might sail from the ports of Normandy and Brittany, but it would sail without naval escort unless a fleet came up the Channel to cover it. Most of Britain's foreign trade (the Baltic trade excepted) came up and down the Channel. If the main fleet cruised to the westward off the mouth of the Channel it was well placed to cover convoys outward and homeward bound, to watch the main French naval base at Brest and intercept fleets coming and going from it, to guard against any attempt to invade Ireland, and to block, or at least pursue an enemy fleet entering the Channel. In developing this principle Vernon was one of the most important theorists, and Anson, as commander-in-chief of the Western Squadron for most of 1746 and 1747, the most influential practitioner.[48]

The principle of a Western Squadron was one of the most valuable and enduring legacies of Bedford's Admiralty, and in one shape or another it formed the core of Britain's naval strategy for a century and more. The practical application of the policy, however, always aroused disagreement, and did so between the members of the Board. If the squadron stayed at sea together for as long as possible, it increased its chances of fighting a decisive action if it met an enemy fleet, but it increased the wear and tear on the ships, especially if it stayed out in the autumn, the season of the equinoctial gales, but also of the rich convoys coming home from the West and East Indies. An autumn cruise might protect the trade at the cost of crippling the squadron for months. If the ships were dispersed in small groups on cruising stations trade might be better protected, but there was a risk of defeat in detail. If the squadron lay in port it kept in the best condition to meet the enemy, but the worst position to do so. The choice of port was also controversial: Spithead or St Helen's (off Portsmouth) were convenient but too far up Channel; Torbay was dangerously exposed either to enemy attack or to a south-easterly wind; Cawsand Bay at the mouth of Plymouth Sound was a cramped and exposed anchorage, while the Hamoaze off Plymouth Dockyard itself took far too long to get in and out of. If the Western Squadron attempted a blockade of Brest, where should it take station? To lie off Brest itself in south-westerly winds was very dangerous, and arguably unnecessary when the French could only sail on an east wind; but to lie, say, in Torbay until the wind veered might give the enemy two hundred miles' start.

These questions continued to be debated as long as warships were driven by the wind and Britain and France regarded one another as potential enemies. There were no absolute right or wrong answers to them, and in different circumstances different admirals and Admiralties adopted different approaches.[49] It is nevertheless interesting to observe what Sandwich thought in this early stage of his long career at the Admiralty, about problems which he was to face at intervals over the next forty years. Vernon argued for keeping the main Western Squadron at sea 'in Soundings' (meaning the Western Approaches), with a force of smaller ships to guard the Narrow Seas against invasion:[50]

> I have always looked upon squadrons in Port, as neither a Defence for the Kingdom, nor a security for our Commerce; and that the surest means for the preservation of Both, was Keeping a strong Squadron in Soundings, which may answer both these Purposes, as covering both Chanels and Ireland, at the same time it secures our Commerce.[51]

Anson agreed, but rather favoured keeping the main force in port until the enemy were known to be preparing to put to sea, and not risking dispersal until he had been met and defeated – for which he was attacked by commercial interests for neglecting their trade.[52] 'The French can never be so much annoy'd', he wrote, nor this Kingdom so well secured, as by keeping a strong Squadron at home, sufficient to make detachments, whenever we have good intelligence that the French are sending ships either to the East or West Indies.[53]

Sandwich argued strongly that concentrating either at sea or in port threw away the opportunity to damage the enemy by intercepting his trade, that detachments could be made while still leaving a sufficient force together for any emergency, and that it was not necessary to allow the threat of invasion to paralyse all offensive measures.

> By immediately recalling them [cruisers], we shall fall into the same trap which has, during the whole war, been so successfully laid for us, of giving way to every sudden alarm, and by that means have missed every opportunity fortune would have thrown in our way.[54]

In other words, he argued for running greater risks than Bedford or Anson, but arguably put a lower priority on winning a decisive victory. In practice it was Anson's opinion which was dominant, and his policy which led to the two naval victories of 1747. We cannot know what might have been the consequences of Sandwich's bolder but more risky, and perhaps more short-sighted policy.[55] What is clear is that he had intelligent ideas of strategy, evolved at a critical period in British naval history, in debate with Anson, Vernon and others whose views carry great weight.

Hitherto we have been discussing Bedford's Admiralty Board as a unified body reaching collective decisions, as an Admiralty Board was supposed to do. In practice it could only do so by extensive correspondence, for after its first few months it hardly ever met complete. In January 1745 the new Board held thirty meetings, and Bedford, Sandwich and Anson attended every one. In February and March they held twenty-five and twenty-six respectively, of which Bedford missed four, Anson two and Sandwich one. Thereafter the duke's initial enthusiasm began to fall away, and by June he had adopted what became his usual working week. On Wednesday mornings he came up from Woburn, and on Thursday afternoons he returned.[56] While he was in the country he expected to be consulted by post on all important decisions, including everything to do with patronage.[57] Otherwise he was happy to leave the running of the Admiralty to those, like Sandwich, who enjoyed it. Bedford's indifference to routine and distaste for administration, his deep reluctance to be drawn from the pleasures of the country to attend the Cabinet even in the most pressing emergency, were a source of

frustration to every government to which he belonged, but for Sandwich they were something of an opportunity. He had always been
a hard worker who mastered his subject; now he had a subject of
absorbing interest and outstanding importance, and in Anson he had
a colleague whom he liked, and whose professional qualities he
deeply admired. The duke's absence left them much freedom, not
to take major decisions which were almost always referred to him
if not the Cabinet, but to develop policy. How, indeed whether, the
two of them divided their responsibilities when they were together
at the Board we cannot easily tell, but Anson was at sea part of the
summer of 1745 and large parts of 1746 and 1747, and the evidence
suggests that he concentrated on the discipline and training of the
Sea Service, while Sandwich worked on the Navy Board and the
civil administration of the Navy. The other members of the Board
were not ciphers, but it is clear that Anson's professional authority,
and Sandwich's position as the duke's close friend and the second
on the Board patent, allowed them to dominate its activities.

This control was interrupted in the autumn of 1745 by the Jacobite
rebellion. Initially it was not taken very seriously as a military threat,
and the Admiralty concentrated on watching the French as well as
intercepting supplies going to Scotland. When the rebels crossed
the border, having defeated every body of regular troops standing
between them and London, attitudes began to change. The king's
son the Duke of Cumberland was hastily recalled from Flanders with
as many of his troops as could be drawn away in the face of the
French army which had just won the battle of Fontenoy. To augment
the woefully small regular army several great magnates offered to
raise private regiments. The offer was regarded with misgivings;
such forces could not be effective for months, the proprietors would
expect to nominate the officers, and the officers would expect half-
pay for life when the regiments were disbanded. In the crisis of the
Forty-Five, however, all doubts were suspended, and the Duke of
Bedford among others raised a regiment. Sandwich joined as one of
his officers, leaving Anson to run the Admiralty over the winter. In
December 1745 he was on campaign in the Midlands when he fell
dangerously ill at Birmingham. Both his wife and his friend Lord
Halifax hastened to help him, and Halifax wrote an interesting
account of what he found:

> The Terrible Lowness of his Spirits makes him take such strange
> notions into his head, as are not to be accounted for, & by Force of
> Reason Impossible to be removed. He fancys the Expence attending

his new Commission, tho' not amounting to £200, has utterly ruin'd him, & that he is undone in his Circumstances, tho' even by his own account they appear noways impaired. These ill founded notions are continually preying upon him; he figures to himself the miseries of Poverty & Distress, & his Disposition is as much affected by them, as if they really existed. No weakness of mind, no want of judgement appears in his Conversation upon any Point, but that single one of his Circumstances, which possesses him in such a manner, as harrasses him to Death. Tho' he has Draughts upon the Bank, and Draughts upon his Agent, he expresses himself in the most extreme Want of money . . . Lady Sandwich is here with My Lord. I was in hopes her Company might in some Degree relieve him, but I don't find it to be the case.[58]

This letter is interesting for what it reveals of Sandwich's fears. No man recovering from a dangerous fever is expected to be entirely rational, but it may be suggested that his unreasonable terror of poverty reflects something he really felt but seldom expressed, something perhaps deriving as much from the personal insecurity in which he had grown up as from his financial situation. In due course Sandwich recovered, and after a convalescence at Hinchingbrooke he was back at the Admiralty on 4th January 1746.[59] The episode left only one lasting consequence. Like the other officers recruited at the time, he was installed on the half-pay lists and remained there, rising steadily in rank, until his notional military career brought him to the rank of full General in 1772[60] – with the result that he sometimes figures in reference books as 'army officer and politician'.

CHAPTER III

An Honest Man Lying Abroad
1746–1748

Not long after Sandwich returned to the Admiralty the ministry was disturbed by a political crisis. Though Bedford and Sandwich were in office, several of the duke's other followers, notably Sandwich's old schoolfellow the Earl of Halifax, were not, and resented it. They appealed to Bedford's honour, and it seemed for a while that he might withdraw from the ministry if they were not satisfied. Bedford's colleagues were alarmed, because they needed the political strength of his party; Sandwich was alarmed, because he did not wish to be obliged to leave office with his patron. In the ensuing negotiations Sandwich played the key part, and when Halifax was pacified with a valuable sinecure, Sandwich reaped much of the credit as a skilful politician, useful to the ministry at large as well as to his department. This reputation opened the door for an unexpected development in his career.[1]

To explain it we need to sketch the situation of the war and the internal politics of the British ministry. In the spring of 1746 the French war had been going for over two years with no great victories to show for it. Two French invasion schemes had failed to take effect, one domestic rebellion had at length been defeated, but the only actual gain had been the unexpected capture in 1745 of the French fortress of Louisbourg on Cape Breton, by a force improvised by the colonials of Massachusetts and the local naval commander Commodore Warren. Nearer home the French army was doing better. In 1744 they had crossed the frontier into the Austrian Netherlands (modern Belgium), and in two years' campaigning they had steadily pushed back the allied army made up of Austrian, British, Dutch, Hanoverian and assorted German troops, which was commanded by George II's son the Duke of Cumberland. The allied army was politically and militarily disunited, and it faced a superior enemy commanded by Marshal Saxe, by common consent the finest professional soldier of the age. The prolonged absence of Cumberland and many of his troops campaigning against the Jacobite rebels had not helped.

In London the ministry was divided in its views on the war. Henry Pelham, the First Lord of the Treasury and leader of the administration in the Commons, was inclined by temperament and ministerial responsibilities to think first of the huge cost of a war which seemed to be getting nowhere. The ministry suspected, moreover, that the Dutch Republic, which was in the anomalous position of being an actual belligerent while technically still at peace with France, would welcome a chance to escape its obligations as an ally and withdraw from the fighting – which would have caused the immediate collapse of the allied war effort in Flanders. Other ministers, led by Pelham's brother the Duke of Newcastle, one of the Secretaries of State, were still optimistic that victories could be won if Britain stood firm. Bedford and his party stood as before for the primacy of a maritime strategy. The capture of Louisbourg they saw as the first of many fruits of it, and they were not prepared to stop at this promising time, still less to offer their prize as a bargaining counter to make up for the losses on the Continent attributable to the incompetence and faithlessness of allies. The administration was planning a great expedition against French Canada, to which Louisbourg was always regarded as the key; this was no moment to be thinking of peace. Politically, however, it was necessary to talk of peace to pacify Pelham and his friends, and diplomatically it was necessary to show the Austrians and Dutch that Britain was willing to consider peace, and not unmindful of the sacrifices they made fighting in Flanders while the British swept up the colonial prizes. The ministry therefore decided to open secret peace negotiations with the French; but at least two-thirds of the ministry determined not to take them seriously.[2]

Sandwich was the person chosen to undertake the discussions. Many observers were surprised at the choice of one without any diplomatic experience or qualifications, other than suitable rank and a good command of French, but it made sense in political terms. The choice of one committed to continuing the war reassured the belligerent part of the ministry that he would not choose to take serious steps towards peace; the choice of one so inexperienced ensured that he could be kept under strict control. In any case inexperience was of little consequence if his only duty was to pretend to be willing to negotiate. In one sense therefore Sandwich's task was simple, but politically it was fraught with the risk of serving a disunited ministry which he could only please by being all things to all men.[3] 'I verily believe Lord Sandwich is well intentioned', wrote

Pelham. 'He has a good capacity, great application, and is naturally
cautious, a quality more necessary for himself, than for the business
he goes upon.'[4] Sandwich was well aware of the risks, but 'I am
naturally of an enterprizing disposition', and, he might have added,
ambitious.[5]

He was still more exposed by the nature of his relationships with
the two Secretaries of State. In mid eighteenth-century Britain, when
the position of prime minister was only beginning to surface
above the turbulent waters of politics, the king's chief ministers in
principle were his two Secretaries of State, who shared equally both
foreign and domestic business. In practice, government (as distinct
from Parliament) interfered relatively little in home affairs, and most
of the Secretaries' work was in foreign affairs, which they divided
geographically. The Northern Department took central and northern
Europe; the Southern Department dealt with southern Europe
(including both France and Spain), the colonies, and the Navy. In
this period the Southern Secretary was usually reckoned the more
important, and the Duke of Newcastle was certainly a more powerful
member of the ministry than the Earl of Harrington. If the ministry
were united, or at least if one Secretary were clearly the dominant
partner, this system could generate a united foreign policy, but the
possibility of disagreement, cross-purposes and intrigue was always
present, and the more so when all ministries were alliances of potential rivals, not united by party discipline or a common programme.[6]
Sandwich was going to open his negotiations at Breda in the (technically neutral) Netherlands, part of the Northern Department, so he
received his instructions and made his reports to Harrington, the
weaker and more pacifist of the two Secretaries. At the same time
he was receiving private instructions in a more belligerent sense from
Newcastle, who carried much more weight in the ministry, and who
(unbeknown to his colleague) was getting the king's approval for
what he wrote. Moreover Sandwich was also receiving instructions
and advice from Bedford his patron, whose views differed from
those of both the Secretaries.[7]

In such circumstances it would need great adroitness to satisfy all
parties, and the correspondence necessary to do so was extremely
complex and laborious. The diplomatic convention of the time was
that correspondence between the Secretaries of State and British ministers abroad was conducted in a series of layers: an official despatch
(which might on occasion be disclosed to Parliament or even the
public), was accompanied by a private but official letter amplifying
it (which could be shown to the king and the Cabinet), and often

by one or more secret and private letters (to be shown to selected persons only). That was the bare framework, but in practice, particularly for Sandwich, things were much more complicated. He was conducting a simultaneous correspondence not only with Harrington and Newcastle, but with Cumberland, who was a party to his negotiations, and with Bedford, Anson and other political colleagues. Each of these was in several layers, sometimes as many as four or five, with private letters carefully designed to be 'ostensible', say to the king, or the Cabinet, or to one person only, or to no one but the recipient. Sometimes the most secret letters had to be accompanied by innocuous cover letters which could be produced in case their existence was suspected. In all this it was essential not to confuse the various series of letters 'private', 'very private', 'secret', 'most secret', 'separate' and 'apart' (to say nothing of the crucial distinction between (official) folio and (private) quarto paper); never to forget for whose eyes any one letter was really intended, and apparently intended; what the readers actually knew, and what they were supposed to know. Furthermore all this correspondence had to be kept secure though all governments regularly tampered with diplomatic mail and maintained sophisticated cryptographic offices, and the British Post Office often read the mail of politicians who might be rivals to (sometimes even members of) the ministry.[8] All correspondents therefore took precautions:

> Pray observe & tell me if my letters are looked into, if I write too freely give me a hint, & I will for the future be as innocent & insipid as the Gazette.[9]

It was not unknown for the Postmaster-General to find his own mail opened,[10] while even Newcastle as Secretary of State had to be careful:

> I make use of a safe conveyance of Mr Bentinck's to send you this letter; But I dare say, I need not give you a Caution not to write to me, at any Time, under Mr Bentinck's Cover; For you know the Curiosity of the Post Office.[11]

In the Dutch Republic the post offices were civic or provincial rather than national employments, open to interference by foreign powers – as the British well knew, having several of the key Dutch postmasters in their pay and enjoying regular access to diplomatic mail passing through the Republic.[12] Much of Sandwich's correspondence was therefore sent in cipher, though some letters were evidently designed to be read by unauthorized eyes, while the most confidential matter was only entrusted to messengers – private or unofficial messengers, if it were necessary to keep the existence as well as the contents of the letter secret.

To help him with this complex correspondence, as well as the actual diplomatic business of his mission, Sandwich had his private secretary Robert Keith, and two official secretaries, his cousin Edward Wortley Montagu and the Duchess of Bedford's younger brother Richard Leveson-Gower. Neither knew anything of diplomacy; moreover the Duchess had sent her brother and Lady Mary Wortley Montagu her son in the identical hope that hard work and Sandwich's example would cure them of idleness and extravagance.[13] The young men were well enough to shine at an ambassador's ball,[14] in due course they acquired some useful experience, (and Wortley Montagu, who had studied at Leiden, was the only one on the embassy staff who knew any Dutch) but they could not be trusted with any confidential business.[15] Much of the very voluminous correspondence of Sandwich's mission, including virtually everything of any secrecy, is in his own hand, and he had to do much of his own ciphering and deciphering.[16] Frequently he left a diplomatic meeting in the evening to stay up long into the night writing despatches.[17]

Sandwich began his mission by travelling to the Hague in August 1746, and then to Breda to meet the French representative the Marquis de Puyzieulx, whom by coincidence he had met in Naples on his travels.[18] To travel to Breda sounds simple, but nothing was simple in the world of diplomacy. To maintain George II's credit Sandwich had to find somewhere to live appropriate to his new station, in a pretty but very small town. He was lucky to be offered by the Prince of Orange a 'pavillion' in the grounds of Breda Castle.[19] He had to contrive to arrive there neither before the French plenipotentiary, which would have conceded precedence, nor afterwards, which would have conveyed an insult: he managed to enter the town within an hour of Puyzieulx.[20] He had to supply himself with the retinue needful for a major embassy. He was lucky to be able to obtain one of the best cooks in the country from the Hanoverian minister in the Hague; Keith his secretary later recalled that 'I never saw things better nor in better order'.[21]

Though Sandwich knew the diplomatic situation only in general terms, the French ministry was divided along similar lines to the British, with one party emphasizing the promising military position in Flanders, the other (represented by Puyzieulx) the growing financial crisis. In order to reach a swift decision, Puyzieulx argued that

France and Britain should settle terms between themselves and present their allies with a *fait accompli*. Sandwich, whose business was to delay matters, had instructions to demand the admission of all the allies to the conference. Both sides took it for granted that discussions involving the varying interests not only of France and Britain, but of Spain, Austria, Sardinia, Genoa and the Netherlands (possibly also Prussia and Bavaria) could not fail to be protracted, and might never be completed. Initially Sandwich found it easy enough to stall, but his dealings with his Dutch fellow-diplomats were complicated by the internal politics of the republic, with its complex and highly decentralized constitution and its two bitterly opposed parties. The 'Republican' party then in control represented the neutralist if not pro-French party most likely to make a separate peace, and in fact already planning to do so, though Sandwich did not yet know it for certain.[22] The supporters of George II's son-in-law the Prince of Orange stood for the anglophile, and in the present context belligerent policy which they and the British regarded as the natural and proper one for the republic. They hoped to have the chance to restore the prince to the office of Statholder,[23] the elective quasi-monarchy in which his ancestors William the Silent, Frederick Henry and William III had led their country to victory over the invader. Sandwich had therefore to maintain official relations with the party whom he had every reason to distrust, and private connections with the opposition without, if possible, arousing distrust.

The foreign diplomats who encountered Sandwich for the first time at Breda knew him only as a young politician who had made his name as an opposition speaker. They found him modest and self-possessed, giving away little.[24] Puyzieulx was angry to find he had been drawn into negotiations which threatened to get nowhere, and condemned him as an ignorant amateur, but d'Argenson the French foreign minister offered a rueful tribute to the skill with which he had played his hand,[25] while on cooler reflection Puyzieulx also was impressed:

> Lord Sandwich has an agreeable, almost shy manner. He is laconic and very reserved, self-possessed and shrewd. He is also knowledgeable, but having recently come to diplomacy he has little experience of public affairs.[26]

Throughout the autumn and early winter of 1746 Sandwich's negotiations at Breda continued as unfruitfully as he and his part of the ministry desired. In the autumn Lady Sandwich and his young children arrived to keep him company and preside over the numerous entertainments a diplomat was expected to provide.[27] In October Lord Harrington was blamed for a blunder which disclosed to the Dutch more of Sandwich's instructions than they were supposed to know, and at the same time found out about Newcastle's secret correspondence with Sandwich, and resigned in disgust. He was replaced by the Earl of Chesterfield, a surprising choice as he was identified with the pacific party in both Britain and the Netherlands (where he had long been ambassador) was no friend to most of the ministers, and could not have been under any illusions about the degree of real authority which he would have.[28] Sandwich's parallel correspondence with Newcastle continued as before. In November he became British ambassador to the Hague in addition to his task at Breda, and added another set of correspondence to his responsibilities. By December, with the Austro-Sardinian army advancing into southern France, and plans well advanced for Cumberland to take the field in the spring with a crushing superiority, Newcastle was full of optimism that the diplomatic charade need not be kept up much longer, while even Chesterfield agreed that 'your drinking champagne with Monsieur Puisieux will I believe . . . be your chief business at Breda'.[29] Leveson-Gower for one enjoyed this kind of diplomacy, describing Puyzieulx as 'a very well-bred man, and has the best champaign I ever tasted'.[30] Presently the recall of Puyzieulx and his replacement by Du Theil, one of the senior clerks in the French foreign office, allowed Sandwich to waste some more time by claiming that the appearance of a commoner insulted his rank, and refusing to be mollified until Du Theil received full powers as a plenipotentiary, accompanied by a spurious noble genealogy.[31]

In February 1747 a new dimension to the conferences opened with the arrival of the eccentric Spanish diplomat Melchior de Macanaz, claiming to speak on behalf of the Spanish government, in spite of vigorous denials by the French and no proper credentials. Macanaz, wrote Sandwich, was

> one of the most extraordinary personages I ever met with; he is 77 years old, but of a surprizing vivacity, tho' from what opinion I have as yet been able to form of him I cannot say that I have as yet discover'd any marks of superiour ability . . . he made use of an immense profusion of words in a very unintelligible language half French, & half Spanish . . .[32]

His arrival allowed Sandwich to delay the public negotiations yet further, while opening a private discussion aimed at detaching Spain from her ally and drawing her into a private peace.[33] This made good progress, and by March Sandwich was able to offer his masters the prospect of a diplomatic triumph bought by returning Gibraltar. Discerning observers, especially sea officers, had always thought 'the Golden Image of English Idolatry'[34] vastly over-valued by the British public, and Sandwich agreed, but he realized that his proposal would probably be politically unacceptable and was not without hope that he could persuade Macanaz to give up even Gibraltar for an immediate peace.[35] Meanwhile the negotiation had at least sowed distrust between France and Spain and gained more time. In April he wrote to Henry Pelham,

> I shall allways consider the having delayed the conferences by means of Maccanaz till the opening of the Campaign without putting ourselves in the wrong in point of argument as a very essential circumstance in our favour.[36]

In the same month Anson won a convincing victory over the French fleet, and the diplomatic prospect seemed encouraging everywhere.

For nearly a year Sandwich had played a diplomatic delaying game with a skill and confidence remarkable in one so young and inexperienced. Even Pelham and Chesterfield were now convinced that it had been right to hang on in the hope of victory, and the ministry looked forward eagerly to the opening of the new campaign, and further victories to strengthen their position.

Very soon their hopes began to dissolve. The French armies counter-attacked in Provence and drove back the Austro-Sardinians. In Flanders Marshal Saxe had now overrun almost the whole of the Austrian Netherlands and stood poised on the frontiers of the Dutch Republic. On 17th April, before Cumberland was ready to start his offensive, the French declared war on the Republic and invaded its territory. The immediate consequence was an upsurge of Orangist sentiment leading to a domestic revolution and the installation of the Prince of Orange as Statholder.[37] This was an enormous encouragement to all the British ministers, who expected that the Republic would now appear in the field with all the military strength and vigour that it had displayed under the prince's ancestor William III fifty years before. 'We promise ourselves', Newcastle wrote,

> All the good Consequences, that can be expected from it; a perfect Union, and good Correspondence between the two Nations; and a

Firmness, and Stability, in Measures, which the Republic has never been able to maintain, ever since the late War.[38]

Sandwich was deep in negotiations with the prince's chief adviser Count William Bentinck, and relayed to London encouraging news of a vigorous rearmament programme. Cumberland was unable to take the offensive, the Dutch proved incapable of properly defending the fortresses under French attack, but if the immediate prospect was uncertain, the British were at least confident that things would soon get better.

The conferences at Breda had been suspended when the French declared war on the Republic and the town was no longer neutral or safe. In June and July Sandwich was in England fighting the general election. On 2nd June Cumberland was defeated at the battle of Lafeldt, ending any further hopes of a victorious offensive in 1747. The following month Saxe made an apparently unofficial proposal of peace terms. In September Sandwich had a secret meeting with Puyzieulx in a convent on neutral ground near Liège and agreed to convene a formal peace conference in the imperial city of Aix-la-Chapelle.[39] Meanwhile he was very busy arranging with the Dutch and other allies for an army of unprecedented size to take the field in 1748 and reverse all Cumberland's disappointments. In London, however, disquiet was growing. Newcastle remained firmly optimistic, ignoring the element of caution which had for some time been appearing in Sandwich's despatches,[40] but virtually all his colleagues were in varying degrees now disenchanted with the war, unhappy at the rejection of what Saxe had offered, and sceptical about the size of the forces which the Dutch would really contribute to the allied army in the spring. As a natural result they became cautious about Newcastle's optimistic and belligerent tone, and about Sandwich's reports on which it was based. A divided ministry could not agree on the line to take, and Sandwich returned to the Continent without clear orders.[41] 'We have no plan for either war or peace', Chesterfield wrote,

> The least favourable event inclines us to the former, the least check to the latter, so that we are always either at the top or at the bottom of the house, and the middle floor is always to be let! . . . Far from [Sandwich] having drawn up his own instructions, I can hardly say that he has any; such is our indecision still.[42]

Chesterfield had already sent a personal representative to the Hague – to spy on him, as Sandwich concluded. Much depended on whether Newcastle and Sandwich were right in their assessment of the strength of the Republic. Sandwich as the man on the spot and the close friend of Bentinck had the best opportunities to know. For the moment they carried some conviction; if they were wrong, it would be better to sacrifice Sandwich for a bad peace than blame the Duke of Cumberland. 'This is the time', Newcastle wrote, 'when Men of Art will have the advantage of plain dealers, & plain Speakers'.[43]

In February 1748 Sandwich was formally appointed the British representative at the forthcoming conference at Aix-la-Chapelle. In the same month Chesterfield resigned, Newcastle moved to the Northern Department to supervise the peace conference, and Bedford took over as Southern Secretary. Almost at the same moment Bentinck's brother Charles arrived in London to present the ministry with a devastating document, setting out in appalling detail exactly how bad the Republic's military situation was, and why it needed a loan of a million pounds before it could do anything.[44] Such a loan was out of the question, and the document made Sandwich and Newcastle look complete fools to have committed the British government to another year of war at enormous expense on illusory promises. It was now clear, Bedford wrote, that Dutch finances were worse than British, which were 'in a state very little distant from bankruptcy'.[45] Henry Legge, on his way to take up a diplomatic appointment in Berlin, wrote from the Hague that the Dutch had no idea how many troops they had:

> not that their numbers exceed all Arithmetick, but because they really don't know where they are, who they are, or whether they have any at all. The present tense is utterly unknown in this Country, they still talk altogether in the future, & whenever you press to know the state of their Army the answer always is that provided such & such Events happen (which are not likely) why then by such a time (which will be too late) they shall have a certain number of men in the field.[46]

The diplomatic situation was transformed. Far from holding out for victory, the British had now to conclude as quickly as possible before things got any worse, and everyone was ready to blame Sandwich. Cumberland alone was generous enough to admit that he too had been deceived.[47] It was too late to replace Sandwich at Aix, but he was now regarded in London as a fool, and by Newcastle as the man who had made him look a fool. In characteristically hysterical terms he reproached Sandwich:

> The Mischief is done. The Secret is out. We have depended upon the Prince of Orange's doing That, which He either could not do, or would not do; and what My Lord Chesterfield, and Those who differed from you & I, always, (to do them justice,) said, He could not. But My Lord Chesterfield, Himself, never represented Things so low, as They now appear to be . . . When My Lord Chesterfield affirmed, (as He always did) That the Dutch would not bring 30,000 Men into the Field, I own, I attributed it to prejudice, Passion, and personal Pique, and Resentment. When he told me, that there were but Three Men in all Holland for these Measures, I thought, That proceeded from the same Cause; But now I find, the Dutch can't bring 10,000 Men together, and That the Government seems quite to give itself up, to be protected by their Friends, or, (what I am afraid is most likely,) to be destroyed by their Enemies . . . I own, I think, we have all been in a Dream; for it does not appear to me, That the Republic has an Army at all; or any, That It will, or can, employ. You know, and Every Body here knows, The Dependance upon the boasted Assistance, which we were to have, this Campaign, was the principal, nay the sole, Cause of our Rejecting Marsl. Saxe's Proposals, and Engaging in the immense Expence of this Year . . . You must forgive Me, My Dear Lord, if I am a little warm: I am much provoked with your Dutch Friends. I have stood the Brunt for Them; I have gone thro' what no one Man ever did, from a blind Dependence upon Them; and now I shall be sacrificed for my Ignorance, Obstinacy, and Credulity . . . You will think my letter a Rant, and in some measure, It is so; But when People are hurt, They are not always discreet. Hurt I am; exposed to the Triumph and Derision of my Enemies, and the Good Nature, and Pity of my Friends.[48]

Sandwich had offended one of the most powerful and sensitive men in British politics, and aroused the distrust of the whole ministry. There was no concealing the fact that it was largely his own fault: 'I own I have been in great measure the dupe of those whom I wished to serve'.[49] He now faced an extremely difficult diplomatic task on behalf of a minister and a ministry who expected a great deal from him to redeem his confident assertions, and were ready to blame him for whatever might go wrong.[50] 'If, by any backwardness of yours', Bedford warned, 'a favourable opportunity of concluding a peace should be lost, your country would be undone, and you would be the victim to her resentment'.[51] Almost everything seemed to be against him. The French representative, St Severin, was a wily Italian professional diplomat, and the French armies were soon advancing to the siege of Maastricht, the fall of which on 10th May opened the way for the whole Republic to be overrun. Newcastle, now in an acute panic, begged him to sacrifice anything and everything to make peace at once.[52] The allies were obstructive. The Austrians, who with some justice felt that they had borne the brunt of a war from which Britain alone had benefited, were not inclined to allow Sandwich to negotiate on their behalf, and were already thinking of reaching a private accommodation with France. The Dutch were represented by a delegation of four persons speaking for different parties, of whom only Bentinck was agreeable to him.

In fact Sandwich's position was not quite as weak as it looked, for France's financial crisis laid heavy pressure on St Severin to settle before a new campaign should gather such momentum that the soldiers could not be stopped.[53] Sandwich was shrewd enough to realize it, and bold enough to resist heavy pressure from Newcastle and the other ministers to sign at once on whatever terms he could get.[54] Throughout April he engaged in long and tense negotiations, and finally on 29th he signed preliminary articles of peace. To reach agreement Sandwich had had not only to give up Louisbourg, which had long been inevitable, but several of the interests of his Austrian and Sardinian allies, who were presented with a *fait accompli*. Understandably, he was extremely nervous about the reception his work would receive in London.[55] But the ministers were by now so frightened that they, and more importantly the king, greeted the terms he had achieved as a triumph, which in many respects they were.[56] Though Britain gained no territory by the war, France's enormous conquests were all to be surrendered. What Louis XIV had spent a long reign trying to achieve and Louis XV had actually won, the whole of the Austrian Netherlands, was to be returned to regain the single fortress of Louisbourg.[57] Ministers could not yet see how slight the value of Louisbourg was to prove, but they could already see that they had won a good bargain, and Sandwich's reputation as a diplomat now rose again almost to its former height.[58] 'As decent a peace as could be expected', Legge commented from Berlin, 'not at all worse than we might have had last year; and considering how much worse our pretensions have grown since that time, I think his Lordship has shown great dexterity in bringing us off so well.'[59] Another diplomat, Sir Charles Hanbury Williams, was full of praise:

I can't conclude my letter without declaring my very high opinion of Lord Sandwich's character. It is impossible to behave better than he does, & that behaviour meets with the greatest respect. He is, to a Stranger, visibly the Superiour Minister at this Court. He has great coolness & great fire in him, both subservient to great sense. Count Chavanne, who has here a very good Character and is an amiable and sensible man, talk'd to me of him in raptures, and said he did not believe it possible for a young man, so new in affairs, to have acted so thoroughly both like a man of business & Parts. He must be a great man.[60]

Sandwich was extremely relieved: 'never was comfort more necessary than it was to me when I received your letter,' he wrote to Cumberland, 'for my agitation of mind was such that I was unable to enter into any business'.[61]

By the Duke of Newcastle, however, he was not forgiven; he was still responsible to the duke, and the preliminary articles had to be turned into a definitive treaty. At this juncture the situation was further complicated by George II's insistence that he would visit Hanover that summer, war or no war. In such a case one of the British Secretaries of State had to accompany him, and it was agreed that Newcastle would go. The rest of the ministry were unhappy that their errant colleague should monopolize the king's ear all summer, and Sandwich had particular reason to be uneasy at the prospect of receiving rival instructions from London and Hanover. It was a situation to bring out all the worst in Newcastle's unique character. It has been said of him that he 'combined three characteristics which are seldom found in an individual: he was an extrovert, a hypochondriac, and a paranoiac'.[62] Timid and flustered in manner, insanely vain and jealous, he had yet a long experience of diplomacy, some political gifts, and an insatiable appetite for work, or at least paperwork. His colleagues knew him well and so long as he was among them were able to keep him under control by ceaseless flattery. As soon as he overcame his terror of damp beds and sea travel sufficiently to set out for Hanover he was out of control, and he could speak with the authority of the king.

Even before he arrived at Hanover in the summer Newcastle had taken steps to control Sandwich by the appointment of a colleague to negotiate with him. Sir Thomas Robinson was an experienced diplomat, but his real function was not to assist but to counter Sandwich. Knowing what his master required, he fed Newcastle with sycophantic letters enlarging on the folly of Sandwich, the wisdom of the duke, and the necessity of an experienced and judicious person such as himself to take charge.[63] In the opinion of foreign diplomats, Robinson was considerably less competent than Sandwich,[64] but the necessity of working with him, at least in public, imposed further burdens on Sandwich. Already his task, a large part of which was making the arrangements for the evacuation of the Austrian Netherlands, was acutely complicated by a breakdown of relations with the Austrians. Sandwich had little sympathy for Austrian indignation at the sacrifices they had been forced to make in the Preliminaries, and suspected them of secret dealings with the French. In fact by this time he was convinced that the French were more trustworthy than the Austrians. Events were to prove that he was right, but Newcastle was a devoted adherent of the Austrian alliance and would admit no possibility of bad faith on their part. In effect he insisted that the negotiations must be held up until the Austrians were completely satisfied, which they showed no sign of ever being.[65]

The ministry in London were appalled by Newcastle's behaviour and did all they could to modify it.[66] 'I own, Brother, it has given me great concern', Pelham wrote on 11th August, 'to see you run so fast into declaring, that we will do nothing without the court of Vienna, let them be never so obstinate'.[67] Lord Hardwicke the Lord Chancellor added his characteristic sweet reason:

> We all agree in the end:- to bring in the Court of Vienna. The difference of opinion is about the means of doing it. And is not this a question concerning which, in a transaction so difficult and delicate, with so interested, obstinate and impracticable a Court, men of integrity and abilities may reasonably differ without any disrespect to each other?[68]

But Newcastle was not reasonable, he had the king's approval, and all the ministers in London could do was encourage Sandwich to retrieve the situation somehow. Sandwich offered the duke submission but not servility, justifying his actions and refusing to be browbeaten.[69] He was helped when it became clear that the Austrians had indeed been negotiating secretly with France,[70] and finally in October he was able to conclude the definitive treaty.

From almost all the ministers he received heartfelt congratulations.[71] Even the public generally approved of the treaty,[72] indeed this was the only peace signed by a British government between 1688 and 1815 which did not bring down the government concerned.[73] In a long and latterly a difficult and dangerous negotiation he had acted boldly throughout. Inexperience and over-confidence had badly betrayed him, but he had kept his nerve, played a weak hand with skill, and recovered the situation. 'I am of Ld Anson's opinon', Bentinck wrote, 'you will tumble on your Legs', and so he had.[74] Only Newcastle was not mollified.[75] He convinced himself and attempted to convince everybody else that he alone had made the peace in spite of the blindness and folly of Sandwich and all his ministerial colleagues.[76] In tones of nauseating egoism he congratulated himself to everyone who would listen (a rapidly diminishing number), and condemned Sandwich as fulsomely as he had formerly praised him. Home from the Continent for the Christmas of 1748, Sandwich found himself the hero of the hour in every quarter but one.

CHAPTER IV

A Great Young Man
1746–1751

Sandwich was well aware of the political risks he ran in undertaking the embassy to Breda and Aix-la-Chapelle. Quite apart from the inherent dangers of a formidable task in which it would be easy to offend and difficult to satisfy, a prolonged absence from the centre of the political world was very undesirable for an ambitious young man. He would have to depend on his friends to advance his interests, though in the political world of the day with its constantly shifting alliances, it might be hard to tell from a distance who were still his friends. He would have to depend on them for information by letter, which would certainly involve delay and was fraught with many possibilities of deception, confusion, and indiscretion. 'It is of immense use for one in my situation', he wrote, 'to be apprized what is going on at the fountain head, for without such intelligence a Foreign minister is often obliged to grope his way in the dark.'[1] The reason he undertook the embassy was undoubtedly not for the pleasure of diplomacy as such, though he threw himself into it with the restless energy which marked every activity he engaged in, but for the advantage of attaching himself to Newcastle, one of the most powerful men in politics, and for the chance to distinguish himself by succeeding. The risks involved were considerable, and Sandwich, who was never foolhardy, weighed them carefully, but once he had made up his mind he acted with determined boldness. It was a characteristic which was to mark his whole career.

All the while he was abroad, he was continually working to advance himself, and because he was abroad and obliged to deal in writing, we are well informed about his activities. It is clear, and had no doubt been clear to his friends from the start, that his ambition was to succeed the Duke of Bedford as First Lord of the Admiralty. Bedford was in office from duty rather than inclination or talent; Sandwich had early displayed diligence and ability, and young as he was his hopes were by no means unreasonable. In November 1746 he described it to Bedford as 'the favourite point of my life . . . I am very much mistaken with regard to myself if, after I once get there, I shall ever be solicitous to obtain a remove'.[2] The difficulty was to advance his suit at a distance, and one part of the difficulty was the risk that the duke, always unpredictable and unwilling to work either in political or administrative harness, might resign his position on a whim and retreat to the sylvan pleasures of Woburn. It was essential to Sandwich that the duke should stay at his post until the ground was prepared for him to succeed.[3]

Another key element in Sandwich's plan was his close relationship with Anson. Together they represented a combination of political, administrative and professional qualifications which carried very strong claims; but without Anson, Sandwich would be exposed as a noble amateur in the midst of a war which called for the highest naval abilities; while without Sandwich, Anson would be unlikely to carry sufficient political weight to dominate any Board. Moreover they needed each other for the same reason that they were both so much away from the Board, Sandwich in the Low Countries, and Anson at sea. Anson had therefore the same reason as Sandwich to keep Bedford chained to the oar until they were ready to take over from him, and the same reason to be alarmed when he heard rumours in December 1746 that the duke meant to resign – to be succeeded, very likely, by some third party disagreeable to both of them:

> tho I have long known that your Grace intended to leave Ld Sandwich your Successor I must own that he is the only Person after your Grace that I would act with and cannot help declaring that ever since your Grace made me acquainted with him I have had the greatest esteem and friendship for him, not so much for his Parts, which are equalled by very few but from a thorough conviction that he will upon all occasions act upon the same honest Principles for the good of his Country that your Grace has ever acted, and therefore being no great Politician myself, shall take him for my Pilot and be wholly directed by him.[4]

The relationship of Anson and Sandwich is one of great importance, not only to their political careers at this juncture, but to the modern understanding of what happened to the Navy in the mid-eighteenth century. We have seen that Bedford's Admiralty Board had embarked on a number of important changes and reforms, all of which were under way while Sandwich was on the Continent and Anson was often at sea, and in which they were as fully involved as they could be by post. 'You see tho' I am this distance,' Sandwich wrote from the Hague, 'I cannot help meddling in sea affairs, and indeed I must own that there are my inclinations, & that that is my favourite object'.[5] There has been a tendency among naval historians to give Anson sole credit for these developments, and to speak of him as an honest professional sailor untainted by involvement with sordid politics.[6] This is to misunderstand completely the nature of the system in which he was operating, as well as his relationship with Sandwich. There was no place on an eighteenth-century Admiralty Board for the simple sailor. Anson certainly had high professional merits, which had been the foundation of his success and were still an important component of his political strength, but he sat at the Admiralty and operated on his own and Sandwich's behalf as a politician and not a sea officer. As a politician he has often been underestimated, not least by his contemporaries who found him taciturn, unclubbable and apparently ignorant of the polite world. In fact he was an effective politician, trusted by those with whom he worked, and with a growing consequence of his own. His naval successes had made him wealthy enough to engage with freedom in national politics; in May 1747 after the battle of Finisterre he was made a peer; and in April 1748 he married Elizabeth Yorke, daughter of Lord Hardwicke the Lord Chancellor who formed a vital element of stability and wisdom in every administration for over twenty years. In short he was rising in the political world almost as rapidly as Sandwich, with the same ambition to reach high office, though more talent in concealing it. Moreover it was obvious that his ambitions and talents pointed him towards the same office, First Lord of the Admiralty, as Sandwich was aiming for.

They did not become rivals for several reasons. Neither of them was yet ready to make a push for the top, so they needed to co-operate in keeping Bedford in place. While they were both absent so much from the Board, they had more to fear from others than from each other, and there was one other in particular who was regarded by both Anson and Sandwich as a dangerous rival. Lord Vere Beauclerk had been seldom at sea since he had been a junior officer, but he had been an active Lord of the Admiralty since 1737, and the son of a duke could never be a negligible figure in politics. Moreover he was on the spot, and they had to rely on others to counter his intrigues.[7] Finally it is clear that they genuinely had a high regard for one another's abilities.[8]

In March 1747 Sandwich was still emphasizing in his letters home, that the Admiralty is the point I have allways had in my view, & to which all my purposes both of interest & ambition are directed & I can never be at ease when any thing comes across my road to that favourite object. . . . what I have during my whole life been endeavouring to render myself capable of, & I must own most thoroughly set my heart upon.[9]

Very soon, however, another desirable object presented itself to view (if it had not done so already). His dazzling success as a diplomat, of which the latest example was the Dutch revolution which took place in April, had suggested to the Duke of Newcastle that the young man, still at that point his favourite, might be a possible Secretary of State. The duke had always found it difficult to find Northern Secretaries who could bring to the job the combination of administrative ability, political dependency and personal sycophancy which he required, and it was already clear that Lord Chesterfield was not the ideal candidate. Sandwich was too young to cause trouble, and his success abroad provided a reasonable excuse to talk about his promotion. The prospect of reaching the highest public office before he was thirty would have dazzled a less ambitious man than Sandwich, and he was very willing to entertain the idea. By the end of April 1747 Newcastle was offering encouraging hints in his letters,[10] and Bedford was happy to advance his protégé. In June Sandwich was home in England and the attempt was made.[11] Rumours of his succession appeared in the papers – in an attempt to unseat him, Chesterfield thought.[12]

All this was too much for Newcastle's colleagues. However high their opinion of Sandwich, they did not care to advance the duke's power by installing at his behest so young and so ambitious a client, one who might easily become a rival to any one of them, and whose rise was already provoking jealousy. The high point of confidence in the situation on the Continent and in Sandwich's ability to handle it was by now passed, and ministers did not care to remove Sandwich until he had finished the job. He therefore returned to his post, leaving Chesterfield still in office, but increasingly discontented with Newcastle. 'You judge very right', Chesterfield told a friend, 'in thinking that it must be very disagreeable to tug at the oar with one who cannot row, and yet will be paddling so as to hinder you from rowing'.[13]

When he finally resigned in February 1748 Sandwich's friends made another attempt to push him forward. Newcastle and Bedford were

backed by the Duke of Cumberland, who had conceived a high
opinion of Sandwich while working with him, but opposed by most
of the rest of the ministry.[14] As Anson explained, he was unpopular
mainly because he was seen as an obstacle to peace:

> My sole motive is the esteem I have for you and the great desire I
> have that all the world should think of you as I do, which the last
> contest for Secretary of State has convinced me is not at present the
> case, for there never was more oposition to your advancement in the
> State, which has come only to my knowledge since my coming to
> town, many of your old Freinds opposed you thro Envy, your new
> allies furnished a Competition who would certainly have been the man
> if the D of Bedford had not accepted the Seals, It was not pretended
> that any part of the opposition was from a dislike to Ld Sandwich but
> to the warlike measures he had pursued in which no body else is
> embarked but the D of Newcastle, who it's said have both agreed to
> treat our Generall with another Campaigne before they think of treat-
> ing for peace in good earnest, this rumour does your Credit great hurt
> here, where most people think this country must be ruined if we
> should be obliged to raise the same Supplys for another year, I think
> it will be a dangerous experiment and therefore hope you will not put
> it to the tryall, for I am convinced your putting your hand to a tolerable
> peace will be the rightest and most popular thing you can do.[15]

Those who disliked him worked to refuse him without offending
Bedford and his friends: "twould be pitty to loose them, yett, the
takeing in this man, who is only their freind, will be the ruin of
you'.[16] When it became clear to Newcastle that he was only damaging himself by pushing an unpopular candidate, he managed to effect
a compromise by persuading Bedford to take his post of Southern
Secretary while he moved to the Northern Department. Sandwich
took over as First Lord of the Admiralty in his patron's place, and
Bedford assured him that he was only keeping the seat warm until
Sandwich returned from Aix to be Secretary of State.[17] Anson
appears to have had a large share in securing this solution.[18]

One interesting aspect of this episode is the violent jealousy Sandwich showed for one of his junior Admiralty colleagues, Henry
Legge, who, he was told, had worked on behalf of a rival candidate
for the Secretaryship. Anson pointed out that Legge was only supporting the party to which he had long belonged, as he was bound
to do in honour, and that he showed no personal hostility towards
Sandwich. Sandwich's extreme sensitivity allows us a glimpse

behind the mask of urbanity which he customarily wore.[19]

Meanwhile Lord Vere Beauclerk used the crisis to make another bid to be at the head of the Admiralty Board, putting Anson in an awkward position.[20] Though he was immeasurably superior in professional achievements and merits, he was five years Lord Vere's junior as a member of the Board and two days his junior on the list of flag officers. 'Your Lordship will easily conceive', Anson wrote,

> How disagreeable my situation must be upon the D of Bedfords remove and your Lordships absence, to act under Lord Vere, who I find is determined to continue at the Board, and seem'd pleased with the Change as he imagined your continuance there would not be long.[21]

Anson still needed Sandwich's support, and Sandwich needed him to run the Admiralty for him in his absence. This was the context of a letter from Sandwich to Anson which has sometimes been quoted to suggest that Sandwich was no more than a figurehead at the Admiralty while Anson actually controlled it.

> I would not lose a moment to desire that you would consider yourself as in effect at the head of the Admiralty; that you would not only write to me your sentiments, as to any measures you would wish to have executed, and where my assistance is necessary, but that you would always make use of my name wherever it may be necessary . . . I shall beg you would suffer everything I do to go through your hands, as it is my meaning to throw my share of the power, and the direction of the whole, as much as possible, into your hands.[22]

A fortnight later Sandwich wrote again:

> I am sorry Ld Vere remains at the board if that is in any way disagreeable to you, but I think that so far from his being able to make a cypher of you that you must put him absolutely in that situation himself. I have allways told you that whenever I got to the head of the Admiralty it should except in the name & shew of it be the same thing as if you was there yourself.[23]

But this did not mean that Sandwich was content to be made a cipher. Confident, able and ambitious, he was not the man to allow anyone, however trusted, to take his job over, and for all his genuine confidence in Anson, he was anxious to be home as soon as possible. For this reason he wanted a suitable colleague who could be left at Aix with the mechanical part of negotiating the definitive treaty, without stealing any of his credit, while he returned to the Admiralty. Instead he got Sir Thomas Robinson, and between him, Newcastle and the Austrians he had no possibility of returning to London until the peace was concluded.

Not until 1749, as the Navy was rapidly demobilized, were Sandwich and Anson back together at the Admiralty. We no longer have any significant correspondence between them, and it is necessary to infer from indirect evidence their respective shares in the Board's activities. What is clear is that the reforming impetus with which they had taken office in 1744 was not in the least spent. 1749 was to see the introduction of three important measures, aimed at three of the eighteenth-century Navy's most serious weaknesses. The first of these was the revision of the Articles of War which was brought forward in Parliament as soon as it resumed after Christmas. The Articles provided the basis of naval discipline, and the charges listed in them were the only possible grounds on which a court martial could be brought. They had their origin in a code issued by the English republic in 1652 with the object of cementing the doubtful political loyalties of its officers, and they were in many respects ill-adapted to the needs of the Navy a century later, but the Admiralty did not attempt a complete replacement of them.[24] The new bill proposed a significant tightening of the Admiralty's control in two respects. The latitude allowed courts martial to vary or avoid the penalties prescribed in the act, which had been so openly abused by some of the recent courts ('led away by their private prejudices or narrow principles, to the discredit of themselves, & to the ruin of their profession'),[25] was sharply decreased, so that, for example, cowardice in the face of the enemy was automatically punishable by death (it was this clause which Admiral Byng was later to fall foul of). Secondly the bill included a provision making officers on half-pay liable to trial. This was probably suggested by a similar provision in the army Mutiny Act which was going through Parliament at the same time, and which was strongly supported by the Duke of Cumberland. In both Services the object was to prevent officers escaping trial by resigning their commissions.

This provision aroused a storm of protest. It was alleged that it would allow a future Admiralty Board to compel officers under threat of court martial to accept whatever service was offered them, however disagreeable or dangerous. It has been explained that the concept of honour, as understood by officers of the day, obliged them to serve only in circumstances in which they could sustain their honour with a fair prospect of success. Many officers felt, or at least professed to feel, that a Board made up of enemies personal or political would use this power to ruin their careers. They must also have been aware that it would make it more difficult to feign sudden ill-health on the receipt of unwelcome orders, something to which both Anson and Sandwich were extremely hostile. A chorus of protest arose, directed and encouraged by Captain Augustus Hervey, a young member of the Prince of Wales's coterie. Since, as usual in the eighteenth century, the Prince was on poor terms with his father, and offered a safe haven for politicians who could not otherwise oppose the king's government without appearance of disloyalty, this meant that opposition politicians were exploiting the issue against the government. The connection with Cumberland, with his 'sinister reputation for unconstitutional designs on the throne',[26] encouraged the idea of tyranny which Englishmen naturally associated with the army.[27] Petitions and counter-petitions were raised, attempts at compromise failed,[28] and finally the strength of Parliamentary opposition persuaded the government to withdraw the offending clause.[29]

So Sandwich's Board failed to get as far as they had hoped in reforming the discipline of the Navy. Meanwhile they had turned their attention to a still more critical problem: manpower. Many of the characteristics, and many of the problems of eighteenth-century navies arose from the fact that, unlike armies then or navies today, they were largely demobilized in peacetime. The ships spent years decaying slowly, or not so slowly, in reserve; the officers, especially the senior officers, spent years ashore forgetting their profession; and the seamen dispersed to their usual employment in merchant ships. No state contemplated interfering with the mechanisms of the free market to make seamen, beyond the encouragement of certain trades (notably the Newfoundland fisheries) which were conventionally regarded as 'nurseries of seamen'. Since a skilled deep-sea sailor was the product of years of training, usually from early boyhood, it was too late on the approach of war to begin training fresh men, and the supply available to any navy was the number created by the peacetime demands of the merchant fleet. Every naval power found this number inadequate to meet wartime demands, and none discovered a solution to the problem. Shortage of skilled manpower was always the most serious constraint on naval expansion for all navies. The French, with the traditions and resources of an absolute monarchy, had established a system by which the seafaring population of coastal districts was registered for compulsory naval service, in theory in rotation. In practice full mobilization required all the men who could be found, and merchant shipping was at times halted altogether. Such arbitrary tyranny, such interference with the rights of commerce, was unthinkable in Britain, where the haphazard tyranny of the press gang reflected the weakness of government and its inability to impose any regulated system on the labour market for seafarers.[30]

Though the French system did nothing to increase France's total stock of seamen, it did work faster and more smoothly in the initial stages of mobilization, and it was well understood to confer a limited but important advantage. Throughout the eighteenth century British Admiralties hoped to find some scheme, politically acceptable and administratively practical, which would at least give the British Navy an equivalent advantage in the opening stages of a war. Sandwich's Board was the latest to tackle the problem. In April a bill was proposed which would have established a species of naval reserve. The Navy Estimates for the year proposed a force of 17,000 men, and the bill suggested that a further 3,000 should receive a retainer of £10 a year to hold themselves available. Since the Navy's maximum strength in the previous war had been nearly 60,000 this was a small step, but it would have been the first and most difficult step, the precedent on which later increases might have been founded. It was for just this reason that it was opposed in the House of Commons as a dangerous assault on English liberty, as a design to make so many slaves and dependents, to be followed in due course by many more. The administration decided that the time was not ripe for so contentious a measure, and the bill was dropped.[31] Another aspect of manning the Navy to which Sandwich turned his mind was the Marine regiments, now under Admiralty control but still on their old, unsatisfactory footing. With the powerful backing of the Duke of Cumberland, he floated the idea of replacing them with a corps without a regimental structure but made up of individual companies.[32] This too proved to be an idea whose time was not yet ripe; the marine regiments were disbanded, but the new, permanent Corps of Marines was not established until the approach of the next war in 1755.

In its attempts to improve the manning and discipline of the Navy the new Admiralty achieved little, but while it was engaged in these attempts its attention was also turned to the civil side of the Navy, and in particular to the management of the dockyards. Henry Pelham as finance minister was working to reduce the national debt, raised to alarming heights by the war, and putting the Admiralty under heavy pressure to save money. Newcastle, estranged from his brother and anxious to recruit Cabinet allies, even made friendly references to Sandwich when writing to those whom he thought would agree:

> We have now (without a compliment) at the head of the Navy a very able and a very honest man, diligent and understanding in his business; and I doubt not but he will take the best measures to answer our ends in this respect: but money is wanting for this, as for all other necessary expenses; and I hear *the Treasury* complain already, that the expense of the fleet *only*, for the ensuing year, amounts to three shillings in the pound, Land Tax; which (common report says) is all that is to be laid upon the land.[33]

This political pressure for economy reinforced the Admiralty's desire for administrative reform. The Board's bruising encounters with the Navy Board in 1745 had left them more cautious but no less determined to enforce some measure of control and some increase in efficiency. In March 1749 Sir Jacob Acworth at last died and Captain Haddock was persuaded to retire; the war was over and the time was ripe for another attempt. It must already have been clear to Sandwich that the Navy Board's monopoly of information was the key to its position. Years later he remarked that,

> In the various offices in which I have had the honour of serving the Crown, I have always found that 'til I understood the business thoroughly myself, I was liable to imposition, and fearfull of taking any thing upon myself; and therefore I have ever made it my first Object to get free from these Shackles, as fast as I could, by making myself Master of what I was to undertake. I then acted without fear, and probably have not exposed myself so much as I should have done, if I had not acted upon that foundation.[34]

So the Board decided on a simple but revolutionary move. On 9th June 1749 their Lordships,

> taking into their consideration the number of Men Borne in the several Dock and Ropeyards, the great Expence Attending the same, And that the Works are not carried on with the Expedition that might be expected from them, which must arise from the remisness of the Officers, or Insufficiency of the Workmen, or both,[35]

decided to visit the dockyards themselves. Since even the Navy Board never visited the yards as a body, and seldom went further than Deptford and Woolwich as individuals, this gave the Admiralty the opportunity to outflank the Navy Board's superior experience with first-hand knowledge. It might be thought that on a pre-arranged visit they would have seen only what they were supposed to see, but it was not so. At Woolwich they 'Walked around the Yard to Observe the Workmen, many of whom were Idle, which the Officers were directed to take Notice of, found the Timber and Plank not regularly sorted, in many Places that which had been longest in Store, being undermost'.[36] Visiting the ships in reserve they found them,

> in very bad Condition little or nothing having been done since they were Paid Off; In some of the Great Cabbins were Fires, and Victuals cook'd in them, and not only Inhabited by the Officers, but Women and Children also, contrary to the many Standing Orders, none of which were hung up in any of the Ships as directed, and on Enquiry amongst the Officers of the Ships found the Officers of the Yard, had not been to View or Muster them, and that the Moarings had not been Overhawled in three years. Intending to Discourse with the Master Attendant on the bad Condition the Ships and Moarings lay in, found him Incapable of Business, or Performing any Sort of Duty.[37]

At Deptford they found the victualling stores falling down and most of the senior officers away; at Sheerness the chaplain of the yard had been absent without leave over twelve months and the Storekeeper was too gouty for duty; at Chatham they saw shipwrights 'carrying out Top Ends and Slabs [of timber], in the Officers presence, not-withstanding the strict Orders to the Contrary'.[38] Everywhere they found buildings and docks decayed, stores in confusion, yard officers too old or ill to do their duty, accounts long in arrears, ships in reserve neglected, and artificers diverted from their proper work to the offices, if not to the private houses of the officers.[39] They also found some things to praise: at Woolwich the Storekeeper and the Master Ropemaker had their departments in excellent order, and at Portsmouth things were generally satisfactory.[40]

One theme concerned the Admiralty at all the yards; task work. Most men in the yards were paid by the day, but Sandwich and his colleagues were very interested in the possibility of improving productivity by going over to piecework, and at every yard they questioned the yard officers on the subject. At Woolwich they saw men working by task work in the stores doing as much work in four and a half days as day labourers did in ten.[41] At Plymouth,

Lord Sandwich, Lord Barrington and Lord Anson discours'd the Builder Mr Slade about employing the Workmen by Task Work. Lord Sandwich said, as it is now, it was impossible to come at the True Value of Building a Ship. Lord Anson said it would be better to build New Ships than to lay out a great deal of Money in repairing Old Ones, and that if a Ship wanted more repair than a Quarter of her Value, he would be for Pulling them to Pieces.[42]

The result of the Admiralty's visitation was a series of detailed orders to the Navy Board issued in November.[43] They caused consternation among the yard officers whose privileges were to be curtailed:

Not a labourer or waterman to come within your doors or to send a boat anywhere upon private business; to be dismissed from your employment upon the least information of breaking that and many other such orders. Storekeeper's and Clerk of the Survey's boats taken from them. Poor Phillipps running mad for the loss of the yachts.[44]

In the long term, however, the effectiveness of these orders was very little. In December 1751 the Navy Board had still not responded to several of them, and it did not respond to the reminder.[45] It reissued its standing orders, but ignored instructions to supplement them, and did little or nothing to reduce the costs or increase the efficiency of the yards.[46] Admiralty orders that bricklayers, joiners and sailmakers should work by task were ignored or evaded, and in 1752 the Navy Board bluntly declared that it was 'against any innovation, more especially the attempting to build any thing whatever by Task'.[47]

In spite of the opportunity to appoint its own men to key positions, the Admiralty found that it was no match for the entrenched conservatism of the Navy Board, but Sandwich had at least found a method which potentially could outflank that Board's expertise. It seems reasonable to attribute it to Sandwich and not Anson, since Anson spent eleven years as First Lord, five of them in peacetime, without once visiting the yards. All we know of their respective interests and competences suggests that this Admiralty's initiatives in the fields of discipline and manning were at least in part owing to Anson's knowledge and enthusiasm, but that he was never especially interested in the running of the yards. It may be significant that in May 1748 Anson wrote to Sandwich:

you have almost brought the office of Admiralty to be a sinecure for all our last orders are sent so that there remains nothing but to dis-

ma[n]tle our ships, a greivous affair to me for I shall never live to
see so well disciplined and compleat a Squadron as we have to the
Westward.[48]

Sandwich never thought the peacetime Admiralty was a sinecure,
but when Anson became First Lord in 1751 the Admiralty's efforts
to reform the yards were allowed to run down. Sandwich had added
considerably to his own unpopularity with Pelham at the Treasury
by his efforts to keep up the strength of the peacetime fleet,[49] but
Anson was more accommodating. It has been strongly argued that
in the five years which elapsed before the outbreak of the Seven
Years War the ships of the Navy were neglected, and that Anson's
undoubted triumphs as a fleet commander and a wartime leader of
the Navy have obscured the fact that like most admirals he was
neither knowledgeable nor interested in its civil administration.[50]

As First Lord, Sandwich had made a promising beginning, but he
had done more to reveal the difficulties than to solve them. In part
this was because of the weakness of his political position. He had
risen on the patronage of Newcastle, who was now his enemy, and
of Bedford, whose idle and unbusinesslike management as Secretary
of State (to say nothing of his pacifist and francophile views) infuriated both his colleagues and the king. He had risen so fast, and at
such a young age, that he had inevitably aroused a great deal of
jealousy; 'an ambitious, interested, warm young man', people called
him, 'ready to make his court at any rate.'[51] In June 1748 he was
warned that,

> you are look'd upon as a man of too much Weight, & Consequence
> to be left at Liberty near the Throne. . . . of late it has been the echo
> from their [the Pelhams'] dependents and table deckers – 'that Lord
> Sandwich is a great young man & no doubt will make a great figure
> in the Governmt but it seems rather too soon for him to be setting
> up for himself & making parties of his own'.[52]

He had also become a friend of Cumberland, who was unpopular
in several quarters, particularly the Prince of Wales's circle. All these
factors left him exposed, but so long as Newcastle was still at odds
with the rest of the Cabinet he felt reasonably secure.

'Upon the whole I am perfectly easy in my situation & tho' I know
that there is one preson in great power, who will never forgive me,
yet his present behaviour to me plainly shews that he finds me to
be out of his reach.'[53]

The situation became much more dangerous when Newcastle and his brother were reconciled in January 1751.[54] Bedford's colleagues were now resolved to be rid of the duke, but he refused to go unless his young follower could replace him as he had originally intended. This was no longer politically feasible, as Sandwich could see clearly, and he worked hard to persuade the duke to resign before worse befell. His fears were justified; the Pelhams decided to dismiss Sandwich as a means of getting at Bedford, who duly took the bait and resigned in fury at the insult.[55]

Sandwich had fallen as swiftly as he had risen. In wartime he had been able to make opportunities for himself; in peacetime they had evaporated. In seven years he had passed from obscurity to high office and back again. His brief and spectacular career perfectly illustrates what could and could not be done in eighteenth-century politics with ability alone.[56] So long as he was useful to great men, he was favoured and advanced, but when he had served his purpose he was expended as a pawn in a political gambit. Lacking the wealth and great estates which made leading politicians even of such unpromising material as Bedford and Newcastle, Sandwich aroused envy rather than loyalty, as his former colleague Bentinck commented:

> Sandwich has ruined himself in the eyes of the public by revealing a limitless ambition to which he has sacrificed everything, with no scruple in his choice of methods. Moreover he is not a great enough magnate to support a party in the way that the brothers Newcastle and Pelham can with their great estates, their connections, the great number of their friends, and above all their personal character and the confidence of the public.[57]

It is not necessary to take these suggestions of bad faith literally; they were the inevitable penalty of success in an age when intrigue was the usual mechanism of politics,[58] but the penalty was real enough nevertheless. Ambition and ability without broad acres and wealth were indecent reasons for claiming high office.

CHAPTER V

Expense of Spirit
1751–1763

Out of office, Sandwich returned to Hinchingbrooke in June 1751. It was not a grand house, and had no park to speak of, but it was comfortable and attractive, and he took pains to fit it up.[1] 'I am not surprised that Hinchinbrook pleases you so well,' wrote one of his cousins,

> or that you are of opinion that it is capable of being made a fine place, it stands upon an eminence and commands a fine prospect, which those that made the Terrass well knew. The venerable old elms in the road are very ornamental, and the wood at the bottom of the garden is pretty as is also the plantation in the Park.[2]

Horace Walpole thought the same:

> a very commodious, decent, irregular old House, much of it built in the time of Queen Elizabeth . . . not an ugly spot for Hunting-donshire.[3]

Here Sandwich retreated with his young family. He now had four children. His first child, John, was born in December 1742 and died soon after. His eldest surviving son (also John), who as his heir took the title of Lord Hinchingbrooke, followed in January 1744. Thereafter came Edward, born in June 1745, his only daughter Mary in February 1748, and William Augustus in February 1752.[4] Sandwich had hopes that Edward ('a complete beauty' his godmother called him) might go to sea with his godfather Lord Anson, but he died at the age of seven.[5] Lady Sandwich had for some time been worried about 'dear little Monty's' cough, so his complaint was probably the same consumption which was to kill his younger brother.[6] She and the children ('with whom', wrote Sandwich, 'I have too much private comfort to wish to live in a state of separation')[7] spent two years following their father's diplomatic career on the Continent. They joined him at Breda in the autumn of 1746,[8] and stayed until two months before Mary's birth, returning by a hazardous mid-winter voyage.[9] In June 1748 Lady Sandwich returned to Aix,[10] holding assemblies every evening; 'the fatigue of business makes them think amusement the more necessary, and they are extremely gay here'.[11] The round of diplomatic entertainments was a competitive business:

> The Sunday before last there was a most magnificent gala, a dinner, supper and ball at the French ambassador's on account of St Louis's day, where I assure you I was much charmed by the unaffected liveliness and gaiety of the French . . . Last Sunday we had a second part of the same comedy by the Dutch on account of the Prince of Orange's birthday; besides a dinner and supper, there was a ball at the Maison de Ville, which of itself is very magnificent, and was finely decorated by Mr Vanharen.[12]

The strain was such that Lady Sandwich was obliged to part with 'one of the greatest comforts of my life, my Dear Hinchy', not being able to look after him properly.[13] He was sent to board with his father's old master Dr Dampier at Eton, at four years old, and he remained there even after his parents had returned to England.[14]

This seems curious behaviour in a mother who always wrote of her children in terms of the warmest affection, and perhaps it was the first sign of something wrong in the Sandwich household. Hitherto, as we have seen, they had been regarded as a model couple to be imitated, and in 1749 there is an admiring reference to Lady Sandwich's devotion in rushing back to London from Tunbridge Wells on hearing that her husband was ill,[15] but by the summer of 1751 her pregnancy was regarded by their friends as 'a very extraordinary piece of news'.[16] That September Sandwich wrote her a long letter which shows that their marriage was under strain:

> I wish anything I could say had any Probability of removing those fatal Prejudices which frequently occasion so much Uneasiness to both of us, if that could be effected, I am very certain I could make you happy, & the Consequence of that would be that I should be very happy myself . . . Suppose me never so much in Fault what can it avail you to have it said that you have been illused, & that all the Misfortunes that your Family is brought into are owing to my bad Conduct, & not to yours; that is the only Satisfaction you can expect from the continuance of your present Behaviour to me; for I don't pretend to disguise it, the Supposition of my having used you ill, &

being upon very ill terms with you prevails very generally, & is the chief Weapon in the Hands of my Enemies, & without your Assistance nothing that I can say or do can prevent the ill Consequences of that Report, & however I may be satisfied in my own Conscience that my Conduct is, & has been irreproachable, the World can never see it in that Light, since the Part you are now acting continues all the Appearance against me . . . It is my Request that all subject Matter of Complaint may be buried in Oblivion on both sides . . . that we may take the only sure Method of convincing the World that we live well together, which is by really doing so . . . I do declare that I still love You sincerely, & that I am convinced that a little Condescension now & then on your Side to my Humours, & the Proof of an Inclination to please me, will in a very short time give you that entire Empire over me that your many good & valuable qualities deserve.[17]

The letter tells its own painful story, or at least part of its own story. What it does not reveal, and was probably not yet clear to those involved, is that Lady Sandwich's mind was failing. In the summer of 1751 she was oppressed by an unnamed trouble which might have been relations with her husband, or the illness of her son Edward: 'I can give you no good account of the welfare of a person without whose welfare and happiness I can never hope to have any real pleasure. We have great hopes given us but truly I see little if any amendment: this melancholy prospect goes very deep'.[18] There is some suggestion that the trouble started with what is now called 'post-natal depression', and after the birth of William Augustus her brother took her away to the country, from 'an apprehension of an immediate shock on her spirits and a desire to prevent it'.[19] It is certain that the illness was for many years intermittent and did not prevent her from keeping up lucid correspondence at least as late as 1758,[20] but she refers to the violent headaches which seem to have been a symptom of her trouble, and in oblique terms to, 'a terrible weakness remaining in the part [the head] that I always wish the strongest, & more particularly so when I attempt to converse with you'.[21] In 1755 the couple parted for ever. Lady Sandwich was initially granted an apartment in Windsor Castle with her unmarried sister, near to Eton where her sons were at school, but her daughter remained with Sandwich at Hinchingbrooke.[22] Lady Sandwich's mental condition continued to decline. A number of formal letters from Sandwich written in 1764 and 1765 about financial business show that by then she was incapable of handling her own affairs and needed constant supervision.[23] By September 1766 the doctors had abandoned hope for her, and in 1767 she was formally declared by the Court of Chancery to have been insane for upwards of two years, and made a ward of court.[24]

Throughout these melancholy developments, Sandwich's relations with his brother-in-law, who had become Lord Fane on his father's death in 1744, remained good. A lawsuit between them over the terms of the father's will seems not to have bred bad blood; probably like many Chancery suits it was rather an appeal to the court to set up a trusteeship than a real dispute.[25] When Sandwich lost office in 1751 Fane granted him an annuity of £1,000 a year, and their dealings at the time Lady Sandwich was finally confined remained friendly:

> Your Lordship may be assured that from principles of humanity, as well as from the respect & gratitude I shall ever bear your Lordship and your Family, every degree of attention will be shewn by me to this unfortunate person, & that I may be the more certain of doing nothing but what is right, allow me most earnestly to sollicit your advice, which you may be assured shall be the rule that shall direct my Conduct.[26]

In September 1765 Sandwich sent him a long account of his sister's condition:

> I am sorry to tell you that I see no appearance of poor Lady Sandwich's amendement in any particular, but I fear she is if anything, more intractable & unfortunate in her disposition than ever . . . I flatter myself I need not tell your Lordship how much this shocking scene distresses me . . . No care or attention is wanting towards her, she has a very decent house, & every necessary in it; proper servants to attend her who are directed to let her want for nothing.[27]

His wife's condition was not only a private grief for Sandwich but also a shadow on his family's future. In September 1765 he confided to a close friend that he was oppressed by two considerations:

> the state of Lady Sandwich & the consequences of it, & the present state of my finances. As to the first I find no appearance of her growing better, and I perceive the impression that I allways feared it would make on the world has had its effect; I have a scheme of a very proper and advantageous match for my son (which possibly may take place) which if it did would make him well in the world & extricate me out of all my difficulties, but the situation of his mother and of some of her near relations is mentioned as an objection, indeed I do not wonder at it, tho' there is not the least appearance in his disposition of anything like the turn of mind of the female line of his family.[28]

Even his cousin and old schoolfellow Lord Halifax might hesitate to marry his daughter into a family with insanity on both sides. However the match between Hinchingbrooke, now twenty-two, and Lady Betty Montagu did in fact take place the following year.[29] Like Sandwich's own marriage, it started auspiciously and ended in tragedy. Lady Hinchingbrooke died in 1768, leaving an infant son John George. He married in March 1790 and was dead in eight months, within the lifetime of both his father and grandfather, leaving no heir. Hinchingbrooke was married a second time in 1772, to the daughter of the Duke of Bolton, who bore him two sons before dying in 1779. The one who survived, George John, was eventually to inherit and transmit the earldom.[30] Sandwich's youngest son William Augustus, after what appears to have been a wild youth, settled down as a lawyer and showed great initial promise, but developed consumption and died at the age of thirty.[31] Sandwich therefore had three legitimate sons, two grandsons and one great-grandson, but only one of each generation survived to carry on the family, and three of the six died in his lifetime.

Sandwich's other worry in 1765 was the state of his finances, and they remained a worry throughout his life. Like most men of property, he had inherited his estates 'entailed', so that he could enjoy the income but not touch the capital. Those in this situation who needed to raise capital to invest or improve their properties, and those who needed to pay off debts, had little alternative to borrowing, usually on mortgage, and enormous debts were commonplace among the great landowners. Newcastle, whose estates brought in about £27,000 a year, spent his whole long career in acute financial difficulties, and died owing over £114,000.[32] The Duke of Marlborough owed the Duke of Bedford £60,000 in the mid-1750s.[33] People with money were willing to lend because the land represented an excellent security even if could not be sold for a generation, and the rental was a good cover for the interest in the meanwhile. The same was true of credit from tradesmen and suppliers. In an age when wages and salaries were paid quarterly in arrears at best, the giving of credit was a normal part of any business, and the landowner, however embarrassed for ready money, was a good credit risk in the long term.

It is not absolutely clear if Sandwich's estates came to him from his grandfather already mortgaged, but there were certainly mortgages going back to 1740, immediately after he came of age, and in 1751 his Huntingdonshire estates were carrying a mortgage of £8,000 from

the great Jewish financier Samson Gideon, which probably represents an inherited burden.[34] This was serious for him because his
property was, for an English earl, very small. His private income in
1748 was only about £3,500 a year, quite insufficient for a peer with
a rôle in public life.[35] His friend the Duke of Bedford, by comparison,
had an income at this date of about £56,300, and Bedford's brother-
in-law Lord Gower enjoyed rather over £20,000.[36] Near the end of
Sandwich's life the Huntingdonshire estates were valued at £61,082,
producing £6,470 a year,[37] but another valuation at almost the same
time reckoned the annual income at only £4,980. 14s. 5d., which
after forty years of rising prices was less in real terms than in 1748.[38]
He often asserted that, 'though I have not much, thank God I have
enough for a private man; and I know by experience I can live very
contentedly upon it'.[39] His problem was that he had no desire to
remain a private man.

For this reason his income as ambassador at Breda and Aix was
of acute concern to him. Eighteenth-century ambassadors received
what were, on paper, very large salaries, but out of them they had
to pay most of their staff and the entire expenses of their embassies,
including the obligatory lavish entertainments.[40] It was usually
reckoned that an ambassador rather lost than gained by his employment – and Sandwich urgently needed to gain. Furthermore as the
king's representatives, ambassadors were paid from the Civil List,
and George II had not forgotten Sandwich's attacks on his beloved
Hanover.[41] The result was that he spent his two years abroad in a
continual struggle to get a salary adequate to maintain his position,
to say nothing of two establishments, one at the Hague as ambassador, and one at Breda, later Aix, as plenipotentiary. His house at
Aix alone cost nearly £800 a year.[42] Because the king denied him the
service of silver plate normally allowed an ambassador, he had to
make do with some of his own and some borrowed from his brother-
in-law, and even then he had to scrounge more whenever he had a
large company to dine.[43] His total earnings from his diplomatic mission were £14,850, but his outgoings were evidently higher.[44] In
January 1748 he reckoned his total salary to be £7,000 a year, of
which £1,500 was as a Lord of the Admiralty, but his diplomatic
expenses were greater than £5,500.[45] The result was that having 'lived
tolerably well during the whole time of the congress', he still gave
foreign diplomats the impression of meanness.[46] In August 1748 he
wrote to Anson, 'I hear one of your messengers is gone off with
£800. I hope it is not with my salary, for I am poorer than ever I
was in my life'.[47]

It was for this reason if no other that he was attracted by the prospect of becoming Secretary of State, for the Secretary earned at least twice as much as the First Lord. In moving from one to the other in 1762 George Grenville claimed to have dropped from over £8,000 to only £2,000 a year.[48] This was perhaps exaggerated; a more careful calculation by his successor put the Secretary's income at £7,480 less the wages of his clerks, while the First Lord usually received £3,000, but the difference was still substantial.[49] So was the difference between public and private life, for just as First Lord Sandwich was nearly doubling his private income.

It was not until 1757 that 'that everlasting Grandmother of yours'[50] in Paris finally died. In spite of her distaste for his politics she left everything to him, but he had difficulty in obtaining her property in Paris, as it was wartime and French law consigned the whole property of enemy nationals to the Crown. Through the good offices of the Marquis de Puyzieulx, Sandwich had long since obtained an order exempting him from this *droit d'aubaine*, but he had great trouble getting it enforced.[51]

His grandmother's will was one of Sandwich's few pieces of financial good fortune. His wife's insanity was an unmixed disaster. Her establishment cost £600 a year, which was more than her join-ture, so that both her brother Lord Fane and her husband were paying to support her.[52] As a married woman her fortune would normally have been at her husband's entire disposal, saving whatever was secured to her as a jointure by her marriage settlement, but as a lunatic she was a ward of the Court of Chancery. This mattered because, against expectations, she became a considerable heiress. Lord Fane died childless in 1766, by which time two of his sisters had also died single, and as a result Dorothy and her married sister Mrs de Salis inherited the whole Fane estates. This was just the opportunity Sandwich needed to realize some capital and pay off his debts, but his wife's condition prevented it. Chancery allowed him only an income of £1,500 a year, for which he had to account in detail.[53] A private act of Parliament was needed to sell Fane's Berk-shire estate in 1771, which raised £22,840, worth about £1,000 a year, out of which he had to pay £840 a year in settlements to the two sisters.[54] Even this manoeuvre was nearly wrecked when his half-brother Henry Seymour (son of his mother's second husband), one of the trustees of the estate, took offence at something said by Lord Hinchingbrooke in the House of Commons, resigned the trust and brought a Chancery suit against Sandwich.[55] The much more valuable Irish lands of the Fanes, worth £5,190 a year, remained in trust, and yielded Sandwich only £1,800 when Lady Fane and Mrs de Salis had had their shares.[56]

Sandwich's other financial hopes mostly came to nothing. His cousin Edward Wortley Montagu, who had talked of leaving him his property (much of it originally Sandwich's grandfather's), left him only £1,000.[57] His son's marriage to Halifax's daughter was equally a disappointment to him. He had hoped to take her fortune himself, pay off his debts, and in return settle his estate on Hinching-brooke, but Halifax would not consent, and he was obliged to settle a rent-charge of £2,000 a year on the couple instead (which they complained was too little to live on). To pay for the wedding he had to borrow £2,500 from Halifax.[58] This debt caused a crisis when Halifax, needing to recoup his losses in the Northampton election, suddenly demanded it back in 1769,[59] and when he died in 1771 he left little to his son-in-law and grandson.[60] Hinchingbrooke's second marriage to Lady Mary Powlett brought £22,000, most of it in trust, and eventually a further inheritance, but none of this benefited Sandwich personally, and much of it only reached his family long after his death.[61] Thus Sandwich's attempts to raise capital came to nothing, and he suffered recurrent financial crises. In 1758 he borrowed £20,000 on mortgage from the Earl of Bath.[62] When Bath unexpectedly foreclosed on his mortgage in 1764, Sandwich was lucky to be able to persuade Sir Laurence Dundas to take it on, together with further mortgages for another £10,000, at 4 per cent rather than 5 per cent.[63]

It is surprisingly difficult to be sure why Sandwich's financial position was so poor. He himself referred to having damaged his fortune by 'indiscretions', but this need mean no more than misjudgements, and we do not know of what kind.[64] The most obvious and likely explanation is simply that he continued to live the life of a public man on the income of a country squire. In 1761, for instance, he was trying to dispose of the lease of his London house in Pall Mall, which cost £420 a year including rates and taxes[65] – a necessary luxury for the would-be Cabinet minister, but hardly one he could afford. At Aix in 1748 he had excused the excesses of young Leveson-Gower with a reference to 'the impossibility for a man of spirit to make a proper figure without unlimited credit at home',[66] and to make a proper figure in public life was expensive. This leads to the consideration of public life's most characteristic activity in this period, gambling. 'I did not design to play at all,' Bedford once wrote to his wife from Bath, 'but without it there is no possibility of knowing how to employ one's time'.[67] Short of retirement to a hermitage, there was no way of avoiding gambling. For a diplomat it was a professional necessity; at Breda and the Hague 'we have assemblys every night where whist is the only fashionable game'.[68] Everywhere social life revolved around the gaming table:

> Cards, betting, dice, opened every nocturnal orgie with an *éclat* of expectation, hope, ardour, and fire, that seemed to cause a mental inflammation of the feelings and faculties of the whole assembly in a mass.[69]

'Extravagance, Luxury & Gaming', wrote an officer in 1771,

> are all the fashionable vices of the town & it will astonish you on your return to see the vast Improvement of the Age. The Coterie, Macaroni's, White's, Almac's &c are in the most flourishing state, & cards in all companies are the only things worth living for – A man of taste must play all the morning or at least four or five games before dinner, which is shortened to give time for the exquisite pleasures of Quinze & Vingt-Un.[70]

We could therefore take it for granted that Sandwich gambled, even if we did not have occasional references to confirm it.[71] 'They are going on here in pretty much the same numbers as last year,' a friend wrote from Hinchingbrooke in the summer of 1756,

> & in just the same manner of gambling; tho' hitherto our meeting has been quite sober. I don't mean that as any reflection upon any person that is absent, I believe the reason is our having been many of us out of order, for the day your Grace left us at Woburn, both Vernon & Waldegrave were taken ill, and Lord Gower tells me he had been out of order too in Staffordshire, so that Sandwich's Claret seems in a fair way of being spar'd this year.[72]

What seems unlikely is that Sandwich played for high stakes. It was an age of extravagant losses, when 500 guineas in a night was unremarkable, and 3,000 quite possible, when a midshipman could lose £100,000 and win back £90,000, and when the brothers Stephen and Charles Fox lost £32,000 between them in three nights.[73] 'It is dreadful,' wrote Sir George Lyttelton,

> to see not only here, but in almost every house in town, what devastations are made by that destructive fury, the spirit of Play! The time, the fortunes, the honour, and the consciences of our nobility and gentry, both male and female, are all falling a prey to it.[74]

In such a climate commonplace imprudence scarcely attracted notice, and it is not conclusive that Sandwich's contemporaries, some of whom were prepared to repeat, and even to believe, the most unlikely charges against him, did not accuse him of gambling to excess, but it is suggestive. It is significant that he did not join those who played for high stakes when they seceded from White's club to found Brooks's in 1764; he only became a member of the latter in 1785 when it had become the headquarters of the Parliamentary opposition.[75] We can be fairly sure that had he lost much or often the fact would have been recorded, but we cannot rule out smaller losses.[76]

With the parallel fashion for wagers we are on surer ground, since they were so often recorded. We find Sandwich laying bets of a few shillings with neighbours on the distances between places in Huntingdonshire, and twenty-four guineas to twenty with the Duke of Bedford on the outcome of an election.[77] He wagered fifty guineas that the transvestite French diplomat and spy the Chevalier d'Eon was not a woman, and five guineas against fifty that Edmund Burke would never become a Privy Councillor.[78] In forty-four years as a member of White's he figures in the crowded betting book three times; once for twenty guineas, once for an unnamed sum, and once participating in a twenty-guinea sweepstake.[79] This was not the way to acquire a reputation as a gamester in the eighteenth century, nor to dissipate even a modest fortune.

What references we do have suggest that he usually gambled in the natural course of other activities which were his real enthusiasm. Cricket, for instance, (described by a modern authority as 'a full-blooded financial brawl') was usually played for money and always accompanied by betting.[80] In 1741 Bedford noted, 'Lord Halifax and Lord Sandwich play the counties of Huntingdon and Northampton against the county of Bedford for 1 guinea a man and 10 guineas over 11 of a side'.[81] When the Old Etonians with Sandwich as captain played All England at Newmarket in 1751 for £1,500 a side, there was alleged (rather improbably) to be £20,000 in side bets on the match.[82] It was the same with cock-fighting,[83] and of course it was the same with politics. In 1750 Horace Walpole reported that Sandwich,

> goes once or twice a week to hunt with the Duke [of Cumberland]; and as the latter has taken a turn of gaming, Sandwich, to make his court – and fortune, carries a box and dice in his pocket; and so they throw a main, whenever the hounds are at fault.[84]

This must be what one of Sandwich's closest friends meant by saying that he did not enjoy gambling, but only its effects.[85]

It remains to consider the circumstances of the invention of the sandwich, which modern works suppose to have been designed to sustain its creator through long nights at the gaming table. The origin of this story seems to be a passage in Grosley's *Tour to London*:

> A minister of state passed four and twenty hours at a public gaming-table, so absorpt in play, that, during the whole time, he had no subsistence but a bit of beef, between two slices of toasted bread, which he eat without ever quitting the game. This new dish grew highly in vogue, during my residence in London: it was called by the name of the minister who invented it.[86]

Grosley's book is a piece of travel literature of a kind not unknown today; based on a brief visit to the country and no knowledge of the language, it combines some shrewd comments with many absurdities. There is no supporting evidence for this piece of gossip, and it does not seem very likely that it has any foundation, especially as it refers to 1765, when Sandwich was a Cabinet minister and very busy. There is no doubt, however, that he was the real author of the sandwich, in its original form using salt beef, of which he was very fond.[87] The alternative explanation[88] is that he invented it to sustain himself at his desk, which seems plausible since we have ample evidence of the long hours he worked from an early start,[89] in an age when dinner was the only substantial meal of the day, and the fashionable hour to dine was four o'clock.[90]

In 1751, however, Sandwich had no work to do. The collapse of his career and his marriage more or less simultaneously seems to have robbed him of personal as well as financial stability. Up to 1751 he was often cited as a model of respectability, and throughout his life he lived frugally,[91] but once out of office he began to acquire the reputation as a libertine which never left him. It is clear that it was not altogether unjustified. As early as 1752 he had a brief affair with Sarah Nailour, the daughter of a Huntingdonshire gentleman whose elder daughter Charlotte was married to Sandwich's brother.[92] This was immediately followed by a longer, but apparently platonic relationship with a third sister Maria (there were nine Nailour children in all).[93] This complicated an already difficult situation, for Captain Montagu brutally ill-treated his wife, who had fled back to her parents. They were terrified by his threats, and Sandwich was doing his best to force his brother to leave both her and them in peace. He failed, because Mrs Nailour insisted that her daughter return, and she was only delivered from her sufferings by her husband's death in 1757.[94]

Throughout these years Sandwich's name was linked in gossip with a number of mistresses amateur and professional.[95] However little these rumours may be believed, his own papers show sufficient evidence of numerous irregular attachments. Leaving aside the begging letters, the blackmail attempts, and the proposals from strangers offering their services more or less explicitly, there are several correspondences with women whose claims Sandwich acknowledged.[96] Though discreet in all these affairs, he made no secret of them among his equals:

> I have never pretended to be free from indiscretion, and those who know me have been . . . long accustomed to forgive my weaknesses, when they do not interfere with my conduct as a public man.[97]

It is an open question whether this weakness did interfere with his conduct as a public man. It would not have occurred to his contemporaries that immorality was dishonourable; a man might treat women with much less regard than Sandwich did and still be taken as a gentleman of his word, and any reputation he had for untrustworthiness did not come from this source. It is sometimes suggested that his private life made him unsuitable for high office, at least in the eyes of George III, whose own married life was a model of rectitude. The king certainly disapproved of Sandwich's private life, but he was prepared to appoint the Duke of Grafton as Secretary of State and Lord Halifax as Lord Lieutenant of Ireland, and Sandwich's amours were discreet by comparison with theirs. He belonged to a generation and class in which these things were widely accepted;[98] his own upbringing, virtually as an orphan, had given him little experience of the comforts of family life; and his wife's insanity had cut him adrift from the only moral anchor he had ever had.

It is in this context that we must judge his involvement, if he was involved, in the 'Hell-Fire Club', if it ever existed. The name can be disposed of at once: there was a club of that name in London in the 1720s,[99] but it has nothing to do with the body known to contemporaries as the 'Order of St Francis' or 'The Monks of Medmenham'. The subject is unfortunately one which attracts cranks and repels scholars; one of the few serious historians to have examined it comes close to concluding that it never existed and that the whole story is the product of over-heated imaginations.[100] This is going too far, for it is certain that the Buckinghamshire landowner and Tory politician Sir Francis Dashwood (later Lord Le Despencer) did establish some sort of private club in the early 1750s. He was fond of boating, and kept several craft on the lake in front of his house at West Wycombe, but the Thames offered better opportunities, and he rented a riverside house six miles away at Medmenham. It was a Tudor house built on the remains of a Cistercian monastery and already ruinous. Dashwood seems to have patched it up to a standard somewhat better than a summerhouse but still rather primitive, adequate for summer weekends when he and his friends used the place as a base for river picnics in their barge.[101] Besides boating, we know that they sometimes dined there, drank very moderately, it seems, and kept musical instruments, chess, backgammon, and a small library of commonplace light reading.[102] A contemporary description makes it all seem rather genteel:

> every one being allowed to amuse himself, according to his own disposition, either in reading, writing, play, or conversation. They, however, always meet in one general sett at meals, where, for the improvement of mirth, pleasantry, and gaiety, every member is allowed to introduce a Lady of a chearful, lively disposition, to improve the general hilarity . . . The Ladies, in the intervals of their repasts, may make select parties among themselves, or entertain one another, or alone, with reading, musick, tambour-work &c.[103]

It seems, however, that the 'ladies' were not ladies, nor needlework their only employment at Medmenham. They appear in fact to have been prostitutes – 'nuns' in the contemporary slang – imported from fashionable London 'nunneries', and taking no vows of chastity.[104]

This is all that we can say with any confidence about activities at Medmenham, and almost certainly all there is to say. In the 1990s they would be thought very tame, and the fact that they continue to attract horrified denunciation from historians can only be a tribute to the purity and chastity of the academic world. It must also spring from an anachronistic view of the 'monks' considered as a secret society. It is not clear that the title Dashwood gave them went much beyond a pun on the origins of Medmenham and of its female visitors, but there are unreliable suggestions of dressing up in mockery of real monks. This was a thoroughly respectable activity, located squarely in the great English tradition of anti-Catholicism, but it was also one with implications which churchmen found uncomfortable. Dashwood and his friends were representatives of the Enlightenment as it affected the English upper classes of the day. Their contempt for Papistry sprang not from Protestant orthodoxy but from scepticism towards religion in general, or at least orthodox religion. It is significant that Dashwood prepared a version of the Book of Common Prayer which virtually eliminates the Trinity and is strongly influenced by Deism; the contemporary view of God as almighty in principle, but remote and unconcerned with the world in practice.[105] Another aspect of the Enlightenment among the upper classes was a strong interest in secret, or at least private societies. Freemasonry was a notable example, and both Dashwood and Sandwich were freemasons.[106] There are obvious points of resemblance between the rituals of masonry and those of societies such as the Dilettanti, which Dashwood helped to found, and Sandwich's Turkish club, of which he was a member.[107] This is the context in which to place whatever dressing up the 'monks' may really have indulged in. A later generation, bred up on the delicious horrors of the Gothick novel, associated ruined abbeys with black masses and satanism, (and this particular ruined abbey later became an inn, whose landlord doubtless encouraged its notoriety),[108] but such things would not have occurred to, or interested, Dashwood and his friends:

> Notwithstanding the general Contempt of Religion among the fashionable World, the uninformed Reader is not to imagine, that the present Age is deep in the Speculations of Infidelity. No such Matter: for that would imply a certain Attention to these Subjects; a certain Degree of Self-Converse and Thought; and this would clash with the ruling Manners of the Times.[109]

What certainly did occur to them was the indulgence of 'natural' pleasures. 'Nature' was a favourite word for the men of the Enlightenment, and it conjured up ideas of the innate rightness and goodness of the natural passions, the unnaturalness of chastity, as preached by Christianity, and above all of celibacy, as professed by monks and nuns. Here the ideas of the Enlightenment coincided with the views of all Protestants on the unnaturalness of the monastic life. In the eighteenth century and for long afterwards, lurid exposés of the 'real' activities of monks and nuns provided the pornography of popular Protestantism, just as the literature and art of the classical world provided the pornography of the gentleman – a principal reason why ladies were not supposed to learn Latin. Medmenham neatly combined these tendencies, with its garden of classical statuary adorned with nothing but suggestive Latin verses, and its active parody of the evils of celibacy.[110] 'The garden, the grove, the orchard, the neighbouring woods,' wrote Wilkes, 'all spoke the loves and frailties of the younger monks; who seemed at least to have *sinned naturally*'.[111]

It seems that Dashwood and his friends held one or two 'Chapters' a year, at which they all assembled, and that smaller groups occasionally met there at other times. What evidence we have suggests that Sandwich was not involved until, probably, the summer of 1763.[112] This was soon after the society had been disrupted by the activities of one of its leading members, John Wilkes, in mounting political attacks on Dashwood and other members.[113] Since much of our 'information' about Medmenham comes from Wilkes, who had no regard for truth and was out to make his political fortune, it needs to be treated with the utmost reserve.[114] In any case Wilkes's descriptions are largely innuendo; most of the colourful detail in modern accounts of Medmenham is taken from Charles Johnson's picaresque novel *Chrysal*,[115] whose success inspired the author to produce an expanded edition in 1765 full of obvious references to people who had become prominent in public life since the first issue. This is prefaced with a disclaimer stating that the contents were pure fiction. The author's object was obviously to sell as many books as possible without being sued for libel, in which he was successful. It is possible to say in general terms that *Chrysal* draws on contemporary gossip, and that gossip sometimes has a foundation of truth, but virtually nothing it offers can be verified, and as a historical source it is useless. Besides Wilkes and *Chrysal*, we have one contemporary description (quoted above), and some uninformative passing references in the poems of Paul Whitehead and Charles Churchill, both of whom were involved.[116]

It appears that after Wilkes's expulsion by the summer of 1763, and the break-up of the original society, which was by 1766 at the latest,[117] Le Despencer (as he had now become) revived it in some form, at least occasionally. There seems to have been some activity up to about 1770,[118] and in that year he wrote to Sandwich inviting him to a meeting,[119] but in 1776 a newspaper reference spoke of it as something long vanished.[120] It was evidently an activity Sandwich was involved in from time to time, and it agrees with what we know of his private life. Modern readers are at liberty to be shocked, so long as they do not imagine that his contemporaries were.

We have the opportunity to judge Sandwich's character and

morality through the eyes of one contemporary who was exceptionally well placed to describe them. Lady Mary Fitzgerald was the
sister of his friend Augustus Hervey. She was married, but long
separated from her husband. For some years in the early 1760s they
carried on a strange relationship which began as a sort of teasing
gallantry, and matured into a serious friendship.[121] Possibly Sandwich began it in the hope of a conquest, but if so he soon realized
that Lady Mary was an easy match for his charms. To begin with
she judged him clever and plausible:

> Can't you be content that I do justice to your Head w.out persisting
> in wronging my judgement by supposing I want the very small degree
> of penetration necessary to see you are & allways have been acting a
> part. I own you are an excellent actor, Garrick is not a much
> better . . .[122]

Eighteen months later she had changed, 'from thinking you a com-
pound of allmost every quality wh. makes a man equally dangerous
as a friend or enemy, to believe you a warm friend & candid
enemy'.[123] She came to believe in his 'disinterested regard & affection
(so different from the libertinism you were allways represented to
me to profess)', and he paid her the compliment of discussing politics
seriously with her.[124] At some point she composed (in French) what
purports to be a self-portrait of Sandwich. As the shrewd and candid
judgement of one who knew him as well as anyone, it is worth
summarizing. His friends tax him with ambition and vanity, but he
regards these as qualities necessary to succeed. His intelligence is
penetrating rather than quick, and he excels in perception of character
and in accommodating himself to those he has to work with. He
has excellent judgement and foresees difficulties, but once he under-
takes a great work he pushes it forward untroubled by doubts. He
does not care to dissemble, but knows how to do it if necessary. He
likes flattery but is never deceived by it, and wishes to be known
for who he really is. He tends to be either too formal or too familiar.
He is happiest when his head rules his heart.[125]

It is a striking portrait, consistent with everything we know about
his public and private life. It shows us a man of outstanding abilities,
equally capable of handling people and things; a man of resolution
and self-knowledge; but one who guarded himself more than he
might have done if his upbringing had encouraged him to develop
further his powers of generosity and self-sacrifice.

CHAPTER VI

Country Life
1755–1763

Sandwich was a big man, tall and slightly awkward in manner, with a reputation for breaking china, and a shambling gait which gave rise to a witticism about his appearing to walk down both sides of the street at once.[1] He told against himself the story that the dancing master he had engaged as a young man in Paris asked him as a particular favour when he took his leave never to reveal of whom he had learnt to dance.[2] Though ungraceful, he was strong and athletic, and all his life enjoyed outdoor activities. 'Stretching out his strong arms and legs, whilst playing at skittles, Lord Sandwich would exult amazingly, if by chance he was able to knock down all nine'.[3] His taste for boisterous horseplay sometimes disconcerted elegant visitors to Hinchingbrooke,[4] and a friend who had the misfortune to fall ill while staying with him remarked ruefully that 'His Lordp's is a good house for the Robust & the Jolly, but a very bad Hospital'.[5] He was, however, never an enthusiast for the conventional pursuits of the upper classes. There are passing references to him hunting and shooting,[6] and in 1757 he briefly owned a racehorse,[7] but the impression given by his correspondence is that these were activities undertaken to make acquaintance with those who enjoyed them, rather than for any pleasure Sandwich himself took in them. The same was true of his rare ventures into agriculture, one of the few 'scientific' subjects of the day in which he had no real interest.[8] His friends were not deceived: 'As to your Farming and Grazing you will excuse my telling you I believe you know as little about them as our present Ministers do of Politicks'.[9]

What Sandwich did enjoy were games like skittles[10] and tennis[11] (meaning real tennis, for lawn tennis was not yet invented). Above all he was passionately fond of cricket. Sandwich and Bedford were prominent among the small group of noblemen who were early patrons of the game, and the first cricketing poem in English, printed in 1744, was dedicated to him. The game was just coming into

favour among the upper classes, and Sandwich had learnt to play it
as a schoolboy, but it was still far from being entirely respectable.
Moralists disapproved of the promiscuous mixing of the classes,[12]
and violence was common. A women's match at the Artillery
Ground in 1747 caused a riot, as matches often did. Casualties among
players were frequent, dogs and spectators a major hazard.[13] The
contemporary atmosphere is well caught by this notice of a match
played on Walworth Common in 1744:

> The gentlemen who play this match have subscribed for a Holland
> smock of one guinea value, which will be run for by two jolly wenches
> . . . They are to run in drawers only, and there is excellent sport
> expected. Capt. Vinegar, with a great many of his bruisers and bull-
> dogs, will attend to make a ring, that no civil spectators may be
> incommoded by the rabble.[14]

There is no doubt that Sandwich's enthusiasm for cricket was genuine, but it was also of great political value to him, as a passion shared
with his patron Bedford. Contemporary cartoonists and satirists usually presented Sandwich with a cricket bat, and they meant it as
a political rather than a sporting instrument.[15] Cricket matches
drew the party and its adherents together, and a taste for cricket
might advance men in politics, or even (it was suggested) the
church.[16]

Yachting was another enthusiasm which Sandwich and Bedford
shared. They both owned yachts, which they raced and cruised in
the Thames, and on occasion well out to sea.[17] Sandwich was also
fond of voyaging on the inland waterways of the Fens, 'labouring
at an oar' as well as under sail, and he sometimes met his fenland
neighbours Joseph Banks and Lord Orford for fishing and sailing
parties on the open water of Whittlesea Mere.[18] Sometimes he cruised
up the Thames, and at the very end of his life was looking forward to
reaching the Severn by the newly-opened Kennet and Avon Canal.[19]
Fenland voyaging was usually combined with fishing and wild-
fowling.[20] Sandwich, whose simple tastes in food were the despair
of his elegant friends,[21] was extremely fond of fish, both sea and
fresh-water, and loved fishing.[22] Another of his fenland pursuits was
punting,[23] and in the winter of 1776 when Whittlesea Mere was
frozen, he and Banks tried out an ice-yacht.[24]

Outdoor pursuits were not the only things he had in common
with his patron. Sandwich, Bedford, and the Prince of Wales, to
whom they were politically related in the 1740s, were all keen on

cricket, sailing, music, and amateur theatricals.[25] The Duchess of Bedford, a woman of ability and ambition whom many people regarded as the true leader of the party, was especially fond of acting, and plays involving the duke's friends and adherents were prominent activities at Woburn and Hinchingbrooke in the 1740s and 1750s.[26] In an age when theatres, actors, and especially actresses were disreputable, amateur theatre flourished in great houses, often on a considerable scale.[27] When Arthur Murphy's play *The Way to Keep Him* was acted for two nights at Hinchingbrooke in 1760 by a company consisting of 'several persons of distinction', four hundred tickets were distributed.[28] Sandwich became a close friend of David Garrick, who assisted in putting on their plays, and of other actors and dramatists of the day.

Garrick was well known in literary society and had many respectable friends, but Sandwich's intimacy with other actors tended to confirm his rakish reputation, and so did the sensational marriage in 1754 of his widowed sister to the actor William 'Gentleman' Smith, the original Joseph Surface of *The School for Scandal*.[29] Smith was an Old Etonian but his profession made him completely unsuitable as a peer's brother-in-law. The match not only brought Sandwich into further disrepute, but obliged him by the terms of his late brother-in-law's will to take care of his sister's children.[30] Further scandal was caused by his membership of the theatrical club the Society of Beefsteaks, which met in a room over Covent Garden Theatre, and of which he was the only nobleman member.[31]

This ability to associate on easy terms with people of varying social background was one of the keys to Sandwich's formidable powers as an electoral manager. There was no such thing as a professional politician in the eighteenth century; politics was simply the activity of men and women in public life, at national or local level, and there was hardly anyone who could be said to earn a living by it. But Sandwich came as near to being a professional politician as a nobleman well could do, and he showed it by his skill and dedication. He was certainly not the only peer with the common touch, but very few cultivated the people of his town and county with such assiduity.[32] 'Electioneering, he boasted, was a trade that he had been bred to, and he did not like to do things by halves'.[33] As an electoral manager he had few equals, and his skill aroused reluctant admiration even from his enemies.

My Lord Sandwich is entire master both of this town and county. He has so rivited his interest, that I believe nobody will venture to oppose as long as he lives. He is really a very great young man, with great talents, and many amiable qualities.[34]

'As indefatigable in the election of an alderman, as in a revolution of state',[35] in Walpole's words, Sandwich spared no pains to attend to everything and everybody. No detail was too trivial, no elector too insignificant for him. 'As we have allready begun to talk of Elections,' he wrote in 1752, 'I am obliged to receive every rec-ommendation that come [*sic*] to my hands, & to be eternally troub-ling my friends in favour of some Huntingdonshire man or other'.[36] 'The great master of electioneering politicks in Huntingdonshire', wrote a contemporary, 'has taught me that no attempt is to be omit-ted where there is a bare possibility of making a vote'.[37] Sandwich's alert eye was quick to spot any possibility of useful connection. In 1769, for example, the great landscape gardener 'Capability' Brown, who had bought a small estate in Huntingdonshire, was 'pricked' to serve in the onerous office of sheriff. Sandwich at once arranged with his friend Lord Gower that Brown should be relieved of the burden, and that the relief should come as a favour from Sandwich: 'it might not be amiss if you was to send Mr Brown to apply to me, as it might occasion the beginning of a Huntingdonshire connection between us'.[38] It did: Brown became a loyal follower, his son was elected MP in Sandwich's interest, and his control of the county was further cemented.[39] In the recent election, a visitor wrote in 1741,

> He gained his point by mere good management, which has contributed a good deal to his character in the world as a very able man . . . I never saw anyone so engaging and affable towards the common people.[40]

Engaging affability and endless hard work were the key to success in local politics. 'Junketting with the Aldermen of Huntingdon and their wives and daughters'[41] was essential, not merely at election time, but at regular intervals every year. At the municipal celebra-tions Sandwich was expected to provide venison for the Council to feast upon – which, having no chase of his own, he regularly begged from the Duke of Bedford:

> My friends of the Corporation of Huntingdon who are very honest fellows, & deserve to be crammed up to the throat with venison, flatter themselves with the hopes of a buck from Woburn Park at the Mayor's Feast on Michaelmas Day.[42]

When Hinchingbrooke came of age in 1765,

a large ox, weighing 140 stone, will on Monday be roasted whole, upon Huntingdon Common near his Lordship's seat, when 4000 loaves and several hogsheads of beer will be distributed to the public . . . on Tuesday there will be a grand ball.[43]

Huntingdon Races were an important scene of such activity. In every county race meetings were the natural assemblies of the local gentry and farmers, and the perfect theatre to display gifts of sociability and charm, to invite 'the freedom that every body had with Ld Sandwich at Huntingdon Races when he bestowed upon us all, me amongst the rest, both his good victuals & drink, & his Jokes and Pleasantry.'[44]

Sandwich's powers as an electoral charmer aroused the envy of the powerful, such as Henry Pelham, who:

is not a little offended at this beating up for voluntaires for Huntingdon Races, & told me, 'if Sandwich provokes I can give him a kick in that County, for all his vain pretended popularity'.

Bedford's reply was:

Good God what can I do? Sandwich is so popular that I cant help it. People will crowd in upon us whether we will or no.[45]

The result of Sandwich's charm and diligence was an electoral control of the borough of Huntingdon out of all proportion to the natural influence of his estates. In the fifty years from 1741 to his death, through ten general elections, he returned both members of Parliament for the borough without contest.[46] During his career he fought twenty-four contested elections in three constituencies, and never failed to return at least one member.[47] As late as 1788, when he was seventy and his son was forty-five, he still managed Hinchingbrooke's election personally 'with great energy and care'.[48] Right up to his death his control of the borough of Huntingdon was unshaken:

The interest of the Earl of Sandwich is so powerful as always to return two Members; and this he effects, not by weight of property, for his Lordship has but one house in the whole town, but by his popularity, and the obligations which he was enabled to confer on some of his principal friends during his connexion with Lord North's Administration.[49]

More remarkable than controlling the borough was Sandwich's influence over the county of Huntingdon, where he had many

potential rivals with larger estates than his own, in particular his
cousin the Duke of Manchester at Kimbolton Castle. Manchester
and Sandwich were always opposed both politically and personally.
'There is no place in England,' Sandwich wrote in 1780,

> where the parties are more at variance than in Huntingdonshire; we
> could not dine together on the election day, and the two members
> could not agree to give a joint ball to the ladies; and as a personal
> mark of enmity to me, the Duke of Manchester has thrown up his
> trust in Lady Cork's separate maintenance, giving it as a reason, that
> he could not concern himself any longer in her affairs because her
> uncle was so inimical to him.[50]

Yet even when he was in opposition Sandwich managed to ensure
that they co-operated to return one MP each without the dreaded
expense of a contested election.[51] When he was in office Sandwich
was careful to ensure that all the favours government had to bestow
in the county were seen to come through his hands.[52] In 1775 he
assured his son:

> you will allways bring in, at least three out of the four members that
> our town & County send to Parliament; but to do that it is absolutely
> necessary that the people who are to look for favours from Govern-
> ment should expect them thro' the medium of the house of Hinch-
> ingbrook.[53]

With such help Sandwich achieved some remarkable electoral
coups, none more remarkable than in the general election of 1747.
Until a few days before it he was on the Continent unable to do
anything in person. At the last moment his brother's erratic
behaviour persuaded him to drop him as candidate in favour of his
cousin Edward Wortley Montagu, who was a complete stranger to
the county, owned no land in it, and would normally have been
regarded as an impossibility with any amount of preparation.[54] It
proved to be none too soon to drop 'Mad Montagu', who became a
considerable embarrassment both personally and electorally. Besides
drunken frolics in the streets of Huntingdon and insulting the mayor,

> He has of late . . . much reflected upon your Ld.ship's Honour in
> Several mixt Company's by charging you with debauching Mr Nail-
> ours family and particularly Maria and saying that she was an whore
> and you made her so.[55]

In 1748 Sandwich was planning to put in another cousin if his half-brother Courtenay should die:

> it is the first principle of my Huntingdon Politicks never to let a gentleman of the County into that Borough. Besides Captain Montagu is a seaman, & I think it much for the advantage of the profession, and a point that you & I ought allways to be attentive to, to get as many of our bretheren as we possibly can into the H: of Commons; and I have still another reason in favour of him that I am afraid it must be by his means[56] that I must forward my very favourite point of having one of my family make a figure in the Sea Service. . . .[57]

To keep the county out of Huntingdon borough, and to retain his own influence over the county, would have been a considerable achievement even with deep pockets, and it was an extraordinary one on Sandwich's slender resources. He achieved it largely by personal attention, and it is significant that his only major defeat was the 1751 Mitchell by-election in Cornwall, where he was exercising his half-brother Courtenay's electoral interest at a distance. Even here his two candidates were elected at the poll, and only unseated on petition by a hostile Pelhamite majority in the Commons.[58] On his home ground he wrung every ounce of advantage from whatever patronage he had to bestow, and ingeniously financed his elections by raising loans from his MPs. Henry Seymour was brought in for a loan of £1,000 and £800 towards electoral expenses. When he changed his allegiance he was replaced by George Wombwell for £1,000 contribution plus £1,000 loan.[59] In 1776 Lord Mulgrave was brought in for a loan of £2,000 and not more that £300 in expenses,[60] but by 1782 Sandwich asked only £500, or £1,000 in the event of opposition, which he was confident would be sufficient, 'as there must be no bribery, and can be no treating till after the Election is over'.[61] By such means Sandwich maintained a dominant local influence on completely inadequate resources.

The same dedication, charm and attention to detail which made Sandwich such a formidable politician in Huntingdonshire was applied to any situation in which he found himself. In 1752, for example, he was considering a forthcoming election for a fellowship at Eton:

> I know of no candidate that I have any personal reason to wish to support, my only part is to take care that the person elected shall owe his success to your Grace & me, & have no connections that shall interfere with his acting hereafter in a proper manner when you or I have any point of consequence to pursue in the College.[62]

Such elections were by no means trivial even in national politics, for they represented the distribution of some attractive patronage.[63] What is noteworthy about Sandwich's attitude is that he plunged into the contest, not to advance any particular client or respond to any request, but simply to build up a bank of influence which might be of use in the future. In just the same spirit he allowed himself to become involved in the politics of the Fen Corporation, though he had no land in the Fens and no natural interest there: 'I wish it may be practicable for I would not willingly have the thing slip thro' my fingers, as I am sure that if I have time I can turn it to advantage'.[64]

The greatest of all Sandwich's non-geographical political interests was the connection which he built up from 1768 onward in the East India Company. He never had any interest in the affairs of India itself, but he was extremely interested in the influence on British politics conveyed by the company's wealth and importance. By the mid-1770s he personally wielded an influence at East India House which was reckoned the equal or even the superior to that of the government as a whole.[65] 'With consummate ability,' wrote an observer at the time, 'Lord Sandwich had constructed a species of political citadel within the Ministerial lines which acknowledged hardly any other commander or comptroller than himself'.[66]

By such means the care and skill which Sandwich applied to local politics could be converted into weight in national politics, as of course he intended it should be. But he was well aware that no amount of local influence would restore him to national office without friends. Modern historians have remarked that the Bedfords were unusually well organized by the standards of the day, and that Sandwich had an unusually clear grasp of the importance of party discipline.[67] Unfortunately none of this came from the duke himself. His obstinacy, impracticality and want of political sense were the principal reason that Sandwich fell from office in 1751, and the risk had been clear for some time before. In May he complained to a friend that the duke,

> who was his friend, lacked the talent to keep a party together and did not know how to exploit his weight or make it felt; that he, Sandwich, was seriously thinking of withdrawing, from necessity rather than choice, because he did not think he could hold his ground.[68]

A month later he was out of office. As a natural result he began to be less closely allied to the duke's party, though they remained on good terms personally. Bedford, who neither needed nor wanted office, could afford to take an Olympian attitude which sorted very ill with Sandwich's condition. He therefore moved towards the Duke of Cumberland, who had inherited much of the opposition leadership exercised by his older brother the Prince of Wales until his death in 1751. Cumberland and Sandwich had worked closely together and were on good terms, so the alliance was a natural one. At the same time Bedford and the rest of his party also moved towards Cumberland. Their problem was that Cumberland's position as the king's son precluded open political activity, and that all of them could only act in conjunction with an effective politician in the House of Commons. Cumberland's ally was Henry Fox; an able manager and excellent speaker, generally agreed to have great prospects before him. Unfortunately for Sandwich, Fox had much more to offer him than he could give in return. He was in the same dilemma as he faced all his career: three MPs counted for something, but even combined with administrative ability and local political consequence they were insufficient to force him into office, and being outside the House of Commons he stood on the margins when ministries were being constructed.[69] It is in this sense that we should interpret a remark often quoted, made by George II to Bedford when Sandwich was dismissed: 'I don't know how it is, but he has very few friends'.[70] Personally Sandwich had many friends, but politically he commanded few allies.

Cumberland and Fox had their opportunity when Pelham died in 1754, leaving the ministry with no one to take the crucial rôle of finance minister and leader of the Commons. This was their opportunity to force Newcastle out of office and form their own ministry, but Newcastle had not lost his skill at neutralizing his enemies, and he persuaded Fox to accept office as a colleague. Thus the opposition was divided, and Sandwich and his friends were left out.[71] He had his opportunity the following year, but it only showed how little weight he carried even when nominally allied to the new Fox–Newcastle administration. He was proposed for the sinecure office of Chief Justice in Eyre North of the Trent, deprived of it to satisfy a claimant of more political weight, and eventually accommodated with a one-third share, already refused by somebody else, in another sinecure, Vice-Treasurer of Ireland. There was no suggestion of offering him any position of 'business', in the contemporary term. His abilities and experience were well enough known, but they were of no political consequence, and he was valued only as a minor follower of Cumberland, Bedford and Fox.[72]

The disasters of the opening stages of the Seven Years War, especially the fall of Minorca in 1756, discredited Newcastle and opened the way for both Fox and his Commons rival Pitt to attempt to form a ministry. At this time there appeared a well-known cartoon showing Fox as a recruiting sergeant beating up for recruits, among whom appears Sandwich in a threadbare coat carrying a cricket bat.[73] Fox's hopes foundered on Pitt's refusal to co-operate, and opened the way for a short-lived ministry composed exclusively of Pitt and his numerous relatives. This in turn gave way in 1757 to an uneasy coalition of Newcastle and Pitt. This unnatural ministry (in the eyes of contemporaries) fought the Seven Years War with success, and its triumphs pushed Sandwich and his friends even further from real power.[74] Nominally connected with government by his sinecure, Sandwich seems in practice to have withdrawn in despair from national politics and plunged once more into country pursuits: 'This conclusive stroke will I think at last make me give up everything relative to home Politicks & grow a country gentleman in good earnest.'[75]

The mould of politics was broken by the death of the old king in October 1760. His grandson George III was twenty-two years old, a student of the British constitution and a devout believer in the orthodox simplicities of political language without any experience of its practicalities. Convinced that all party was 'faction' and wicked, believing that his grandfather had been the prisoner of designing men manipulating power for their own advantage, he determined to rise above party and choose administrations from good men of any connection or none.[76] In principle everyone agreed; in practice men like Sandwich with political experience knew , 'that this country must be governed by combinations of people'.[77] For his new chief minister the king chose the one man whom he knew and trusted, his old tutor the Earl of Bute. Bute was not a fool, but he was almost as inexperienced as his master – they have been described as 'twin babes in the dangerous wood of politics'[78] – and as a Scot he was exposed to virulent prejudice. In particular he was connected with Jacobitism and arbitrary government, and it was freely suggested that his designs had been advanced by seducing the king's mother. George III's attempt to rise above party succeeded only in creating the potent myth of a young king imprisoned by an all-powerful minister. This myth was accepted even by the soberest and best-informed observers, and continued to distort British politics throughout the 1760s. Bute himself did not have the stamina for high politics, and retreated with a nervous breakdown after fourteen months as Secretary of State, but he continued to haunt successive ministries in the improbable character of the spirit of arbitrary power, and even twenty years later at the height of the American War, when Bute himself was no longer a credible threat even for the most paranoid, opposition politicians were claiming to have sighted the old ghost in one shape or another, still drifting noiselessly along the corridors of power.

Sandwich fully shared the general hostility to Bute, and refused to desert Cumberland and the opposition to take a share in his ministry.[79] When Anson, still First Lord of the Admiralty, died in June 1762 he was widely talked of as the obvious successor, and the choice of Halifax, whose powers were visibly failing, caused some astonishment. 'It is plainly a stop-gap,' wrote Newcastle, '& shews a great want of hands; however as I hope . . . he will be directed by Cleveland, he may do tolerably well'.[80] Next month Sandwich's name was mentioned as a possible Secretary of State.[81] These suggestions did not arise from any sudden realization of his talents, but from the need to reconstruct the ministry by recruiting from the opposition. It was rightly judged that Sandwich and Fox, being needy and ambitious, were the most likely to be open to offers. At the end of October Fox offered him the job of joint Postmaster-General,[82] but the alternative of ambassador to Madrid was also proposed, and it was this which he decided to accept.[83] On 10th November he wrote a painful letter to Cumberland explaining that his straitened circumstances obliged him to accept office, and received a generous reply, though the loss of Fox and Sandwich had effectively reduced Cumberland's party to vanishing point.[84] At the end of November 'the intended ambassador for Spain' was busy planning his mission.[85]

CHAPTER VII

The Secretary of State
1763–1765

In the spring of 1763, as Sandwich prepared to leave for Madrid, the process of reconstructing the ministry was going on. Though Bute was now out of office, he was still taking the leading rôle, and the new chief minister George Grenville was presented with his ministers rather than choosing them himself.[1] One of those who were chosen was the brilliant but erratic Charles Townshend to be First Lord of the Admiralty. He accepted, but only on condition that his follower Peter Burrell should have a seat at the Board. Since all the vacancies were already disposed of this was refused, and when he learnt that he could not have his way, Townshend resigned in a huff. So it was necessary to find a substitute in a hurry, and Sandwich's name was suggested. The three leading ministers discussed him with the king, and 'nothing was said against him but an insinuation that they hop'd he would be oeconomical'.[2] With this pallid recommendation Sandwich returned unexpectedly to the office he had left twelve years before.[3]

The Navy was in the throes of demobilization after a victorious but debilitating war. We do not know directly what Sandwich thought of Anson's management of the Admiralty, but he must have been aware that in the 1750s Anson had allowed it to sink below the strength for which he had fought, and he was certainly aware how slowly the fleet had mobilized in 1755, as it was one of the subjects the Board began by studying: 'Thus it appears that 39 ships of the line and 474 men over is all that can be raised in the first year in addition to the numbers of the peace establishment'.[4] Sandwich's Admiralty was therefore looking at one of the fundamental weaknesses of the eighteenth-century Navy. Sandwich must also have been aware that the fleet he had inherited included a disproportionate number of ships built in haste during the war to make up for peacetime neglect, and he must have suspected if he did not already know that this was laying up a problem of decay for the future. What the Navy needed was a long-term shipbuilding programme with sufficient funds to keep up a fleet of a given size by regular replacement, building at deliberate speed with seasoned timber to give the ships the longest possible working lives. To this end the Admiralty called for estimates of the total value of the ships of the Navy with all their stores, and of the annual cost of replacing them in cycles of between twelve and sixteen years.[5] Another calculation was 'An Estimate of the Expence Necessary for the Repairs of his Majts. Fleet, with the Time requisite for Accomplishing the same at single days work, by the Number of 3000 Shipwrts. being 200 more than are now Established . . .',[6] which shows that Sandwich had not forgotten the subject of task work. Nor had he lost his old enthusiasm for seeing for himself and mastering the technicalities of his subject. Soon after he arrived at the Admiralty the Board went down to inspect the hull of a frigate in dock which had spent a commission in the West Indies experimentally sheathed below the waterline with copper plates.[7]

It is interesting but profitless to speculate what might have happened if Sandwich had been selected on merit to be First Lord, by a ministry aware of the Navy's need for long-term reform and determined to support it. In practice he had been chosen more or less by accident by men who expected of him chiefly that he should keep the Navy Estimates down, and he was about to lose his job almost as quickly as he had gained it, to suit another ministerial reshuffle. The precarious situation of a ministry chosen by Bute who was out of office, and unpopular with the king who had been forced to part with him, soon induced a crisis. In August secret negotiations with Pitt were in progress. As usual he pitched his terms impossibly high, demanding the dismissal of most of the existing ministry.[8] This was too much, and the failure of the alternative strengthened the ministry. George Grenville, the First Lord of the Treasury, was now able to consider himself the real head of it, and dispose of departments as he wished. By the end of August Sandwich knew that he was in consideration for Secretary of State.[9] Lord Egmont took over the Admiralty ('which I think considering all things is tolerably well');[10] and on 9th September Sandwich took up the seals of office of the Secretary of State for the Northern Department. Henry Fox, now Lord Holland, who was Paymaster-General in the Grenville ministry, kindly allowed the new Secretary to take his official residence in the Pay Office, without which Sandwich would have had nowhere to live in town.[11]

The change of ministers was made necessary by the death of Lord

Egremont, the Southern Secretary, who was replaced by moving
Halifax across to his department. Halifax had markedly declined
from the keen young man who had been at school and university
with Sandwich, and was drinking too much.[12] Egremont had originally been chosen as 'a very good and proper man' for Secretary of
State because of his wealth and social standing, unsupported by any
experience of public office.[13] He had been ill for some time, and ten
months before he died was evidently not fit for business;

> If your Grace had seen the poor man after dinner as I did to day, you
> would feel nothing but compassion for him. He seems in a confirmed
> lethargy, the instant he has dined, he drops asleep and all his efforts
> to prevent it are to no purpose, notwithstanding that Lord Halifax, at
> whose house we dined, and Sandwich, myself, and three or four more
> made rather more than our usual uproar.[14]

Egremont and Halifax had been responsible for the early stages
of the prosecution of John Wilkes. It has been remarked that a Secretary of State's duties were primarily concerned with the king's
proper business of foreign affairs and war, but he had domestic responsibilities as well, and as this one was to become one of the most
celebrated incidents in Sandwich's career, it is worth examining in
detail.[15]

John Wilkes was a young MP and man about town who had run
through a large fortune by the usual methods and was looking about
for some means to recoup it. In the violent dissension surrounding
the Bute ministry he saw his opportunity.[16] Anti-Scottish prejudice
was everywhere, so Wilkes launched a scurrilous newspaper called
the *North Briton*, attacking Bute, the ministry, and all Scotsmen with
unrestrained abuse. Englishmen had been outraged by the phrase
Bute had introduced into the young king's first speech, in which he
declared that he 'gloried in the name of Briton' – instead of 'Englishman', as Lord Hardwicke had written in the first draft.[17] In English
ears 'Briton' was little better than a cant word for 'Scotch', and all
things Scots were tainted with barbarism and tyranny. The ministerial paper the *Briton*, edited by the Scots journalist Tobias Smollett,
further fastened the popular identification of 'Briton' with 'Scots'.
This was the vein which Wilkes worked with such enthusiasm. In
No.45 of the *North Briton* he excelled himself, attacking the king's
speech from the throne at the opening of Parliament in terms which
plainly accused him of lying in order to support a Scots despotism.[18]

He had already accused the king's mother of being Bute's mistress, the Archbishop of Canterbury of buggery, and the Bishop of Gloucester's wife of professional prostitution. Such suggestions might conceivably attract prosecution today, and even in the more tolerant climate of the eighteenth century they had aroused notice. The attack on the king decided the ministry to attempt prosecution, if they could not silence Wilkes by more direct means.

To set up as an opposition journalist and make so much trouble as to be worth being bought off was a traditional tactic, and ministers knew that Wilkes had his price. He had already offered his services to Bute, demanding the characteristically outrageous price of Governor of Canada.[19] As Bedford had acted as intermediary in this transaction, Sandwich no doubt knew about it, and in any case it was obviously his business if possible to avoid trouble and recruit an effective publicist to the ministry. As soon as he came to office he therefore made it his business to open communication.[20] We do not know what was offered or demanded, but Wilkes's price was evidently still too high, and the negotiation lapsed.

It is a matter of interest to know if Sandwich's offer should be understood as an office of friendship, since it was alleged by Wilkes, and has been widely believed, that they were intimate friends. We can take it for granted that they knew one another, for in the little world of London politics and society everyone knew everyone else. The evidence that they were close friends, however, is thin, and much of it is traceable to the claims of Wilkes himself. Since Wilkes was a habitual liar with every motive for fiction, his testimony is valueless without support. He said himself, 'give me a grain of truth and I will mix it up with a great mass of falsehood so that no chemist will ever be able to separate them';[21] he frequently dispensed with the grain of truth. It is usually said that Wilkes and Sandwich were intimates together of the Monks of Medmenham. They were certainly both members, but Wilkes was made unwelcome there by the *North Briton*'s attacks on his fellow-member Hogarth (in No. 17 of 25th September 1762), and on Dashwood, who was Bute's Chancellor of the Exchequer from May 1762 to April 1763. He appears to have been expelled by the summer of 1763,[22] which is probably when Sandwich became involved.[23] The one club where they certainly did meet is the Society of Beefsteaks, of which they were both members. We know they dined in company on one occasion when Boswell was a guest,[24] and there were probably others, but Sandwich had been a member for less than two years in 1763, and we have no reason to think them particular friends. Horace Walpole put it about that Sandwich was expelled from the club after the prosecution,[25] but it is clear from Wilkes's own list that Sandwich remained an ordinary member until 1769, then became an honorary member until his death.[26] At its dissolution in the mid-nineteenth century the club still possessed Sandwich's portrait.[27] Such evidence as there is suggests that it was Wilkes rather than Sandwich who was at this period unpopular with the club for his attacks on his fellow-member Hogarth.[28] It is certain that in the 1770s he often dined there,[29] and there is some slight evidence that he and Sandwich met on friendly terms in later life,[30] but there is hardly anything to suggest that they knew one another well in 1763. It is significant that among the tens of thousands of Sandwich's letters which survive, the only correspondence with Wilkes is a formal note from him about East India Company politics.[31] One further piece of evidence, if it may be called that, which is often adduced to prove their friendship, is a piece of repartee along these lines:

> *Sandwich:* 'I don't know whether you will die of the pox or on the gallows.'
> *Wilkes:* 'That depends, my Lord, whether I embrace your mistress or your principles.'[32]

It is a good story, and like many good stories, migratory. The only witness who claims actually to have heard it himself firmly attributes it to the actor and wit Samuel Foote, whom Sandwich certainly did know.[33]

Whatever ties of friendship Sandwich may have acknowledged, his duty as a minister was clear. There was now no alternative to pursuing the prosecution begun by his predecessor. The king demanded it; the Lord Chancellor and the highest legal authorities regarded it as essential for the maintenance of the rule of law; Grenville had made it the new ministry's immediate priority. Sandwich certainly shared their views, and with his acute political sense at once perceived that there were advantages to be gained for the ministry in a prosecution 'which is our strong and popular point'.[34] He set to work with his customary enthusiasm to master his brief.[35]

Halifax and Egremont had bungled the initial prosecution. They had allowed Wilkes to seize the initiative and present himself as a martyred hero of English liberty, and they had made some serious errors.[36] In particular Philip Carteret Webb the Solicitor-General, who was managing the legal case, had had Wilkes arrested on the original general warrant used to take up everyone involved in the publication of No.45 of the *North Briton*. General warrants (meaning warrants which did not name individuals) were used in such cases to arrest and interrogate witnesses, seize papers and generally to gather evidence which could be used to frame proper charges against those actually responsible. The small fry of printers and messengers had been duly released, but Wilkes had been arrested on the original general warrant rather than on a specific warrant naming him and his offence. This was to prove a serious mistake, but as Sandwich studied the papers early in October it was not yet clear how serious.[37]

The issue of general warrants was to be the first, but by no means the last example of Wilkes's genius for lighting on questions of real constitutional significance. He himself was never interested in the issues except as a means of personal defence, but they, and consequently he, attracted many serious supporters who cared for English liberties and recognized Wilkes as their defender. In the early autumn of 1763, before the legality of general warrants had clearly emerged as an issue, it was not yet clear how successful Wilkes was to be in raising serious constitutional questions, but it was already probable that this was the line he would take. Sandwich's problem, and his opportunity, was the dichotomy between Wilkes the man and Wilkes the issue. Those who knew the man knew him as charming but completely disreputable. Edward Gibbon described him as, 'a thorough-going profligate in principle as in practice, his life stained with every vice and his conversation full of blasphemy and indecency'; but he nevertheless, 'scarcely ever met a better companion. He has inexhaustible spirits, infinite wit and humour and a great deal of knowledge'.[38] With the effrontery and skill in publicity which never deserted him Wilkes had cloaked his private character in the purple robes of a martyr of English liberty, and even those who knew him personally as 'an impudent worthless fellow', disapproved of 'dismantling the fences of our liberties' to punish him.[39] Sandwich's business was to strip that cloak away and expose Wilkes as the man whom no respectable man could support.

The legal situation was awkward. As a member of Parliament Wilkes was immune from prosecution for felony, and could only be convicted for seditious libel if it could be classified as a misdemeanour, which was uncertain. A surer way was to have him expelled from the House of Commons before prosecution, but much would be needed to persuade MPs to violate the immunity of a member. Time was short, for Wilkes had brought an action for false arrest in

the Court of Common Pleas which was due to be heard on 6th
December, and ministers feared that Chief Justice Pratt and a London
jury would certainly bring a verdict against them.[40] There was less
than two months left to reverse public opinion, expel Wilkes from
Parliament and complete the action against him in the Court of
King's Bench. With some reason, Wilkes was confident that it could
not be done.[41]

Studying the voluminous papers which had been seized from
Wilkes's lodgings, from the printer of the *North Briton* and elsewhere,
Sandwich found several interesting items. He read a crudely offensive
parody of 'Instructions to Lord Sandwich', written some months
before when he was destined for Madrid, but never printed. Among
many other insults, this accused him of cowardice, something no
gentleman could afford to overlook and still retain the character of
a man of honour.[42] He also read the copy for the unpublished No. 46
of the *North Briton*, which contained further personal attacks.[43] None
of this can have warmed whatever feelings of friendship for Wilkes
he may have had.

Among the papers Sandwich found references to Wilkes's having
printed a bawdy poem called *The Essay on Woman*. By some slightly
underhand means, Webb obtained a copy from the printer. Wilkes
assiduously put it about that Sandwich already knew the piece well,[44]
which is not impossible in itself, but appears to rest solely on his
word and the record of that malicious collector of rumour, Horace
Walpole.[45] There is every reason to suspect information from these
sources, and no necessity to believe that Sandwich had any more to
go on than his acute political instincts and the clues in Wilkes's
papers.[46]

What Webb's men obtained was a printed text of the first part
of an obscene parody of Pope's *Essay on Man*, ornamented with
mock-learned notes attributed to Bishop Warburton of Gloucester.
The poem, probably written about 1750 by Thomas Potter, is of
the sort which might today command an audience among boys of
about thirteen, and which intelligent men of the eighteenth century
apparently found amusing.[47] The notes, probably added recently by
Wilkes, are genuinely funny and a clever parody of the humourless
learning of the bishop. With the *Essay on Woman* were a number of
other indecent verses, several of them crudely blasphemous.[48]

These poems offered Sandwich the opportunity he needed. The
lawyers were of opinion that printing technically constituted publication and laid Wilkes open to prosecution for blasphemy. Much
more valuable for Sandwich, however, they laid Wilkes open as the

man he was, and provided a means to explode his public reputation. The trap was laid in great secrecy and sprung with devastating effect. On 16th November, as Grenville was speaking in the Commons to a motion to expel Wilkes, Sandwich rose in the Lords to expose him in a speech which included excerpts from the *Essay on Woman* read at length. In the Lords the piece was voted a scandalous attack on a member of the House (Bishop Warburton); outside it the revelation had the effect of destroying Wilkes's support at a stroke. For some time his supporters had been uneasy at the violence of the *North Briton*'s language and the disreputable nature of their hero's private life. Now he stood exposed as a crude blasphemer it was impossible for public men to identify with him. Obscenity might have been overlooked, but direct assault on Christianity in the most offensive terms could not be. Former supporters like William Pitt, who is known to have read and enjoyed his bawdy verses, hastened to condemn him in extravagant terms:

> The author did not deserve to be ranked among the human species – he was the blasphemer of his God and the libeller of his King. He had no connexion with any such writer. He neither associated nor communicated with any such . . . He knew nothing of any connexion with the writer of the libel.[49]

Nor did anyone else by the time the news spread. The Commons swiftly expelled the delinquent, and long before Chief Justice Pratt delivered his expected verdict, Wilkes had been condemned in the King's Bench and had fled the country. Sandwich had achieved one of the most spectacular political victories of the century.[50] Even his enemies were forced to admire it:

> This bomb was certainly well conducted, and the secret, though known to many, well kept. The management is worthy of Lord Sandwich, and like him. It may sound odd for me, with my principles, to admire Lord Sandwich; but besides that he has in several instances been very obliging to me, there is a good humour and an industry about him that are very uncommon. I do not admire politicians; but when they are excellent in their way, one cannot help allowing them their due. Nobody but he could have struck a stroke like this.[51]

Wilkes lived to fight another day, and to win victories against other opponents, but Sandwich was not involved in them and we need not pursue them. The legacy he was left with was a reputation as a political tactician of ruthless skill, and a treacherous hypocrite who had destroyed his former friend. We have seen that their friendship is very doubtful, and this aspect of the story seems to owe more to Wilkes's skill as a propagandist than to the facts of the case. At the same time Sandwich did have a reputation as a libertine, not altogether unfounded, and the stories were plausible enough to gain currency. It was at this time that the nickname 'Jemmy Twitcher' was first applied to him, from the character in Gay's *The Beggar's Opera* who betrays his colleague. Much of this, however, has been viewed and often is still viewed in the distorting mirror of Victorian morality. As Sandwich read out the *Essay on Woman* to an appreciative audience in the House of Lords, Le Despencer is reported to have remarked that he had never before heard the Devil condemn sin. This has been repeated as though it were an exclamation of pious horror, rather than a piece of easy banter in the intimate atmosphere of the Lords, whose active membership was only a few score all of whom knew one another well.[52] Le Despencer had never made any secret of his activities as 'St Francis' and could not have feigned to be shocked without consummate hypocrisy, but he had no need to pretend to be amused. The situation was full of humour. Quite apart from the contrast between Sandwich's private reputation and his public duty, the position of the Bishop of Gloucester was piquant. Warburton was a self-educated pedant of massive but unsound learning whose theological opinions were regarded by many as heretical, and whose violent and abusive controversial style aroused disgust even in an age of invective. Such a man was not the ideal defender of charity and orthodoxy. He had himself published an edition of Pope's *Dunciad* adorned with notes parodying the great scholar Bentley, which left him in a poor position to resent the 'diabolic monster' Wilkes's effrontery.[53] Lastly there was the rumour, known to at least some of those present, that Thomas Potter, the probable author of the *Essay on Woman*, was also the probable father of Warburton's only child.[54]

The members of the House of Lords undoubtedly had an entertaining afternoon, and with the exception of the bishops and the pious Lord Lyttelton, we need not imagine that as private men they were unduly shocked.[55] As public men, however, they had a clear duty to repel an assault on the king, the Church and the state which no defender of the British constitution could view with indifference. None of them would or could have acted in Sandwich's place in any other fashion than he did, though few of them could have handled the case with such skill. Wilkite propaganda was successful in attaching to Sandwich the reputation among the general public of a hypocrite, but among those who mattered to him, in the political world and in Parliament, the episode restored him after a long absence to the status of a politician of the first rank, a valuable friend and a dangerous enemy. He had returned to the Cabinet after twelve years largely because of his convenience to others rather than any positive claims of his own; after the Wilkes affair he commanded attention for his own abilities.

The prosecution of Wilkes was a serious distraction from the usual business of a Secretary of State, and in particular from foreign affairs. Sandwich dominated the ministry's handling of diplomatic issues by his energy, ability, and long experience.[56] His colleague Halifax was by now idle and complaisant; 'as to abilities and character . . .' an opponent wrote, 'dead and rotten before his Body actually died'.[57] Once the Wilkes affair was dealt with, Sandwich took the lead in formulating policy.[58] He was hampered by the Wilkes business itself, which did great damage to Britain's standing overseas. Foreign powers, nearly all absolute monarchies in which such activities would not have been tolerated for a day, took it for granted that a house divided against itself could not stand, and that Wilkes's career marked the weakness of British government. It was an impression shared by many British observers, particularly as a rapid succession of British governments chased one another in and out of power during the 1760s.[59]

Sandwich's diplomatic ideas were essentially those he had learnt in the 1740s. Like most British statesmen of the day, indeed of the century, he assumed that France was Britain's permanent and most dangerous enemy, and that she would probably be seconded by Spain. He took it for granted that Britain could and should acquire Continental allies to resist the might of France, and that European powers would naturally share Britain's views and wish to join her. By the 1760s these views were ceasing to correspond with the reality of the diplomatic situation.[60] The relative decline of France, and the spectacular victories of Britain during the Seven Years War, made Britain rather than France the object of fear and envy, at least among maritime powers. On the Continent France no longer appeared so formidable and French policy was unexpectedly quiescent. Just as Britain turned increasingly outwards towards colonies and maritime warfare, the centre of gravity within Europe was moving eastward with the rise of Russia. Here was the new region of instability where alliances were to be sought and found. The question was whether

Britain needed that sort of alliance, or needed it enough to pay whatever price was demanded.

Sandwich began his efforts with a hopeless attempt to interest
Austria in a revival of the 'Old System'; investigated the chances of
a Prussian alliance, (nil, as he soon concluded); then spent the bulk
of his time on negotiations with Russia. It proved possible to renew
a trade treaty, since both sides had good reasons to foster the Baltic
trade, but much more difficult to reach agreement on an alliance. The
basic problem was that the Russians wanted money and promises of
assistance against Turkey which represented far too high a price for
Britain to pay to secure the assistance of a power so remote from
the parts of the world where she expected to need help.[61] Sandwich
saw the problem clearly. 'There is one fundamental error', he told
Lord Buckingham in St Petersburg,

> which the Court of Petersburg seems to have taken up, and which we
> know for certain has been a favourite maxim with the minister, that
> the exigency of affairs in this country makes an alliance with Russia
> so absolutely necessary that we shall be glad to accept of it upon their
> own terms, whereas the real fact is that the present situation of Great
> Britain is so entirely free from any embarrassing engagements that no
> foreign power could wish for more favourable a period to enter into
> an alliance with us.[62]

Neither Sandwich nor his successors were able to overcome this
obstacle, and given the divergence of British and Russian interests,
it is doubtful if anyone could have. It has often been argued that
Britain's failure in these years to construct a system of Continental
alliances was a root cause of defeat in the American War fifteen years
later. This argument has been attacked from both sides: the alliance
in question was not available at any price which it would have been
reasonable to pay, and in any case British difficulties during the
American War arose from entirely different factors.[63] It can certainly
be said with hindsight that Sandwich's conventional ideas were no
longer adequate, but no amount of vision could have altered the
fundamental limitations of Britain's position, and in practice his
shrewd handling of affairs achieved as much as could be achieved.

Britain's strength, both diplomatic and military, lay chiefly in her
navy. It was this which had won her the Seven Years War, and on
which she had to rely during the peace.[64] This meant that the British
government had to be alert to foreign naval developments, and ready
to threaten whatever use of naval force was necessary to deter foreign
aggression. It also required keeping up British naval strength in spite

of the acute pressure for economy. In 1764 the Cabinet approved a scheme presented by Lord Egmont, Sandwich's successor at the Admiralty, for a long-term rebuilding project at Portsmouth and Plymouth to equip the dockyards for larger fleets.[65] Ministers were careful to keep foreign fleets under observation. Both Britain and France at this period kept their naval intelligence services at a much higher level than had previously been thought necessary in peacetime, and as early as 1763, the year of the Peace of Paris, the French were collecting information for the invasion of Britain.[66] Sandwich did not neglect other European navies, and instructed the British diplomats in his department to collect information on the fleets of the countries to which they were accredited, warning them that, 'there is a great deal of Difference between the real Strength of a Navy, and the Figure it makes when delivered in upon Paper'.[67]

Grenville and Sandwich agreed on the necessity of naval preparedness, and were ready to act on it as necessary. When a French warship occupied one of the Turks Islands in the West Indies the ministry's firmness had the intended effect.[68] Even the pacifist Bedford accepted the need for deterrence: 'I do most fervently agree with you, that the Eyes of all Europe are fixed upon us, to see whether we will brook such an injury or not'.[69] In such cases the diplomatic game had to be played with boldness, a quality Sandwich always excelled in. If the French retreated, an observer predicted,

> our Secretarys will plume themselves upon their spirited dispatches and will be looking out with eager expectations for popular applause, but if there is the smallest appearance of a rupture with that court, there is not a man among them except Lord Sandwich who would presume to take the lead in so dangerous a conjuncture.[70]

Diplomats who had to deal with Sandwich at this period carried away the impression of a businesslike and agreeable minister:

> An excellent Man to do Business with, and always speaks to the Purpose . . . I know not why the World has been so severe to him. I protest in all that I have seen, and lately I have seen his Lordship a good deal, there was not the smallest Trifle the Most rigid Moralist cou'd blame. I passed the last week at Hinchingbrook, where every thing breathed gaiety, Freedom, and good humor.[71]

Besides the main lines of policy, Sandwich had to deal with the many and varied incidents which came to a minister who dealt equally with home and foreign affairs. He had to cope with the crisis caused by the sudden insanity of the British minister in Copenhagen,[72] and parry the prosecution of the French ambassador in London – just the sort of incident which foreign observers agreed could never happen in a well-regulated state.[73] He had to advise on the appointment of bishops ('dignified divines are so long lived, that vacancys are extremely scarce; they are like cats & have nine lives each'),[74] and on the royal prerogative of mercy to condemned criminals ('you can't think how it distresses me to be put to a momentary decision where a mans life is concerned').[75] He also had to discharge the usual political obligations of a leading minister. He secretly managed 'Anti-Sejanus', the pen-name of the Reverend James Scott, who was one of the best political journalists of the period and who did a great deal to present the ministry's case to the public.[76] As Grenville's most capable colleague he helped in Parliamentary management. In September 1763 he wrote, 'I have been employed allmost this whole day with Mr Grenville in canvassing the list of the house of Commons'.[77] This was one of the most difficult and critical skills in an age of weak party structure, and notwithstanding his absence of experience in the Commons, it was one Sandwich excelled in.[78] Two years later Horace Walpole was teasing his successor for his mistakes: 'Sandwich was more accurate in lists, and would not have miscounted 25'.[79] It was at this period that Sandwich revived the practice of weekly Cabinet dinners for the despatch of business.[80] This was particularly apposite because George III was not averse to playing off his ministers against one another, and their political position was not as strong as it seemed in view of the disunity and feebleness of the opposition.[81]

For most of his time as Secretary of State Sandwich had one particular concern in domestic politics. In the autumn of 1763 it became clear that old Lord Hardwicke, the greatest living English jurist and doyen of successive ministries for twenty years, was dying. Among his offices he was High Steward of Cambridge University. This was an office of prestige rather than power, but it behoved the ministry to have a candidate ready. Sandwich and Halifax were the only Cambridge men in the Cabinet, and Sandwich made a private agreement that he would go for the High Stewardship while Halifax would be the candidate to succeed the Duke of Newcastle (then aged seventy) as Chancellor.[82] This presented the king and the rest of the ministry with something of a *fait accompli*, and they agreed without enthusiasm that Sandwich should be their candidate.[83] Aware of the danger in all electoral matters of starting late, Sandwich began his canvass before Hardwicke was dead, and as early as 29th November wrote, 'I have canvassed most of the principle people of the University of Cambridge, and have great reason to think I must meet with success'.[84] To begin canvassing before the vacancy occurred was not unusual in university politics,[85] but it was tactless, and contributed to the impression of ministerial power being deployed rather too forcefully and nakedly.[86] Especially in the aftermath of the Wilkes affair, Sandwich would have been wiser to have been less ruthlessly efficient, and he subsequently regretted the attempt.[87] As it was, he persuaded Newcastle and the opposition to put up the new Lord Hardwicke to stand against him. Hardwicke was a dull and timid candidate, but he was respectable, and provided a home for those offended by Sandwich's approach. The result was a long and close-fought contest ending in an exact tie and an appeal to the courts which was eventually decided in Hardwicke's favour.[88]

By this time, as Hardwicke later noted, 'Lord Sandwich was on the point of being dismissed, & neither he nor the Court were the least concerned about the issue of the Cause, & as little mortified at it as I was elated'.[89] In the summer of 1765 the ministry encountered a series of crises. The first and most spectacular was the weavers' riots of May 1765. Incensed by a vote the Duke of Bedford had given in favour of allowing imports of French silk, a mob of several thousand silk-weavers from Spitalfields surrounded and besieged Bedford House while a Cabinet meeting was going on within. The mob very nearly stormed the house, but at the last moment the ministers were saved by the arrival of the cavalry. Even then the Bedfords stood a siege of three days with a garrison of seventy soldiers.[90]

This sort of thing happened in the eighteenth century because government in general was weak, not because any particular administration was. The real troubles of Grenville's administration were not caused by popular riots or even votes in Parliament but by the disapproval of the king. He had not forgotten the expulsion of Lord Bute and had come to dislike Grenville intensely. He therefore worked behind the scenes to find an alternative. In May and June 1765 the crisis came to a head with a scheme for Pitt to form a ministry, but the reconciliation of Grenville with his brother Lord Temple, Pitt's closest ally, frustrated it, and Grenville was apparently restored to power stronger than before.[91] His triumph was short-lived. In July George III, with the help of his uncle the Duke of Cumberland, finally found the administration he sought, made up by the Marquis of Rockingham mainly from the followers of New-castle.[92] Once again Sandwich was in opposition, his reputation enhanced by two years in office, but his hold on power apparently no stronger than before.

CHAPTER VIII

Hope Deferred
1765–1770

Sandwich put a brave face on his dismissal: 'Jemmy Twitcher died like a Cock'.[1] He and his colleagues in the parties of Bedford and Grenville hoped that Pitt and his followers would soon join them, and were confident that the new administration would be weak and transient.[2] Its real head the Duke of Cumberland was obliged by his situation as a royal prince to remain in the background, while the nominal first minister, the Marquis of Rockingham, hardly seemed suitable to supply his place. The size of his estates made him a natural leader of society in Yorkshire, and he commanded a faithful following at the Jockey Club, which was well represented in his administration, but he was otherwise ignorant of public life, timid, and incapable of public speaking.[3] Weak as Rockingham's party and the new administration was in men with any experience of public life, and weaker still when Cumberland died on 31st October, it leaned considerably on the two admirals Sir Charles Saunders and Augustus Keppel. They were eminent at least in their own profession, and there were few in government who could claim as much. Nominally no more than junior members of the Admiralty Board of which Egmont remained First Lord, they occupied a position of political influence out of proportion to their offices, or indeed their experience;[4] 'wrongheaded admirals,' one of Sandwich's friends called them, 'a species of animal I admire upon their own element, but not amphibious enough ever to judge right on shore'.[5] They also brought an unusually political approach to their professional affairs. At the Rochester by-election of December 1765 they led the full Admiralty Board down to hold a formal session there. Newcastle, no stranger to the political arts, was scandalized by this naked manipulation of the dockyard vote: 'The same Thing might have done without that *Eclat*; Sir Robert [Walpole] dared not do *That*'.[6] As a whole, Rockingham's 'administration of boys' as George III later called it,[7] gave an impression of incompetence which delighted their opponents. Sandwich sarcastically summed up their arguments;

> that the late ministers are rogues, rascals, and idiots, and that they sold employments, and were governed by Lord Bute; that the present people are extremely popular, and likely to be able ministers, if their unkind and cruel adversaries will but give them time to learn their trade.[8]

Unfortunately for Sandwich, the unkind and cruel adversaries were not as united and formidable as he wished. Pitt was as always wayward and unpredictable. The Grenville and Bedford parties remained allied but distinct, while the Bedfords were themselves only a loose connection of which Sandwich was not the centre. It was always difficult to be sure who actually ran the duke's party; at various times Sandwich, Richard Rigby, the duchess, and even the duke himself were identified as the true leaders.[9] What became painfully clear to Sandwich was that his political position was not much stronger than it had been in the 1750s. Two years as Secretary of State had enhanced his ministerial reputation, but that had aroused jealousy as much as admiration. Lords Gower and Weymouth, Sandwich's less able colleagues in the Bedford party, regarded him as a dangerous rival.[10] His little group of four MPs gave him some consequence,[11] but he still did not carry enough weight to command office by himself, and he was not important enough to his party colleagues for them to demand it for him.

After twelve months Rockingham's ministry was replaced by one formed by William Pitt, now Earl of Chatham, without Sandwich being much nearer returning to power. On 17th July 1766 he wrote to his Grenvillite friend Augustus Hervey full of hope: 'you know I am not unreasonable, impracticable or improperly ambitious, but it would hurt me to be quite neglected'.[12] Two days later he was still hoping to be restored to the Admiralty,[13] but it was soon clear that Chatham had no immediate use for the old political 'factions' which he affected to despise. Sandwich had to be content with rural life, and a pretence of indifference to politics which deceived none of his friends. He had hopes in October when the Madrid embassy had to be filled and Chatham was extending feelers to Bedford, but they came to nothing.[14] The duke agreed with Weymouth, Gower and Rigby that the four of them must be 'reinstated in employments of magnitude, and that the rest who had suffered upon our account should be, as occasions offered, provided for'.[15] Sandwich was one of 'the rest'. In November he had wind of another negotiation between Chatham and Bedford, and wrote to remind the duke of his claims:

> We country gentlemen receive news of resignations among those con-
> cerned in the Political world without understanding what they mean,
> or what they are likely to end in . . . I flatter myself your Grace will
> consider me among the number of your friends, whither attack or
> defence is the plan you mean to pursue. I will only add one word
> more, which is that I find, that views of ambition are not so violent
> after a man is past 48 as before that period; & that therefore I shall not
> be so burthensome to you, as I should have been while the blood in
> my veins flowed with greater warmth.[16]

Bedford duly 'mentioned Lord Sandwich as one who might be of use to the King's affairs',[17] but his only demands were as before on behalf of Weymouth, Gower and Rigby.[18] The Bedfords did not regard the restoration of Sandwich as a high priority, and in any case Chatham was not prepared to make any concessions to buy their support. In the midst of the negotiations he appointed Sir Edward Hawke First Lord of the Admiralty without even mentioning it to Bedford, and the discussions collapsed.[19]

Sandwich returned to Hinchingbrooke to resume his frustrating wait:

> I am grown so mere a grazier that I scarce enquire how matters go in
> the Political world, but I think whenever any spirited measures are in
> agitation my friends will let me hear from them, & I shall then allways
> be ready to quit my grazing on a very short notice.[20]

During the spring of 1767 the Bedfords moved closer to the main body of the Rockingham group. In March Grenville had a 'Project of a Ministry to be formed if Ld Chatham should go out', combining his followers with the Bedfords and Rockinghams, making Sandwich or Gower Secretary of State.[21] Sandwich smelled a change of ministry ('I am not often mistaken in matters of this sort'),[22] but the grand design foundered on the Rockinghams' refusal to ally with the Grenvilles, Bedford's refusal to abandon them, and the unwillingness of either duke or marquis to take second place.[23] In July the Bedfords and the Rockinghams held a political conference to try to agree terms on which they might unite. Bedford, Weymouth, Rigby and Sandwich represented their party; Newcastle, Rockingham, Keppel, the Dukes of Richmond and Portland and others represented

theirs.[24] Sandwich and Weymouth were 'very reasonable and desirous to bring things to a happy conclusion', but after a promising
start, the conference foundered on the Rockinghams' surprise proposal to advance their follower Henry Seymour Conway.[25]

By the autumn the Bedfords had given up hope of building a united
opposition capable of forcing its way into power, and decided to
offer their services to the Duke of Grafton, who was effectively in
charge during the prolonged illness of Chatham. As a mere group
of individuals hungry for office their negotiating power was weak,
and what they had was reserved for the benefit of the party leaders.
The inexperienced, drunken and indolent Weymouth became Secretary of State. Sandwich was offered a half share in the Postmaster-
Generalship. The weakness of his position was obvious to all: he
badly needed office for political and financial reasons, he was neither
especially valuable to the leaders of his own party nor dangerous to
any other, and he would have taken whatever was offered.[26] The
Chatham administration had strengthened its position by splitting
the opposition and securing useful allies, and in Sandwich's case they
had paid a very cheap price to do so.
   The Postmaster-General was not an insignificant figure in an
eighteenth-century administration, for the postal system represented
a substantial part of the government's provincial patronage. For this
reason he was forbidden to engage in electioneering, a restriction
Sandwich found very irksome.[27] There was work to be done in
the actual administration of the Post Office, and Sandwich, taking
alternate months with his colleague Lord Le Despencer, took the job
seriously. Together they introduced a number of reforms tending to
reduce the cost and increase the efficiency of the postal service.[28] But
Anthony Todd the Secretary was an efficient manager, and there
was no disguising the fact that alternate months at the Post Office
hardly provided sufficient occupation for Sandwich's ability and
ambition:

> There is so little business that requires our attendance, & we have the
> good fortune to agree so perfectly well in every thing that requires
> our opinion, that there is very little occasion we should put ourselves
> to any inconvenience by a personal attendance.[29]

It is scarcely surprising that Sandwich was not 'thoroughly easy in
my present situation', as he put it in a letter to Grafton in October.
Some office like Lord Privy Seal, he hinted, would, 'enable me by

my situation to do more effectual service in the support of his [the king's] measures', and 'restore me to that rank in government which my former services give me some foundation to hope I may think myself entitled to look to'.[30] But there was no easy way to convert former services, or present abilities, to political advantage. Moreover idleness did not bring out the best in Sandwich. In August 1768 he considerably embarrassed his old colleague Bentinck by an unexpected appearance in Holland:

> the truth is that I am with a party of out of the way people of both sexes, who came to sea on a scheme of fishing, & out of a frolick, took it into our heads to pass a few days in this country, we have no cloaths but those on our back.[31]

He was in Amsterdam again in the autumn of 1769:

> I fear your Grace will think me a very idle man for passing my time as a boy at twenty does who goes to see the world as it is commonly called; but indeed I have nothing else to do, & cannot help saying that of all the scenes of life I ever was engaged in, the present is the most disagreeable.[32]

Frolics like these were ostensibly the reason why Sandwich did not realize another of his political hopes, to be Lord Lieutenant of Ireland. For a long time this had been a largely honorific and social position requiring only intermittent residence; 'a place wherein a man had business enough to hinder him from falling asleep, and not so much as to keep him awake', as Lord Chesterfield put it when he accepted the office in 1745.[33] In the 1760s, however, Anglo-Irish relations were becoming more delicate, and in 1767 the ministry were looking for an active statesman who would reside in Dublin.[34] Sandwich applied for the job, and it looked for a while as though he might get it.[35] It is usually said that he did not because the king disapproved of his private life, but George III's letter to Grafton gave equal weight to political objections from members of the administration,

> who are already jealous of the weight the Bedfords have in administration [and] I fear would be much hurt if so very great an Employment was given to Lord Sandwich, besides his Character is so well known in both Kingdoms that it would sully Administration; as to give him hereafter a more lucrative Employment I shall not object to that but cannot think his constant teazing can be sufficient grounds for placing Him where his Private Character must disgrace Me & administration.[36]

Five months later the king again advised that if a new Lord Lieutenant had to be chosen to replace Lord Townshend, he should be 'of at least as blameless a character, therefore must desire you will not give any encouragement to Lord Sandwich, who is as well known in Ireland as here'; and, the king went on to hint, whose advancement would strengthen the Bedford faction over Grafton's own.[37]

There is no doubt that George III's 'censorious chastity and sobriety'[38] was genuine, which makes it all the more difficult to take these remarks at their face value. The Duke of Grafton, to whom they were addressed, had spent his whole period of office absorbed in an extremely public affair with the professional courtesan Nancy Parsons, attended with ostentatious cruelties to his wife, to the neglect of his duties and the scandal of even the most tolerant members of society. This had then been concluded by a sensational divorce and the remarriage of both parties.[39] The whole business had brought the king's government, and by extension the king himself, into contempt throughout Europe. In the circumstances the king's reflections on Sandwich's (comparatively discreet) private failings were singularly ill-timed. In anybody but George III one might suspect sarcasm, but it seems more likely that he was merely erecting a flimsy screen around remarks which were essentially political. Grafton's ministry was disastrously divided, adrift in a sea of crises both foreign and domestic. The duke's priority in all this was to strengthen his faction at the expense of the others.[40] The king for his part was never entirely unhappy to see his ministers divided and his own freedom of manoeuvre enhanced. Read in this light his remarks seem to have a political rather than a moral significance. Certainly George III had been willing to see Halifax as Lord Lieutenant install his mistress as hostess of Dublin Castle,[41] and he had appointed and sustained Grafton. Ever since he had forced Grenville out of office he had presided over a succession of weak and fumbling ministries which had done grave damage to the country's standing abroad, and allowed destructive antagonisms to awake in domestic and colonial affairs. It was a bad time for a responsible sovereign to be quibbling about the private life of one of his ablest servants.

Furthermore there were many aspects of Sandwich's private life which were regular and even admirable, and several tastes he had in common with the king himself, notably music. A shared enthusiasm for opera as well as spoken drama had always been one of the things Sandwich and Bedford had in common,[42] but over time Sandwich's tastes moved towards concerts and oratorio. By 1759 at the latest he was holding regular musical meetings at Hinchingbrooke.[43] The pattern as it developed was for a whole week at Christmas and another in the summer to be dedicated to an ambitious and exhausting programme of music centred on the oratorios of Handel. The performers were a wide circle of Sandwich's friends and acquaintances with a stiffening of professional musicians, particularly for the solo parts. Many of the most eminent performers of the day came to the Hinchingbrooke meetings,

> where lord Sandwich is entertaining the county and University with Musick for a whole week; he has Giardini with him, and Leone, the Jew, who is said to have a wonderfully fine voice; I have been pressed to go to these Oratorio's, but have my hands, as usual, so full of work, that Orpheus himself could hardly tempt me to leave college.[44]

By 1767 Sandwich was assembling sixty or seventy performers[45] and tackling six different oratorios in six days, besides other music:

> Every Oratorio, which was performed in the evening, was rehearsed throughout in the morning. After dinner catches and glees went round with a spirit and effect never felt before, till everybody was summoned by a signal to the opening of the performance. This always lasted till supper was on the table: after which catches and glees were renewed with the same hilarity as in the earlier party of the day; and the principal singers generally retired to rest after a laborious exertion of about twelve hours. His Lordship constantly animated the whole by his own personal assistance; submitting himself at the same time to the discipline of the orchestra, with the most scrupulous obedience.[46]

The discipline required to sustain twelve hours' singing a day was not negligible, and a jocular poem describing the Hinchingbrooke music meetings refers to Sandwich whipping in stragglers who had slipped out for a walk:

> Lord Sandwich meantime, ever active and steady,
>   Eyes the drums with impatience, and cries, 'Arn't you ready?'
>   Knows who are the alert, and who always ask pardon,
>   And who are the men must be fetched from the garden.[47]

As this extract indicates, Sandwich himself always played the drums in the Hinchingbrooke orchestra. (His descendants still preserve his copy of the tympani parts of the Handel oratorios, with annotations in his hand.) We know nothing about his musical education, but he gives the impression of one who had come to an enthusiasm for music in adult life. He had little time to encounter it as a child at home, and little chance to at Eton, where musical instruments were actually forbidden to the scholars on the foundation.[48] As a young man he apparently tried to learn the harpsichord,[49] but in later life he confined himself to the drums, and singing. He evidently had a good general knowledge of the grammar of music, 'though he set up no pretensions to reputation, either as theorist, or as a performer'.[50] It is true that one person who knew him claims that 'he had not the least real ear for music, and was equally insensible of harmony and melody',[51] but it is hardly credible that anyone would spend so much time, enthusiasm and money over so many years on music, who was really incapable of appreciating it. His library contained a large quantity of vocal and instrumental music (some of it still in the family's possession),[52] and in private company he enjoyed singing.[53] Always a convivial host, he was at his most animated and charming in musical company, as even his enemies agreed:

> By the way (to quit a subject which vexes me and proves how little pretensions I have to Stoicism) Lord Sandwich appears to me a wonderfully pleasant man in society; he is quite what the French call *aimable*, and possesses in a high degree the art of putting all around him at their ease. I never saw so much of him before: I like his conversation and his musick, but fear that his politicks and ours would not make good harmony.[54]

Out of Sandwich's enthusiasm for music and from the circle of amateur and professional musicians he gathered at Hinchingbrooke arose several organizations which were to have an influence on the musical life of the nation, and one of which survives today. The Noblemen and Gentlemen's Catch Club, which he founded in 1761, existed and still exists to sing and to promote the writing of canons, catches and rounds. In a sense it was a musical outgrowth of the convivial societies like the Dilettanti, the Divan and the Turkish Club which Sandwich had been so much involved with in the 1750s. It met seriously to make music, but the members certainly had a good time in the process. They balloted for the prize-winning catches, and they balloted for the best claret. They sponsored and sang much sacred music, but they also enjoyed the classic catches of Purcell and other seventeenth-century composers in which, 'a judicious placing of rests in the parts ensured that words which had no connection with the written text would be heard in a new association which could give rise to more than one interpretation'.[55] The professional members who performed the prize pieces included such eminent musicians as Dr Arne, while the noblemen and gentlemen were many of them the same who attended the Hinchingbrooke music meetings.[56]

Sandwich remained a faithful attender at the Club almost to his death, but in musical terms it represented the early and less sophisticated phase of his musical enthusiasm. More directly inspired by the Hinchingbrooke meetings, and much more influential, was the Concert of Ancient Music, founded by Sandwich and his Welsh friend Sir Watkin Williams Wynn in 1776. As patron of the Catch Club and the Ancient Concerts, Sandwich exercised a powerful influence on English musical life, and he has been described as 'arguably the most important musical amateur in late eighteenth-century England'.[57] The idea of 'ancient music' was not a complete novelty; there had been an 'Academy of Ancient Music' founded in 1726 by Oxford Tories chiefly to preserve Latin church music,[58] but in an age when composers had not yet abandoned their public, all secular music was contemporary music. Sandwich and his friends were proposing something revolutionary;[59] to revive and preserve the music of the remote past, 'such solid and valuable productions of old masters as an intemperate rage for novelty had too soon laid aside as superannuated'.[60] The remote past meant specifically music written at least twenty years before, and above all the music of one man who had died in 1759, and who, they feared, was already half-forgotten: George Frederic Handel. The Concert of Ancient Music opposed the fashionable concerts of composers in the new 'galant' style like C. P. E. Bach with performances, which rapidly became equally or even more fashionable, of Handel, Glück, J. S. Bach, Purcell, Corelli, Pergolesi, Wilbye and others – but above all, Handel.[61] The Ancient Concerts,

> are conducted in the most magnificent stile. The Band is quite perfection and the best music is performed there, the presence of the Royal Family, and all the State Court attendants make the room look Grand. The Room is beautifully lighted, the Subscribers in number three hundred are all people of high rank and fashion.[62]

There was in this a social and even a moral dimension. The preservation of ancient music went with the preservation of the social order, and for many subscribers to the Concerts it was identified with the revived piety of the early Evangelical movement.[63] Sandwich was no Evangelical, but he was in the manner of his generation an enthusiast for the perfection of the British constitution, and he had perhaps some need to identify himself with the dignity and propriety associated with ancient music. This was not for him a matter of conscious calculation;[64] for all his powerful mind, he was always a conventional and unreflective thinker. His enthusiasm for Handel was straightforward and genuine, but there was nevertheless a significance belonging to the Ancient Concerts which spread beyond music.[65]

The Concerts were actually directed by the organist and conductor Joah Bates,[66] whose career owed a great deal to Sandwich's patronage. His father was parish clerk and landlord of the Ring o'Bells in Halifax. He was taught to play by the church organist at Rochdale, and went on to school in Manchester where there was a more celebrated organist. He then became a scholar at Eton – a bold step in an age when life on the foundation was so hard that it was difficult to find parents willing to risk their boys, or boys tough enough to survive it. Musical instruments were forbidden to the scholars, but Bates found a sympathetic master with a harpsichord. He emerged from Eton to become first a scholar and then a fellow of King's College Cambridge, where he became the tutor of Sandwich's younger son William Augustus. He was already prominent in university music-making, and his talents as musician and scholar recommended him. He became Sandwich's private secretary, followed him to the Admiralty in 1771, and after years of efficient hard work received the conventional reward for a First Lord's private secretary of promotion to the Victualling Board. Meanwhile his life as a musician proceeded in parallel with his career as a public servant. From directing university concerts at Cambridge he graduated to the orchestra at Hinchingbrooke, and from there to the Concerts of Ancient Music.[67] By this time he was probably the best-known keyboard player and orchestral director in England – director is the correct term, for he always eschewed the new-fangled French custom of having a conductor 'to beat the time, either with a roll of paper, or a noisy *baton*, or truncheon',[68] and directed even the largest forces from the keyboard. This had been the invariable custom of Handel, and Bates was the greatest Handelian of his day. In 1766 he organized and directed a performance of the *Messiah*, the first oratorio ever heard in the North Country, to celebrate the commissioning of a new organ in the parish church of his native Halifax. (On this occasion Dr Herschel the future Astronomer Royal played first fiddle in the orchestra.)[69] Sandwich's 1769 trip to Holland was in part undertaken to give Bates a tour of the great Dutch organs.[70]

In 1780 Bates married Sarah Harrop, whose career was one of the most remarkable in eighteenth-century music. She is said to have been a Lancashire mill-girl,[71] and sang in a women's choir, a North-Country innovation disapproved of by traditionalists.[72] In 1772, when she was seventeen, she was one of a group of Lancashire singers who took part in the Three Choirs Festival at Gloucester, where she attracted the attention of the eminent musician Dr Howard of Leicester, and was introduced to the annual music meeting there patronized by Sandwich's friend Lord Denbigh, and directed by Bates.[73] From there she proceeded via the Catch Club to be the principal soloist of the Ancient Concerts, making her London debut in *Judas Maccabaeus* in 1777. She was soon regarded as the finest soprano of her age, an unequalled interpreter of the great Handelian rôles. Married to Mr Commissioner Bates, she continued to sing at private concerts, and on several occasions before the king and queen: 'Mrs Bates is now and then sent for to the Queen's House to sing to their Majesties, but she never attends their Concerts except at their requests, and that on the footing of a gentlewoman and without any reward'.[74] It was a remarkable rise from obscure origins, and Sandwich's knowledge and enthusiasm played a significant part in it.

Sandwich also became a friend and supporter of the musical scholar and historian Charles Burney. He helped Burney's tours on the Continent by providing introductions to ministers and noblemen, and when Burney's great work *The History of Music* appeared he subscribed for five sets himself, and collected twenty other subscriptions from his friends.[75] As with Bates, Sandwich's musical enthusiasm intersected with his public career. Dr Burney's son James joined the Navy: in 1771 they were both invited to Hinchingbrooke to meet Captain Cook, then just about to set out on his second Pacific voyage.[76] Young Burney sailed with Cook and a recommendation from the First Lord, and duly returned an acting lieutenant. He sailed again on the third voyage, by which time he was not only one of the handful of Englishmen who could speak Polynesian, but was able to help Sandwich elucidate a problem which greatly interested him, whether the South Sea islanders did or did not understand harmony and counterpoint. Burney was able to produce actual examples of Polynesian music which he had written in his journal.[77] The correspondence incidentally shows that Sandwich had a good understanding of the grammar of music, as well as providing an example of the musical influence on his public life.

The musical influence on his private life centred on Martha Ray. About the year 1762, in circumstances variously stated in several accounts, none of them very reliable, Sandwich took as his mistress a seventeen-year-old milliner's apprentice.[78] She had a fine voice which he had trained by several of the best teachers of the day (in particular the retired *prima donna* Catherina Galli), and she sang most of the female solos in the oratorios at Hinchingbrooke.

> I have frequently enjoyed the pleasure of hearing her sing at Hinchinbroke, and as well for that as her personal accomplishments and engaging manner allways thought her the most accomplished woman I have seen. Her behaviour on those occasions, on which for six nights together, she alone supported all the female parts in different oratorios and did the honours of Ld. S's house to everyone's satisfaction, was surprising, and (if any thing) might in some measure apologize for his attachment. In short I look on her as a second Cleopatra – a woman of thousands and capable of producing those effects on the heart which the poets talk so much of and which we are apt to think chimerical.[79]

She and Sandwich lived together for seventeen years, during which she bore him five children (one source says nine children of whom five lived).[80] As far as discretion and propriety allowed – which is to say, in private among tolerant friends – they lived openly as man and wife. Divorce was only possible in the eighteenth century by private act of Parliament, and was effectively accessible only to those who did not need to think either of money or public opinion. For Sandwich, Martha Ray represented the nearest he could get to the happy marriage he had lost for ever. As far as we can tell she provided him with the happiness and stability which he badly needed, and his 'London family' formed the centre of his affections. It is significant that the correspondence from Robert Montagu, his eldest son by Martha Ray, is warm and affectionate in tone, while his relations with his heir Lord Hinchingbrooke were always strained. Moreover Hinchingbrooke resented his father's alternative family and Sandwich had to try to ensure that they never met.[81]

This was part of the problem which troubled his relationship with Martha Ray in 1772. Sandwich had refused to make her any financial settlement, no doubt because of the precarious situation of his finances. She was perturbed by the fate she foresaw for her and her children if Sandwich should die and leave them to Hinchingbrooke's mercy. She also realized that her voice could earn her a large income on the stage, so that she was not without some means of independence.[82] She was clearly a woman of character, not easily

browbeaten, and Sandwich's refusal to make her a settlement caused
a brief crisis, during which Sandwich turned for advice to his friend
Lord Loudoun.

> I will not conceal from you that nothing can be a greater calamity to
> me than the loss of Miss Ray, but as things stand at present unless
> you can interpose I see very little probability of preventing it; giving
> way to a woman in unreasonable points never does any good, besides
> I never did nor never will make a settlement, it is too foolish a prop-
> osition to tell the reasons against it.[83]

Loudoun firmly advised that Sandwich ought in honour and prudence to make her a settlement: 'she is a fine woman whom you
debauched very young who you tell me has lived with you eleven
years I see she still possesses your fondest wishes'.[84] It is not clear
on exactly what terms, but the quarrel was resolved and their domestic life resumed on its old footing.[85] There is no doubt that they
were deeply fond of one another, and yet even by eighteenth-century
standards, and even allowing for his financial situation, Sandwich's
conduct towards her seems ungenerous. It must also be said that
enough survives on paper to prove that he was not entirely monog-
amous during these years.[86]

It is an open question whether the same was true of her. In 1771
she made the acquaintance of a young army officer named James
Hackman, in Huntingdonshire with a recruiting party. They were
attracted to one another, and Hackman at least entertained some
hopes of marriage. In order to prosecute them he threw up his military career and took orders, intending to carry Martha Ray off to a
country vicarage.[87] Whether a clergyman could really have married
a cast-off mistress and still have hoped for a living is uncertain, and
it is equally obscure how much encouragement he received from
her. Much of the evidence is contained in a series of letters purporting
to be love letters between them, which was published soon after her
death. Contemporaries agreed that they were obviously spurious,
and there is no doubt that the letters as then published contain numerous passages added by the editor to bolster his argument in an un-
related literary dispute. The modern editor of the correspondence,
however, believed the letters, stripped of their additions, to be genuine.[88] They certainly had a good provenance and contain nothing
which is obviously impossible. One interesting detail in the letters
is Martha Ray's suspicion of Omai the Polynesian, then staying at
Hinchingbrooke: 'Omiah's simplicity is certainly very diverting, but

I should like him better, and take more pains with him, if I did not think he suspected something'.[89] We know from another source that he did observe something.[90] If the correspondence is genuine, Martha Ray's attachment to Hackman was longer and deeper than Sandwich ever discovered.[91] She was strongly tempted by the prospect of a secure, respectable marriage, and held back only by the thought of losing her children: 'My poor, innocent, helpless babes! Were it not on your account, your mother would not *act* the part she does'.[92] At least, that is the impression she gave Hackman, to whom she would hardly have stressed a continuing love for Sandwich. All accounts agree that he made a final approach to her in 1779, when he had probably not seen her for some time, and was refused. Hackman's letters give an impression of an unstable young man, and it is curious that he twice relates to her stories of men who killed their lovers.[93]

If the letters are genuine it was a warning. On the evening of 7th April 1779, while Sandwich worked late at the Admiralty, Martha Ray went in his coach to the opera at Covent Garden, accompanied by Signora Galli who lived in the household as a companion or chaperone. As she was stepping into the coach at the end of the performance, Hackman came up to her with a pair of pistols and shot her through the head. He then fired the second at himself and missed.[94] They brought the news to Sandwich late that night:

> His Lordship stood, as it were, petrified; till suddenly seizing a candle, he ran up stairs, and threw himself on the bed, and in an agony exclaimed, 'Leave me for a while to myself – I could have borne any thing but this!'.[95]

Very early the next morning he scribbled a note to his friend Captain Walsingham:

> My Dear Walsingham, For Gods sake come to me immediately, in this moment I have much want of the comfort of a real friend; poor Miss Ray was inhumanly murthered last night as she was stepping into her coach at the playhouse door.[96]

It was a long time before Sandwich was willing to move in society, but at length Walsingham persuaded him to dine with him:

> All passed off exceedingly well for a while, and his Lordship appeared more cheerful than could have been expected; but after coffee, as Mr and Mrs Bates were present, something was mentioned about music, and one of the company requested that Mrs Bates would favour them

with 'Shepherds, I have lost my Love'. This was unfortunately the very air that had been introduced by Miss Ray at Hinchinbrook, and had been always called for by Lord Sandwich. Mr Bates immediately endeavoured to prevent its being sung, and by his anxiety increased the distress; but it was too late to pause. Lord Sandwich for a while struggled to overcome his feelings, but they were so apparent, that at last he went up to Mrs Walsingham, and in a very confused manner said, he hoped she would excuse his not staying longer at that time, but that he had just recollected some pressing business which required his return to the Admiralty.[97]

Thus for the second time in life Lord Sandwich was cruelly deprived his domestic happiness. After Hackman had been convicted of murder and condemned to death, he

desired Lord Sandwich's pardon, without wch he could not die in peace; Lord Sh sent him word as he 'look'd upon this horrid action as an act of frenzy he forgave it, that he received the stroke as coming from Providence wch he ought to submit to, but that it had robb'd him of *all comfort in this world*'.[98]

'I suppose you have heard of the late accident,' he wrote to a friend about this time, 'pray God keep you and yours from such severe trials'.[99] When Sandwich's private failings are remembered, as they so often are, his sufferings should also be remembered, and something allowed for the fact that twice in his life he had been cut adrift from his moorings and driven out to sea.

CHAPTER IX

The Admiralty and the Navy
1770–1774

During the years from 1765 to 1770, while Sandwich sought solace in music from the trials of unemployment and underemployment, the standing of the country abroad had fallen to a degree which seemed extraordinary to everyone who in 1763 had watched a triumphant Britain dictating terms of peace to France and Spain. Weak and unstable, the ministries of Rockingham, Chatham and Grafton had observed but failed to control a series of foreign and domestic crises. The career of Wilkes as a popular gadfly reached a new pitch of confusion and tumult with his disputed election as MP for Middlesex in 1768, further impressing foreigners with an idea of the weakness of British government, while the rapid succession of ministries confirmed their prejudice that only autocratic, monarchical government could provide stability and order.[1] The Secretaries of State who conducted, or failed to conduct, foreign policy during these years did not inspire respect. Grafton was young and inexperienced; Conway hesitant; Halifax and Weymouth each drunken and idle; Shelburne clever but bitterly distrusted and not on speaking terms with his colleagues; Rochford an experienced diplomat but volatile, indiscreet, and suspected of abusing his position to manipulate the stock exchange for private profit.[2] Grenville's ministry had handled foreign affairs firmly and had not hesitated to threaten force. The contrast with his timid and indecisive successors was striking. The 1766 dispute with Spain and France over the possession of the Falkland Islands was the first revelation to French and Spanish ministers, and above all to Choiseul the French foreign minister, that their position was not so weak as they had supposed. Though British naval power was still unequalled, warships frightened nobody in the hands of a government unable to take the decision to mobilize them. Thus the weakness of the Chatham ministry, that 'tesselated pavement without cement', as Burke called it, converted a strong position into a serious diplomatic defeat.[3] The story was repeated on a larger scale with the French annexation of Corsica in 1768. Choiseul was emboldened by his previous success, but he did not confuse ministerial weakness with military weakness, and it is probable that France could have been deterred by a British show of force. Instead Britain made a show of vacillation and division, and the French ministry gained both a diplomatic triumph and a significant strategic advantage in the Mediterranean.[4] Detached observers in Britain were appalled by the damage done to the country's international standing. 'Fuimus Troes; fuit Ilium', wrote the Under-Secretary Edward Weston in 1769, recalling the fate of Troy.[5]

Recovery from this humiliating condition had much to do with the rise of a British politician who never held a diplomatic office or dealt directly with foreign affairs. Lord North became Chancellor of the Exchequer in Grafton's government in September 1767, and leader of the House of Commons soon after. His competence in both rôles was immediately obvious; though Grafton remained First Lord of the Treasury, he was glad to leave his colleague to run the Board.[6] When Grafton resigned in January 1770, his ministry irreconcilably divided over domestic and colonial policy, the king invited North to succeed him. North's triumph in simultaneously constructing and defending an administration in the most unpromising circumstances was the first of what turned out to be many examples of his mastery of the House of Commons. Much of the instability of the previous ministries had arisen from their lack of convincing leadership in the Commons. North was the first prime minister since Grenville five years before to be able to manage the Commons himself, and with the combination of his unequalled skill in that arena, and a support from the king which Grenville had soon lost, North was soon presiding over a ministry with prospects of stability not seen for years.[7]

To achieve it he needed a ministerial team of his own choosing, capable of working effectively together. His chance came with another crisis in foreign policy. In September 1770 came news that Spanish troops had expelled the British garrison in the Falkland Islands. Weymouth as Southern Secretary took an intransigent line, but the Spaniards proved to be equally firm, and ministers faced the prospect of war. Foreign powers were by now persuaded that British governments would always retreat. The problem was how to change their minds without actually precipitating a war, and Weymouth's colleagues came to suspect that his inflexible attitude was an obstacle to real negotiation. Initially without Weymouth's knowledge, North began to take private diplomatic soundings to see if there were any hopes of peace. When the Cabinet backed North's approaches the crisis came to a head, and in December Weymouth resigned. North had to find a successor quickly; one who would be beholden to North himself for his office, one who had the ability and experience to discharge it better than Weymouth. Since it was important to conciliate Weymouth and retain his support, his views were taken seriously. Weymouth proposed that his Bedfordite colleague Sandwich should replace him as Secretary of State, while his place at the Post Office was taken by Weymouth's brother as a demonstration that he continued on friendly terms with the administration. The scheme had advantages for North which Weymouth perhaps did not appreciate, for it permitted North to detach Sandwich from the Bedfords, who had done so little for him in recent years. North, who had arrived in power unprovided with political followers, now had an ally of proven ability, and he had deprived the Bedford connection of its most valuable member. The duke himself died a few weeks later, hastening the disintegration of his group. George Grenville had died in November, and most of his followers likewise joined North's following. The result was a stable ministry enjoying substantial support in Parliament and from the king, facing a feeble and divided opposition.[8]

Yet again Sandwich had reached high office because he formed a convenient element in someone else's political scheme rather than because his abilities were in demand for their own sake. The difference was that in attaching himself to North he had for the first time in his career chosen a patron who came to understand and value his skills, and one whose own position was neither a threat to Sandwich nor threatened by him. North was not a conventional politician who had risen with the help of a party of his own. Until he became prime minister he had no party, and his claim to high office was his skill in finance and Parliamentary politics. He was not vulnerable to the conventional politics of faction and intrigue by which Sandwich had pursued his career, and consequently he had no need to feel jealous. He could appreciate and employ Sandwich's very different skills, because they complemented his own, rather than threatening him. For other politicians Sandwich remained a dangerous rival: 'where there are great acknowledg'd public talents they will always raise little low opposition,' a friend warned him; 'reputation is like fruit: the birds picking at it shows both its excellence & maturity'.[9] For him the difference was that he now belonged to a stable ministry which was willing and able to use his talents.

The paradox was that in spite of his experience as Secretary of State and his obvious qualifications for the place, neither North nor he had been looking in that direction. Sandwich's eyes had long been fixed on his favourite object of ambition, the Admiralty. He had good reason to think himself well qualified for it, and he was aware of rising dissatisfaction with the effectiveness of Sir Edward Hawke as First Lord. Hawke was an eminent sea commander but had never been entirely at home with administration or politics, and he was not well equipped to make the best of Grafton's divided and hesitant administration.[10] He himself admitted that the Navy Estimates under Grafton were insufficient: 'the late peace establishment will not keep up fourscore ships of the line in perfect repair, especially when it [is] clipped ten or twelve thousand every year by the Minister'.[11] This implied that the real strength of the fleet was at least twenty ships of the line less than it appeared to be. Hawke's health had for some time been poor, and those ambitious for his office watched it with interest, but he was rumoured to refuse any hint of resignation unless he were paid off with a peerage. In August the Navy was described by Augustus Hervey, admittedly a highly partisan witness, as, 'a ruined service . . . I have the particulars of many instances of neglect very alarming to this country, but when ignorance and obstinacy are predominant at that Board, it is of little consequence to represent'.[12] Another prejudiced but well-informed observer was the Duke of Grafton, who hoped to return to public office as First Lord, and was fed with information damaging to Hawke by his protégé Thomas Bradshaw, Secretary of the Treasury, and by Captain Cockburne the Controller of the Navy.[13] When Cockburne died in July Bradshaw was alarmed that Hawke would make an unsuitable appointment, though, 'from the weakness of the Admiralty, it was doubly necessary that the Comptroller of the Navy should be a man of ability & diligence'.[14] The progress of the mobilization ordered in the autumn of 1770 aroused further misgivings in Hawke's colleagues. Some of them suspected that the Admiralty's reports concealed more than they revealed.[15] Bradshaw complained that,

> The Admiralty have already most miserably *bungled* the business, & they are not only tardy, but every step they mean to take, is already, as well known as it will be, when carried into Execution – from what I have already seen of that office, I not only pity the Country, but the Minister who is to work with such Implements.[16]

All these were partisan comments, though made by men in a position to be well informed. Modern research suggests that Hawke handled the mobilization itself with energy and speed, but that the Admiralty was taken by surprise by the poor condition of the ships in reserve.[17] What is certain is that the mobilization soon acquired a momentum of its own. So much depended in eighteenth-century naval warfare on gaining an initial advantage, that the power which gained it was under the strongest pressure to use its advantage by going to war at once. The situation was analagous to the 'war of timetables' of 1914, with the dockyards taking the place of the railway system. By the beginning of December Britain had a clear lead, and the belligerent Weymouth was driving towards war. On 17th December, the day Weymouth resigned, Bradshaw wrote that 'I believe there is not a glimmering of Hope, that we shall have peace, in the mind of any one person, who knows the real state of things'.[18]

The chances of peace were saved, not only by the resignation of Weymouth, but by a similar political change which took place a week later in France. Ever since the end of the Seven Years War the Duc de Choiseul had been following a policy of building up the French navy for a war of revenge which should retrieve all the disasters and humiliations of that conflict.[19] Now his Spanish allies were drawing France into a war long before the French navy was ready for it, he struggled to avert the possibility. The prospect of being dragged into war generated a political crisis in France for much the same reasons as it did in England, and on Christmas Eve 1770 Choiseul was dismissed. Three days later Richard Phelps, one of the Under-Secretaries of State, minuted on an intercepted and deciphered despatch from the fallen minister:

> the Court of France in dismissing Mr de Choiseul have turn'd out an able and active Minister, and who certainly has meditated nothing but war (when he found a favorable occasion) ever since the last peace.[20]

The removal of both Weymouth and Choiseul opened the door to peace negotiations. The French at first disbelieved British sincerity, but when the French chargé d'affaires in London called on Lord North after dinner and found him 'drunk as a cabbie' but still taking the same line, they concluded he must be sincere.[21] Once Paris and London understood one another, Madrid was obliged to come to an accommodation, and one hour before Parliament reassembled on 22nd January 1771, an agreement was signed.[22]

The same day, the Earl of Halifax kissed hands as Secretary of State for the Northern Department. The prospect of peace had wrought another revolution in Sandwich's career. So long as war seemed imminent it was difficult to dispose of a great naval hero like Admiral Hawke, but as soon as the crisis had passed there was a reaction against him. North and his colleagues felt that the mobilization had revealed serious problems with the Navy, and that the elderly and sickly Hawke was not the man to deal with them. So the admiral was retired with his peerage, and North turned to the man best fitted to succeed him – and best fitted to exclude the rival claimant, Grafton, who as the recent chief minister would not have been so agreeable a Cabinet colleague.[23] After three weeks as Secretary of State, Sandwich returned for the third time to be First Lord of the Admiralty. Nominally it was a demotion, and actually involved a fall in salary, but there is no reason to disbelieve what he wrote to his son: 'It is not I that have accommodated administration but administration that has gratified me in my request to change my department'.[24] The Admiralty had long been the object of his ambition, North had agreed the previous August that he was the best qualified candidate,[25] and with so much to be done, appointment to the Admiralty, 'in the present critical conjuncture, is the highest Mark of His Majesty's Goodness, and Confidence in me, that I could possibly receive'.[26]

To see what had to be done, we need to step back from 1771 to look at the situation of the Admiralty and the Navy in the mid-eighteenth century, and at what had changed since Sandwich had last had a real opportunity to influence naval affairs twenty years before. The key to many of the Navy's problems, and an essential factor in almost all of them, was mobilization; so often taken for granted in the eighteenth century, and so often forgotten today. The fact that in peacetime the majority of the Navy's officers, especially its senior officers, were unemployed, meant immense problems in recreating the professional skills, discipline, cohesion and physical fitness which they had possessed ten or fifteen years before. The fact that in peacetime the majority of the Navy's ratings dispersed to employment in the merchant service or elsewhere meant that in wartime the supply of skilled manpower always fell far short of the demand, and could be made up only very slowly and painfully. The fact that in peacetime the majority of the Navy's ships, including almost all the battleships, were laid up in Ordinary, presented great difficulties in peacetime maintenance, and imposed an impossible strain on the yards at the outbreak of war.[27]

The first problem which Sandwich had to address, the problem which had been thrown into sharp focus by the 1770 mobilization, was the relationship between shipbuilding and repair, the size of the fleet and the size of the dockyards. By the end of the Seven Years War the fleet had grown by sixty-five per cent in twenty years to a theoretical size of nearly 150 ships of the line,[28] but with the limited exception of Portsmouth and Plymouth, the dockyards remained virtually unaltered from Queen Anne's reign. Not only were the available docks, building slips and stores supporting a greatly increased load, but they were facing a changed strategic situation. The requirements of the sixteenth and seventeenth century had given the Navy a concentration of yards to the eastward. Four of the six major yards were in the Thames or Medway, only two were on the south coast, and only one, Plymouth, was well placed to support the Western Squadron which had come to be the centrepiece of British naval strategy. Although Plymouth had undergone some recent expansion, it fell far short of the demands which had lately been placed on it, and probably would be placed again in a future war. Of the eastern yards, Woolwich, Deptford and Sheerness all suffered from cramped sites which inhibited expansion; Chatham was shoaling badly; and Sheerness, which alone had ample deep water and easy access to the open sea, was affected by malaria above water and shipworm below. For all these reasons, much of the Navy's capacity to build and repair ships was in the wrong places. Even more critical, in some respects, was the distribution of the victualling yards, which were still more heavily concentrated to the eastward. Since the prevailing winds blow from the South-West, the Western Squadron's supplies had to come up from far to leeward, with the inevitable result of long and unpredictable delays. The result had been a victualling crisis in 1758 when the Western Squadron under Hawke first attempted the blockade of Brest.[29] Taking all the yards together the resources were clearly no longer adequate to build, maintain and support a fleet of the size which actually existed.

Although the general nature of the problem was evident to informed contemporaries, it was extremely difficult for them to grasp it in detail. The design and construction of ships were questions of great complexity, far beyond the understanding of most politicians. Even sea officers, who knew about handling ships and often held strong opinions about their qualities, were entirely dependent on the naval architects to realize them. The management of the yards, each of which individually was about ten times the size of the largest private enterprises of the time, presented problems of management which were equally outside the experience, and often the comprehension, of even well-informed outsiders. These factors provided the

Navy Board with much of its inherent advantage in dealing with unwelcome proposals of innovation.

There were further factors which made it very difficult even for the experts to estimate the true situation. Wooden ships were always vulnerable to decay, and it was all too easy for ships in reserve to rot without anybody noticing. Even if the shipkeepers and the yard officers were alert, which was by no means always the case, the ships' massive hulls easily concealed decay which only became obvious when they were taken in hand to be commissioned, and sometimes not until they got to sea. Frequently ships listed as being in good condition proved on inspection not to be so. Less often the reverse happened, with ships supposed to be in a poor state discovered to be sounder than had been feared. For these reasons navies' own lists of their real, effective strength were always approximate, and their intelligence of foreign naval powers even more liable to error. Mobilization was often the occasion for surprises, usually unpleasant surprises. One thing was constant, that a proportion, sometimes even a majority of the ships nominally on the list were not in practice capable of being sent to sea, or not in any reasonable time. But this was another source of confusion and variation in lists, for which ships could and could not be repaired for service was not an absolute, but a matter of judgement in given circumstances. If the yards were not too busy, a ship might be taken in hand which at busier times would have been laid aside in favour of more urgent work, and very likely have been too far gone in decay by the time her turn came for the dock. 'At present', as Sandwich explained,

> when ships are laid up in Ordinary they are divided into three Classes (exclusive of those in good condition) namely such as require small, middling, & great Repair. – Those that are nearest being brought into condition for service must naturally be first taken in hand, & while they are in the Dock the others grow worse & worse, & before there is any room for them many of them successively become past Repair, & must be broke up or sold; whereas were their docks sufficient, more of them would be taken in at the same time, & many valuable ships saved from destruction which would in process of time fully repay the Expense of the additional Docks & other Requisites.[30]

In this way the yards' resources to repair ships directly affected the number which could be kept available. When the fleet had outgrown the yards, as it had long before 1771, its size could only be kept up by allowing ships to decay before the notional end of their useful lives, and building more ships to replace them. Since the yards were as short of building slips as of docks for repairs (and the biggest ships were best built in dock anyway), this extra construction could only be undertaken by contract in merchant shipbuilding yards. Since contract-built ships were by universal consent of inferior workmanship and shorter working lives, this in turn increased the repair burden and worsened the overall position of the fleet.

The repair problem also reacted directly on another prime cause of confusion, misinformation and ignorance in naval affairs, the system of naval finance. Parliament voted Estimates for the Navy in terms not of money but of a number of men, which by a traditional formula was converted into money terms. The formula had long ceased to bear any relation to reality, but it continued to cause confusion to those who interpreted an increase in 'men' as a sign of mobilization, when it was equally or more likely to represent extra shipbuilding, arrears of repairs or discharged debts.[31] That part of the estimate which covered repairs to ships, and which ostensibly specified how much was to be spent on each named ship during the financial year, was in practice the prisoner of unpredictable circumstances. No one could know in any detail what works the yards would be able to undertake during the year, what accidents and emergencies would occur, which ships would prove on examination to be the most urgent cases and which the least promising, what estimates of the cost of repair would prove to have been accurate and what to have been wildly wrong. The result was enormous discrepancies between theory and practice. Between 1774 and 1783 fifty-two estimates for repairs to 74-gun ships were presented to Parliament, but only thirty-nine of them were actually taken in hand. Eleven other ships not mentioned in the Estimates at all were repaired instead. £36,972 was voted over four years to repair the *Dragon*, but none of it was ever spent on her. Sums were voted to build at least two ships which were never begun.[32] The Navy Board and the yard officers had in fact long ceased to pay much attention to the notional breakdown supplied in the Navy Estimates,[33] and could not in any circumstances have regarded it as fixed and binding, but many politicians were ignorant enough to take it as a real statement of what was, or ought to be happening. Hence a famous scene in the House of Commons when something of this had been explained, and Burke in an affected passion threw at the Treasury bench the 'fine gilt book of Estimates, calculated to a farthing, for purposes to which the money granted was never meant to be applied'.[34]

There was a further reason why the Navy Estimates did not closely reflect what was actually spent on the Navy, for they were not the only source of naval finance. The Navy and Victualling Boards paid for what they purchased in the usual fashion by writing bills of exchange, but Navy Bills were not simply payable within the customary ninety days. They were numbered and paid in strict sequence, and when naval finance was under strain the 'Course of the Navy' (the delay between issue and payment) was allowed to increase. Since bills of exchange were negotiable, and Navy Bills bore interest after six months, the Navy was in effect issuing its own negotiable securities; a private national debt outside the control of Parliament or the Treasury. Navy Bills traded at a discount to their face value which reflected the Course of the Navy, and both discount and Course were printed daily in the financial press. In practice Navy Bills were regarded as an investment, or rather a speculation, for specialists with deep pockets. The naval supplier looked up the current price of Navy Bills in the paper, adjusted his price accordingly, and when he received his bill took it down to the Exchange to sell it for cash to one of the bill brokers who dealt in them. The system of payment 'in course' inflated costs, as all systems of borrowing do, but it gave the Navy a large measure of flexibility to spend either more or less than Parliament had granted. Naturally the difference was usually on the side of greater spending, and at intervals, especially after each war, the Admiralty obtained Parliamentary grants to pay off part of its debt, or fund it into government stock. This means that there is a very large difference between tables of Parliamentary votes for the Navy, with their occasional sudden peaks when debt was paid off, and tables of actual expenditure whether on vote or credit.[35]

For all these technical and financial reasons, it was difficult even for the most expert contemporaries to arrive at exact knowledge of the situation. It was easy for men who really were, or had some pretence to be experts, to differ widely in their estimates of the situation, even if they were not influenced by political considerations. For the Admiralty, always to a considerable extent the prisoner of the Navy Board's information, a determined effort was needed to come to grips with the situation.

Lord Egmont, who succeeded Sandwich as First Lord in 1763, seems to have been the first to appreciate the problem, and to draw up a scheme to tackle it.[36] Egmont had constant and generally unsuccessful battles with Grenville over the Navy Estimates, but in 1765 he was able to obtain approval for a long-term plan to expand the capacity of the yards, though for financial reasons the improvements were restricted to Plymouth and Portsmouth, at a cost of £352,240 and £379,170 respectively.[37] This building programme was very slowly advanced during the 1760s. At the same time no administration provided sufficient funds to maintain the existing fleet. In September 1764 it was reckoned that the total fleet at the end of the war the previous year had been 149 ships of the line, including those under construction. Of these, nine had since been scrapped, nineteen were not worth repair, and forty-one had been completed or made ready for service, leaving not less than eighty ships awaiting attention. To repair them and replace the nineteen – that is to make up a fleet of 140 ships – would need £2,003,785.[38] Six months later in March 1765 the Navy Board reported that twenty-two out of a total fleet of about 140 ships of the line were in commission and only twenty-five more in good condition. By working overtime all summer they hoped to increase the number of ships in good condition to sixty-three by the end of 1767. That is to say that one-third of the fleet was ready for service, and they hoped with nearly three years of effort to increase that proportion to 45 per cent. By this time the yards depended on working overtime throughout every summer. Their capacity had long ceased to suffice without it, and the workmen had come to expect the extra earnings.[39] In November 1765 the Navy Board informed the Admiralty that with the existing number of shipwrights, 3,150, it would be possible to keep up a fleet of ninety sail of the line providing they were allowed to work overtime all summer as a matter of routine. To keep up the 140 which in theory existed would require a one-third increase, to about 4,200 men. No attempt was made to attain such a figure, although the Rockingham ministry increased both the naval vote and the repayment of naval debt. With a supportive ministry and an able First Lord, the best that could be achieved was to keep up two-thirds of the fleet.[40]

Under the Grafton ministry true naval expenditure was maintained at about the same level, but late in 1767 the Secretary of the Treasury drafted a speech which proposed that a further four years would be needed to put the fleet into a satisfactory condition to face the prospect of war. Hawke prepared a memorandum arguing from the experience of the Seven Years War that manpower would suffice only to man thirty-nine ships of the line in the first year of war, and that seven years had been needed to reach the maximum figure of 84,770 men, equivalent to about 130 sail of the line.[41] The implicit argument was that it did not matter how slowly the dockyards prepared ships for service, nor how many of those on the list proved to be beyond repair, so long as there were always ships ready to receive as many men as could be raised. It was equivalent to an argument that resources for shipbuilding and repair were free, and that it was of no consequence to what extent they were wasted.

From the beginning Sandwich had a quite different idea. It was clear to him that to sustain a real, effective fleet at anything like the number of ships which the strategic situation demanded, with the amount of money Parliament was willing to provide, would be impossible unless the working lives of ships could be increased, and the burden of maintenance on the yards reduced. The critical problem was the rate at which ships decayed, and the large emergency programme of ships built during the Seven Years War, almost all of green timber, were responsible for a sharp increase in the rate of decay. Virtually all the ships between seven and twelve years old in 1771 were in poor condition:

> As the decay of the Fleet, has been infinitely more rapid of late years, it has been my principal study how to remedy that Inconvenience . . . In a Fleet thus circumstanced, the Decay will always outrun the Repairs, nor is it practicable to keep a large Fleet in good Condition, unless some means are found to make the ships more durable.[42]

To achieve this he needed to undertake fundamental reforms, and for them he needed information. Beginning in 1771, the Admiralty began a programme of annual inspections of the yards. They had last been visited by the Admiralty exactly twenty years before, when Sandwich was last in charge. Neither Anson, nor Egmont, nor Hawke had imitated him.[43] Under Hawke the Admiralty had ordered the Navy Board to make inspections and to reissue its standing orders to the yards, but it had done nothing to enforce the orders, nor was there much it could do from a distance.[44] The standing orders were in any case equally useless as an instrument of reform, or an aid to good management, being a vast undigested mass of miscellaneous instructions, many of them more than a century old, unusable as a collection and in many cases irrelevant to contemporary conditions.[45] To achieve real reform it was no good issuing bland exhortations from a safe distance; it was necessary for the Admiralty to acquire for itself the sort of detailed knowledge on which decisions could be grounded and orders enforced.

The visitations which began in 1771 display the same energy and enthusiasm, the same voracious appetite for fact, the same determination to see and understand everything for himself, which had marked Sandwich's first visits to the yards. There was, however, one significant difference. In 1749 and 1750 the Admiralty Board visited the yards in a body, leaving the Navy Board in London. In 1771 Sandwich visited the yards in a mixed company, varying from yard to yard but including members of both boards. The difference reflects in part the effects of twenty years in clearing away the old men of the 1740s and replacing them with younger and more flexible characters. The change may also reflect Sandwich's own experience of the minimal gains achieved by frontal assault; the politics of confrontation were to be replaced with those of co-operation.

The range of concerns and interests displayed in the minutes Sandwich compiled of these visitations is remarkable.[46] He and his colleagues ordered reports on the utility of worming rigging and whether masts were best left standing or unstepped and put in store; they investigated the depth of water at Chatham (now too shoal for large ships to lie without grounding at low water); they inspected the results of a trial of anti-fouling compounds at Sheerness; at Portsmouth they saw in action and approved a type of pump newly designed by Captain John Bentinck (the son of Sandwich's old diplomatic colleague), as well as his 'new invented Method of leading the Tiller rope in a sweep & Groove to prevent it's slackening, which is universally approved, & will be brought into general use in the Navy'.[47] This is a small but typical example of Sandwich's concern to master the technicalities of the naval service. The device may sound trivial, and doubtless would have done to almost all civilian politicians of the day, but it represented a considerable advance in the efficiency of steering-gear, and hence in the safety of navigation.[48] The fate of ships and lives often turned on such devices. To understand them put Sandwich in a position to do his job much more effectively, and made it difficult for admirals, or the Navy Board, to impose on him.

Continuing at Portsmouth, they viewed the great naval hospital at Haslar, and inspected the Royal Naval Academy where a small number of young gentlemen were educated for the Navy, making the obvious point that fees equal to those of Eton 'naturally excludes the children of Sea Officers'. Touring the remains of the wooden buildings burned in the serious fire of 1770, Sandwich commented on the importance of replacing them in brick, and of finishing the programme of new works which was still creeping slowly forward.[49] At Plymouth they inspected a model of the yard made by the Foreman, and ordered similar models made for the other yards; they saw the Master Mastmaker's models of improved 'made' masts (the largest masts were made up of a number of smaller sticks fitted together); they viewed the Master House Carpenter's invention of a tidewheel to work the ventilators which kept dry the holds of ships in Ordinary; and they 'directed that each ship's name be hereafter written on her Stern'.[50] Besides the dockyards, Sandwich and his colleagues visited hospitals, victualling yards, ropeworks and merchant shipyards where ships were building by contract. Everywhere he personally inspected all the ships lying in Ordinary. On Sunday 14th June 1772, not an exceptionally busy day, he visited thirty-four ships at Portsmouth.[51]

In all the minutes he compiled of his annual visitations Sandwich's dominant concern was the timber problem. 'Unless we can find means by a sufficient seasoning to make our ships last longer, our strength at sea must in a few years be reduced to a state, that carries with it very alarming Reflections'.[52] From the beginning he aimed to have three years' supply of timber always in stock, so that it could have so much seasoning before being used. By this means the fleet of eighty effective ships of the line in 1771 (out of 123) could be increased without extra expense.[53] He sought a rational, standard policy on timber stocks, rather than leaving it to the choice of the Surveyor of the day:

> frequently when a new one has been appointed, it has been his Practice to imitate the Misconduct of Builders of Political Structures, and to proceed upon a System without considering whether it is a good, or a bad one, provided it differs essentially from that of his predecessor.[54]

For want of an adequate building programme before the Seven Years War, the fleet had had to be increased by an extensive emergency building during it. For want of stocks of seasoned timber the ships had been built of green timber with the inevitable consequence of rapid decay. If war had come in 1770 just as these ships were falling to pieces the problem would have been compounded:

> for we could not have built fast enough to make up for the rapid decay with which we were threatened; and those ships which would have been run up at an immense expence in all the King's and Merchants yards in the Kingdom, would few of them have lasted more than 6 years.[55]

The problem of premature decay revealed by the 1770 mobilization grew rapidly more serious as Sandwich investigated the state of the fleet he had inherited. Out of eighty-six ships shown as being in good condition in December 1770, seven were condemned as being beyond repair during 1771. By 1778 only half of them were still in service, and only seventeen had not required large repairs.[56] Sandwich's figures for 1771 showed a real total of only seventy-five ships of the line, of which thirty-one were in commission, thirty in good condition, and fourteen building or repairing. In 1773 thirty-six were in good condition, but the number needing repairs had risen to thirty-eight.[57] Among them were some appalling examples of the costs of hasty wartime construction. The *Ardent* 64, built at Hull in 1764 for £23,000 and never once commissioned, in 1771 needed a £17,000 repair.[58] The *Cornwall* 74, built in 1761 at a cost of £29,000, was in 1773 estimated to need £23,000 to fit her for service. In the same year the *Mars*, launched in 1759, was reckoned to need repairs costing £20,000. This one ship had in fourteen years cost £56,000, enough to build two battleships, each of which, if built of seasoned timber, might have been expected to last twice as long.[59]

Dry rot is a problem to which the twentieth century has found no solution, and in the eighteenth the only hope of reducing decay, which could never be eliminated, was by building with seasoned timber, and by trying as far as possible to ensure that the hull, both on the stocks and afloat, was kept well aired and dry. Not that the Admiralty neglected alternatives: there was a continuous if unsystematic programme of research going on to test the efficacy of different methods of preserving timber. Trials were conducted of steeping timber in lime water (recommended for casks by Mr Thrale the great brewer); pickling it in brine (as practised by the Dutch navy); and boiling, but none of these was successful.[60] The necessity of new building slips in the yards was evident,

> but neither this or any thing else that can be devised, will enable us
> to keep up the proper number, unless it is contrived to give them a
> greater duration than that which we have experienced of late years,
> nor is it in my opinion possible for any Nation to keep up a Fleet so
> built; the Experience of the late War fully evinces this proposition; we
> set out in the year 1756 with 69 ships of the line, we ended in the year
> 1761 with 81, 12 were taken from the enemy and employed during
> the war in the King's service, & tho' we built as fast as possible in the
> King's Yards, and employed all the Merchant Yards that could build
> a ship for us, it is to be observed that we finished with exactly the
> same number with which we set out.[61]

There was no escaping the fundamental necessity of seasoned timber, but there were some serious obstacles in the way of getting it. Firstly, seasoned timber was by definition timber left for some years. Such stocks could only be built up by suspending, or at least reducing, the ordinary consumption while timber was allowed to accumulate and season. At a time when many ships of the fleet were decaying rapidly, the implication was that the size of the fleet would fall sharply while the stocks were built up. Next there was nowhere in the yards to put the seasoned timber. Everywhere the largest timbers, which were also the scarcest and most valuable, lay about in the open exposed to the rain. Most serious of all, there was an acute shortage of timber on the market, especially in the largest sizes, and it was widely thought that no more could be had.[62] When Sandwich took office early in 1771 the timber famine in the dockyards was so great that shipwrights were actually idle for want of materials to work up.[63]

All these problems Sandwich tackled systematically, beginning with the supply of timber. The dockyards' stocks of timber had been falling steadily for many years, and at the end of 1770 amounted to 18,277 loads, or less than four months' consumption by the usual reckoning.[64] He appreciated that the problem of supply was more accurately a problem of supply at a price which the Navy Board were willing to pay. Transport costs were always a large component of the price of timber, and in practice trees growing more than fifteen miles from navigable water were prohibitively expensive for naval purposes. The argument that the demands of shipbuilding, iron-works or other industry consumed the forests of England is disproved by the existence of oak forests not much less extensive today than they were two hundred years ago.[65] It was accessible, suitable timber that was scarce. It was said in the eighteenth century that a tree growing in the forests of Poland was worth five shillings felled, twenty-five shillings floated down the Vistula to Danzig, and five guineas delivered at an English dockyard – more than 95 per cent of the cost was freight.[66] Even at this rate it was often cheaper to buy abroad than at home. In 1771, for example, Sir William Bagot offered the Navy Board a large parcel of timber from his park near Uttoxeter in Staffordshire at just under £5 a load (a load was 40 cubic foot rough or 50 sided). The transport costs were reckoned at 22s. 2d. a load for the nineteen miles to the river at Burton-on-Trent, 17s. for wharfage and carriage to the port of Gainsborough, and 20s. by sea from there to the dockyard. This was one-third more than the carriage charged by the timber merchants.[67] At this date the Navy Board allowed 38s. a load for the transport cost of timber from any source, and with Scandinavian softwood as with English oak the supply near enough to water to be shipped for this price was falling fast.[68] Sandwich's first and simplest move was therefore to increase the freight paid on timber, which immediately increased the supply.[69] He also secured a limitation on the number and size of the ships of the East India Company, the only merchantmen large enough to compete directly with ships of the line for large timber.[70]

The next component of the timber problem to be tackled was the supply of timber from abroad. The Navy imported softwood planks and deals from Scandinavia and large pines for masts from the Baltic lands and North America, because in both cases there were no sufficient supplies in Britain.[71] It imported oak from various German and Baltic ports not so much to ease an absolute shortage as to provide an alternative source of supply. There were few timber merchants with the contacts and financial resources to deal in the Navy's very large contracts, and the Navy Board perforce dealt with a small circle of contractors who knew one another well. Sandwich fully shared the Board's traditional suspicion of cartels colluding to force up prices. He also believed the merchants forced the East India Company to buy more timber than it required.[72] Whether the 'timber ring' really existed is uncertain, but it very easily might have done, and building up alternative foreign sources of supply provided a ready means of preventing it.[73] Five hundred loads a year were ordered from Hamburg and Stettin, not because there was an immediate need for the supply, but because it, 'keeps our own timber merchants in order, and may be again, as it has already, be [sic] of the utmost use in times of emergency'.[74] One source of foreign timber which Sandwich declined was the offer made in 1775 by the Greek merchant who supplied the French Mediterranean dockyard of Toulon with oak from Albania, to turn over his existing contract to the British, delivering the timber for the same price to Port Mahon.[75] The Navy did not need the timber and could not use it at Port Mahon where no shipbuilding was done, while the government was trying to maintain good relations with France and had no desire to make such a provocative gesture.

British shipbuilders had very strong prejudices against foreign oak, and in due course Sandwich was to be accused of ruining the Navy by using it. Palliser later admitted that 'the first foreign timber which we purchased was very bad stuff indeed, but we soon found out the best market to go to and the best method for obtaining the best kind, and we afterwards got it of the best quality'.[76] Sandwich approached the question with his usual sceptical detachment. The condition of French prizes made him doubt that their timber was inferior, and a number of ships were ordered to be built wholly of foreign timber to see if they lasted less well.[77] The same approach was applied to winter-felled timber[78] (usually considered the hardest), and to some of the proprietary systems of preserving timber.[79] None of these trials conclusively proved anything; it would have been necessary to have built in much larger numbers over a long period to have produced statistically useful results, and it cannot be proved that the shipwrights' prejudices were wrong, but Sandwich's cautious scepticism looks the more rational approach. He learnt things from the experts which must have reinforced his scepticism. At Portsmouth in 1771 Thomas Bucknall the Master Shipwright told him that the *Royal William*, built by John Naish in 1719 out of seasoned timber, had been largely unemployed, and very nearly broken up, because of Sir Jacob Acworth's prejudice against the work of the shipwright who had been his master when he was an apprentice.[80] The ship was afloat until 1813. Sandwich was also at pains to inform himself of the facts by historical research. He borrowed from the king a 1698 survey of the dockyards to study their development over seventy years.[81] He learned by studying the manuscripts of Samuel Pepys that warships had lasted thirty years in the seventeenth century, and it renewed his determination to do as well himself.[82] He had been told that timber could not be had, and proved it to have been an artificial scarcity. He was assured that timber could not be held in stock in quantity for want of sheds to cover it, nor the sheds built for want of room; 'I went to the spot, and showed them where they might be placed'.[83] Thus the practical knowledge acquired on visitation allowed Sandwich to outflank the objections of the experts.

Sandwich achieved his goal of three years' stock of seasoned timber within three years of taking office. In the summer of 1773 he wrote:

> I cannot help observing with unspeakable pleasure, that the difficulties that at first appeared in the getting the Fleet into proper repair, have by the Measures that have been taken and firmly pursued, diminished by degrees and may be now said to be totally conquered; for a very few years more of repose from War, will have brought every thing into so good a train, that our Ships will be all built & repaired with seasoned timber; and consequently that enormous expence in renewing them 6 or 7 years after they have been built will at a period not very distant be no longer known. It was necessary to lose some time in our

building & repairs, in order to let the ships remain a considerable time on the Stocks in order to season, and if I had not at the same time that that order was given, directed that several new ships should be set up in the Merchants Yards, that delay would have been severely felt.[84]

When Joseph Banks visited Chatham in 1775, he commented that,

nothing could be more pleasing to any one who is fond of order than the great exactness neatness & regularity with which all kinds of stores were here arranged every store house as neat & clean as a private house & every kind of store so laid as to be got at without removing any other, every piece of timber mark'd & numbered so that none can be us'd which is not sufficiently season'd & an abundance of that & every other store which imply'd a moral impossibility of want of any kind.[85]

Seasoning the timber before building only addressed part of the problem of decay. It was equally necessary that hulls should season while they were under construction, for rapid construction even with seasoned timber invited trouble.[86] In 1772 the standard contract for ships building in merchant yards was altered to require them to stand in frame on the stocks for six months, and in October 1773 all new ships of the line were ordered to stand in frame twelve months.[87] Sandwich's ideal scheme was for each building slip to have on it a complete ship ready for launching, with the complete frame of another stored nearby, ready to assemble, and the remainder of three years' stock of timber already 'converted' (meaning sided, or roughly cut to shape) and seasoning under cover. Whenever a ship had to be replaced a new ship could be launched, and a new frame set up on the slip to replace her.[88] This ideal was never completely achieved, for even with three years' seasoned timber and regulations ensuring that new ships were seasoned on the stocks, Sandwich knew he was still many years away from the complete fleet of durable ships which was his ultimate ambition. In 1774 he wrote:

I have no doubt that many of the ships that now stand upon the Serviceable List are far advanced in their decay; some years hence, when they have been worn out, and their place supplied with ships built upon the new plan, his Majesty will have a fleet upon the durability of which there may be some dependence.[89]

This was both the strength and weakness of Sandwich's approach. For the first time a First Lord had conceived a programme of fundamental reforms aimed at the causes, and not simply the symptoms of the Navy's problems. But the plan was in its nature an extremely long-term one, which called for consistent government policy and support over at least fifteen years. It also called for a long period of peace.

CHAPTER X

The Dockyards and the Navy Board
1774–1776

The problems of building a new fleet of seasoned timber were compounded by the poor condition of the fleet Sandwich had inherited, for repairs competed with building for the timber and manpower of the yards. On average 74-gun ships between 1770 and 1786 took two years eight months to undergo a large repair. Between 1770 and 1777 it took twelve months for a middling repair to a 74, and five months for a small repair. In both cases the times were slightly less in wartime.[1] At this rate it did not take many battleships under repair to absorb virtually the entire capacity of a dockyard. For these reasons Sandwich appreciated that the size of the fleet, both nominal and (to a lesser extent) real, was bound to fall during the first years of his administration. It was an unavoidable consequence of the condition of the fleet he had inherited, made worse in the short term by his search for a long-term cure to the problem of decay.

To meet this problem Sandwich was obliged to let some contracts to build ships in the early 1770s, while the dockyards were building up their stocks of seasoned timber and new building slips were being laid down. He also relieved the yards by contracting out repairs to some frigates.[2] The problem with contract building, and still more contract repairing (which had never hitherto been permitted), was controlling the quality of workmanship and materials. Private shipbuilders were relatively small businesses, almost invariably undercapitalized. They could not afford to carry stocks of timber to season, and were dependent on progress payments to carry on their contracts. They were subject to heavy penalty clauses for late delivery. All this gave them strong incentives amounting at times almost to compulsion to skimp on the quality of workmanship and materials for the sake of speed, and explains why contract-built ships were reckoned to last at best only two-thirds of the lives of dockyard-built ships.[3] Even if the shipbuilders were honest and competent, which was not always the case, they walked a precarious path between bankruptcy and shoddy construction. The Navy Board's only control was the presence of the overseer, a senior shipwright sent to stand by a ship building in a merchant yard to enforce the standards of quality laid down in the contract. The further he was from a dockyard, the more exposed an overseer became to corruption and pressure. From Liverpool it was reported that, 'The Superintendents live well with the Builders & are neither so skillful or so clear sighted as they should be'.[4] This was one of the main reasons why the Navy Board preferred to confine its contracts to Thames shipbuilders and a few in the vicinity of Portsmouth.[5] The Thames was the biggest centre of English shipbuilding and included most of the few private yards capable of building large warships, and here it was possible for members of the Navy Board or senior yard officers to visit ships building to check and support the overseers.

It is surprisingly difficult to tell whether, or to what extent, the universal prejudice against merchant shipbuilders was justified. The experts who voiced it were the Surveyors of the Navy and the master shipwrights of the yards, who were implicitly comparing their own work with that of their professional rivals. Sandwich approached their claims with his usual inquisitive scepticism, and was inclined to suspect that the badness of contract-building was exaggerated if not invented.[6] Some rather crude figures, calculated from the working lives of ships of the line built in dockyards and private shipyards, would suggest there was a real difference, but that it was smaller than contemporaries believed:

	NUMBER		MEAN LIFE (YEARS)	
	Dockyard	*Contract*	*Dockyard*	*Contract*
1720–44	82	19	28.2	24.5
1745–54	24	7	35.5	21.1
1755–70	43	14	37.9	33.7
1771–82	20	38	36.8	31.5[7]

However these figures need to be treated with great caution, if only because many of the numbers involved are too small to be statistically reliable. They take no account of the differing circumstances in which ships at different dates spent their working lives, nor of the resources available to keep them in repair. In principle it would be more revealing to compare the 'life-cycle cost' of different ships by adding their initial building cost and the total cost of repairs and maintenance over their working lives; this would balance the lower initial cost of contract building (on average 7.7 per cent lower in 1772)[8] against the cost of maintenance over a ship's working life.[9] (In modern warships the building cost is typically about a quarter of the 'life-cycle cost'.) Something along these lines might be attempted, but so many of the eighteenth-century statistics which would have to be used are inaccurate to the point of fiction that it is very doubtful if any useful results could be obtained.[10] In any case the exercise would be of only notional value, for Sandwich, like his predecessors and successors, was driven to build by contract not from any sophisticated analysis of costs, but because there was no other way to obtain enough ships.

Speaking in the House of Lords in February 1775, he claimed that,

> When he came to the Admiralty Board, the Navy was in the most ruinous condition; so much, that within the last four years there were no less than forty line-of-battle ships broke up, and even six in the course of the last year; that there was not six months timber of any kind in the yards, and in some, he believed, not £50 worth . . .[11]

He could reasonably claim to have achieved a great deal in four years. What he did not explain in public was how much more there was still to do. Between 1770 and 1777 the Navy actually completed twenty-two ships of the line, and disposed of twenty-one. By comparison thirty-one had been completed between 1763 and 1770, including the end of the wartime emergency building programme.[12] Sandwich had more or less kept pace with decay, but only by building six of the twenty-two new ships by contract.[13] Half of the ten ships of the line which were laid down after Sandwich resumed office in 1771, and completed by the end of 1775, were built in merchant yards.[14] His timber policy had laid the basis for a better situation in future, but to maintain the size of the fleet in the meantime he had been driven to a building programme which compromised it. Surveying the situation in 1774, he concluded that if war broke out, there would again be no alternative to an emergency programme of building by contract.[15] The dockyards were still a long way from being able either to build or to maintain the fleet which Sandwich hoped before long to have in existence.

By 1774 the dockyards had three years' supply of seasoned timber in store, and a number of new building slips had been constructed.[16] It was now possible to recommence building in the yards, using seasoned timber and allowing hulls to season on the stocks – but this was only the beginning of a solution to the overall problem.

Sixteen of the twenty-seven building slips in the dockyards could carry a ship of the line.[17] If each ship stood three years on the stocks, which was the absolute minimum needed to satisfy the new regulations for seasoning in frame, the yards could only launch five ships of the line a year at best. This would just suffice to keep up a fleet of eighty sail of the line if each ship lasted sixteen years. Sandwich hoped in time to have a fleet of ships which lasted thirty years, but he must have known that in 1774 the actual figure was much less. Moreover building work proceeded in practice only to the extent that the yards had labour to spare. Some slips were unoccupied for long periods, while others were occupied by the same ship for much longer than three years. The biggest ships of the line were regarded by the yards as 'stock' jobs on which men could be employed at quiet times like neap tides when the docks were sometimes empty. In wartime the pressure of repairs eliminated such time almost completely, with the result that building times of ten years and more were not uncommon among the first and second rates. The dockyards laid down only sixteen ships of the line between 1770 and 1776, each of which stood on average 6.4 years on the stocks. From 1777 to 1782 only ten ships of the line were laid down, though they spent a mean of only 4.4 years on the stocks.[18] Over the whole period only twenty-six ships of the line were laid down in the yards, two a year, each of which took on average 5.6 years to build. On the highly optimistic assumption that each ship lasted thirty years, the building rate of the yards would suffice to keep up a fleet of sixty sail of the line. It was out of all possibility to imagine that they could keep up eighty or a hundred sail.

One obvious way to increase the yards' capacity would have been to build a completely new yard in addition to the expansion of the existing yards which Sandwich had inherited and pushed forward. Sir Thomas Slade, who as Surveyor was the joint author of Egmont's 1765 scheme for Portsmouth and Plymouth, had made a proposal to build a large new yard adjoining Sheerness, but the scheme had to be abandoned because of the marshy ground and the discovery of shipworm infesting the anchorage.[19] Sandwich's colleague Lord Rochford made a similar suggestion in 1771, but Sandwich pointed out that his existing programme of works needed over £300,000 and several years to finish it, and there was no prospect of getting even more money.[20] The political reality was that Sandwich was under great pressure to reduce the running expenses of the yards, which could only be done by reducing the size of the workforce. He was favoured in the first three years by the level of international tension, but even so the number of men in the yards was falling slowly, and had been falling for a long time. Between 1730 and 1790 the dockyard workforce as a whole fell by 8 per cent while the fleet to be maintained nearly doubled.[21] In March 1774 the Admiralty was obliged to discharge shipwrights, and by 1775 the pressure for economy was becoming irresistible. What Sandwich and Palliser wanted was an increase to match the size of the fleet which they had to maintain, but they had to live with the prospect of an enforced reduction.[22] The only possible means of reconciling the two was a large increase in the productivity of the dockyard workforce.

To achieve it Sandwich returned to task work, which he had vainly attempted to institute more than twenty years before. Workmen in private shipyards were almost all paid by this method, and it was certain that they earned more than their counterparts in the dockyards, particularly in wartime. It seemed certain to Sandwich and his contemporaries that they worked faster when they were paid by the piece rather than the day. It seemed certain to the Navy Board and the yard officers that the quality of their work suffered as a result. Sandwich was convinced that task work properly supervised would yield a large increase in efficiency without loss of quality. As late as 1782 he was claiming that work could be done by task one-third faster and at half the expense of day labour. This was certainly too optimistic; Palliser calculated that once the initial rates had been raised the saving in money was small, but the saving in time was real.[23] Modern scholars agree that the cost saving must have been largely offset by the need to buy the men's acceptance with higher nominal wage rates, but the gain in efficiency, which was the essential object, remained.[24]

It was only possible to implement the 'bold and imaginitive'[25] scheme of task work because relations between Admiralty and Navy Board were so much better than they had been before, and because many, though not all, of the senior yard officers were converts to its virtues. For all of them the new scheme called for a great deal of extra work. Sir John Williams the Surveyor spent a whole year working out a scale of works for a 74-gun ship, setting down a time and price to work up and assemble every individual timber in the ship.[26] This was ready in March 1775, and task work was introduced into all the yards that spring. The rates had been set to allow the men a large increase in their wages, and Sandwich was confident that the scheme would meet an enthusiastic reception.

Instead it met widespread alarm and tumultuous strikes at Portsmouth and Plymouth. The Admiralty had failed to make sufficient allowance for the complexities of forcing this radical change onto a highly traditional working system. From the shipwrights' point of view, task work seemed to present a number of threats. It offered high wages to those willing and able to work hard, but it threatened to leave behind the elderly, the inexperienced, and the idle. The shipwrights were supposed to be 'shoaled' into gangs containing the same proportion of men of different ages and abilities, but the shoaling, like the inspection of work, was done by the yard officers, and both offered many opportunities for favouritism and corruption. In any case, shoaling in its nature discriminated against fit and able men. The scale of works drawn up by Williams differed greatly from those drawn up by the several Master Shipwrights, and was completely revised twice in its first year of use, which only emphasized how much room there was to disagree on how long it ought to take to do any particular job properly. The increase in wages offered by task work was very large set against existing nominal wage rates, but much less compared with real earnings, inflated by more or less fictitious overtime. The usual day wage was 2s. 1d. in winter, 2s. 8½d. in summer (with an extra 'tide' of two and a half hours), but two tides extra increased earnings by day work to 3s. 4d. The average wage by task was initially 3s. 10½d.[27] The whole scheme took the men by surprise, and it was left to the yard officers to explain and justify it. Particularly in yards where the Master Shipwrights, like Israel Pownoll at Plymouth, were lukewarm or hostile, the result was violent opposition.[28] Going on his annual visitation in the summer of 1775, Sandwich found himself trying to reason with angry mobs of shipwrights at Portsmouth and Plymouth.[29]

In September 1775 the Woolwich shipwrights petitioned to be admitted to task work,[30] and in the 'River' yards it was generally accepted. In time the rumour had its effect that shipwrights there were earning 5s. 3d. for a twelve-hour day – more than a shilling over day wages for a day and two tides, or seventeen hours' work. After the end of the war Portsmouth and Plymouth accepted task work, and by the mid 1780s it was general in all the yards.[31] Even in the long term, however, it did not achieve as much as Sandwich had hoped. In the context of an undisciplined system with entrenched trade privileges and weak authority, it was almost as liable as day work to be perverted to the mutual convenience of the men and their officers. At bottom task work was a scheme to get men to work harder, or at least more efficiently, but even higher wages will not elicit more work without some discipline, and dockyard management was very weak.[32] In the short term the introduction of task work was highly disruptive. The 1775 strikes halted work in the two biggest yards for several weeks and poisoned relations for long afterwards. To enforce its authority the Admiralty felt obliged to dismiss 129 shipwrights just when it wished to recruit more, but by subsequently readmitting all but a few ringleaders, and abandoning any idea of forcing task work on the unwilling, it effectively admitted how weak its position was.[33] 'In this country of liberty,' as Sandwich put it, 'the idea of forcing people to work in a manner they dislike would not be generally approved, and might occasion great uneasiness, possibly general commotions'.[34]

Sandwich deserves credit for his courage and determination in introducing task work, but its fate demonstrates that the problem was much more complex and intractable than it seemed. It may also be said that in concentrating on task work Sandwich neglected some less radical but more practical means of increasing the efficiency and size of the dockyard workforce. The yards had always been lifetime employers, offering stability and security. Boys joined them as apprentices, and many of them continued to work there into old age. Private shipyards, by contrast, were essentially employers of skilled but casual labour, taken on for as long as necessary to do a particular job. In wartime they paid much more than the fixed rates in the yards, and even in peacetime they offered the fit and hard-working the opportunity to earn more by task than the day wages of the dockyard artificers, but there was no security. The Navy Board's system of lifetime employment had rather grown up over time than been adopted as a conscious act of policy, but it was not necessarily irrational. Loyalty and experience are valuable assets in any workforce, and even the degree of underemployment which was admitted to exist in peacetime could be justified as providing a hidden margin of spare capacity to meet the demands of war.[35] The problems arose from lack of attention to the retirement of the elderly and the recruitment of the young.

The logic of the dockyard employment tradition was that men would be attracted by the prospect of security in their old age in spite of relatively low wages. In practice this was frequently achieved by employing men who were long past efficient work, or any work at all. This was still a normal situation in official jobs of all sorts at every level; it was as true of commissioners of the Navy like Acworth as of working shipwrights. Many senior officers of the yards were too old to do their duty, but it was still considered highly improper to force them into retirement if they did not choose to go.[36] For the artificers and labourers of the yards, there was a scheme of super-annuation instituted by Egmont in 1764 and extended by Sandwich in 1771, but it provided only a fixed number of places for which men were to be nominated by the yard officers.[37] Like the equivalent scheme for the officers of the Navy, it was regarded as a reward for a deserving minority, not an entitlement earned by long service, nor a means of removing those no longer able to work. Moreover its effectiveness depended a good deal on Sandwich's own eye reviewing the men individually on his summer visitations. When the American War broke out and he was no longer able to visit in person, the numbers recommended for superannuation fell away.[38] In 1773 the minutes of the Admiralty visitation record that, 'We have the plea-sure to observe that the late extention of the superannuation will shortly ease us of all the useless hands',[39] but the scheme was too limited to achieve anything like as much. Neither the Admiralty nor the Navy Board was sufficiently radical to propose unlimited superannuation, which alone would have removed all the incapable.[40] There were virtually no precedents, and given the wartime shortage of labour when men superannuated could not easily be replaced, yard officers were reluctant to lose anyone who could still be of some use.

There were in principle two levels at which the yards might recruit skilled labour, but adult shipwrights, already qualified, were nearly impossible to obtain in wartime against the lure of higher wages in private yards. Sandwich always considered that there was no point in raising wages when private employers could always outbid the dockyards and maintain their differential:

There is a line which the exertions of every country cannot pass. We cannot, nor ever could, do more than employ all the shipwrights that this country affords; the law does not allow compulsion upon any race of men but common sailors; and if the trade of this country is to go on, the merchants will and always must give more for shipbuilding than the Crown. The increase of wages without increase of work in the dockyards would be exactly so much money thrown away, as the merchants would rise in proportion. Therefore, according to my reasoning, there is no possibility of alluring the men by profit or getting them by compulsion; and it is on this account that no mode has yet been found out of extending our naval construction but by making contracts with all responsible persons who have a capital, sufficient materials at hand, and a proper place to build in, for as to going on with building in the King's yards (Chatham excepted, and

Deptford and Woolwich to a small degree), it must always be nearly
at a stand in time of war on account of the constant employment of
the artificers in refitting the ships that come from sea.[41]

He might have added that there was no chance of obtaining Parliamentary approval for an increase in dockyard wages. Though we
can now say that prices were rising steadily in the 1770s,[42] the concept
of inflation was still virtually unknown, and it would have been
impossible to persuade MPs that a wage sufficient in their fathers'
time was no longer adequate.[43]

This left the recruitment of apprentices to supply the yards' future
requirements for skilled labour. Here the problem was that the
number and distribution of 'servants' or apprentices was not governed by the requirements of the yards at all. Servants' wages went
to their masters, and they were assigned as a reward to those who
were deemed to deserve extra wages. It was not unusual for them
to be allocated to shipwrights who were freemen of the borough,
in return for their votes.[44] Sometimes they were given as a substitute
for a retirement pension, or even a widow's pension. Carpenters in
the Navy were allowed two servants each, but took only one to sea,
leaving the other in the yard. Overall the number of apprentices was
far too small, and many of them were allocated to the wrong masters.
Working shipwrights, deserving of encouragement and ready to pass
on their skills to a new generation, were denied servants; while boys
whose masters were absent, or incapable of work, or dead, had no
one to train them. It was not until 1782 after four years of war that
Sandwich turned his full attention to this problem.[45]

It was undoubtedly a failure on his part not to concentrate more
on the linked problems of superannuation and apprentices. He was
aware of the situation, and it may be suggested that he simply had
not sufficient time and energy to attempt to reform them at the same
time as he was introducing task work. Moreover these were at best
slow and partial solutions to the problem of the inadequate capacity
of the yards, which called for a drastic and rapid remedy. Sandwich
was by temperament attracted to the bold and sweeping measure. It
was one of his greatest strengths as a minister that he thought in
large terms, that he had both the skills to work out and the courage
to push through grand reforms – but in this and perhaps in other cases
he would have been well served by relatively modest and humdrum
(though certainly not easy) initiatives.

In looking at Sandwich's reforms of naval administration, both successful and unsuccessful, there are lessons to be learned by comparing his first period at the Admiralty in the 1740s with his service a quarter of a century later. Then he had formed part of a close-knit and generally harmonious little group at the Admiralty which had attempted to force change on a reluctant Navy Board. Seven years of more or less open warfare had achieved very little, and his successor Anson had tacitly abandoned attempts to reform the civil administration of the Navy. Back in office in 1771, Sandwich adopted a completely different approach. In marked contrast both with his own earlier practice, and with the practice of his successors at the Admiralty, he worked in close co-operation with the Navy Board as a whole, and with three successive Controllers in particular. In part this was a matter of finding men with whom he could work easily, but in one case it involved working with a talented but extremely difficult man. This was not the obvious or automatic approach for Sandwich or any First Lord, and he deserves credit for what was achieved by this effective co-operation between Admiralty and Navy Board, which would not have been achieved by hostility between them, and was not before or after his time.

The Controller in office when Sandwich returned to the Admiralty in 1771 was Captain Hugh Palliser.[46] He had recently been appointed by Hawke and had no previous connections with Sandwich, but they soon formed an excellent relationship, and all Sandwich's work in the dockyards from 1771 to 1775 was planned in close co-operation with him. He also acted as a naval adviser on many matters outside the Navy Board's competence, rather as if he were an unofficial Lord of the Admiralty. Palliser was a Yorkshireman of an obscure family, son of a captain in the army who had died when he was very young, leaving him to make his own way in the world. He had risen in the Navy by his own merit, and became in turn the patron of others who had their way to make in the Service, notably James Cook, who came from the same corner of the North Riding. Although appointed by Hawke, Palliser became the most prominent of a small group of officers who attached themselves to Sandwich and served him at the Admiralty or the Navy Board. He was made a baronet in August 1773 when the king visited Portsmouth, and in April 1775 he made the very unusual leap from the Navy Board to the Admiralty. For the next four years he was Sandwich's principal professional colleague at the Admiralty. It would be a mistake to see him as First Sea Lord in the modern style, for no such position was recognized by eighteenth-century convention, but even a First Lord as knowledgeable as Sandwich needed a seaman's assistance, and in the spring

of 1775 Sandwich lost his only naval colleague when his former
friend, now rather his rival, Augustus Hervey, succeeded to the
Earldom of Bristol and resigned on failing to make good his claim
as an earl to be Sandwich's second and deputy at the Board.[47] From
1775 to 1777 Palliser was the only sea officer at the Admiralty Board.
Much of his work was essentially political: as a peer, Sandwich
needed a spokesman for the Board in the House of Commons, and
his preference was always for someone who could speak with the
confidence born of that real understanding of the issues to which he
always aspired himself. Palliser, 'who had risen from an obscure
origin . . . wanted the advantage of education, as well as those of
manner, deportment and external grace, in all of which he was
wholly deficient'[48] – but he did know what he was talking about.
There was a conventional division in Admiralty Boards of the day
between the mere placemen, who were there to draw an income in
return for their signatures, and the working Board members who
took a share in Admiralty business and spoke for their department
in Parliament. Palliser was clearly a working member, and so was
John Buller, who spoke seventeen times on the Admiralty's behalf.[49]
It is characteristic that it was these two who were running the Admiralty over Christmas 1775 when Sandwich was making music at Hinchingbrooke, and he was content that they should issue urgent orders
in his absence.[50] By contrast Charles Fox never spoke in two years
at the Admiralty,[51] and Bamber Gascoyne, who sat from 1779 to
1782, once offered to come to town if needed; 'not that I am vain
enough to think that my presence is useful at the Board; other than
my signature may be convenient'.[52]

Palliser is typical of those whom Sandwich singled out for favour.
Obscure in origin, friendless except insofar as his professional merits
had won him friends in the Navy, he proved to have outstanding abilities as a naval administrator. Sandwich protected and favoured him.
In 1771 he was a half-pay captain of twenty-five years' seniority; in
1773 he was a baronet, in 1775 a rear-admiral and member of the
Admiralty Board, and by 1778 a vice-admiral and third in command
of the main fleet. It was a sudden rise for an officer not favoured by
birth, and an unusual one, in that service in the civil administration of
the Navy did not often lead to a return to sea command. Palliser had
certainly earned his promotion, and Sandwich had every right and every
reason to advance him; yet it did not necessarily make either of them
popular with officers who had risen by more conventional means.

Another of Sandwich's naval protégés was Captain Constantine
Phipps, who led the 1773 Arctic expedition. Phipps was of good

birth, heir to an Irish peerage, but he was not particularly rich or prominent in the Navy, and as an MP he usually supported the opposition to North's administration. The experience of working with Sandwich evidently impressed him, however. In February 1774 he delivered an unexpected speech in praise of Sandwich in the Commons,[53] and late in 1775 their mutual friend Joseph Banks brought them into contact. 'I am the more desirous to come closely to the point,' Sandwich wrote to Banks,

> & to know, whither if he could come into Parliament without obliga-
> tion to any one but to me, he would be disposed to embark with me
> as a Politician; his abilities would be of great use to me, and the footing
> I have got in the world would be of no disservice to him.[54]

At this time Sandwich was 'so unfortunate as to be obliged to tell you' that his younger son William Augustus was dying; 'it is proper to be prepared for the fatal event', he wrote, with a candidate to replace him as MP for Huntingdon.[55] In October they met and agreed terms for Phipps's election. Thereafter Lord Mulgrave (as Phipps became on his father's death that year) remained a close political ally of Sandwich's, and in December 1777 he joined the Admiralty.[56] Well before then he was acting as an unofficial spokesman for Sandwich in the House of Commons. In October 1776 Sandwich was urging him to come to town for the opening of Parliament,

> as there never could be a moment in which I can have more occasion
> for your advice and assistance than the present; the management of
> the navy during the Summer will undoubtedly be a principal subject
> of discussion, my situation is very ticklish, as I have many enemies
> besides those of the Opposition; & unless I have an able friend and
> advocate in the house of Commons my interest & reputation may
> suffer considerably.[57]

Mulgrave was an officer in the mould Sandwich preferred: able, diligent, a master of his profession, he carried conviction as a speaker in the Commons by knowledge rather than eloquence, while his tedious delivery and undignified speaking voice were the subject of some satire.[58] Sandwich, Palliser and Mulgrave formed the inner circle at the Admiralty, which planned the naval aspects of the first part of the American War. In December 1777, for example, they met before a critical Cabinet meeting:

> At our dinner to day it was agreed that a meeting should be held on

Thursday morning next to consider and determine upon the carrying
into execution the plan which I had given in writing, relative to the
mode of conducting the naval war in America the next year; and that
your Lordship & Sir Hugh Pallisser should be desired to attend that
meeting to give your sentiments upon that subject. . . . I will appoint
Sir Hugh Pallisser to meet you that we may confer together & take
care to be in the same story; & if that happens, we may manage this
matter entirely in our own way.

   This is a very material point towards establishing our credit as a
board of Admiralty & it was with that view I proposed that the two
Sea Officers of the Board should be called to give their opinion.[59]

This is a good example both of the harmonious way Sandwich
worked with his professional colleagues, and the political skill with
which he handled naval business in the Cabinet.[60]

When Palliser was elevated to the Admiralty in April 1775, Sandwich
chose Captain Maurice Suckling to replace him. He seems to have been
another of Sandwich's favourite type of sea officer: able, hard-
working and somewhat obscure, capable of doing the job, and not
closely linked with any obvious political rivals.[61] As Palliser had done
when he was Controller, he functioned not only as the effective head
of the Navy Board but as a professional adviser to Sandwich on matters not confined to civil administration.[62] It is difficult to say more as
no serious study of Suckling's period at the Navy Board has ever been
undertaken, and by January 1777 he was already seriously ill.[63]

   Surveying Sandwich's naval followers, a modern scholar has
commented:

   They were not of particularly distinguished birth, they had no record
   of parliamentary service nor of any considerable administrative experience and they were all comparatively junior men in their profession.
   On the other hand, it is clear that Sandwich chose them with care, for
   all proved to be seamen of outstanding ability and to be equally successful as administrators.[64]

These choices served to make Sandwich's department more efficient,
and to make Sandwich's own political position stronger. They surrounded him with obvious ability, and in the invariable fashion of
eighteenth-century sea officers who held official posts and sat in
Parliament, his followers exerted their abilities for professional and
political purposes alike. There was nothing in this which previous
First Lords had not done, but not many had done it as well, and no
civilian First Lord in living memory had built up a naval following

Right: The young traveller in Turkish dress at Constantinople, by Liotard (detail)

Below: Another of the 'Turkish' portraits, this one by Joseph Highmore, with the dome and minarets of Haghia Sophia in the background

Right: The young Turk newly returned to England, attributed to James Northcote. No other picture so well captures the lean and hungry look which frightened many of Sandwich's contemporaries

The young diplomat triumphant, by Jean Fournier. This official portrait, painted to celebrate the conclusion of the peace of Aix-la-Chapelle, still hangs there in the Old Town Hall where the Congress was held

Right: Sandwich in his peer's robes, probably for the coronation of George III in 1760, by Reynolds

The Secretary of State, by Zoffany. This is an informal portrait of Sandwich the public man, suave and self-assured

Martha Ray, by George Dance. This was the painting Sandwich kept to remember her by

Nos. 10 and 11 Storehouses at Portsmouth Dockyard, part of the dockyard
expansion scheme which Sandwich inherited and pushed forward

A range of timber seasoning sheds at Chatham Dockyard. This modest
building is almost the last survivor of hundreds like it which formed an
essential part of Sandwich's timber programme

in this way. In a sense Sandwich was crossing the invisible barriers erected by the Navy to preserve sea officers' powers of patronage, which were their means of control of the inner working of the Navy. Senior officers had always had to exercise these powers in alliance with the First Lord of the day, but when the First Lord was a civilian they expected to have the advantage over him of expert knowledge of the profession, and personal knowledge of the men. A civilian peer was supposed to recommend on political grounds; he was not supposed to play the admiral and build up a professional following of his own, still less to do so with skill and effectiveness. Sandwich's naval following enabled him to manage the Admiralty and the Navy more effectively, but this did not endear him to flag officers who preferred their civilian First Lords to be remote and ineffectual. The recruitment, and the rapid advancement, of men like Palliser, Mulgrave and Suckling generated a sense of unease among senior officers who had nothing personally against them; it was another example of Sandwich roaming the corridors of power with a lean and hungry look, when his less capable colleagues preferred to have men about them who were fat.[65]

Suckling died on 17th July 1778, just as war with France broke out. The choice of a successor had never been more critical, and the choice Sandwich made was an unexpected one, not altogether fitting the pattern he had established. Captain Charles Middleton was an obscure Scotsman with an undistinguished career behind him. His recent dealings with Sandwich had not obviously recommended him. As captain of a guardship he had figured among Sandwich's correspondents asking for leave rather more often than was decent, and with some curious excuses, including the suggestion that his commander-in-chief was mentally unbalanced.[66] He had tried to get his brother appointed his purser in a highly irregular fashion, and had been rebuffed.[67] His interest in agriculture, his involvement in the 'Clapham Sect' and the nascent Evangelical movement, his campaigns for the abolition of the slave trade, all seemed to mark him as an officer busy in retirement.[68] Unlike Sandwich's other naval followers, Middleton was not unconnected politically, being a member of the Dundas family, so prominent in Scottish politics, as well as a relative by marriage of the Pitts.[69] Lord Chatham died in May 1778, so that this connection was no obvious threat to Sandwich, but neither was it a recommendation, especially when there was a rival candidate for the Controllership who combined long experience as Commissioner of Chatham Dockyard with close connections in Huntingdonshire politics.[70] It is possible that Middleton was suggested as a candidate for Controller by his brother-in-law Captain Gambier, the Commissioner of Portsmouth Dockyard, and Middleton refers to having been urged to think of it before Sandwich had made the offer.[71] It is certain, however, that Sandwich already knew him as a proprietor of East India Company stock, and that they had had dealings about East India Company politics.[72] He was also a subscriber to the Concerts of Ancient Music, where they must have often met.[73] Most likely Sandwich, with his discerning judgement of men, had himself identified Middleton as the naval administrator he needed.

Arguably this was the single most important decision Sandwich took in his entire career. Beneath Captain Middleton's frankly unpromising exterior, Sandwich had discerned the genius who was to do more than any other man to reform the civil administration of the Navy. For nearly thirty years Middleton exercised a decisive influence on the Navy, as Controller from 1778 to 1790, as a member of the Admiralty Board, as member and adviser of successive committees and commissions of enquiry, as unofficial naval adviser to the younger Pitt, and finally as First Lord of the Admiralty in 1805 during the Trafalgar campaign. Middleton resembled Sandwich in being a first-class administrator with a voracious appetite for paperwork. In every other respect they were completely unlike one another. Sandwich was polite, urbane, detached, with the tolerance born of indifference to religion and scepticism towards all universal claims. Middleton was narrow-minded, intolerant, priggish, and devoted to the novel and alarming doctrines of the Evangelical movement. Long experience as a politician and diplomat had given Sandwich a deep knowledge of men and affairs; Middleton was content to know the mind of God. Sandwich was an excellent judge of men including himself, familiar with their weaknesses as well as his own, accustomed to delegate and to manage. Middleton was the type of reformer whose remedy for every evil is to take the business concerned into his own hands. He viewed the conduct of most of those with whom he had to deal with unconcealed contempt, and his own conduct with unconcealed admiration. No doubtful transaction ever shook his conviction that he was right, and God was with him. Just as Sandwich epitomizes many of the virtues and some of the vices of the eighteenth century, Middleton seems to step from the pages of Samuel Smiles with all the irritating merit of a great Victorian.[74]

The work which Middleton took on as Controller would have been very great even if he had not inherited Sandwich's reforming schemes, nor taken office on the outbreak of a major war. The constitution of the Navy Board, of which the Controller was the only permanent naval member, directed to him a huge amount of business, much of it trivial, and left some of his colleagues underemployed if not unemployed. Robert Gregson, a Navy Office clerk who sometimes assisted the Secretary of the Board, described the situation in 1789:

> Sir Charles Middleton the Comptroller is the most indefatigable & able of any in my time. The load of business he goes through at the Board, at the Treasury, Admty, & his own House, is astonishing, & what I am confident no other man will be able to execute. There is talk of his leaving us for a Flag; if he does we are ruined. . . .
>
> Upon the whole the weight of business falls upon a few, & of those few, chiefly upon the Comptroller & Secretary, who have piles of Papers before them a foot high, to digest & Minute, while two or three at the Board are looking on or reading Newspapers, who if they were to assist, the business would go on smoother & easier: some I believe, conscious that their stile & manner would expose them, chuse not to meddle with things, but it is a terrible thing, my Lord, that such men should be at a Board where from the extent, weight and importance of its business every hand should be employed.[75]

Ambrose Serle, who became Secretary a few days after that letter was written, described his work next year in a letter to Middleton:

> the real business is done by two or three members at the head of the table, and they must do the whole, or suffer arrears to come on, and they must do it cursorily, superficially and imperfectly. The direction at the head of the table must be conveyed to me at the bottom, and I ought to have as many ears as Argus has eyes to know sometimes what you are saying, and am happy to guess your meaning, from the conversation of the gentlemen at leisure about me . . .[76]

To do all this work required in the Controller a combination of qualities summed up by Middleton himself:

> As the whole conduct of the Board must naturally depend on his exertion, he in his professional line should have a comprehensive knowledge and extensive abilities; in his principles he should be conscientious and upright; in his conduct impartial, firm and decisive; in the expenditure of public money, provident and liberal; in receiving information open, and in giving a fair trial to whatever promises improvement, candid and patient. In short, as in [on?] the management of this department, the serviceable state of the whole Navy and the

expenditure of public money required in it depends, his knowledge and his care must extend to everything connected with it, and therefore to his professional line he must join great application and method, and a general knowledge of business and accounts.[77]

This may be compared with the sketch of Middleton offered by one of Sandwich's anonymous informants:

> Naturally industrious & persevering, with an high reputation for integrity, this gentleman adopts no plan without persuing his object with unremitting assiduity & indefatigable labour, his natural disposition being in this respect assisted by the pertinacity derived from certain religious opinions.[78]

The story of Middleton's career as a naval reformer belongs largely to the period after the American War, when Sandwich had left office.[79] To an extent Sandwich's reforms, as well as the impact of a lost war, cleared the way for Middleton's work, but Sandwich was only indirectly involved, as the man who first chose and appointed Middleton. Working with Sandwich during the war, Middleton like him was a frustrated reformer who could see a great deal which needed to be done as soon as he had a moment to do it. Meanwhile he was fully occupied with an immense load of administration, as well as with acting as a general naval adviser to Sandwich when his Admiralty colleagues were away at sea. A large book would be needed, indeed is needed, to tell the full story of the administration of the Navy during this war, and all that can be done here is to examine how Sandwich and Middleton worked together.[80]

In moments of irritation Middleton was apt to present their relationship as that of the devoted, indefatigable administrator cursed with an idle, dilettante superior.

> If I, my lord, who am a professional man, find myself unequal to the duties of the office I am in, with an application of twelve hours six days in the week, how is it possible that your lordship can manage yours, which is equally extensive, in three or four? Indeed, my lord, it cannot be. The two offices are so nearly connected, that I must be wilfully blind not to see the sad management that prevails at present, and the ruin that accompanies it . . .
>
> In short, my lord, for want of plan, for want of men of professional knowledge used to business to assist at the Admiralty, and for want of method and execution, one error has produced another, and the whole has become such a mass of confusion, that I see no prospect of reducing it to order. All I can do at the Navy Office will avail but

little if the Admiralty continues what it is at present. It is, indeed, so wretchedly bad, that, if I waited for official orders and kept within the mere line of duty, without pressing or proposing what ought to come unasked for, we must inevitably stand still. These, my lord, are a few of the many observations I have made on naval management since I have been in office; and I must own I feel such a despondency from the impression they make, that I scarce know how to act. I know the king's fleet to be equal to any service, if it is properly employed; but is it possible, my lord, that gentlemen who are at an office one day, and following their amusements or private concerns another, can carry on a line of business that requires not only great practical knowledge, but the closest application and attention?[81]

A century ago Victorian historians, who found Middleton a congenial figure, were prepared to accept these judgements at face value, but it has long been clear that they cannot be taken as statements of fact, nor even of Middleton's settled opinion. Though Sandwich's responsibilities as a Cabinet minister in wartime were far wider than just administration, he habitually worked long hours at his desk; 'He rose at an early hour, and generally wrote all his letters before breakfast. It was a common expression with him, "that he was not a letter in arrear"'.[82] 'Lord Sandwich might serve as a model for a man of business. He rose early, and till a late dinner, dedicated his whole time to business'.[83] 'No naval Officer who stated his Demand to the First Lord of the Admiralty, with becoming brevity, ever waited for an Answer; and he was accustomed to say, "If any Man will draw up his Case, and put his Name at the foot of the first Page, I will give him an immediate Reply. Where he compels me to turn over the sheet, he must wait my Leisure"'.[84] 'He was very active and regular in business . . . whoever addressed him by letter, was sure of receiving an answer by the post the day after it had been received'.[85] Even his enemies conceded this: 'to give him his due, he is seldom backward, I believe, in *answering* letters; howmuch soever he is disinclined, at the moment, to comply with the Requests they contain'.[86] On one occasion, admittedly a crisis, he wrote for thirteen hours, and on another a friend recalled him receiving seventy letters in one day when on holiday.[87] There are many examples among his correspondence of letters written early in the morning, or after midnight.[88] Middleton, for his part, insisted even at the height of the war on a weekend off (in an age when Saturday was an ordinary working day).[89]

It is true that Sandwich knew how to relax, and some of his contemporaries professed to be scandalized. In May 1776 David Hume met Sandwich, Denbigh, Banks, Mulgrave and 'two or three Ladies of Pleasure' staying for three weeks' fishing in an inn at Spine Hill near Newbury; 'Lord Sandwich in particular had caught trouts near twenty Inches long, which gave him incredible Satisfaction'. Hume was astonished,

> that the First Lord of the Admiralty, who is absolute and uncontrouled Master in his Department, shou'd, at a time when the Fate of the British Empire is in dependance, and in dependance on him, find so much Leizure, Tranquillity, Presence of Mind and Magnanimity, as to have Amusement in trouting during three Weeks near sixty Miles from the scene of Business, and during the most critical season of the year.[90]

The fate of the Empire, however, did not depend on Sandwich's presence in London. There was a crisis in America, but the Admiralty's share in it was confined to an enormous logistical effort, which had been going on for five months and was in the very capable hands of Palliser and Suckling. Had Sandwich been needed he could have reached London in half a day. Knowing with hindsight how many disasters have been caused in modern war by exhausted men who did not know how to delegate or relax, we may see some virtue in Sandwich taking a holiday when the opportunity offered.

Middleton's diatribe is equally unreliable as a guide to his normal working relationship with Sandwich. There is much correspondence between them in print,[91] and much more unprinted, which shows two very different men co-operating cordially in their work. Middleton was frequently asked for his opinion, and frequently volunteered it unasked. Occasionally in moments of stress he lapsed into the sort of wild and insulting language quoted above. He never apologized, but Sandwich never altered his calm and reasonable tone. Under provocation which would certainly have aroused almost any other cabinet minister or peer of the day to dismiss Middleton, Sandwich remained firm but friendly. Middleton was subsequently to serve under and with a series of First Lords, naval and civilian, some of them among the most talented of the century. Keppel, Howe, Chatham and Spencer differed in many respects, but they agreed in finding Middleton impossible to work with; an ungovernable subordinate, an offensive adviser, a disloyal colleague, a meddler and intriguer. Relations between the Admiralty and the Navy Board, which had been close and cordial under Sandwich, broke down in the late 1780s and never entirely recovered.

Middleton certainly was a political intriguer who was disloyal to Sandwich as well as to his successors. He habitually maintained secret connections with opposition or rival politicians, and attempted to play them off against the First Lord. His object was in part to further his great ambition to raise the Controller to the Admiralty Board and make him the First Lord's chief professional adviser. In such a position, controlling both the administration of the Navy and the professional advice offered to the Cabinet, he would have been in all but name a Minister of the Marine in the French style. Middleton's connections with Sandwich's Cabinet colleague and rival Lord George Germain were close, and Germain flattered Middleton's hopes of 'an executive First Lord acting under the marine minister and that Lord a professional man. He was so partial to me as to wish that I might be the person'.[92] Middleton must have realized that he was being used to undermine Sandwich's position. Middleton's capacity for self-deception is not to be under-estimated, and perhaps he had persuaded himself that he was acting honestly, but this was one subject which apparently embarrassed him, and about which he never spoke with his usual candour.[93] He was, however, quite willing to threaten Sandwich openly with the political consequences of not doing as he wished.[94] When Sandwich left office Middleton behaved in the same way to his successors. He used his long connection with Lord Shelburne to go behind Keppel's back. He undermined Lord Howe by dealing directly with Pitt.[95] In 1788 when it seemed that Pitt's government would fall, he opened secret contact with Sandwich again.[96]

To harness Middleton's unequalled talents while restraining the destructive and ignoring the offensive sides of his character called for a combination of qualities which only Sandwich possessed.[97] 'Sandwich released in Middleton great springs of activity and initiative, which Keppel and Howe would not have permitted, and Chatham would not have evoked'.[98] Within eight months of Sandwich leaving office Middleton was already regretting him:

My altercation with the noble Lord . . . was on public ground, and notwithstanding I found myself obliged to contend with him on such occasions, yet as a private Man, and as a duty incumbent on me in return for his taking in good part whatever remonstrance I made respecting the public service, I think myself obliged to preserve for him every mark of attention, and do him every act of friendship in my power.[99]

Looking back on his service under Sandwich with the experience of later and less happy relationships, Middleton came to regard it as something like a golden age. In 1794 he told his cousin Henry Dundas that, 'I had the full confidence of Lord Sandwich, and I flatter myself I did not abuse it . . . I directed both departments under a man of great abilities and discernment'; in 1805 he advised him,

> With a land lord at the head of the Admiralty, he [the Controller] must be his dictionary, and with a seaman he will be his right hand. Lord Sandwich was the only First Lord in my time who understood this, and if I had been of a disposition to consider self, there is nothing he would not have gratified me in.[100]

It was characteristic of Middleton to assume that he was really 'directing both departments', and it is instructive to see what happened when he actually tried. He and Sandwich had a number of serious disagreements, but one of the most revealing occurred in 1781 when Middleton attempted to claim for the Navy Board the right to appoint senior officers to the dockyards. This power had always been vested in the Admiralty, but the Navy Board was obviously in a position to make expert recommendations, and did so. With Palliser and Suckling at the Navy Board, Sandwich had easily and amicably settled on the best candidates, and for three years Middleton made no difficulties. By 1781 Sandwich was in a weaker political position, and it looks as though Middleton saw an opportunity to gain power for his board, and of course for himself, at the Admiralty's expense. He had mistaken his man.

It is important to be clear that the issue was one of power. In an age when the Admiralty, like government in general, had weak powers of coercion, its authority rested essentially on its ability to reward. Had it lost the right to appoint the senior officers of the yards, it would have lost all real power to enforce obedience. For Sandwich, the veteran of power struggles with Sir Jacob Acworth in the days when Middleton was only a midshipman, this was obvious; and it is equally obvious to the modern reader who is familiar with eighteenth-century society. It suited Middleton's purpose and character, however, to present the issue in essentially moral terms, as a contest between his disinterested virtue and efficiency, and Sandwich's devious and partial approach. He was too clever to accuse Sandwich openly of corruption, but he was a man with acute political instincts, and both the substance and the timing of his arguments were clearly designed to dovetail with opposition charges that Sand-

wich corruptly disposed of the offices in his gift; arguments 'calculated with a peculiar spirit for Parliamentary Enquiry & have much
the language & air of Opposition & Independence, both of your
Lordship's Board, & of the Court of Admiralty'.[101]

There are few aspects of Sandwich's administration which were
more relentlessly attacked at the time, or have been more thoroughly
investigated by modern scholars, than his handling of patronage,
and we are well placed to judge the accuracy of the opposition
charges, and the real grounds of his differences with Middleton.[102]
As early as 1773 Sandwich was accused by an opposition newspaper
of selling the place of a Commissioner of the Navy for £2,000. The
charge was sponsored by Captain John Luttrell and the publisher
John Almon, who evidently thought they had found a case of Martha
Ray using her influence for money. They had failed to check their
facts, and were easily discomfited in court, but they had taken precautions to avoid personal risk, and it was their unfortunate printer
John Miller who was abandoned to pay £2,000 in damages.[103] This
case has a small place in legal history as the last employment of the
ancient charge of *scandalum magnatum* or defamation of a peer, and
it is a witness to Sandwich's strong sense of tradition that he should
have used this charge when the evidence would easily have supported
a conventional accusation of libel.[104]

Modern scholarship has confirmed that Sandwich's handling of
dockyard appointments was honest and impartial. When money was
offered him, he refused it with contempt: 'I never was, nor ever will
be concerned in the disposal of any Office in which I have even the
most distant suspicion of any pecuniary transaction relative to the
filling the vacancy'.[105] Though energetic and successful as an electoral
manager, ever alert to the disposal of the minutest piece of patronage,
Sandwich did not allow political considerations to interfere with his
dockyard appointments. There are more than three hundred applications for yard offices entered in Sandwich's appointment books, of
which thirteen make political claims to advancement, of which four
succeeded.[106] Samuel Hogsflesh, Foreman Smith at Sheerness, was
refused promotion to Master Smith in spite of controlling four votes
in Rochester.[107] Sandwich was quite willing to make political capital
from the advancement of men whose capacities justified the choice,
but he would not break the established rules.[108]

An example of his approach is the 1782 promotion of Jacob Pownoll from Storekeeper of Gibraltar to Plymouth. Pownoll was the son
of the former Master Shipwright of Plymouth, and the brother of
Captain Philemon Pownoll, one of the most brilliant and beloved

officers in the Navy, who had recently met a gallant death in action.[109] Sandwich's reasons for choosing him in spite of Middleton's opposition were four: Pownoll's family connections with Plymouth Yard; the respect due to the memory of his late brother; the fact that the existing Storekeeper Philip Justice, whose incompetence made it highly desirable to replace him, had probably only agreed to resign in favour of Pownoll (his brother-in-law); and finally that Pownoll's experience and abilities were fully equal to the job.[110] This was the second occasion on which Middleton buttressed his argument by quoting from 'Sir William Pepys':[111]

> . . . the office of a storekeeper in the Navy is an employment of very great trust and such a one as, whatever it calls for of integrity, calls for no less experience in the business of the Navy; and therefore [I] do in all humility hope on his Majesty's behalf that with regard his Majesty may be pleased to have those who by many years' education and labour in his service have qualified themselves above all others for his favours herein.[112]

Sandwich had known Samuel Pepys's manuscripts for years, but did not allow himself to be provoked into saying so.[113]

Insofar as there was a real ground of difference between Sandwich and Middleton other than the question of who was master, it lay in Sandwich's respect for tradition. He placed a high value on seniority and experience, where Middleton was more willing to upset the established order by advancing men who were still quite young. Sandwich appointed the 63-year-old John Smart Master Joiner of Woolwich, for example, against Middleton's candidate who was only 34 years old.[114] There were things to be said in favour of both approaches, but it is certain that Middleton's would have been highly divisive, and the height of a major war was not the time to try it. In an age when office was still regarded as a sort of personal property and the aged or incompetent had to be tempted to retire, Sandwich's persuasive charm combined with his conservative use of existing conventions were much better adapted to achieve results than Middleton's thoughtless abruptness. In 1773 for example, Sandwich persuaded John Harris, Master Shipwright of Chatham, to retire on the promise of preferment for his son.[115] Harris had served long and loyally but was too ill to continue and had never been of outstanding ability.[116] Middleton would no doubt have disapproved of Sandwich's approach, but there was no other available which would have achieved the desired result of easing the old man out of office. Perhaps Middleton's essentially nineteenth-century approach might have yielded greater efficiency, but it is very unlikely that it could have been made to work in eighteenth-century conditions.

Moreover Middleton's argument that only the Navy Board could know the yard officers well, and that its authority needed to be buttressed by controlling their appointments, ought to be treated with scepticism. In practice the Navy Board was little better equipped than the Admiralty to form an independent judgement, and much more open to potentially corrupt relationships with the yards. Sandwich had many independent sources of information, and knew of just such dealings, for example between George Marsh as Clerk of Acts and the officers of Chatham Yard.[117] We know that the vehemence of Middleton's argument was sharpened, and the whole quarrel may have been precipitated, by a private relationship of his own: he had promised promotion to John Cleversal, Master Joiner of Sheerness, and was embarrassed not to be able to fulfil his engagement. Cleversal had revealed some corrupt practices in his yard and no doubt deserved a reward, but the relationship, which Middleton was careful to keep secret, was just the sort of connection which in other hands could easily have been perverted to corrupt ends.[118] He may have had a private connection of another kind with William Shrubsole, Master Mastmaker of Sheerness and Huntingdonian preacher.[119] Furthermore Sandwich, as a frequent visitor to the yards, had personal knowledge of the senior officers which even Middleton could not match.

> I may safely venture to say, that there is not an Officer in any of the Dock Yards, whose character I am not thoroughly acquainted with, and as they all know that their Promotion depends entirely upon their Behaviour, they vie with each other in recommending themselves by a strict discharge of their duty.[120]

This was even more true of appointments directly from the Sea Service, such as Joseph Gilbert, master of the *Resolution* on Cook's second voyage, who was a great success as Master Attendant at Portsmouth.[121] Middleton, as he admitted, found it difficult to find out about such officers even by report.[122]

One incident may be quoted as a commentary on Middleton's dealings with yard officers. On Christmas Eve 1781 he wrote to George White, Master Shipwright of Portsmouth, in these terms:

As the master-joiner of Woolwich yard is become too infirm to carry
on the business of his office, I was naturally led to enquire into the
character of the leading man in that branch. The answer not coming
up to my expectations, I enquired who placed him there, and, to my
great surprise and disappointment, found it to be Mr White.

I now perceive that all my endeavours must end in nothing; for if
you, to whom I have said so much on this subject, will put men into
places of trust who are incapable of performing the duties of them,
and thereby act unjustly by those who are, to the prejudice of the
king's service, what am I to expect from others who have not fallen
so immediately under my notice?[123]

Knowing as we do that White's ability and integrity had been praised
by Middleton himself, by Mostyn and Palliser, two of his predecessors as Controller, by the Surveyor Sir John Williams, by Captain
Hood the Commissioner of Portsmouth, by Anson and Boscawen,[124]
we might be inclined to suspect that there was another side to this
episode, and there is. White had been Master Shipwright of Woolwich for thirteen months from March 1778 to April 1779, during
which time he doubtless exercised influence over promotions within
his department – but the appointment of foremen and quartermen
rested with the Navy Board, not the yard officers,[125] and if there
was blame for any such appointment made during that time, it rested
primarily with the Navy Board, and with Middleton who presided
over it. Furthermore the leading man in question, Samuel Lyon,
Foreman Joiner, had in fact been appointed before White came to
Woolwich.[126] The most charitable comment that can be made is that
Middleton was under great pressure and acted in haste on inadequate
information. The evidence would bear the interpretation that
he was trying to cover his own mistakes by shifting the blame onto a
subordinate. Either way it casts an unflattering light on his handling of patronage, and illustrates one good reason for Sandwich to
keep the appointment of the most senior yard officers in his own
hands.

The argument between Sandwich and Middleton was not one
between two opposite points of view; it was one between Middleton's intransigent demands and Sandwich's reasonable compromise.
He never denied the Navy Board's right to make recommendations,
and even to expect most of them to be adopted. In fact, thirteen of
the nineteen senior yard offices filled in this period followed the
Navy Board's suggestion.[127] Sandwich only insisted that the ultimate
authority must rest with the Admiralty:

I shall adhere firmly to my resolution of not discussing by letter the points on which we have differed. You will probably retain your opinion and I mine; but I have some hopes from the contents of your last letter that our friendly intercourse and connexion may not be discontinued, notwithstanding this difference of opinion; and I am ready on my part to renew and continue it with the same cordiality as before existed.

When next we meet not a word shall drop from me of the disagreeable matters that have lately passed, and I shall continue to ask information from you, as I have done ever since you have been Comptroller of the Navy, in matters both within and without the cognizance of the Navy Board. It has been my method in every branch of business in which I have been concerned to gain knowledge from men of ability who I thought were likely to give me useful instruction; no one comes more fully under that description than yourself, and my conduct shows that the instruction I have received from you has been much attended to by me.

As to the particular official dispute about recommendation to the offices in the dockyards, I think it would be unfair not to appraise you that the Board of Admiralty are united in their opinion on that subject, and that, if it was my inclination, it would not be in my power to prevail on them to vary from the ground they have taken . . .[128]

The contrast between Middleton's extravagant language[129] and Sandwich's patient courtesy is marked.

CHAPTER XI

Rewards and Favours
1771–1782

'It is highly disagreeable to a generous mind', wrote Commodore
Sir George Collier in March 1780, 'to say anything of one's services'.[1]
It was only the seventh time in as many years that he had managed
to overcome his finer feelings sufficiently to represent his claims.
He asked for various employments, for promotion and for higher
allowances; he complained at the lack of royal favour (nothing but
a knighthood), and of missing the chance to carry a lucrative 'freight'
of government money. 'Aggrieved as I think myself, it would be
meanness to be silent'.[2] Yet Collier was the most restrained of pet-
itioners. Not many senior officers presented their suits so modestly,
or so seldom, as he, and not many had such good claims to favour,
for as temporary senior officer in North America for part of 1779
he had acted with vigour, and won a small but crushing victory over
a rebel squadron in the Penobscot River. If every senior officer had
been a Collier, Sandwich and his ministerial colleagues would have
had an easier time. As it was, the distribution of promotion, employment and distinction in the Navy was without doubt his most vexatious single responsibility.

A contemporary moralist defined honour as 'The Desire of Fame,
or the Applause of Men, directed to the end of public Happiness'.[3]
Sandwich could certainly have vouched for the first part of the definition, but might have wondered how often public happiness came
into it. As a politician directing a professional service he stood at the
point of collision between two different systems of values. In the
Navy, as in society at large, the relations between men with power
and men with ambitions were regulated by patronage. In both, great
men formed followings of lesser people who served themselves by
serving their patrons. In society at large the 'merit' by which men
supported and advanced their claims was greatly, often entirely
founded on birth and wealth, either in the claimant or his patron.
Ability and hard work were recognized as having their place, and

in certain circumstances might confer a respectable claim, but they constituted only one element among the qualities which might bring success. Within the machinery of government, there were many positions, some of them quite senior, which were understood as being posts of 'business' for which abilities would be required of candidates with suitable influence, but there were virtually none to which a man could hope to make his way without possessing, or acquiring, appropriate social connections. The system of patronage was thought of as part of the fabric of society rather than of the machinery of government.

Most of this was equally true in the Navy, but there were two critical differences. Naval followings were constructed on professional criteria. Though social and political influence was often employed, there were hardly any positions in the Sea Service (and not many in the civil administration of the Navy ashore) which did not require a minimum level of professional experience and ability. Birth and social influence often advanced the careers of men of ability faster than those of their less fortunate contemporaries, but in this uniquely complex and dangerous profession they could not make up for the absence of talent. The other important peculiarity of the naval system was that it was self-contained. Naval patronage was controlled by senior officers, not by men of weight in outside society, and only to a limited extent by the Admiralty. In a system with weak authority at the centre, and poor powers of discipline, patronage provided the cement which bound the Service together, conferring on senior officers the power to command, and teaching juniors to look to them for reward. Admirals could and did use their naval connections to serve themselves in politics, but they jealously guarded the naval system against interference from outside. Politicians and men prominent in public life could not be allowed to interfere in naval patronage, not only because they would not understand the importance of professional ability, but because their interference threatened the admirals' monopoly of the real power in the Navy.[4]

This was the main reason why almost all the successful eighteenth-century First Lords had been admirals. Standing at the head of their profession, officers like Torrington, Wager and Anson had naturally combined authority within the Service with standing in the political world. Civilian First Lords like Winchelsea and Temple had found it difficult to establish real control over a service which they did not understand, and where they had no connections. Sandwich's position was unprecedented. Three times First Lord, by the end of the

American War he had been familiar with the Admiralty and the Navy for nearly forty years. He had known even senior officers since their youth; he knew at least as much as they did about the people in the Navy, and a great deal more about its civil administration. In many respects he was able to play the admiral to effect; 'not bred a sailor, yet he governs the department in every minute sense of it, as well as any sailor that ever presided at the board!'.[5] This made him a threat to the independent power of senior officers. Though his own professional following was small, the fact that it existed at all aroused unease – yet it was too small to fill more than a few senior positions. Anson had established his unequalled authority over the Navy partly by installing his own numerous and talented followers in most of the key positions. Sandwich's were too few to do the same. He could only work through senior officers who instinctively distrusted his position, even if they respected his abilities.

If Sandwich was too close to the admirals for their comfort, he was not close enough to his peers in public life. As First Lord, he had to apply the naval standards in the disposal of patronage, standards not accepted or even understood in the political world. But for his contemporaries Sandwich was pre-eminently a politician, a skilful and at times ruthless operator of the machinery of electoral politics. He was not the man to carry easy conviction when he proclaimed that he was adhering to an alien professional code. Twenty years before Anson had taken the same line, and aroused much grumbling among great men whose attempts to apply their influence had been abruptly rebuffed – but Anson was not one of them. Sandwich was, and many of his contemporaries and social equals simply refused to believe that he could or would betray his class and upbringing by adopting a different system of values. Men whose birth or position entitled them to look for favour from the king's ministers regarded Sandwich's references to ability, experience and sea-time as trifling excuses covering political or personal enmity. Indeed, the preferring men of obscure birth over 'men of fashion' was inherently a corrupt practice, or at least a suspicious one. Gentlemen helped one another on a basis of social equality; the obvious reason for preferring the low-born was that they could not stand independently of their patrons, in short they were natural tools of ministerial power. The Rockingham Whigs in particular, an aristocratic group with conservative social views and an acute fear of government tyranny, deeply distrusted any policy which might tend to remove power of any sort from men like themselves to which it naturally belonged. The very fact that government employed men who depended on their salaries for their living was in their eyes dangerous, and their attempts at political reform were directed at abolishing as many government offices as possible, and removing the rest from contact with the electoral system. Himself notoriously a man who needed money, Sandwich controlled the patronage of tens of thousands of government jobs, and insisted on disposing of them on criteria of his own which seemed to ignore or devalue the rightful claims of the leaders of society. In this perspective Sandwich's espousal of the naval standards which he had learnt from Anson in the 1740s looked very like corruption.[6]

This is the background to a series of clashes between Sandwich and the noble or influential patrons of officers in the Navy who expected that their 'interest' would carry as much weight there as it would have done anywhere else. Lord Robert Manners, for example, was a son of the Duke of Rutland, and expected to be treated as such. Sandwich had to explain to an unreceptive elder brother that, 'I am thoroughly disposed to give every assistance in my power to Mr Manners, but he cannot, according to the fundamental rules of the Navy, be made a Lieutenant till he has served six years and passed an examination'.[7] As soon as he became a lieutenant he was demanding to be promoted again, and again meeting unaccountable resistance. This was 'trifling too much with one of the first families in the kingdom',[8] and it had political consequences. Sandwich's colleague Lord Mansfield explained that the young man was genuinely keen on the Navy, but 'the same ambition makes him impatient of being humbled, mortified & kept back', and he would quit the Service if he were obliged to wait for his promotion.

> He & the whole family will feel it as a personal injury, and there are [those] who will rejoice to exasperate, & ascribe his being neglected to false motives & call it by false names . . . I conjure your Lordship to consider how prejudicial so bitter an alienation of so considerable a family may be.[9]

A week later Mansfield again explained the young man's position:

> He wishes to continue in the Profession from Ambition & not for Bread. If he is to rise by the same slow Degrees by which every Cabin Boy may be advanced, there is no Prospect worthy of Ambition, & the same spirit which makes him desire to pursue the Profession, must make him quit from Despair of being early enough in a Rank, which will enable him to make a figure.[10]

Manners was then a lieutenant of eighteen months' seniority. In naval terms he needed much more experience to have a claim on a command; in social terms he had every right to a rank which would 'enable him to make a figure'. The family were already 'very sore & much mortified',[11] and if Sandwich could not speedily find a way to gratify their expectations both he and the government could expect to suffer for it. He was able to do it by persuading Admiral Rodney to take Lord Robert with him to the West Indies. On over-seas stations promotion could be fast, and none rose faster under Rodney's command than the sons of the powerful. Less than one month later Manners was a post captain. Before the end of the American War he was dead, mortally wounded at the battle of the Saintes.

Sandwich was lucky with Lord Robert. He was able to find an expedient within the accepted conventions of naval promotion, and the young man was really a good officer in spite of his inexperience. It was not always so easy. The Duke of Leinster also had a brother in the Navy, and the state of Irish politics, which threatened to follow the American example, was delicate enough to make it even more important to gratify Irish dukes than English. Moreover Admiral Keppel, who also had to be conciliated in the spring of 1778, took an interest in the young man.[12] In November of that year Leinster was asking for his brother to be made commander after six months as a lieutenant,[13] but the real difficulty for Sandwich came in September 1780, by which time Lord Charles Fitzgerald was already a post captain, and Irish politics were in crisis. 'Upon a very urgent sollicitation from the Duke of Leinster,' wrote Lord Buckingham the Lord Lieutenant,

> I wrote last night to Lord Sandwich expressing his wish that his brother should be appointed Captain of the *Belle Poule* frigate. It was my duty to recommend the measure earnestly. The name of Fitzgerald, ever of consequence in Ireland, is at this juncture a material object.[14]

Sandwich explains the difficulty this put him under in a letter to Lord Mulgrave, who had at the same time been pressing for the advancement of his follower Captain Pakenham:

> I have already written to Ld Longford upon his brother's subject, and must entreat of you not to press me to do more than what I propose to do in that business, which is to expect, that before he gets a frigate of a larger class he should for some time (which need not be very

long) command one of 28 guns. There are many young men of fashion now in the service, their friends are very importunate & their requests frequently very unreasonable, my language to them must be uniform or I shall involve myself in difficulties very unpleasant to me, and very prejudicial to the service. I have within this fortnight resisted the applications of the late and present Lord Lieutenants of Ireland & the Duke of Leinster in behalf of Lord Charles Fitzgerald, & have given him only the command of the *Sybil* tho' his views were much higher; if I do not withstand these applications I shall have very improper people forced upon me, and the able & deserving officers of rank and service kept in ships of inferior rates. This can only be resisted by uniformity of conduct, & tho' I have the highest opinion of Captain Pakenham's merit I shall not be able to convince the Duke of Leinster & many others that their sons & brothers have not equal pretensions. In this situation I must once more beg of you not to urge me any farther upon this point, Captain Pakenham shall certainly have no reason to complain of me, but if I am put out of my rules, my situation in this office will become so burthensome & disagreeable that I shall be fairly tired out at last.[15]

Adherence to rule was the guiding principle of Sandwich's handling of patronage, and his chief defence against importunity. Only by sticking inflexibly to standards could he hope to parry the many and powerful voices which clamoured for his attention. Invariably he refused to make any promises about jobs which were not yet available[16] or ships which were not yet ready; 'I told him I never would promise that or any ship that was so far from being ready, but that when she was fit for sea he would have as good a chance of her as any other person if he was on the spot'.[17] When Lord Scarsdale asked him to advance his son to lieutenant after three and a half years at sea instead of the regulation six,[18] or his colleague Charles Jenkinson put forward a political connection, Sandwich could hope to avoid making another enemy only if he had stuck closely to the regulations, and been seen to do so:

As soon as ever you inform me that Mr Bentley has passed his exmination he shall be made a Lieutenant, but I am fearfull from your letter that he has served only four years which will be an invincible bar to his promotion, as they must be six years in the Kings service before they can be examined.[19]

'The Candidates for promotion in the Navy are so numerous', Sandwich wrote to Lord Berkeley, that it is absolutely necessary for me to hold the same language to all who address themselves to me upon that subject, and I am obliged to have the most strict attention to the seniority of those who either by themselves or friends sollicit preferment.

The rule of seniority indeed usually gives way in cases where officers have the good fortune to distinguish themselves in battle, but I cannot agree with your Lordship that exertions on harbour duty tho' very meritorious should give the same pretension.

There are many young men of fashion in the Navy who are equally sollicitous for preferment and their friends are equally pressing; your Lordship will find on enquiry that my answer to all of them is the same, whatever their connections may be.[20]

That was the source of much of the trouble. Adherence to regulations 'that are not inconsistent with what I think for the good of the service, & necessary for my own ease and comfort in office'[21] might be Sandwich's only plausible defence, but it was an offence in the eyes of those for whom rules applied to other people. 'A total relaxation of discipline, and the Rule laid down by a great Man, that we are all alike, must in the end be productive of bad Consequences',[22] complained Vice-Admiral Barrington. Old Lord Hawke agreed: 'the thinking all men are alike in the service, must bring the Navy to destruction at last'.[23] For different reasons, both admirals within the Navy and great men without felt Sandwich's policy of impartiality was outrageous.

They did not conceal their indignation. Reading the begging letters which reached Sandwich every day one is repeatedly struck by how many of them were not in fact begging, but demanding, often in tones of anger or insolence.[24] 'I must be stupid and have lost all sensibility', wrote Rear-Admiral Digby, 'to be comforted by your giving me to understand that you have difficultys in satisfying those you don't consider as your friends and that you expect those you do to remain satisfied under every neglect'.[25] Young and not so young gentlemen took it for granted that they conferred an honour upon Sandwich by serving in the Navy, and had a right to corresponding favours in return. Lieutenant Thomas Lewes informed the First Lord that he had only consented to serve upon the understanding that he would speedily be promoted. Now he gathered that Sandwich would not promote officers who had quitted their ships and were on half-pay in wartime; 'that you "enter into no engagements with any officer for promotion, and that you can give no officer rank who is not in actual service"'. Evidently, Lewes concluded, Sandwich was a personal enemy; unless he were immediately promoted, he would leave the Service forthwith, and his patron Lord Carlisle would draw the appropriate conclusion.[26] Unlike many other young officers with aristocratic patrons, Lewes actually had respectable seniority, being a lieutenant of twenty years' standing in 1781; the difficulty was that he had spent very little of that time at sea. It was not a difficulty that impressed his patrons:

> the same objection will hold good against every Lieut in the Navy, that is not immediately in Your Lordships eye . . . I have been well enough acquainted for many years with the common course of things in the Navy, to know what several of your Lordships predecessors have don, & what has been don by your Lordship, & what you can do, & what you will do again, & I dare say during this war, your Lordship will find opportunities to promote those have been at sea, hardly half the time that Mr Lewes has been a Lieutenant, without one of his abilities.[27]

In this and in many similar cases Sandwich found it impossible to persuade people that he meant what he said:

> Nothing that I desired Lord Lisburne or any other person to convey to you could contain anything like an *absolute promise* of preferment; it is my intention to keep clear of all promise or engagement whatsoever, & I must hope that you will attend to the words of this letter which is what alone I mean to abide by.[28]

Lewes replied that he understood that Sandwich could not go beyond 'general professions', but was confident that his advice to continue in service was 'in all respects adequate to an absolute promise'.[29]

It was nothing of the kind, but Lewes was only one of many well-connected officers who assumed that Sandwich's talk of rules was only a smokescreen concealing the usual political manoeuvres; that a plain statement actually meant the opposite of what it appeared to mean. When they found out that Sandwich had really meant what he had said, they accused him of betraying the promises which they were confident he had 'really' made. The processes of patronage were an almost perfect recipe for making enemies. This was not peculiar to the Navy: 'By making one Peer, ten enemies are made, & twenty claimants';[30] but it was probably a more divisive factor there than ashore. Not many officers imitated Commodore Mackenzie, who 'went to the Admiralty with loaded pistols to demand why the promotion of flags stopped at him',[31] but most of them

reckoned they had grievances. In wartime there was never enough
to give away, and in peacetime there was hardly anything;[32] 'Naval
news there is none, all goes on quietly', wrote Augustus Hervey in
1772, 'many suitors and little to bestow'.[33] Those who were told to
wait assumed that they had been refused; those who received something complained that it was too little or too late; all of them blamed
their disappointment on personal enmity. Lord Bristol pestered
Sandwich for months to promote an old follower:

> You distress me exceedingly by pressing me on a matter in which it
> is impossible for me to comply with your request without drawing
> myself into inextricable difficulties; was I to break the ice with regard
> to promotion at home I could not remain where I am with any ease
> or comfort.[34]

At length Sandwich was able to promote the man, but by then it
was too late: 'I have made Lieutenant Foulkes a Master & Commander, but by the enclosed note from Ld Bristol you will see he
is determined to be angry with me which I am sorry for, but could
not prevent'.[35] In 1781 Sir Harry Heron wrote in a fury to resign
his commission. If after sixteen years a lieutenant and four a commander, in spite of all the efforts of his patron Lord Huntingdon,
he was still commanding an obscure convoy escort in the North Sea,
it could only be because Sandwich had become a personal enemy.[36]

A common cause of displeasure was Sandwich's refusal to allow the
well-connected to avoid service in the unhealthy West or East Indies.
Lady Waldegrave took it for granted that if Sandwich had been
willing to give her son a ship, he would be willing to exchange him
to another to avoid three years in the East Indies. 'There are different
ways of granting favours, either in a pleasing, or a disagreeable
manner', she wrote on learning her mistake.[37] Lord Paget desired
that his brother might avoid the West Indies by retiring to harbour
service, and Sandwich hardly needed Lord Dartmouth to point out
the political risks of refusal:

> I heartily wish yr Lordp may think fit to adopt this or some other
> expedient, without which it will be impossible to convince Ld Paget
> that he is not designedly ill used, & I am sure yr Ldp sees as I do, that
> it is of some consequence at this moment to satisfy Lord Paget.[38]

At least in these cases the officers concerned were actually willing
to serve – when and where it suited them. Many of Sandwich's

correspondents assumed that the Navy existed to supply their private convenience. Titled gentlemen and their wives expected to cruise in the king's ships for their health or pleasure, even in wartime.[39] Edward Stratford wrote in 1777, assuming rather than asking that his brother would very shortly be a post captain, and requesting that Sandwich would give him a ship in the Mediterranean in order that they might take a grand tour together, 'having a rage for travel & classical Ground, which I cannot do with such satisfaction to myself, as in a Brother's ship'. He also mentioned that it would be proper to have his brother made a baronet.[40]

With many of these requests an already fraught relation was made worse by politics. Sandwich's colleagues in government operated on the same assumptions as everyone else. 'My view, when I undertook his cause was to bring him forward in his profession as fast as other young gentlemen of his rank & fashion', Lord North wrote of a client whom he wished made post after seventeen months as a commander.[41] By conventional standards North had every right to make such requests, and no one knew better than that master of electoral politics Lord Sandwich how important it was to grant them if the administration were to be sustained. In this and every case when they conflicted with his rules, Sandwich refused, but he understood that refusal undermined both the strength of the ministry as a whole, and his standing with his colleagues. In 1775 Henry Dundas wrote on behalf of his friend Sir George Home, still a lieutenant after twenty-one years.[42] He was eventually promoted, but not till four years later. By 1781 Dundas was leading a faction within the administration trying to eject Sandwich; his principal motive was certainly self-preservation rather than old grievances about patronage, but the Home incident was a perfect example of how to alienate one's colleagues, for what they would regard as a trifle.

Even Mulgrave, bred up from boyhood to the standards of the Navy, expected Sandwich to break them for an Admiralty colleague. 'I have the fullest confidence in your friendship that you will find some expedient for gratifying me', he wrote, asking for someone to be made purser of his ship (a line-of-battleship) who had never served in the Navy before.[43] 'What you say to me about the Purser of the *Courageux* distresses me beyond measure', Sandwich replied,

> I have so repeatedly pledged my word that I would never make a Purser for the first time who did not go to Sea in a Sloop, that not only my comfort in Office, but my honour is so closely concerned in my adherence to this regulation, that I must rely on your friendship

not to press me farther upon the subject: if the person for whom you interest yourself will take a cruize or two as Purser of a Sloop, I will in a very short time bring him by regular steps into the *Courageux*, but it would bring me into such inextricable difficulties, and load me with such just accusations of inconsistency that I am sure your friendship will not allow you to urge me upon so delicate a subject.[44]

It was the same story with the privilege of taking key members of a ship's company to serve in a new ship, which frequently resulted in disabling a ship fit for service to furnish one still in dockyard hands. Mulgrave requested the favour for his nephew Lord Hervey:

I must again entreat you not to press me about the *Daphne*'s men, I cannot give them without breaking my word with half the Captains in the Navy; I mentioned the names of Edwards & Macbride only as two recent instances out of innumerable others; it was but yesterday that I gave Captain Lutwidge a flat refusal of any more than ten men out of the *Yarmouth*, & it has been my invariable regulation to be firm on this ground, without which the ships in actual service would be perpetually disabled, to accommodate those which cannot be ready for sea in many months. Was I to give the same indulgence to Ld Hervey as was given to Captain Macbride, it would not be 50 men as you suppose, but a tenth part of the complement of the *Daphne*, which was the proportion taken from the *Bienfaisant*. Be assured, my dear Lord, that I bear every proper attention & goodwill to Lord Hervey, but I must at the same time consider my own comfort & consistency, which would be considerably broken into if I was to give way upon this proposition.[45]

Mulgrave wanted a follower promoted early, and when Sandwich complained that even his friends laid such burdens on him ('have I not a little reason to complain that my friends, instead of feeling for my distresses, will help to multiply them?'),[46] Mulgrave replied with hurt incomprehension:

I did not expect that Mr Allen would have been upon a footing in your Lordships opinion with above half the first Lieutenants of the Fleet or that your Lordship thought my Application ought to be postponed to that of every friend you have & that of every Person in Authority in Government; I can only say that if Half the first Lieutenants in the Fleet have better Pretentions than twenty years constant & meritorious Services as an Officer give to Mr Allen the country is very well off; & if your Lordship has many Friends who from their Regard & attachment have better Claims upon you than myself I dont think your Situation is such as you ought to be tired of, or to give you reason to complain I don't feel for your distresses.[47]

Of course Sandwich's willingness to offend his political allies to preserve the Navy from interference did nothing to endear him to officers connected with the opposition. Determined as he was to extinguish faction in the Service, anxious as he was to employ the best men if they could be had, Sandwich went out of his way to be as accommodating as possible to officers who had identified themselves as his enemies. None of Admiral Keppel's more partisan followers suffered for their behaviour in the violent controversies of 1778–79 except Captain Leveson-Gower who refused to serve.[48] Some opposition officers, however, clearly took Sandwich's advances as a sign of weakness, and an invitation to respond with contempt. Captain Cornwallis presented a string of unreasonable demands couched in petulant and impertinent terms.[49] Sandwich replied as always with temperate courtesy, ('I fear we shall never settle the points between us in writing, particularly as I by no means agree with the manner in which you have stated them'), and repeated his willingness to oblige.[50] Two years later he was describing Cornwallis as 'one of the most distinguished officers in the King's service', and going out of his way to attend to his followers.[51] Cornwallis at least knew how to apologize,[52] and refrained from openly invoking politics. More violently partisan officers like Captain James Luttrell started with the blunt assertion that only politics governed Sandwich's actions, and proceeded to threaten him with the political consequences of not serving them.[53] By dealing fairly with men like Luttrell, Sandwich aroused the resentment of government supporters who saw the 'Sons & Brothers of Noblemen, & Gentlemen, who have constantly and violently thwarted & opposed Government in every measure' favoured over their own relations,[54] or regarded their loyalty as conferring a right to insist on what they wanted.[55]

It comes almost as a surprise after reading so many thousands of letters to Sandwich complaining, demanding and threatening, to find that he had a few correspondents who were actually grateful, and even contented. Captain Timothy Edwards was happy with his ship the *Cornwall*; 'she is finely manned and in every respect an English man-of-war ready for sea on the shortest notice'.[56] So was Captain Bazely who took over the *Apollo* from the lamented Philemon Pownoll: 'I find myself comfortable and happy in my command, officers and ships company united as one family'.[57] There were even a very few disappointed applicants who appreciated his 'fair frank yet obliging treatment' and apologized for pressing him too hard,[58] but it was the rarest of sentiments.

It is pleasant to record also that there was one group of officers who remembered Sandwich with gratitude long after his fall from power. Without regimental structure, and almost without access to the general staff, Marine officers found their careers severely hampered by comparison with their brethren in the army, which was particularly painful when they were operating as part of the army ashore in America in 1776. In the face of the king's indifference and the active hostility of Lord Amherst, Sandwich was a steady advocate of their interests, and managed to secure many improvements in their status.[59] It must have given him pleasure to hear of the celebrations in 1787 for the hanging of his portrait in the Marine officers' mess at Plymouth, when the officers,

> assembled together with Major General Collins at their head to Celebrate their Day, and ordered a Dinner with Wine to the Non Commissioned Officers; and Beer to the Marines, to do the same. When after Dinner; on your Health being drunk, Three Vollies were fired by the Company of Grenadiers who were drawn up on the pleasing occasion.[60]

Just before he died Sandwich heard from a friend who had rented a house belonging to a Marine officer, 'and the first object that presented itself upon my entering the best parlour to view the House was your Lordship in full Length and elegant Frame'.[61] Amidst the violent politics of the American crisis, one group of officers did not forget their old patron.

Sandwich himself had not forgotten how to be a politician when he went to the Admiralty. He was perfectly willing to take political credit for whatever promotions and advancements were within his rules.[62] There were positions, particularly in the civil administration ashore, in which personal or political influence was admissible to a greater degree than they were among sea officers. 'My Uncle Sir Roger Burgoyne has been long a very useless officer at the Victualling Board',[63] wrote North in 1779, asking that Burgoyne's son might succeed, and Sandwich duly recommended him to the king: 'he is a young man of capacity & promises to make a better officer than his father'.[64] Another vacancy at the same board was filled by the Storekeeper of Woolwich; 'Mr Lance has passed all his life in the service as Purser & Storekeeper, and will in Ld. Sandwich's opinion make a very good commissioner he is strongly recommended by Lord Dudley'.[65] Lance had backing, as civil officers usually did, but he had ability and experience as well, and he was preferred over a Huntingdonshire applicant who would have done Sandwich's own political interest good.[66] Similar considerations applied at the Sick and Hurt Board. Lord Hinchingbrooke had a protégé named Corbett, for whose sake Sandwich was in 1777 'endeavouring to find a pretext to add a commissioner of Sick & Hurt to the present number', but only on condition that Corbett was prepared to be a working commissioner, not a sinecurist.[67] When a vacancy arose in 1781 for which Mulgrave urged a candidate, Sandwich explained that,

> I was indispensably obliged to appoint Mr Walker Surgeon of the *Cambridge* to the last vacancy at the Sick & Hurt Office, as he is not only a remarkable good man in his profession, but was the principal cause of my carrying the Election at Callington for Mr Stratton during the last Parlaiment [sic]; and chusing two Members for that Borough at the last general Election.[68]

This combination of political and professional qualifications was usual for this sort of post.

The same was true to some extent with the 'civilian' officers afloat like surgeons and pursers. Thus in 1774 Sandwich wrote to Cornwallis, 'there is on board your ship a surgeon's mate, named Thong, whose relations at Huntingdon are my particular friends. I cannot, therefore, at their intercession avoid recommending him to your protection'.[69]

In all these cases Sandwich was willing to follow precedent and reap whatever political advantage was to be had without damaging the Service. Sometimes the advantages applied to his home ground of Huntingdonshire, but he was particularly sensitive to the charge of improper political influence in this context. 'Can you imagine', he reproved Rodney in response to another irregular promotion,

> That after I have refused confirmation to officers in North America and the Leeward Islands under similar circumstances, I would make a distinction at Jamaica because one of the persons promoted had connections in Huntingdonshire, & the other was the son of one for whom I have a very particular esteem? You know me very little if you imagine I can act so inconsistently.[70]

There were Huntingdonshire men in the Navy, like Captain Hayward, 'a good man, and has besides the merit of being born in the county of Huntingdon',[71] or Captain John Brown, son of Lancelot 'Capability' Brown who had settled in the county. Sandwich took an interest in him, and his brother became one of the MPs of his connection, but his career was no more or less favoured than that of dozens of other young officers with much less powerful connections.[72]

When Samuel Bentham was referred to the Navy Board on applying for a senior post (for which he lacked the qualifications and experience), his brother Jeremy commented 'What everybody is agreed about is that the place would have been within the Department of the Admiralty if Sam had been a freeholder of Huntingdon'. In fact no applicant to Sandwich for a dockyard position, who mentioned being a freeholder of Huntingdon, ever succeeded.[73] Moreover we have his lists of the Huntingdon freeholders compiled in canvassing at general elections, from which we can tell exactly what patronage Sandwich bestowed upon them. Of one hundred and five resident burgesses in 1779, one, a postman, was an employee of government. The one hundred non-resident burgesses included twenty-three public servants, plus two of Sandwich's naval friends (Palliser and Sir Richard Bickerton) who had no doubt been admitted freeholders in compliment to him. But these twenty-three, most or all of whom had certainly been appointed by Sandwich's influence, were for the most part in the humblest jobs. The most senior were two chaplains and an official of Greenwich Hospital, an unestablished extra clerk in the Admiralty, a lieutenant in the Navy, and another in the Marines. Otherwise they included dockyard labourers, porters, messengers, clerks, a tailor, two warrant officers, a rating and three private soldiers.[74] The 1782 canvass showed a very similar pattern, save that in three years the number of government employees had fallen from twenty-four to fifteen.[75] No burgess of Huntingdon was ever advanced by Sandwich to a senior position. It would be difficult to find a single other minister of his day who could have made such a claim, least of all one who maintained such a hold on his constituency.

To find something like a real abuse of the Admiralty for political purposes in Sandwich's time it is necessary to descend to a very low level. In connection with the 1780 general election he privately arranged for a man valuable to Lord Clive's election at Ludlow to be discharged from the Navy ('but not on any account to apply to him *in my name* for his vote'), and for a Marine officer to have leave to attend the election ('and I wish you would find some means of applying to him as desired as it would be very indiscreet in me to apply to him myself').[76] It was not a transaction Sandwich wished to have known, but it can hardly be described as a major abuse.

Perhaps the most political of Sandwich's uses of patronage concerned Sir John Borlase Warren, a young Devon landowner and baronet who entered the Navy. This was highly unusual for a man in his position, and Sandwich early marked him as a follower, in the Navy and in Parliament. Warren had made his choice very late in life (about the age of nineteen), and was anxious to catch up with his peers. Sandwich was prepared to cut some corners on his behalf, including bearing his name on the books of one of the royal yachts in harbour to gain 'sea-time', but this was an accepted device to allow young men to get some formal schooling ashore, and Sandwich would not break the six-year rule.[77] Like Mulgrave, Warren expected the rules to be bent for him, and he was not subtle in invoking the political advantages of doing so:

> I was very happy in being able to comply with your Lordship's wishes in being in town time enough to attend the debate on Monday. I am sure your Lordship cannot doubt of my personal attachment to yourself or desire of concurring in any measure where you think your own interest concerned.
>
> On the other hand I hope your Lordship will not think me unreasonable in requesting an immediate and public proof of your Lordship's approbation, by giving me a *frigate* and a station in the spring, either, in the *South Sea* or off Lisbon.[78]

This sort of approach did not yield results with Sandwich,[79] but as the North administration grew weaker in the course of the American War, Warren grew more exigent. By March 1782 his requirements were a relief captain to fit out his ship for him, followed by a cruise in the best station to pick up prizes, but near enough to home to allow him to see his wife frequently.[80] This was his final demand, or rather threat, for he was already preparing to desert 'your Lordship who has brought me forward in the Service & always behaved to me with *Candour & honour*'.[81] A few days later Sandwich enclosed Warren's letter announcing his defection with the remark 'I believe you will join with me in opinion that the writer of the enclosed is not only a rat but an idiot'.[82] So the most 'political' of all Sandwich's acts of patronage was perhaps the least successful, at least in political terms.[83]

Because commanders-in-chief abroad disposed of so much of the

available patronage, and had to be trusted with a latitude pro-
portional to the slowness of communications, they often had better
opportunities than the First Lord of the Admiralty to make speedy
promotions, and Sandwich like Anson before him needed to cultivate
close relations with them for the advantage of both sides.[84] When
it was politically necessary to make promotions on the margin of
respectability, the quick and discreet way to do it was by arrangement with a commander-in-chief overseas, especially in this war
when so large a proportion of the fleet was in the West Indies.
Rodney was sometimes useful in this respect, as he was with Lord
Robert Manners. In January 1782, for example, Sandwich was
anxious to keep on good terms with Mr Wells the shipbuilder and
Huntingdonshire landowner, but 'it is utterly impossible for me to
give promotion at home to so young a Master & Commander' as
his son, so he turned to Rodney, who duly obliged.[85] In return
Sandwich was prepared to push as far as the unwritten rules allowed
to favour Rodney. In 1772 he mentioned that the captain of the *Ferret*
sloop was due to be relieved; 'if I can manage it, I will send her out
to you under the command of a Lieutenant, in order to give you an
opportunity of making your first Lieutenant a Master & Commander, which in that case will be confirmed'.[86] The problem with
Rodney was that his notorious weakness for breaking the rules was
liable to disrupt a process which depended on his not overstepping
them: 'let me entreat you to do it upon a regular vacancy, for if he
comes to me with a disputable title it will make things worse, and
draw me still into greater difficulties'.[87]

Sandwich helped his own son Robert, Martha Ray's eldest child, by
sending him to the East Indies with Sir Edward Hughes. Hughes
was a friend, but his praise of this 'very good young man capable
in his profession a diligent officer',[88] goes beyond conventional pol-
iteness and is clearly sincere, and Robert rose fast enough to have a
chance to show his real abilities.[89] But this treatment was strictly
within the rules, and Sandwich rejected an expedient proposed by
Palliser to allow the young man to be examined for lieutenant before
he had served the required six years at sea.[90]

Captain Luttrell was not the only member of the opposition to be
deceived by his own propaganda into thinking that Sandwich dealt
in bribes. One or two people directly offered him money,[91] while
at least two enterprising brokers traded on his reputation and their
clients' credulity by claiming secret influence, usually with Martha
Ray.[92] Others, including an admiral, were unwise enough to make

direct approaches to her,[93] though 'that Lord immediately abandons any person who thinks to make an Interest thro' that Channel',[94] while some officers attempted blackmail.[95] All these approaches at once destroyed any hopes of the applicants' success. It is also worth noting that Sandwich was firm in repelling the pretensions of two people to whom he owed money.[96]

The only admiral who attempted blackmail was James Gambier, whose obscure and oily prose was usually employed for the grossest flattery. The incident is not without humour, and tells us a good deal about both parties. In 1774 when Gambier was Commissioner of Portsmouth, Sandwich stayed with him while visiting the yard, and at a social occasion met a young lady from Chichester whom, as he confided to Gambier, he would be glad to meet again:

> You will think me made of very combustible matter if I own to you that even at my time of life I am capable of receiving very strong impressions from a few hours acquaintance with a very agreeable woman . . . but the fear of her being offended or laughing at me prevented my saying half what I had in my mind . . . I must own that after 55 a man in love is but a ridiculous being.[97]

Gambier replied with friendly enthusiasm, promising to do his best to arrange another meeting.[98] There is no evidence that one took place, and the matter slept until 1781, by which time Gambier had convinced himself that his supposed professional disappointments took their rise from his refusal to act as a pimp for the First Lord. 'Fortunately for me, the proof of this transaction is still in my hands', he wrote, and he would show it to the king if not satisfied.[99] Gambier was not the most intelligent or attractive flag officer of the day, but it still requires an effort of the imagination to believe that he could have been so foolish. So far as the letters go, they show Gambier an eager participant in Sandwich's not very wicked design. Even if he had been able to show himself an innocent observer of a serious crime, any attempt at blackmail would have destroyed his character for ever, not only with the king but with every member of polite society. It would also have exposed him to universal derision, for he was well known as the adulterer who had had to pay heavy damages for seducing a brother officer's wife.[100] The worst that Sandwich had to fear, as he pointed out with his usual urbanity, was looking rather silly:

> it will probably occasion some ridicule upon me; but I have never pretended to be free from indiscretion, and those who know me have

been so long accustomed to forgive my weaknesses, when they do not interfere with my conduct as a public man, that I have no sort of apprehension, from any communication of this letter that you may think proper to make.[101]

Sandwich turned the situation very easily by showing the correspondence to 'some of your friends and Brother Officers'.[102] They presumably explained to Gambier what he was too stupid to see for himself, and at the last minute he withdrew his head from the noose he had made for it, and submitted with abject apologies.[103]

Though adherence to rule and precedent was Sandwich's great defence against importunity, he was in some respects an innovator, laying down stricter standards than Anson had done. Mulgrave wanted to get some leave in 1777 by allowing his ship to go to sea under an acting captain; 'this was frequently done in the last war upon account of Health or particular business'.[104] Sandwich's reply was plain:

> I cannot consent to her going to sea without her proper Captain: I know this method has been practised in the late War, but it is a method I much disapprove, & shall allways discourage, and you must see that if this indulgence was shewn to your Lordship, it would be impossible for me ever to refuse it to any other person.[105]

Sandwich was notably stricter than Anson had been with promotions by commanders-in-chief overseas of their sons and kinsmen. No self-respecting First Lord could have tolerated Rodney's flagrant abuses, which included advancing a son of fifteen from midshipman to post captain in six weeks,[106] but Sandwich was equally firm with the more discreet misdeeds of admirals like Man, Montagu and Young.[107] Unlike his predecessors he would not allow pursers to serve by deputy, which 'can never be allowed without total ruin to this branch of the Service'.[108] Admiral Hardy's secretary Peter Osborn was one of many who tried to get round this requirement:

> The letter I have received from you is not an answer to the question I desired Mr Wright to ask you, which was simply this, *whether if you was appointed purser to the Union you would do your duty on board her in person, and would relinquish her if hereafter you should choose to go to sea with Sir Charles Hardy or any other Admiral?* My reason for making this condition is from a fixed determination that no purser shall with my knowledge do his duty by deputy.[109]

He was equally strict in forbidding them to enter direct into big ships without first gaining experience in sloops – a rule which both Mulgrave and Middleton tried unsuccessfully to evade.[110] Even chaplains, regarded by all but a few eccentrics as the persons who could most easily be spared from a ship's company, were kept to their duty:

> I fear the attending in London upon a literary business and the duty of a sea chaplain are incompatible, especially as he can receive no pay but in consequence of his attending musters regularly on board his ship: if a fortnight's leave of absence would enable Mr Stockdale to finish his pamphlet, I could strain a point to make it easy to him; but I could not go any farther without subjecting you who recommended him, and myself who have appointed him, to a good deal of well-founded abuse.[111]

Many examples have been given, and many more could be given, to establish the spirit in which Sandwich tackled the vexatious business of patronage, but it is also worth examining it overall, and thanks to the books in which Sandwich recorded every application he received, it is possible to do so systematically.[112] From 1771 to 1782 (omitting 1779) he received 923 applications by or on behalf of post captains for promotion or favour. Of these 203 came from noble or influential patrons, of which 73 were successful.[113] Only about a fifth of those officers made post had either influential sponsors outside or kinsmen within the Navy.[114] Of 426 lieutenants or unemployed masters and commanders who applied for commander's commands 146 were successful, of whom 58 were supported by significant 'interest'.[115] The proportions were much the same among the 1,812 young gentlemen who applied for commissions as lieutenants; 762 were successful, 318 having interest, plus another 22 recommended by commanders-in-chief overseas.[116] Of 323 would-be lieutenants backed by noblemen, 123 (38 per cent) succeeded; compared with 195 out of the 440 (44 per cent) backed by commoners.[117] These figures are no doubt inexact, and influence is by its nature not easily measured, but they are still very striking. There can have been very few if any areas of eighteenth-century public life in which well-connected candidates would not have fared better. It is probable that if we had similar evidence of the practices of Anson and possibly Wager, we should find a similar pattern, but in following their example Sandwich was deviating sharply from what was expected of him by his colleagues and contemporaries. Many reasons have been advanced for Sandwich's isolation during the later stages of the American War, but this was undoubtedly the most obvious.[118] Nothing was better calculated to arouse fury than disappointing the expectations of the privileged.

CHAPTER XII

Home and Abroad

1771–1775

As First Lord of the Admiralty, Sandwich was only at leisure to think about long-term reforms in the intervals of the everyday responsibilities of his office. Eighteenth-century government departments were not large, and ministers were expected to handle in person a mass of extremely detailed administration. Partly this was because the appointment and promotion of even very junior officers and employees represented patronage and was of political consequence, but mainly it reflected a system which did not clearly distinguish overall policy from routine business, and offered ministers very little shelter from administrative pressures, or incentive to think in the long term. This no doubt was why none of Sandwich's predecessors had grasped the full extent of the timber problem, but he was just as much involved in matters of detail as any of them. A single letter may be quoted to give an idea of the sort of business to which every First Lord, and every Admiralty Board, devoted most of their time. It was written to the Deputy Secretary of the Admiralty from Hinchingbrooke in October 1773, and is typical of scores of such letters written when Sandwich was away from the Admiralty, and tens of thousands of such decisions taken when he was there:

> The Chaplain of the *Cerberus* should of course have leave to resign his warrant, and the Captain of the *Salisbury* be ordered to proceed without loss of time to Spithead.
>
> Lieutenant Thomas may have the leave he asks for, and by the return of the Messenger I will send you the name of another officer to supply his place in the *Albion*.
>
> I am at a loss what answer to give to Captain Macbrides letter about the Marines on board the *Orpheus*, but if she is not yet sailed to Plymouth, can think of no other way of disposing of the men than by landing them, & letting them march to their division: there may however be objections to this scheme which at present I am not aware of.

It seems to me proper to agree with the Navy Board, and in consequence of their opinion, to order Bassett & the other four drudgermen
to be discharged.

The case of Thomas Berry as represented by Captain Douglass is a
very compassionate one & I think Mr Seddon should be directed to
take the affair in hand, and to do what the Law will authorize him to
make the creditor repent of his cruelty.

Coll: Bell does not say whither he approves of the four Lieutenants
having leave of absence; if they are none of them near sea duty, and
there is no objection at quarters to their being absent, they have my
consent.

The case of the Smiths of Deptford yard should be referred to the
Navy Board before we give any opinion.

For the reasons mentioned in Coll: Bells letter Lieut: James Stuart
should have leave to go on half pay, but not till he produces a certificate
from some medical person that the state of his health is as represented;
& Lieutenant Charles Stuart if he is in prison should be put on half
pay at all events; as he may be employed again if he chuses it as soon
as he obtains his release.

It seems to me that the person who commanded the *Gibraltar* should
be paid as Captain for the time of his service, and not Sir Thomas
Rich; such leave of absence as he had was unprecedented, & certainly
ought to be discouraged.

You will forward the enclosed letter to his Majesty in a box, & if
there is any answer to it will send it by a messenger.[1]

At the same time as he dealt (often from memory) with the cases of
individual officers, ratings and dockyard employees, a First Lord
took a large share in forming a government's foreign policy. This
was especially true of Sandwich because of his long experience, and
because of the circumstances in which he had returned to office.
Without European allies, Britain depended more than she had
formerly done on the Navy as an instrument of prestige, deterrence,
and if necessary coercion. A succession of weak administrations had
so damaged the country's reputation that North's ministry had to
work hard to restore it. The Falklands crisis of 1770 had shown
evidence of government firmness, but it had equally given fresh
evidence of the inherent division and instability of the British constitution. Radical leaders like Wilkes, now installed as a City magis-
trate, and his colleague Brass Crosby, having loudly called for
mobilization against Spain, had done all in their power to impede
pressing within and without the City boundaries.[2] Opposition newspapers were always willing to print stories of ministers sold to the
enemy, and foreign ministers often believed them. They even

believed the savage invective of the anonymous letters of 'Junius', with his allegations that North and his colleagues were manipulated by Bute and the Princess Dowager.[3] At the height of the crisis opposition speakers had virtually invited a French invasion, and in 1771 they were encouraging Spain to attack Minorca and Gibraltar, and pointing out how best to do it. Lord Chatham had declared that he would not oppose an enemy invasion: 'I had rather be a slave to France, than to a fellow-subject'. This was mild compared to the hysterical and violent language often used in Parliament. 'There must be blood, I say there must be blood,' cried Edmund Burke in 1771, 'to atone for the misconduct of those who transacted this dark affair'.[4] All this confirmed the prejudices of foreign observers that Britain was only one step removed from that epitome of all weakness, division and delay: a republic. Confident in the strength and stability conferred by absolute monarchy, French and Spanish ministers looked across the Channel with increasing pity and contempt. Even Nero, Vergennes thought in 1775,

> did nothing more horrible than the members of the Opposition are doing now. Without pity they tear at the bosom of their mother country, merely to satisfy their thirst for power. You may be sure I do not pray for England's success, but I blush for humanity to see spirits not simply unnatural and cruel, but for the most part so weak and foolish as to dignify the extreme of treason and wickedness with the titles of virtue and patriotism.[5]

French ministers were at the same time much more aware than their potential enemies that in the long term the balance of strength was moving in their direction. The fact that France was no longer seen as a threat to her neighbours had the effect of denying Britain her customary alliances, which in turn meant that it was naval power by which France and Spain had to be measured against Britain. The British with few exceptions viewed this situation with more complacency than was prudent. In two wars against France and Spain the Royal Navy had emerged victorious, and in the most recent, overwhelmingly triumphant – but victory was not as simple or inevitable as many Englishmen imagined. In the first war Britain had fought Spain alone for five years before France openly intervened, while in the next it was France that had been decisively defeated before Spain declared war. Had the allies opened the war together the situation would have been more difficult, and had they exploited their well-known advantage in early mobilization they might have been able to obtain a decisive advantage in the critical early stages of a war.[6] Furthermore both French and Spanish fleets were steadily improving in numbers and quality. The Spanish fleet, in particular, was the subject of watchful attention from the few in Britain who appreciated the growing threat it presented.[7] In France Choiseul had spent seven years and large sums of money building up the strength of the French fleet, not only in ships but in less obvious yet more important capacities like iron gunfounding.[8]

The fall of Choiseul caused an immediate relaxation of French, though not Spanish, naval expansion, and the ill-judged administrative reforms of Bourgeois de Boynes in 1774 spread chaos and demoralization.[9] At the same time the diplomatic situation in the early 1770s was more favourable to Britain than it had been for some time. The North administration was at least more stable than its predecessors, foreign observers gave Sandwich credit for increasing the real strength of the Navy, and British foreign policy was better handled.[10] This showed in the successful resolution of two overseas disputes which might easily have ended in further humiliation. In the West Indies Sir George Rodney, the new commander-in-chief at Jamaica, arrived to find that the schooner *Sir Edward Hawke* of the squadron had been seized by the Spanish authorities. Sandwich and his colleagues in London evidently guessed even before they saw the detailed reports that she had been engaged in some activity which it would be impossible to avow, and intended to close the matter with a civil apology from the Spanish authorities. They were, however, alarmed by the thought of what Rodney might do. One of the ablest junior admirals of the Seven Years War, he had a reputation for aggression which was not entirely encouraging in the circumstances, and a reputation for greed and dishonesty which was thoroughly alarming. The Jamaica station was a favourite spot for rich prizes in the event of war, and ministers feared that Rodney would start a war to line his own pockets. This was a delicate situation which called for Sandwich's acknowledged skill in handling difficult characters, but fortunately Rodney was less reckless than had been feared, the Spanish authorities were conciliatory, and the affair blew over.[11]

Meanwhile another and more serious threat to British interests had been developing on the other side of the world, where French forces in Mauritius were building up to an extent which seemed to presage some intervention in India. The British East India Company's affairs were troubled and vulnerable, India was too far away to be supported on news of an attack, and in March 1771 Sandwich sent out a reinforced East Indies squadron. Early the next year more ships were sent out. The level of tension in the East remained high while in

Europe naval movements were made, or threatened, over French involvement in Swedish politics, which seemed to risk a Baltic war. This caused a mobilization of fifteen ships in 1773, and it was not until the summer of that year that tension eased sufficiently to recall most of the ships from the East Indies and pay off those at home.[12]

This background of international tension and risk of war was a distraction for Sandwich from his long-term plans of reform, but it was also a means of keeping the naval budget higher than it would otherwise have been. The North administration, like governments in every age, had to balance financial and military security. The Seven Years War had left an enormous debt, and retrenchment was politically and financially indispensable. At the same time North was supportive of Sandwich's work, and prepared to spend money on naval reforms.[13] The international situation provided good reason to obtain money from Parliament, much of which went into the dockyards. North also raised no objections to a steady increase in the Navy debt. In the three years 1771 to 1774 £8,870,655 was voted for the Navy, compared with £6,676,014 from 1767 to 1770 (both figures including debt repayment). At the same time the Navy debt, which had fallen by nearly four million pounds between 1762 and 1769, increased from £1,200,000 in 1771 to £2,700,000 at the end of 1775.[14] Total expenditure from all sources was £6,982,943 from 1767 to 1770, and £9,532,400 from 1771 to 1774 – an increase of more than a third.[15] This increase was not painless, and it was a source of constant worry to North. In 1772 he made a determined attempt to reduce naval expenditure, which Sandwich was able to parry, using his superior diplomatic knowledge to survey the dangerous international scene.[16] The need for economy obliged Sandwich to husband all his resources. He refused to support even his favourite Pacific exploration without a special vote from Parliament,[17] and he at least acquiesced in the rejection of the 1773 petition to increase captains' half-pay, for which Lord Howe gained considerable backing in the House of Commons.[18]

The continuing diplomatic tension during the early 1770s helped Sandwich to develop and demonstrate his ideas about the guardships. By the 1770s it had become an established feature of British naval policy in peacetime to maintain a force of what were called guardships, meaning battleships in commission in port. In theory they were there to guard the dockyard ports from any sudden attack, but their real function was to make up for Britain's acknowledged weakness in mobilizing manpower. Every man mustered aboard one of the guardships was one less man to recruit on the approach of hostilities, and the guardships formed, or might form, a squadron ready for immediate use on the outbreak of war. In practice much depended on the condition as well as the number of the guardships. The name might cover anything from a ship ready for sea at a few days' notice to one hardly more forward than those lying in Ordinary. She might be manned with nothing more than a complete set of officers and a few score men, or she might muster a full war complement. Since the guardships were the only means of mobilizing a squadron quickly, they were the principal naval deterrent, and diplomatic considerations dictated what decisions about them should be made and what decisions should be made public. It was common for the guardships to be below their public establishment of manpower, which allowed for a measure of 'hidden mobilization'· if necessary, but at the expense of a hidden deficiency.[19]

The mobilization of 1770, which had hardly got beyond the guardships, had called attention to their condition, and the combination of Parliamentary disquiet and the unsettled international situation allowed Sandwich to make changes which considerably improved the real strength of the force. Firstly the number of guardships was restored to twenty, the notional size of the squadron which in recent years had actually varied between fourteen and eighteen.[20] Instead of being docked to have their bottoms cleaned once a year, in the spring, the guardships were ordered to be cleaned twice a year in rotation, and provided with a complete armament and outfit of stores.[21] Most importantly, their crews were increased from 180 to 350 for a third-rate, being from one-quarter to one-half their full war complements. A half complement was sufficient to navigate the ship safely, which permitted the institution of regular training cruises in the summer months. In practice a smaller squadron was usually sent to sea with full complements made up by borrowing from other guardships.[22] The guardship squadron was now reckoned to need only three or four weeks to make up to full complement and put to sea. The effect was to nullify the advantage in early mobilization which the *système des classes* gave the French navy.[23] The king calculated, perhaps optimistically, that it even gave Britain an advantage of about three months.[24] The opposition, mindful of their duty to oppose, dismissed it as 'a mere job of the Admiralty; the Admirals Saunders and Keppel showed the extravagance of it as a peace establishment, and its insufficiency as a war establishment',[25] but there is no doubt of its real effect. In the summer of 1772 the situation in the Baltic was sufficiently alarming for the government to order ten guardships to mobilize and assemble in the Downs.

After three days the order was cancelled, but it was reckoned that in only four more the ships would have been ready.[26] In 1773 ten guardships sailed three days after receiving their orders.[27] Sandwich also took steps to improve the readiness of the much larger number of ships in Ordinary. Instead of lying as bare hulls, their lower masts and rigging were set up, and their topmasts, spars and other gear stowed aboard. This not only saved time when they were needed, but avoided the possibility of devastating losses like the Portsmouth dockyard fire of 1770,

> by which all the stores and furniture of 25 capital ships of the line were destroyed; every mast, yard, sail, cable, cordage &c appropriated to those ships were destroyed, consequently those ships were for a time useless.[28]

At regular intervals the guardships' bottoms were cleaned, and their sides and decks scrubbed, scraped and caulked.[29] Sandwich was particularly anxious that ships in Ordinary should be well ventilated. When Joseph Banks visited them in 1775:

> The condition of these ships I could not but admire, instead of the visible marks of rotting which formerly I have seen every part of them was found as dry & airy as an inhabited house nor could I tho I examined several very thoroughly find a damp timber except in one which provd to be merchant built & therefore had probably some green timber in her.[30]

At Portsmouth he found the guardships,

> as dry or even dryer than Ld Sandwich's most sanguine expectations could have hop'd by means of a frequent use of Windsails & Ventilators . . . every one I talk to agrees that our children will bless the day when such precautions were taken to season timber & consequently make our ships more durable.[31]

In improving the readiness of the guardships, and in all his schemes to reform the Navy, Sandwich had a significant strength which had been denied to his predecessors, and to himself in his earlier period of office. Under Sandwich's guidance George III was developing an informed enthusiasm for his fleet which none of his predecessors had shown since James II a century before, and which he himself had not hitherto displayed. The king was not intellectually distinguished, but he was conscientious and hard-working, and he set to work to learn as much as possible about the complex and advanced

technology of the naval world. Sandwich arranged for him to see a
ship launched at Deptford, and sent him large quantities of plans,
perspectives and models of ships and dockyards. The Surveyor of
the Navy attended at the Palace to instruct the monarch in the essentials of ship design.[32] 'I give you infinite trouble,' the king wrote,
'but it is from a desire of being a little au fait of ship building'.[33]

The climax of this royal interest came in the summer of 1773. The
mobilization of most of the guardships in response to the diplomatic
crisis gave Sandwich the opportunity to suggest a royal visit to Portsmouth to view the dockyard and the fleet.[34] Nothing like this had
happened in England for nearly a century, and this very public demonstration of royal interest and approval served several purposes.
Firstly it advanced the king's own knowledge; 'I do not mean a visit
of empty parade, but to come back au fait of the mode of conducting
so complicated an affair as the fitting out a ship'.[35] It provided a
public demonstration of royal interest in and support for the Navy,
and by extension for the First Lord of the Admiralty. It also showed
off the reality of British naval power and the speed with which it
could be mobilized to foreigners like the French ambassador, who
was invited to see the assembled fleet (though not to go round the
dockyard).[36] The 1773 royal visit to Portsmouth was a grand and
spectacular affair. The king's desire to keep protocol to a minimum,
at least within the dockyard, did not prevent a great deal of cere-
mony[37] – nor an awkward dispute over precedence between the
senior officers of the guardships and the members of the Navy
Board, which turned in part over whether Palliser, as a captain on
half-pay, was to be regarded as a civilian official or a military officer.[38] The quarrel pointed, not for the first time, to the ambiguous
position of naval commissioners. It also revealed Palliser to be
unusually touchy even among men always sensitive to their honour;
in his words, it showed,

(and not for the first time) a formd designe by an evious [*sic*] artfull
few, to put a bar to my ambitious pursuits in his Maj. Service in the
millitary line, by procuring a determination that might be construed
into a declaration by Admty that accepting an employm: in this branch
of the Naval service for the benefit of the income as I was uncivilly
told in your Lordships presence, should take away my pretensions
and make me unworthy of a place amongst them had they made a
remonstrance in the terms of good manners the real designe against
me and the contumelious attack on the office of the Navy Board would
not have been so strongly marked.[39]

Palliser was made a baronet on this occasion, but he was not entirely mollified.

At the back of the organization of the guardships and their mobilization was the eternal manning problem which hung like a black cloud over every eighteenth-century naval plan. After the failure of the 1749 naval reserve scheme Sandwich does not appear to have contemplated any fundamental reform, nor is it clear what reform there could have been which was politically or administratively possible, but this did not mean that he had lost interest in the subject. One of his first actions when visiting the yards in 1771 was to order the abolition of the old system of 'petty-warrant' victualling, which had the effect of serving the crews of ships in port with worse food than those at sea. Since the work in port was often very hard, this was unreasonable, and it encouraged desertion from the guardships. For the same reason the guardships' men were allowed extra pay for working aboard other ships.[40] When it came to recruiting, Sandwich always disliked impressment and did not despair of one day developing an alternative to it,[41] but in the meantime vigorously defended it as lawful and essential: 'tho' odious in many particulars, [it] is I am positive the only method in these times by which there is any possibility of manning the Fleet'.[42] He encouraged the guardships to keep a proportion of landmen among their ships' companies, in order to be continually training fresh men, 'and I perceive it to be the opinion of many of our best officers that a ship so filled is better manned than if she had nothing but able seamen on board'.[43] He was always open to proposals from any quarter, and among his papers are many schemes of more or less merit to do with manning the Navy.[44] He was strongly in favour of the traditional methods of recruitment by individual captains for their own ships:

> Such a mode of procuring men creates a confidence between the commanding officer and the seaman. The former is in some measure bound to act humanely to the man who gives him a preference of serving under him; and the latter will find his interest and duty unite, in behaving well under a person from whom he is taught to expect every present reasonable indulgence, and future favour. These, and other instances of a similar nature which have come to my knowledge, have enabled me to point out one thing that might, in my opinion, be the means of furthering the naval service; that is, trusting less to the assistance of the Admiralty board, and giving every possible encouragement to the captains appointed to the command of ships to complete their own crews.[45]

On two matters he held particularly clear opinions. The 1758 Navy
Act, commonly known as 'Grenville's Act' from its chief sponsor,
enforced regular payment of wages to the crews of ships in home
waters. Formerly several years' pay had been withheld in wartime
to discourage the men from running away; 'it was then the Interest
of their Creditors (mostly Alehouse Keepers) to prevent their Desertion, by which they would forfeit their Wages, & consequently the
means of paying off their Scores'. Now it was in theory illegal for
arrears of pay to exceed six months, which was much less than
seamen could expect from a merchantman in advance wages for a
long voyage, they 'must be kept almost entirely a float to the great
prejudice of their Health, & to the diminution of their Comfort in
the Service'.[46] There is statistical evidence tending to confirm that
Grenville's Act encouraged desertion.[47]

Sandwich had equally strong views on the admission of criminals
into the Navy. There was a history of conflict on this point. In an
age with no long-term prison system, Parliament and magistrates
wanted some means of punishing vagrants, petty thieves and ne'er-
do-wells, intermediate in severity between whipping and transportation, and preferably having the effect of removing them from
society. The officers of the Navy wanted nothing to do with criminals of any kind except debtors, who were harmless, and smugglers,
who had valuable skills.[48] An act of Parliament of 1744 had made it
possible for magistrates to offer naval or military service as an
alternative to punishment for 'rogues and vagabonds' and 'idle and
disorderly persons', but it did not oblige the Navy to accept them,
and Sandwich firmly opposed doing so.[49] The question had to be
settled at the highest level when men condemned to death were
reprieved by the king (on the advice of a Secretary of State), usually
on condition of being transported. Hawke had allowed a number of
murderers into the Navy, but Sandwich flatly refused to do the same,
'as such persons may not only bring distempers and immoralities
among their companies, but may discourage men of irreproachable
characters from entering H.M.'s service, seeing they are to be ranked
with common malefactors'.[50] When the American rebellion closed
the usual channel of transportation the pressure from his colleagues
grew intense, but he still resisted. In October 1777 he wrote privately
to Lord Weymouth:

You will receive an official letter concerning some convicts that have
been pardoned on condition of serving in the Kings ships, to which I

cannot avoid adding my private & earnest request that you would not press this disagreeable business upon us.

I am in my conscience convinced that receiving these wretches into a ship crowded with men is excessively dangerous to the health of the crew, & will occasion desertion and villainy to encrease; besides the Captains and officers are against receiving them, & allmost the first word that passed between Admiral Keppel & me was his desiring that when his ship was commissioned he might not have any jail birds sent on board. Add to this that it is generally known I have set my face against the measure, & you remember that the opposition, tho' very unjustly, found fault with the Admiralty for manning the fleet with convicts; they will of course triumph if it should now be allowed.[51]

But later in the war as the pressure from his colleagues grew intense he was forced to accept some convicts.[52]

Much later, after the war, a suitable destination for transportees was at length obtained with the establishment of the colony of New South Wales.[53] Sandwich had nothing to do with this, but he was indirectly a parent of European settlement in the Pacific as one of the great patrons of exploration. European exploration of the Pacific restarted in the mid-eighteenth century, after a lapse of more than a century, for a combination of scientific and commercial reasons. The Enlightenment, with its simple faith in the power of reason to unlock secrets and benefit mankind, found ignorance of so large a part of the globe intolerable; the spirit of Nature abhorred the vacuum of knowledge. At the same time the rise of colonial and naval power persuaded practical men that it was worth investing the small amount called for by a modest expedition, to forestall the profitable discoveries which other powers might make. The main obstacle was Spain, which pretended to control the whole Pacific, and resented the presence of foreigners. The undoubted value of Anglo-Spanish trade was for a long time sufficient to outweigh speculation as to what might be won by Pacific discoveries.[54] The first eighteenth-century British proposal to explore the Pacific was made by Sandwich in 1749. The scheme was to send two sloops to investigate 'Pepys Island', supposed to lie near, or possibly to be identical with, the Falkland Islands. From there they were to round the Horn and sail westward across the Pacific for three thousand miles, and then back the same way, covering a broad tract of unexplored ocean between 10° and 25° South latitude. First the Pacific part and then the whole scheme was abandoned in the face of Spanish objections, made just as an Anglo–Spanish commercial treaty was under negotiation.[55]

Lord Egmont revived the scheme fifteen years later, when Captain Byron was sent with two sloops to explore the South Atlantic and thence cross into the Pacific. He was followed in August 1766 by Captain Wallis, sent into the South Pacific to look for the unknown Southern continent, Terra Australis, so beloved of the geographers.[56] The Royal Society's ambition to observe the Transit of Venus from somewhere in the Pacific on or near the Equator gave the impetus for another expedition in 1768, which was commanded by Lieutenant James Cook.[57] Sandwich had nothing to do with this expedition or with the selection of Cook, but he was in office when Cook returned in 1771.

He took an immediate and close interest, both in Cook and in exploration in general. The popular hero of the expedition, the man generally assumed to have been its real leader, was Sandwich's Fenland neighbour Joseph Banks, the noted botanist. As a landed gentleman he occupied a position in society which eclipsed that of any lieutenant in the Navy, even had Cook been of high birth. Sandwich was an old friend of Banks,[58] but he was not deceived by popular admiration into taking him for the real leader of the voyage. In August 1771 Cook was promoted unsolicited to the rank of Master and Commander and presented to the king,[59] and when he submitted a memorandum in February 1772, proposing an expedition to the Pacific to clear up for good the existence of Terra Australis, Sandwich was immediately receptive.[60] Lord Hillsborough the Colonial Secretary also supported the idea.[61] The preparations for the expedition went ahead, and two vessels were selected. They were initially to be named *Drake* and *Raleigh*, but on a hint from Lord Rochford the Southern Secretary they were replaced by two names less likely to irritate the Spaniards, *Resolution* and *Adventure*.[62]

The fitting out of these ships gave rise to an incident, well known but still worth looking at for the light it throws on Sandwich's management of business and people. Banks intended to sail on the new voyage, accompanied by a suite of servants and scientists appropriate to his status. Like the public, he seems to have assumed that he was the real commander, or at least the most influential member of the expedition, and that his demands would be met unquestioningly. At first they were, and an entire deck of cabins was added to the *Resolution* to accommodate him and his followers, but as soon as she was tried at sea it was obvious that the seamen's misgivings had been fully justified. The ship, formerly an admirable seaboat, was now unsafe and unmanageable, and there was nothing to do but remove the additions and restore her to her original state. Banks was obliged to retrench his suite to the modest size which could still be accommodated. He refused to do so, withdrew in dudgeon from the expedition, and threatened to make all the very considerable trouble which his rank in society would permit.[63]

Sandwich had taken a close interest in the voyage from the beginning and several times visited the ships fitting out. He was thoroughly briefed by Captain Palliser (Cook's old patron as well as Controller of the Navy), and took the advice of all the experts.

> Mr Hunt the Master Builder at Sheerness, whose knowledge and ability is undeniable, told me, that if he had been directed to build a Ship for the purpose for which the *Resolution* is intended, he would have constructed her exactly with the same Body & Dimensions.[64]

Confident of his ground, he secured the backing of the king and applied all his emollient skills to pacifying Banks. Meanwhile public opinion was hostile. It was obvious that the demands of a gentleman like Banks must be reasonable, and that only 'dirty manoeuvre', 'jobbing and meanness', could explain the preferring the opinions of low persons like dockyard officers.[65] If Banks chose to take his case to the public he was assured of a sympathetic hearing. Sandwich therefore prepared a rejoinder, 'more urbane but more deadly',[66] intended to appear in the newspapers anonymously. In the event it was not needed. Banks had the sense to retire from the contest; in time he and Sandwich were reconciled and continued good friends.[67]

The episode well illustrates several of Sandwich's skills. On the practical level he always insisted on seeing for himself. Having visited the ships several times already, he and Palliser came aboard for the last time, to be sure that all was well, as Cook was heading down Channel and they were returning from visiting Plymouth Dockyard: 'It is owing to the perseverance of these two persons,' Cook wrote in his journal,

> that the expedition is in so much forwardness, had they given way to the general Clamour and not steadily adhered to their own better judgement the Voyage in all probabillity would have been laid aside.[68]

Sandwich's determination to take a rational decision on the basis of accurate knowledge may seem unremarkable, but it has never been the universal method of conducting public affairs, and in this case it distinguished him from Banks and the generality of public commentators. Cook's comment was that his personal interest was 'a laudable tho rare thing in a first Lord of the Admiralty'.[69] Having made up his mind he firmly stood his ground, and applied all his tact and charm to win over the recalcitrant Banks. At the same time he was prepared for a political battle, if it had been forced on him. He was, and remained, a real friend of Banks – but had he been driven into enmity, Banks would have found him a dangerous opponent, armed and ready. It is characteristic of the element of calculation in Sandwich's character which helped to make him so formidable a politician, but which on occasion also helped to make him feared and distrusted.

While Cook was in the Pacific, Sandwich sponsored another voyage of exploration, intended to clear up a geographical uncertainty which was in its way as important as the existence of Terra Australis. Many scientists, including Banks, argued that sea water could not freeze, that all sea ice must be made from fresh water, and consequently must come from land. The southern ice which Cook had sighted on his first voyage was therefore an argument for the existence of a southern continent. The same logic suggested that if, as was widely (and correctly) believed, there was little or no land around the North Pole, the sea there should be ice-free, and might offer a quick route to the East. To test this hypothesis Captain Constantine Phipps with two ships sailed for the Arctic in the summer of 1773. He got as far as the northern tip of Spitzbergen, and extricated himself from the ice with difficulty. His expedition is usually forgotten today, because its discovery was a purely negative one, and anyway did not convince the enthusiasts for the 'ice-free Arctic' theory. Nevertheless it was intelligently conceived and skilfully executed, with great attention by Sandwich to the detail of its preparation. It broke new ground with the publication of the official narrative, which is not only lavishly printed, but consists of a brief account of the voyage followed by ample appendices of scientific discoveries. It marks a significant stage in the movement from exploration and travel literature to scientific research and analysis.[70]

Captain Furneaux in the *Adventure* lost company with Cook off New Zealand and returned in July 1774. With him came Mae, usually called Omai or Omiah in England, a native of the Society Islands who rapidly installed himself in English society. His natural courtesy charmed and flattered the Enlightenment's expectations of a noble savage, while his genuine good nature made him many friends.[71] He formed a link between several of the circles of Sandwich's life. For much of the autumn and winter of 1774 he stayed at Hinching-brooke, and became something of a friend to Sandwich, who learned enough Polynesian to assist communication.[72] Banks and James Burney, who spoke the language fluently, were often of the company, and Omai accompanied them both on a visit to the Yorkshire home of Captain Phipps. When he left to live in London, Sandwich wrote 'I am grown so used to him and have so sincere a friendship for him that I am quite depressed at his leaving me'.[73]

Cook returned from his second voyage in the summer of 1775, when Sandwich was in the middle of his annual visitation of the dockyards, accompanied in the yacht by a party of friends including Omai and Banks.[74] With him he brought the knowledge that settled the essential geography of the Pacific and dissolved for ever the phantom of Terra Australis which had haunted geographers for two thousand years. Sandwich hastened back to London, but Banks, who evidently felt some embarrassment, stayed away, and missed a celebratory dinner aboard the *Resolution*. Banks's friend Dr Solander, the Swedish botanist, who had not disdained a cramped cabin, and shared the renown of a triumphant voyage, described the day:

> Our Expedition down to the *Resolution*, made yesterday quite a feast to all who were concerned. We set out early from the Tower, reviewd some of the Transports; Visited Deptford yard; went on board the *Experiment*, afterwards to Wolwich, where we took on board Miss Ray & Co and then proceeded to the Galleon's where we were wellcomed in board of the *Resolution* – and Lord Sandwich made many of them quite happy.[75]

Cook was promoted post captain by making him captain of a line-of-battleship for the day. This was an early example of promotion 'for rank', an administrative fiction which Sandwich seems to have been the earliest First Lord to use to any extent. Sandwich described the visit to the *Resolution* in a characteristically tactful letter to Banks, approaching the subject indirectly with mention of a hornets' nest, a chameleon, and 'One of Miss Rays new paroqueets', before mentioning that,

> We had a very pleasant party before I left London on board the *Resolution* at Galleons reach, Dr Solander was of our party; we saw the New Zealanders head part of which had been broiled & eaten by one of his countrymen.[76]

Sandwich went on to mention that a third voyage was in prospect, with one of its objects being to return Omai to his native land: 'I feel that I shall be really concerned at losing him'. The more serious aims of the new expedition had to do not only with still unknown areas of the Pacific, but with completing the Phipps' expedition by attempting an approach to the Polar seas from the other side, to be sure that there was no open water away from land.[77] At this point the commander of the new voyage was not settled, and it was not until January 1776 that it was known that it was to be Cook again. Cook's first biographer Kippis has left us an anecdote of a dinner party at which Sandwich skilfully (but, the implication is, unscrupulously) fired him up to volunteer for what no one could decently ask him to do.[78] The book acknowledges help from Sandwich, and the story may be true, but other information Kippis fathered on him certainly is not,[79] and this may be doubted. Cook was restless in his comfortable but idle berth as one of the Captains of Greenwich Hospital (something usually reserved for officers much more elderly than he), and we do not need to assume that he had to be put under any pressure; 'the limits of Greenwich Hospital,' he wrote within a week of his return in August 1775, '. . . are far too small for an active mind like mine . . . whether I can bring myself to like ease and retirement, time will shew'.[80]

Cook never enjoyed ease and retirement, and by the time the third expedition returned both it and the Admiralty were under other command. But Sandwich's successors did not share his personal interest in exploration, and it was left to him to preside over a committee which edited and saw through the press the journals of Cook's last voyage. The publication of voyages was a subject in which Sandwich had by this time a good deal of experience, some of it hard-won. Cook's first journal had with the best of intentions been entrusted to Dr Hawksworth, an experienced scholar and writer, recommended by Dr Burney, who promised to be able to produce a much more acceptable literary work than Cook could have done.[81] Unfortunately Hawksworth's high polish took off much of the interest and not a little of the meaning of Cook's original. Cook, Sandwich and the public were dissatisfied, and when it came to the second voyage Sandwich evidently decided that the captain would be able to do the job better than anybody else.[82]

This generated trouble of another sort, for the German botanist Johan Reinhold Förster, who had succeeded Banks as one of the two principal scientists on the second voyage, conceived himself to have been promised the task, and a very large sum of money for doing it. Sandwich was willing to allow Förster to contribute scientific material, and to see him well paid, but he would not tolerate Förster taking over Cook's narrative, and he insisted that his ungrammatical English should be corrected. Förster, who has been not unfairly described by a modern writer as 'remarkably disagreeable, grasping and dishonest',[83] then severed all connection and withdrew in a fury to make as much trouble from a distance as he was able.[84]

By comparison the task of editing and seeing through the press the journals of Cook's third voyage was almost straightforward, though it required a great deal of work. Sandwich presided over the editorial committee which took the main decisions, including how to share out the profits of the work among those who had contributed to it.[85] He also undertook a great deal of detailed and scholarly editorial work, such as revising the place-names which Cook had bestowed in the Pacific.[86] Sandwich found that Cook had used the names 'Sandwich', 'Hinchingbrooke' and 'Montagu' more freely than he thought decent, and the name 'Cook' not at all. He therefore inserted the Cook Inlet for a large unnamed body of water in Alaska, struck out a fair proportion of the 'Sandwich's, and replaced them with members of the royal family. Prince William Sound in Alaska is one of those he renamed.[87]

All this was far in the future when Sandwich was sending out Cook's second and third voyages, at a time when he was much too busy running the Admiralty and the Navy to have leisure for detailed scholarship. He did however have other uses for an exact mind and a capacity to take pains. One of the responsibilities of the Admiralty which called for extra attention in a period of international tension was intelligence. The British government had long maintained the Rotterdam espionage organization, now run by Richard Wolters' widow, which still furnished regular reports to the Admiralty and the Secretaries of State. There were in addition other, independent sources of information, some of them of great importance. The British diplomat George Cressener spent much of his career accredited to various minor German courts, largely as a cover for 'controlling' a very highly placed agent at the French court. When he was appointed British Resident at the court of the Prince-Bishop of Liège in 1747 Lord Chesterfield, the Secretary of State, remarked that a salary of £600 a year, 'seems a very reasonable one, considering that the King has no occasion for any such minister there'.[88] Sandwich was closely involved in establishing this agent in 1746, and again in retaining his services in 1763.[89] In Paris, Lord Stormont, the British ambassador from 1772 to 1778, built up an extremely

efficient espionage network of his own.[90] The Post Office
deciphering branch and the Hanoverian post office continued to produce frequent intercepts from the diplomatic mail, of which in the
1770s the most secret were restricted to a circulation of four: the king,
Lord North and the two Secretaries of State.[91] Neither Sandwich nor
Lord Dartmouth, the new American or Colonial Secretary, automatically saw the most secret papers.

This emphasizes that foreign intelligence had its political as well
as its diplomatic aspects. It did no harm for a First Lord of the
Admiralty to develop his own private sources, independent of the
Secretaries, and Sandwich did not neglect to do so. He cultivated a
contact with Samuel Swinton, a former naval lieutenant who had
ruined his career by an intemperate quarrel with his captain in 1759,[92]
and since turned to journalism. Swinton published the *Courier de
l'Europe*, an English rival to the established French-language newspapers published in Holland, which exploited the relative freedom
of the press in these countries to print foreign news for readers
all over Europe. Swinton's correspondents in Paris and elsewhere
included a secretary in the Minister of Marine's office who produced
valuable information, though Swinton warned Sandwich that he was
known to be retained as a correspondent, and might be used as a
channel of misinformation.[93] After the outbreak of war Swinton
apparently made a number of secret visits to France.[94]

Sandwich also had a spy of his own. John Walker was a former
army officer fallen on hard times, who in 1771 wrote to Sandwich
and the chairman of the Secret Committee of the East India Company proposing a simple but effective scheme. Many English
smugglers were settled in Breton ports, and Walker would join them,
settling in Morlaix, on the main road to Brest, and visiting the
French East India Company's port of Lorient to buy india goods to
smuggle.[95] His boats would carry his letters, addressed to the home
of a clerk in the Navy Pay Office who would deliver them to the
Admiralty. For this he asked £600 for his initial outfit and the same
amount annually thereafter.[96] Sandwich accepted, and Walker
installed himself as planned. He provided a steady stream of accurate
and rapid intelligence up to the outbreak of war in 1778, when he
presumably returned.[97] He must have been back in England by April
1779 when Sandwich's former colleague Augustus Hervey (by then
his opponent Lord Bristol) mentioned him by name in a debate in
the House of Lords, and in December of that year he was referred
to as one who, 'has distinguished himself under very hazardous &
difficult circumstances in favour of Government'.[98]

All this activity was at least matched by French espionage in England. Choiseul had spies reporting on potential invasion areas within a few months of the end of the war in 1763,[99] and his staff collected much useful information from newspapers and Parliamentary debates. By 1768 the French embassy in London controlled a spy network with agents in the Navy Board and at Portsmouth and Plymouth, and in the 1770s it was expanded.[100] From 1770 the French Navy printed for internal use monthly statements of the strength of the British fleet.[101] The British ministers knew about the espionage network by 1775 at the latest, but permitted it to remain in operation for much of the war.[102] Not until 1781 was the principal agent H. F. de la Motte arrested, followed by other spies.[103] One of these, David Tyrie, a Portsmouth dockyard clerk, has the melancholy distinction of being the last man in England to be hung, drawn and quartered for treason.[104] Besides these conventional spies there was a shadowy world of double agents. It appears that during the American War the French were deceived by more than one British double agent. One of these, using the ironic cover name 'Montagu Fox', persuaded the French ministers that he came as an envoy from traitorous leaders of the Opposition, and so convinced were they of the unnatural vice of Parliamentary politics that they believed him, even though the letter he produced, allegedly signed by Richmond and Shelburne, was an obvious forgery which bears clear marks of having been written by a Dutchman with an uncertain command of English.[105] Much about this affair still remains obscure, but if Fox was being controlled from London (which is not certain), Sandwich may have been responsible.[106]

If so, his motive might have been to lay a trap for secret traitors among the opposition as much as for open enemies abroad. But this cannot be understood without going back to the beginnings of the American crisis – or, as we may more properly describe it, the last British civil war.

CHAPTER XIII

The American Rebellion
1776–1777

Lord North's ministry brought to the country the stability which it had sorely lacked for ten years. Securely based on the esteem of the king and the support of a growing majority in both Houses of Parliament, it faced an opposition fragmented and discredited, and a situation at home and abroad more favourable than any since the end of the Seven Years War in 1763. It was this happy situation which gave Sandwich the opportunity to undertake his reforming schemes in the dockyards. His problem was that he needed a long period of suitable conditions to achieve all he hoped for. His reforms were to some extent at the mercy of uncontrollable events abroad; a premature war would have wrecked them, but an unduly peaceful international scene threatened to starve them. In effect, the French indirectly provided much of the support for Sandwich's reforms, by stirring up international tension, but they suffered a financial crisis during the early 1770s which did their own navy much harm.[1] As the French threat seemed to fade and international tension eased, the Navy's claims to unusual financial support weakened. The Admiralty's real expenditure was falling slowly all the time, and by 1775 the risk of war seemed so remote that Sandwich found it impossible to stave off North's pleas for economy.

But at the very moment when the dockyards were discharging shipwrights, a situation was coming to a head across the Atlantic which was in the fullness of time to involve the Navy in a desperate war against odds which it had not faced for two hundred years, to overthrow the government of Lord North and the career of Lord Sandwich, and to subject the British constitution to a profound crisis. So much has been written about the American War of Independence that it would be unnecessary, indeed impossible, to use this book as an occasion to retell it all, but there are still things which it is very necessary to say if the situation as it faced Sandwich and his colleagues in the 1770s is to be rightly understood. Almost all of what

has been written about the War of American Independence assumes
that that is what it was: a war fought over the issue of independence
for the thirteen colonies. It is of course natural and reasonable for
historians, especially American historians who form so large a majority of those who have written about the subject, to assume from the
vantage point of two hundred years later that no other consequence
of this war, and few other events of this century, were as important
as the emergence of the new republic. The mistake is to see the
responsibilities of British ministers of the day from a perspective
which was neither reasonable nor possible for them. Even today
most American historians assume that the only issue British ministers
had to deal with was the colonial crisis, and that all other problems,
and all other enemies, deserve mention only insofar as they influenced the situation in America. A recent survey states baldly that
'Historians of the American Revolutionary War divide roughly into
those who argue that America won the struggle, and those who
believe that Britain lost it';[2] those who think that France, Spain and
the Netherlands were involved do not figure at all. Moreover serious
historians still write books on the assumption that Britain fought a
war against America between 1775 and 1782. This doubly falsifies
the reality of the time. It puts America on a pinnacle which it actually
occupied for barely two years, between the autumn of 1775 when
the American rebellion arose to dominate the concerns of government, and the autumn of 1777 when it was pushed aside by the
imminent onset of a French war. Before 1775 America was a departmental problem to be left to the ministers concerned; by 1778 it
was a strategic issue of secondary or tertiary importance to British
ministers who faced a threat to national survival. Furthermore the
common assumption of historians is still very often that Britain
fought America; in other words that two distinct nations, one independent and the other nearly so, faced one another on equal terms.
The implicit standard of comparison is the wars of conquest of the
French Revolution, or for many recent American historians the
Second World War against Germany or Japan, and for the most
recent of all the war of the United States in Vietnam.[3] Their ideas
of the strategy which ought to have been employed are those appropriate to a war of national survival between two societies with
radically different values. But even if eighteenth-century wars had
been fought in this way, which they were not, the military operations
in America were a civil war, not a contest between nations. This
was an internecine struggle in which Englishmen fought one another,
a war without frontiers and conventions. It was a war fought not

for the control of territory but to resolve an internal political crisis, which turned on the sources, nature and extent of the authority of government. The military strategies which might have been appropriate to an international war in the eighteenth century, still more the twentieth century, were irrelevant to the situation which presented itself to North's government in the 1770s. Ministers' problem was not to conquer a foreign enemy, but to re-establish the authority of the Crown at home. Troops might be needed, as they were often needed in that age of popular disorder without a police force, but the object of using them remained exclusively political. British ministers could not and did not think that they were fighting a foreign enemy, or an enemy at all. They were trying to reduce the king's deluded subjects to their natural obedience, to restore to them the blessings of the only constitution which could secure their rights and liberties. The virtual independence of the thirteen colonies, the starting point of so many modern studies of the subject, was the one factor which North and his colleagues could not take into account.

The possibility of political dialogue between British ministers and American dissidents was largely nullified by the growth of a colonial political language and mythology which reversed or perverted the settled usages.[4] An older generation of historians accepted that rebels in America and opposition in Britain shared a common cause in resistance to royal power which, in the words of Dunning's famous motion of 1781, 'had increased, was increasing and ought to be diminished'. Nowadays there are very few historians prepared to argue that George III in the 1770s acted in any way unusually or unconstitutionally.[5] The Americans adopted the ancient convention which reconciled opposition and loyalty to the Crown by the only possible means, which was to proclaim a constitutional crisis.[6] In reality there was, from a British perspective, no crisis, only the application to the colonies of the most routine of constitutional mechanisms, Parliament's power to levy taxation. George III was quite right when he claimed to be 'fighting the battle of the legislature',[7] for it was Parliamentary, not royal, sovereignty which the Americans were attacking. By doing so they struck at the root of the Revolution settlement of 1689, and at the foundation of all British liberties. The most fundamental of all British political assumptions was that liberty had to be preserved against the only thing which seriously threatened it, which was the arbitrary power of the Crown.[8] The centrepiece of the 1689 settlement was Parliament's power to grant or withhold taxation, which limited the king's power to control military and foreign policy. An attack on this power was an attack on liberty.

The American suggestion that the Crown should raise taxation in the colonies on the authority of colonial legislatures was a direct appeal to the mechanisms by which the Stuarts had played off the Parliaments of England, Scotland and Ireland against each other.[9] The Americans seemed to be using the language of liberty to advance the arguments of tyranny and absolutism. For men of Sandwich's generation this perversion of truth was highly reminiscent of Jacobite propaganda, and to all observers in Britain it seemed that the Americans were espousing doctrines which were both archaic and absurd – but still dangerous. The impression they created was of corrupt colonial oligarchs seeking to establish their own power by subverting their countrymen's liberties. In Britain people concluded that reform of colonial government was urgently needed, lest the decay of colonial politics infect the whole body. No one seriously thought that the colonies could stand alone, and an attack on liberty from one side of the Atlantic threatened the most perfect of constitutions at every point. Long before the Americans had secured the assistance of France, British opinion was psychologically prepared to expect it, for men who were so abandoned as to attack the authority of Parliament which was the only foundation and security of their liberty, were the natural allies of absolute governments everywhere.[10]

These assumptions united virtually everybody who was active even on the most radical and eccentric fringes of British politics. It suited opposition groups to proclaim their friendship for the Americans, but the degree of real support which they offered to the colonial cause was effectively a function of the extent to which they could not, or would not, recognize what the Americans were claiming. The Rockingham Whigs represented the government which had passed the Declaratory Act affirming British sovereignty. Lord Chatham and his followers were prepared to concede almost anything to the colonials, but only on the assumption that concessions would expose an underlying common position.[11] Even the radicals who argued for some sort of Parliamentary reform, who espoused extra-Parliamentary action, and who professed themselves to be Americans in sentiment and conviction, stood for the strengthening of Parliament, not its overthrow. For them America was a convenient symbol and a source of slogans, not an issue in which they were seriously interested.[12] All the opposition groups found themselves in an insoluble dilemma. All more or less committed to the myth of arbitrary royal power, because none of them could face the fact that it was their own incompetence and unpopularity which excluded them from office, they professed to support the Americans, but none of them accepted the central proposition by which the Americans justified their opposition to Parliamentary authority. Their position was hopelessly compromised, and the fact became ever more obvious as the American crisis deepened.

So many modern historians write about the American crisis with sympathy for the American point of view that it is still easy to forget just how unpopular it then was in British politics. North's position had been strong even before the American rebellion broke out, but the actions of the Americans and the antics of the opposition rendered it impregnable.[13] 'I do not remember ever to have seen so remarkable a tone of Vexation and Disappointment among the Leaders of the Opposition', wrote William Eden in 1778. 'There never was less appearance of instability in the government'.[14] Independent members of Parliament who normally opposed government on principle rallied to sustain its authority, and public opinion everywhere was disgusted by what they took to be the selfishness and disloyalty of the minority of politicians who rejoiced at American successes, and who advanced dangerous and incoherent doctrines in a futile attempt to restore themselves to power.[15] The support of established charlatans like Wilkes only discredited the American cause still further.[16]

Sandwich fully shared the views of his contemporaries on the American issue. Though quick, intelligent and curious, he was, as we have already seen, never an original thinker, and accepted the conventional wisdom in which he had been brought up. By this time he was almost an elder statesman; 'a very old practitioner in business and I fear a very old man, for yesterday was my 54th birthday',[17] as he put it in 1772; and 'one of the old, if not the oldest member' of the House of Lords: 'I have sat here these seven and thirty years'.[18] He had been a Cabinet minister when North was a schoolboy at Eton and Lord George Germain a subaltern in the Guards. After the death of Lord Chatham in 1778 he was the last survivor of the generation who had entered politics when Sir Robert Walpole was in power. He brought to the American crisis the perspective of one who had taken the field against the Jacobite rebels in 1745. Within North's Cabinet, he was one of those arguing for more forceful measures, but it is a mistake to imagine any deep division between the belligerent and the pacifist. The differences between him and even the most mild of his colleagues were small, and the government had no difficulty in reaching common decisions.[19] Nor would any less determined policy have been accept-

able to Parliament or the king, for all respectable political opinion
was in agreement.[20] When Sandwich opposed the repeal of the Stamp
Act in 1766 it was still possible for reasonable men to take either
side, but by the time he spoke warmly in favour of the Massachusetts
Government Bill in 1774, and acted as teller against Chatham's Conciliatory Bill the following year, he was speaking for the overwhelming majority.[21] Like most experts, Sandwich had a low opinion of
colonial troops, and said so in a speech describing them as 'raw,
undisciplined, cowardly men', which he subsequently had cause to
regret.[22] But North's ministry did not send troops to Boston in 1775
because they thought it would be easy to restore order; they acted
because public opinion demanded it, and they could see no alternative.[23] All other avenues seemed to be exhausted, and their duty as
ministers of the Crown and as Englishmen was to uphold the most
perfect of all constitutions in the face of a sinister conspiracy to
subvert it.

Their attempts to do so during the next seven years were to bring
to the fore one of the less clear aspects of the constitution: the
relationship of ministers to one another and to the king. It was a
well-established principle that ministers were responsible to the king
for their own departments, and in normal circumstances they were
not supposed to bring up matters for discussion among their Cabinet
colleagues without the king's prior leave.[24] They invariably saw the
king alone, and he never discouraged them from complaining about
their colleagues. All this did not promote solidarity among ministers,
nor did the age expect it. On the other hand George III made no
attempt to force his opinion on ministers:

> The K[ing] himself . . . thinks as you do, but always will leave his
> own sentiments, and confirm to his Ministers, though he will argue
> with them, and very sensibly; but if they adhere to their own opinion,
> he will say, 'Well. Do you choose it should be so? Then let it be.'
> And sometimes he has known him add, 'You must take the blame
> upon yourself'.[25]

If ministers formed a common opinion and could sustain Parliamentary majorities to back it, they had nothing to fear from him.[26] The
problem lay in settling how and when ministers ought to reach a
common view, and what rôle, if any, the chief minister played in
the process. Though in modern eyes the Cabinet needed a permanent
chairman with the authority, or at least the force of character, to
enforce collective decisions, the eighteenth century was slow to see

the disadvantages of a system in which only the king in person united all the strands of government. Without agenda, papers or secretariat, in theory without business to discuss except by the king's leave, and with no established leader, an eighteenth-century Cabinet was naturally an indecisive body, and always had been. In 1747 Pelham complained that,

> he did not know where the government lived; that there was none; they met indeed, and talked, and then said, 'Lord! it is late; when shall we meet to talk over this again?' and that the King was quite insensible, and would do nothing, saying it was their business.[27]

It used to be said that the elder Pitt during the Seven Years War had acted as a dominating prime minister and war leader, but modern research has made it clear that he did not usually step outside his departmental responsibilities as Secretary of State, and that there were many divisions within the ministry. What he did achieve was the fruit of a unique political position and a fortunate strategic situation rather than any constitutional development.[28] Back in office in 1766, he failed to establish a united ministry: 'He made no attempt to weld together the collection of individuals who composed his Cabinet. They were heads of executive departments, not makers of a common policy'.[29] We need not therefore be surprised that Lord North followed the established constitutional convention; it would indeed have been extraordinary if he had not,[30] and it was arguably not until the nineteenth century that prime ministers can be said to have presided over their Cabinets in the modern style.

The strains of the American War were nevertheless to reveal some of the deficiencies of the old system, not least to North himself, who combined a thorough knowledge of politics with an acute sense of his own unworthiness. His conclusion in 1782 was:

> There should be one man, or a Cabinet, to govern the whole, and direct every measure. Government by departments was not brought in by me. I found it so, and had not the vigour and resolution to put an end to it. The King ought to be treated with all sort of respect and attention, but the appearance of power is all that a king of this country can have.[31]

The same idea had long been held by everyone who was familiar with the mechanism of government. As early as 1777 John Robinson, the Secretary of the Treasury, warned Sandwich that,

War can't be carried on in departments; there must be consultation, union, and a friendly and hearty concurrence in all the several parts which set the springs at work and give efficacy and energy to the movements, without which the machine must fail.[32]

In September 1779 Sandwich was urging North to take command of his Cabinet:

Will your Lordship in this place allow me to lament the state of our Cabinet meetings, & to point out to you how absolutely necessary it is that you should take the lead among us, & not suffer any question to be agitated there that is not decided & carried into execution.[33]

When Lord Stormont became Secretary of State the following month he was advised to revive the habit of keeping Cabinet minutes, neglected by his predecessor Lord Weymouth:

In the imperfect Constitution of our Cabinets (which form unfortunately a Government by Departments and not by a Superintending Minister) you will find it of essential use, not merely for the ease of your own Mind, but for the real [energy?] of the public service, to take regular Minutes . . . The ill Consequences which followed the neglect of those minutes have to my certain knowledge been very mischievous to the public Interest.[34]

All these quotations display awareness of the problem, but they also hint at the difficulty of solving it. North's own temperament was part of the problem. An eighteenth-century chief minister who sat in the House of Commons discharged three duties each of which is nowadays the business of one or more people. As First Lord of the Treasury he was the minister of finance. He acted as leader of the Commons, manager of all government business and principal speaker in many of the debates. Finally he was chairman of the Cabinet, insofar as the position was recognized. North was extremely good at the first two parts of his job, and only failed in the last under the acute strain of the worst crises of the war; in Dundas's words, he 'lacked only one quality to render him a great and distinguished statesman, I mean, a more despotic and commanding temper'.[35] This want was a source of intermittent difficulty to his colleagues, and of disruption to the war effort. In 1778 he tried to resign, urging the king to replace him with,

one directing minister, who should plan the whole of the operations of government, & controul all the other departments of administration so far as to make them co-operate zealously & actively with his designs even tho contrary to their own.[36]

Whether George III could have found such a person who shared North's talents, and had any hope of maintaining Parliamentary majorities, is very doubtful. At all events, he did not try, and by 1779 North's indecision brought the ministry to the point of grave crisis. The difficulty was not directly in the conduct of the war effort, but in the political management of the ministry. From June 1778, when Lord Suffolk had a stroke, until his death in March 1779, the Northern Department was paralysed, and all the business of state fell on the idle and unbusinesslike Southern Secretary Lord Weymouth. North lacked the resolution to impose on his colleagues' rivalries.[37] Robinson's letters, the king confided to Sandwich in October,

> shew too clearly that indecision in the composition of his principal [North], that keeps me in cruel uncertainty and to which most of the misfortunes of the present hour are to be attributed; I fear this evil is so much a part of him that He cannot rectify it; but if he would cast of[f] his jealousy the other might be contrived to be less detrimental; I mean by getting two active Secretaries of State, and when He cannot decide letting others do it.[38]

But the position of the Secretary of State was itself one of the crucial constitutional ambiguities, and arguably presented more difficulty for the conduct of a war than the diffidence of a prime minister who as yet had no established constitutional rôle. The Secretaries of State were still the only proper channel by which the king's commands were conveyed to government, but their position in relation to the First Lord of the Admiralty was both vague and shifting, and the situation had been complicated by the creation in 1768 of a third Secretary of State for the colonies. In principle the three Secretaries were equal, and any or all of them were the proper channel by which the diverse affairs of government might be united.[39] The Southern Secretary remained responsible for military and naval affairs, except the army in the colonies.[40] This exception was to be a source of continual trouble during the American War. The First Lord of the Admiralty was in principle subordinate to the Southern Secretary. Major operations were governed by orders to the Admiralty issued by the Secretary in the king's name; combined operations were controlled directly by the Secretary of State with the Admiralty merely kept informed. In practice the growing political and professional authority of First Lords, above all Anson, during the two previous

wars, had raised them to a position almost equal to that of the Secretaries of State. The records of the orders issued by them to the
Admiralty during the later eighteenth century show a steady decline
in the incidence first of real, and later of formal instructions, until
by the Napoleonic War they consist of routine inter-departmental
correspondence conducted on a footing of equality.[41] This process
still had some way to run in the 1770s, but there is no doubt that
only an inexperienced or supine First Lord, which Sandwich was
not, would have expected to be under any real control by a Secretary
of State. It is significant that the instructions for Cook's second and
third voyages – just the sort of operation big with implications for
diplomacy which a Secretary of State needed to supervise – were
issued by the Admiralty.[42]

The relationship of the First Lord of the Admiralty and the Secretary of State for the Colonies was of critical importance to the conduct of the American War because of the nature of the war, and
because of the personalities involved. When the crisis broke in 1775
the Colonial Secretary was North's pious half-brother Lord Dartmouth, but in November of that year he was replaced by one better
qualified to handle the deployment of troops. Lord George Germain
was a professional soldier whose career had been ruined by his conduct at the battle of Minden in 1759. As commander of the British
cavalry, he had failed to obey an order from his commander-in-chief
Prince Ferdinand of Brunswick in circumstances which led to his
being court-martialled and dismissed from the army for cowardice.[43]
There is little doubt that he was not a coward, but like so many
officers of the eighteenth century, he allowed the cloak of 'honour'
to be cast over personal resentments, rancour and ambition. The
effect was to add to the isolation of a man whose natural character
was cold and arrogant. Germain was an able administrator and Parlia-
mentarian, thoroughly familiar with military affairs, and at one with
the king in his determination to crush the American rebellion if
necessary by the most ruthless means. He was also a difficult and
disloyal colleague, who habitually worked in secret to undermine
his fellow ministers. Though never on friendly terms with Sandwich,
Germain was not primarily working out personal enmities, but trying to establish himself as the dominant war minister. To do so he
had to subvert the authority of the Admiralty, the Southern Secretary, and Lord North, but of the three it was Sandwich who was
the most formidable obstacle to Germain's hopes. In Cabinet he
professed cordiality, but in private he lost no opportunity to spread
the idea that every reverse and disappointment in the war was the

fault of other people's failure to co-operate with him.[44] Naturally he was not liked, and his isolation was increased by the rumour that he was homosexual. In any circumstances this would have aroused distaste, and especially so when the circle about him included the personable young American Benjamin Thompson, who was suspected of being a French spy.[45]

Germain's equivocal constitutional position impinged at every turn on the conduct of the war. He alone was empowered and obliged to impose administrative unity on disconnected departments, especially on the diverse collection of military and civil organizations which made up the eighteenth-century army. The task was very necessary, but Germain used it as a means to divide and rule rather than to unite and assist.[46] The result was repeated disasters as British armies in America failed to support one another. It was also Germain's business to co-ordinate army and Navy, but it was impractical and improper to do so in any other way than by cordial co-operation with the First Lord of the Admiralty. Cordial co-operation was not Germain's style, and he spent a great part of the war attempting by various underhand means to remove operations or responsibilities from the Admiralty's control to his own. Germain complained to his Under-Secretary William Knox (and no doubt intended Knox to spread abroad), that:

> It is in vain to argue upon the operations or destinations of fleets when it is impossible to know the true situation of our naval force. If Lord Sandwich proposes or fully approves any policy, we seldom want resources; on the other hand, if he does not heartily adopt what other ministers think right, official difficulties occur, and the state of our fleet is such that no new measure can be pursued.[47]

This passage has often been quoted at face value, but it perhaps reveals more than Germain intended. Undoubtedly the reason why he wanted information about 'the true situation of our naval force' is that knowledge is power, in this case the power to interfere in his colleague's department. Ignorant of the real complexity of naval administration (to say nothing of the real inaccuracy of naval statistics), his suspicious mind interpreted every difficulty as disloyalty. Many modern historians have tended to take his side, partly no doubt because his papers were published long before Sandwich's, but mainly because they were predisposed to agree with Germain on the strategic issue which divided the two men. We shall see that after the entry of France into the war in 1778 the American fighting

became a strategic backwater. Germain never accepted this strategic
logic, nor the political consequences which flowed from it, for if
France and Spain were the principal enemies, the principal ministers
responsible were Sandwich and the Southern Secretary of State. Germain's continual campaign to undermine his colleagues was intended
equally to promote the American War, the American Department,
and the American Secretary.

North's real failure as a war minister was his failure to impose a
common policy and exact a loyal support of it. To do so he would
have had to step beyond precedent, to stretch the conventions of
Cabinet government, to call forth extraordinary powers which he
did not possess. He can hardly be blamed for not doing so, but the
need was nevertheless there, and he himself saw it as clearly as anyone. In consequence the government never sustained a coherent strategy for any length of time, and ministers, including Sandwich, were
forced to spend much of their energies on internal politics rather than
the conduct of the war. This is the context in which they invoked the
doctrine of collective responsibility. It was no novelty to claim that
administrations stood collectively bound by their major decisions.[48]
In a sense the idea flowed logically from the convention that the
king was not personally responsible for the actions of government,
so that his 'confidential servants' in a body stood as surrogates for
their sovereign. Thus Pelham reproached his brother in 1748 for
using his access to the king in Hanover to appropriate the authority
of the whole administration:

> I don't think it's very decent for some Few of us to give an Opinion
> upon a national Question, when we are all equally entrusted by his
> Majesty here. Private Advice such as a Minister gives to the King in
> his closet, is of one nature; but a formal Opinion in writing, possibly
> to be transmitted to the Plenipotentiaries at the Congress, is of a very
> different one.[49]

It was only with explicit permission that a minister could reveal the
king's personal opinion, even in confidence.[50] For ministers in
trouble collective responsibility was an obvious defence,[51] and frequently invoked as such by Sandwich as well as his colleagues: 'he
could not deserve censure; he acted ministerially; the measures were
deliberated upon elsewhere; and if he did his duty, as obeying the
orders he received, he was by no means responsible for the events'.[52]
Sandwich was consistent in appealing to collective responsibility; he

referred to it in 1775 in response to what was then a purely hypotheti-
cal question about sending the main fleet to relieve Gibraltar: 'the
question would not turn on what I, in my official capacity, wished
to do; but what the majority of his Majesty's ministers had really
decided'.[53] North took the same line defending Germain: 'If censure
were due, he laid his claim for part; they were measures of state,
originating in the King's councils, and were of course no more
the noble lord's measures than they were of any other member of
the cabinet'.[54]

The doctrine was naturally handy for ministers in difficulties, but it
was a constitutional reality as well as a political expedient. During the
American war the formal approval of ministers absent from Cabinet
meetings was sought in writing for all major decisions,[55] and on one
occasion when the Cabinet outvoted Lord Amherst, the commander-
in-chief, on a military matter, the king's personal approval was
sought to back the decision.[56] Even if a Cabinet were actually disunited, government could not be carried on unless its members were
prepared to stand together in public. This is relevant to criticisms
which have been directed at Sandwich, who, as we shall see, was at
some critical points overruled by the majority of his colleagues.
Solidarity with them made it impossible for him to defend himself
in public with more than hints of disagreement, even when the event
had proved him right and them wrong:

> His lordship supposes that I said early in the last session, that I would
> undertake, at all times, to have a naval force equal to cope with, or
> superior to, any which the united efforts of the House of Bourbon
> would be able to bring against us. I confess that these amount pretty
> nearly to my words . . . I am still of the same opinion, that we ought;
> nor do I hold myself responsible, as an official man, that we have not.
> I act merely ministerially, under the direction of his Majesty's councils,
> and can never therefore be deemed farther responsible, or bound by
> any engagement, than so far as I am enabled to perform it.[57]

Contemporary opponents, however, refused to accept that the
Cabinet could take any collective responsibility off a minister's
shoulders,[58] while modern historians tend to discuss the war at sea
as a personal responsibility of Sandwich's, with the implication that
he should have stood out for the right decisions in despite of his
colleagues. The difficulty with this argument is if, as virtually everyone agrees, the North cabinet needed leadership and unity, it needed

ministers who were prepared to compromise in the interests of a united strategy.

All these considerations must serve as background to the strategic decisions which faced the Cabinet in 1775. Royal authority had broken down in the colony of Massachusetts Bay, and something had to be done to restore it. Two alternative policies were suggested. The obvious course was to send troops to back the Governor, but Lord Barrington, the Secretary at War, proposed as an alternative that the task be left to a naval blockade of the port of Boston.[59] Barrington's motive was doubtless to avoid entangling his small army in a thankless and quite possibly limitless commitment. The ministry chose troops rather than ships, as they were bound to do given their objectives. Royal authority could only be asserted by men on the spot. Ships hull-down on the horizon might impose suffering on the commercial classes of the colony, but would rather support than undermine the political strength of the rebels. Modern historians have tended to emphasize how grave a mistake it was to neglect blockade, particularly since the colonials were almost completely dependent on imported munitions.[60] This is true, and ministers knew it, but they could only have relied on blockade alone if they had been fighting another country. Blockade was an effective military weapon, but their problem was a political one. They might have judged differently had they known that the troops sent to Boston in 1775 were not going to succeed in restoring order, and that within two years a substantial rebel army would be in the field disputing the authority of the Crown.

Even if ministers had decided to impose the most rigorous possible blockade, it is doubtful if they could have made it effective. The North American squadron under Vice-Admiral Samuel Graves was too small to cover the numerous harbours and inlets of New England even if it had had nothing else to do.[61] In practice it was almost completely occupied in burdensome tasks which nobody had foreseen. The troops, instead of controlling the province, needed the support of ships to hold just the port of Boston. Instead of the province feeding both army and Navy, there was an acute shortage of supplies of all sorts, made worse by an unexpected famine in Canada.[62] There was also an acute shortage of seamen in the squadron.[63] Much of the colonists' imports of munitions came through the West Indies, where the Dutch in the island of St Eustatius were accommodating middlemen, and merchants in most of the British islands were tied by sentiment and trade more closely to New

England than to old.[64] Here too the local squadrons were too small to achieve real success, and much of the trade was covered by foreign flags, so that the problem was as much diplomatic as military.[65] Indeed the whole problem of blockading the rebellion was only really soluble if French and Dutch shipping could have been stopped and searched, and European ports blockaded. These were acts of war, and a European war would – in the event did – remove any hope of suppressing the rebellion. What is clear with hindsight is that both Graves in America and Admirals Young and Gayton in the West Indies needed many more ships than they had. In July 1775 Palliser calculated that Graves needed fifty ships of various sizes, which was nearly double what he actually had.[66] As the situation became clear in London reinforcements were ordered, but of course all this took time. One to three months were needed to carry a message across the Atlantic, and one or two to bring forward a frigate from Ordinary. Inevitably Graves received too few ships, too late, to meet his unexpected demands. Inevitably his performance was criticized, and the complaints were loudest from Germain and the army, anxious to lay the blame for failure at some other door than their own.[67] An anonymous letter, which was shown to the king, attacked 'Sandwich's perverse obstinacy' in not replacing Graves with someone who 'reasons more weightily from his lower tere than from calm councels under a heavy periwig'.[68]

In this connection Sandwich was and has since been criticized on grounds plausible in themselves, but mutually contradictory. He has been accused of appointing an incompetent admiral, and refusing to remove him long after it had become necessary. He has also been accused of offering Graves up as a scapegoat to save his own skin.[69] In short he was too loyal, and not loyal enough. Much the same criticisms were later made of his dealings with other admirals. The truth in this case is that he recognized that Graves was in an impossible position, and defended his performance both privately to the king, and publicly in Parliament; 'my best friends were of opinion that I persisted longer than was consistent either with your interest or my own to keep you in that command'. What he did not do in public was explain in detail how difficult Graves's position had become, for to do so he would have had to expose the misjudgements of the ministry, and of Germain, the responsible minister, in particular.[70] Nor could he sustain Graves indefinitely against the complaints of those the admiral had to work with in Boston, and Sandwich had to work with in London.[71] Once the king had made up his mind further resistance was useless,[72] and in September he was recalled:

I own I am not convinced that Mr Graves has been deficient in any part of his duty, but I believe the business will go on better under the direction of a more active & more sensible man, especially as he is thoroughly apprized of the disposition of people at home, and knows that it is not likely he should be blamed for pursuing vigorous measures.[73]

As some compensation for the loss of his command, Sandwich arranged for Graves's numerous nephews to be promoted.[74] To relieve him was sent Rear-Admiral Molyneux Shuldham, already nominated as second-in-command, who took over in January 1776.

In December news reached London that a rebel army had invaded Canada and laid siege to Quebec. It was feared that help would inevitably be too late, but Sandwich and his colleagues reacted with vigour, and over Christmas Sir Hugh Palliser worked out a scheme.[75] A small squadron led by Captain Douglas of the *Isis* was assembled with great effort, in spite of a very hard winter. 'For gods sake get the *Isis* down to Blackstakes the next spring tide', Sandwich urged, 'your being ready to leave the land early in February is of the utmost importance to the publick service, I think the fate of Quebec depends upon it'.[76] On 7th February the *Isis* got down the Medway, Mr Hammond the Master Attendant piloting her in a full gale.[77] On arrival in the St Lawrence, Douglas found the river still largely frozen, and with 'unspeakable toil' forced his ship through the ice under full sail for nine days.[78] Finally the *Isis* reached the city on 6th May, at the very moment the besiegers were making their final assault. The Americans were completely defeated and retreated, leaving their general dead on the field. It was a momentous victory, arguably more significant than the original capture of 1759, and Sandwich could take much of the credit for the energy with which the relief expedition had been mounted.[79]

Meanwhile a much greater effort was being mounted to transport another and larger army to America. The events of 1775, culminating in the evacuation of Boston in March 1776, had demonstrated that the colonial crisis was much worse than anyone had suspected, and that only a large army would suffice to crush it. To transport this force, and another for Canada, Sandwich and his colleagues had to assemble a larger fleet of transports than had been employed at the height of the previous war. On 26th December Germain issued a first order to prepare 10,000 tons of transports.[80] In February Sandwich was informed that a total of 77,200 tons would be needed for the four principal forces.[81] By July the total had risen to over 95,000 tons in five months. On 8th Sandwich noted 'I am at this moment full of Comfort, & rather exulting at my having got rid of this Burthen by the sailing of the last transports from Spithead about a fortnight ago'.[82] By then the Navy Board had taken up 146,189 tons of transports (including victualling transports, ships locally chartered in America, and those engaged before December 1775). This was 46,471 tons more than at the height of the last war, and it had been achieved in peacetime, without the use of impressment.[83]

Carrying the army to America, however, was only the beginning of the transport problem. Already in December 1775 Palliser had been daunted by the problems unfolding:

> It seems the demands from the small army now in America are so great as to be thought impossible to be furnished. The wagons and draught cattle is prodigious. If this is the case, what will it be when we have another army there of above 20,000 men, if they can't make good their quarters, and command carriages and cattle, and subsist and defend themselves without the aid and defence of the fleet, who whilst so employed can perform no other service? I think some people begin to be astonished and staggered at the unexpected difficulties we are in.[84]

The repeated failure of the British forces in America to take and hold a region large enough to supply food and fuel meant that their supply line ran straight back across the Atlantic. The British found themselves with a logistical problem on a scale which was not to be repeated until the Second World War.[85] The machinery of government was not well equipped to handle it.[86] Four different transport services were involved: the Navy Board, for naval stores and troops; the Treasury, for army victuals; the Victualling Board, for naval victuals; and the Ordnance Board, for Ordnance and Engineer troops, guns and ammunition. The Navy and Victualling Boards had long experience of their business and conducted it with professional skill and frugality. The Ordnance Board had long experience but valued its independence and suffered from an inefficient Secretary.[87] The Treasury had virtually no experience, and its transports were in effect conducted by Germain, whose guiding principle was to do everything a different way from the Navy. The Admiralty and Navy Board arranged convoys for their transports; Germain complained about the delay and the loss of stragglers, and insisted his transports sail singly but heavily armed.[88] The Navy Board tendered for transports at a fixed price; Germain outbid them and cleared the market. The result was confusion, delay, and resentment. Germain was an efficient administrator (though his staff was far too small to keep track of all his responsibilities); his fault was not in his policies, many of which were defensible, but in refusing to co-operate and compromise, and in disdaining expert advice on matters with which nobody in his office or the Treasury was familiar.[89] In co-ordinating the different transport services, which was unquestionably Germain's right and duty, his performance was lamentable.[90] The obvious solution would have been to amalgamate all the transport services under the Navy Board, which alone had the skill and experience to conduct such an enormous task. Middleton, ever alert for an opportunity to reform something else by taking it over, proposed just this,[91] but it was too radical a scheme for the time, and would have represented a large transfer of power to Sandwich. All that was achieved (over Germain's devoted opposition) was for the Navy Board to take over the Treasury service in 1779. At the same time the Victualling Board took responsibility for the victuals of the army, with a considerable gain in efficiency and economy.[92]

Very early in 1776, while Palliser was labouring to assemble a great fleet of transports to carry General Sir William Howe's reinforcements to America, the ministry decided on a combined military and political campaign for the 1776 season. The army was to make a direct attack on the rebel forces to crush armed resistance, while at the same time General Howe was empowered as a peace commissioner to open negotiations with the rebels. To assist him in both tasks his brother Vice-Admiral Lord Howe was to assume command of the North American squadron. Thus the ministry decided to replace Shuldham before he had even taken over his command. Again Sandwich found himself trying to placate an offended admiral. It was not an age in which the spirit of duty impelled men to serve wherever they were ordered; honour obliged officers to take only those employments in which they might distinguish themselves and make their fortunes. The fate of the 1749 Navy Act had secured in law what was well understood as a moral right. There was nothing Sandwich or any other First Lord could do about it. Shuldham was a capable officer who had been hard done by, and his compensation was an Irish barony and promotion to vice-admiral.[93]

On 3rd July 1776, while Shuldham was still in command, General Howe's army landed on Staten Island. From there they moved to

Long Island, captured New York in September, and crowned a series of successes with the capture of Rhode Island in December. Though General Howe's caution allowed the bulk of Washington's army to escape from a trap, the Navy could congratulate itself on complete success in some of the largest and most complex amphibious operations ever carried out by British forces.[94] Much ink has been spilt over the rôle and priorities of the Howe brothers in all this. It used to be argued that they allowed their position as peace commissioners to override their duties as commanders-in-chief; that is, that they deliberately did not press military operations to a decisive victory because they preferred to conciliate rather than to conquer. It seems unlikely that this was true; like ministers in London, they thought only defeat would force the rebels to negotiate. Undoubtedly they overestimated the consequences of capturing the biggest city in North America, and undoubtedly General Howe failed to make as much as he could of his large army and the superior mobility conferred by sea power, but it was a failure of understanding and execution, not of will.[95]

A related controversy revolves round Lord Howe's failure to institute a strict blockade of the rebel colonies. He had orders to do so, but except briefly over the winter of 1776–77 he made no serious attempt to obey. This has been interpreted as political opposition to government, or as a preference for conciliation over victory,[96] and Germain, after his fashion, made it the occasion for snide remarks about naval efficiency.[97] It seems clear that the real reason was simple. Ministers desired Howe to mount a blockade, but it was not their or his first priority.[98] He had been appointed commander-in-chief primarily to work with his brother in combined operations. The object was still to crush the rebellion and open the way for a political settlement; ships were no better able to do that than they had been in 1775, and the Navy's task was to support the army. Large-scale amphibious operations called for huge numbers of small vessels, barges and boats, and men in proportion. Whatever was left over could properly be employed on blockade, but in practice not much was. Sandwich accepted the situation, and even when a squadron of rebel privateers put to sea in May 1777 and briefly caused much damage (and political embarrassment), he did not reproach Howe with neglect of orders,[99] though he did complain in private

that if Ld Shuldham had been left in command, it would have been full as well managed as it has been since; & I should think that with his vigilance & attention to every part of his extensive command, he would not have suffered twenty sail of Privatiers to sail from Boston to molest the English Channel.[100]

In the light of hindsight it is easy to see that a blockade would have done the rebels much damage, but it is not likely that Howe could have mounted one and supported the army's operations, and in view of the government's priorities it is hard to argue that he should have done.[101]

The Navy's share in the ministerial strategy for 1776 and 1777 was carried out efficiently, and Sandwich could reasonably claim to have done what had been asked of him. Though the Navy's commitment, especially in transports and manpower, was by 1777 very large, it remained subservient to a military and political campaign. The American rebellion was essentially a departmental problem for Germain to solve. He had proposed and the Cabinet had accepted a strategy for dealing with it; Sandwich had loyally provided the support which it was the Navy's business to offer. It was during the 1777 campaign that Germain's strategy finally fell to pieces. General Howe's army in New York and General Burgoyne's coming down from Canada were to co-operate to cut the rebel colonies in two. Instead Howe went off in the opposite direction, taking his army by sea, by the longest possible route, to attack Philadelphia.[102] He was rewarded by the capture of the rebel capital, but meanwhile Burgoyne's army was stopped in the wild country of upper New York and forced to surrender at Saratoga. A small naval and military force pushed far up the Hudson to save him, but with the bulk of the army elsewhere it was insufficient. Though neither general emerges from this disaster with credit, and much must be allowed for the huge distances and slow communications involved, it was Germain who was supposed to control and co-ordinate the campaign. Certainly the major decisions had to be taken by king and Cabinet, but this was a departmental, not an inter-departmental problem, and it was for Germain to present the situation and lay out the choices. It is clear that he did not himself appreciate what was happening, nor explain it to his colleagues. He had always insisted that the American problem belonged to his department and that he could solve it. Now his colleagues faced the bankruptcy of the policy which he had proposed and they had accepted.[103]

For three years the Navy had played an important but subsidiary rôle in the attempt to suppress the American rebellion. As a member of the Cabinet as well as the minister responsible for the Navy and for the bulk of the transport effort, Sandwich had been closely involved – but the centre of his attention was always elsewhere. America was a serious and growing problem, but it was essentially Germain's. Much nearer home, only just across the Channel, lay the threat which was the first concern of Sandwich and the Navy. For any eighteenth-century minister, but especially for Sandwich with his long experience, the Navy existed chiefly to preserve the country from the ever present danger of foreign invasion, and that danger could only come from France, possibly supported by Spain. A younger generation, their experiences shaped by the Seven Years War, were apt to think the Navy as the arbiter of colonial warfare. Sandwich, who had started his political career as a young 'Patriot' demanding a colonial, naval war instead of a profitless Continental commitment, understood such language, but for him the first essential was always to be strong at home. The Western Squadron, in whose development he had himself had a share, had been the key to success overseas in both the great wars of his lifetime. Only by dominating the Western Approaches could Britain at once guard against invasion at home, and open the way for successful expeditions overseas. For him the essential dimension of the American crisis was the risk that France would exploit it to threaten British naval supremacy.

This set him at variance with his Cabinet colleagues. North was anxious to economize, both for financial reasons and because increased expenditure could not easily be carried through Parliament. He was even more anxious to preserve what seemed, in 1775, to be an unusually peaceful international scene. An essential part of British policy towards America was that the crisis must be resolved quickly, before foreigners were tempted to exploit it for their own ends. Sandwich fully agreed, but all his long experience taught him that only real force actually available would deter a potential enemy. North and the majority of his colleagues stood for appeasement. The result was a running debate within the Cabinet as Sandwich repeatedly urged the necessity of increasing naval strength, and North replied with the necessity of preserving the peace. North would have been justified if Germain's schemes had worked as quickly and decisively as every year he assured his colleagues they would; but with each year of disappointment they grew more dangerous.[104] Sandwich was acutely aware of the difficulty of mobilizing seapower, and the risks of falling behind in preparations. He also had an experience of foreign policy which neither Suffolk nor Weymouth, the Northern and Southern Secretaries, could equal.

The divergence of views was evident from the summer of 1775. Lord Rochford, Southern Secretary until November of that year, refused to take a French threat seriously.[105] In June the decision was taken to allow limited impressment, and in September and October to increase the strength of the Navy (or rather, the number of men voted in the Navy Estimates) from 18,000 to 28,000, but these increases were entirely to meet the needs of the North American station.[106] At the same time the number of shipwrights in the yards was actually being reduced. In March 1774 it had been 8,114; in September 1775 the number had fallen to 7,543, and it did not climb back above eight thousand until 1778.[107] Already Sandwich was receiving warnings of French preparations. In September 1775 Walker the spy wrote from Morlaix reporting that the French naval minister Sartine was on a tour of the dockyards; 'wherever he acts your Lordship will find in him a most formidable adversary'.[108] At this stage the French could probably have been deterred by a timely display of force. The (quite illusory) prospect that North might fall and be replaced by Lord Chatham aroused much alarm at Versailles, where ministers were far from ready for war.[109] In Madrid there was even less enthusiasm. Spain had lately put down her own American rebellion and had no sympathy with the colonials.[110] She was besides preoccupied with assembling a major (and in the event, disastrous) expedition against Algiers, and with a territorial dispute in South America which threatened war with Portugal.[111]

The opportunity was passed by, and all Sandwich and his colleagues could do was to keep a watchful eye on the situation. 'I have taken notice', wrote Palliser in January 1776,

of the several articles in the foreign mails relative to armaments in Spain and France which your Lordship has; and am constantly thinking (when other matters that require immediate attention do not possess my mind) what would be the best plan immediately to adopt upon any sudden alarm from those quarters, whilst we have so many seamen in almost the whole of our frigates employed at such a distance and such a body of our troops in such a situation. Indeed a plan of measures to be adopted in case of such an event is necessary, and I hope is prepared against it may happen.[112]

It was not until the summer of 1776 that Sandwich's wary observation of France turned to real alarm. In June he presented a paper to the Cabinet arguing that France and Spain already had more ships in commission in Europe than Britain, and would draw rapidly ahead unless something was done. He also pointed out that all available frigates, including the small 50-gun two-deckers, were in America. He proposed increasing the number of guardships from twenty to twenty-four, and bringing forward another twelve ships of the line ready to receive men, which would equal French preparations 'as far as the preparation of ships in the Dock Yards; for it is to be apprehended that they can raise Seamen to a certain number much faster than we can'. The Cabinet agreed to increase the number of guardships but after heated debate refused the extra twelve ships of the line.[113] Soon after Sandwich received more news from Morlaix: 'except during the altercations with Spain about Falklands Islands, there has been no such movement as at present since the peace at Brest'.[114] In July he had intelligence

> of so serious a nature that I must beg once more to lay my sentiments on this subject before your Lordship. I think the last letters from Lord Stormont mention that 23 ships of the line are preparing at Brest, and 7 at Toulon; the Spanish have at least 10 sail of the line in commission and many more in readiness to be commissioned; and I own I dread the consequences, and cannot help thinking we shall have much to answer for, if they are allowed to have a fleet of 50 sail in Europe ready to receive men, when we have not above half that number in the same degree of preparation.[115]

North returned an emollient reply, and later the same day Sandwich returned to the charge:

> If they have a fleet ready for service double to ours, their advantages and our danger will be such that I tremble to think of it . . . If the French go on preparing their ships for receiving men, baking bread, and collecting provisions, as they have a register and classes of seamen which they can call in at a very short notice, they may have a fleet at sea much superior to anything we can bring against them (especially when joined by the Spaniards) for a considerable time; and if they really mean anything hostile to this country, may attack us when we can resist them only with an inferior force.
>
> I am sure your Lordship will forgive my troubling you so much on this important business, but I know so much of the state of the fleet from want of preparation at the time of the dispute about Falkland Islands that I think it my duty, as a firm friend of your Lordship's administration, to point out the danger of being again taken in the same unprepared situation.[116]

This time the Cabinet approved, and by October the twelve ships were ready to be commissioned.[117]

Meanwhile in France a decision to give secret help to the American rebels had been taken in April, and naval preparations were increased. The French navy was still far short of readiness, but ministers well understood that their decision made eventual war very likely.[118] Twenty ships of the line were ordered to be ready in October, in August the French navy received a large supplementary grant, and by September the dockyards were in full mobilization.[119] This time the evidence was alarming enough to persuade the British Cabinet. Late in October Sandwich received approval to start impressment of seamen, man the guardships to their war complement, commission the twelve further ships which were now ready, and bring forward more to replace them.[120]

By March 1777 Sandwich was again agitating for further mobilization. Ships had been detached to reinforce Lord Howe without their places being supplied. On his calculations, the Navy had thirty-six sail of the line in commission at home (four of them under orders for America), against forty-nine French and Spanish ships.[121] But this time North was not convinced, and in the fashion which was to become common with him, he retreated from a difficult problem into indecision. In April Vergennes, the French foreign minister, commented that Britain's difficulties offered a tempting possibility of revenge for the humiliation of the previous war: 'the opportunity would be seductive and it would be a sublime effort of virtue to refuse it'.[122] In July he took the final decision for war.[123] It was not until late August that the British ministry as a whole finally accepted the urgency of the situation. By that time, according to British intelligence, forty-three British ships of the line in commission faced twenty-three French and forty-one Spanish. The Spanish fleet, already mobilized against the Algerines and Portuguese, formed the majority, but many more French ships were preparing.[124] Now even North admitted that war was 'every day more probable'.[125] On 1st November Walker the spy reported from Morlaix, 'the French Navy was never in so good order, nor the Magazines of every kind so compleated, nor the Sea Officers so disposed for action, to recover (as they acknowledge themselves) their lost honour'.[126]

Never before had Britain found herself so much at a disadvantage in the decisive factor of mobilization. French preparations were at least as advanced, the Spanish fleet much more advanced, and there was a serious risk that they would begin the war together. Not only was Britain largely outnumbered in ships of the line available, but the dockyards' capacity to bring more forward had been affected by the untimely reductions in manpower. Worst of all, a high proportion of the stock of seamen was committed to the fleet and transports in America, and manpower was always the critical factor in every mobilization.

A further difficulty was the shortage of frigates. It was usually regarded as safe to keep only a reduced force of these smaller warships in peacetime, since they lasted less well than ships of the line, but could be built in numbers in merchant yards. It took only nine months to build a frigate, compared with at least eighteen to commission the bulk of the battlefleet, so an emergency wartime building programme usually sufficed. The American rebellion, however, presented an unusual situation, which had drawn into commission every frigate and 50-gun ship available, without any corresponding mobilization. In the thirteen months from June 1775 to July 1776 the Navy commissioned for America one 64-gun ship, one 60, six 50s, three 44s, fifteen 32s, thirteen 28s, one 24, six 20s, twelve sloops, and seven other small warships.[127] Sandwich was unable to build many more frigates for the same reason that he could not secure agreement to commission ships of the line. Between 1775 and 1778 only seventeen frigates were ordered (compared with twenty-seven in the first three years of the previous war), though there were as many as twenty-six already building in 1775.[128] Only four ships of 50 guns and under were launched in 1775; there were eighteen in 1776, seventeen in 1777, twenty-four in 1778, twenty-nine next year, nineteen in 1780, twenty-one in 1781 and eighteen in 1782.[129] Overall these figures compared well with those for the previous war – but that took no account of the enormously increased demand for small ships generated by the fighting in American waters. Moreover the fighting had spread to European waters by 1777, with American privateers operating from French, Spanish and Dutch ports. Though the losses inflicted by Gustavus Conyngham, John Paul Jones and the others were numerically insignificant, they were politically damaging, and their activities exposed to the world the fact that there was little left in home waters but battleships.[130] Probably the most damaging consequence of the shortage of frigates was in the West Indies, where American privateers and neutral shipping worked together to promote American and damage British trade. Here if anywhere a blockade might have been effective, had the government been prepared to risk war by searching French and Dutch shipping – and had there been ships to conduct it with effect.[131]

By the autumn of 1777 repeated disappointment in America, and the increasing threat from France, were already turning ministers' thoughts towards a naval strategy. The news of Burgoyne's surrender provoked a political crisis which tipped the balance. North, so often more perceptive and less resolute than his colleagues, realized that the ministry's policy over the past three years had completely failed, that war was inevitable, and that he was not equipped to direct it. Not for the last time he begged the king to release him, but in vain. The new situation urgently called for a new policy, for Germain's had collapsed. In December the Cabinet agreed on a strategy for the war in America. The army was to be confined to holding a few key ports, while a naval blockade reduced the rebellion.[132] At the same time Sandwich begged again for further naval mobilization. The policy of blockade would call for more ships in America, the situation in Europe was more threatening than ever, and still full mobilization was deferred.[133] Finally in January 1778, after more than eighteen months of repeated pleas from Sandwich, and fifteen months behind the French, the Cabinet accepted the need for unlimited mobilization. It was too late to avoid a general war. The French saw before them the opportunity which for eighty years they had longed for, the chance to catch the British fleet at a decisive disadvantage.[134] In March the French government admitted the existence of a treaty of amity and commerce with the rebels, which was tantamount to an act of war.[135] At the same time the Cabinet decided to relegate the American campaign to a minor rôle, sending most of the troops to the West Indies. They accepted Sandwich's argument that with war against France now certain, the colonial rebellion had become a sideshow.[136]

For the country and the ministry the situation was now very grave. For Sandwich personally it was both a disaster and an opportunity. It was a disaster because the ministry's policy of appeasement had left the Navy to face a European war weaker in relation to its enemies than in any year since at least 1588. It was an opportunity because Germain's American, land-based strategy was discredited. The effect of Saratoga was to give Sandwich his chance to show that the Navy could do better against France than the army had done against the colonials – but the odds against victory over the combined fleets of France and Spain were now very high.

CHAPTER XIV

The American War
1778–1779

In the spring of 1778 both Britain and France saw a strategic opportunity opening before them. For the British there was the chance to fight the French fleet while the Spaniards still stood aloof. In April it was estimated that the French had between thirty-three and forty-three ships of the line available at Brest and Toulon together, against fifty-five British on 15th March, of which forty were ready for sea and fifteen still wanted men. In June twenty ships were detached to America in pursuit of the Toulon squadron, leaving only twenty to match the Brest squadron, but by the time the Comte d'Orvilliers put to sea with thirty-two sail in July, the Western Squadron had risen to twenty-nine, and its higher proportion of three-deckers gave it rough equality in weight of fire.[1] For the French this was the long-awaited opportunity to meet the British fleet on equal terms, before the slow but certain process of British mobilization began to tell.[2] Both sides therefore had reason to long for a decisive action. Looking back to the smashing victories of the later stages of the Seven Years War, the British hoped, and needed, to do the same again, and would not be satisfied with anything less. For the French a drawn battle would look something like a victory by comparison, but their strategic situation demanded a real victory.

Undoubtedly both sides over-estimated the chances of achieving one, for the obstacles to decisive victory in an eighteenth-century naval battle were high. The only possible fighting formation for warships mounting their armament on the broadside was the line ahead, but a line of battle was an extremely unwieldy instrument. Ships of different size and design, some recently docked to clean their bottoms and others months 'off the ground', were very hard to handle in company even with long practice and highly-trained officers, let alone when hastily assembled at the outbreak of war and commanded by captains who had spent many years ashore. Flagships tended to be slower than the rest of the line of battle; Keppel's flagship the *Victory*, now at sea for her first wartime campaign, remained the favourite of generations of admirals because, unlike most three-deckers, she could keep up with the best ships in the fleet: 'the *Victory* meets with no disgrace as yet, which is a great deal to say for a ship of her size, near fifteen months off the ground with tons of mussels upon her bottom'.[3] Signalling up and down a line was inherently difficult, and became nearly impossible in action with thick clouds of smoke and increasing damage aloft. On the British side the signals available were few and ambiguous, and consisted essentially in directing attention to paragraphs of the *Fighting Instructions*, which were themselves a haphazard collection reissued by successive admirals in constantly changing forms. The French system was by comparison complex and sophisticated, but it too referred to a fixed set of orders directing particular manoeuvres.[4] No admiral could convey anything like a normal message except by sending a boat or a frigate, and in the British fleet this was the only way of obtaining a reply. Flagships alone were issued with a full set of signal colours, and others were confined to a tiny repertory of urgent signals conveyed by combinations of guns and ensigns. Frigates might be issued with a set of colours and stationed on the disengaged side of the line to repeat an admiral's signals, which helped captains to see them, but did not make them more intelligible.

The line of battle itself, once formed and held, was a formation very strong in the defensive and very weak in the offensive. Like trench warfare, it usually produced a stalemate, even if both sides were determined to fight. In practice French doctrine held that an admiral should not be distracted from the task in hand even by the prospect of victory; 'It is a principle of warfare', one of them wrote in 1781, 'that much is to be risked to defend one's own position, and little to attack the enemy's'.[5] Often the British found themselves trying to force action on an unwilling enemy, which was nearly impossible with prevailing tactical ideas. The more aggressive side was likely to be first disabled by damage aloft, and even a modest action soon produced sufficient damage to masts and yards to oblige both fleets to return to port. Mutual retreat gave each side the excuse to claim a victory, often with equally little gained. So long as two fleets of roughly the same size both formed their lines and held them, the chances of achieving victory were small. 'I have often told you', wrote Captain Jervis of the *Foudroyant*, 'that two Fleets of equal Force, never can produce decisive events, unless they are equally determin'd to fight it out, or the Commander in Chief of one of them, bitches it, so as to misconduct his Line'.[6] All the British naval

victories of the century had been gained over fleets which never
stood their ground in a coherent line, or formed one but were heavily
outnumbered. Even in these circumstances victory required a degree
of skill in handling ships in company which was never attained on
the outbreak of war. Only after years of practice under admirals
who were conscious of the need for it (which some were not) did a
fleet develop real efficiency.

The choice of a commander-in-chief was of course critically important, and invariably difficult. At the outbreak of war the choice lay
usually between admirals who were too old and those who were too
inexperienced, all of them being completely out of practice. Both
Britain and France had attempted to deal with this problem in the
1770s by sending out training cruises to practice simple manoeuvres.
These undoubtedly gave useful experience to a selected few, but
handling five or six ships for a few weeks in summer is not the same
as handling twenty or thirty for a wartime cruise.[7] The necessity of
employing battleships to cruise against American privateers in 1777
had given many British captains useful practice at sea, but not of
handling their ships in line. On the French side the senior officers
of the Seven Years War had been so discredited that commands
were given to officers of an older and more glorious generation like
d'Orvilliers (aged sixty-eight in 1778) and de Guichen (aged seventy
in 1782), or to those from different backgrounds like the former
army officers d'Estaing and Bougainville, or the Bailli de Suffren
from the navy of the Knights of Malta.[8] On the British side the great
admirals of that war were either dead, like Anson, Boscawen and
Saunders, or retired, like Hawke and Pocock. Only Keppel and
Howe, young commodores at the end of the last war, had experience
of handling squadrons and were still available.

Howe was in North America in 1778, and the choice of Keppel
to command the Western Squadron (often referred to in this war, at
least by younger officers, as the Channel or Grand Fleet), was inevitable. Like Byng, chosen to command in the Mediterranean in 1756,
he was the only officer with the necessary seniority and experience.
Nevertheless the choice was difficult, and in the light of hindsight,
unfortunate. The least of the problem was that Keppel had been
ashore for fifteen years, he was no longer young and fit, and had
anyway been a specialist in combined operations who had never
handled fleets in line of battle. The real difficulty was what he had
been doing during that fifteen years. Other admirals spent their years
of half-pay in the conventional pursuits of the gentleman, but Keppel
had taken a path unusual among sea officers; he had become more

or less a full-time politician. He and his friend Saunders were leaders of the Rockingham Whigs, distinguished throughout the 1760s and 1770s by the strength, or at least the immoderation, of their views.[9] Keppel was therefore an old political opponent of Sandwich. It is a matter of judgement to what extent Keppel the politician could be said to be acting for himself, but his correspondence gives an impression of a weak man manipulated by unscrupulous friends; 'he was as it were a weak man, and he lacked understanding mightily!'.[10] Long before the American War developed, long before Sandwich became First Lord of the Admiralty, Keppel had learnt, or been taught, to judge even professional matters by political criteria. When Saunders was nominated to command the fleet in the event of war in 1765, Keppel discussed with him the choice of officers and his relations with Lord Egmont in almost exclusively partisan terms, referring hardly at all to the naval requirements of the moment.[11] When Keppel's name was mentioned in 1774 as the obvious commander-in-chief, his cousin the Duke of Richmond, whose extreme views placed him well on the left wing of the Rockinghams,[12] urged him to treat Sandwich with the utmost distrust:

> I do not see how you could refuse your service. Let me, however, advise you to insist upon your own terms . . . I would advise you to have the condition of each ship examined by your own officers, and assented to by the Admiralty, in writing. I would insist upon having so many seamen to each ship, and the most distinct and clear orders before I went to sea.[13]

Moreover it had already occurred to Keppel that if war broke out, 'the unheard of before Errors, in the direction of this once Glorious Country' might help him back to the Admiralty.[14] He had therefore a direct interest, not in defeat as such, but in fixing the blame for failure on Sandwich. When he was offered the prospective command a newspaper imagined him telling the king that he would obey him, but 'that he would receive no orders from Lord S, for he knew nothing of that gentleman'.[15] This was not what he actually told George III when he accepted in March 1778,[16] but it may not have been so far from his real thoughts. Lord North likened the opposition to barnacles slowing Keppel down,[17] but they might better have been described as deflecting his course from the line of duty.

Furthermore Keppel, like most admirals, conceived that he had professional grievances against those who had failed to recognize his merit as it deserved; or, worse still, had recognized the merit of others. In 1775 Sandwich had bestowed the vacant position of Lieutenant-General of Marines on Palliser. The Marine general ranks were sinecures given to flag officers not by seniority but as a reward for good service. Keppel was infuriated that his junior should benefit, and a correspondence ensued, emollient on Sandwich's side, acrimonious on Keppel's, ending with a veiled threat: 'what is to follow time will discover'.[18] Early in 1776 he found further ground of complaint with the promotion of his junior Lord Howe. Howe's ability he admitted, but he should 'follow me and not go before me'.[19] The actual situation was that in 1770 Keppel was a Vice-Admiral of the Blue and Howe a Rear-Admiral of the Blue, three steps behind. On 31st March 1775 they were promoted to the same ranks in the White Squadron, still the same distance apart. In February 1776 Keppel, still declining to serve, rose to be Vice-Admiral of the Red, and Howe, about to become Commander-in-Chief North America, was raised to Vice-Admiral of the Blue – only two steps behind. This was what Keppel called having a junior promoted over his head. In January 1778 there was a further promotion of flag officers, which carried Keppel to Admiral of the Blue, but because the Rear-Admirals were announced a few days before the Vice-Admirals Keppel had time to complain that he was being slighted on political grounds.[20]

In modern eyes these complaints may seem almost unreasonable, but it must not be thought that they would have surprised contemporaries. Gentlemen of nice honour were expected to be alert to slights, and ever ready to vindicate their reputations. For First Lords of the Admiralty, and for all who had patronage to bestow, it was a fact of life which had to be lived with. A similar case arose with Sandwich's former friend and discontented rival Rear-Admiral Lord Bristol. Bristol was asked to hoist his flag as one of the junior admirals in Keppel's squadron. Having failed to get the Mediterranean command, Bristol accepted, demanding that the *Royal George* be held ready for him until such time as his health would permit him to go to sea. Sandwich declined to tie up the ship indefinitely, and when Bristol was ready she had already been allocated to Rear-Admiral Harland.[21] The result was another admiral nursing another grievance against Sandwich.

Although on professional grounds Keppel was the unavoidable choice for commander-in-chief, his political position obliged Sandwich to treat him with great caution. He had to work hard, and be seen to work hard, both to establish mutual trust between the admiral and himself, and to demonstrate to opinion at large that he was doing so. Had success in North America and prompt mobilization against France placed Sandwich and the ministry beyond criticism, he could have ignored the political dimension, but as it was it was necessary that uncommitted members of Parliament should be persuaded that Sandwich was playing fair with the admiral. Had Keppel been an avowed friend, or one among a number of strong contenders for the command, his requests could have been treated on their merits, but as it was Sandwich had to conciliate him by every available means. He had to accede to his numerous and increasingly unreasonable demands for special promotion and privileges for his relatives and followers.[22] He had to attend to his cautious strategic ideas. Keppel urged that the Navy had to stand on the defensive, 'that detachment & separation is dangerous & risks too much',[23] that not only America but the East and West Indies would have to be abandoned; 'The defence of England and Ireland, with Gibraltar . . . is all my poor judgement allows me to expect'.[24] Keppel was well aware of the threat posed by the Spanish fleet,[25] and hence the need for speedy victory over the French, but he approached the task in a mood of pessimism. Admittedly he had a great deal to be anxious about, and it is fair to say that some great fighting admirals like Hawke showed to worst advantage in such circumstances, but the gloomy and corpulent admiral is a sad contrast with the bold young captain of thirty years before. His correspondence, not only with Sandwich[26] but with his most intimate friends, is permeated with a defeatism at times almost reminiscent of the letters of Admiral Byng.[27] He sought guidance on whether to fight if he met the enemy in overwhelming force, on where to retreat if forced to, on how to defend against invasion with a disabled fleet; it was clear that all these possibilities were in the forefront of his mind.[28] Far from that resolution to conquer in spite of all odds which marks the great commander, Keppel approached 'the most anxious and critical situation that ever an officer who had character to preserve was placed in' in a spirit of despondency.[29]

Sandwich found Keppel's mood irritating and worrying, and he certainly could not have collected any lucid strategy from the admiral's obscure prose, but it is nevertheless arguable that Keppel was right to press for concentration. Keppel was the favourite follower of Anson; for him as for Sandwich the rise of the Western Squadron was a formative experience. Both of them approached the strategic situation of 1778 with a general sense that there should be a powerful main fleet to the westward. What neither of them possessed, what was not worked out until the end of the nineteenth century,[30] was a coherent body of naval strategic thought which would have made clear to them, and allowed them to make clear to others, exactly why it was important to concentrate at the decisive point, and how concentration might be expected to bring victory again as it had done before. As it was Keppel and Sandwich had the right instinct, but neither of them seem to have appreciated the true importance of what they were proposing.

Keppel returned from his first cruise in June, just as a number of valuable convoys were coming in, on a report that the French fleet in Brest might be superior to his own, though it had not put to sea. His orders gave him discretion and he was not openly reproached, but in private the king and his ministers were furious. His additional instructions permitting retreat in the face of heavy odds had been issued in response to his own plea that he was exposed by the detachment of so many of his ships to America; now he seemed to have turned them to a political end.[31] It was easy for ministers to suspect that Keppel's priority was less to gain a victory than to embarrass the government by stressing the inferiority of his fleet.[32]

When the two fleets actually met off Ushant on 27th July, after four days of manoeuvring in search of an advantage, the affair was as indecisive as might have been expected. In the opinion of many British officers the French line was better handled than the British:

> The want of Attention to the Signals that were made occassion'd all the Confusion that happend. . . . Its a general observation of the Officers of the fleet, that no ships could be fought better or better managed than the Enemies ships were, there line was formed very exact.[33]

It was certainly sufficient to repel the British attack and retreat in good order to Brest.[34] Keppel's squadron suffered no loss but was heavily damaged aloft, and returned to Plymouth in search of new masts. His political friends, including a number in the fleet, industriously put it about that only the poor condition of the ships had robbed their hero of victory.[35] The charge was privately rejected by Keppel at the time,[36] and has been decisively refuted by modern scholarship.[37] The only serious problem, apart from the perennial constraint of manpower, was a shortage of spare 'made masts' for the lower masts of battleships damaged in the action. There was a large stock of 'single sticks' for topmasts and yards, but such extensive damage to lower masts was unprecedented, and it took some time to make up replacements.[38] 'The object of the French', Keppel wrote, 'was at the masts and rigging, and they have crippled the fleet in that respect beyond any degree I ever before saw'.[39] When the fleet put to sea again in the autumn many lower masts had to be temporarily repaired for the cruise. Keppel had very few frigates to scout for the enemy, and it proved to be a fruitless search for d'Orvilliers, though a number of valuable convoys returning from the West and East Indies were covered safely into port.

The French, who had feared the worst, regarded Ushant as a great triumph.[40] For Sandwich and his colleagues, it was a great disappointment. He had succeeded in getting out an adequate fleet in spite of the lateness of the mobilization, but his hopes of speedy victory were dashed. He did not blame Keppel even in private:

> It is unfortunate that the affair was not more decisive, but I am persuaded it was out of our power to make it so. The object now to be attended to is to get the fleet out again as soon as possible otherwise our trade will be ruined, and the French will claim the victory, which as things now stand is I think clearly on our side.[41]

Though Keppel was not blamed, Sandwich declined to offer him the public praise for a great victory which he felt he deserved. The admiral returned in October, fretful, ill and querulous.[42]

With a great deal of effort Sandwich had managed to maintain good relations with Keppel throughout the year. One of the keys to this success was undoubtedly the appointment of Sir Hugh Palliser as third-in-command of the fleet. It was usual in the eighteenth century for naval members of the Admiralty Board qualified by age and seniority to serve afloat in wartime, and it was not therefore odd that Palliser hoisted his flag as a vice-admiral, nor that Mulgrave took command of a battleship. In spite of the resentment aroused by Palliser's appointment as Lieutenant-General of Marines, he and Keppel were old friends and colleagues, and joint beneficiaries of Saunders's will.[43] Palliser was able to act, and undoubtedly was meant to act, as a bridge between the First Lord and the commander-in-chief.[44] There was a brief disagreement between the two admirals in August, when the fleet was at Plymouth refitting after the battle of Ushant, but it was soon smoothed over.[45] Although it was the inability of Palliser's division, which was the most heavily engaged and damaged, to get back into line, which prevented

Keppel renewing the battle, he did not publicly reproach his junior.

Unfortunately, while the fleet was at sea in the autumn, Keppel's friends were at work to poison relations between the two admirals. When they returned, both tired, ill and disappointed, Palliser read in an opposition newspaper a paragraph written by an officer in Keppel's flagship accusing him of losing the chance of victory, and hinting at cowardice or a political motive.[46] This letter was probably written by Keppel's nephew Lieutenant George Berkeley, and it was natural to assume that the letter reflected his uncle's opinion, if not his instructions.[47] Keppel's friends industriously embroidered the story, suggesting that Sandwich had worked up Palliser to wreck the battle in order to spoil Keppel's career.[48] In the fevered atmosphere of the hour no charge was too absurd to lose credibility.[49] It was known that the Pallisers had once been Catholics, and that some of them still were, so it was even suggested that Sandwich and Palliser were in secret league to overthrow Protestantism and liberty.[50] In the House of Commons Keppel hinted at cowardice.[51]

Even the most easy-going gentleman could not afford to overlook a suggestion of cowardice, and the 1773 episode had shown Palliser to be sensitive to slights. A man of his humble origins, without the easy social connections of Keppel (brother of an earl) and his political allies of the Rockingham connection, had to be doubly sensitive to his honour, for his character as a gentleman was all he had to sustain himself. He therefore proffered to his commander-in-chief a statement exculpating him from the allegation of cowardice. Keppel refused to sign it, thus in effect associating himself with the charge. Palliser published the statement anyway, and the quarrel between the two admirals became open and violent. Though Palliser and to some extent Keppel refrained from translating personal to political, and Sandwich kept silent, Keppel's friends seized on the quarrel as an opportunity for the most savage attacks on Sandwich.[52]

The affair was already highly damaging to the Navy, to Keppel and Palliser, and to Sandwich. For him it was the return of scenes he had witnessed thirty years before, as he explained in the House of Lords:

An enquiry, he said, would be of as bad consequence as a defeat, because it would divide the officers and seamen into factions and private cabals . . . Such precisely were the consequences of the miscarriage of Matthews and Lestock, in the Mediterranean; the navy was split into parties and factions, the absence of the principal officers,

present or absent on that day, was necessary, either as judges or witnesses, by which the naval armaments were neglected, or suffered to
stand still; the enquiry raised a kind of commotion in the nation; and
at the conclusion no one good purpose was answered.[53]

But it was impossible to smooth the affair over unless the principals
showed some willingness. The fatal stroke was Palliser's formal
demand, made on 9th December, for a court martial on Keppel for
misconduct in the battle. 'The moment there was a Court Martial
there was an end of knowing any true opinion, for it became a Party
affair'.[54] No correspondence between Sandwich and Palliser survives
between 9th November and 12th December.[55] We do not know if
Sandwich knew in advance of Palliser's intention, but we can be sure
that he would have tried hard to dissuade him from such folly. It
might have seemed impossible for any action to inflame the situation
any further, but this did. The wording of the articles of war was so
remote from the actual situation that the charges had to be framed
in terms of cowardice or treachery.[56] These carried the death penalty,
and were the precise charges under which Byng had been shot. From
vindicating his own honour, it seemed, Palliser had passed to
attempting his commander-in-chief's life. The most moderate
opinion was shocked:

> I have not the least guess what will be the consequence of all this
> bustle; but I know this; that when Men become angry, they do things
> they would never have thought of doing in their sober senses. Who
> is in the right, or in the wrong, it is hard to say out of the profession;
> but if Palliser cannot make good his charge, he must be inevitably
> ruined.[57]

In the Navy, where Keppel had always been one of the most admired
and popular of officers,[58] Palliser's charges had the effect of completely isolating himself, and throwing the darkest suspicion on
Sandwich. A memorial deploring the charges and signed by various
admirals, mainly of the opposition but including Hawke, was presented to the king.[59]

Sandwich's dilemma was what to do with Palliser's charges. All
precedent suggested that an officer could not be refused the opportunity to vindicate his honour. Both justice and policy seemed to insist
that junior officers had to be able to bring charges against their
seniors if misdeeds in high places were ever to be punished. Sandwich
could not forget that after the battle of Toulon Lieutenant Hugh

Palliser and his fellow officers of the *Essex* had accused their captain of cowardice, and that he had confirmed the charge by fleeing the country rather than face it.[60] In the present case Palliser was the aggrieved party, however he might have over-reacted; moreover he was an honest and deserving servant of the Crown; and the follower of a man who did not desert his friends. Yet the damage which would be done by allowing the court martial to go ahead was too obvious. Violent passions had already been aroused and would be still further inflamed. It would be impossible to escape the imputation of partiality, and further alienate moderate opinion within and without the Navy. If Keppel were court-martialled, it would be represented as an attempt at judicial murder; if the court martial were refused, he would complain at being denied the opportunity to vindicate his honour. It has been suggested that Sandwich should have refused Palliser's request and instead brought a court martial against him – but this would have been both unjust and illegal, and it is hardly likely that it would have mollified Keppel and his friends. Moreover they brought a motion in the House of Commons demanding a court martial on Palliser, which immediately made it a political issue.[61] Probably the least damaging outcome would have been if Palliser had asked for a court martial on himself, before the Rockinghams demanded one. Once Palliser accused Keppel in public, the affair was out of control, and there was very little Sandwich could do but ride out the storm.[62]

The court assembled early in the new year. According to law, the prisoner and the trial should have been held aboard ship, but Keppel pleaded ill health, and it was no moment to appear vindictive, so the government reluctantly consented to an act of Parliament permitting the court to sit ashore. The president and members of the court acted with flagrant partiality, brow-beating witnesses, denying Palliser a hearing and manipulating the evidence. The court, ashore in Portsmouth, was crowded with Keppel's aristocratic friends, cheering points in his favour and hissing those few brave enough to testify for Palliser.[63] None of this was necessary, for an impartial court would certainly have acquitted Keppel of the charges. However anxious he had been before the battle, he had done nothing during it to justify any accusation beyond incompetence, at worst. His real crime was to allow himself to be used for political purposes to destroy the career of his fellow admiral – but there was no charge in the articles of war to cover that.

Keppel's acquittal was followed by an outburst of popular enthusiasm. The Rockingham Whigs were down at Portsmouth in force,

revelling in the unaccustomed sensation of popularity. No expense
was spared by Keppel's friends, no expense was forgotten by the
Portsmouth inn-keepers, which could contribute to a memorable
day.[64] A procession carried the admiral through the streets of Portsmouth led by a band playing 'See the Conquering Hero Comes'.

> The whole concourse and ladies from the windows supplied the vocal
> part, and the crowd closed each period of the harmony with a choral
> cheer . . . It is impossible to paint the joy that possessed every face.
> Holiday was expressed in every look, and the hearts of the people
> were in their eyes.[65]

In London a mob led (if we can believe Horace Walpole) by several
of the younger members of the Rockingham group including Charles
Fox, attacked the Admiralty, gutted Palliser's house and burned the
contents in the street.[66]

By now it was inevitable that Palliser would have to be court-
martialled as well. Once again the charges of misconduct in action
which were brought bore little relation to the real issue of Palliser's
relations with his commander-in-chief. Even a hostile court could
hardly find him guilty of cowardice, but he was reprimanded for
failing to signal his damages to Keppel; a 'censoriously acquitting
sentence', as one officer called it.[67] By now Palliser had no defenders
left. Even those who remembered his long and talented services to
the Crown, lamented his folly and saw the necessity of his dismissal.
The king's verdict was balanced:

> Perhaps there never was a more general run than against poor Sir
> Hugh Palliser, and that not only from a faction but moderate men are
> shocked and with reason at his bringing a capital charge and yet not
> having proved the smallest appearance of ground for such a grievous
> charge; therefore I should hope that Mr Fox having withdrawn his
> very severe motion is some proof that men are a little returning to
> their senses and will at length see that though Palliser's conduct is
> alone to be accounted for by the passion that attended the very
> unguarded attack he met with, yet that his services to the public make
> him deserve a little indulgence.[68]

Only Sandwich held out in favour of his follower, long after the
battle was clearly hopeless.[69] Finally Sir Hugh was forced to resign
his seat in the Commons, his offices of Lieutenant-General of
Marines and Governor of Scarborough Castle, and retire to obscurity. In the light of history, he is a figure out of Greek tragedy,

destroyed by his own faults of character in spite of all his noble qualities. He never understood the share he had had in his own downfall, but blamed it all on the

> party rage, faction, injustice & envy of those who are professedly in opposition to the King's ministers, and are your Lordship's avow'd enemys, not mine, for I had no enemys but those who became so because of my steady zeal and attachment to his Majesty's service and government, & because of my serving in office with your Lordship & being honor'd with your friendship & confidence.[70]

Sandwich, who had suffered nearly as much from the affair, never reproached him with his folly, and remained a steadfast friend in spite of the political cost.[71] In May 1780 he aroused further attacks by appointing him Governor of Greenwich Hospital, and in November brought him back into Parliament on a by-election in Huntingdon.[72] We have seen that Sandwich could be ruthless, and that an element of watchful suspicion formed one of his strengths as a politician, and one of his less likeable qualities as a man; it is fair to remember this other side of his character, as someone whose loyalty clearly overcame his political judgement. Perhaps a greater statesman would have accepted the necessity of Palliser paying the price of his rashness, but the treacherous Jemmy Twitcher depicted by Wilkite propaganda would not have stood by his friend.

For Keppel the affair represented a tumultuous climax to his reputation. His sea service was over, for relations between him and the Admiralty had broken down entirely.[73] Even so he refused to resign his command, and ministers were naturally reluctant to dismiss him, but he complained of his treatment to the king in angry but vague terms,[74] laid down to the Admiralty the offensive conditions on which he would serve, and the ministry was glad to construe his language as a resignation.[75] Among the public, and even the opposition, he had already done himself a good deal of damage by parading as a conquering hero, 'for tho' he had done as well as he could yet there was nothing very great done'.[76] Independent political opinion was not prepared to join him in denouncing an administration whose policies were still popular, least of all when a French invasion threatened.[77] As early as January 1779 those with long memories were comparing him with Vernon;[78] in October Archbishop Cornwallis warned his naval brother: 'As to your Friends Leveson, Admirals Keppel & Harland; I find it to be the general opinion of all unprejudiced minds, that their names ought no longer to remain in the List of Admirals & Captains; Admiral Keppel, who was the Idol last January is now very unpopular'.[79] Rodney's victory over a Spanish squadron in January 1780 gave rise to pointed comparisons between the two:

> The Cause like others you did not betray,
> Who faintly Fought and almost Ran away.[80]

By 1782 Keppel was being accused of losing the battle of Ushant deliberately,

> Lest Sandwich should the honor share
> Or North remain Prime Minister,
> Or Britain end its 'ruinous war';[81]

and identified in cartoons by the words 'He that fights & runs away, May live to fight another day'.[82] Distaste for Keppel's antics was not the same as approval of Palliser, yet as early as February 1780 he had friends besides Sandwich prepared to speak for him in Parliament, and in December he aroused a good deal of sympathy with a long and boring speech in his own defence.[83]

Before the political tide turned, the Keppel–Palliser affair came close to removing Sandwich from the Admiralty. In Parliament he had to face an attack on his management of the Navy led by Lord Bristol, a few days after the murder of Martha Ray.[84] The administration won this debate, but the thinking of Lord North and the king was that his unpopularity among officers had made him a liability in the Navy. If he could be replaced by Lord Howe, who returned from America in the middle of the trials, tranquillity might be restored to the Navy, and Sandwich's acknowledged talents and experience could be exploited by promoting him to the vacant Secretaryship of State.[85] This scheme foundered mainly on the price demanded by Howe:

> If Lord Howe would have come cordially into the Admiralty it might have been a popular appointment; but as he has added conditions that it would be disgraceful to grant, I am clear Lord Sandwich fills the Admiralty much better than any other man in the kingdom would.[86]

'I cannot have the least doubt of the propriety of keeping Lord Sandwich in his present employment', the king continued in a later letter, 'and even saying that at this hour no person is so well qualified for holding it'.[87] In the autumn there was a further crisis; 'If you are thoroughly acquainted with the present state of the political system', wrote Robinson to Sandwich, 'I think you must be well informed indeed, for if I mistake not the clouds lower, are gathering, and thicken fast'.[88] The immediate problem was the Secretaryship of State vacant ever since the death of the Earl of Suffolk in March 1779; the real difficulty was as usual Lord North:

> It would surprize your Lordship to be informed of the various turns of his Mind in the Course of yesterday on this Subject, and what difficulties I had to bring him to decision – at first in the Morning all vigour for endeavouring to make up an administration and go on, soon afterwards doubtful, hesitating and diffident, then clearly that it wd. not do, and that Ld Stormont would not accept and that all attempts wd. be in vain; and at last abt 4 o'clock when pressing him closely to decision, telling me that seeing things as he did, that he was unequal to the task, that the King's Buss. cd. not be done by him, that no good administration cd. be formed while he was first Lord of the Treasury, for that people wd. not act with him; that the Govt wd. be overturned in the first or Second Week in Parliament, that he cou'd not govern, that he had no Weight, that he sent intelligence gave his advice and opinion, wished to have persons employed who he tho't cou'd essentially serve the publick, and it was disregarded, and yet he was deemed responsible for Events . . .[89]

'We shall feel the want of your assistance most grievously at the opening of the sessions', Sandwich wrote to Mulgrave,

> where I suppose our department will again be a principal object of attack; I know not what we shall do without you, especially as I do not see the spirit of decision & firmness in administration that is to be wished; god knows how it will end, but I must say I do not like the present appearances.[90]

Secret discussions with the opposition in December failed because .they like Lord Howe demanded far too high a price, in this case the dismissal of Germain, Sandwich and North himself.[91] No ministry, least of all one with a Parliamentary majority, could be expected to commit suicide to please its opponents. The same thing happened in July 1780, when the opposition insisted only on the replacement of Sandwich by Keppel. George III's comment then was:

> As to Lord Sandwich whatever his private failings may be, I know no man so fit for his department, he has now got out the finest fleet

this country ever possessed, I cannot think it therefore either wise or just to remove him and the more in favour of one who would renew faction and overthrow every means of conducting that department with propriety.[92]

The faction which the king referred to was the most serious consequence of the Keppel–Palliser affair. The political tide turned in due course and Sandwich's reputation recovered, at least as far as the course of an unsuccessful war permitted, but the divisions introduced into the Navy took much longer to heal.[93] There had always been a small group of officers with connections to the Rockinghams who took their politics seriously and stirred up as much opposition to Sandwich as they could.[94] One of them, Captain John Leveson-Gower, assured a friend that Sandwich 'never had any decency & shocking as it is yet it is most true that he concealed the account of his Sons death two or three days that it might not stop the amusements at Hinchinbroke'.[95] The story is quite untrue: the long-expected news of William Augustus Montagu's death in Lisbon arrived on 10th January 1776 when the music at Hinchingbrooke was over and Sandwich was busy at the Admiralty.[96] Already in the autumn his son's illness had caused him to send his apologies for missing the Leicester music meeting, 'being much out of spirits'.[97] The story shows, however, that there were already officers prepared to believe and eager to spread anything to his discredit. Among them were men like Captain John Blankett who made it their business to supply the opposition press with as many naval secrets as they thought would discredit the First Lord.[98] After the courts martial their number grew considerably.

The immediate loss was the resignation of Keppel, Vice-Admiral Harland, and Captains Leveson-Gower and Lindsay. Much more serious was the creation of two bitterly-opposed parties, inevitably nicknamed the 'Montagues' and the 'Capulets', among senior officers, particularly in the Channel Fleet. This caused great damage to discipline and efficiency, and the eradication of it was one of Sandwich's dominant concerns for the rest of the war.[99] The problem, however, ought not to be exaggerated; it was largely confined to the Channel Fleet (on the North American station 'Keppelite' came to mean 'dilatory' or 'troublesome'),[100] and the number of violent partisans of either party was never large. In November 1778 a secret analysis of the admirals and captains prepared for Sandwich suggested that about five might be considered partisans of Keppel and another eleven inclined towards him; one was strongly and five

generally favourable to Palliser, and twelve remained neutral. The
report is clearly founded on personal knowledge and has the appearance of impartiality. It does not make any equation between political
and professional virtues; Captain Jervis, for example, is, 'a good
officer, but turbulent & busy, and violent as a politician attached to
Mr Keppel'.[101] This survey was taken before the trials came on to
inflame opinion, but it seems always to have been the case that the
neutral officers outnumbered those 'warm' on either side. When a
number of captains petitioned the king in February 1779 to dismiss
Palliser from the Service, it aroused the disgust of people who were
not friends of Palliser or Sandwich:

> What a glaring proof is this, my Lord, of the malevolence and rancour
> of party; and what presumption to attempt to prescribe to his Majesty
> who he shall or shall not employ. Let Sir Hugh's fate be what it may,
> the King never had a more brave and able officer, or a more zealous
> and faithful servant.[102]

The following month Vice-Admiral Campbell, a close friend and
follower of Keppel, 'condemns Admiral Keppel greatly for mixing
politics with his profession; acknowledges that Government cannot
go on if military people are to point out who shall or shall not be
the King's ministers, & is very ready to serve whenever Your
Majesty thinks proper to command him'.[103] About May Captain
Walsingham, who was both a supporter of Keppel and a close friend
of Sandwich, claimed that 'We are as quiet here as if we had never
had a court martial; these violent party affairs soon subside'.[104] In
September 1779 Mulgrave referred to,

> the remains of Admiral Keppel's party the chief of which are Jervis,
> Macbride & perhaps Sir John Ross tho' the latter is not violent: upon
> the whole he thinks the temper of the fleet as good as can be
> expected.[105]

After a visit to Portsmouth the same month Sandwich considered
the fleet 'in perfect good humour, as much as it can be, while the
remains of Admiral Keppel's party exists'.[106]

The American war was the most politically charged and divisive of
the eighteenth century, and given that a number of officers were
irreconcilably opposed to the administration, it seems unlikely that
Palliser's rash action would have had any less disastrous results whatever Sandwich might have done or said. Possibly a naval First Lord

would have been better placed to mollify the turbulent admirals, but the unpopularity subsequently aroused by Keppel's extreme partiality as First Lord in 1782–83, and Howe's austere impartiality in 1784–88, suggest otherwise. 'I do aver', Sandwich declared in the House of Lords in 1782,

> that no Naval Administration could be formed that would not have more of these difficulties to struggle with. Sea officers are apt to be discontented if everything is not done according to their wish; they are exceedingly jealous of one another, and ready to find fault with everybody's conduct but their own. But yet they will do their duty, and I do not believe any instance can be produced where orders have been wilfully disobeyed under this Admiralty, or where a want of confidence has appeared on the part of the officers employed more than at any other period. To be sure Admiral Keppel and all those who are connected with them have no confidence in the Admiralty, nor the Admiralty in them, but their number is inconsiderable and is daily diminishing, and I own I can never think it for the good of this country to bring them forward to conduct the naval affairs; and though I acknowledge there are some very good officers and very good men among them, they have suffered politics to lead them so totally that the good of the service is a very secondary consideration with them.[107]

The courts martial and the political crises of 1779 would have been enough to have occupied any minister, but this was also the year of the worst military crisis of Sandwich's lifetime, when a foreign invasion seemed to be imminent and the Channel Fleet less able to prevent it than ever before. In France the 1778 campaign had produced elation among those who claimed Ushant as a great victory, and alarm among those who soberly considered the strategic situation. Already manning and other difficulties suggested that the French navy was approaching its maximum strength, and the odds in 1779 promised to be about sixty-six sail of the line against ninety British.[108] Sandwich agreed, and was full of confidence as long as Spain did not enter the war; 'for our fleet is in excellent condition & greatly superior to that at Brest, and I hope in equal forwardness as to getting to sea'.[109] The Spanish alliance was vital to France, and the Spaniards were well aware of the fact. They set their price high, including French participation in a scheme of invasion of Britain about which the French had grave misgivings. The two fleets were to rendezvous off Corunna and come up the Channel in overwhelming force to cover landings on the Isle of Wight and around Portsmouth.[110] Both fleets fell far behind their schedule. D'Orvilliers did not sail from Brest until the first week of June, even then ill-prepared, and when he arrived at the new rendezvous off Cape Finis-terre the Spanish ships had not sailed. By the time the Spaniards joined on 23rd July the French had been waiting six weeks and were becoming sickly. Further time was lost instructing the Spaniards in the French signal system, and it was not until the middle of August that the Combined Fleet of sixty-six sail of the line at last entered the Channel. Already d'Orvilliers was acutely short of provisions and water, and the mounting numbers of dead included his own son.[111]

Meanwhile Sandwich in the aftermath of the courts martial had been at work fitting out the Channel Fleet, and finding a commander-in-chief for it. The obvious replacement for Keppel was Lord Howe, whose reputation as a tactician had been enhanced in 1778 by his skilful defence of Sandy Hook against d'Estaing's much superior fleet. He was in principle not unwilling to serve, but he and his brother the general had returned from America with few successes to claim, and many grievances against the administration. In particular Sir William and Lord George Germain blamed one another for the lack of success in 1776, and the disaster of Saratoga in 1777. Lord Howe and Sandwich had no serious reasons to quarrel, but the admiral took his brother's part against the administration in general, and regarded himself as unfairly loaded with the blame for failure:

> He said, It was a little hard, that after a man had devoted his whole time and talents (however poor the latter might be,) to the service of his country, that the *event*, and not his conduct, should determine his character; that to be *unsuccessful* and guilty should be the same thing, and that he should be held up as a public criminal, for not doing what could not be done![112]

The real difficulty with Lord Howe was that he set a price on his services which was high even by the standards of an age in which officers were expected to look after themselves. In December 1775, when Palliser was appointed Lieutenant-General of Marines, Lord North had forgotten that he had promised it to Lord Howe.[113] This generated a minor crisis: 'We are brought into a situation of great distress . . .' Robinson wrote, 'Something must be done with[ou]t loss of time or all will be blown up'.[114] Howe's appointment to the North American command is said to have been part of the price of pacifying him, but it seems more likely that he was offered the command on merit, and mollified for his disappointment with the promise of being made Treasurer of the Navy at the next vacancy. When this occurred in 1777 Howe was still abroad, but he clearly felt aggrieved at not receiving the lucrative sinecure, and 'the Howes were not easily placated when their honor was concerned'. Honour, in this case, was worth £4,000 a year.[115] Howe was willing to serve as commander-in-chief, but his price was not only promotion and reward for himself, but the complete rehabilitation of his brother and the disgrace of Germain. Hindsight may lead the modern reader to think that promoting Howe and removing Germain would have done much for the war effort, but the idea was politically impossible. Even the ablest admiral could not expect to break up the ministry to satisfy his family pride, and Howe's terms were refused. Thereafter the Howes moved into opposition – but the admiral's refusal to serve arose primarily from demanding too high a price rather than from political motives or personal dislike of Sandwich.[116]

The loss of Howe's services was a further blow to Sandwich, for he was by far the ablest candidate for the Channel Fleet, and the one who commanded the widest professional support. The choice of officers to replace him was distressingly narrow. Among the younger admirals it was hard to see one available who was not too deeply involved with the Montagues or Capulets, or whose advancement would not raise jealousies. In the end the choice fell on Sir Charles Hardy, an Admiral of the White then aged about sixty-three.[117] Hardy had had a respectable though not brilliant career, with much experience as second-in-command of large fleets. His seniority put him beyond the reach of jealousy, and his popularity and relaxed manner were well calculated to calm the heats of faction. This last was probably the key factor, for few things were more urgent in the spring of 1779 than to restore unity and cohesion to the Channel Fleet.

In fact only one thing was more urgent, and that was to defeat the most formidable invasion threat the country had faced since 1588. When Hardy sailed on 16th June with thirty sail (increased to forty-two during the next six weeks) and orders to blockade Brest,[118] there was still hope that Spain would stay out of the war, but as soon as the Spanish declaration of war was made the strategic situation changed completely.[119] When the Combined Fleet entered the Channel on 15th August Hardy faced odds of roughly two to one. This was a very perilous situation. It was generally agreed that to go into battle even five ships fewer than an enemy fleet was dangerous, because the longer line could stretch ahead or astern to double on the van or rear and overwhelm it, thence working up the line with ever-increasing advantage. To face an enemy thirty ships stronger was by all conventional standards a complete impossibility. In the face of this crisis Sandwich's colleagues and professional advisers were divided. One argument, advanced strongly by Middleton, was to adopt Fabian tactics, avoid immediate action and draw the enemy up Channel.[120] Like the Spanish Armada two centuries before, the Combined Fleet would be moving further into confined and dangerous waters, and further to leeward of its bases. So long as Hardy kept his fleet intact an invasion would be too risky, and the longer the Combined Fleet stayed at sea the stronger he became, and the better the chance that by disorganization or accident it would give him a chance to fight with advantage. Other voices, notably Mulgrave's, were alarmed at any suggestion of retreat. What the nation and the fleet needed, he argued, was a battle now; nothing would so powerfully restore morale and discipline even if the result were not a complete victory. The Combined Fleet was far too large to be handled effectively, and a well-trained squadron of thirty sail could defeat an unwieldy mass of sixty.

> I own I was much concerned to see any orders for retreating without a battle, as I think our present situation equal to meeting anything, both from the strength of the ships, for their number, and the great superiority of our discipline to that of the Spaniards till they have been a considerable time at sea. The last is an advantage I should be sorry we lost, especially as it must lessen every day.
>
> Thirty sail is as great a number as I think can be brought properly to action in a line. More ships will undoubtedly be useful as a reserve; but I should be sorry to see them in the line when we have them, as they must probably in that situation impede our motions and prevent a general close action, which is what we have to wish for whilst our ships' companies are healthy and the days long . . . Unless you expect a very considerable reinforcement very early I see no advantage that can be gained by retreat.[121]

Sandwich entirely agreed:

> As you very rightly judge, delay can do us no service; our ships are now healthy and in compleat condition, sickness and accidents may disable them, quarrells & disunion may happen among you, and as the blow must be struck, it will be for our advantage that it should be decided while every body is able & willing to use their utmost exertion in their country's cause.[122]

To the Cabinet, looking at the situation as a whole, and of course not unmindful of their political position, it seemed essential to retreat no longer but to fight. Any result short of serious defeat would be less damaging to the morale and unity of both fleet and nation than continued inactivity. This was also the king's view:

> It must be self evident, if so great and so well disciplined a fleet retires into port without having done everything that prudence, a knowledge of the profession, and a spirit equal to the necessity of the times could suggest towards distressing at least, if not defeating, the fleet of our enemies and protecting the extraordinary number of rich merchantmen now upon their return, that not only the greatest disgrace must fall upon the commanding officer and those who recommended him, but what is of infinitely more serious consequence the whole nation must either be so intimidated or so disgusted as to produce universal confusion.[123]

Sandwich argued strongly for giving battle on both military and political grounds:

> You judge very rightly that it is impossible to give positive orders to a Commander in Chief to fight at all events against an apparent superiority, but the orders that are now gone to Sir Charles Hardy are as near that as I think can be given by any set of men who have not entirely lost their senses, for he is told that the combined fleets are at sea with an intention to invade either England or Ireland, which he must endeavour to prevent, and not to return into Port except in a case of *absolute necessity*. I enclose to you in the utmost confidence a copy of a private letter which I have written to Sir Charles which will give you an insight into my sentiments; to which I will add that from the first man in the kingdom to the last I do not believe that there is one who will not be dissatisfied if you do not seek an action.
>
> I own I shall be very uneasy while you are so near our own Ports; if you do not immediately get to the Westward, it will give the utmost advantage to our own internal enemies who are watching every opportunity to discredit the fleet, and those who have anything to do in the management of it either at sea or on shore; and if you come into Port & any blow is struck during that time, the torrent will most probably be too strong to be resisted.[124]

In this crisis the first man in the kingdom had no doubt of what to do: 'I own I have not the smallest anxiety if the ships already under the command of Sir Charles Hardy can bring the combined fleet of the enemies to a close action'.[125] George III was not a clever man, and he did not concern himself with strategic subtleties, but he had all the qualities of leadership and moral courage which his chief minister so badly needed, and in the supreme crisis of his reign he was ready, indeed eager to stake his kingdom on a battle against fearful odds. Hardy for his part was prepared to fight in circumstances of his own choosing, but intended to draw the enemy up Channel first. In the event the two fleets spent a month in light airs and frequent fogs, several times near one another but never able to engage. On 11th September the Combined Fleets returned to Brest, crippled by sickness.[126]

It was some time before it was known in England that the enemy had withdrawn, and anxiety remained high. In mid-August Sandwich wrote to Mulgrave:

> I own I dread your coming in without an engagement, a drawn battle, or even a retreat with some loss would in my opinion be better than the return of the whole fleet without striking a blow: such a return would occasion great convulsions in the political world, where the fabrick I fear stands upon a very loose foundation.[127]

When Hardy brought the Channel Fleet in to Spithead at the beginning of September it alarmed the administration and many of the officers (including Mulgrave). There seemed a considerable risk that the fleet might be attacked at anchor, and a certainty that the administration would be accused of another retreat. In the face of intense pressure to return to sea at once, Hardy insisted on getting his ships properly stored before he would sail. Sandwich obtained the king's permission to go down to Portsmouth himself to hasten the work.[128] Before Hardy was ready to sail again, however, it became known that the allies had also gone into port, and Hardy did not sail again until 22nd October for an autumn cruise to guard against the allies renewing their invasion project, as intelligence suggested they would.[129]

Hardy's performance in the summer of 1779 has traditionally been judged harshly. He has been presented as elderly, timid and incompetent, the 'safe' choice of a politician frightened of risk.[130] Much of this rests implicitly on the assumption that there were better alternatives available. It also rests on criticism from one or two sources which have been published, notably the letters of Captain Richard Kempenfelt and of Germain's young protégé Benjamin Thompson. Kempenfelt was an extremely able officer, only slightly younger than Hardy but far his junior, who was appointed Captain of the

Fleet (a sort of admiral's assistant) to provide Hardy with some of the intelligent advice it was evidently felt he would need. Kempenfelt was a friend of Middleton, who drew many of his ideas from him.[131] He too was a reformer, but of the tactics and signalling of the sea-going squadrons. Throughout this war, under successive commanders-in-chief, Kempenfelt was at work experimenting with new ideas and methods. By the end of the war, largely thanks to him and Lord Howe, British fleets were adopting new practices which were in time to transform the tactical possibilities open to admirals, and help to break down the old tyranny of the line of battle. There is no doubt of the value of Kempenfelt's work, and moreover on the one occasion when he was given his own command, in 1781, he showed that he knew how to translate theory into practice. What he has to say deserves to be treated with respect – but not credulity. Throughout history clever subordinates have been fretting at the excessive caution of their commanders-in-chief, and making no allowance for their responsibilities. Hardy did not always follow Kempenfelt's advice, and in moments of exasperation Kempenfelt damned him for an old fool. Kempenfelt was a naval intellectual, a historian's admiral, a man whose correspondence was published early. Historians have found him agreeable and plausible, and have allowed too little for the bias inherent in his position, and the awesome responsibility which Hardy carried, and he did not.[132]

It is less easy to explain the attraction of Thompson, other than that his letters to Germain have been published,[133] and that they flattered the prejudices of an older generation of historians. Thompson was allowed to make a cruise with the Channel Squadron that summer to make some experiments in ballistics, and favoured his patron with inside information on the state of the fleet – which no doubt was the real purpose of the cruise, at least for Germain. Thompson's letters have two themes. The first, and by far the most prominent, is the extraordinary brilliance of Benjamin Thompson, superior in knowledge and talent to everybody with whom he came into contact, infinitely better qualified than any sea officer to handle a ship or a fleet. For Thompson this delightful theme never palled, but occasionally he introduced more general observations on the incompetence of the Navy and its officers which are clearly intended to tell Germain what he wanted to hear, and to provide him with the ammunition to undermine his colleague for which he was always looking. Historians may regret that an intelligent observer with Hardy's squadron did not make better use of his opportunities, but it is rather surprising that they should have used what Thompson actually wrote as a source of fact.

Hardy can be and has been judged from different standpoints. Contemporaries like the king who 'sigh after a close action with the united fleets of my enemies',[134] and modern historians for whom a naval battle is the only decent conclusion to a campaign, have been inclined to accuse Hardy of caution and timidity. Since Hardy never in fact had a fair chance of a battle, and was only one day in sight of the enemy, these are largely theoretical complaints, resting on his declared intention to lure the enemy up Channel to fight at best advantage. For officers like Walsingham the cruise was an acute disappointment: 'I wish with all my *heart and soul* we may have the good fortune to meet the fleets. I am full as sanguine as your Lordship on the subject, and think we really are a match for *anything*.'[135] For Middleton and the advocates of delay, Hardy was too willing to fight against heavy odds. 'The captains in general', his secretary assured Sandwich, 'look on an action as the most improper step Sir Charles can take; the same opinion prevailed when in sight of the French fleet'.[136] For Kempenfelt and Mulgrave, he withdrew too far and too fast, and was insufficiently receptive to their advice. From the political point of view, of which Sandwich for one was extremely conscious, his return to port with the enemy supposed to be close behind was an embarrassment as well as a danger, and his decision to come right up to Spithead to take in stores the faster was risky. On balance it must be said that Hardy at least achieved the necessary minimum of deterring invasion – not a trivial service, even if the failures of the enemy contributed as much as British skill. Given the baffling weather during the short time the Combined Fleet was in the Channel it is not clear that even the most belligerent admiral could have forced an action. It must also be said that Hardy's calmness in the face of alarming odds, his refusal to be bullied by Kempenfelt or Sandwich into a rash and possibly fatal battle, might be cited as evidence of moral courage. The greatest of modern authorities on naval strategy regarded Hardy's cruise as a masterpiece of skilful defensive tactics.[137]

As a peacemaker Hardy seems to have been very successful. For most of the summer he was praised by his subordinates.[138] Mulgrave thought well of his professional abilities:

Sir Charles's Dispositions for forming his Fleet Expeditiously & disposing his Force properly appear to me exceedingly proper & he has just issued some Orders to prevent the Probability of Seperation that

I think will have great Effect – I own my Expectations are so Sanguine and my mind so full of everything that can possibly contribute to our success that I may trouble you with too much upon the subject – but with the Reinforcement which I confess I had no notion your Exertions could have produced but which if you are properly seconded in the subordinate Branches we shall have before we can meet I think the situation of this Fleet not only very Important but Flattering.[139]

It was only on the autumn cruise, which many of them thought was a mistake, that discontent began to surface and accusations of incompetence to be proffered. 'He is good-natured, honest, has many private virtues which I esteem him for', wrote Kempenfelt, 'but as an officer, you know my opinion . . .'[140] By October Walsingham was reported as saying 'that every officer looked upon Sir Charles Hardy as extremely inadequate to the command, though a very honest, well meaning man';[141] and Mulgrave was exasperated with him: 'I am forced to be very cautious in giving Him Advice & never do it but on his own motion; He is jealous of being managed, fickle & irresolute & does not brook contradiction';[142] Jealousy of being managed, it may be remarked, has been a characteristic of all great commanders, and indeed of all who did not choose to have their authority usurped by their juniors.

Sandwich's own performance during 1779 has been criticized by impartial historians. His old energy and administrative ability did not flag, but it has been argued that his nerve began to fail under the repeated blows of the Keppel–Palliser affair, the Parliamentary debates on the Navy in February and December, and the murder of Martha Ray. So far as it explains the choice of Hardy, this is a weak argument unless a better candidate can be named; but in his dealings with Hardy, it is suggested that he resorted to unofficial correspondence in order to avoid responsibility.[143] This too seems unreasonable: all commanders-in-chief who enjoyed any relationship of trust with their ministers expected to be kept informed of the government's thinking and the political situation more fully and candidly than was possible in official orders, and Hardy would have had good reason to complain if he had not received private information. 'I cannot think', Sandwich explained to Mulgrave,

that the orders which have been communicated to you by your Commander in Chief convey a wish that you should retreat from the enemy; but a discretion must be allowed to those who are upon the spot, and when intelligence is given that you may be attacked by a force very superior in numbers, no superiors can order you absolutely to give battle let the superiority be never so great. I am sure the wish of every one here from the highest to the lowest is that you should risque an engagement, tho' the numbers should be against you; and if you do retreat, whatever the numbers may be you will be blamed by both friend & foe; but this opinion cannot be given out in orders, & you will consider what I now write to you as the sentiments of a private friend, and not as those of an official man.[144]

Eighteenth-century admirals had to be given a considerable degree of latitude in their orders, when communications were slow and the unexpected was always likely to occur. For a First Lord, private letters of explanation were as much an assumption as an avoidance of responsibility; they were less likely to be quoted in public, but they could not be covered with the cloak of collective responsibility. Sandwich had always trusted commanders-in-chief this way,[145] and so did every minister of his day who had any cordial relationship with his subordinates. The same was true of personal conversation. When Sandwich proposed to visit Portsmouth in September he suggested to the king that, 'if Lord Sandwich goes there he can enforce any ideas your Majesty may have . . . without committing your Government by official correspondence at so critical a time.'[146] This could imply some sinister private plot between Sandwich and the king, but it has not been suggested what such a plot might have been. Most likely the phrase means simply that Sandwich would be able to explain much about the strategic and political situation which was worth Hardy knowing, but which could not be dealt with in official correspondence, or (in some cases) freely discussed in Cabinet. It must be said, too, that the cogency of the argument that Sandwich sheltered from responsibility is not improved by arguing simultaneously that he sheltered from official correspondence behind private letters, and that he sheltered from private commitment behind the collective responsibility of the Cabinet.[147]

Where Sandwich can be criticized is in the heavy emphasis he placed in his private correspondence with Hardy on the political risks of the situation. He was always alert to the political dimensions of everything he did, it was one of the qualities which made him so effective a politician, but as a rule he maintained a clear division between the political and the professional. Arguably he put Hardy under unnecessary pressure by stressing fear of public opinion when he had quite sufficient professional worries, and Sandwich should himself have carried the political burden. Against this it may be said that this is a twentieth-century distinction, that in the eighteenth century Hardy was as much exposed to political risk as Sandwich, and had a right to be warned. In correspondence with Mulgrave, who was an Admiralty colleague and consequently a member of the administration, it was very proper for Sandwich to deal at large with the political situation. Nor was Sandwich one of those who panicked at the risk of invasion or feared the outcome of battle, but it can certainly be argued that he allowed more of his natural anxiety as a member of a fragile and at times tottering administration to percolate through to the commander-in-chief than was altogether fair.

The same anxiety showed in his unwillingness to break the law by pressing men protected by Acts of Parliament to man the fleet in the summer crisis.[148] His colleagues assured him that afterwards they would obtain a Parliamentary act of indemnity, but he was reluctant to expose himself, and perhaps doubtful of their ability to obtain what they promised. Englishmen of Sandwich's generation, including the independent members of Parliament who would have to decide his fate, held the law and the authority of Parliament in reverence as the bulwark of their liberty – it was after all what they were fighting a war in America to preserve – and if he had been willing lightly to break through it, they might not have been willing to forgive him. So the events of 1779 showed Sandwich to be in fear of public opinion to some extent, which he never had been before. It is a matter of judgement how far this can be described as a weakening of Sandwich as a man under the repeated blows of fate, and how far it simply reflects his weaker position as a member of a government in growing difficulties.

CHAPTER XV

The World War
1780–1782

Few subjects are more complex and controverted than the grand strategy of the American War. Because rather than in spite of the number of books which have been written about it, it remains difficult to discern the outlines of the problem as it presented itself to British ministers. The fundamental question was one of priorities: British, French and Spanish ministers had to weigh the competing claims of European waters, America, the West and East Indies. But most of the books are written about the fighting in America, and even those which view the world war as a whole, take the American crisis as their point of reference. The effect is to prejudge the central issue of the war, to ignore the most difficult decisions ministers had to take, and to distort understanding of the rest. Moreover putting America first has the same effect of distorting our understanding of politics within the North Administration, for the strategic issue of America or the world was an aspect of the political issue; Lord George Germain or Sandwich. To start from the assumption that America was the most important issue facing British ministers is to assume that Germain was the most important war minister, to whom his colleagues were, or ought to have been subservient. Germain has received in recent years a number of serious biographies, most of them sympathetic and all of them naturally concentrating on him.[1] By far the best general history of the war from the British standpoint is friendly to him,[2] and tends to take America as its point of reference. Sandwich, by contrast, has never had a serious biography (though the publication of his papers did something to compensate). The result has been that America has dominated the strategic picture.

This in turn exacerbates a tendency to determinism which marks many studies of the American War. Starting from the easy and in many ways proper assumption that nothing else about it was as important as the independence of the United States, historians have slipped insensibly into the idea that American independence was inevitable, and that it had evident causes with inescapable effects. If the independence of the United States was a God-given blessing for the world, as an older generation of writers tended to assume, it could hardly have come about by a series of accidents. Modern historians are less likely to invoke the will of God, but just as willing to see what actually happened as inevitable, as the only possible outcome of preceding events. In a sense this is the logical consequence of a proper reluctance to speculate about what might have been; if, as many historians believe, nothing useful can be said about what cannot be known, the only proper subject of discussion is what actually happened, and it becomes in effect (if not in logic) the only thing which could have happened. The result in incautious hands is to present as evident what is seen, with hindsight, to have been certain, and to blame the men of the eighteenth century for resisting the irresistible and ignoring the obvious.

Thus the manifest destiny of the United States to be independent has imposed a frame of reference which completely distorts the real strategic issues facing Sandwich and his colleagues. So in another way have anachronistic ideas about the rôle of naval power. The weight of the great American naval historian Mahan, writing a century ago, is still felt in many studies which assume that the Royal Navy existed to win battles and to control the sea, using certain hallowed techniques of which blockade was the best known. These ideas were evident and immutable, and if they were not adopted during the American War only the stupidity of ministers was to blame. We now know a great deal which makes these old interpretations untenable, though it has by no means made them extinct. Much of the doctrine Mahan expounded was his own synthesis, and often simplification, of British naval practice evolved during the 'Great War' against France between 1793 and 1815. Many of these doctrines did not yet exist during the American War, nor if they had would they necessarily have been applicable to an entirely different strategic situation. The 'time-honoured' doctrine of blockade was in fact a range of practices, some of them novelties and others not yet developed, applicable in different ways in different circumstances. The close blockade of enemy bases, which is usually what general historians refer to as 'blockade', called for a superiority in numbers which the Royal Navy did not have during the American War.[3] Modern studies of the working of naval warfare emphasize that there were no simple and universal strategies, that the accidents of wind and weather and the slowness of communications often reduced operations to matters of chance rather than plan, and that 'the

strategy of attrition . . . was more often than not the characteristic
form of naval warfare'.[4] In any case, strategy is a luxury available
to the side with the initiative. Just as American historians naturally
tend to see Americans as moving the events of the American War,
the characteristic weakness of British historians is to assume that
Britain's natural rôle is to lead, and that the business of foreign
powers is to oppose or conform to British initiatives. In the American War it was the other way around. Late mobilization meant that
for most of the war the Royal Navy was fighting on the defensive
against heavy odds. In such circumstances it is rarely possible to
dictate the course of events. As Chatham admitted in 1770, 'we can
no more command the disposition than the events of a war. Wherever we are attacked, there we must defend.'[5]

British strategy has often been criticized as uninspired and reactive,
but this is the nature of a defensive war against odds. Inspired origin-
ality is the privilege of those who have forces to spare from essential
tasks. During this war British ministers were only able to find such
forces on a small scale. They did plan operations such as the Fullar-
ton–Humbertson expedition to the South Seas[6] or Mulgrave's attack
on Flushing,[7] which would have been daring and original had circumstances permitted them to go ahead, but they were on too small
a scale to affect the outcome of the war. There were only two points
in the war when Britain had forces at sea sufficient to support the
initiative: 1778, before Spain had entered the war, and 1782, when
at last the Navy's strength had built up to match that of France and
Spain together. Criticism of the naval strategy of Sandwich and his
colleagues is best directed at what they did in 1778, and what they
planned to do in 1782 had they not fallen from power. Only in these
years did they have a real possibility of taking the initiative.

Much criticism of British strategy during the American War rests
implicitly or explicitly on a comparison with the Seven Years War.
At its crudest this is presented in terms of personalities; the elder
Pitt was a great genius, but North, Germain and Sandwich were
fools. More often it is expressed in constitutional terms; Pitt by force
of character overcame the weaknesses of eighteenth-century British
government and imposed a unified strategy on king and Cabinet.
We know now that he did nothing of the kind. Pitt and his colleagues
fought the Seven Years War with exactly the same departmental
style of government as their predecessors had employed in the 1740s,
and their successors used during the American War.[8] The essential
difference between Pitt and North was not genius but circumstances.
So far as abilities are concerned, North's financial and political skills

– both of which Pitt markedly lacked – were essential to a successful war, and might have earned him as great a reputation as Pitt's had he had the good fortune to deploy them in the favourable circumstances of the 1750s. Pitt certainly was a gifted strategist, with enough if not too much of the domineering personality Lord North lacked, and by the middle of the Seven Years War he and his colleagues enjoyed the luxury of the initiative, but they fought that war by very much the same processes of improvisation and adaptation as North's administration used twenty years later. Fighting a world war with slow communications, outnumbered on every front, George III's ministers had no choice.

Nor did they have any real choice in the form of government to which they belonged. Historians who used to think that Pitt had overturned the British constitution by force of character naturally lamented that North had not done the same, and drew support from the clarity with which North himself pointed out what needed to be done. But there was a wide gap between seeing what needed to be done, and actually being able to do it. To set up a dominant prime minister able to enforce a consensus Cabinet policy required a considerable evolution of machinery and attitudes, such as could not have been achieved quickly. It was in the event, and probably always had to be, a matter of slow development over many years, not of hasty improvisation in wartime. The administration in which Sandwich worked was essentially a departmental one, moderated by the idea of collective responsibility, and the convention that the king's personal views were not named in public. Loyalty to colleagues and decency towards the Crown often made it impossible for ministers to explain themselves properly. It has been remarked that in his defence of his administration which Sandwich made in the House of Lords early in 1782 he spoke with confident command of his administrative reforms, and only faltered when he came to the strategic conduct of the war.[9] This was not only because he had done much better at one than the other; it was because he himself was responsible for naval administration, but the government as a whole for the management of the war. It is naturally difficult to defend collective compromise, especially if one does not agree with it and events have proved it to be unsuccessful. But Sandwich's contribution to the war effort, like the performance of the government as a whole, can only fairly be assessed in relation to what might have been; to the decisions which ministers might reasonably have taken, with their knowledge and their objectives; to the achievements which were within their grasp, with the forces available to them.

To condemn Sandwich it must be plausibly arguable that he might have found better choices available within his own departmental responsibilities, or better opportunities to influence his colleagues. It is not enough to say that as a member of the ministry he shared the responsibility of failure, if success was not within their reach. Without showing how he could have done better, to blame him for being associated with failure is little better than condemning him for not having been born a different man in a different age.

Studies of the handling of the American War at sea are equally prone to the weaknesses of determinism and hindsight. Lacking foreknowledge, with insufficient forces to be strong everywhere, ministers were often forced to choose what seemed to be the least dangerous alternative. When things went wrong, as they often did, both contemporary and later critics have accused them of misjudgement or folly.[10] Implicitly the argument is that there was a 'right' decision available which would have avoided loss or gained victory, and the fact that things went wrong proves that the wrong decision was taken. This does not logically follow: it may be, and often is in a war against odds, that there is no prospect of complete success, and the best choice available can only minimize loss. It is easy to show that things went wrong, but it does not follow that they might have gone better. It is easy to say that if this or that task had been allocated a greater proportion of scarce resources, it might have yielded success or avoided defeat. Seldom do critics ask where the ships and men would have to have been taken from, and with what results. Failure attracts attention, while success is taken for granted. Sandwich has often been criticized, for example, for keeping the Channel Squadron cruising too late into the autumn, with the result that ships were disabled by the autumnal gales and could not be repaired in time to sail early for the next year's campaigns. This is not an unreasonable argument taken in isolation, but to carry real force it has to consider the gains bought by cruising late, in particular the safe arrival of the rich convoys from the West and East Indies which usually came home in August, September or October. These brought the wealth which was critical to the economy, and provided the liquid capital which floated government loans and sustained the war. Because North's skill kept the machinery of government finance working well through the worst crises of the war, it has received little attention, but ministers could not take it for granted. If Sandwich had called in the Channel Fleet in the summer and major convoys had been lost, as they were twice in the war when the fleet was absent, government credit might have collapsed. Strategic advantages in next year's campaigns would have been purchased at the price of inability to carry on the war at all.

These questions cannot be discussed without speculation and are not susceptible of proof, but historians must be prepared to discuss what might have been if they are realistically to assess the judgement of ministers all of whose decisions had to be based on estimates of what might be. It will not do, for example, to state that it was only fear of the political consequences of losing a convoy which drove Sandwich to keep the fleets out, with the implication that convoys had no intrinsic worth which would justify the exercise. There certainly would have been political consequences, as Sandwich was well aware – no government could be expected to suffer so great a loss at sea and remain unscathed in Parliament – but to imply that Sandwich allowed politics to divert him from the war seems to rest on the idea that commerce and finance are subjects beneath the notice of the profession of arms.[11]

Sandwich has frequently been accused of a defensive mentality[12] – the most serious charge possible under the Mahanian code – but the most cogent criticism of the naval strategy of the war is the one which was, and is, seldom made; that it was not defensive enough. Throughout the war Sandwich was under intense pressure from his Cabinet colleagues, from the king, and from his professional naval advisers, to take 'offensive measures', by which they meant to send squadrons overseas to the areas where fighting was taking place on land. 'I see the difficulties of the times', the king wrote,

> but I know nothing advantageous can be obtained without some hazard; I very clearly see that if we alone attend to home security that every valuable possession will be lost before any effort is made to any other tendency but making the country secure against foreign invasion . . . Perhaps no man in my dominion has a mind more ready to bear up against misfortunes, but then I must feel that all that could have been done has; it is by bold and manly efforts nations have been preserved not pursuing alone the line of home defence.[13]

This was moral courage and leadership indeed, but it was strategic folly of a high order. Sandwich was deeply reluctant to dissipate his forces overseas, and wanted to reinforce the West Indies at the expense of America, not Britain.[14] He has been criticized since as he was then for his 'defensive mentality' and reluctance to take risks. But the reason for maintaining the maximum possible concentration of force in home waters was not primarily to defeat invasion, essential though that was. Anson and his colleagues had developed the idea of the Western Squadron thirty-five years before not as a defence against invasion, but as a means of command of the sea. A large proportion of French naval strength was based at Brest and Rochefort. Nowhere in the world were French squadrons more likely to be met with, and more likely to be divided, than in the Western Approaches and the Bay of Biscay. This was the place to find them, and to fight them with advantages, and if they could be defeated there the benefits would be felt all over the world. This was the strategy which had yielded the victories of the two previous wars. It was thoroughly 'defensive', if by that is meant that it kept the bulk of forces concentrated in the critical area, which was near home, until decisive results were obtained – but it had led to crushing victories. Only then were great expeditions overseas mounted, when they could proceed under the distant but certain cover of a superior Western Squadron.[15]

This strategy was as sound in 1778 as it had ever been. Slow mobilization faced the Navy with alarming odds, but decisive victory was still the only way to redress them. The task was more difficult, but it was not less essential, and the unwisdom of French strategy continued to present fruitful opportunities. Sending d'Estaing's Toulon squadron to America in 1778 was an example of the usual French practice of sending out individual squadrons 'en mission' rather than massing a fleet at the decisive point. It invited defeat in detail, and offered an inferior but concentrated fleet the chance of local superiority. If the Toulon squadron had joined d'Orvilliers in 1778, the French would have had a united fleet; by waiting until d'Estaing was known to have sailed Sandwich gained in principle the chance of a great victory over d'Orvilliers which would have changed the war. The same argument held true even after the entry of Spain into the war. A concentrated force in the Western Approaches was the most likely to intercept the French squadrons, none of which were larger than twenty sail and mostly smaller, as they came and went to the Americas. It was also best placed to catch the French component of the Combined Fleets of 1779 and 1781 before they joined. Operating from home bases, the Western Squadron could be kept in the best condition, and under the closest strategic control. Certainly this strategy would have led to initial losses overseas, as it had done in the previous war. Very likely the American war ashore would have had to be more or less abandoned, and certainly some sugar islands would have been lost – but once superiority at sea was gained, there would have been ample time to recover all these.

The basic fault was one familiar to British naval historians; the doctrine of the mindless offensive, which has so often scattered ships in the places where they were least likely to meet the enemy. By sending out squadrons like Byron's, and even by maintaining large fleets on distant stations, the government in effect abandoned control of the war. Being human, Sandwich and his colleagues could not know what was going to happen, and usually they did not know what actually was happening overseas until too long after the event to be useful. Eighteenth-century communications were too slow to make it possible to conduct a world war from London, or anywhere else. Plans might be formulated, but most often they were overtaken by events, and even in home waters commanders-in-chief had to be allowed wide latitude to interpret orders which often turned out to be irrelevant to the situations as they actually developed. During the Seven Years War the British had succeeded by 1758 in imposing sufficient control of European waters to prevent large enemy forces escaping overseas. This gave them the luxury of conducting operations in America and the West Indies without disturbance. With the Western and Mediterranean Squadrons isolating France from her colonies, it was possible to plan operations and launch them from London with some assurance that they would not be disrupted. In the circumstances of the American War, it was simply not possible to exercise competent control over forces spread so widely and so far. As a result it was little better than chance when, where and in what force the enemy might be encountered. So far as the dispositions and knowledge of the Admiralty went, Graves might equally have met de Grasse at the Chesapeake with superior forces, or Rodney have been inferior at the Saintes.[16] Fighting the war overseas reduced it to a lottery, in which the advantage would naturally go to the side with the most tickets.

Sandwich had been closely involved in the establishment of the Western Squadron in the 1740s, and should have been better able to expound its value than anyone in the government. Whether he could have overborne the united voices of his colleagues, the king and most of his naval advisers is doubtful, but he certainly should have tried. It does not appear that he did, at least with clarity and on paper. It has been remarked that at the very outset of the Western Squadron, Sandwich's strategic ideas about it had been clever but somewhat confused, and perhaps they still were.[17] It is clear that he had a general sense of the importance of a concentration in home waters, but he did not defend it explicitly as a means to victory at sea. He has repeatedly been condemned for keeping the Channel

Fleet 'aimlessly cruising', but he did not point out that this was just
the process of loose blockade by which the French and Spaniards
had been defeated in the previous wars. Politicians had always complained about autumn and winter cruising; Newcastle had written in
1747 that 'I don't much taste your friend Anson's long, unsuccessful,
Dangerous, Winter Cruize'.[18] Late in the season, however, was when
enemy squadrons often came home and sometimes sailed, and that
was then they had to be met and defeated; it was in November that
Hawke had won the great victory of Quiberon Bay.[19] It did not
happen in this war in spite of a great deal of cruising, partly no doubt
because of bad luck, partly in all likelihood because of a shortage of
scouting frigates in the early stages of the war, and possibly, as the
king complained, from inadequate intelligence. But it was still the
right thing to do, and no colonial distractions should have been
allowed to dissipate it until victory had been won. Though close
blockade was not initially possible, and was in any case a controversial novelty, it was in the Western Approaches that the war at
sea could have been won, and there alone that Britain had the chance
to take and hold the strategic initiative. Sending forces overseas, too
far away to be effectively controlled, abandoned the initiative to the
enemy, and the outcome to chance.

Given that command of the sea, which could only have been won
in home waters, was not won, and that the war was largely fought
across the Atlantic, there was a dimension to it which ministers did
not properly appreciate. Novel though the problem was, experienced
men like Sandwich should have realized the disadvantages of the
Navy's traditional structure of 'stations'. Dividing the waters overseas into areas each with its own autonomous squadron and commander-in-chief made sense if there was sufficient control of home
waters to minimize interference, but carried considerable disadvantages in a fluid war of rapid movement over long distances, when
powerful squadrons might appear without warning and disappear
no one knew whither. If each British admiral had orders confining
him to his squadron and his station, he would be ill-placed, indeed
unable, to cross into another station to support a colleague. The
institutional structure of command needed radical change to accommodate a new strategic situation, and ministers do not seem to have
realized it.

The physical structure of overseas bases also needed to change,
and here it was largely too late to do what would have needed long

years of investment in peacetime. The fact that each British squadron overseas had a naval yard to support it had been one of the strengths of British naval operations in previous wars, but the yards were quite insufficient to cope with the demands of the American War. A little careening yard like English Harbour at Antigua was sufficient for a squadron of a dozen frigates regularly relieved, but quite incapable of keeping twenty or thirty sail of the line in repair. Only a regular naval yard with dry docks could do that, and the only British docks overseas were in the East India Company's yard at Bombay. Only the East Indies Squadron, therefore, was properly maintained. The practice in the past had been to send ships, especially big ships, home in rotation from the overseas squadrons to be refitted – or condemned as past repair. In this war the situation was so desperate, and the centre of operations in the West Indies so remote, that many ships were kept on station until they literally fell to pieces. There was nothing that the Admiralty could do in the short term but send out as much naval stores as possible and rely on ships' companies patching their ships to keep them going as long as possible. To supply the dockyards which were needed would have been the work of many years, and was not in fact attempted for another century. In spite of all Sandwich's work in reforming the dockyards, they were not in the right place to do all that was needed in this war – though they would have been, had British strategy been sounder.

All these considerations have to be borne in mind if Sandwich's contribution to the strategic direction of the war is to be fairly assessed. Another book is wanted to do so thoroughly; all that can be attempted here is to discuss some key strategic issues in which Sandwich was deeply involved, and use them as illustrations of his contribution to the direction of the war. The first is the crisis which arose in the spring of 1778, as the French moved towards war without having formally declared it, and Keppel's squadron was assembling at Spithead. As always, the geography of France with her three sea-coasts presented British ministers with problems. In principle a sufficient Western Squadron could cover the French naval bases of Brest and Rochefort while at the same time protecting British trade in the Western Approaches and guarding against invasion of Britain or Ireland. What it could not do was cover the French Mediterranean base of Toulon, or any of the Spanish bases. To intercept the Toulon squadron a force would have to be sent into the Mediterranean, or at least as far as Gibraltar. The danger of doing so in any but overwhelming force was obvious, for if French ships escaped from the northern bases, or the Spanish fleet intervened, the squadron sent

to the southward risked being caught and overwhelmed by an enemy
concentration. This was exactly the problem in 1778. A force of
twenty ships under Vice-Admiral Byron was made ready to be
detached from Keppel's fleet to intercept the Toulon squadron under
d'Estaing, but Sandwich strongly opposed risking Byron in a situation in which he might be caught between two fires, especially if
the Spaniards entered the war. Germain naturally took the opposite
line, fearful that d'Estaing's squadron, if left unopposed, would sail
to America and overwhelm Lord Howe's fleet of smaller ships –
which would have ended the American War, if not the world war,
at once. Not for the last time, the Cabinet hesitated between the
two, backing first Germain, then Sandwich. The result was that
Byron did not sail until it was known for certain that d'Estaing
actually had gone to America, by which time Byron was too late to
catch him.

Sandwich has been heavily criticized for opposing Germain and
his American policy. Historians who know that d'Estaing was going
westward have attacked Sandwich, who did not, for being over
cautious, and praised Germain for his correct assessment of the situation. But Germain was simply backing his department, arguing
that the fleet ought to save his bacon rather than someone else's. If
Byron had sailed early for North America, d'Estaing's orders could
easily have been changed. Seapower is inherently flexible, and the
French had won a victory at the opening of the previous war by just
such a last-minute alteration of plans. No responsible minister could
ignore the danger of invasion, which was on any rational assessment
infinitely more serious (though perhaps less likely) than the risk to
Lord Howe. Nor could Sandwich ignore the chance of defeat if
Byron had been sent south to Gibraltar and caught between two
French fleets. A decisive defeat early in the war would have been
disastrous, and the loss of America would have been the least of the
consequences to be feared. Above all, sending Byron threw away
the chance of decisive advantage in home waters, where it really
mattered, for an uncertain hope of achieving something in America.[20]

Sandwich (and Keppel) with their reluctance to detach ships from
the main fleet, had the right instinct, but in the absence of a naval
strategic doctrine they were unable to formulate it with sufficient
clarity. In practice ships had been detached in the previous wars well
before decisive command was achieved. From the twentieth century
it is easy to point out that circumstances were different with only
one enemy to face, and that the Western Squadron had always been
kept clearly superior to the enemy. There were no precedents for

Sandwich to draw on which would have supported a complete refusal to reinforce overseas squadrons, and yet with the balance of forces in 1778 nothing less ruthless would have sufficed to make victory possible. The situation was novel, and rigorous analysis was called for to expose its essentials. There is nothing in Sandwich's papers to show that he appreciated them with the necessary clarity.

Byron sailed late, and to save time risked the more direct route straight across the North Atlantic, where he encountered violent storms which damaged and scattered his squadron. D'Estaing reached North America early and found Howe's much weaker force unprepared. A bold attack might have changed the course of the war, but d'Estaing was not bold. With great tactical skill, Howe arranged his little squadron in a strong defensive position behind the island[21] of Sandy Hook off New York, and d'Estaing would not risk taking his big ships across the shoal water of the bar to attack them. Instead he sailed on to the West Indies, where much the same thing happened again. The British commander-in-chief in the Leeward Islands, Rear-Admiral Barrington, had only lately arrived himself, and had no idea that d'Estaing was coming, but he found in General Grant a kindred spirit, and together they had mounted a rapid and successful attack on the French island of St Lucia, strategically placed to provide a base to watch the French headquarters of Martinique. They had barely done this when d'Estaing appeared, and hesitated long enough to allow Barrington to moor his little squadron in a strong defensive position. This time the French did attack, and were repulsed. So St Lucia was held, but Barrington was too weak to prevent the French in turn from capturing Grenada, and Byron was too late. Like d'Estaing, he appeared just after the enemy had completed landing on the island. D'Estaing chose to fight under sail, Byron launched a bold attack which went wrong, and but for the caution of his opponent might have ended in a real defeat. D'Estaing went on to mount an attack on Savannah in Georgia which was driven off with loss, while Byron returned direct. At the end of 1779 both admirals were back home with very little achieved.[22]

Holding Byron back until it was clear that the French were not planning a concentration in home waters risked America for the sake of higher priorities at home. 'The object of the war being now changed, and the contest in America being a secondary consideration',[23] Byron's place was at home. The logic of the decision which the ministers had half-taken when France entered the war was that America was not worth so large a diversion of forces.[24] By sending d'Estaing's squadron across the Atlantic the French were running a

big risk which might have been exploited. If Howe had been left to
fend for himself, which in the event he had to do anyway, and
Byron's ships had remained with Keppel's fleet as Sandwich and
Keppel wanted,[25] the balance of naval power in home waters would
have been transformed. The battle of Ushant, had it been fought,
would have been fought at odds of at least five to three in Keppel's
favour. Had d'Orvilliers stayed in port, which is perhaps more likely,
Keppel could have established a loose blockade of Brest. Either way
the naval war would have taken a potentially decisive turn in Britain's
favour, much earlier than it had done in the previous war. This
was the decision indicated by logic and tradition, this was the bold
concentration which might have yielded early victory.

It did not happen because ministers, like modern historians, could
not get America out of their mind. If the king had been prepared to
admit the logic of abandoning most of America until France was
defeated – and the logic of abandoning Germain which went with
it – the French folly in splitting their fleet when they might have
united it would have opened the chance of a decisive victory before
Spain could enter the war. True, decisive victory early in a war was
rare, but at the available odds it was far from impossible, and it was
the best chance of retrieving their error in mobilizing late. Instead they
imitated the French, sending Byron's squadron on a costly wild-goose
chase half across the world. With him vanished the only chance of
driving France out of the war and depriving the American rebels of
support. Evacuating most of America would certainly have allowed
the rebels to consolidate and the loyalists to suffer, but in the long
term it was probably the only hope of establishing conditions by
which the rebellion might one day have been defeated. Unfortunately
for North and his colleagues, neither Parliament nor the king would
have been prepared to support a government which abandoned
America altogether, even in the hope of recovering it later.

What was worse, the campaign in America was unexpectedly favourable. This is ironic, since the success derived from the naval
strategy which Sandwich, Palliser and Mulgrave had developed in
December 1777 and persuaded the Cabinet to adopt.[26] This assumed
that America would be largely evacuated, with troops holding only
a series of naval bases from which to carry on a cruiser war in
American waters. One of these was needed in the south; from this
idea developed the biggest and most successful British amphibious
operation ever mounted, the great expedition which in May 1780
captured Charleston, took a large part of the rebel field army and
opened a new theatre of operations in the southern states. It allowed

Germain to argue that victory was just around the corner, and persuaded ministers to divert resources back to America, now the least important and least promising of their responsibilities. But Sandwich always remained unconvinced. For him America was a strategic backwater.[27] It presented the Navy with an enormous administrative and logistical problem, but it was not a likely theatre for decisive fleet action. The bulk of the ships, and the best of the talent, were reserved for home waters and the West Indies. This of course increased Germain's resentment and redoubled his efforts to undermine his colleague.

Sandwich's principal naval scheme for 1779 combined the relief of Gibraltar, under siege by a Spanish army, and the reinforcement of the West Indies. As soon as the Combined Fleet left the Channel and Hardy's fleet had returned to port, a squadron was made ready which in December sailed under Vice-Admiral Rodney. The operation was a triumphant success. Coming down the coast of Spain, Rodney met a Spanish squadron in the night, and in an action fought by moonlight in a rising gale, close inshore, he captured six ships of the line. He then went on to relieve Gibraltar and arrived in the West Indies early in 1780.

Here it is necessary to digress to explain why Barrington was no longer commander-in-chief in the Leeward Islands, and how Sandwich came to lose the services of another talented admiral. When the news of Barrington's action at St Lucia reached England by unofficial channels, Sandwich at once wrote a letter of congratulation. The official Admiralty letter was written later than Sandwich's, when Barrington's despatches had been received, and it was less fulsomely worded than Barrington had expected. It appears that Philip Stephens the Secretary of the Admiralty, overworked and ill, had delegated the drafting to a subordinate and failed to check it before it went out. The two letters reached Barrington together. A second private letter from Sandwich was written on 5th August, after Barrington had left the West Indies, and must have crossed with him in mid-Atlantic. He chose to interpret the Admiralty letter as a deliberate slight, and refused to believe that Sandwich's second letter had ever been written. When another copy was sent him he denounced it as a forgery; when Sandwich arranged for a backdated replacement Admiralty letter in eulogistic terms, he dismissed it as inadequate.[28] This mattered, for Sir Charles Hardy died on 18th May, and Barrington was the obvious successor. Unfortunately he had now taken so violent a dislike to Sandwich that he refused to serve again.

The loss of Keppel, Howe and now Barrington, serious though it was, proceeded from no common cause. Keppel's alienation was the result of political activities going back twenty years, exacerbated by Palliser's rash attack. Howe had no political objections to serving if the ministry had been prepared to pay his price. Though he later went into opposition to justify himself, his true motive was honour, or ambition, or greed – the reader may choose the appropriate term. With Barrington the explanation must be sought in his difficult character.

> Admiral Barrington will allways be found to be a dark, troublesome, & impracticable man; his turn is towards complaint both in great & little things, & tho' I do not believe that he has any particular disinclination to this administration, he is very likely to be drawn in by flattery properly placed (to which he is very open) by Admiral Keppel's faction.[29]

He did not stand out for anything for himself, apart from praise, and his political connections were with the government in which his brother was a minister, but he was a hard man to please. 'I never perceived in him the least disposition to faction of any sort', his brother wrote,

> and whenever he is not pleased it is on a ground of his own. He is much attached to his friends, but is to the full as likely to differ from them in opinion as they were his enemies. He certainly loves me as much as any man in the world, but not having the least influence on his mind I may fairly conclude no other man has any.[30]

His reasons as given in private are incoherent.[31] His explanation to Sandwich is best given in Sandwich's words:

> The death of Sir Charles Hardy has occasioned many embarassments; our first scheme was to let the command of the fleet devolve to Barrington; in which idea I sent for him to town, when after a conversation of above an hour & my having used every argument to prevail upon him to take the command, he obstinately declined it on the single ground of his unfitness, and unalterable determination never to command in chief: however in the course of our conversation I got out of him that he thought the fittest person in the Kingdom to command the fleet was Admiral Keppel. You well know my opinion is that the fleet cannot well be commanded by an enemy to government,

therefore in pursuance of that idea the command is given to Admiral Geary who with the help of Kempenfelt will I hope do at least as well as your late commander.[32]

'Charming, spirited, honest Captain Geary'[33] was one of the best known and best-liked sea officers of his generation, and over the years successive senior officers had found him the ideal second-in-command.[34] A fine seaman and a gallant officer, Geary could be trusted to carry out unambiguous orders with the minimum of fuss. What had not hitherto been detected in him was the independent initiative needed in a commander-in-chief. 'Though my friend Geary is a stupid fellow', Boscawen had written twenty-five years before, 'he is a good officer and will do his duty without noise, confusion or puffing himself after'.[35] 'A Brave, Honest, good temper'd Man', was Hawke's verdict; 'I am only afraid of his being too Easy, and that he will subject himself to be blamed as Sir Charles Hardy was, for letting the discipline of the Fleet come to nothing'.[36] Geary was in many ways another Hardy, and he has been condemned on the same grounds, with the complaints of the same commentators, especially Kempenfelt. Once again the root of the complaint was Geary's refusal to be managed by his subordinates. One of the few modern commentators to have examined the Channel Fleet's operations in the summer of 1780 concludes that Geary's handling was skilful and effective.[37] Had he had the good fortune to meet the enemy and fight a successful action he would no doubt have been praised as an inspired choice. As it was he did all that he reasonably could have done, and he was well suited to carry on the essential work of unifying and reconciling. Where he may be faulted, and Sandwich for choosing him, is in being too old (he was about seventy, though he lived another sixteen years in good health) and comfortable to bring the fleet to the high state of efficiency which was badly needed – but as always this objection has force only if a better alternative commander-in-chief can be pointed out.

Barrington was the obvious choice, and he came to the fore again in August when Geary fell ill. As the second-in-command, Barrington was ordered to take the fleet to sea in his chief's absence. He refused to carry out the orders. This was no better than mutiny, and left the Admiralty no choice but to dismiss him.[38] In his place the Channel Fleet was given to Vice-Admiral George Darby. Darby was one of a younger, less experienced generation of senior officers to whom, perhaps, Sandwich should have turned earlier. Modest, able and apolitical, Darby proved to be the commander-in-chief the

Channel Fleet had long needed. Though forgotten to naval history because he never fought a great battle, he can be cited as one of the best sea officers whom Sandwich identified and advanced. He calmed the spirit of faction which Barrington had reawoken, while supplying the professional drive which was equally needed.[39] 'I never saw an officer who took such proper pains to make himself agreeable to those under his command, without sacrificing the discipline of the Service,' wrote Mulgrave,

> I have seen many instances of steadiness and temper in his behaviour that showed his fitness for employment and nothing to make me doubt of his acquitting himself in every situation of service with honour to himself and advantage to his country. I say this the more freely, as I have never been consulted in his measures, which, I believe, are generally taken as they ought to be from his own judgement, which is very sound, or when that is proper, by the advice of the flag officers serving with him.[40]

'There is a manliness and plain firm sense about Admiral Darby that will make him do everything for the best', Mulgrave wrote on a later occasion, adding significantly that it was wise of this 'plain but valuable man' to have given Kempenfelt command of a division rather than taking him as a First Captain, which 'would have had an appearance of being managed'.[41] Evidently Kempenfelt's character was well understood by his colleagues.

The whole subject of Sandwich's choice of flag officers has been bedevilled by misconceptions. It has been argued, or assumed, that the pool of talent was infinitely large, or that it can only have been his fault if Keppel, Howe and Barrington refused to serve. It has also been assumed that he alone could choose commanders-in-chief. This very issue caused a violent dispute in Cabinet in 1777 when Germain tried to exercise a veto on Sandwich's choice of admirals for the American station:

> From what passed between us this morning, I guess that I am to be sacrificed to Lord George Germain's intrigues; I am sorry for it, on my own account, & much more so on account of the cause which I have firmly supported under Ld North, & to whom I have ever shewn every proper attachment . . . if Lord George Germaine is to canvass the conduct & appointments in my department I have a right to claim the same power in the land part of the American war, which I can shew has been at least as injudiciously administered as the naval arrangement . . .[42]

John Robinson's reply to this letter is revealing. He assured Sandwich that 'every thought of your being sacrificed to the intrigues of Lord George Germain is totally groundless', and proceeded to hint at the political unwisdom of choosing admirals like Sir Peter Parker, whose qualities were not approved 'in the opinion of the world, of Lord North, and of the Cabinet'; or like Graves and Shuldham, 'equally objectionable from these gentlemen's not carrying with them popular opinion or confidence'.[43] When the Secretary of the Treasury, North's political manager, spoke of 'popular opinion', he was not referring to sentiment in the country at large, still less to expert opinion within the Navy, but to votes where it mattered, in Parliament. The essence of his objection was that Sandwich was choosing flag officers on professional grounds, at political cost.

> If persons are appointed who do not carry with them public opinion, dissatisfaction will arise, even before anything happens; murmur and discontent will prevail, and it will at last break out into a flame that must destroy the fabric . . . War can't be carried on in departments; there must be consultation, union, and a friendly and hearty concurrence in all the several parts which set the springs at work and give efficacy and energy to the movements, without which the machine must fail.[44]

In the name of Cabinet solidarity, Sandwich was obliged to accept the Cabinet's right to consider the appointment of admirals, and on several occasions officers were appointed in whom Sandwich had no confidence. This was notably the case with Commodore George Johnstone, who commanded the naval side of the abortive 1781 expedition to the Cape of Good Hope. Johnstone was an enemy of Sandwich (also of Germain, with whom he had fought a duel)[45] but an independent politician with a support sufficient to buy North's alliance and command his choice of employment.[46] Sandwich would rather have entrusted the expedition to Sir Robert Harland, one of the Capulets who had repented and offered his services, 'but for God's sake how is it to be taken out of the hands it now is in?'[47]

It is too often assumed that the North American station was the centre of naval activity, which deserved the best available admirals. In fact after 1778 it was a strategic backwater in which only small forces of ships of the line were maintained, and it was the least likely part of the world in which to fight a fleet action. What was needed there was primarily an experienced naval administrator to run the immense logistical effort required to support the army. This is the background to the appointment of Marriot Arbuthnot to be commander-in-chief North America in 1779. Few admirals have been more severely criticized,[48] and yet he had many of the needful qualities for the job, and achieved a great deal in the face of severe difficulties. 'A judicious as well as zealous officer',[49] he was a man of initiative, who was not frightened of big decisions.[50] He had to co-operate with General Sir Henry Clinton, who had talents as a tactician but little strategic judgement and a paranoid suspicion of everyone around him.[51] No senior officer of either service ever managed to keep up a working relationship with him for long, and it is much to Arbuthnot's credit that he preserved cordiality long enough to mount the great Charleston expedition, an amphibious triumph which alone would entitle him to be taken seriously as an admiral.[52] In spite of his age, he showed great determination in the difficult blockade of the French squadron at Rhode Island during the winter of 1780–81; he acted with speed and decision when they escaped in March, and the resulting battle, mishandled and indecisive in itself, saved the army under General Arnold which the French intended to trap in the Chesapeake.[53] It is true that Arbuthnot was sixty-eight and his health was failing; it is also true that the breakdown in relations with Clinton may have contributed to the British failure to mount an attack on Rhode Island in 1780 – if Clinton meant the idea seriously, which is not certain.[54]

Much of the criticism of Arbuthnot, however, springs from an incident which deserves more attention. On 14th September 1780 Sir George Rodney, commander-in-chief in the Leeward Islands, arrived off Sandy Hook without any warning, announcing that he had come to take over Arbuthnot's station. He had come to avoid the hurricane season, and because of intelligence, which proved to be incorrect, that a French squadron was coming north from the West Indies. This at once exposed a glaring weakness in British command arrangements, for no mechanism existed by which Rodney could legally assume, or Arbuthnot legally resign, the command of the North American station. Modern historians have universally assumed that Rodney, being the senior of the two admirals, had an automatic right to command wherever he pleased, and this was precisely what he claimed: 'the Commission I bear intitled me to take the supreme Command, which I ever shall do on every Station where His Majesty's and the Public Service may make it necessary for me to go'.[55] He had no legal foundation whatever for this. A commander-in-chief commanded by virtue of orders from the Admiralty, founded on the king's order conveyed by a Secretary of State. As a matter of course a commander-in-chief was always the senior officer of the squadron, but it was by virtue of his orders and not his seniority that he commanded. In certain circumstances a more senior officer might be present without interfering with his command. This often happened in the Leeward Islands, for ships going to Jamaica (for much of the eighteenth century the more important of the two commands), had to pass through the Leeward Islands to get there. A relief commander-in-chief Jamaica might therefore pass through the Leeward Islands station without disturbing the authority of the local commander-in-chief, his junior but not his subordinate. Rodney's orders as commander-in-chief in the Leeward Islands explicitly confined him to his station, and contained no permission to leave it under any circumstances. He was allowed to send ships to reinforce the Jamaica squadron if necessary, but his responsibilities were limited to whatever attacks on French or Spanish colonies might prove possible, and 'the general protection of His Majesty's Possessions and the Trade of His Majesty's Subjects within the Limits of your Station (which must always be the principal objects of your care & attention)'.[56] Only the arrival of a successor bearing orders to relieve him, and orders to him to hand over, could absolve him of his responsibility. Barrington had had the same orders before him.[57] A commander-in-chief was empowered, sometimes ordered,[58] to assist neighbouring stations by sending them reinforcements, but he had no authority himself to leave his own station or enter anyone else's. When the Admiralty intended any such authority, it always wrote it specifically into a commander-in-chief's orders. Arbuthnot, for example, had permission to enter the Newfoundland station, 'notwithstanding it is out of the Limits of your command', in pursuit of a French squadron if necessary – but even in this case, he did not assume command of the station, but left the local commander-in-chief (who would invariably be junior to him) in local command.[59] If a French squadron entered the North American station, he was to 'follow & pursue it with the whole or such part of your force as you shall judge necessary wherever you shall be informed it is most likely to be met with within your command', but if it left for the West Indies he was to remain on his station and detach his second-in-command in pursuit.[60] His predecessor Lord Howe had orders in the same vein to pursue the enemy 'within the limits of your Lordship's Command', and to detach ships to the Leeward Islands to serve under the commander-in-chief there.[61] Byron's flying squadron, belonging to no station, sailed under special

orders which empowered Byron to take command of the Leeward
Islands station on arriving there if he should be senior to the local
commander-in-chief, as in the event he was – but this was a special
case, specially provided for, and even so Byron tried to leave the
ordinary duties of the station to Barrington.[62] There was nothing to
cover Rodney's unexpected action. 'I am not qualified to decide as
to the powers of a superior officer, under your situation, having
quitted his station, by his own authority, and endeavoured to super-
sede an Admiralty Commission, and in a great measure obstructed
the execution of the powers the King has vested in me', Arbuthnot
wrote, with justice.[63]

Yet Rodney had real and good reasons for what he did. The hurricane season was not itself a strong argument, for the big ships of
the Leeward Islands usually avoided it by going south to the Spanish
Main rather than far north to America,[64] but if French squadrons
were going to pass between North America and the Caribbean, the
British had to be prepared to do the same, and there might be circumstances in which a commander-in-chief needed to come himself
rather than send a part of his squadron under a subordinate. Any
other admiral would have openly avowed that he had used his initiative and broken his orders in the name of an unforeseen strategic
necessity. But Rodney was not a normal admiral; there was in his
character an element of gratuitous deceit which often led him into
dishonesty when honesty would have been the best policy. With all
the very considerable art of which he was capable, he set about
claiming that his seniority gave him a natural right to take over
Arbuthnot's command. To every influential correspondent he sent
letters congratulating himself on his wisdom and virtue, and accusing
Arbuthnot of greed and spite.[65] This was the usual tenor of Rodney's
views on everybody, and must have been familiar to his regular
correspondents, but on paper Rodney's smooth insinuations still
carried more conviction than Arbuthnot's blunt expostulation,
though there is no doubt that on every point of substance Arbuthnot
was right.[66]

The question naturally arises why Rodney did not rest his defence
on strategic necessity, his best and strongest point. The question
would not have occurred to his contemporaries. Even in an age when
officers joined the Navy to make their fortunes, and when gentlemen
were expected to look out for their own interests, Rodney had an
evil reputation for rapacity. They would have taken it for granted,
as Arbuthnot did, that his object was to add the prize money of a
second station to his own. Any prudent and selfless admiral, even

Right: Captain Maurice
Suckling, Sandwich's first
appointment as Controller
of the Navy

Left: Sir Hugh Palliser,
Sandwich's leading naval
follower, by George Dance

Right: Sir Charles
Middleton, painted some
years after he worked
with Sandwich

Left: Martha Ray, from a portrait in Admiralty House

Right: The first Lord of the Admiralty, by Gainsborough. This was painted after he had left office, for the Greenwich Hospital collection; the buildings appear in the background, and he is holding the plan of the new Infirmary which he added

Left: A sketch of Sandwich by C. Bretherton soon after leaving office in 1782; though visibly aged by the strains of the American War, he seems already to have recovered much of his former buoyancy

Below left: the orchestra and choir gallery constructed at the west end of the nave of Westminster Abbey for the 1784 Handel Commemoration. Joah Bates is seated at his keyboard in the middle, below the organ

Below right: The Royal Gallery (*above*) and Director's Gallery (*below*) against the choir screen of Westminster Abbey at the 1784 Handel Commemoration. The Directors are visible, holding their wands of office

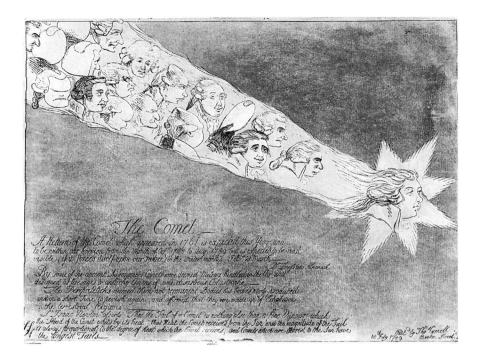

Above: Sayers' cartoon 'The Comet' showing the Prince of Wales and his followers falling out of the political sky at the end of the 1788 Regency Crisis; Sandwich is near the end of the tail, at the top

Right: The last portrait of Sandwich, painted by Thomas Beach in 1790

without Rodney's reputation to live down, would have made his first action on arriving at New York a declaration that he would not interfere with either the patronage or the prize money of Arbuthnot's squadron.[67] This was the first essential if he was to have any hope of co-operation from the other. It would have taken superhuman forbearance in an eighteenth-century admiral, however firm his sense of duty, to accept the authority of another commander-in-chief whose motive for taking over appeared to be no more than theft. Rodney did nothing to dispel, and everything to confirm the idea. Leaving Arbuthnot the exhausting and dispiriting task of blockading Rhode Island, he settled himself comfortably ashore at New York and devoted his attention to amassing as much money as possible.[68] When he left, he immobilized the transports by impressing their crews, took with him two of Arbuthnot's frigates and nearly all the naval stores in the yard.[69]

As soon as Rodney's and Arbuthnot's letters started arriving in England it should have been obvious to Sandwich and Germain that they had opened an issue which would have to be dealt with. Either commanders-in-chief had to be strictly confined to their stations, in which case Rodney was as Arbuthnot claimed, a deserter,[70] to be disavowed and punished, or arrangements must be explicitly made to regulate how and when station limits might be crossed. There was much logic in the suggestion, made for their respective services by both Rodney and Clinton, of a single commander-in-chief for both North America and the West Indies.[71] Against it was the fact that communications made it no easier to control such a vast area from New York than from London, but at least the question needed to be addressed. All Sandwich did was to warn Rodney not to interfere with other people's patronage in future. He backed Rodney against Arbuthnot, but avoided the substantive issue, and left other admirals in the future to work out local arrangements as best they could.[72] Defending himself in 1782, he claimed that 'it was a measure taken . . . that the whole of the Leeward Islands fleet should move to join Admiral Graves', and a marginal note in his papers added, 'Standing orders were given to this effect in 1779, and repeated in succeeding years, but though moved for by Lord Sandwich, not pressed for prudential reasons'.[73] What this is meant to mean is unclear, but there were no standing orders allowing a commander-in-chief to leave his station, nor was Rodney *ordered* to go north in 1781, though he was 'recommended' to do so in certain circumstances.[74] The only 'standing order' was the occasional general exhortation to stations to support one another, of which the first was issued in December 1779.[75] In September 1780, for example, while Rodney was actually at New York (though the fact was not yet known in England) the Secretary of the Admiralty wrote that:

> Their Lordships command me to remind you that they consider the whole of His Majt. Possessions on the Continent of America, as well as in the Islands, as requiring the attention of the Commanders of all His Fleets in those Seas, and that therefore they conclude you will act for the Defence of the whole according to such Information as you receive of the motions of the Enemy.[76]

Without powers and orders to act, this was nothing but a platitude, and whatever Sandwich may have urged in private, he did not achieve any clarification of this crucial issue. From orders issued in December 1779 by the Admiralty at Germain's direction to Rear-Admiral Hyde Parker, who was left in command of the Leeward Islands when Byron and Barrington went home, it looks as though Germain thought that Parker had inherited Byron's orders, and was at liberty to pursue d'Estaing north to Savannah.[77] In fact Parker was Barrington's successor as station commander-in-chief, but even if he had inherited Byron's powers, it did not follow that all succeeding commanders-in-chief in the Leeward Islands would do so, nor did Byron's orders provide for this situation.[78] This confusion was in a way the counterpart of Germain's repeated neglect to establish clearly which, if any, of the generals in North America was the commander-in-chief to whom the others reported – but Sandwich should have tried to clear up Germain's confusion. This is one of the most critical failures of the North administration, for the failure to settle command arrangements would have made it impossible to carry out a unified strategy had it existed. Here it could fairly be said that 'the want of Courage that has marked the Resolutions of the Cabinet in all their Acts since the Year 1774, may be considered as the chief reason why Things have been attended with so little success in the execution'.[79] Very likely Sandwich could never have carried a decision on his own, for it would have been highly contentious, but he certainly should have raised the question, and it does not appear that he ever did. His long official memory went back to the time more than thirty years before when Sir Peter Warren had proposed a unified American command.[80] He was better equipped than any of his colleagues to face the issue.

All this is relevant to the events of the autumn of 1781, when it was French and British squadrons sent unexpectedly into North America waters which decided the issue of the American War on land, and indirectly the fate of the North ministry and the political career of Sandwich. In the summer Rodney was still the commander-in-chief in the Leeward Islands, and faced the same decision as he had the previous year. He had intelligence indicating that the French squadron would send at least part of its force northwards before the hurricane season, and there were indications which he might have interpreted to suggest that the whole French force was going together. But this was a surprising idea, involving abandoning French convoys homeward bound from the West Indies to concentrate on the periphery, and Rodney ignored it. He also failed to pass on what information he had either to the commander-in-chief in North America, or to his own second-in-command Sir Samuel Hood whom he detached with half his squadron to reinforce Arbuthnot.[81] Rodney, in short, decided not to repeat the previous year's controversial experiment. We cannot tell how far he was influenced by the consideration that he could not hope to take the extra prize money a second time; he was certainly ill and anxious to spend a winter ashore in England rather than in America.

After the event Rodney falsified the record in an attempt to show that with his customary brilliance he had foreseen the French move and kept the commander-in-chief North America fully informed of it.[82] In fact it was only the arrival of Hood which brought the first, partial news of what was afoot, to add to the excellent local military intelligence which Clinton possessed, though he did not correctly assess it. The situation with the command of the station was now in a state of confusion which flowed naturally from the Admiralty's and government's failure to sort out who commanded what. Arbuthnot had gone home, leaving the command in the hands of Rear-Admiral Graves,[83] who had brought out reinforcements from the Channel. Arbuthnot's relief Vice-Admiral Digby arrived just as Hood did, but declined to take command in the instant emergency. The combined squadron therefore sailed from New York under Graves, with Hood as his second-in-command, to face an emergency created by the unexpected concentration of the whole French West Indies squadron under de Grasse, the whole Franco-American army under Rochambeau and Washington, and a large British army under Lord Cornwallis. Cornwallis had set out from Charleston the previous year on an independent campaign which had at length brought him to the southern shore of Chesapeake Bay. There was very little co-ordination, or even communication, between Cornwallis and Clinton, and Germain had failed even to make clear which was in overall command. Once arrived on the banks of the York River, Cornwallis experienced a mysterious paralysis, and made no attempt to evade or to break up the enemy armies which were very slowly concentrating against him. Nor did Clinton attack the army marching south across New Jersey, presenting a vulnerable flank to him in New York. Instead both generals remained inactive, and Cornwallis allowed himself to be besieged within makeshift defences at Yorktown.

This would not have mattered if Graves had come to the rescue, as Arbuthnot had rescued Arnold six months before. The big difference was that Graves had to deal not only with the small French squadron from Rhode Island, but with a much larger one from the south – bigger than his own force, and much bigger than he had any reason to suspect. Moreover he had shortly before received orders from London to cruise for a French supply convoy heading for Boston, which had left his squadron in need of repairs and delayed his move south.[84] Off the Chesapeake on 5th September Graves and Hood met what they took to be the combined French squadrons coming out to meet them, and fought an indecisive action marred by the failure of Hood's division to come into proper action. Hood was a gifted tactician with a successful action in the West Indies to his credit; he was also a gifted publicist with many friends in high places, whose version of events, laying all the blame on Graves's ambiguous signals, has been generally accepted. There is a strong counter-argument. Graves came from the Channel Fleet where he had been involved in Kempenfelt's tactical reforms. He was an excellent manager of men associated with the new ideas of initiative and delegation which were to be the key to future tactical development; 'very knowing in his Profession, distinct and clear in his understanding'.[85] Hood had spent most of his recent career ashore as Commissioner of Portsmouth Dockyard, and the rest serving under Rodney, who stood for an uncompromising autocracy in which the commander-in-chief took every decision and subordinates, including subordinate flag officers, were allowed no liberty to think or act for themselves.[86] With the primitive and ambiguous signals available this had already proved to be a recipe for confusion and recrimination.[87] Graves had only a few days in which to meld squadrons accustomed to different signalling systems, different Fighting Instructions, and above all different traditions of command. He would have been very lucky to have achieved outright victory in the circumstances. Moreover he did not know that Cornwallis was going to do nothing and allow himself to be trapped,[88] nor did he know that he had fought only de Grasse's force from the West Indies – in other words that the French were about to be largely reinforced by the squadron from Rhode Island. He therefore had no reason to believe that the situation was urgent or getting worse, and no incentive to run extraordinary risks by, for example, trying to slip into Chesapeake Bay behind de Grasse as some armchair critics have suggested. It is well he did not, for Cornwallis's fate was largely decided by his own inaction, and if Graves's squadron, damaged after the battle, had allowed itself to be trapped in the Chesapeake by a French fleet half as large again, it would probably have led to the loss of both fleet and army.[89]

The surrender of Cornwallis's army was the fault of the Navy in the sense that the North American squadron might in other circumstances have been able to retrieve the generals' blunders and evacuate the troops. As it was, the battle of the Chesapeake gave the French local command of the sea for the crucial few weeks, and brought about a victory which led directly to the independence of the United States. In Britain the news finally precipitated the fall of Lord North's government and the installation of a ministry led by the Marquis of Rockingham and determined on peace with America. In France it reached ministers who had already secretly determined to abandon their American allies and seek an accommodation with Britain before the balance of power swung any further against them.[90] At the last possible moment, against long odds, the Yorktown campaign rescued the sinking rebellion. The French navy and General Washington could fairly take most of the credit for a daring, even desperate strategic move which just paid off.[91] Sandwich could and did claim that the Admiralty had done what it could, that enough ships were available in the Americas just to match the French, if the admirals had taken all the right decisions – but this avoided the crucial issue of command and control.[92] To say that 'the American stations must support each other and consider the whole as a joint service; the enemy pursue that conduct, and we must do the same'[93] was very true, but did not explain why the Admiralty had not issued any orders to make it possible. In December 1781, after the news of Yorktown had reached England, the transatlantic commands were ordered more explicitly to co-operate and reinforce one another without waiting for orders, but still the question of authority was not cleared up.[94] Had North and his colleagues confronted that question earlier, there might not have been so much resting on the decision of a relatively junior officer deprived of most of the necessary intelligence.[95]

For the Americans, Yorktown came just in time, but for the French, it came too late. Slow, painful, grievously delayed though it might be, British mobilization had by the end of 1781 produced a fleet the equal of the French and Spanish together.[96] Vergennes, one of the most clear-sighted ministers of the day, could read the signs.[97] By the spring of 1782 they were evident to all.[98] On 9th May Rodney at last won the great victory in the West Indies which had so often eluded him. It is true that the Saintes owed as much to French tactical weakness as to British brilliance, and that it was nothing like as crushing as it might have been had it been properly followed up, but its moral effect was enormous.[99] On both sides, it was seen to restore the two fleets to their positions of twenty years before. A new confidence and unity began to be felt on British quarter-decks, while among the French, recrimination, hatred and mutual court martial ensued in a fashion strongly reminiscent of the Keppel–Palliser affair.[100] In terms of numbers, the allies were still at least equal, and the Spaniards, the only belligerents whose campaigns in America had been uniformly successful,[101] were flushed with victory and determined to press on to the recapture of Jamaica and Gibraltar.[102] But the French saw the writing on the wall, and it seemed to say that yet again their fleet had been weighed in the balance and found wanting.

In European waters the Cabinet's decision in December 1780 to declare war on the Dutch had added another enemy. The reason was to make it possible to cut off the flow of naval stores carried from the Baltic in Dutch merchantmen, and from Holland into France by inland waterways. At the cost of mounting a blockade of the Dutch coast, and adding a dozen or so ships of the line to the enemy total, there was a prospect in the medium term of crippling the French fleet. This was a bold policy which Sandwich took the lead in drawing up.[103] It is also virtually the only occasion on which we have an account of the progress of a Cabinet meeting. Since policy and strategy were decided in Cabinet, and we have no record of its discussions, nor even of the conclusions in many cases, it is not possible to speak easily of Sandwich's personal rôle in such decisions, though we can infer his opinions from other sources. In this one case we have a description of the course of the meeting which took the momentous decision to break one of Britain's oldest alliances and declare war on the Netherlands. The meeting was held over dinner, and foreign affairs came round with the port, with the natural results:

The Ministers who met were Lord North, the Chancellor, President, three Secretaries, Sandwich and Amherst. The first and third fell asleep as soon as the business was opened – Lord Hillsborough nodded and dropped his hat; Lord Sandwich was overcome at first, but rubbed his eyes and seemed attentive. Lord Amherst kept awake, but said nothing. Lord Stormont, the reader of these important papers, the Chancellor and Lord George Germain only gave them consideration, but when the others awoke they approved of what was proposed.[104]

This needs to be treated with scepticism, however. The narrator is William Knox, Germain's Under-Secretary, who must have had the story from his master. Germain undoubtedly wanted it to reach the king and as many other people as possible, to make his Cabinet rivals look foolish. It is not to be taken as an impartial narrative of what actually happened on this occasion, nor of the Cabinet's usual working methods.

In this case Sandwich himself, with the longest diplomatic experience of anyone in the Cabinet and the closest concern with the question of naval stores, took the lead in its bold decision. The even bolder naval strategy adopted at the end of 1781 was primarily the work of his professional advisers. The events of the summer of 1781, when another Combined Fleet had paraded the Channel in strength too great for Darby to risk giving battle, without achieving any result of consequence, had encouraged Middleton and Kempenfelt, among others, to develop a radical and daring strategy.[105] The North Sea had become a theatre of war, obliging the Admiralty to find ships for yet another squadron to blockade the Texel. The new scheme was in effect to abandon the Western Squadron except for a force of about twenty fast ships of the line. It was calculated that they would be adequate to make any invasion scheme impossibly difficult. The bulk of trade would be diverted northabout into the North Sea, where a strong squadron would watch the Dutch and cover trade into both the Atlantic and the Baltic. The forces thus freed would go to the West Indies to secure there a crushing superiority and decide the issue of the war. If North's government had not fallen in March this strategy would have been adopted in 1782.

This strategy was as unsound as ever in 1782, and decisive victory was still most likely in the Western Approaches. The fact that such highly capable and experienced officers as Kempenfelt and Mulgrave were prepared to concentrate British strength in a remote quarter of the world, far away from the Admiralty which might control the ships or the dockyards which had to maintain them, shows how difficult it would have been for Sandwich to insist on a sound strategy in the teeth of his professional advisers as well as his colleagues. The only argument in favour of the new strategy is that with large French and Spanish squadrons already in the West Indies, and Jamaica threatened with imminent invasion after which the rest of the British West Indies would have followed, it was perhaps too late to concentrate at home. The enemy had been allowed to choose the decisive theatre of war, and had naturally chosen that least advantageous to Britain. It could be argued that it was now too late to seize the initiative in home waters; for both military and political reasons the enemy had to be checked in the Caribbean. Nevertheless the chances of victory were certainly much lower there than they would have been in home waters, and the chances of the unexpected and the uncontrollable were much higher.

Sandwich has often been criticized for not having sufficient naval advice to hand,[106] with his Admiralty colleagues often away at sea, but the evidence suggests that he depended very closely on them, especially on Mulgrave.[107] The new policy of concentrating in the Caribbean was adopted on the advice of Mulgrave, 'whose opinion as to the making our great effort in the West Indies was what I shall allways acknowledge as one of the principal causes of our adopting that measure'.[108] Sandwich might be accused of depending too much on the admirals and not thinking sufficiently deeply for himself, but he cannot be fairly charged with ignoring them. When he did go against professional advice, for example over the appointment of Sir Samuel Hood to a sea command over the objections of Lord Mulgrave,[109] the event did not necessarily vindicate the admirals. But on strategy Sandwich did not usually resist his advisers, and not until the great enemy fleets of 1779 and 1781 had paraded the Channel and achieved nothing were admirals prepared to take the unprecedented and still very risky step of leaving the Channel largely uncovered. A growing sense of their own power, and a growing realization of the weakness and disunion of the enemy, tempted them into greater daring.

So did a technical development which did more than anything else to redress the balance of naval power between 1778 and 1781. To describe it we must return to Sir Charles Middleton and the dockyards. Two severe restraints hampered the operation of wooden ships, one in warmer waters, the other throughout the world. In the tropics, and sometimes in home waters where it had been brought by returning ships (notably at Sheerness), the shipworm, *teredo navalis*, ate away submerged woodwork leaving the outer surface intact and the inside a honeycomb. The result was that ships could only be kept operational in the West Indies by sheathing their bottoms in several thicknesses of fir plank, which were regularly eaten by the worm and had regularly to be renewed. This levied a heavy penalty in lost time and increased weight, and at best was never more than a partial protection. Everywhere the bottoms of ships were covered by marine plants and shellfish which slowed them down. In practice the length of time a ship had been 'off the ground' (meaning since she had last been docked to clean her bottom) determined her speed far more than the skill of captain or designer. Naval operations were severely affected by the need to dock ships regularly, which sharply reduced the amount of time each ship was available for service.

The first experiment with sheathing a ship's bottom with copper plates was tried with the frigate *Alarm* in 1762, and covered only her keel. This was sufficiently encouraging to lead to the complete coppering of three small vessels in 1764, the *Tartar*, *Dolphin* and *Tamar*. The results of these trials showed that copper not only protected against the worm, which was the object, but that by a process not then understood, it remained smooth and clean. The result was that a coppered ship had no need to be docked regularly to have her bottom cleaned and held a large margin of speed over uncoppered ships. The trials also showed that the presence of copper caused severe corrosion to the iron bolts and fastenings in the underwater hull, including the rudder irons. This presented a considerable difficulty, and the Navy Board does not appear to have taken note that the *Dolphin*, fastened with copper bolts, had avoided the corrosion problems of the other two.[110] Further experiments were undertaken.[111] In 1770 the *Hawke* sloop was sent to the East Indies, coppered and with the heads of the iron bolts capped with lead. She returned in 1775, the experiment a great success in all respects except that her ironwork was much corroded. Sandwich inspected her on his tour of the dockyards, which may have awakened his interest in coppering.[112]

It certainly engaged the powerful attention of Charles Middleton, who set to work to develop a method of avoiding corrosion. Middleton's method consisted essentially of coating the bare hull in layers of waterproofed brown paper before the copper plates were fastened on top. So long as a watertight seal was preserved, copper and iron could not react against one another. The problem with this method was that wooden hulls were inherently flexible, and the chances of the paper seal remaining long intact as the hull 'worked' in a seaway were poor.[113] But Middleton's talents at self-persuasion were unequalled, and after perfunctory trials he convinced himself that the problem was solved. He then convinced Sandwich, and in 1778 the momentous decision was taken to copper the entire fleet. An immense industrial effort was needed simply to obtain the copper required and hammer it into sheets of the desired thickness. For three years the dockyards laboured to copper every ship as she came in for refit, until by 1781 virtually the entire fleet was copper sheathed.[114] At the end of that year Sandwich claimed to have coppered 82 ships of the line, 14 50-gun ships, 115 frigates and 102 sloops.[115]

The results astonished even the most sanguine. Captains found that the slowest ships with copper bottoms could outpace the fastest without.[116] Admirals found that a coppered squadron was so comfortably faster than one without that it was safe for a small force to hang about a much larger one, harassing and teasing it, in the confidence that only by the grossest blunder could they be caught. For the dockyards, the effect of coppering was to reduce enormously the burden of docking and cleaning, just as the fleet grew to its largest. The number of refits carried out on 74-gun ships was seventeen in 1776, thirty-one in 1777, twenty-seven in 1778, thirty-one in 1779, thirteen in 1780 and 1781, and only eight in 1782, when the fleet was at its maximum size.[117] The average ship of the line was docked 0.87 times a year between 1770 and 1777, but only 0.52 times a year from 1778 to 1782.[118] In the short term, at least, coppering provided what Sandwich had long been looking for; a means of keeping up a much larger number of ships with the existing yards. By saving the necessity of frequent docking, copper in effect increased the size of the active fleet as ships were able to spend so much more of their time in service. Uncoppered ships spent an average of one-quarter of their time docking and refitting.[119] If coppering had saved all of that time, it would have been equivalent to a one-third increase in the size of the fleet, which Middleton claimed it was.[120] It permitted ships to be employed in the West Indies in winter and at home in summer, with no lengthy refits in between.[121]

The immediate result of coppering was to make it even more difficult to handle a fleet in company. Hardy, for example, had seven coppered ships, which meant seven ships which could only with great difficulty be made to sail as slowly as the rest of the fleet. As soon as they experienced the results of copper, every flag officer wanted their ships coppered, above all in the West Indies. 'To bring an enemy to action', Rodney wrote after the Moonlight Battle, 'copper bottom ships are absolutely necessary'.[122] By 1781 British squadrons everywhere enjoyed a huge advantage in speed over the enemy fleets, in which only a few ships were coppered. It was this which made Rodney's victory possible at the Saintes, and it was this which made Kempenfelt's 1782 strategy conceivable. Only a coppered squadron, in the presence of uncoppered enemy fleets, had the margin of speed to make it safe to cruise in the presence of a superior enemy.

The policy of coppering the fleet, undertaken in haste without adequate experiment, was daring and risky. It was characteristic of Middleton that having persuaded himself and Sandwich of the rightness of the plan, he would admit no doubt of its perfection. Yet unknown to him, serious problems were developing. The paper seals were not reliably watertight. Since coppered ships did not need to be often docked, and many of them were anyway years away from home and docks, there was no opportunity to examine what was going on under their copper. Ships on a wooden bottom had to be regularly docked, when defects in their bottoms would naturally be noticed. The problems of copper bottoms were invisible. By 1781 officers were becoming aware that coppered ships began to develop major defects, often with alarming suddenness, after about three years at sea. At the battle of the Chesapeake,

> We felt severely the danger of keeping coppered line of battle ships long out without looking at their bottoms, as the *Terrible*, one of the finest seventy-fours we had, by her exceeding bad state even before she left the West Indies, and by the firing of her own guns, and the enemy's shot in the action, was found in so desperate a state that she was ordered to be scuttled and set on fire, which was done the night after we lost sight of the French fleet, it being thought impracticable to keep her above water until we got into port.[123]

Her loss prompted this reflection from the same witness, the captain of the *Resolution* in Hood's squadron:

> Next month the ship will have been three years coppered and out of dock, which is the usual time of their service; and from the loss of the *Terrible*, and the very bad state of the ships of the same standing, it is probable they will go home at nearly the same time. It is remarked that copper-bottomed ships, when they once begin to show their defects, drop all at once, which is the case of the *Invincible*, who is now in as bad a state as the *Terrible* was, and several others, which they are afraid even to trust home.[124]

It is clear in retrospect that the problem was electrolytic corrosion affecting the iron fastenings. A number of ships which foundered in the closing year of the war, including the famous *Royal George* (coppered two years seven months before her loss in August 1782), may have been affected by it.[125] It is certain that the end of the war came fortuitously for the coppering process, allowing ships to be paid off and examined at leisure which otherwise would have been driven on until they fell apart. As it was Middleton for long refused to believe any evidence of corrosion and dismissed the enquiry which was set on foot in 1782 as useless.[126] In the end the solution was discovered: bolts and fastenings of a hardened copper alloy. An expensive programme of replacement was set on foot, and by the 1790s the whole fleet was copper-bottomed and copper-fastened, ready for another war against a French fleet which was still struggling to overcome the technical problems of coppering.[127]

In almost every respect the coppering programme was a triumph for Sandwich. Undoubtedly he was misled by Middleton's over-confidence, and was running greater risks than he knew, but he was lucky in this (if not in any other) respect that the war ended when it did. Meanwhile copper had transformed the performance of the British fleet and contributed enormously to restoring, or even reversing the balance of power at sea.

It had one other effect, which did not become evident until long after Sandwich's time. Regular docking was not only a chance for a ship's bottom to be inspected for defects, but also a chance for the ship's company to have leave. During this war, 74-gun ships refitting spent on average thirty-eight days preparing for the dock, three weeks actually in dock, and another forty-three days preparing for sea afterwards – over eleven weeks in all, with good prospects of leave especially during the three weeks in dock when there was little for the ship's company to do.[128] Copper allowed the ship to be driven like a machine for months or years at sea, and the exigencies of a war against odds, with many of the ships deployed overseas where there were no docks, enforced the same ruthless pace of work. But ships cannot sail without men, and they too were driven much harder than had been necessary or possible before. Copper, introduced during a desperate war in which every ship was needed, must have been the major factor in reducing or eliminating regular leave. Some captains welcomed it precisely because they never had to land their men or suffer desertion.[129] Hitherto leave had been natural, relatively painless, almost automatic.[130] Now it meant disabling a ship which could otherwise be in service. The greater the reliability of the ships, the harder the strain on the men. It is not fanciful to trace a direct link between coppering and the great mutinies of 1797.

Another technical innovation which Middleton persuaded Sandwich to adopt, and Sandwich then pushed through against opposition, was the type of light but powerful gun called the carronade. Mounted on the upper decks in place of the small pieces hitherto mounted there, carronades enormously increased the weight of fire ships could bring to bear on an enemy's decks without any increase in weight, or of men needed to man the guns. They contributed significantly to the victory of the Saintes, and helped to spread among the French the impression of resurgent British power. Their adoption had to be forced through against the opposition not only of the Ordnance Board which supplied the Navy's guns, but of Lord Mulgrave, Sandwich's principal naval adviser.[131]

The American War was in some respects the worst crisis in the Navy's history, when the country came nearest to a complete defeat at sea. It survived at least as much because of the blunders of the enemy as the good judgement of its leaders. The attention of the king and most of his ministers was firmly fixed on the periphery of events, and Sandwich lacked both the clarity of thought and the strength of position to call them back. On the matters entirely within his department – administration, shipbuilding, and patronage – he could claim an excellent record. On strategy and policy, which he had to share with the king and his colleagues, the results were very much more mixed. It seems certain that Sandwich could have had clearer and better ideas on them than he did. We can never tell whether he would have been able to get them adopted, but it would have been well to have tried. All this, however, is the wisdom of hindsight, on a subject about which able judges with complete knowledge still cannot agree. It should not surprise us that ministers with incomplete knowledge of what was going on, and none at all of what was going to happen, made mistakes in dealing with novel and perplexing difficulties. In the end they failed in one part of the task they were set, the suppression of the American rebellion, but it must be doubted if success in the terms they sought was really available. However talented a British ministry might have been at making war, the political situation in the colonies had moved beyond the point at which a lasting restoration of royal authority was feasible. The best they might have achieved would have been a peace imposed by force of arms, leading to a political settlement stopping short of immediate independence. In the other and more important part of their duty, where success was possible but very difficult, Lord North and his colleagues had certainly turned the corner to victory by 1782. At the least they had preserved the country and almost all its possessions outside North America, which intelligent observers like Keppel thought impossible in 1778. Time was to show that what seemed like a disastrous defeat had cost the country very little but money and prestige, and preserved for it the means of future power and greatness. First among these was a rebuilt and revivified Navy.

CHAPTER XVI

Music at the Close
1782–1792

The news of Cornwallis's surrender at Yorktown arrived in December 1781, and set in train a political crisis which led to the downfall of North's administration. The immediate consequence was disunion within the ministry, as some of its members sought to save their position by jettisoning their most unpopular colleagues. The two pointed out were the two most involved in running the war, Germain and Sandwich. The opposition sought to exploit the disaster by launching a Parliamentary enquiry into the management of the war, and especially into the war at sea. Sandwich spent January working hard on his defence in Parliament, and attempting to buttress his position with his colleagues.

> Lord Sandwich said he feared nothing from that enquiry unless there should be a party among the friends of government who wished a change of administration, and meant to effect that purpose by forcing out the First Lord of the Admiralty, who probably they considered as a principal outwork, which must occasion the surrender of the place; that he knew he could prove to demonstration that the exertions while he had been at the head of the department had been carried on to the utmost extent that the strength of this country would admit of, and had infinitely exceeded anything that was ever done before.[1]

He had to devote much attention to persuading North and other colleagues that his defence of the management of the Navy stood on as firm ground as he said it did; he and Middleton had a three hour meeting with the chief minister early in January.[2] As the minister with the longest experience and the strongest nerves, Sandwich remained more confident than his colleagues. Until the news of Yorktown their Parliamentary position had been good, the opposition weak, divided and lackadaisical. He believed that the administration could surmount this defeat as it had surmounted others.[3] Informed observers agreed. Horace Walpole, no supporter of

Sandwich, noted in January that he 'has numerous foes too, but more friends'.[4] Those in a position to know shared Sandwich's confidence that the Parliamentary enquiry would damage rather than assist the opposition: 'The Public is big with expectation upon it: but it is the name which beguiles, for they have no Grounds to go upon within their reach to mature into a Charge'.[5] But Fox, leading the attack in the Commons, avoided discussing the strength and condition of the fleet, on which Sandwich's ground was strongest, and concentrated on its employment. The ministry's majority was reduced to only twenty-two votes; 'Lord N horrid sick'.[6] In spite of the sacrifice of Lord George Germain, who resigned in February, the ministry's position continued to weaken. As late as 15th March Sandwich had not given up hope: 'From what I have heard to-day I am persuaded that if Lord North did not despond and talk of giving the thing up, matters would not yet be irretrievable'.[7] But by this time they were. North's efforts were now directed to persuading the king to yield gracefully and to send for the opposition leaders, Rockingham and Shelburne, who alone could form a new government. On 20th the North ministry resigned.[8]

It is conventional to regard this as the end of Sandwich's public career, and virtually the end of the American War, but he had seven years of active politics ahead, and the war was not concluded for twelve months.[9] The fall of Lord North ended twelve years of stable government, and ushered in two years of confusion and intermittent crisis. A succession of weak and transient ministries attempted to end the war and secure their own position on the basis of hesitant support from king and Parliament. Sandwich, who had seen all this often before in his long career, had no reason to despair of returning to power. His party in the House of Commons, carefully nurtured over twelve years in office, was second only to North's own when the ministry fell. No one knew better than he that it had been built up with the help of the patronage available only to a minister, and would not indefinitely survive in opposition, but so long as power seemed to be within his reach he could and did retain the support of his followers, and the strength of a man whose favour was worth obtaining. 'At present my Parliamentary interest is very considerable', he told North a few days after they resigned. 'Your Lordship knows that it is so without my naming names, but if I am reduced by my circumstances to live in absolute retirement, that interest will soon sink to nothing, and my means of doing any service to this distressed country be utterly annihilated'.[10] In November and again in February 1783 he reckoned to command twelve or more MPs.[11] In February nine followed his lead in voting against the peace terms, and in March John Robinson reckoned his party to number eleven.[12] Even after the 1784 general election he still had three or four – a significant party by eighteenth-century standards – and was worth the cultivation of leading politicians.[13]

Meanwhile the new administration showed few signs of strength or stability. Within a month of its taking office its members were concluding 'that the jealousies are too great for this Administration to hold long'.[14] In the summer Grafton considered that 'The Circumstances are such that I look with the utmost Diffidence on the Probability of the present System continuing any Time';[15] and Sandwich wrote that 'I do not think this administration can stand without much additional strength, but I am well assured that they have procured no such strength as yet'.[16] Rockingham remained ineffectual as minister or politician, and in July he died. His successor Shelburne was preferred by the king but hated and distrusted by virtually everybody else in the political world. Intelligent and excellently informed, he was completely unable to build working relationships with his colleagues.[17] He undermined Keppel, the new First Lord, by dealing secretly with Middleton behind his back.[18] Charles Fox, the ministry's best speaker in the Commons, resigned after Rockingham's death.[19] By December, with Keppel and Richmond openly opposing the peace terms put forward by the government, the Shelburne ministry was publicly disintegrating, while Lord North 'appeared throughout the whole debate not only pre-eminent in talents of every description, but as the arbiter of the scene'.[20]

Sandwich's MPs played an essential part in the February 1783 defeat (by sixteen votes) of the Shelburne ministry's peace terms.[21] 'There never was any political measure in which I more pointedly took the lead than in the present, nor by which I have gained more Political consequence', he wrote.[22] The result was a new and to contemporaries extraordinary coalition ministry formed by North and Charles Fox, representing the majority of the Rockingham Whigs. This seemed to be Sandwich's opportunity to return to office.[23] The strength he had to offer was considerable; his difficulty was that he was tainted by association with an unsuccessful war, and not popular with enough of his prospective colleagues. Furthermore the constitutional reforms pushed through by the previous government had considerably reduced the number of offices available, and consequently increased the difficulty of reconciling different interests. After prolonged negotiations during April, the best offer Sandwich could obtain was the sinecure of Ranger of the Royal Parks.[24] He explained to Mulgrave his reasons for accepting; the

> late political negociations . . . have indeed been very unpleasant, and Lord North's desertion of my interests is what I shall never forgive. I am very unwilling to throw myself into an Opposition headed in one house by Lord Thurlow & in the other by Mr Pitt; such an engagement is neither suited to my time of life, to my natural disposition nor I believe to my interest & that of my friends . . . what Lord North had to dispose of is gone among his own relations & immediate dependants, and his principal friends are left to shift as they can. Was my fortune affluent, the part I should take would be to support government without an office, but I am sorry to say (which you will conceive I do in the utmost confidence of friendship) that an addition of income is very necessary to me, & that I have not time to set Ministry at defiance . . . I am offered a sinecure office, which with some douceurs that will be added to it . . . will tolerably answer my immediate purpose.[25]

Thus Sandwich returned to government, if not to power, just over a year after he had left it. But the Fox–North coalition proved to be not much more stable than its predecessor. The king worked actively for its downfall, and a crisis arose in December over its bill for reforming the East India Company. This was highly contentious in itself, and was used by George III to encourage opposition to the ministry which he so much disliked. On 18th December he dismissed the coalition, and invited the young William Pitt to form another ministry.[26]

Sandwich remained loyal to the coalition, voted for the India Bill, and when his colleagues were dismissed, resigned his office of Ranger of the Parks. Undoubtedly he hoped, as the others did, that the king's new 'mince-pie' administration would last no longer than Christmastide. Lacking a Parliamentary majority, with no ministers of consequence and experience, it seemed impossible that Pitt at the age of twenty-five could hold together a lasting ministry. These reasonable hopes were falsified. Pitt not only survived, but in April fought a general election which left him with a comfortable majority. He was to remain prime minister for the next seventeen years.[27] Fox, North and Sandwich retreated once more to opposition. Resignation and the general election disposed of the bulk of Sandwich's following. Several of them lost their seats, though he held both Huntingdon seats against the general trend.[28] Some, including his own son

Hinchingbrooke and his closest naval colleague Mulgrave, accepted office under the new government and parted company with him.[29] It was hard for younger men with a career to make to accept opposition whose position looked every bit as hopeless as the Rockinghams' had done twenty years before. Sir Hugh Palliser held to the old maxim that no honest man could oppose his sovereign's chosen ministers, and gave up his Parliamentary seat rather than be forced to choose between Sandwich and the king.[30] Of North's former close colleagues, few remained loyal to him. John Robinson, for so long his Parliamentary manager as Secretary of the Treasury, moved rapidly to serve first Shelburne and then Pitt, earning the nickname 'Jack Renegado the Ratcatcher'.[31] William Eden's defection in 1785 created a furore, and contemporaries repeated with relish Sandwich's terse reply to his letter announcing it: 'Sir, your letter is before me, and will presently be behind me'.[32]

When Rockingham and Shelburne took office in March 1782 they at once set on foot negotiations for ending the war with the Americans. It was Shelburne's private approaches, undertaken without the knowledge of Fox the Foreign Secretary, and following a quite different policy from his, which led to Fox's resignation in the summer. Meanwhile, however, the war continued on all fronts, and there was no immediate intention of seeking peace against France, Spain and the Netherlands. With a great Franco-Spanish force mustering in the Caribbean to attack Jamaica, the Spaniards preparing for a final assault on Gibraltar, and another Combined Fleet intending to enter the Channel to support an invasion scheme, the new ministry faced one of the worst crises of the war.[33] It has been explained that North and his colleagues had agreed to adopt a very daring plan to counter it, by which almost everything would have been risked to obtain a crushing superiority in the West Indies. The new ministry reverted to a cautious position. Without actually abandoning the West Indies, Keppel refused to reinforce them at the expense of a concentration at home. Only with the greatest reluctance did he consent to send the Channel Fleet to relieve Gibraltar.[34] Lord Howe, who replaced Darby as commander-in-chief, conducted a masterly defensive campaign in the face of a superior enemy, but the relief of Gibraltar was the only positive achievement possible.[35]

Though the new ministry planned to evacuate America and use the troops to take the initiative in the West Indies, they had no conception of the practical problems involved. Co-operation between Keppel and Middleton was non-existent, and the Controller learned of the evacuation plan when he read about it in the newspapers. At once he proposed a scheme for carrying it out, but his ideas were ignored; the possibility of an offensive was lost and the army spent another year in America doing nothing because the new ministers were too preoccupied and incompetent to manage the move.[36] Keppel's incapacity aroused the indignation of the king,[37] and the annoyance of his colleagues. In the face of a possible invasion his 'anxiety & uneasiness were beyond Description'.[38] Moreover his handling of patronage was foolish and vindictive. From the first his object seemed to be to revive all the divisions which Sandwich had laboured to heal, and impartial observers deplored. Putting Howe and Barrington in to command the Channel Fleet was uncontroversial, except in the price he had to pay to secure Howe (promotion to full admiral, an English peerage, and his brother's appointment as Lieutenant-General of the Ordnance),[39] and it could be justified by results. Otherwise Keppel's appointments seemed to be based chiefly or only on political allegiance. He dismissed George Jackson the Second Secretary of the Admiralty, the first such dismissal since 1690.[40] His unsuccessful efforts to eject Palliser from the Governorship of Greenwich Hospital, if possible without bearing public responsibility for the act, aroused general disgust.[41]

Above all he made himself look very foolish with the replacement of Rodney. In itself this was defensible; the admiral was untrustworthy, ill and bitterly unpopular. Unfortunately for Keppel the order to haul down his flag had no sooner been sent than the news arrived of his great victory at the Saintes. In fact unofficial news reached Keppel in time to recall the order, but he declined to do so.[42] The result was acute embarrassment for the government, and much pleasure for Sandwich:

> it is indeed a glorious event, the value of which I think is by no means diminished by the blow that it gives to this Administration, whose measure of recalling Sir George gives universal discontent. I have received congratulations from all sorts of people, and the world seem unanimous in giving the merit of it to the late Board of admiralty to whom it is certainly due.[43]

The contrast between Rodney's barony and recall after two great victories, and Keppel's new viscountcy and promotion to First Lord after a disappointing skirmish, was an obvious target for satire.[44] What made it worse was the choice of Hugh Pigot to relieve Rodney. Admiral Pigot's political links with Keppel were warm (and he was Howe's brother-in-law), but he had last been employed, as a captain, in 1770, and his unremarkable sea career had in effect ended at the peace twenty years before.[45] He had declined the chance to serve in 1778.[46] Moreover Pigot shared Fox's passion for gambling, and it was rumoured that he had been given the command to satisfy a debt of £17,000 which Fox could not pay.[47] As commander-in-chief he was amiable, corrupt and idle. The rigid discipline established by Rodney disintegrated, and the defeat of the Franco-Spanish invasion of Jamaica was left largely to their own disunity.[48]

In strategy as in politics, 1782 and 1783 was a tale of what might have been for Sandwich; the great victories which might have been possible for a fleet at last restored to the peak of its strength and recovering its old confidence and cohesion. With peace concluded at last, and Pitt's ministry secured by the 1784 election, Sandwich's hopes of once more holding high office began to fade. He remained an active politician, taking the lead, for example, in opposing Parliamentary reform,[49] and to the end of his days he retained the esteem, so characteristic of his generation, for the British constitution as the most perfect in the world. Addressing the Huntingdonshire Grand Jury in 1791, he contrasted the happy position of England with the distracted state of France racked by revolution:

> I . . . congratulate you and the rest of my countrymen upon the happy state in which we find ourselves under the best constitution, and the best government that the ingenuity of man has ever formed. While other nations are involved in intestine troubles, & threatened with bankruptcy, civil war, & every other calamity that an unhappy people ever experienced, England is governed by mild & gentle laws, made & executed by ourselves; laws that ensure our property & our liberties, and under which a person who is not contented to live, cannot I am sure be contented any where.[50]

But before this he had had one last chance of regaining high office, in the crisis caused by the king's illness in 1788. This was the first of the severe attacks of what contemporaries regarded as madness, and has now been identified as porphyria.[51] Fox and the opposition, now gathered around the Prince of Wales in the traditional Hanoverian fashion, rejoiced (very indecently in the case of the Prince and his disreputable friends) at the prospect that a regency would have to be declared. This they assumed would easily and automatically make the Prince the effective sovereign, and themselves the new government. Sandwich had been cultivating the prince for some years, and at the height of the crisis the prince, who called him 'the

first *Marine Minister* that ever this Country had',[52] promised him the
Admiralty in the administration he expected soon to form. This
caused a rift within the opposition, whose leaders had not been
consulted, and under heavy pressure the prince was obliged to
withdraw his offer. So Sandwich's last hope evaporated, followed
almost at once by the hopes of the whole opposition, as the king,
amidst the rejoicing of his subjects, recovered his sanity and resumed
his reign.[53]

It is easy enough in retrospect to see that Fox, the Prince of Wales
and his friends never had so strong a position as they imagined, and
that Fox handled the crisis disastrously.[54] It was clear as a result of it
that Sandwich remained too controversial a figure among politicians
most of whom had been in opposition throughout the American
War, to retain a hope of returning to office, at least by that route.
Yet from the perspective of the Navy Sandwich looked a much more
attractive First Lord in 1788 than he had in 1782. Keppel as First
Lord from March 1782 to January 1783, and again under the
Fox–North coalition in 1783, had been incompetent and vindictive.
Lord Howe, First Lord from January to April 1783 and again under
Pitt from December 1783 to July 1788, was austere and impartial,
but his relations with his Cabinet colleagues were extremely poor,
and his refusal to allow politics to influence his handling of patronage
aroused exactly the same anger that Sandwich had experienced.
'Patronage', Howe complained, as Sandwich could have warned
him,

> was not so desirable as might be imagined. Whenever a vacancy in the
> appointments in his nomination happened, there were always twenty
> candidates for it, at least. He was sure therefore to disappoint nineteen,
> and was not always certain of pleasing the twentieth.[55]

A promotion of admirals in 1788 generated so much heat that the
friends of the disappointed mounted a Parliamentary attack on the
First Lord. On this occasion Sandwich, although he was in opposition and might fairly have resented the treatment he had received
from Howe, spoke in his support, and recalled his part in the establishment of the 'yellow admiral' scheme nearly forty years before.[56]
By this time some sea officers had come to remember Sandwich
with nostalgia:

> I never have nor do I ever expect to receive a favour from you; at the
> same [time] I must add that I never knew any one who acted with

more disinterestedness, ability & honour to himself & country than your Lordship during your presiding at the board of Admiralty.[57]

Where Howe was 'austere, morose and inaccessible', Sandwich was 'courteous, affable and easy of access . . . a most perfect master of Naval etiquette'. He was 'full of liberality, sound sense and penetration', in contrast to his successor 'enveloped in mystery, and perplexed with errors'.[58] When the fleet mobilized in 1790 under Howe's command, he was extremely unpopular. There were violent quarrels and resignations; 'party runs very high and they are sadly disunited'.[59]

From one quarter in particular Sandwich received warm encouragement. Sir Charles Middleton had spent the years of renewed peace elaborating the administrative reforms which the experience of the war had suggested. In Pitt he had found a sympathetic minister who provided the Navy in peacetime with the votes needed to continue much of the work of rebuilding which Sandwich had begun.[60] What he had quite failed to find was a First Lord who appreciated his talents. To Keppel and Howe, he was a meddling Scotsman who had failed in the Navy and was now trying as a civilian to interfere with their authority. Neither of them cultivated a working relationship with the Controller, or enjoyed the support of their Cabinet colleagues. Neither took an interest in the management of the dockyards, supported Middleton's reforming schemes, or protected him from political interference in dockyard appointments.[61] Lord Howe was replaced in July 1788 by Pitt's elder brother Lord Chatham, who was amiable and had the merit of 'connecting the department of the Admiralty with the rest of the Administration, which has never yet been the case under Pitt's Government, even in the smallest degree',[62] but was incurably idle and indifferent to Middleton's enthusiasms. With the experience of six years under three different First Lords, Middleton was able to estimate Sandwich at his true value, and he longed to have him back:

It is generally said that your Lordship may have the Admiralty if you chuse it, and that you deliberate on the acceptance of it. If your Lordship hesitates from a remembrance of former times, I have only to say – That the Military part of the Service have since that time been brought to distinguish between your Lordship's conduct & those that followed you in office – and the Civil Branch is in that State as to secure your Lordship the full Credit of restoring that Navy which you had so great a share in raising.[63]

Reading this letter must have been a melancholy satisfaction to Sandwich, who already knew that he had failed in his hope of returning to office.

Melancholy, however, is the wrong word to describe Sandwich in his last years. Though he remained the complete politician, for whom loss of office was always a deprivation and the hope of regaining it always a stimulus, he seems to have experienced the fall of North's ministry as something of a private liberation. We have little evidence for his personal life during the war years. Concerts, clubs and dinners seem to have been severely curtailed by the burdens of his work. His trouting expedition to Newbury in June 1776 was apparently his last holiday, and Christmas 1776 was the last of the Hinchingbrooke music meetings. The night Martha Ray was murdered, and probably most other nights as well, he was working late at the Admiralty. Not only his duties but the violent passions of those years provided a reason to stay indoors. Sandwich received several death threats,[64] and narrowly escaped with his life when his coach was attacked during the Gordon Riots in 1780.[65] Freed from the exhausting and dispiriting business of managing an unsuccessful war, he was able to return to the pleasures of private life – and he had not lost his zest for life. He resumed reading for pleasure – in October 1782 he read six volumes of Livy's Roman History in a fortnight.[66] 'I could not but look with admiration at the Earl, who at our age can enter into any pursuits and find them amusing! It is pleasant to have such spirits . . . after going through such busy political scenes',[67] wrote Horace Walpole in 1785, after Sandwich had come to breakfast with the Reverend Mark Noble, a clergyman who had published a promising but inaccurate history, *Memoirs of the Protectorate-House of Cromwell*.[68] Sandwich took both author and work in hand, supplied numerous corrections, introduced Noble to people with relevant manuscripts, solicited subscriptions for the second edition, and finally helped the young man to a better living.[69] Nor were reading and historical research his only vigorous activities. In 1786, when he was actually sixty-seven, he admitted to his friend George Coleman the dramatist that he was the 'wrong side of sixty-five – but Sexagesima Sunday, tho' after Xmas, yet comes before Lent'.[70] His public image was certainly not lenten and penitential. The author of a satirical pamphlet of 1782, proposing to reform the constitution and pay off the national debt at a stroke by auctioning the members of the House of Lords, imagined Lord North knocking down Sandwich in these terms:

A Man of gallantry, a *quondam* minister of *integrity*; and, to sum up his perfections, a lot of incomparable *virtu*. Old, yet not decrepid; a debauchee, yet warm as beauty could wish to fancy him; with a penny in his pocket, yet careless, and exulting as the deity who guards him from the skirmishes of unequal love, and secures him from the destined hazards of impeachment. At the n–y board, or at a catch club, absolute, and unrivalled. In his senatorial, or his domestic capacity, inimitably wonderful; in this house, great, in Mother –'s, greater: In address, incomparable; in undress, ravishing![71]

The innuendo was not entirely unjustified.[72] In 1787 Major Arabin, one of the Prince of Wales's court, wrote proposing a new actress for Sandwich's revived theatrical company: 'She has played publicly six Times, but not by her own name. She is hardly twenty, stage mad, a pretty voice, and has always lived with her parents'.[73] One cannot help wondering exactly what part she was expected to play. Sandwich himself no longer appeared on stage, but he wrote prologues.[74] When the Prince of Wales visited Hinchingbrooke for Christmas 1789, the entertainment included not only concerts, catches and glees, but productions of old favourites such as *Love à la Mode*, *The Mock Doctor*, *The Virgin Unmasked*, and *High Life below Stairs*.[75] In London he appeared regularly at the Catch Club; in 1791, the year before he died, he attended three-quarters of the meetings.[76]

Of all his old enthusiasms, music remained the deepest. Amidst the trials of a lost war and a collapsing career, with society shaken, political life in turmoil, and the country driven for ever (as it seemed) from the ranks of the great powers, only Handel recalled the happier days of Sandwich's youth and Britain's greatness. 1784 was thought to be the centenary of Handel's birth,[77] which suggested to the circle who directed the Concerts of Ancient Music the idea of a Handelian celebration to mark the occasion.[78] This developed into the great Handel Commemoration, 'in some ways the most important single event in the history of English music during the eighteenth century'.[79] Sandwich was the patron, organizer and moving spirit of the Commemoration, and Joah Bates was its musical director. Under their leadership, with the enthusiastic patronage of the king, the Commemoration grew to a scale which had never been seen before in England. The whole Broad Aisle, the western part of the nave of Westminster Abbey, was fitted up by the architect Thomas Wyatt with elaborate wooden galleries for musicians and spectators, in

Gothic style to match the Abbey.[80] The choir and orchestra were banked up at the West End, with the galleries for the royal family and the directors facing them against the choir screen, and galleries for spectators down either side. There was seating for 4,500 people, and so many demanded to be admitted that the original programme of three concerts (including one of secular music in the Pantheon in Oxford Street) had to be extended by repeating two. Five hundred and twenty-five performers were directed by Joah Bates. In order that Bates should see all his forces, his keyboard was 19 feet horizontally and 27 feet vertically below the organ, connected to it by mechanical linkages.[81]

> The Organ a very fine one built for Canterbury Cathedral was in the *center* & by a contrivance of the Organ builder, your Brother was brought near the front of the Orchestra, eighteen feet from the Organ he played, by which means he could see the whole band, and they could see him, and had no time beater which is a terrible eyesore, but was wholly conducted by the motion of his head or his holding up a hand, & it was the wonder of the world that a band consisting of 500 performers should go more perfectly together than was heard before.[82]

A choir and orchestra on such a scale had never been seen before, and experts like Charles Burney thought it impossible that they could be brought to keep time, but the result was a triumph both of music and organization. Even the most sophisticated were overwhelmed by the grandeur of the occasion and the music. *Zadok the Priest*, which began the first concert, starts quietly with an instrumental introduction before the choir enters suddenly. Skilfully managed, it is a dramatic moment even with a few singers; on this occasion 'the force and effect . . . almost took me off my legs, and caused the blood to forsake my cheeks'.[83]

Burney was one of the modern scholars who were not uncritically enthusiastic about Handel, but in the face of Sandwich, Bate and George III he became deeply involved. The king had always been 'very fond of old music, particularly of Corelli. I don't like the present compositions. They are too quick and hurrying.'[84] Burney found him 'full as *intoleratingly* fond of the old Saxon as B[ate]'.[85] In a moment on enthusiasm Burney agreed to write the official account of the Commemoration, which involved him in much more work than he had anticipated, especially as he found that he was expected to forgo his royalties in favour of the musicians' fund for which the Commemoration was being held.[86] He also had reservations about

Sandwich's fondness for drums, and for archaic curiosities like trombones, which proved to be nearly impossible to find,[87] and in Burney's opinion by no means delightful to hear:

> At the Commemoration of Handel, the double drums, double cartels, tromboni, &c. augmented his lordship's pleasure, in proportion to the din and stentorophonic screams of these truly savage instruments; which, in so wide a building as Westminster Abbey, and softened by so powerful a chorus of voices and instruments as were assembled at the Commemoration, had, occasionally, a fine effect; but in a more confined space, the almost incessant use of the tromboni, and perpetual roll of the double drums, annihilate all the pleasing effects of mellifluous harmony.[88]

Less sophisticated observers were impressed by 'such prodigious kettle drums, that most powerful instrument the trombone'.[89]

The Commemoration was a celebration of national reconciliation, a healing of wounds opened by war and politics.[90] For the first time since 1708 the monarch attended a concert in person. The first programme included the Dettingen *Te Deum*, celebrating the victory at which George II had taken command, and the anthem *Zadok the Priest* written for his coronation. The third consisted of the *Messiah*, already acquiring the status of a national work uniting every strand of Protestantism. The Evangelicals so prominent at the Ancient Concerts, Methodists and bishops happily united in praising the great work[91] (though Cowper objected to profaning a sacred building with a concert).[92] The Commemoration was described by one clergyman as 'a great act of national assent to the fundamental truths of religion';[93] another considered that Handel's music 'furnished the best idea we shall ever obtain on earth of what is passing in heaven'.[94] At the fifth concert, the second performance of the *Messiah*, the king himself stood to demand that the Hallelujah Chorus be repeated.[95] It was, one spectator remembered,

> the triumph of Handel, the commemoration, and of the musical art. Now, as the orchestra in Westminster Abbey seemed to ascend to the clouds, and unite with the saints and martyrs represented on the painted glass in the west window, which had all the appearance of a continuation of the orchestra, I could hardly refrain from imagining that this orchestra was a point or segment of the celestial circles: and perhaps no band of mortal musicians ever exhibited a more imposing appearance to the eye or afforded more ecstatic and affecting sounds to the ear than this.[96]

The 1784 Handel Commemoration was followed by others in which Sandwich was as deeply involved. The king's illness in 1788 effectively ended them as an annual series, but by then they had had their effect in installing Handel, and above all the *Messiah*, in the centre of national musical life. Other baroque composers like J. S. Bach enjoyed a limited revival in the nineteenth century, and many have again become popular in the twentieth, but Handel alone received in England an enduring popular devotion. The hundreds of amateur choirs which, two centuries later, perform the *Messiah* every year in parish churches throughout England, are the inheritors of an unbroken tradition which can be traced back through the great 1784 Commemoration to the Hinchingbrooke music meetings of the 1760s. This was not all Sandwich's work; a powerful influence was the church music festivals like the Three Choirs Festival and the annual Festival of the Sons of the Clergy (of which Sandwich was a steward in 1773);[97] but Sandwich is the single most important figure in it, and arguably the English Handelian tradition is his most enduring monument.[98]

It would have been happy for Sandwich had he been able to pass a serene old age illuminated by the music of Handel and untroubled by the cares of the world, but he was not a man to be indifferent to the world, and there was one care which he could not escape. As soon as he lost office his financial problems again became acute. He told the king that his fortune had been damaged by twelve years in office,[99] and the salary of a First Lord of the Admiralty was certainly little enough to carry the obligations of high office. Like several of his colleagues, he asked for, and apparently obtained a civil list pension, but it can hardly have been sufficient to make a real difference.[100] The income of Ranger of the Parks, which he enjoyed for nine months, amounted to about £1,500 a year, mostly from farming the pasture.[101] The result was that he was nearly as much indebted as he had been before he took office. The £30,000 on mortgage which he owed Sir Laurence Dundas in 1765 had fallen by 1785 only to £22,000 to his son Sir Thomas.[102]

The financial situation was made much worse by a loan of £25,000 taken in September 1784 from a syndicate of financiers led by Robert Burton.[103] There is no direct evidence of why the money was borrowed, but it was not used to pay off any existing debts, and it looks overwhelmingly likely that it was connected with the general election. For two years Sandwich had been sustaining a large political party on an income which would hardly have supported a single seat. Like all his colleagues, he hoped very soon to be back in office, and his chances of returning would be poor unless he could keep up his political position. He had probably incurred debts to do so during the two years out of office, and fighting a general election must undoubtedly have cost a lot of money. It was a gamble, and it failed disastrously. The opposition lost heavily in the election, and Sandwich was left owing another £25,000 on penal terms to unscrupulous usurers. Under the terms of the mortgage, if he failed to pay the interest he forfeited a bond for £50,000, which was at least the value of his entire Huntingdonshire estates.[104] In effect he had staked and lost his own political position and his family's future. In September 1783 he reckoned to need some money just for a short time until the maturity of a new scheme, presumably the Burton mortgage, 'which operation is certain of success, & will only want a few months to be brought to perfection'.[105] It was a disastrous miscalculation.

He spent the remaining years of his life in a succession of desperate attempts to evade the consequences. Like so many landowners in his position, he had good prospects in the long term if only he could buy time. 'My conduct has for some time past been brought to the disagreeable situation, of gaining as much time as possible in expectation of events that may better my situation'.[106] The death of Lady Sandwich was what he had to hope for, releasing a half share in the Fane estates. If he could hold on until then, the family would survive. In the circumstances he had to be optimistic, particularly with creditors. In 1785 he assured one of them that 'in a few months more I shall cease to be troublesome to my friends';[107] in January 1789 he was 'on the eve of rising again in the world, & becoming once more usefull to my friends as well as to myself';[108] while in 1791, 'if I could by any means raise £400 we could pay every shilling of interest now due, & then the future payment would become regular and easy'.[109] At this date he had total mortgages on the Huntingdonshire estates of £49,900.[110]

His numerous creditors may be roughly divided into the benevolent, the neutral and the hostile. Burton was hostile, and attempted to use his debt to blackmail Sandwich into electing him as MP for Huntingdon in the place of his eldest grandson John George Montagu, who died in November 1790. When Sandwich refused, Burton in 1791 moved to foreclose on his mortgages.[111] Neutral creditors included those who simply needed their money back, like Sir Thomas Dundas who recalled his mortgage in 1785,[112] or Sandwich's steward John Painter who suddenly called in his floating debt of

£9,000–10,000 in 1788.[113] He seems to have been put off, but by 1791 he would wait no longer.

> I am sorry to tell you that I think I see plainly that Mr Painter means to desert me . . . it is to no purpose to expatiate upon his falseness & ingratitude, or to conceal from you the unfavourable light in which things appear to me at this time . . . if Painter leaves me to shift for myself in the month of June, I must acknowledge that I know not how to extricate myself.[114]

Shortly before Sandwich died Painter obtained a distraint order, and he was not yet buried when the bailiffs were removing the furniture of his London house.[115]

Sandwich had loans of various sums from a wide variety of friends and official contacts. They included the Prince of Wales,[116] Philip Stephens the Secretary[117] and George Jackson the Second Secretary of the Admiralty,[118] John Robinson the Secretary of the Treasury,[119] John Slade of the Victualling Board,[120] the former Agent-Victualler John Michie,[121] the Reverend John Cooke, Chaplain of Greenwich Hospital and his future biographer,[122] Admiral Rodney,[123] the Society of Dilettanti,[124] and several East India contacts.[125] A number of loans for electoral purposes came back to haunt him when the MPs concerned either lost their seats,[126] or changed sides in politics. This was the background to Mulgrave's demand in May 1784 (six months after he had joined the Pitt government) for the repayment of £2,000 lent in 1776.[127] By contrast, two of his old naval followers showed conspicuous generosity to him when he needed it. When Sandwich asked Shuldham for a loan of £5,000 in January 1784, he replied with £8,000 and a promise to remember Martha Ray's children in his will:

> I look upon it as one of the most fortunate circumstances of my Life to have it in my power to manifest to your Lordship the Gratitude of my Heart for the numerous instances of your Friendship to me, by disposing of part of that Fortune which I owe to your Benevolence, to your Lordship's use.[128]

Even more striking was the support of Sir Edward Hughes, who spent most of the American War as commander-in-chief in the East Indies, where his campaigns against the great French admiral Suffren form one of the epics of naval history. Even before he had returned, in January 1784, Lady Hughes lent Sandwich money,[129] and a year later Sir Edward followed it with a further sum, apparently of about £14,000,[130] refusing a mortgage as security.[131] In February 1788 when the withdrawal of Painter threatened to 'oblige me to retire out of the world to pass the remainder of my life in indigence and obscurity', Sandwich appealed to Hughes again:

> After the astonishing proofs of friendship that I & my family have received from yourself & your worthy Lady, I feel such a repugnance at endeavouring once more to have a recourse to your goodness that my hand trembles while I write, what I am sure I could not have courage to mention to you in an interview. Necessity however has no law, and in the unexpected difficulties in which I find myself . . .[132]

Hughes's reply was simple: 'If ten thousand pounds will relieve your Lordship I will bring it soon as I can get it'; he asked no security.[133]

Sandwich's other main support in his last years was his 'man of business' or agent Ousley Rowley. 'I must acknowledge', he wrote in one occasion, 'that considering the disagreeable business you & I have to transact together you are the most pleasant correspondent I ever met with, as your sole object seems to be kindness & accommodation'.[134] Rowley managed the delicate but essential business of conciliating Lord Hinchingbrooke, whose relations with his father, never very good, were reduced to breaking point by the family's financial crisis. Since it was impossible to raise capital on entailed estates without close co-operation between father and son (and Hinchingbrooke also had large debts of his own),[135] Rowley's efforts were vital.[136] Through his good offices Sandwich was able secretly to sell the family's Northamptonshire estates for £20,000, and repay Burton without giving him the opportunity to foreclose.[137]

By such manoeuvres Sandwich was able to stave off the worst, but his last years were evidently made miserable by the perpetual search for money. In March 1790,

> I never in the whole course of my life was so distressed for ready money as I am at this moment . . . I have allso payments to make the beginning of next month, which embarrass me exceedingly & lower my spirits in a very great degree.[138]

In January 1792 Hinchingbrooke described his father as 'too much oppressed both in body and mind'. By then he was seriously ill, and it would hardly be surprising if worry had contributed to it. By April he was 'going very fast'. [139] On 28th he addressed a note to

Hinchingbrooke, recommending his faithful servants, and ending 'Adieu, probably for ever', to which another hand added 'My Lord desires me to add that he is going to sleep'.[140] On 30th he died, at the age of seventy-three. After funeral expenses his entire personal estate was worth £624. 5s. 1d.[141]

He must have known that his death was the best hope of saving the family estates, and so it proved. Friendly creditors at once began a Chancery suit designed to establish a scheme of trusteeship, which had the effect of preserving the situation until old Lady Sandwich at length died in 1797.[142] In time the Powlett and other inheritances came to retrieve the situation, and in the nineteenth century the Sandwiches once more enjoyed modest affluence, but they never again produced a public man of the character and talent of the fourth earl.

CHAPTER XVII

Conclusion

As a politician, Sandwich had too few of some and too many of other things necessary for success. His relative poverty was a critical disadvantage in an age of expensive politics, with no national parties to bear the expense. A fortune barely sufficient for a private gentleman was quite inadequate to support the career of a leading politician. But lack of money was less damaging in itself than by implication; for a man in his position poverty was not only inconvenient but disgraceful. Peers in the nature of their privileged position in public life were supposed to be satisfied. They as individuals and the House of Lords as a constitutional feature were there to balance the British constitution by preserving it against the opposite evils of popular and royal despotism. The justification of their position and the means of carrying out their duty was the same; independent wealth, which placed them beyond the temptation of avarice. A peer who needed money was not independent. His desire for employment because he needed the money was itself corrupt, or at least a strong ground of suspicion.

> His Fortune, which did not altogether correspond with his high rank, and habits of gratification or expence, was supposed to lay him open to seduction; or at least to render him capable of listening to propositions, that a more independent man might have disdained.[1]

There was in addition something damaging in his easy affability. 'English Ministers, in general, are as inaccessible as the Peruvian Mountains',[2] one of his correspondents wrote; it was not simply a defence against importunity, but an expression of social superiority. Sandwich's easy approachability, his association with actors, his patronage of men of obscure birth, his willingness to correspond with almost anybody who would write to him, not only exposed him to ceaseless demands, but seemed indecent to many who valued the status of a nobleman and gentleman. The sense that he was a player among gentlemen may explain some of the disdain and contempt with which he was sometimes addressed.

He also aroused distrust by his ability and ambition, as he well understood. He was always anxious not to appear as 'the interested, ambitious, and ungratefull person that I am most unjustly suspected to be'.[3] The lean and hungry look has never been popular among the comfortable and the second-rate, and the English have always preferred the casual amateur to the ostentatious expert. In the eighteenth century a gentleman was not expected to display expert knowledge, and ran some risk of lowering his status if he did so. Henry Legge as Chancellor of the Exchequer was sneered at by the *Gentleman's Magazine* for his 'clerk-like knowledge of finances';[4] and twenty years later Lord Shelburne's expertise in the same subject was felt to be in poor taste.[5] The very ability which in modern eyes seems Sandwich's strongest claim on high office was in his own day something of a disqualification. Combined with ill-concealed ambition, it did a great deal to damage his reputation. Men not of noble birth could very properly display ability and diligence; it was their natural claim to preferment, and there were many positions in government, 'posts of business', which called for such qualities. But Sandwich was aiming for Cabinet posts, which did not. It was understood that every ministry needed at least one capable minister to lead in the Commons and take charge of financial affairs which were peculiarly the Commons' business – this was the position which was in process of maturing into the modern prime minister – but the majority of ministers were usually peers, and invariably chosen for their weight in society not for their abilities. Bedford, the First Lord of the Admiralty who hated to come to London, and Chatham, the First Lord who never answered letters; Grafton, the First Lord of the Treasury who understood nothing of money, and Suffolk, the Secretary of State who spoke no French, these were typical ministers of their time.[6] They had claims on high office which Sandwich could not match, and which ability and ambition could not replace.

In some ways his political skills also made his position worse. As an electoral politician he had few equals, and the skill with which he controlled Huntingdonshire politics with the frailest of natural assets was a foundation of his position in national politics. But part of his skill, which was also part of his skill in judging and handling people, was an element of calculation which people found unsettling. He was sometimes accused of being treacherous or deceitful, but this is usually supported by reference to the Wilkes case, and is difficult to sustain without it. The truth seems to be that he was loyal to his followers and dependents even at the cost of considerable damage to himself. But he was a hard man to surprise. He thought ahead and took precautions; though he did not betray others, he was always alert to the possibility that they might betray him. Perhaps his upbringing, in which school effectively replaced family, had taught him that reserve which comes naturally to sensitive characters who have suffered in boyhood. The 'jolly, hearty, lively man' whom Boswell encountered,[7] the 'talents for wit and humour, a frank and lively temper, and an insinuating address' which others recalled,[8] were not the whole story. To his closest friends he could reveal a sensitivity, even an anxiety, which betray fragile self-esteem. He cared a lot about how men, and women, regarded him. 'You used to tell me', he wrote to Bentinck in 1749,

> that I was the vainest man in the world, why then will you pique my vanity by telling me that my friends would rather go to Paris than to London? as often as you tell me that, I must answer you that you are mistaken; for you know I never can allow that any woman of judgement who can come where I am will chuse to go elsewhere.[9]

Lady Mary Fitzgerald, who knew him better than anyone, implied that his affability and imperturbability were a mask. We may conjecture that behind it there was a lonely man, whose hopes of love and domestic security were repeatedly dashed, and whose upbringing had taught him to seek in physical pleasure some substitute for the true happiness which he never found.

If so it may account for some of the distrust which he encountered. He never lacked true friends, in good fortune or adversity. His 'talents, his munificence, his steadiness in friendship, and his literary endowments, it is impossible to deny: the Reminiscent found him on every occasion a warm and active friend'.[10] He had none of the heartless egoism of Wilkes or Fox. Yet he was too good a politician, in an age when politics and intrigue were intimately linked, to be completely trusted. There is an instructive comparison to be drawn with Lord North, another young peer driven to ambition and high office partly from poverty.[11] Being the heir to the parsimonious Earl of Guildford, who lived until his son was old and blind, North passed his whole career in the Commons, and perhaps Sandwich in the same position might have been able to make as much of it. We may doubt it, however, and not only because he lacked North's easy wit and was not particularly an expert in finances. North, with his

careless classical learning and his only partly affected idleness, was
the ideal gentleman amateur, almost concealing a first-class mind
behind his bland and corpulent exterior. Sandwich, by contrast, was
serious and methodical; 'I must have pen and ink, and write down,
and ruminate: give Lord North a bundle of papers, and he'll turn
them over, perhaps while his hair is dressing; and he instantly knows
their contents and bearings'.[12] But there was a more fundamental
difference. In North there was a lovable quality which set him apart
from his contemporaries. 'Among his political adversaries, he had
not a single enemy'.[13] North's childhood had been almost as disturbed as Sandwich's, but in adult life he found true contentment.
Secure in one of the happiest marriages of the age,[14] he faced savage
invective in the Commons not merely with imperturbable affability,
but with an inner peace which contemporaries did not detect in
Sandwich. The example of North shows that it was possible, for a
different man, in a different House and a different fashion, to rise in
politics without arousing distrust.

For Sandwich, the man he was in the situation he was, it is less
surprising that he encountered distrust and spent long periods out
of office, than that he received as much favour as he did. Part of the
reason may be that he came to be considered as a specialist in the
Navy. 'Capacity is so little necessary for most appointments', Henry
Fox wrote in 1757, 'that you seem to forget that there is one where
it is absolutely so – viz. the Admiralty', and later he added that 'the
First Lord of the Admiralty must needs be a man of real ability and
great application'.[15] Sandwich had as good claims to be considered
as an expert diplomat, but expertise of any kind was regarded as
much less necessary in a Secretary of State. The Admiralty was as
near to a 'post of business' as the Cabinet offered, and it was as First
Lord of the Admiralty that he made his most important contributions
as a minister.

Before the American War, contemporaries were united in their
praise for his work there. 'The Admiralty, most assuredly, cannot
be under the direction of a more *able* or a *more active* man than Lord
Sandwich; and the national advantage would be infinite if every
department was filled up by one as equal to the charge as he is to
that'.[16] Horace Walpole, a malicious enemy whenever he thought he
could get away with it,[17] recorded that :

> The Admiralty, at which he had formerly presided with credit, was
> the favourite object of Lord Sandwich's ambition; and his passion
> for maritime affairs, his activity, industry, and flowing complaisance,

endeared him to the profession, re-established the marine, and effaced great part of his unpopularity. No man in the Administration was so much master of business, so quick or so shrewd, and no man had so many public enemies who had so few private; for though void of principles, he was void of rancour, and bore with equal good-humour the freedom with which his friends attacked him, and the satire of his opponents.[18]

'Your old friend, Lord Sandwich, is activity, industry, and knowledge in person', he wrote subsequently, 'and the most proper man in the world to be at the head of the marine'.[19] It was the course of the American War which made him unpopular:

Lord Sandwich was unquestionably industrious, zealous, indefatigable, enlightened and in every point of view adequate to the duties of his station, but he could not surmount the augmenting weight of war and calamity which, between 1775 and 1782, pressed upon the country.[20]

His work at the Admiralty may be divided into peace and war. Undoubtedly his most lasting contribution was as a reformer of naval administration. He could fairly claim to have tackled many issues which his predecessors had not identified or not addressed. He saw and attempted to remedy the fundamental problem that the fleet had outgrown its dockyards. The investment in docks and buildings which he promoted played a critical part in sustaining the Navy through the great wars against Revolutionary and Napoleonic France. Yet in many respects Sandwich failed to get to the bottom of his problems. His faith in task work proved to be naive, and it could be argued that the whole idea of getting more work out of the dockyards without paying for it was a chimera, a politician's solution. If so it is an illusion which is still being pursued as keenly in the twentieth century as it was two hundred years ago. It seems clear that there was no practical possibility of a large increase in the dockyard workforce or the number of yards, and his only way forward was increased productivity however difficult it might be to achieve it. He can be accused of over-optimism, but at least he tried.

Perhaps his greatest achievement was to choose Sir Charles Middleton and to evolve a working relationship with him. The experience of the 1740s had taught him about sterile confrontation with the Navy Board, and the 1770s showed what could be achieved by a First Lord and Controller working in harness. Perhaps the old system never worked to better effect than it did in these years. It

certainly never worked to better effect again. Sandwich's successors
returned to the path of confrontation. Keppel and Howe despised
the Controller, Chatham ignored him and St Vincent regarded the
Navy Board as an enemy power to be 'crushed'.[21] Throughout the
Great Wars relations between the two boards remained indifferent,
and finally in 1830 the Navy Board was abolished altogether. The
consequences were momentous for the Navy, and in many respects
deplorable. It is just possible that if Sandwich had been able to remain
in office longer he might have established a durable pattern of co-
operation between the two boards. What he actually did was to push
forward a process of reform, started in company with Bedford and
Anson in the 1740s, which led on eventually to the much more
drastic changes of the nineteenth century. Sandwich was far from
being revolutionary, but his drive to improve set in train developments which were in time to transform the Navy's administration
out of recognition. There is an irony here in the relationship of
Sandwich and Middleton. It is easy and obvious to contrast them as
the man of the eighteenth century and the premature representative
of the nineteenth, and in some ways it is true. But it is equally true
that Middleton's system of reform by concentrating everything in
his own hands was an early example of a pattern which was to recur
frequently in British naval history, almost always with unfortunate
results. Middleton knew a lot about things, but Sandwich understood people, and preferred to work with them rather than against.
The difference showed in his management of dockyard patronage,
and in many other ways. It can hardly be doubted that Sandwich,
who worked hard but knew how to delegate, who learnt a great
deal about the Navy but never ceased to ask the experts for their
opinions, who insisted on 'method' and consistency, was better
equipped to run a complex organization than Middleton, who tried
to do everything himself and believed he knew everything – with
results which in the case of coppering came close to catastrophe.

Sandwich might be called the first modern First Lord of the Admiralty. Before his time the successful First Lords had virtually all been
admirals, who alone were in a position to combine professional
knowledge and political standing. This was a solution which was
only possible so long as the senior ranks in the Navy were thoroughly
politicized. The drive to reduce political distortion of naval promotion and increase the professional spirit of the officers which
Anson did so much to forward, and which Sandwich enthusiastically
took up, pointed in the direction of the sense of duty as it came to
be understood in the nineteenth century. Flag officers in Sandwich's

day, as he knew to his cost, were by no means slaves of duty, but it was already becoming clear what difficulties attended the double rôle of leading politician and leading admiral.[22] The naval First Lords who followed him, Keppel and Howe, were neither of them a success, and Lord St Vincent was something like a disaster. It was civilian First Lords like Lord Spencer and Lord Melville who provided the leadership the Navy needed during the Great Wars. None of them ever matched Sandwich's technical knowledge or his voracious enthusiasm for discovery, but they knew how to manage men and affairs, and they connected the civil and the military, the political and the professional, better than the admirals were able to do. In this sense Sandwich was a modern minister born out of his time, and it was Middleton whose ideas of one man controlling everything were archaic.

Both of them, in fact, were to a much greater extent than they realized the prisoners of the eighteenth century's haphazard statistics. Sandwich aimed to achieve a stock of three years' consumption of timber, and believed he had succeeded. Only after the war when Middleton had leisure to re-examine the Navy Board's estimates did he discover that the figure for a year's consumption had been grossly underestimated. The reserve Sandwich achieved was probably little more than two years' stock.[23] It was enough, with efficient management; at the worst crisis of the war the yards never ran short of seasoned timber, and the stocks of all sorts of naval stores remained ample.[24] The fact remains that the figures on which both Sandwich and Middleton based their calculations were extremely misleading. Further errors were introduced in the timber figures by the difficulty of expressing stocks of sided timber in terms of rough. Worst of all, the stocks of all sorts of naval stores were only checked when one dockyard Storekeeper took over from another, which might happen once in thirty years. In between the clerks tallied items going in and out, but they never counted the total – with the natural result that very large cumulative errors might arise. John Greenway, the efficient Storekeeper of Portsmouth, took a 'cursory survey' of his timber stocks in 1782 and found a net deficiency of 8,722 loads. Half his compass-timber and a third of the straight timber was not there, but in other categories he had an unexpected surplus. 'The evil is a serious one, for the balance of my accounts will never agree with the state of real timber in the yard . . . I apprehend other yards must have found this inconvenience'.[25] Other yards did, on the rare occasions when anyone had the time to undertake such a survey. In 1777 the Clerk of the Ropeyard at Plymouth was short 110 tons of hemp; the following year the Storekeeper of Deptford found 670 beds in stock when his accounts showed 4,649.[26] After the war Middleton devoted much time and energy to tightening up the accounting system, and achieved some improvements, but it is doubtful if he ever appreciated the full scale of the problem, let alone solved it.[27] He certainly never noticed what seems the most remarkable statistical error of all; the number of ships in the Navy was consistently overestimated. The Admiralty's lists of ships in commission, and the Navy Board's of ships in Ordinary or building were added but never compared. Not until 1805 was it discovered that for half a century some ships had been appearing in both. Eighteen ships appeared twice in 1775, fifty-eight in 1779, and ninety in 1783, including twenty-eight ships of the line.[28] For fifty years a phantom battlefleet cruised on paper between the Admiralty and Navy Board without anybody noticing.

This puts in perspective the detailed knowledge which Sandwich and Middleton worked so hard to acquire. Their knowledge certainly was formidable by the standards of their time, but it was little better than superficial by any absolute measure. Hard work and efficient management achieved a great deal, but they were working within an ancient system which needed radical reform before it could be capable of being controlled as precisely as they hoped. It is fascinating but profitless to speculate on what might have happened if North's government had not been troubled and eventually overcome by the American crisis, and the team of Sandwich and Middleton had enjoyed fifteen or twenty years to reform the dockyards. As far as timber and shipbuilding went, even twenty years would hardly have established the virtuous cycle Sandwich aimed for of building only in the king's yards, only with seasoned timber. In practice the Navy survived the American War as it survived the Great Wars by making up for the yards' inadequate building capacity with a large and expensive programme of building in merchant yards.[29] Sandwich never reached his target; nor did any of his successors. He did, however, achieve a great deal. The fleet which went to war against Revolutionary France in 1793 was larger and in a better condition than ever before, and the credit belongs in about equal measure to Sandwich, Middleton, and Pitt, a prime minister who regarded the strength of the Navy as 'a part of our policy, if possible, as essential as that of our Treasury'.[30] In 1818 the First Lord of the Admiralty, looking back over thirty years and more, sadly contrasted a Service exhausted by the struggle against Revolutionary and Napoleonic France, with its flourishing condition at the end of the American War.[31]

It must be concluded that as a naval reformer Sandwich thought he could achieve, and thought he had achieved, more than was really possible, yet he was the best First Lord of the Admiralty in the eighteenth century considered as a naval administrator. If only he had been able to secure the early mobilization he strove for, the Navy would have been better prepared for war in 1778 than ever before: 'If we had been early enough in our naval preparations, and by that means had had a fleet ready for sea and superior to the combined force of France and Spain, little danger (except to our finances) would in my opinion have been to be apprehended'.[32] If Sandwich had really been a timid and pliant minister, who saw what needed to be done but failed to argue it for fear of unpopularity, it would be right to blame him for the failure to mobilize. Besides the repeated and vigorous arguments which he put forward, however, we have the evidence of his handling of patronage. The man who repeatedly rebuffed and antagonized men of power and influence, those whose enmity he had to fear or whose friendship he needed to preserve, those to whom he owed favours and those to whom he owed money, was not a time-server. He might be called rash or quixotic, but he can hardly be called cowardly. Within his own department, where he had liberty of action, he guarded his independence and that of the Navy.

Considering him as a strategist during the American War the picture is less clear. Here he operated in Cabinet, which was necessarily the sphere of compromise. Responsibility for what was decided was diffused between him and his Cabinet colleagues, while much of what he proposed was the work of his naval advisers. Though he has often been criticized for not adhering to a model of 'offensive' naval strategy which has proved disastrous every time it has been applied, neither his position nor his ideas were strong enough to insist on the right strategy, which would have been a concentration of force at the decisive point until victory had been won, only then followed by the dispersal of strength to distant waters to exploit it. The result was compromise, and weakness at all points in the face of a superior enemy. Not until 1782 did the Admiralty, which in this case meant Sandwich's naval advisers, feel confident enough to propose a real concentration, and then it was in the West Indies rather than the Western Approaches. It was a very dangerous scheme, and perhaps only copper could have justified it.

Had it come off, the result might have been a decisive victory at last. If the troops from America could have reached the West Indies in time to work with a superior fleet, there would have been the

opportunity of real gains. As it was British naval strength in the end
reached, and probably somewhat passed, the point of balance with
the fleets of France and Spain. Given the initial failure to mobilize
in time, which Sandwich did all he could to oppose, this was a
considerable achievement. Moreover it had considerable results.
Modern accounts of the American War tend to conclude with the
flat statement that the Americans won and the British lost. This is
true, but by no means the whole truth. Britain failed against the
Americans, but against France she virtually held her own. None of
the three Combined Fleets which entered the Channel in superior
force in 1779, 1781 and 1782 succeeded in covering an invasion, or
indeed in achieving anything at all. In the West Indies British losses
were nearly outweighed by the gain of St Lucia. In the East Indies
Sir Edward Hughes fought Suffren to a standstill and saved British
India. Spain alone of all the European belligerents could claim real
territorial gains, but Minorca and the two Floridas were a poor substitute for Gibraltar and Jamaica, the prizes she was hoping for.
In all these cases what actually happened was much less serious
for Britain than might have been expected given the forces on
either side.

It is also worth considering the achievement of the Americans
from the perspective of what might have been. What we know now
suggests that the political situation in the colonies made independence
sooner or later inevitable. But independence in some form would
certainly have come anyway, as it came to all British colonies, and
if a few more ships had been present in Graves's squadron, if a few
accidents had fallen out favourably to the Navy in that campaign,
Cornwallis's army might have been retrieved to fight another
day, and the French decision to abandon their allies have had
time to work out its consequences. For all the avoidable blunders,
the British naval effort might very easily have prevented American
independence.

To some extent it did. There was nothing inevitable about a republic of the thirteen colonies. There were nineteen colonies in British
North America, not counting the West Indies, and in economic and
geographical terms they formed a unit stretching from Labrador to
Barbados. There were many good (from the rebel point of view,
essential) reasons to expect them to sink or swim together. The
fact that Canada, Newfoundland and Nova Scotia in the North, the
Bahamas and the West Indies in the South, remained British, is a
consequence of the partial success of British sea power. The survival
of French Canada as a British colony is directly traceable to the relief

expedition organized by the Admiralty in the winter of 1776. It is this which is the decisive event in the modern history of Quebec, not the conquest of 1759. If Saunders and Wolfe had not succeeded in that year someone else would have done so sooner or later; the French garrisons and the French navy were much too weak to sustain a colony so far away. But if the Americans had stormed Quebec the day that the *Isis* arrived, it is most unlikely that they could have been dislodged. The whole geography and modern history of the Americas is indelibly marked by the partial success and partial failure of British seapower two hundred years ago. If it is true, as in a certain sense it is, that Sandwich as the responsible minister for the Navy was the man who lost the American War, it must be true in the same sense that he was the man who saved Canada, India and the West Indies.

This would be sufficient to make Sandwich interesting, but it is far from being the only interesting thing about him. As a man, he is both a representative of his age and an exception to it. Always a conventional thinker, he accepted the opinions of his day, and only began to stand out in old age because by then he represented an earlier era. He never set out to do anything revolutionary. He stood for piecemeal improvement within the existing system; nothing more was possible in so excellent a system. 'The noblest constitution the human mind is capable of framing', George III called it; 'the wisest of human institutions' in the opinion of Junius; 'that perfection of human wisdom, that noblest work of mankind', according to Wilkes:[33] no other subject could have united the four of them. But in applying pragmatic solutions to practical problems, Sandwich set in train developments which form the naval counterpart to the secular changes which transformed British society during the Great Wars and after. Arguably he made the old system work better than it had ever done before, and inadvertently showed that without radical reform it was incapable of working as well as necessary. That restless urge to take the watch apart to see if it was working which has marked British naval administrators for nearly two centuries was quite foreign to him, and yet in a way he started it.

It was the same with his musical life. Like the men of the Renaissance, he set out to revive the lost glories of a classical era, and succeeded in founding a new tradition. It is certainly his most enduring monument. Of his naval work only some docks and buildings now survive. The great fleets which he laboured to create and preserve have vanished; besides the *Victory*, ordered and built under Anson though first commissioned by Sandwich, nothing survives as a witness to the age when the fate of navies and nations turned on the conquest of dry rot. But the Handelian tradition remains thoroughly alive. Though Sandwich's connection with it is forgotten, it preserves into our own century a lively image of his life and his world. 'I know that my Redeemer liveth', the air that Martha Ray excelled in, is as close a link as we shall ever have to Sandwich and his lifetime, and the best, because it has not lost its power to move. The other causes that Sandwich worked for and the events in which he engaged are things of the past now. Though he is in some ways a sympathetic character, it requires an effort of the imagination to sympathize with him when his life and work seem so remote. His reputation has unfairly suffered by being associated solely with the American War. For his enemies then, and those who have taken their part since, he became a personification of folly and wickedness. Discovered as a man, he proves like other men to have been imperfect, but his life is full of significance and interest. Lord North summed him up as a public man in 1782:

> He has certainly been a very diligent and a very able, and a very faithful servant; his situation naturally drew upon him many enemies, and made him the object of persecution on the part of the Opposition, but Lord North believes that his merit will be known when he is gone.[34]

It is surely time it were.

Abbreviations Used in the
Notes and Bibliography

AHR *American Historical Review*
AN *American Neptune*
BC Russell, *Bedford Correspondence*
BFP Scott, *British Foreign Policy*
BIHR *Bulletin of the Institute of Historical Research*
BM British Museum (now British Library) Department of Manuscripts
BNA Baugh, *British Naval Administration in the Age of Walpole*
Bodley Bodleian Library, Oxford
CG3 Fortescue, *Correspondence of George III*
EHR *English Historical Review*
ERO Essex Record Office
FNAI Dull, *The French Navy and American Independence*
HEH Henry E. Huntington Library, San Marino, California
HJ *Historical Journal*
HLQ *Huntington Library Quarterly*
HMC Historical Manuscripts Commission
HRO Huntingdonshire Record Office
HS Historical Society
IHR *International History Review*
JBS *Journal of British Studies*
JICH *Journal of Imperial and Commonwealth History*
JMH *Journal of Modern History*
KCC King's College Cambridge, Rowe Music Library

MC Mulgrave Castle
MM *The Mariner's Mirror*
MPS Mansfield Papers, Scone Palace
NDAI Tracy, *Navies, Deterrence and American Independence*
NMM National Maritime Museum
NRS Navy Records Society
NS New Series; New Style
NUL Nottingham University Library
OS Old Style
PH *Parliamentary History*
PRO Public Record Office
PRONI Public Record Office of Northern Ireland
RAW Royal Archives, Windsor
S Sandwich
SM Sandwich MSS, Mapperton
SP Barnes & Owen, *The Sandwich Papers*
SRB Suffolk Record Office, Bury St.Edmunds
SRO Staffordshire Record Office
SZ Sausmarez Papers
TRHS *Transactions of the Royal Historical Society*
VCH Victoria County History
WA Woburn Abbey
WC Lewis, *Walpole Correspondence*
WLC William L. Clements Library, Ann Arbor, Michigan
WRO Warwick County Record Office

Notes

INTRODUCTION

1 W. C. Sellar & R. J. Yeatman, *1066 And All That*, (London, 1930 &c) p. 120.

2 Edinburgh, 1974, p. 1130. The 1990 edn. has a much longer entry to exactly the same effect.

3 For astronomy, Cradock, *Memoirs*, I, 140–41. For numismatics, BM: Add.MSS 52362 f. 16, Minutes of Egyptian Society; NMM: SAN/V/12 pp. 15–146, S to W. Montagu, 16 Jul 1764. Sandwich, *Voyage*, p. iii.

4 Sir Edward Warner's introduction to his 1976 list of the papers, prepared for the Historical Manuscripts Commission.

5 A list of these arranged in chronological order has been deposited in the Historical Manuscripts Commission and the National Maritime Museum.

6 *The London Magazine or Gentlemans Monthly Intelligencer*, XLVIII (1779) pp. 291–92.

7 Quoted in *SP*, IV, 272.

8 *The European Magazine and London Review*, XXV (1794) p. 193. *The Scots Magazine*, (1792) p. 207. *The Gentleman's Magazine*, (1792) p. 482.

9 E.g. John Adolphus, *The History of England from the Accession of King George the Third to the Conclusion of Peace in the Year 1783*, (London, 1802, 3 vols) II, 185–86. Wraxall, *Memoirs*, I, 398–99. Coxe, *Pelham*, II, 108.

10 *The Private Papers of John, Earl of Sandwich . . . 1771–1782*, ed. G. R. Barnes & J. H. Owen (NRS Vol. 69, 71, 75 & 78, 1932–38).

11 Work on it has now been resumed by Dr R. J. B. Knight.

12 Those by Knight, Morrison, Phillips, Usher, Wickwire and Williams listed in the bibliography.

13 Those by Breen and Jamieson in the bibliography; there are a great many more of lesser significance.

14 Those by Crimmin, Davies, Morgan and Webb.

15 Those by Haas, Johnson & Massie.

16 James and Mahan are antiquated though still useful for operations; Dull is excellent from the French point of view; Syrett is also excellent but deals only with American waters; G. J. Marcus, *A Naval History of England; The Formative Centuries*, (London, 1961) summarizes the received opinions of sixty years ago.

CHAPTER I

1 *Complete Peerage*, XI, 434–36.

2 WA: Vol. XXVIII f. 99, S to Bedford, 10 Sep [1753], mentioning that he has known Eton 'above 28 years'.

3 Christopher Hollis, *Eton, A History*, (London, 1960), p. 156.

4 *The Marlborough–Godolphin Correspondence*, ed. Henry L. Snyder, (Oxford, 1975, 3 vols, continuously paginated), I, 399 n. 5 & II, 732.

5 *VCH Huntingdonshire*, II, 34.

6 *Complete Peerage*, XI, 434–35.

Halsband, *Letters of Lady Mary Wortley Montagu*, III, 223 n. 6. Cork, *Orrery Papers*, I, 50 n. 1. Cruickshanks, *Political Untouchables*, p. 39.

7 *VCH Huntingdonshire*, II, 14. Sandwich, *Hinchingbrooke*, pp. 10–18.

8 Clark, *English Society*, p. 51 n. 27. Langford, *Polite and Commercial People*, p. 83.

9 Cole, *Journal*, p. 85.

10 *WC*, XVII, 231 n. 8, & XIX, 388.

11 Climenson, *Elizabeth Montagu*, II, 113.

12 PRO: C 11/1793/28 & C 38/411, Sandwich con Seymour.

13 Wallbank, 'Eighteenth Century Public Schools', pp. 3–10.

14 Various figures for the proportion who went to school are offered by Wallbank, pp. 1–2; J. V. Beckett, *The Aristocracy in England 1660–1914*, (Oxford, 1986) p. 99; and Cannon, *Aristocratic Century*, pp. 40–41.

15 Quoted in *BC*, I, xxi.

16 M. L. Clarke, *Classical Education in Britain 1500–1900*, (Cambridge, 1959) pp. 55 & 58.

17 Crimmin, 'Admiralty Administration', p. 70.

18 Wallbank, 'Eighteenth Century Public Schools', pp. 7–10.

19 BM: Add.MSS 32811 f. 174, S to Newcastle, 16 Feb NS 1748.

20 Jesse, *Celebrated Etonians*, II, 55.

21 Gerretson & Geyl, *Briefwisseling van Bentinck*, II, 110.

22 Sandwich, *Voyage*, p. iii.

23 NMM: SAN/F/49/160, cf. Mk. 10:46.

24 HEH: Misc. MSS, S to Revd Mr [T. Dampier?], 23 Sep 1771.

25 Sandwich, *Voyage*, *passim*.

26 Sandwich, *Voyage*, p. 137.

27 Sandwich, *Voyage*, p. 158.

28 Jeremy Black, *The British and the Grand Tour*, (London, 1985) pp. 23 & 50.

29 E.g. Frederick Lewis Norden, *Travels in Egypt and Nubia*, trans P. Templeman (London, 1757) pp. 147–48.

30 Sandwich, *Voyage*, p. iii.

31 NMM: SAN/F/50; SM: V/110–11.

32 Sandwich, *Voyage*, pp. iii–iv.

33 Taylor, *Marmor Sandvicense*.

34 John Sweetman, *The Oriental Obsession: Islamic Inspiration in British and American Art and Architecture 1500–1920*, (Cambridge, 1988) pp. 62–63.

35 BM: Add.MSS 52362, Minutes of Egyptian Society, ff. 1–33. W. C. Lukis, ed., *The Family Memoirs of the Rev. William Stukeley, M.D.*, (Surtees Soc. Vols. 73, 76 & 80, Durham, 1882–87) I, 55 & 326. W. R. Dawson 'The First Egyptian Society', *Journal of Egyptian Archaeology*, XXIII (1937) pp. 259–60. M. Anis, 'The First Egyptian Society in London (1741–43)', *Bulletin de l'Institut Français d'Archaeologie Orientale du Caire*, L (1952) pp. 99–105.

36 NMM: SAN/V/113.

37 Cust & Colvin, *Society of Dilettanti*, pp. 55, 74, 82–83, & 248.

38 *WC*, XXXVII, 33–34, H. S. Conway to H. Walpole, 10 Sep 1737 OS.

39 *HMC 68 Denbigh*, V, 216, W. Bristow to Lady Denbigh, 10 Jun 1737.

40 *Complete Peerage*, XI, 436.

41 NMM: SAN/V/12 p. 270, S to Fane, 19 Oct 1765. PRO: C 211/23/94 gives her portion in 1767 as £2,680 in the Old South Sea Annuities; it was certainly not £5,000 as contemporary rumour had it, still less £5,000 a year as stated by Haas, 'Rise of the Bedfords', p. 13.

42 Climenson, *Elizabeth Montagu*, I, 87, E. Robinson to her mother, 20 Oct 1741.

43 *HMC 27 Beaufort*, pp. 203–4, T. Dampier to W. Windham & Lord Haddington, 30 Jul 1741.

44 *HMC 28 Charlemont*, I, 179, E. Murphy to Charlemont, 4 Apr OS 1747.

45 NMM: SAN/V/50 p. 189, Lady Sandwich to S, 10 May 1748.

46 *HMC 68 Denbigh*, V, 216, W. Bristow to Lady Denbigh, 10 Jun 1737: 'qui a un bon sens et merite infini'.

47 For the domestic political situation see Owen, *Rise of the Pelhams*; Speck,

Stability and Strife; Cannon, *Aristocratic Century*.

48 John Cannon, ed., *The Whig Ascendancy: Colloquies on Hanoverian England*, (London, 1981) is a useful collection of pieces on 'party-politics' in this century.

49 *BC*, I, 88, H. Legge to Bedford, 3 May 1746.

50 Pares, 'American versus Continental Warfare', is still the best introduction to this large subject. See also Rodger, 'Continental Commitment'.

51 Ehrman, *Younger Pitt*, p. 313.

52 Quoted by Namier, *American Revolution*, p. 304.

53 *BNA*, pp. 14–15.

54 Mimler, *Der Einfluss kolonialer Interessen*; Niedhart, *Handel und Krieg*.

55 Clark, *Waldegrave Memoirs*, p. 8.

56 McCahill, *Order and Equipoise*, pp. 1–12. Cannon, *Aristocratic Century*, p. 155.

57 P. D. G. Thomas, ' "Thoughts on the British Constitution" by George III in 1760', *BIHR*, LX (1987) pp. 361–63, at p. 362.

58 Thomas, *Stamp Act Crisis*, pp. 244–45. See also Simmons & Thomas, *American Debates*, II, 338.

59 Barbara English & John Saville, *Strict Settlement, A Guide for Historians*, (Hull, 1983, Univ. of Hull Occasional Papers in Economic & Social History No. 10).

60 Speck, *Stability and Strife*, p. 35.

61 Pares, *George III and the Politicians*, p. 6.

62 *Common Sense*, quoted by Cannon, *Aristocratic Century*, p. 171.

63 The most recent study is O'Gorman, *Voters, Patrons and Parties*.

64 O'Gorman, *Voters*, pp. 82 & 149–50.

65 Paul Langford, 'Property and 'Virtual Representation' in Eighteenth-Century England', *HJ*, XXXI (1988) pp. 83–115.

66 Namier & Brooke, *House of Commons 1754–90*, I, 344–45.

67 O'Gorman, *Voters*, pp. 158–60.

68 *VCH Huntingdonshire*, II, 43.

69 O'Gorman, *Voters*, p. 113.

70 Owen, *Rise of the Pelhams*, p. 81. Haas, 'Pursuit of Political Success'.

71 Haas, 'Rise of the Bedfords', p. 7.

72 Johnson, 'Bedford Connection', pp. 46–51.

73 Haas, 'Rise of the Bedfords' pp. 8–9.

74 Coxe, *Pelham*, I, 121.

75 Cork, *Orrery Papers*, II, 178. *WC*, XVIII, 356.

76 Haas, 'Rise of the Bedfords' p. 28.

77 Sandwich, *Voyage*, p. xxx. Robert Bisset, *The History of the Reign of King George III to the Termination of the Late War*, (London, 1803, 6 vols), II, 218. Adolphus, *History of England*, II, 186. Good examples of his speeches at this period are in Cobbett, *Parliamentary History*, XII, 601–10, 1059–61 & 1071–83.

78 Cobbett, *Parliamentary History*, XII, 1072. This is taken from *The Gentleman's Magazine*, whose reporter was Johnson.

79 Jeremy Black, 'The House of Lords and British Foreign Policy, 1720–48', in Jones, *Pillar of the Constitution*, pp. 113–36, at p. 127.

CHAPTER II

1 McCann, *Richmond–Newcastle Correspondence*, No. 238 p. 160, Newcastle to Richmond, 8 Dec 1744.

2 WA: Vol. LVIII f. 86, S to Bedford, 16 Jun 1769. NMM: SAN/V/47 pp. 199–201, 18th-century copy of Haddock's narrative of the loss of the *Royal James*, in 1672.

3 Here and throughout this book I refer to the inner or effective Cabinet rather than the larger outer Cabinet which at this date was still formally in existence.

4 *BNA*, pp. 61–76 describes the Admiralty's functions in detail.

5 *BNA*, pp. 77–81.

6 *BNA*, pp. 68–69. For the battle of Toulon and the ensuing courts martial see Richmond, *Navy in the War in 1739–48*, II, 1–57.

7 *BNA*, pp. 29–48 describes the Navy Board.

8 *BNA*, p. 67.

9 Lavery, *Ship of the Line*, I, 75. Pool, *Navy Board Contracts*, p. 79.

10 *BNA*, p. 48.

11 BM: Add.MSS 15955 f. 276, A. Geddes to Anson, 5 Dec 1748.

12 Lavery, *Ship of the Line*, I, 75–90.

13 Lavery, *Ship of the Line*, I, 83. Baugh, *Naval Administration 1715–50*, pp. 199–200.

14 Lavery, *Ship of the Line*, I, 81. Baugh, *Naval Administration 1715–50*, pp. 197–98. Jean Boudriot, *The Seventy-Four Gun Ship*, trans. David H. Roberts (Paris, 1986–88, 4 vols), describes French ships of the line in great detail but does not attempt comparisons with foreign designs.

15 SZ: Undated draft, P. Saumarez to Admiralty [13 Feb 1746/7].

16 PRO: ADM 106/2073, 31 Dec 1744, 12 & 23 Feb 1744/5. ADM 106/2114, 6 Aug 1745. ADM 3/49 f. 244 & ADM 3/51, Admiralty Board Minutes 8 Feb 1744/5, 7 & 20 Jun 1745. *BNA*, pp. 251–52. Baugh, *Naval Administration 1715–50*, pp. 200 & 225–35. Lavery, *Ship of the Line*, I, 93–95.

17 The development of British battleship design over the past twenty years was well summarized in 1774 by the then Surveyor Sir John Williams in a paper for George III, printed in *CG3*, III, 57–59, & Hattendorf, *Naval Documents*, No. 289.

18 WA: Vol. XI f. 34, H. Legge to Bedford, 6 Mar 1745/6; printed in *BNA*, pp. 89–90.

19 This paragraph is based on Robert Gardiner, 'Frigate Design in the Eighteenth Century', *Warship*, Nos. 9–12 (1979) pp. 3–12, 80–92 & 269–77. His *The First Frigates: Nine-Pounder and Twelve-Pounder Frigates, 1748–1815*, (London, 1992) appeared too late to be used here.

20 WA: Vol. XVI f. 73, G. Anson to Bedford, 17 Apr 1747.

21 NMM: AGC/13/25, B. Slade to Anson, 10 Nov 1747. SRO: D 615/ P(S)/1/9/21 & 22, B. Slade to G. Anson, 31 May & 21 Jul 1747. BM: Add MSS 15955 f. 119, W. Bately to Anson, 5 Jun 1747 (Bately was Slade's assistant).

22 PRO: ADM 106/2073, 16 Jan, 27 Feb & 14 Mar 1744/5, 29 Mar 1745; ADM 106/2114, 2 May, 13 Jul, 23 & 24 Aug, & 3 Sep 1745; ADM 106/ 2115, 9 & 27 Jan & 4 Mar, 1746/7, 26 & 31 Mar, 13 May, 13 Jun 1747. NMM: ADM/B/130, 28 & 29 Aug, 3 & 11 Sep & 9 Oct 1745; ADM/B/ 134, 2 Feb 1746/7; ADM/B/135, 11, 16 & 18 Mar 1746/7.

23 No answer was received to many of the demands, in spite of reminders; see PRO: ADM 106/2116, 14 Dec 1751.

24 PRO: ADM 106/2114, 2 May 1745. NMM: ADM/B/129, 7 May 1745. *BNA*, pp. 88–89 & 268–69. Pool, *Navy Board Contracts*, pp. 105–8.

25 *BNA*, pp. 90–92. Baugh, *Naval Administration 1715–1750*, pp. 21–23.

26 Tunstall, *Naval Warfare*, pp. 97–100. Corbett, *Fighting Instructions*, pp. 216–17. Barrow, *Anson*, p. 405.

27 PRO: ADM 3/49 f. 259, Admiralty Minute 14 Feb 1744/5.

28 SRO: D615/P(S)/1/10/24, T. Anson to Anson, 24 Jul [1748?].

29 PRO: SP 42/30, f. 89, Admiralty Board to Harrington, 31 Jan 1745/6.

30 *BNA*, pp. 142–44. Richmond, *Navy in the War of 1739–48*, II, 54–57.

31 *BNA*, pp. 7–8. Barrow, *Anson*, pp. 126–27.

32 PRO: SP 42/30 f. 362, Admiralty Board to Newcastle, 16 May 1746.

33 SZ: Box 75, J. Blackwood to P. Saumarez, 14 Nov [NS] 1746.

34 Richard Harding, *Amphibious Warfare in the Eighteenth Century: The British Expedition to the West Indies, 1740–1742*, (Woodbridge, Suffolk, 1991; Royal Historical Society Studies in History No. 62).

35 Ranft, *Vernon Papers*, pp. 434–587. Hartmann, *Angry Admiral*, pp. 180–85.

36 Ranft, *Vernon Papers*, p. 554 prints a

good example of Vernon's use of this sort of language.

37 BM: Add MSS 15955 f. 121, Ld V. Beauclerk to G. Anson, 1 Apr 1747; f. 137, Duchess of Bedford to G. Anson, [4 Apr? 1747], printed incomplete in Barrow, *Anson*, pp. 158–59. Rodger, *Wooden World*, pp. 315–16.

38 BM: Add.MSS 15955, T. Griffin to G. Anson, 7 Feb 1746/7; Add.MSS 15957, ff. 191, 193 & 201, Sir P. Warren to G. Anson, 21 & 31 May & 5 Jul 1747.

39 BM: Add.MSS 15957, f. 10, Sandwich to G. Anson, 14 Apr NS 1747 (printed in Barrow, *Anson*, p. 160); also f. 60, S to Anson 10 Apr NS 1748.

40 *BNA*, pp. 127–141. Baugh, *Naval Administration 1715–50*, pp. 81–84. Barrow, *Anson*, pp. 150–51.

41 Baugh, *Naval Administration 1715–50*, pp. 79–80.

42 BM : Add.MSS 15956 f. 88, A. Keppel to Anson 23 Dec 1747. PRO: ADM 106/2115, 29 Jun 1748.

43 *BNA*, pp. 129–37.

44 PRO: SP 42/60, f. 112, [Carteret] to Winchelsea, 27 Jul/7 Aug 1743.

45 Rodger, *Wooden World*, p. 299. Cobbett, *Parliamentary History*, XXVII, 117–18.

46 SZ: Box 74, T. Brett to P. Saumarez, 15 Aug 1747.

47 Lowe, *Portsmouth Division of Marines*, p. xiv.

48 Richmond, *Navy in the War in 1739–48*, III, 6–8, 20–23, 82–84, 226–29. Ranft, *Vernon Papers*, pp. 436–37, 441, 451–452, & 459. Duffy, 'Establishment of the Western Squadron'.

49 There are excellent discussions in Ryan, 'Blockade of Brest', and Duffy, 'Establishment of the Western Squadron'.

50 Ranft, *Vernon Papers*, pp. 446 & 451.

51 WA: Vol. X f. 35, E. Vernon to Bedford, n.d. [1745].

52 Pares, *War and Trade in the West Indies*, p. 299.

53 WA: Vol. XVII f. 65, Anson to Bedford, 2 Aug [1747].

54 Barrow, *Anson*, p. 155.

55 See the discussion in Richmond, *Navy in the War of 1739–48*, III, 21–23.

56 PRO: ADM 3/49–51.

57 *BC*, I, 36, H. Legge to Bedford, 17 Aug 1745.

58 BM : Add.MSS 15956, f. 3, Halifax to G. Anson, 13 Dec 1745.

59 PRO: SP 42/30 f. 6.

60 Sandwich, *Voyage*, p. vi lists his commissions.

CHAPTER III

1 Haas, 'Rise of the Bedfords', p. 46. Blackey, 'Halifax', p. 18.

2 Lodge, *Eighteenth-Century Diplomacy*, pp. 156–70. Browning, *Newcastle*, p. 145. Massie, 'Defence of the Low Countries', pp. 118 & 180–90.

3 Lodge, *Eighteenth-Century Diplomacy*, pp. 169–72. Coxe, *Pelham*, I, 332 & 365.

4 *HMC 38 Buckinghamshire*, p. 149, H. Pelham to R. Trevor, 12 Aug OS 1746.

5 Add.MSS 32806 ff. 81–82, S to Newcastle, 17 Oct NS 1746.

6 Horn, *Great Britain and Europe*, pp. 13–16.

7 Lodge, *Eighteenth-Century Diplomacy*, pp. 172–73.

8 Ellis, *Post Office*, pp. 62–68.

9 BM: Add.MSS 35363 f. 94, P. Yorke to J. Yorke, 25 Aug 1745.

10 *SP*, I, 9, A. Hervey to S, 13 Aug 1770.

11 Add.MSS 32809 f. 256, Newcastle to S, 27 Aug 1747.

12 Ellis, *Post Office*, p. 75.

13 Lodge, *Eighteenth-Century Diplomacy*, p. 325. NMM: SAN/F/48/1, Duchess of Bedford to S, 11 Apr 1748. Halsband, *Lady Mary Wortley Montagu*, p. 240.

14 BM: Add.MSS 35363 f. 228, J. Yorke to P. Yorke, 21 Oct/1 Nov 1748.

15 BM: Add.MSS 32810, f. 324, S to Newcastle, 22 Dec NS 1747.

16 BM: Add MSS 35461 f. 20, S to R. Keith, 22 Mar NS 1748. In NMM: SAN/V/59–68, original despatches from the Secretaries of State 1746–48, are numerous examples of deciphers in Sandwich's own hand.

17 BM: Add.MSS 32810, f. 172, S to Newcastle, 31 Oct NS 1747, written 'past two in the morning'.

18 NMM: SAN/V/52 p. 45, Puyzieulx to S, 10 Mar NS 1748. BM: Add.MSS 15957 f. 326, [P. Yorke] to Anson, 5 Jul NS [1748].

19 Krämer, Supplement to Bussemakers, *Archives ou Correspondance Inédite*, No. 78, W. Bentinck to Orange, 30 Aug 1746 NS.

20 Lodge, *Eighteenth-Century Diplomacy*, p. 178.

21 *HMC 45 Buccleuch & Queensberry*, I, 412, R. Keith to Cardigan, 29 Sep NS 1747.

22 BM: Add.MSS 32808 f. 217, a copy in S's hand of minute of Secreet Besogne (of States-General) 2 Jul 1746. Lodge, *Eighteenth-Century Diplomacy*, p. 164.

23 Strictly, offices, provincial rather than national.

24 Krämer, Supplement to Bussemakers, *Maison d'Orange-Nassau*, Nos. 78, 79 & 83.

25 J. V. A., 6th Duc de Broglie, *Maurice de Saxe et le Marquis d'Argenson*, (Paris, 1891, 2 vols) II, 28–33. E. J. B. Rathery, ed., *Journal et Mémoires du Marquis d'Argenson*, (Paris, 1859–67, 9 vols.) IV, 351.

26 'Le comte de Sandwich est d'un caractère doux et même timide. Il est fort laconique et très réservé, assez pénétrant et maître de lui-même. Il sait beaucoup de choses: mais, ne s'étant appliqué aux négociations que depuis peu de temps, son expérience dans les affaires générales n'est pas fort étandue'. André & Bourgeois, *Instructions aux Ambassadeurs, Hollande*, p. 147. This description was written by Puyzieulx when foreign minister in 1748, for his successor's information, and is obviously based on his experience at Breda. Mirepoix repeated almost the same description for the ambassador to London in 1749; Paul Vaucher, ed., *Receuil des Instructions données aux Ambassadeurs et Ministres de France: XXV-2 Angleterre III (1698–1791)*, (Paris, 1965) p. 349.

27 HEH: MO 1651, Lady S to Mrs E. Montagu, 8 Nov NS [1746].

28 Lodge, *Eighteenth-Century Diplomacy*, pp. 175–78, 185–89. Lodge, *Chesterfield–Newcastle Correspondence*, pp. xli–xlii. Massie, 'Defence of the Low Countries', p. 193. Haas, 'Rise of the Bedfords', p. 52. BM: Add.MSS 32806 f. 166, Newcastle to S, 29 Oct 1746.

29 Dobrée, *Chesterfield Correspondence*, III, 837, Chesterfield to S, 23 Dec/3 Jan 1746/7.

30 *BC*, I, 144–45, R. Leveson Gower to Bedford, 6 Oct 1746 NS.

31 Lodge, *Eighteenth-Century Diplomacy*, p. 225. Massie, 'Defence of the Low Countries' p. 204. Dobrée, *Chesterfield Letters*, III, 860 No. 1085, Chesterfield to S, 6 Feb OS 1747.

32 BM: Add.MSS 32807 f. 37, S to Newcastle, 7 Feb NS [1747].

33 Lodge, *Eighteenth-Century Diplomacy*, pp. 226–31. André & Bourgeois, *Instructions aux Ambassadeurs, Hollande*, p. 104.

34 Conn, *Gibraltar*, p. 256, quoting Commodore Curtis in 1783.

35 NUL: NeC 464, S to H. Pelham, 14 Mar NS [1747]. Conn, *Gibraltar*, pp. 147–49. Lodge, *Eighteenth-Century Diplomacy*, pp. 238–41.

36 NUL: NeC 465, 11 Apr NS [1747].

37 It is hinted at by Lodge, *Eighteenth-Century Diplomacy*, pp. 183 & 249, and closely argued by Porta, *Joan en Gerrit Corver*, pp. 172–228, that this was a covert British coup d'état organized by Sandwich among others. I hope to examine elsewhere this claim, which I believe to be ill-founded.

38 NMM: SAN/V/53 p. 165, Newcastle to S, 28 Apr 1747.

39 Lodge, *Eighteenth-Century Diplomacy*, pp. 286–89. Rex Whitworth, *Field Marshal Lord Ligonier: A Story of the British Army, 1702–1770*, (Oxford, 1958) p. 162.

40 Massie, 'Defence of the Low Countries', p. 215. BM: Add.MSS 32810 f. 380, S to Newcastle, 30 Dec 1747 NS.

41 McCann, *Richmond–Newcastle Correspondence*, p. 253 No. 381, Newcastle to Richmond, 30 Jul 1747.

42 Dobrée, *Chesterfield Letters*, III, 975 No. 1322, Chesterfield to S. Dayrolles, 31 Jul OS 1747.

43 McCann, *Richmond–Newcastle Correspondence*, p. 249 No. 375, Newcastle to Richmond, 16 Jul 1747.

44 It is in BM: Add.MSS 32811 ff. 235ff.

45 *BC*, I, 341, Bedford to S, 6 Apr 1748.

46 NUL: NeC 561 H. Legge to H. Pelham, 6 Mar 1747/8.

47 NMM: SAN/V/43 p. 184, Cumberland to S, 15 Apr NS 1748.

48 BM: Add.MSS 32812 ff. 11–14, Newcastle to S, 1 Apr OS 1748.

49 BM: Add.MSS 32812 f. 35, S to Newcastle, 21 Apr NS 1748.

50 Massie, 'Defence of the Low Countries', pp. 246–81.

51 *BC*, I, 343–44, Bedford to S, 6 Apr 1748.

52 BM: Add.MSS 32812 f. 45, Newcastle to S, 15 Apr 1748 [OS].

53 Lodge, *Eighteenth-Century Diplomacy*, pp. 327–30.

54 BM: Add.MSS 32812 ff. 51–55, S to Newcastle, 28 Apr NS 1748.

55 Coxe, *Pelham*, I, 496–500, S to Newcastle, 1 May NS 1748 (BM: Add.MSS 32812 f. 104). BM: Add.MSS 15957 f. 63, S to Anson, 30 Apr NS 1748. NMM: SAN/V/51 pp. 53–57, S to Cumberland, 5 May NS 1748. Gerretson & Geyl, *Briefwisseling van Bentinck*, II, 2.

56 Lodge, *Eighteenth-Century Diplomacy*, pp. 339–42. Coxe, *Pelham*, I, 420, Cumberland to H. Pelham, 25 Apr/6 May 1748. BM: Add.MSS

32812 f. 118, Newcastle to S, 26 Apr 1748.

57 Sosin, 'Louisbourg'.

58 *BC*, I, 357, Bedford to S, 28 Apr 1748.

59 *BC*, I, 367, H. Legge to Bedford, 1/12 May 1748.

60 Ilchester, *Fox Letters*, pp. 28–29, Sir C. H. Williams to H. Fox, 6 May NS 1747.

61 NMM: SAN/V/51 p. 53, S to Cumberland, 5 May [NS] 1748.

62 Barnes, 'Pelham and Newcastle', p. 66.

63 Coxe, *Pelham*, II, 8, Sir T. Robinson to Newcastle, 20 Aug NS 1748 (BM: Add.MSS 32813 ff. 302–3). BM: Add.MSS 32813 ff. 329–33, Sir T. Robinson to Newcastle, 24 Aug NS 1748; Add.MSS 32815 ff. 29–31, Sir T. Robinson to Newcastle, 18 Oct NS 1748.

64 Bussemakers, *Maison d'Orange-Nassau*, I, 185 Notes by W. Bentinck of an interview with Marshal Batthiany at Cologne, Nov 1748. Beer, 'Friede von Aachen', pp. 109–10. PRO: PRO 30/50/45 ff. 1–2, deciphered intercept of Sottomayor to Wall, 1 Oct 1748.

65 Haas, 'Rise of the Bedfords', pp. 67–68.

66 *BC*, I, 403 & 520, H. Pelham to Bedford, 7/18 Jul & 15 Sep 1748; I, 504 & 512, Bedford to S, 6 & 11 Sep OS 1748; I, 513–14 & 517, Hardwicke to Bedford, 12 & 13 Sep 1748. Yorke, *Hardwicke*, I, 664–66, H. Pelham to Hardwicke, 8 Aug; & Hardwicke to Newcastle, 12 Aug 1748. NUL: NeC 719, Hardwicke to H. Pelham, 14 Aug 1748; NeC 756, H. Pelham to Newcastle, 9 Sep 1748.

67 Coxe, *Pelham*, II, 17.

68 Yorke, *Hardwicke*, I, 671, Hardwicke to Newcastle, 2 Sep 1748.

69 Coxe, *Pelham*, II, 5, S to Newcastle 19 Aug NS 1748. BM: Add.MSS 32813 ff. 317–18, S to Newcastle, 21 Aug NS 1748; Add.MSS 32814 ff. 192–94, S to Newcastle, 16 Sep NS 1748.

70 Lodge, *Eighteenth-Century Diplomacy*, pp. 348–51. Coxe, *Pelham*, II, 36.

71 *BC*, I, 565, Bedford to S, 17 Oct 1748.

72 Hanbury-Williams, *Works*, III, 79, Sir C. H. Williams to H. Fox, 22 Sep NS 1748.

73 Langford, *Polite and Commercial People*, p. 209.

74 NMM: SAN/V/48 p. 73, W. Bentinck to S, 9 May NS 1748.

75 Gerretson & Geyl, *Briefwisseling van Bentinck*, II, 170, C. Bentinck to W. Bentinck, 5 Oct 1748. Haas, 'Pursuit of Political Success', pp. 61–64.

76 NUL: NeC 720, Newcastle to Hardwicke, 21 Aug/1 Sep 1748; NeC 781 & 782, Newcastle to H. Pelham, 1/ 12 & 9/20 Oct 1748. Barnes, 'Pelham and Newcastle' p. 72.

CHAPTER IV

1 PRO: PRO 30/50/44 f. 19, S to R. N. Aldworth, 4 Sep NS 1748.

2 *BC*, I, 191, S to Bedford, 24 Nov NS 1746.

3 Dobrée, *Chesterfield Letters*, III, 812 No. 980 Chesterfield to S, 21 Nov 1746.

4 WA: Vol. XV f. 74, G. Anson to Bedford, 13 Dec 1746.

5 BM: Add.MSS 15957 f. 29, S to Anson, 14 Nov NS 1747.

6 S. W. C. Pack, *Admiral Lord Anson*, (London, 1960), for example, remarks on p. 1 that 'he was not really interested in politics', before describing a career which would have been impossible to any but an active politician.

7 NMM: SAN/V/49 p. 65, Chesterfield to S, 20 Feb OS 1746/7; SAN/ V/50 p. 210, C. Clarke to S, 4 Mar 1747[48]; SAN/V/53 p. 135, Newcastle to S, 27 Mar 1747. Dobrée, *Chesterfield Letters*, III, 812 No. 980, Chesterfield to S, 21 Nov OS 1746. *BNA*, pp. 78–80. *BC*, I, 282–84, S to Bedford, 5 Nov NS 1747. BM: Add.MSS 32807 ff. 208–9 & 263, S

to Newcastle, 21 Mar & 11 Apr [NS 1747]; Add.MSS 15957 f. 65, S to Anson, 14 Jun NS 1748.

8 *BNA*, pp. 78–80.

9 BM: Add.MSS 32807 ff. 208–9, S to Newcastle, 21 Mar [NS 1747].

10 NMM: SAN/V/53 p. 164, Newcastle to S, 24 Apr 1747.

11 BM: Add.MSS 32707 f. 300, S to Newcastle, 11 Jun [1747]; Add MSS 15955 f. 141, Bedford to Anson, 20 Jun 1747. NMM: SAN/V/48 p. 122, S to W. Bentinck, 5 Jun 1747.

12 Dobrée, *Chesterfield Letters*, III, 942 No. 1260, Chesterfield to S. Dayrolles, 16 Jun 1747.

13 Dobrée, *Chesterfield Letters*, III, 1043 No. 1439, Chesterfield to S. Dayrolles, 23 Oct 1747.

14 Coxe, *Pelham*, I, 390, H. Fox to Sir C. H. Williams, 17 Feb 1747/8. William Coxe, *Memoirs of Horatio, Lord Walpole*, (London, 1802), p. 376. Rose, *Marchmont*, I, 264, (cf *HMC 67 Polwarth*, V, 267). BM: Add.MSS 32811 ff. 197–98 & 213, Newcastle to S, 9 & 12 Feb 1747/8. Haas, 'Pursuit of Political Success', p. 63. Massie, 'Defence of the Low Countries', p. 288.

15 NMM: SAN/V/50 pp. 93–95, Anson to S, 23 Feb 1747/8.

16 McCann, *Richmond–Newcastle Correspondence*, p. 267 No. 400, Richmond to Newcastle, 9 Feb 1747/8.

17 *BC*, I, 323–24, Bedford to S, 12 Feb 1747/8; I, 324–25, Anson to Bedford, 13 & 14 Feb 1747/8. BM: Add MSS 15955 f. 161, Bedford to Anson, 12 Feb 1747/8; Add.MSS 15946 f. 48, Bedford to Anson, 16 Feb 1747/8.

18 *BC*, I, 319 & 324–25, Anson to Bedford, 5, 13 & 14 Feb 1748.

19 NMM: SAN/V/50 pp. 81, 98 & 105–6, Anson to S, 14 & 23 Feb 1747/8 & 10 May 1748; pp. 210 & 215, C. Clarke to S, 4 Mar 1747[48] & 29 Mar 1748. BM: Add.MSS 32812 f. 1, S to Newcastle, 12 Apr NS 1748.

20 BM: Add MSS 15955 f. 79, T. Anson

to Anson, 18 Feb 1748; ff. 219–22, J. Clevland to Anson, 13 Feb 1747[48]. Barrow, *Anson*, pp. 196–202.

21 NMM: SAN/V/50 p. 83, Anson to S, 14 Feb 1747/8, printed at greater length by Barrow, *Anson*, pp. 199–200.

22 BM: Add.MSS 15957 f. S to Anson, 5 Mar NS 1748, printed inaccurately by Barrow, *Anson*, p. 203.

23 BM: Add.MSS 15957 f. 53, S to Anson, 19 Mar NS 1748, printed at greater length by Barrow, *Anson*, p. 204.

24 The 1652 articles are printed in *Letters and Papers relating to the First Dutch War, 1652–1654*, ed. S. R. Gardiner & C. T. Atkinson (NRS Vols 13, 17, 30, 37, 41 & 66, 1898–1930) III, 293–301; those of 1661 and 1749 (as passed) in various editions of the Statutes or in *Articles of War*, ed. N. A. M. Rodger (Havant, 1982).

25 WA: Vol. X f. 112, S to Bedford, 22 Oct 1745.

26 Clarke, *Waldegrave Memoirs*, p. 40.

27 Dobrée, *Chesterfield Letters*, IV, 316 No. 1625, Chesterfield to S. Dayrolles, 9 Mar 1748/9.

28 NMM: SAN/F/1/4, T. Smith to S, 17 Feb 1748 [49].

29 *WC*, XX, 33 & 38, H. Walpole to H. Mann, 4 & 23 Mar 1748/9. Haas, 'Rise of the Bedfords', p. 77. Baugh, *Naval Administration 1715–1750*, pp. 86–87. Erskine, *Augustus Hervey's Journal*, pp. 78–84. Yorke, *Hardwicke*, II, 84–88. Hardwicke's copy of the draft bill, annotated with matters raised in debate, is in BM: Add.MSS 35876, ff. 354ff.

30 Rodger, *Wooden World*, pp. 145–204. David J. Starkey, 'War and the Market for Seafarers in Britain, 1736–1792', in Lewis R. Fischer & Helge W. Nordvik, eds. , *Shipping and Trade, 1750–1950: Essays in International Maritime Economic History*, (Pontefract, 1990) pp. 25–42.

31 Barrow, *Anson*, pp. 221–24. Bromley, *Manning Pamphlets*, p. xxxiv.

32 Barrow, *Anson*, p. 210. Hattendorf, *Naval Documents*, No. 244.

33 BM: Add.MSS 35410 ff. 153–54, Newcastle to Hardwicke, 10 Sep 1749.

34 PRO: ADM 7/662 f. 73, written in 1775.

35 PRO: ADM 3/61, minute of 9 Jun 1749.

36 PRO: ADM 3/61, 26 Jun 1749.

37 PRO: ADM 3/61, 26 Jun 1749.

38 PRO: ADM 3/61, 29 Jun, 5 & 6 Jul 1749; ADM 7/658 pp. 17–18 & 27.

39 Haas, 'Royal Dockyards', pp. 196–97. Middleton, '1749 Visitation'.

40 Haas, 'Royal Dockyards', p. 197. PRO: ADM 3/61, 26 & 27 Jun 1749.

41 PRO: ADM 3/61, 26 Jun 1749.

42 PRO: ADM 174/290, 12 Aug 1749, Journal of Commissioner Vanbrugh; I owe this reference to the kindness of Dr Michael Duffy.

43 PRO: ADM 106/2116, 10 Nov 1749. Haas, 'Royal dockyards' p. 198. Middleton, '1749 Visitation', p. 24.

44 Matcham, *Forgotten John Russell*, p. 306.

45 PRO: ADM 106/2116, 14 Dec 1751. NMM: ADM/B/145.

46 Haas, 'Royal Dockyards', p. 198. PRO: ADM 106/2507 No. 399. Middleton, '1749 Visitation', pp. 26–27.

47 PRO: ADM 106/2186 pp. 129–37 & ADM 3/62, 2 Jun 1752. Haas, 'Task Work', pp. 47–48.

48 NMM: SAN/V/50 p. 109, Anson to S, 10 May [1748].

49 Lawson, *Grenville*, pp. 62–63.

50 Mackay, *Hawke*, pp. 136–37 & 305–8.

51 Yorke, *Hardwicke*, II, 87.

52 NMM: SAN/V/50 p. 219, C. Clarke to S, [Jun 1748] (first page missing).

53 KHA: Bentinck MSS Box 6, S. to W. Bentinck, 6 Nov [NS] 1748.

54 Speck, *Stability and Strife*, p. 254. Haas, 'Pursuit of Political Success', p. 69. Haas, 'Rise of the Bedfords', pp. 71–90.

55 Ilchester, *Fox Letters*, pp. 57–59, S to H. Fox, 30 Mar 1751. NMM:

SAN/F/41/4, R. Leveson Gower to S, 13 Jun 1751. Gerretson & Geyl, *Briefwisseling van Bentinck*, II, 552, 560–62, 572, 595–96 & 602. W. Bentinck's diary, 8 & 13 May, Jun, & 13 Aug 1751. Walpole, *Memoirs of George II*, I, 3, 78, 82 & 106. *WC*, IX, 115, H. Walpole to G. Montagu, 13 Jun 1751.

56 Wellenreuther, *Repräsentation und Grossgrundbesitz*, p. 53 has useful reflections on this.

57 'Sandwich s'est perdu dans l'ésprit du public en montrant une ambition demesurée à laquelle il a tout sacrifi- cié, sans aucune delicatesse sur la choix des moyens, outre qu'il n'est pas assez grand seigneur pour se sou- tenir par lui même, moins encore pour former et entretenir un parti comme les deux frères Newcastle et Pelham le peuvent par leurs grands possessions, leurs alliances, le grand nombre de leurs amis et surtout par leur caractère personnel et la confi- ance nationale'. Gerretson & Geyl, *Briefwisseling van Bentinck*, II, 595.

58 Blackey, 'Halifax', p. 81.

CHAPTER V

1 J. J. Cartwright, ed., *The Travels through England of Dr Richard Pococke*, (Camden Soc NS XLII & XLIV, 1888–1889) I, 77. Sandwich, *Hinch- ingbrooke*, is a history of the house.

2 Climenson, *Elizabeth Montagu*, I, 269, Edward Montagu to Mrs Eliza- beth Montagu, 28 Sep 1749.

3 Toynbee, 'Walpole's Visits to Country Seats', p. 49; cf *WC*, X, 79, H. Walpole to G. Montagu, 30–31 May 1763.

4 Sandwich, *Voyage*, p. v.

5 Climenson, *Elizabeth Montagu*, I, 271. BM: Add.MSS 15957, S to Anson, 30 Jan NS 1748.

6 HEH: MO 1658, Lady S to Mrs E. Montagu, 30 Aug [1749?].

7 NUL: NeC 557, S to H. Pelham, 26 Jan NS 1748.

8 HEH: MO 1651, Lady S to Mrs E. Montagu, 8 Nov [NS 1746].

9 BM: Add.MSS 15957 f. 36, S to Anson, 19 Dec [NS] 1747.

10 NMM: SAN/V/41 p. 93, R. Keith to S, 5 Jun NS 1748.

11 Chatterton, *Gambier*, I, 24.

12 Climenson, *Elizabeth Montagu*, I, 261.

13 HEH: MO 1653, Lady S to Mrs E. Montagu, 18 Sep NS [1748].

14 HEH: MO 1656, Lady S to Mrs E. Montagu, 23 Jul [1749].

15 Climenson, *Elizabeth Montagu*, I, 266.

16 *BC*, II, 102, R. Rigby to Bedford, 20 Aug 1751.

17 SM: F/59c/1, S to Lady S, 26 Sep [1751].

18 HEH: MO 1680, Lady S to Mrs E. Montagu, 4 Aug [1751].

19 SM: F/59c/2, Fane to S, 12 May [1752].

20 Climenson, *Elizabeth Montagu*, II, 103. HEH: MO 1649, Lady S to E. Montagu, 23 Apr 1758; MO 1697, Lady S to Mrs E. Montagu, 5 Dec 1758.

21 HEH: MO 1652, Lady S to Mrs E. Montagu, 7 Apr [1751 or 52].

22 Climenson, *Elizabeth Montagu*, II, 69. SM: F/45a/4, S to Cumberland, 16 Jun 1757.

23 NMM: SAN/V/14 No. 83, S to Lady S, 11 Aug 1764; SAN/V/12 pp. 251 & 253, S to Lady S, 10 & 11 May 1765.

24 NMM: SAN/V/14 No. 84, C. Green to S, 18 Sep 1766. PRO: C 211/23/94, return to writ De Lunatico Inquirendo, May 1767.

25 PRO: C 12/792/4 Fane con Sand- wich. BM: Add MSS 36060 f. 84 are Lord Hardwicke's notes on this case. See also PRO: C 11/2109/18–19 Fane con Salis & C 11/2109/23 Fane con Stanhope.

26 NMM: SAN/V/12 pp. 247–48, S to Fane, 18 Mar 1765.

27 NMM: SAN/V/12 pp. 268–69, S to Fane, 9 Sep 1765.

28 SM: F/53/72, S to Lady M. Fitz- gerald, 9 Oct 1765.

29 *WC*, X, 207, G. Montagu to H. Wal-

pole, 12 Mar 1766, and Osborn, *Political and Social Letters*, pp. 132–33, both describe the wedding.

30 *Complete Peerage*, XI, 436–438.

31 *WC*, X, 209, G. Montagu to H. Walpole, 29 Mar 1766. Cradock, *Memoirs*, I, 154. WRO: CR2017/ C268/39 & CR2017/C243 p. 464, S to Denbigh, 6 Oct 1775, printed in *HMC 68, Denbigh*, V, 297.

32 Kelch, *Newcastle*, pp. 37 & 73.

33 Johnson, 'Bedford Connection', p. 33.

34 HRO: HINCH/2/1 & 2/61.

35 Haas, 'Pursuit of Political Success', p. 56.

36 Johnson, 'Bedford Connection' pp. 21 & 51.

37 SM: F/57/19.

38 HRO: HINCH/5/70.

39 *BC*, I, 245, S to Bedford, 29 Aug [NS] 1747.

40 Horn, *Diplomatic Service*, pp. 61–62.

41 BM: Add.MSS 32810 f. 391, Newcastle to S, 25 Dec 1747.

42 BM: Add.MSS 32810 f. 289, S to Newcastle, 1 Dec NS 1747.

43 BM: Add.MSS 32811 ff. 183–84, S to [H Pelham], 16 Feb NS 1748.

44 PRO: T 38/161 Civil List Accounts Midsummer 1746–47 f. 9, 1747–48 f. 6, 1748–49 f. 6. NMM: SAN/F/ 47/2. NUL: NeC 555.

45 NUL: NeC 557, S to H. Pelham, 26 Jan NS 1748.

46 Bussemakers, *Maison d'Orange-Nassau*, IV, 333 n. 5. *BC*, I, 584, S to Bedford, 1 Dec NS 1748.

47 BM: Add.MSS 15957 f. 78, S to Anson, 7 Aug NS 1748.

48 Thomas, *Stamp Act Crisis*, p. 3.

49 Blackey, 'Halifax', p. 48. Sainty, *Admiralty Officials*, p. 20.

50 NMM: SAN/F/45a/7, Cumberland to S, 16 Aug 1757.

51 *WC*, I, 89, H. Walpole to W. Cole, 9 Mar 1765. BM: Add.MSS 32874 f. 15, S to Newcastle, 12 Sep 1757. SM: F/59a/29, D. Murphy to S, 5 Aug 1757. Cole, *Journal*, pp. 83–85.

52 NMM: SAN/V/12 pp. 270–73, S to Fane, 19 Oct 1765.

53 SM: F/57/6, S to Halifax, 12 Feb 1768.

54 SM: F/57/19. HRO: HINCH/2/16–17. PRO: C 211/23/94.

55 SM: F/61/3, H. Seymour to S, 30 Mar 1771. NMM: SAN/V/12 pp. 285–86, S to H. Seymour, 1 Apr 1771.

56 PRO: C 211/23/94. SM: F/57/19.

57 Montagu Pennington, *Memoirs of the Life of Mrs Elizabeth Carter*, (London, 2nd edn. 1808, 2 vols) I, 436–37. Horace Walpole thought it was £4,000, but his information about wills was frequently wrong: *WC*, XXI, 473, H. Walpole to H. Mann, 27 Jan 1761.

58 SM: F/57/6, S to Halifax, 12 Feb 1768; F/53/73, S to Lady M. Fitzgerald, 12 Dec 1765. Osborn, *Political and Social Letters*, p. 168.

59 SM: F/57/9, Halifax to S, 13 Oct 1769; F/62/7, S to Halifax, 16 Oct 1769.

60 *SP*, I, 19, S to A. Hervey, 13 Jun 1771.

61 SM: F/57/19.

62 HRO: HINCH/2/3–4.

63 SM: F/57/1 & 2, Bath to S, 2 Nov 1763 & 23 Jan 1764. HRO: HINCH/ 2/10. NMM: SAN/V/12 pp. 71 & 73, S to Bath 20 & 23 Jan 1764.

64 NMM: SAN/F/45a/10, S to Cumberland, 10 Nov 1762.

65 BM: Eg. MSS 3438 f. 140, S to Holdernesse, 11 Aug 1757; Eg. MSS 3439 f. 190, S to Holdernesse, 30 Apr 1761. Cust, *Cust Family*, p. 212, Egmont to Sir J. Cust, 3 Nov 1761. I have not discovered when S acquired this house, but it was a 15-year lease, taken out not later than 1756.

66 *BC*, I, 332, S to Bedford, 17 Mar [NS] 1748.

67 *BC*, I, 93, Bedford to Duchess of Bedford, 4 May 1746.

68 HEH: MO 1651, Lady S to Mrs E. Montagu, 8 Nov [NS 1746]. Krämer & Bussemakers, *Maison d'Orange Nassau*, Supp. No. 81, W. Bentinck to Orange, 1 Sep NS 1746.

69 D'Arblay, *Burney*, I, 36–37.

70 NMM: COR/57, J. Blankett to W. Cornwallis, 14 Dec 1771.

71 *BC*, II, 158, R. Rigby to Bedford, 29 Mar 1755.

72 WA: Vol. XXXII f. 39, R. Rigby to Bedford, 29 Jul 1756.

73 *BC*, II, 130 & III, 214, R. Rigby to Bedford, 3 Aug 1753 & 3 Mar 1763. Ashton, *Gambling*, pp. 72 & 75.

74 *Memoirs and Correspondence of George, Lord Lyttelton, from 1734 to 1773*, ed. R. J. Phillimore (London, 1845, 2 vols) I, 420.

75 Boulton, *White's* I, 126–27, 150–52. Brooks's, *Memorials*, pp. xi & 35.

76 Sandwich is not mentioned in such works as Andrew Steinmetz, *The Gaming Table: Its Votaries and Victims*, (London, 1870, 2 vols) & Ashton, *Gambling*. Jones, *Clubs of the Georgian Rakes*, p. 92, says that 'he gambled with caution and he drank without excess'.

77 NMM: SAN/F/49/160. Johnson, 'Bedford Connection', p. 146.

78 NMM: SAN/F/41/63. SM: F/51a/39, Sir G. Colebrooke to S, 25 Jan 1777.

79 Boulton, *White's*, II, 23, 25, 37 & 76.

80 McLean, *Men in White Coats*, p. 24. Langford, *Polite and Commercial People*, p. 574. Buckley, *18th Century Cricket*, passim.

81 Johnson, 'Bedford Connection', p. 17.

82 Altham & Swanton, *History of Cricket*, I, 34–36. *BC*, II, 97–98, R. Rigby to Bedford, 27 Jun 1751, gives an account of this match.

83 WA: Vol. XXXII f. 39, R. Rigby to Bedford, 29 Jul 1756.

84 *WC*, XX, 113, H. Walpole to H. Mann, 31 Jan 1750.

85 SM: F/53/90, undated 'Self-Portrait' [of Sandwich] by Lady M. Fitzgerald.

86 P. J. Grosley, *A Tour to London; or New Observations on England and its Inhabitants*, trans T. Nugent (London, 1772, 2 vols) I, 149.

87 Cradock, *Memoirs*, IV, 171 n. A contemporary use of the word is in Copeland, *Burke Correspondence*, IV, 398, E. Burke to T. L. O'Beirne, 24 Dec 1781.

88 Jones, *Clubs of the Georgian Rakes*, p. 92.

89 Butler, *Reminiscences*, I, 72. Sandwich, *Voyage*, p. xviii.

90 Count Frederick Kielmansegge, *Diary of a Journey to England in the Years 1761–1762*, trans Countess Kielmansegg (London, 1902), p. 28.

91 Cradock, *Memoirs*, I, 153.

92 SM: F/53/1–3, S. Nailour to S, all undated.

93 SM: F/53/4–20, M. Nailour to S, all undated [1752–54] except F/53/13, 5 Nov 1752; F/53/16, ca 16 Aug 1754; F/53/19, 1 Apr 1755.

94 SM: F/53/10 & 16, [M. Nailour] to S, n.d. & ca 18 Aug 1754; F/59b/9, G. Nailour to S, 18 Aug 1754; F/59b/10, S to G. Nailour, 20 Aug [1754].

95 *WC*, XXII, 402, H. Walpole to H. Mann, 1 Mar 1766, & XXXVIII, 394. Horace Bleackley, *Ladies Fair and Frail: Sketches of the Demi-Monde during the Eighteenth Century*, (London, 1909) pp. 17 & 78. *Nocturnal Revels*, I, 269–70.

96 All in SM: F/53, 54 & 54a.

97 NMM: SAN/V/13 p. 280, S to J. Gambier, 1 Jan 1781.

98 Lawrence Stone, *The Family, Sex and Marriage in England 1500–1800*, (London, 1977), pp. 531–33.

99 Allen, *Clubs of Augustan London*, pp. 119–20.

100 Kemp, *Dashwood*, pp. 131–36.

101 Williamson, *Wilkes*, pp. 32–33. Dashwood, *Dashwoods of West Wycombe*, p. 32. The best description of the house is in Toynbee, 'Walpole's Visits to Country Seats', pp. 50–51.

102 Dashwood, *Dashwoods of West Wycombe*, pp. 29–30 & 36. The books and the cellar book are still at West Wycombe.

103 *Nocturnal Revels*, I, Sig. A5–A5v.

104 The best modern descriptions of Medmenham are Williamson,

Wilkes, pp. 32–42; Jones, *Clubs of the Georgian Rakes*, pp. 116–33; Dashwood, *Dashwoods of West Wycombe*, pp. 27–47.

105 Dashwood, *Dashwoods of West Wycombe*, pp. 66–70.

106 S became a freemason in Holland, where the movement was closely associated with Orangist politics: Porta, *Joan en Gerrit Corver*, pp. 208–9.

107 Cust & Colvin, *Society of Dilettanti*, pp. 22–41. NMM: SAN/V/113, 'al Koran'; Minute Book of Divan Club [unpaginated], with list of members.

108 Jones, *Clubs of the Georgian Rakes*, p. 3.

109 Brown, *Manners and Principles*, I, 55.

110 Peter Wagner, *Eros Revived: Erotica of the Enlightenment in England and America*, (London, 1988), pp. 72–86 & 267–69. Roy Porter, 'Mixed Feelings: the Enlightenment and sexuality in eighteenth-century Britain', in *Sexuality in eighteenth-century Britain*, ed. Paul-Gabriel Boucé (Manchester, 1982) pp. 1–27. Charles Vereker, *Eighteenth-Century Optimism, A Study of the Interrelations of Moral and Social Theory in English and French Thought between 1689 and 1789*, (Liverpool, 1967). Jones, *Clubs of the Georgian Rakes*, p. 127.

111 Almon, *Wilkes Correspondence*, III, 62.

112 He is not mentioned in the list of members given by Horace Walpole (Toynbee, 'Walpole's Visits to Country Seats', pp. 50–51.) who was there in June 1763, nor by Wilkes who had by then been expelled, but he is described when elected as 'First Lord', which would put it between April and September of that year; Dashwood, *Dashwoods of West Wycombe*, pp. 36 & 38.

113 Dashwood, *Dashwoods of West Wycombe*, pp. 39–40. Kemp, *Dashwood*, pp. 134–36. Rudé, *Wilkes and Liberty*, pp. 17–19 describes Wilkes's connections with Dashwood.

114 Wilkes's references are printed in: Almon, *New Foundling Hospital for Wit*, pp. 42–46; & Almon, *Wilkes Correspondence*, III, 60–63. In his *Life and Political Writings*, p. 426, Wilkes mentions being at Medmenham in October 1762.

115 [Charles Johnston] *Chrysal: or the Adventures of a Guinea*, (London, 6th edn. 1768, 4 vols) III, 231–55; see also William Davis, *An Olio of Biographical and Literary Anecdotes. . . ,* (London, 1814) pp. 13–21.

116 *The Poems and Miscellaneous Compositions of Paul Whitehead*, ed. Captain Edward Thompson (London, 1777) p. xxxviii. Laver, *Churchill Poems*, II, 382–83.

117 Bodley: MS D. D. Dashwood B. 11/8/9, J. Tucker to Le Despencer, 22 Mar 1766.

118 Dashwood, *Dashwoods of West Wycombe*, pp. 37 & 45.

119 SM: F/51a/13, Le Despencer to S, 19 Aug 1770.

120 Carter, *Banks*, p. 152, quoting the *Morning Post*, of 22 Aug, which is possibly the earliest application of the name 'Hell-Fire Club'.

121 The correspondence is partly printed by Marillier, *Eighteenth-Century Romance*.

122 SM: F/53/40 [Lady M. Fitzgerald] to S, 23 [Dec 1762].

123 SM: F/53/53, M. Fitzgerald to S, 19 Jul 1764.

124 SM: F/53/58 & 71, [Lady M. Fitzgerald] to S, 19 Sep [1764]; S to Lady M. Fitzgerald, 21 Aug 1765.

125 SM: F/53/90, n.d.

CHAPTER VI

1 Cradock, *Memoirs*, IV, 165–66. SM: F/53/90, 'self-portrait' of S by Lady M. Fitzgerald.

2 Cradock, *Memoirs*, IV, 166.

3 Cradock, *Memoirs*, IV, 163.

4 *WC*, XXXVIII, 295.

5 Ribeiro, *Burney Letters*, p. 237; this

was at Hampton Green rather than Hinchingbrooke.

6 WA: Butcher MSS X/44/51, W. Montagu to S, [14 Dec 1752]. MC: VI. 8/39, S to J. Banks, 3 Sep 1775.

7 NMM: SAN/F/45a/9, S to Cumberland, 20 Sep 1757.

8 WA: Vol. XL f. 104 S to Bedford, 20 Sep [1759]; Vol. LV f. 36, S to Bedford, 19 Jan 1767.

9 NMM: SAN/F/41/25, Denbigh to S, 4 Oct 1766.

10 *BC*, III, 314, R. Rigby to Bedford, 5 Aug 1765.

11 *WC*, XX, 155.

12 Altham & Swanton, *History of Cricket*, I, 37.

13 McLean, *Men in White Coats*, pp. 25–38.

14 Buckley, *18th Century Cricket*, p. 18.

15 George, *English Political Caricature*, p. 105. Hanbury-Williams, *Works*, III, 25.

16 Walpole, *Memoirs of George II*, I, 2–3. Haas, 'Rise of the Bedfords', pp. 9 & 13. BM: Add.MSS 5834 f. 213, Commonplace Book of Revd Wm Cole.

17 PRO: ADM 106/2116, 13 Jun & 21 Aug 1751. Ilchester, *Fox Letters*, p. 242, C. J. Fox to Holland, 20 Jul 1765. WA: Vol. X f. 51, S to Bedford, 20 Aug 1745.

18 NMM: SAN/F/41/21, S to A. Hervey, 15 Jul 1766; SAN/F/49/31, Orford to S, 4 Jul 1775. Childers, *Orford's Voyage*. KCC: A. H. Mann Papers, 'Cambridge Musicians Vol. I', H. Bates to his sister, 19 Jul 1778. O'Brian, *Banks*, p. 33.

19 Aspinall, *Later Correspondence of George III*, II, 498 No. 1431, Provost of Eton to Walsingham, 30 Jul 1796. NMM: SAN/F/37b/12, S. W. Loveden [?] to S, 28 Jul 1791.

20 *BC*, III, 314, R. Rigby to Bedford, 5 Aug 1765.

21 Cradock, *Memoirs*, I, 133–35.

22 Greig, *Hume Letters*, II, 319, D. Hume to W. Strahan, 10 May 1776.

23 Almon, *New Foundling Hospital for*

Wit, V, 15. Gruber, *Howe Brothers*, p. 9.

24 MC: VI. 9/1 p. 54, Mulgrave's Diary, 1 Feb 1776.

25 Betty Kemp, 'Frederick, Prince of Wales', in Natan, *Silver Renaissance*, pp. 38–56, at pp. 43–44 & 51.

26 *BC*, I, 18, S to Bedford, 10 Jan 1743/4; I, 21, D. Garrick to Bedford, 11 Sep 1744; I, 582, H. Legge to Bedford, 20 Nov NS 1748. Garrick, *Private Correspondence*, I, 31, Bedford to D. Garrick, 17 Sep 1744; II, 342, S to D. Garrick, 24 May n.y. *WC*, XXXII, 180 n. 10. Sandwich, *Voyage*, p. xxxii. Haas, 'Rise of the Bedfords', pp. 9–13 & 184.

27 Speck, *Stability and Strife*, p. 5. Langford, *Polite and Commercial People*, p. 613.

28 Howard Hunter Dunbar, *The Dramatic Career of Arthur Murphy*, (New York, 1946) pp. 85–86.

29 R. B. Peake, *Memoirs of the Colman Family*, (London, 1841, 2 vols) I, 233–35. Laver, *Churchill Poems*, I, 27 n.

30 SM: F/60/4, Mrs E. Smith to S, 2 Jun [1754]; F/19–40, Chancery Suit Courtenay con Smith, 1754–60.

31 Allen, *Clubs of Augustan London*, pp. 141–43. Arnold, *Society of Beefsteaks*, pp. xvii-xx.

32 Haas, 'Rise of the Bedfords', p. 163. Brooke, *Chatham Administration*, p. 32.

33 Turberville, *House of Lords*, p. 458.

34 Climenson, *Elizabeth Montagu*, I, 240, E. Montagu to Mrs E. Montagu, 30 Jun 1747.

35 Walpole, *Memoirs of George II*, II, 41.

36 BM: Eg.MSS 1721 f. 254, S to W. Bentinck, 24 Oct [1752].

37 Brooke, *Chatham Administration*, p. 32 n. 1, quoting BM: Add.MSS 35638 f. 382, E. Leeds to C. Yorke, 30 Oct 1768.

38 PRO: PRO 30/29/1/14 f. 616, S to Gower, 19 Nov 1769.

39 Stroud, *Capability Brown*, pp. 158 & 204.

40 *HMC 27 Beaufort*, p. 204, T. Dam-

pier to W. Windham & Haddington, 30 Jul 1741.

41 ERO: D/DBy C3/12, H. J. de Salis to R. N. Neville, 6 Mar 1772.

42 WA: Vol. XXVIII f. 67, S to Bedford, 30 Aug [1752].

43 *WC*, X, 151 n. 5, quoting *London Chronicle*, 4–6 Apr 1765, xvii, 336.

44 NMM: SAN/F/13/37, F. Greville to S, 21 Mar 1778.

45 McCann, *Richmond–Newcastle Correspondence*, p. 305 No. 459, Richmond to Newcastle, 27 Jul 1750.

46 Namier & Brooke, *House of Commons 1754–90*, I, 311–12. Sedgwick, *House of Commons 1715–54*, I, 264.

47 Johnson, 'Bedford Connection', pp. 157–60. Namier & Brooke, *House of Commons 1754–90*, I, 311–12.

48 Namier & Brooke, *House of Commons 1754–90*, III, 155.

49 Namier & Brooke, *House of Commons 1754–90*, I, 312, quoting T. H. B. Oldfield, *An Entire and Complete History, Political and Personal, of the Boroughs of Great Britain*, (London, 1792, 3 vols) II, 143.

50 *HMC 20 Dartmouth*, III, 253, S to Dartmouth, 24 Sep 1780.

51 NUL: NeC 461, S to H. Pelham, 2 Oct NS [1746]. NMM: SAN/V/12 pp. 19–22, S to Halifax, 29 Oct 1763; p. 302, S to Manchester, 8 Feb 1773. PRO: PRO 30/29/1/14 ff. 579–81, S to Gower, 21 Nov [1764]; f. 671, S to Gower, 8 Nov 1772. Cust, *Cust Family*, p. 275, S to J. Cust, 24 Jan 1768. Christie *The End of North's Ministry*, pp. 50 & 131. Namier & Brooke, *House of Commons 1754–90*, I, 310–11.

52 BM: Add.MSS 32806 f. 73, S to Newcastle, 13 Oct NS [1746].

53 SM: F/62/24, S to Hinchingbrooke, 27 Jun 1775.

54 *HMC 10 Underwood*, p. 296, Bp of Lincoln to E. Weston, 1 Jan 1747. NUL: NeC 466, S to H. Pelham, 23 May NS [1747]. Haas, 'Rise of the Bedfords', p. 165.

55 SM: F/59b/2, T. Thong to S, 3 Apr 1753.

56 Sandwich had given up hope of his brother distinguishing himself in the Navy.

57 BM: Add.MSS 15957 ff. 43–44, S to Anson, 20 Feb NS 1748.

58 Linda Colley, 'The Mitchell Election Division, 24 March 1755', *BIHR*, XLIX (1976) pp. 80–107. Sir George Forrest, *The Life of Lord Clive*, (London, 1918, 2 vols) I, 231–32. Namier & Brooke *House of Commons*, I, 234.

59 NMM: SAN/V/12 pp. 278–79, S to G. Wombwell, 19 Oct 1770.

60 MC: VI. 9/1 p. 15, Mulgrave's diary 21 Oct 1775.

61 MC: VI. 11/155, S to Mulgrave, 25 Jun 1782.

62 WA: Vol. XXVIII f. 29, S to Bedford, 5 Apr [1752].

63 See Hoffman, *The Marquis*, p. 54, for another example, concering an election for Governor of the Charterhouse.

64 WA: Butcher MSS III/7/51, S to R. Butcher, 15 May [1749]; X/40/32, S to R. Butcher, 14 May [1752].

65 Sutherland, *East India Company*, pp. 178–83, 215–16, 267 & 275–78.

66 Wraxall, *Memoirs*, I, 403.

67 Johnson, 'Bedford Connection', pp. 312–13. Namier, 'Monarchy and the Party System', pp. 36–37.

68 'Qui étoit son ami, manquoit de talents pour soutenir un parti et ne savoit ni profiter de son poids réel, ni le faire valoir; que lui Sandwich pensoit serieusement à se retirer non par choix, mais par necessité, ne sachant pas, s'il pouvoit maintenir son terrein'. Gerretson & Geyl, *Briefwisseling van Bentinck*, II, 561–62, Bentinck's diary, 13 May 1751.

69 Haas, 'Pursuit of Political Success', pp. 69–70. Haas, 'Rise of the Bedfords', pp. 80, 94–106 & 184–86. Bussemakers, *Maison d'Orange-Nassau*, II, 284, notes by W. Bentinck on political situation, 7 Jun 1753.

70 Walpole, *Memoirs of George II*, I, 128.
71 Haas, 'Rise of the Bedfords', pp. 110–12. Langford, *Polite and Commercial People*, p. 227.
72 Haas, 'Rise of the Bedfords', p. 70. Clark, *Dynamics of Change*, pp. 206 & 223. Walpole, *Memoirs of George II*, II, 115.
73 George, *English Political Caricature*, p. 105.
74 Haas, 'Rise of the Bedfords', pp. 124–28 & 140–45. NMM: SAN/F/41/6, H. Fox to S, 30 Oct 1756; SAN/F/41/7, S to Cumberland, 7 May 1757; SAN/F/41/8, S to Cumberland, 27 May 1757.
75 NMM: SAN/F/45a/4, S to Cumberland, 16 Jun 1757.
76 Sedgwick, *Letters of George III to Bute*, Intro. provides an excellent description of the king's views.
77 Namier, 'Monarchy and the Party System', p. 37.
78 Marshall, *Eighteenth-Century England*, p. 311.
79 Namier, *American Revolution*, p. 331.
80 Blackey, 'Halifax', p. 128, quoting BM: Add.MSS 32939 ff. 408–9, Newcastle to Hardwicke 19 Jun 1762. John Clevland was the Secretary of the Admiralty.
81 Brown & Schweizer, *Devonshire Diary*, p. 177.
82 Namier, *American Revolution*, p. 369.
83 Haas, 'Rise of the Bedfords', p. 71. Namier, *American Revolution*, pp. 210 & 383–84.
84 NMM: SAN/F/45a/10, S to Cumberland, 10 Nov 1762; SAN/V/14 No. 1, Cumberland to S, 10 Nov 1762.
85 WA: Vol. XLVI f. 128, R. Rigby to Bedford, 24 Nov 1762.

CHAPTER VII

1 Thomas, *Stamp Act Crisis*, pp. 1–9.
2 Sedgwick, *Letters of George III to Bute*, p. 228, George III to Bute, ca 18 Apr 1763.
3 Sedgwick, *Letters of George III to Bute*, pp. 223–24, George III to Bute, 3 letters all 15 Apr 1763. Copeland, *Burke Correspondence*, I, 169–70, E. Burke to Mrs E. Montagu, [25] Apr 1763.
4 *CG3*, I, 2 No. 3. This note is in the king's hand, but he is unlikely to have initiated research into the subject.
5 NMM: SAN/F/1/32 of October 1763.
6 NMM: SAN/F/1/34 dated 1 Sep 1764; its presence among Sandwich's papers strongly suggests that he originated it, and certainly shows that he was interested.
7 WLC: Lacaita-Shelburne Papers, S to Shelburne, n.d. [Jul 1763].
8 Thomas, *Stamp Act Crisis*, p. 13. Ilchester, *Fox Letters*, p. 179, S to Holland, 26 Sep 1763.
9 PRO: PRO 30/29/1/14 ff. 554–55 & 560, S to Gower, 31 Aug & 6 Sep 1763.
10 NMM: SAN/F/41/10, S to A. Hervey, 7 Sep 1763.
11 Ilchester, *Fox Letters*, p. 190, S to Holland, 14 Oct 1763.
12 Blackey, 'Halifax', p. 101.
13 Brown & Schweizer, *Devonshire Diary*, p. 19.
14 WA: Vol. XLVI f. 140, R. Rigby to Bedford, 26 Nov 1762. This passage is omitted from the version printed in *BC*, III, 159–63.
15 For general accounts of the Wilkes affair see Rudé, *Wilkes and Liberty*, Bleackley, *Wilkes*, Nobbe, *The North Briton*, pp. 239–47, and Hamilton, *Infamous Essay on Woman*.
16 Cannon, *Parliamentary Reform*, p. 58. Hamilton, *Infamous Essay*, p. 45.
17 George Harris, *The Life of Lord Chancellor Hardwicke*, (London, 1847, 3 vols) III, 231. Langford, *Polite and Commercial People*, p. 327.
18 For the text of No. 45 see *A Complete Collection of the Genuine Papers, Letters &c. in the Case of John Wilkes*, ('Berlin', 1769) Supp. pp. 1–15. Wilkes, *Life and Political Writings*, reprints extracts of various numbers.

19 Laver, *Poems of Churchill*, I, xxix.

20 BM: Add.MSS 32951 f. 220, G. Onslow to Newcastle, 29 Sep 1763. Hamilton, *Infamous Essay*, pp. 66 & 105.

21 Hamilton, *Infamous Essay*, p. 45.

22 Jones, *Clubs of the Georgian Rakes*, p. 133. Dashwood, *Dashwoods of West Wycombe*, pp. 38–39.

23 See above p. 83 and note 112.

24 Pottle, *Boswell's London Journal*, pp. 56–57.

25 *WC*, X, 110, H. Walpole to G. Montagu, 20 Nov 1763.

26 BM: Add.MSS 30891 ff. 2 & 9–10.

27 Arnold, *Society of Beefsteaks*, p. 150.

28 Hamilton, *Infamous Essay*, p. 57. [Charles Marsh] *The Clubs of London*, (London, 1828, 2 vols) II, 22. Marsh's information came from Arthur Murphy who was a member at the time.

29 W. P. Treloar, *Wilkes and the City*, (London, 1917), pp. 259–88.

30 *An Asylum for Fugitive Pieces in Prose and Verse*, (London, 1785, 4 vols) I, 283. Butler, *Reminiscences*, p. 75; Butler was a friend of both Sandwich and Wilkes.

31 NMM: SAN/V/14 No. 75, J. Wilkes to S, 9 Mar [1764?].

32 Williamson, *Wilkes*, p. 103. Henry Lord Brougham, *Historical Sketches of the Statesmen who flourished in the Time of George III*, (London, 1839–43, 3 vols) III, 189 is the earliest source attributing it to Wilkes which I have encountered.

33 Brian Connell, *Portrait of a Whig Peer, compiled from the papers of the Second Viscount Palmerston 1739–1802*, (London, 1957), pp. 107–8

34 Ilchester, *Fox Letters*, p. 180, S to Holland, 26 Sep 1763.

35 Hamilton, *Infamous Essay*, pp. 111–12.

36 *An Authentick Account of the Proceedings against John Wilkes Esq*, (London [1763]) prints letters, press comment etc., up to May.

37 Lawson, *Grenville*, p. 167. Thomas, *Stamp Act Crisis*, p. 16.

38 Hamilton, *Infamous Essay*, pp. 9 & 15.

39 Thomas Prowse MP, quoted by Colley, *In Defiance of Oligarchy*, p. 288.

40 Lawson, *Grenville*, p. 170.

41 Hamilton, *Infamous Essay*, p. 106.

42 Hamilton, *Infamous Essay*, pp. 92 & 105.

43 Hamilton, *Infamous Essay*, p. 107.

44 Watson, 'Wilkes and the "Essay on Woman"', pp. 145, 163 & 241.

45 *WC*, XXII, 185, H. Walpole to H. Mann, 17 Nov 1763. Walpole, *Memoirs of George III*, I, 248–49.

46 Watson, 'Wilkes and the "Essay on Woman"', p. 242.

47 The authorship of the poem is discussed by Williamson, *Wilkes*, p. 82; Hamilton, *Infamous Essay*, pp. 188–89; Rudé, *Wilkes and Liberty*, p. 31. Potter died in 1759.

48 PRO: KB 10/34 (pt. 3), King's Bench Indictments Mich. 4 Geo. III, contains the informations in the two cases The King v. John Wilkes, and extracts from the poems and No. 45. Hamilton, *Infamous Essay*, pp. 193–230, prints Pope's original and Potter's parody (with notes) on facing pages.

49 Cobbett, *Parliamentary History*, XV, 1364. Watson, 'Wilkes and the "Essay on Woman"', pp. 143–45.

50 O'Gorman, *Rise of Party in England*, pp. 79–80. Lawson, *Grenville*, pp. 171–73. *WC*, XXII, 181–86, H. Walpole to H. Mann, 17 Nov 1763; XXXVIII, 229, H. Walpole to Hertford, 17 Nov 1763. Blackey, 'Halifax', pp. 159–60. Michael McCahill, 'The House of Lords in the 1760s', in Jones, *Pillar of the Constitution*, pp. 165–98, at p. 171. Ayling, *George III*, pp. 111–13.

51 *WC*, XXXVIII, 231, H. Walpole to Hertford, 17 Nov 1763.

52 J. V. Beckett & Clyve Jones, 'The Peerage and the House of Lords in the Seventeenth and Eighteenth Centuries', in Jones, *Pillar of the Constitution*, pp. 1–19, at p. 3. G. M.

Ditchfield, 'The House of Lords in the Age of the American Revolution', *ibid*, pp. 199–239, at pp. 201–3.

53 NMM: SAN/V/14 No. 69, Bishop of Gloucester to S, 5 Nov 1763.

54 Williamson, *Wilkes*, pp. 82–83. Walpole, *Memoirs of George III*, I, 248. Langford, *Polite and Commercial People*, pp. 263 & 271–72. A. W. Evans, *Warburton and the Warburtonians: A Study in some Eighteenth-Century Controversies*, (Oxford, 1932) pp. 18, 63, 65, 131–32 & 276. Jones, *Clubs of the Georgian Rakes*, p. 98 gives MS authority for Mrs Warburton's infidelity.

55 *A Selection from Unpublished Papers of the Right Reverend William Warburton*, ed. Francis Kilvert (London, 1841), p. 227, W. Warburton to R. Allen, 17 Nov 1763, gives the bishop's account of the debate.

56 BFP, p. 12. Spencer, *Sandwich Diplomatic Correspondence*, pp. 64–66.

57 Copeland, *Burke Correspondence*, II, 219.

58 Spencer, *Sandwich Diplomatic Correspondence*, pp. 64–65. BFP, p. 54.

59 Roberts, *Splendid Isolation*, pp. 4–7.

60 Jeremy Black, 'Britain's Foreign Alliances in the Eighteenth Century', *Albion*, XX (1988) pp. 573–602. Baudi di Vesme, *La Politica Mediterranea Inglese*, p. 105.

61 Roberts, *Splendid Isolation*, pp. 24–27. BFP, pp. 51–63. Michael Roberts, 'Great Britain, Denmark and Russia, 1763–70', in *Studies in Diplomatic History: Essays in Memory of David Bayne Horn*, ed. Ragnhild Hatton & M. S. Anderson (London, 1970) pp. 236–67. Spencer, *Sandwich Diplomatic Correspondence*, pp. 9, 17 & 60.

62 Collyer, *Buckinghamshire Despatches*, II, 133, S to Buckingham, 20 Jan 1764.

63 Baugh, 'Why did Britain lose command of the Sea?'. Rodger, 'Continental Commitment'.

64 *NDAI*, pp. 1–2.

65 Haas, 'Royal Dockyards', p. 211.

66 *BFP*, p. 74. Ozanam & Antoine, *Correspondance Secrète*, I, 196 No. 101, de Broglie to Louis XV, 16 Dec 1763.

67 PRO: SP 75/117 f. 230, S to W. Titley & D. A. S. Cosby, 30 Nov 1764, printed in Spencer, *Sandwich Diplomatic Correspondence*, p. 245. This is the copy addressed to Copenhagen of a circular which went to all missions. See also Roberts, *British Diplomacy and Swedish Politics*, p. 125.

68 Tracy, 'Gunboat Diplomacy'.

69 NMM: SAN/V/14 No. 6, Bedford to S, 16 Aug 1764.

70 *HMC 49 Stopford-Sackville*, I, 95, Ld G. Sackville to J. Irwin, 22 Aug 1764.

71 Ilchester, *Fox Letters*, pp. 197–98, Sir G. Macartney to Holland, 7 Aug 1764.

72 PRO: SP 75/118 ff. 9–11, S to W. Titley, 15 Jan 1765; f. 54, W. Titley to S, 2 Feb 1765.

73 *CG3*, I, 70–71 No. 44, S to George III, [4 Mar 1765].

74 WA: Vol. L f. 200, S to Bedford, 14 Nov 1764.

75 BM: Stowe MSS 259 f. 63, S to R. Phelps, 4 Sep 1764.

76 Walpole, *Memoirs of George III*, II, 191. Brewer, *Party Ideology*, p. 234. Rea, *The English Press in Politics*, p. 100. John Brewer, 'The Misfortunes of Lord Bute: A Case-Study in Eighteenth-Century Political Argument and Public Opinion', *HJ*, XVI (1973) pp. 3–43, at p. 17.

77 WA: Vol. XLVIII f. 102, S to Bedford, 17 Sep 1763.

78 Brewer, *Party Ideology*, p. 58. WC, XXXIX, 79, H. Walpole to H. S. Conway, 18 Oct 1766.

79 *WC*, XXXIX, 79, H. Walpole to H. S. Conway, 18 Oct 1766.

80 Smith, *Grenville Papers*, II, 256, S to G. Grenville, 27 Jan 1764. E. R. Turner, *The Cabinet Council of England in the Seventeenth and Eighteenth Centuries, 1622–1784*, (Baltimore, 1930–32, 2 Vols) II, 71.

81 Ayling, *George III*, p. 105. Spencer,

Sandwich Diplomatic Correspondence, p. 63.

82 NMM: SAN/V/12 pp. 188–91, S to Townshend, 16 Nov 1764; pp. 203–8, S to Bedford, 24 Nov 1764.

83 Smith, *Grenville Papers,* II, 227 & 236.

84 *WC,* XLIII, 186, S to?, 29 Nov 1764.

85 Winstanley, *Cambridge in the Eighteenth Century,* p. 316. Winstanley, *Unreformed Cambridge,* pp. 281–82.

86 Yorke, *Hardwicke,* III, 484–85 & 561.

87 BM: Add.MSS 32982 f. 435, S to Newcastle, 26 Jun 1767.

88 Winstanley, *Cambridge in the Eighteenth Century,* pp. 56–138. Walpole, *Memoirs of George III,* I, 314–15. *WC,* XIV, 131 & 133, T. Gray to H. Walpole, 27 Jan & [18?] Mar 1764; XXXVIII, 363, H. Walpole to Hertford, 5 Apr 1764.

89 BM: Add.MSS 35428 f. 9, Hardwicke's 'Memorial of Family Occurances, 1760–70', Jan 1771.

90 Smith, *Grenville Papers,* III, 168. *CG3,* I, 96–97 & 99–100 Nos. 64 & 67, Halifax to George III, 17 & 18 May 1765. BM: Add.MSS 34712 f. 56, Bedford to Halifax, 19 May 1765. WA: Vol. LI ff. 66, 70 & 102, W. Ellis to S, 17, 17 & 18 May 1765.

91 Lawson, *Grenville,* pp. 211–18. Add.MSS 34713 f. 239, Cabinet Conclusion, 22 May 1765. Bateson, *Newcastle Narrative,* pp. 19–23, Newcastle to J. White, 4 Jun 1765. Smith, *Grenville Papers,* III, 52–62.

92 Lawson, *Grenville,* p. 219. NMM: SAN/F/41/17, S to A. Hervey, 4 Jul 1765; SAN/F/53/71, S to Lady M. Fitzgerald, 21 Aug 1765. WA: Vol. LII f. 4, S to Bedford, 2 Jul 1765. Thomas, *Stamp Act Crisis,* pp. 115–17.

CHAPTER VIII

1 Ilchester, *Fox Letters,* p. 230, G. Selwyn to Holland, 12 Jul 1765.

2 NMM: SAN/F/41/18, S to A. Hervey, 20 Jul 1765. SM: F/53/71, S to Lady M. Fitzgerald, 21 Aug 1765.

Ilchester, *Fox Letters,* p. 242, C. J. Fox to Holland, 20 Jul 1765. WA: Vol. LII f. 4, S to Bedford, 2 Jul 1765; f. 170, R. Rigby to Bedford, 26 Oct 1765.

3 Lawson, *Grenville,* p. 220.

4 Langford, *Rockingham Administration,* pp. 271–72. Bateson, *Newcastle Narrative,* pp. 86, 97, 120, 141, 146, 155 & 161 gives examples of their prominent position.

5 *BC,* III, 313, R. Rigby to Bedford, 5 Aug 1765.

6 Langford, *Rockingham Administration,* p. 93.

7 Langford, *Polite and Commercial People,* pp. 363–64.

8 *BC,* III, 317, S to Bedford, 26 Aug 1765.

9 Brooke, *Chatham Administration,* pp. 30–32.

10 Haas, 'Pursuit of Political Success', p. 73.

11 Namier, *American Revolution,* p. 214.

12 NMM: SAN/F/41/22, S to A. Hervey, 17 Jul 1766.

13 SM: F/54/81, S to [Lady M. Fitzgerald], 19 [Jul 1766].

14 Brooke, *Chatham Administration,* p. 37 n. 3.

15 Wright, *Cavendish's Debates,* I, 592, Bedford's diary 31 Oct 1766.

16 WA: Vol. LIV f. 112, S to Bedford, 28 Nov 1766.

17 *BC,* III, 359, Bedford's memorandum, 1 Dec 1766.

18 Brooke, *Chatham Administration,* p. 40.

19 Brooke, *Chatham Administration,* pp. 64–65.

20 WA: Vol. LV f. 36, S to Bedford, 19 Jan 1767.

21 Add.MSS 42085 f. 11 [23 Mar 1767].

22 WLC: Lacaita-Shelburne Papers, S to Rochford, 22 Mar 1767.

23 Brooke, *Chatham Administration,* pp. 121 & 126.

24 *BC,* III, 382, Bedford journal, 20 Jul 1767.

25 Bateson, *Newcastle Narrative,* pp. 146 & 155, Newcastle to J. White, 21 Jul 1767, & Albemarle to Rockingham,

23 Jul 1767. Wright, *Cavendish's Debates*, I, 605–7.

26 Brooke, *Chatham Administration*, pp. 325 & 331. Haas, 'Pursuit of Political Success', p. 74.

27 Ellis, *Post Office*, p. 10.

28 Betty Kemp, 'Some Letters of Sir Francis Dashwood, Baron Le Despencer, as Joint Postmaster General, 1766–81', *Bulletin of the John Rylands Library*, XXXVII (1954–55) pp. 204–48.

29 Bodley: MS D. D. Dashwood B.2/1/2a, S to Le Despencer, 28 Sep [1769].

30 WA: Vol. LVII f. 194, S to Grafton, 24 Oct 1768.

31 BM: Eg.MSS 1862 f. 252, S to W. Bentinck, [24 Aug 1768]. NMM: SAN/F/47/26, W. Bentinck to S, 28 Aug 1768.

32 WA: Vol. LVIII f. 146, S to Bedford, 6 Sep 1769.

33 Quoted by Stanley Ayling, *The Elder Pitt, Earl of Chatham*, (London, 1976), p. 92.

34 Thomas, *North*, p. 59.

35 WA: Vol. LVIII f. 74, S to Bedford, 29 May 1769; f. 78, R. Rigby to Bedford, 6 Jun 1769.

36 SRB: Ac. 423/535, George III to Grafton, 6 Jun 1769.

37 SRB: Ac. 423/539, George III to Grafton, 29 Nov 1769.

38 Pares, *George III and the Politicians*, p. 64.

39 Langford, *Polite and Commercial People*, p. 375. Smith, *Grenville Papers*, IV, 275–77 & 348, T. Whately to G. Grenville, 22 Apr & 24 Aug 1768.

40 *BFP*, pp. 114–36.

41 Blackey, 'Halifax', pp. 99–101.

42 *BC*, I, 13, T. Brand to Bedford, 3 Jun 1743. Haas, 'Rise of the Bedfords', p. 9.

43 *WC*, IX, 258, G. Montagu to H. Walpole, ca 15 Nov 1759.

44 Cannon, *Jones Letters*, I, 139, W. Jones to Althorp, 1 Jan 1774.

45 SM: F/52/2 is an anonymous song describing a meeting in 1773 and mentioning many of the performers.

46 Sandwich, *Voyage*, pp. xxxiv–xxxv.

47 Mann, 'Mr and Mrs Bates', p. 14.

48 Mann, 'Mr and Mrs Bates', p. 14.

49 *HMC 28 Charlemont*, I, 179, E. Murphy to Charlemont, 4 Apr OS 1747.

50 Sandwich, *Voyage*, p. xxxiii.

51 Butler, *Reminiscences*, p. 72.

52 See the Hinchingbrooke library borrowing book, now at Mapperton.

53 Childers, *Orford's Voyage*, pp. 7 & 34.

54 Cannon, *Jones Letters*, I, 338, W. Jones to Althorp, 13 Jan 1780.

55 *New Grove*, IV, 6.

56 *New Grove*, XI, 193. BM: Music Library H.2788.rr. & ss., Minute Books of the Catch Club, *passim*. Viscount Gladstone, *The Story of the Noblemen and Gentlemen's Catch Club*, (London, 1930, privately printed), pp. 9–13.

57 Weber, *Rise of the Musical Classics*, p. 147.

58 Weber, 'Handel Commemoration', pp. 49–50. *New Grove*, XI, 192–93.

59 Weber, *Rise of the Musical Classics*, pp. 169–70.

60 Charles Burney, *A General History of Music, from the Earliest Ages to the Present Period*, ed. Frank Mercer (London, 1935, 2 vols) II, 1022.

61 *New Grove*, XI, 194. Weber, 'Handel Commemoration', pp. 52–53. Weber, *Rise of the Musical Classics*, pp. 168–88, analyses the repertory of the Concerts.

62 KCC: A. H. Mann Papers, 'Cambridge Musicians Vol. I', [Mrs H. Furey?] to [Grace Bates?] her sister-in-law, n.d.

63 Weber, *Rise of the Musical Classics*, pp. 163–66.

64 Weber, *Rise of the Musical Classics*, pp. 150–51, seems to imply this, but I know of nothing to confirm it in S's correspondence, and his musical interests long predate the Wilkes affair.

65 Weber, *Rise of the Musical Classics*, pp. 143–46.

66 He seems usually to have signed 'Bates' and occasionally 'Bate', his brother Henry the other way round.

67 Weber, 'Handel Commemoration', p. 54. *New Grove*, II, 284. KCC: A. H. Mann Papers, 'Cambridge Musicians Vol. I', notes on Joah Bates. Rees, *Cyclopaedia*, s.v. Bates, Joah [by Charles Burney]. Mann, 'Mr and Mrs Bates', & 'Batesiana'.

68 Burney, *Handel Commemoration*, p. 14.

69 Percy A. Scholes, *The Great Dr Burney*, (London, 1948, 2 vols) II, 63 n. 1. Mann, 'Batesiana'.

70 Mann, 'Batesiana'.

71 But mill-girls would hardly have been able to afford to travel to a musical festival, and she appears to have had connections of respectable social standing (*ex inf.*, Prof. W. Weber).

72 Mackerness, *Social History of Music*, p. 113.

73 Cradock, *Memoirs*, I, 120. *New Grove*, II, 284. Most of the information about her comes from the sources cited above for her husband's life.

74 KCC: A. H. Mann Papers, 'Cambridge Musicians Vol. I', Mrs H. Bates to Mrs Furey, 13 Mar 1783.

75 Ribeiro, *Burney Letters*, pp. 115 n. 8 & pp. 162–63.

76 Lonsdale, *Burney*, pp. 111–12. D'Arblay, *Burney*, I, 269–70. Troide, *Burney Journals*, I, 172–73.

77 NMM: SAN/F/36/98, C. Burney to S, 17 Feb 1784, enc Mrs S. Phillips to C. Burney [SAN/F/36/95]. Susanna Phillips was James's sister, married to Lt Molesworth Phillips of the Marines, another of Cook's officers. See also SAN/F/36/101 & 102, Exeter to S, 17 & 19 Dec 1790.

78 Jesse, *George Selwyn*, IV, 65. Cradock, *Memoirs*, I, 118. *Notes and Queries*, 4th S. III (1869) p. 339. *Case and Memoirs of Miss Martha Reay*, pp. 1–4. *The Town and Country Magazine or Universal Repository of Knowledge, Instruction and Entertainment*, (1769) pp. 561–64.

79 Black, *Cumberland Letters*, p. 228.

80 *WC*, XXIV, 459, H. Walpole to H. Mann, 17 Apr 1779. The existence of the child named Ray mentioned in G. F. Grand, *The Narrative of a Gentleman Long Resident in India*, ed. Walter K. Firminger (Calcutta HS, 1910) p. 10 is unconfirmed by any other source.

81 SM: F/55a/8, M. Ray to S, 24 Jun 1772.

82 Cradock, *Memoirs*, I, 143. SM: F/55a/5, 10, 12 & 13 M. Ray to S, 2 Oct [1766], 22, 26 & 28 Oct 1772; F/55b/3, R. Phelps to S, [27 Oct 1766].

83 HEH: LO 9203, S to Loudoun, 22 Oct 1772.

84 SM: F/55b/10, Loudoun to S, 30 Oct 1772.

85 HEH: LO 6421, S to Loudoun, 30 Oct 1772.

86 SM: F/54a *passim*

87 Hackman's story is given in various forms by: *WC*, XXXIII, 99–100, H. Walpole to Lady Ossory, 9 Apr 1779. Jesse, *George Selwyn*, IV, 67–68. *Case and Memoirs of Miss Martha Reay*, pp. 9–11. *The Case and Memoirs of the Late Rev Mr James Hackman*, (London, 1779). *The Genuine Life, Trial, and Dying Words of the Rev. James Hackman . . .*, (London [1779]). *Nocturnal Revels*, I, 247–49.

88 Burgess, *Love Letters of Mr H. and Miss R.*, originally published anonymously by Sir Herbert Croft as *Love and Madness: A Story too True*, (London, 1780). Oblique evidence of their genuineness in offered by Martelli, *Jemmy Twitcher*, p. 174.

89 Burgess, *Love Letters of Mr H. and Miss R.*, p. 39.

90 Prince Hoare, *Memoirs of Granville Sharp*, (London, 2nd ed 1828, 2 vols) I, 227; the author is surely wrong in reading this as a reference to Lady Sandwich, whom Omai cannot have met.

91 For Sandwich's subsequent enquiries see BM: Add.MSS 35615 f. 202, S to Hardwicke, 11 Apr 1779. SM: F/55c/3, S's examination of C. Galli.

92 Burgess, *Love Letters of Mr H. and Miss R.*, p. 40.

93 Burgess, *Love Letters of Mr H. and Miss R.*, pp. 119–20 & 136–37.

94 All the sources cited above for the lives of Ray and Hackman give accounts of the murder. Jesse, *George Selwyn*, IV, 60–65, collects newspaper stories.

95 Cradock, *Memoirs*, I, 146.

96 PRONI: D. 638/121, S to R. B. Walsingham, 8 Apr 1779.

97 Cradock, *Memoirs*, I, 147.

98 Lady Llanover, *The Autobiography and Correspondence of Mary Granville, Mrs Delany*, (London, 1861–2, 6 vols) V, 424, M. Delany to Mrs Port, 17–19 Apr 1779.

99 To Sir J. H. Cotton, quoted in *WC*, II, 156 n.

CHAPTER IX

1 *BFP*, pp. 119 & 123. Jeremy Black, 'Britain's Foreign Alliances in the Eighteenth Century', *Albion*, XX (1988) pp. 573–602, at pp. 574–76.

2 Roberts, *Splendid Isolation*, pp. 5–7. Their periods of office were as follows. Northern Department: July 1765–May 1766, Grafton; May 1766–Jan 1768, Conway; Jan–Oct 1768, Weymouth; Oct 1768–Dec 1770 Rochford. Southern Department: May–July 1766, Richmond; July 1766–Oct 1768, Shelburne; Oct 1768–Dec 1770, Weymouth; Jan–June 1771, Halifax.

3 Geoffrey W. Rice, 'Great Britain, the Manila Ransom, and the First Falkland Islands Dispute with Spain, 1766', *IHR*, II (1980) pp. 386–409.

4 Nicholas Tracy, 'The Administration of the Duke of Grafton and the French Invasion of Corsica', *Eighteenth-Century Studies*, VIII (1974–75) pp. 169–82.

5 Roberts, *Splendid Isolation*, p. 4.

Weston's reference is to Virgil's *Aeneid*, II, 325–27: 'fuimus Troes, fuit Ilium et ingens/ gloria Teucrorum; ferus omnia Iuppiter Argos/ transtulit: incensa Danai dominantur in urbe.' 'We were Trojans, Troy was great and the Trojans glorious; but now savage Jupiter has taken it all away, and the Greeks control our burning city'.

6 Thomas, *North*, pp. 22–23.

7 Thomas, *North*, p. 37.

8 Thomas, *North*, pp. 46–49.

9 NMM: SAN/F/41/60, Sir J. Marriott to S, 1 Oct 1770.

10 Philip Lawson, 'Parliament and the First East India Inquiry, 1767', *PH*, I (1982) pp. 99–114, at p. 106, gives an example of Hawke's damaging naivety in politics.

11 Mackay, *Hawke Papers*, p. 477.

12 Smith, *Grenville Papers*, IV, 525, A. Hervey to G. Grenville, 4 Aug 1770.

13 Sir William Anson, ed., *Autobiography and Political Correspondence of Augustus Henry Third Duke of Grafton*, (London, 1898), p. 257.

14 SRB: Ac. 423/615, T. Bradshaw to Grafton, 24 Jul 1770.

15 *CG3*, II, 175, 178 & 181, No. 843, Rochford to George III, 6 Dec 1770; No. 846, George III to Rochford, 6 Dec 1770; No. 850, Rochford to George III, 9 Dec 1770.

16 SRB: Ac. 423/617, T. Bradshaw to Grafton, 15 Sep 1770.

17 *NDAI*, pp. 81–87. Mackay, *Hawke*, pp. 327–29. *BFP*, pp. 143–44. Nicholas Tracy, 'The Falklands Islands crisis of 1770; Use of naval Force', *EHR*, XC (1975) pp. 40–75.

18 SRB: Ac. 423/633, T. Bradshaw to Grafton, [17 Dec 1770].

19 Scott, 'Bourbon Naval Reconstruction'.

20 PRO: PRO 30/29/3/2 f. 143 No. 14, R. Phelps to [Gower?], 27 Dec 1770. Since the despatch was to a French diplomat in Hamburg, this intercept must have been made either in a Dutch post office, or by the Hanoverian authorities.

21 'Ivre comme un fiacre': M. C. Morison, 'The Duc de Choiseul and the Invasion of England, 1768–70', *TRHS*, 3rd. S. IV (1910) pp. 83–115, at p. 104 n. 1.

22 *BFP*, pp. 153–54.

23 Williams, 'Sandwich's Naval Administration', p. 9.

24 SM: F/62/9, S to Hinchingbrooke, 21 Jan 1771.

25 *SP*, I, 13, North to S, 24 Aug 1770.

26 MPS: Box 36, S to Stormont, 22 Jan 1771.

27 Rodger, 'Mobilizing Seapower'.

28 *BNA*, p. 530, taking the numbers 'listed' in 1742. *NDAI*, p. 11.

29 N. A. M. Rodger, 'The Victualling of the British Navy during the Seven Years' War', *Bulletin du Centre d'Histoire des Éspaces Atlantiques*, No. 2 (Bordeaux, 1985) pp. 37–53.

30 PRO: ADM 7/659 f. 59.

31 *FNAI*, p. 99 n. 16.

32 Knight, 'Royal Dockyards', pp. 66–68. There are more examples of this sort from the 1784 estimates in Webb, 'Navy and British Diplomacy', pp. 151–52.

33 NMM: SAN/F/3/50, Memorandum by H. Palliser, [1772].

34 Cobbett, *Parliamentary History*, XIX, 726–30. Hattendorf, *Naval Documents*, No. 262.

35 Mackay, *Hawke*, pp. 305–6, prints a most useful table of actual expenditure for each year from 1745 to 1781.

36 Smith, *Grenville Papers*, II, 171–74 & 290–92, Egmont to G. Grenville, 3 Dec 1763 & 16 Apr 1764.

37 *NDAI*, pp. 22–26.

38 *NDAI*, p. 11.

39 *NDAI*, p. 25.

40 *NDAI*, pp. 26–27.

41 *NDAI*, p. 29.

42 NMM: SAN/V/6, s.d. Jun 15.

43 Haas, 'Royal Dockyards', p. 193, mentions a Navy Board visitation ordered by Egmont in 1764.

44 Haas, 'Royal Dockyards', pp. 202–3. Mackay, *Hawke*, pp. 310–11.

45 Knight, 'Royal Dockyards', pp. 42–46.

46 Sandwich's minutes of the visitations are as follows: 1771, PRO: ADM 7/659 & NMM: SAN/V/5; 1772, NMM: SAN/V/6; 1773, PRO: ADM 7/660 & NMM: SAN/V/7; 1774, PRO: ADM 7/661 & NMM: SAN/V/661; 1775, PRO: ADM 7/662 & NMM: SAN/V/9; 1776, NMM: SAN/V/10.

47 PRO: ADM 7/659 ff. 4, 9, 15–16, 33 & 45.

48 The tiller sweep (actually designed by Thomas Pollard the Master Boatbuilder of Portsmouth Yard, and tested by Bentinck) is described by Lavery, *Arming and Fitting*, pp. 20–21. He also describes the Bentinck-Coles chain pump, pp. 72–76.

49 PRO: ADM 7/659 ff. 46 & 51–53.

50 PRO: ADM 7/659 ff. 60, 65, 72 & 82.

51 NMM: SAN/V/6 s.d. Jun 14.

52 PRO: ADM 7/660 f. 12.

53 PRO: ADM 7/659 f. 112.

54 NMM: SAN/V/6, 15 Jun.

55 PRO: ADM 7/661 ff. 80–81.

56 *SP*, IV, 304–306.

57 *NDAI*, p. 33.

58 *CG3*, II, 282, No. 979. PRO: ADM 7/659 f. 2.

59 PRO: ADM 7/660 ff. 48 & 74.

60 PRO: ADM 7/659 f. 76; ADM 7/660 ff. 19, 47 & 71. NMM: SAN/F/2/14, 'The Cause of Timber Rotting . . . by a Shipbuilder'.

61 PRO: ADM 7/661 f. 74. Sandwich here refers to numbers actually in service; 81 compared with 149 notionally in existence in 1763.

62 Albion, *Forests and Sea Power*, p. 134, quoting Navy Board reports of 1768 and 1769.

63 NMM: SAN/F/26/31, Sir H. Palliser to S, 22 Jan 1781.

64 Williams, 'Sandwich's Naval Administration', pp. 284–286. Knight, 'Royal Dockyards', p. 216.

65 Oliver Rackham, *The History of the Countryside*, (London, 1986), pp. 90–92.

66 Albion, *Forests and Sea Power*, p. 151.

67 NMM: SAN/F/2/21, Extract of J.

Slade to Navy Board, 10 Apr 1771.

68 Kent, *War and Trade in Northern Seas*, p. 45 n. 1. Williams, 'Sandwich's Naval Administration', p. 285.

69 NMM: SAN/V/6, 18 Aug.

70 Albion, *Forests and Sea Power*, p. 134. Sutherland, *East India Company*, p. 216.

71 Kent, *War and Trade in Northern Seas*, pp. 40–45. Sven-Erik Åström, 'English Timber Imports from Northern Europe in the Eighteenth Century', *Scandinavian Economic History Review*, XVIII (1970) pp. 12–32.

72 Cobbett, *Parliamentary History*, XIX, 828.

73 Albion, *Forests and Sea Power*, pp. 135 & 161. PRO: ADM 7/662 f. 69. Williams, 'Sandwich's Naval Administration', pp. 288–90.

74 PRO: ADM 7/661 f. 69.

75 NMM: SAN/F/6/77–78, C. Micalopolo to S, 19 Sep 1775.

76 *SP*, IV, 309.

77 NMM: SAN/V/6, 12 Jul, 17 & 18 Aug. PRO: ADM 7/660 f. 73.

78 PRO: ADM 7/661 f. 5.

79 PRO: ADM 7/660 f. 71.

80 PRO: ADM 7/659 f. 42.

81 *CG3*, III, 2 No. 1290, S to George III, 5 Jul 1773. NMM: SAN/F/45c/13, George III to S, 18 Jul 1773. PRO: ADM 106/3568 is a supplement to this survey bringing it up to 1774.

82 NMM: SAN/V/6, 22 Jun.

83 PRO: ADM 7/662 ff. 74–75.

84 PRO: ADM 7/660 ff. 50–51.

85 NMM: SAN/V/11 p. 5.

86 NMM: SAN/V/6 12 Jun.

87 NMM: SAN/V/6 17 Jul. Williams, 'Sandwich's Naval Administration', p. 427.

88 NMM: SAN/V/6 15 Jun.

89 PRO: ADM 7/661 ff. 75–76.

CHAPTER X

1 Knight, 'Royal Dockyards', p. 336.

2 NMM: SAN/V/6, 22 Jun.

3 Knight, 'Building and Maintenance', pp. 37–41.

4 NMM: SAN/F/24/95, B. Gascoyne to S, 30 Sep 1780.

5 John E. Barnard, 'John Barnard the Younger, Shipbuilder of Ipswich and Harwich 1705–84', *MM* LXXVIII (1992) pp. 155–75, deals with one of the few substantial contract builders elsewhere.

6 PRO: ADM 7/662 f. 7.

7 Calculated from the lists in Lavery, *Ship of the Line*, I, 169–82, omitting ships never put in service, those wrecked or otherwise lost in service, and prizes by or from the enemy. Service life is measured from the date of order (deduced in a few cases from that of laying down) to the end of sea service as a ship of the line; seagoing service as troopship, hospital ship etc. is not counted.

8 Haas, 'Task Work', pp. 44–45.

9 Williams, 'Sandwich's Naval Administration', p. 425, gives the Navy Board's 1772 estimates of the cost of building various classes of ship in dockyards and merchant yards.

10 In principle expenditure on repairs can be obtained from the Progress Books in PRO: ADM 180. The modern concept of 'life-cycle cost' is described in Philip Pugh, *The Cost of Seapower: The Influence of Money on Naval Affairs from 1815 to the Present Day* (London, 1986) pp. 120–27.

11 Simmons & Thomas, *American Debates* V, 396–97.

12 Williams, 'Sandwich's Naval Administration', pp. 428–29.

13 Lavery, *Ship of the Line* I, 178–82.

14 Knight, 'Royal Dockyards', p. 405.

15 PRO: ADM 7/661 f. 82.

16 Williams, 'Sandwich's Naval Administration', pp. 52–53 & 427. Coad, *Royal Dockyards* pp. 101–10 describes the dock and slip-building programme.

17 Morriss, *Royal Dockyards*, p. 45, gives the number of slips in the early 1790s; none had been added since Sandwich's time.

18 Calculated from Lavery, *Ship of the Line* I, 178–82.

19 PRO: ADM 106/3568 p. 34.

20 *Calendar of Home Office Papers* III No. 765, S to [Rochford], 15 Jul 1771.

21 Coad, *Royal Dockyards* p. 3.

22 *SP* IV, 311. Knight, 'Royal Dockyards', p. 116.

23 *SP* IV, 310. NMM: SAN/F/31/39, S to North, [rough draft, 9 or 10 Dec 1782].

24 Haas, 'Task Work', pp. 44–45.

25 Knight, *Portsmouth Dockyard Papers* p. xliv.

26 PRO: ADM 7/662 ff. 1–4. Haas, 'Task Work', p. 51.

27 Haas, 'Task Work' p. 58.

28 Knight, 'Royal Dockyards', pp. 157–67. Williams, 'Sandwich's Naval Administration', pp. 402–17. Haas, 'Task Work'. PRO: ADM 7/662 ff. 3 & 59–61.

29 *CG3* III, 227 & 245 Nos. 1671 & 1694, S to George III, 27 Jun & 12 Aug 1775.

30 *CG3* III, 254 No. 1707, S to George III, 8 Sep 1775.

31 Haas, 'Task Work', pp. 66–67.

32 Haas, 'Work and Authority', pp. 420–22.

33 Knight, 'Royal Dockyards', p. 116.

34 *SP* IV, 289.

35 Haas, 'Work and Authority', p. 422.

36 Knight, 'Royal Dockyards', pp. 170–71.

37 Haas, 'Royal Dockyards', p. 200. Williams, 'Sandwich's Naval Administration', pp. 398–99.

38 Knight, *Portsmouth Dockyard Papers* p. xlvii.

39 PRO: ADM 7/660 ff. 10–11.

40 Knight, 'Royal Dockyards', pp. 173–77.

41 *SP* IV, 292–93.

42 Langford, *Polite and Commercial People*, pp. 447–52.

43 Haas, 'Task Work' p. 60.

44 NMM: SAN/F/3/38, C. Proby to S, 2 Oct 1772; SAN/F/3/53 is a return of servants at Chatham & Sheerness granted for electoral reasons 1765–72.

45 Knight, *Portsmouth Dockyard Papers* p. xxxix. Knight, 'Royal Dockyards', pp. 122–30. NMM: SAN/F/30/21–23. PRO: ADM 7/658 p. 21.

46 He changed his signature from Pallisser to Palliser about 1773; for convenience I use the later form throughout.

47 *CG3* III, 190–92 Nos. 1622 & 1626, S to George III, 27 & 29 Mar 1775. NMM: SAN/F/41/78, Bristol to S, 28 Mar 1775.

48 Wraxall, *Memoirs* II, 268.

49 Thomas, *House of Commons*, p. 237.

50 NMM: SAN/F/7/25, G. Jackson to S, 21 Dec 1775.

51 Thomas, *House of Commons*, p. 237.

52 NMM: SAN/F/24/95, B. Gascoyne to S, 30 Sep 1780.

53 Steuart, *Walpole's Last Journals* I, 298.

54 MC: VI. 8/39, S to J. Banks, 3 Sep 1775.

55 MC: VI. 8/44, S to C. J. Phipps, 15 Sep 1775.

56 MC: VI. 9/1 pp. 15, 47 & 50–51, Mulgrave's diary 21 Oct 1775, 17 & 24 Jan 1776.

57 MC: VI. 11/4, S to Mulgrave, 21 Oct 1776.

58 Broomfield, 'Lord Sandwich at the Admiralty Board', p. 10. *The Rolliad, in two parts; Probationary Odes for the Laureatship; and Political Eclogues* . . . (London, 21st ed, 1799), p. 200: 'Sooner shall mackrel on the plains disport, / Or MULGRAVE's hearers think his speech too short . . .'; see also pp. 270–71 'Ode on the New Year, by Lord Mulgrave'.

59 MC: VI. 11/29, S to Mulgrave, 13 Dec 1777.

60 NMM: SAN/F/44/12 is a minute of their submission to the Cabinet.

61 Syrett, *Shipping and the American War*, p. 21.

62 E. g. *HMC 20, Dartmouth* II, 397, S to Dartmouth, 30 Oct 1775.

63 NMM: SAN/F/10/27, M. Suckling to S, 28 Jan 1777.

64 Broomfield, 'Sandwich at the Admiralty', p. 9.

65 Broomfield, 'Sandwich at the Admiralty'. Rodger, *Wooden World* pp. 273–302 & 331–43.

66 NMM: SAN/F/38/34, C. Middleton to S, 23 May 1776; SAN/F/13/64, C. Middleton to S, 8 Apr 1777. He may, however, have been right about Commodore Mackenzie.

67 NMM: SAN/F/10/9 & 17, C. Middleton to S, 13 & 16 Jan 1777; SAN/F/10/22, J. Gambier to S, 21 Jan 1777.

68 Phillips, 'Evangelical Administrator', pp. 22–33.

69 Phillips, 'Evangelical Administrator', p. 11. Chatterton, *Gambier* I, 6.

70 NMM: SAN/F/13/133 & SAN/F/14/9, C. Proby to S, 29 Apr & 4 May 1778. Namier & Brooke, *House of Commons 1754–90* I, 310 & III, 334–35. Proby's nephew Lord Carysfort was a prominent Huntingdonshire landowner.

71 Knight, 'Royal Dockyards', p. 33. NMM: SAN/F/13/12, C. Middleton to S, 8 Mar 1778.

72 NMM: SAN/F/13/64, C. Middleton to S, 8 Apr 1777. Phillips, 'Evangelical Administrator', pp. 35–36.

73 Weber, *Rise of the Musical Classics*, p. 163

74 Mackesy, *War for America*, pp. 164–65.

75 WLC: Shelburne MSS Vol. 151 No. 87, R. Gregson to Shelburne, 20 Dec 1789. Hattendorf, *Naval Documents* No. 267.

76 Phillips, 'Evangelical Administrator', p. 228.

77 Phillips, 'Evangelical Administrator', p. 70, quoting BM: Add. MSS 24135.

78 NMM: SAN/F/25/32, 'Zero' to S, [1781?].

79 For Middleton's reforms post-war see Phillips, 'Evangelical Administrator'; Webb, 'Navy and Diplomacy'; Usher, 'Civil Administration'; Laughton, *Barham Papers*; Morriss, *Royal Dockyards*. There is no modern life of Middleton.

80 Naval administration during the war is dealt with in the theses (all unpublished) of Knight, Morrison, Phillips, Usher, Wickwire & Williams. See also Syrett, *Shipping and the American War*.

81 Laughton, *Barham Papers* II, 3–5, C. Middleton to S, [1779].

82 Sandwich, *Voyage*, p. xviii.

83 Butler, *Reminiscences* I, 72.

84 Wraxall, *Memoirs* I, 398–99.

85 *The European Magazine and London Review* XXV (1794) p. 193.

86 HEH: Howe MSS, Howe to R. Curtis, 29 Jun 1779.

87 Christie *End of North's Ministry*, p. 32. Cradock, *Memoirs* IV, 164.

88 *CG3, passim.* eg. Nos. 2742 [7 a.m.], 2746 [12.15 a.m.], 2942 [midnight], 3327 [7.45 a.m.], 3426 [6.30–8 a.m.]

89 Mackesy, *War for America*, p. 165. NMM: SAN/F/16/43, Sir C. Middleton to S, 30 Sep 1778.

90 Greig, *Hume Letters* II, 319, D. Hume to W. Strahan, 10 May 1776.

91 Chiefly in Barnes & Owen, *Sandwich Papers*, and Laughton, *Barham Papers*.

92 Phillips, 'Evangelical Administrator', p. 68 n. 1.

93 Phillips, 'Evangelical Administrator', pp. 141–43 & 265. *SP* IV, 372, Sir C. Middleton to S, 23 Oct 1780. NMM: SAN/F/23/73, Sir J. Marriott to S, 12 May 1780.

94 Laughton, *Barham Papers* II, 6.

95 Phillips, 'Evangelical Administrator', pp. 299–301. Norris, *Shelburne and Reform*, p. 208.

96 Webb, 'Navy and Diplomacy', p. 184.

97 Knight, 'Royal Dockyards', pp. 11 & 20–21.

98 Phillips, 'Evangelical Administrator', pp. 173–74.

99 NMM: MID/2/26/5, Sir C. Middleton to Keppel, 14 Oct 1782.

100 Phillips, 'Evangelical Administra-

tor', pp. 121 & 173, in both cases quoting BM: Add. MSS 41079.

101 NMM: SAN/F/24/22, Sir J. Marriott to S, 29 Jun 1780.

102 What follows is based unless otherwise noted on Knight, 'Sandwich, Middleton and Dockyard Appointments', and Phillips, 'Evangelical Administrator', pp. 145–52. The essential correspondence is printed in *SP* IV, 375–82, and Laughton, *Barham Papers* II, 8–30.

103 *The Evidence . . . in the Trial wherein the Rt. Hon. John, Earl of Sandwich, was Plaintiff, and J. Miller, Defendant . . .* (London, 1773). NMM: SAN/F/32b *passim*. Werkmeister, *London Daily Press*, p. 113. *HMC 30 Fortescue (Dropmore)* IX, 278, Buckingham to Grenville, 12 Feb 1809.

104 John C. Lassiter, 'The Defamation of Peers: The Rise and Decline of the Action for Scandalum Magnatum', *American Journal of Legal History* XXII (1978) pp. 216–36. William C. Lowe, 'Peers and Printers: The Beginnings of Sustained Press Coverage of the House of Lords in the 1770s', *PH* VII (1988) pp. 241–56, at p. 242.

105 NMM: SAN/V/13/ p. 47, S to J. Slade, 24 May 1777; see also SAN/F/10/102 & 107, J. Slade to Sandwich, 22 & 27 May [1777]. Slade offered 1,000 gns for a seat at the Victualling Board.

106 Knight, 'Sandwich, Middleton and Dockyard Appointments', p. 187. Williams, 'Sandwich's Naval Administration', pp. 278–82, comes to the same conclusion.

107 Knight, 'Sandwich, Middleton and Dockyard Appointments', p. 188.

108 NMM: SAN/F/9/76, C. Proby to S, 29 Oct 1776.

109 Knight, 'Royal Dockyards', p. 79.

110 NMM: MID/1/125/11, S to Sir C. Middleton, 17 Apr 1781.

111 *SP* IV, 382, Sir C. Middleton to S, 13 Apr 1781; the original is NMM: MID/6/5/3. The earlier quotation is

in SAN/F/19/138, C. Middleton to S, 18 Jun 1779.

112 *SP* IV, 382–83.

113 NMM: SAN/V/6, 22 Jun.

114 Knight, 'Sandwich, Middleton and Dockyard Appointments', pp. 188–89.

115 NMM: SAN/V/12 p. 301, S to J. Harris, 16 Jan 1773.

116 NMM: SAN/F/1/37 & SAN/F/4/2, characters of senior shipwrights, [Sep 1772].

117 NMM: SAN/F/7/88, C. Proby to Navy Board, 28 Jan 1776; SAN/F/7/122, C. Proby to Navy Board, 27 Feb 1774, 18 & 22 Jan 1776; SAN/F/9/103, C. Proby to S, 20 Nov 1776.

118 NMM: SAN/F/26/14, C. Middleton to S, 9 Jan 1781. Phillips, 'Evangelical Administrator', p. 152. Usher, 'Civil Administration', pp. 463–64. WLC: Shelburne MSS Vol. 151 Nos. 56–57.

119 W. Shrubsole, *Christian Memoirs; in the Form of a New Pilgrimage to the Heavenly Jerusalem* (London, 3rd edn. 1807) p. xl; I suppose that the 'distinguished and excellent character' is Middleton.

120 PRO: ADM 7/662 ff. 72–73.

121 Knight, *Portsmouth Dockyard Papers* p. xxx.

122 NMM: SAN/F/23/11, C. Middleton to S, 3 Feb 1780.

123 Laughton, *Barham Papers* II, 31. The original is NMM: MID/2/51/1 & 2.

124 NMM: SAN/F/20/56, C. Middleton to S, 17 Aug 1779; SAN/F/1/37, memo on senior shipwrights [1771]. Knight, *Portsmouth Dockyard Papers* p. xxxii n.. *CG3* IV, 346 No. 2644, Sir S. Hood to George III, 29 May 1779.

125 Knight, 'Sandwich, Middleton and Dockyard Appointments', p. 177.

126 PRO: ADM 42/1925–1928, Woolwich Yard paybooks.

127 Williams, 'Sandwich's Naval Administration', p. 282.

128 *SP* IV 376–77, S to Sir C. Middleton, 24 Jan 1781.

129 E. g. his 1779 letter quoted on p. 168.

CHAPTER XI

1 NMM: SAN/F/23/31, Sir G. Collier to S, 3 Mar 1780.
2 NMM: SAN/F/4/68, F/5/26, F/6/59, F/8/80, F/12/50 & F/17/4; G. Collier to S, 26 Jun 1773, 3 Oct 1774 (quoted), 29 Jun 1775, 2 May 1776, 23 Jan 1778 & 25 Nov 1778.
3 Brown *Manners and Principles*, I, 58.
4 Rodger, *Wooden World* pp. 273–343.
5 *WC* XXVIII, 120, quoting the preface to a new version of Shadwell's play *The Fair Quaker of Deal*, written anonymously by Captain Edward 'Poet' Thompson.
6 Pocock, 'The Revolution against Parliament', p. 272. Dickinson, *Liberty and Property*, pp. 170–72.
7 *HMC 24 Rutland* III, 3, S to Granby, 8 Sep 1778. Granby succeeded as Duke of Rutland in 1779, when 'Mr Manners' became Lord Robert.
8 *HMC 24 Rutland* III, 22, Lord R. Manners to Rutland, 15 Nov 1779.
9 NMM: SAN/F/22/55, Mansfield to S, 2 Dec 1779.
10 NMM: SAN/F/22/75 Mansfield to S, 11 Dec 1779.
11 NMM: SAN/F/22/75 Mansfield to S, 11 Dec 1779.
12 NMM: SAN/F/14/60, A. Keppel to S, 15 May 1778.
13 NMM: SAN/F/17/11, Leinster to S, 29 Nov 1778.
14 *HMC 49 Stopford-Sackville* I, 276, Buckinghamshire to Lord G. Germain, 30 Sep 1780.
15 MC: VI. 11/116, S to Mulgrave, 20 Oct 1780. Lord Longford was Captain Pakenham's elder brother.
16 BM: Eg. MSS 2136 f. 74, S to Le Despencer, 1 Jun 1763.
17 MC: VI. 11/107, S to Mulgrave, 31 May 1780.
18 NMM: SAN/F/16/38, Scarsdale to S, 28 Sep 1778.
19 BM: Add. MSS 38217 f. 253, S to C. Jenkinson, 16 Jan 1782.
20 NMM: SAN/V/13 pp. 244–45, S to Berkeley, n.d.
21 MC: VI. 11/139, S to Mulgrave, 9 Nov 1781.
22 NMM: MID/1/9, S. Barrington to C. Middleton, 22 May [1780]; printed by Laughton, *Barham Papers* I, 366.
23 Earl of Rosse's MSS, Letter Book H2 ff. 185–86, Hawke to S. Barrington, Jun 1780. This is an answer to SB's letter of 22 May (Rosse MSS B16) in which he had suggested the phrase.
24 NMM: SAN/F/8/20, J. Montagu to S, 15 Mar 1776; F/13/87, J. Montagu to S, Portsmouth, 13 Apr 1778; F/24/6, R. Digby to S, 2 Jun 1780; F/26/16, Sir G. Collier to S, 11 Jan 1781; F/30/14, J. Wallace to S, 14 Jan 1782.
25 NMM: SAN/F/23/84, R. Digby to S, 26 May 1780.
26 NMM: SAN/F/27/5, [T. Lewes] to S, 3 Apr 1781; F/27/6, Lisburne to S, 4 Apr 1781; F/27/39, Carlisle to S, 3 May 1781; F/28/45, T. Lewes to S, 19 Aug 1781.
27 NMM: SAN/F/11/116, Kensington to S, 20 Dec 1777.
28 NMM: LEW/1/9, S to T. Lewes, 24 Jan 1781.
29 NMM: SAN/F/26/39, T. Lewes to S, 25 Jan 1781.
30 Sir Archibald MacDonald in 1786, quoted by Michael W. McCahill, 'Peerage Creations and the Changing Character of the British Nobility, 1750–1850', in Jones & Jones, *Peers, Politics and Power*, pp. 407–32, at p. 409.
31 Quoted by Spinney, *Rodney*, p. 272.
32 NMM: SAN/F/4/12, S to [Edgecumbe], 4 Mar 1773.
33 Quoted by Spinney, *Rodney*, p. 257.
34 NMM: SAN/F/10/86, S to Bristol, 28 Apr 1777; F/9/9, S to Bristol, 20 Jun 1776.
35 MC: VI. 11/29, S to Mulgrave, 13 Dec 1777.
36 NMM: SAN/F/29/59, Sir H. Heron to S, 27 Nov 1781.

37 NMM: SAN/F/9/24, Lady Walde-grave to S, 11 Aug 1776.

38 NMM: SAN/F/27/50, Dartmouth to S, 10 May 1781.

39 NMM: SAN/F/10/41, M. Howe to S, 18 Feb 1777; F/24/33, Tem-pletown to S, 11 Jul 1780.

40 NMM: SAN/F/10/21, E. Stratford to S, 20 Jan 1777.

41 NMM: SAN/F/9/117, North to S, 4 Dec 1776.

42 NMM: SAN/F/6/57, H. Dundas to S, 28 Jun 1775. He must mean 21 years in the Navy, as Home was a lieutenant of 1759.

43 NMM: SAN/F/22/17, Mulgrave to S, 13 Nov 1779.

44 MC: VI. 11/91, S to Mulgrave, 17 Nov 1779.

45 MC: VI. 11/127, S to Mulgrave, 26 Feb 1781.

46 MC: VI. 11/40, S to Mulgrave, 13 Aug 1778, quoted at length in Rodger, *Wooden World*, pp. 341–42.

47 MC: VI. 11/42, Mulgrave to S, 17 Aug 1778.

48 Williams, 'Sandwich's Naval Administration', p. 250.

49 NMM: SAN/F/9/123, 129 & 134, W. Cornwallis to S, 10, 19 & 21 Dec 1776; SAN/V/13 p. 133, S to W. Cornwallis, 29 Jul 1778.

50 NMM: SAN/V/13 p. 137, S to W. Cornwallis, 30 Jul 1778.

51 *HMC 55 Various Collections* VI, 327, S to W. Cornwallis, 15 & 20 Jun 1781.

52 NMM: SAN/F/9/135, W. Corn-wallis to S, 21 Dec 1776.

53 NMM: SAN/F/15/50, J. Luttrell to S, 25 Jul 1778; SAN/V/13 pp. 135–36, S to J. Luttrell, 29 Jul 1778.

54 NMM: SAN/F/18/45, R. Holt to S, 26 Jan 1779.

55 NMM: SAN/F/26/4, C. Mellish to S, 1 Jan 1781.

56 NMM: SAN/F/12/64, T. Edwards to S, 29 Jan 1778.

57 NMM: SAN/F/25/33, J. W. Bazeley to S, 1 Nov 1780.

58 NMM: SAN/F/19/78, S. Martin to S, 13 May 1779, enc. SM to J. Robin-son, 30 Mar 1779.

59 NMM: SAN/F/35 *passim*; F/46/17, George III to S, 1 Apr 1779; F/35/124, Amherst to S, 14 Feb 1781. Lowe, *Portsmouth Division of Marines*, p. xx.

60 SM: F/51c/6, E. Windus to S, 18 Jul 1787. The picture is still hanging in the officers' mess at Stonehouse Barracks.

61 NMM: SAN/F/31/111, E. Southouse to S, 18 Sep 1791.

62 *HMC 15 Abergavenny* p. 3, S to J. Robinson, 21 Jan 1771.

63 NMM: SAN/F/18/78, North to S, [7 Feb 1779].

64 *CG3* V, 1 No. 2913, S to George III, 2 Jan 1780.

65 *CG3* V, 169 No. 3217, S to George III, 25 Dec 1780.

66 NMM: SAN/F/25/29, W. Peacock to S, 30 Oct 1780.

67 NMM: SAN/F/62/33, S to Hinch-ingbrooke, 15 Aug 1777.

68 MC: VI. 11/126, S to Mulgrave, 24 Feb 1781, answering NMM: SAN/F/26/75, Mulgrave to S, 21 Feb 1781.

69 *HMC 55 Various Collections* VI, 314, S to W. Cornwallis, 29 Oct 1774.

70 PRO: PRO 30/20/20/5 p. 62, S to Sir G. B. Rodney, 16 Sep 1773. See also Rodger, *Wooden World*, p. 326.

71 BM: Add MSS 57810 f. 183, S to G. Grenville, 18 Aug 1767.

72 Stroud, *Capability Brown*, pp. 158 & 204. BM: Add. MSS 69795 f. 32, S to L. Brown, 11 Aug 1772. PRO: ADM 1/5308 ff. 113–34, Court Mar-tial of Lt J. Brown. For notes on Brown's career I am indebted to Dr Peter Le Fevre.

73 Knight, 'Sandwich, Middleton and Dockyard Appointments', p. 188.

74 Proby, 'Burgesses of Huntingdon', pp. 222–30.

75 Proby, 'Burgesses of Huntingdon', pp. 231–36.

76 NMM: SAN/V/117 f. 96, S to [G. Jackson], 8 Sep 1780.

77 NMM: SAN/F/10/36 & F/11/3, Sir

J. B. Warren to S, 6 Feb & 4 Sep 1777.

78 NMM: SAN/F/23/23, Sir J. B. Warren to S, 23 Feb 1780.

79 NMM: SAN/F/24/24, Sir G. Cooper to S, 29 Jun 1780; F/28/83, Sir J. B. Warren to S, 24 Sep 1781.

80 NMM: SAN/F/30/65, Sir J. B. Warren to S, 7 Mar 1782.

81 HRO: HINCH/8/290/2, Sir J. B. Warren to S, 25 Feb 1782.

82 HRO: HINCH/8/287, S to J. Robinson, [18 Mar 1782] (Abergavenny transcript).

83 Williams, 'Sandwich's Naval Administration', pp. 271–72.

84 Rodger, *Wooden World*, pp. 282–94. NMM: SAN/V/13 p. 5, S to J. Young, 27 Jul 1776.

85 PRO: PRO 30/20/21/2 pp. 180–85, S to Sir G. B. Rodney, 9 Jan & 22 Feb 1782.

86 PRO: PRO 30/20/20/5 p. 33, S to G. B. Rodney, 14 Dec 1772.

87 PRO: PRO 30/20/21/2 p. 157, S to Sir G. B. Rodney, 18 Dec 1780.

88 NMM: SAN/F/34/39, Sir E. Hughes to S, 17 Feb 1780.

89 NMM: SAN/F/34/49 & 52, Sir E. Hughes to S, 10 Oct 1781 & 15 Jan 1782.

90 *SP* II, 61, Sir H. Palliser to S, 14 May 1778.

91 NMM: SAN/F/10/102, J. Slade to S, 22 May [1777]; F/35/129, C. Courtenay to S, 30 Sep 1781.

92 SM: F/55b/21, 'Scritch Scratch' to S, 1 Dec 1777. NMM: SAN/F/28/5, J. Bentham to S, 4 Jul 1781.

93 SM: F/55b/20, R. L. to M. Ray, 20 Mar 1776. NMM: SAN/F/10/18, J. Reynolds to S, 17 Jan 1777.

94 Little & Kahrl, *Garrick Letters* No. 896, D. Garrick to W. A. Miles, 15 Mar 1775.

95 NMM: SAN/V/12 p. 311, S to J. Stockdale, 11 Feb 1775.

96 BM: Add. MSS 9344 ff. 116 & 121, S to G. Jackson, 15 Mar 1782 & 24 Apr 1786. NMM: SAN/F/31/100, J. Slade to S, 16 Feb 1790; this is the same person who in 1777 offered Sandwich 1,000 gns for a seat at the Victualling Board (SAN/F/10/102), but I cannot prove that the loan goes back so far.

97 NMM: SAN/F/26/3, J. Gambier to S, 1 Jan 1781, enc. S to JG, 17 Jul 1774.

98 NMM: SAN/F/26/3, J. Gambier to S, 20 Jul 1774.

99 NMM: SAN/F/26/3 & 11, J. Gambier to S, 1 & 8 Jan 1781.

100 George Metcalfe, *Royal Government and Political Conflict in Jamaica, 1729–1783* (London, 1965), p. 136. Gwyn, *Royal Navy and North America*, p. 433.

101 NMM: SAN/V/13 p. 280, S to J. Gambier, 1 Jan 1781.

102 NMM: SAN/V/13 p. 281, S to J. Gambier, 6 Jan 1781.

103 NMM: SAN/F/26/100, J. Gambier to S, 16 Mar 1781.

104 MC: VI. 11/19, Mulgrave to S, 5 Jan 1777.

105 MC: VI. 11/20, S to Mulgrave, 6 Jan 1777.

106 Rodger, *Wooden World* p. 326.

107 Williams, 'Sandwich's Naval Administration', p. 260. *SP* I, 387–90 & 399–402, G. B. Rodney to S, 31 Aug & 7 Sep 1774; J. Young to S, 8 Mar, 25 Aug & 10 Sep 1777. NMM: SAN/F/9/82, J. Young to S, 1 Nov 1776.

108 MC: VI. 11/145, S to Mulgrave, 9 Jan 1782.

109 NMM: SAN/V/13 p. 199, S to P. Osborn, 25 Jan 1780.

110 NMM: SAN/F/10/9 & 17, C. Middleton to S, 13 & 16 Jan 1777.

111 Garrick, *Private Correspondence* II, 173, S to D. Garrick, n.d.; cf. *The Memoirs of the Life and Writings of Percival Stockdale* (London, 1809, 2 vols), II, 102–9.

112 Williams's figures which follow are not definitive for two reasons: he used the patronage books (SAN 1–6) in the NMM but not those (now SAN/V/3–4) then at Mapperton; and he did not realize that some entries were carried over from book

to book, so that there is a degree of double counting. There seems no reason, however, to doubt their general validity.

113 Williams, 'Sandwich's Naval Administration', p. 233.

114 Williams, 'Sandwich's Naval Administration', p. 258.

115 Williams, 'Sandwich's Naval Administration', p. 266.

116 Williams, 'Sandwich's Naval Administration', p. 267.

117 Williams, 'Sandwich's Naval Administration', p. 267 n. 153.

118 Mackesy, *War for America*, pp. 11 & 321.

CHAPTER XII

1 NMM: SAN/V/117 ff. 124–25, S to G. Jackson, 7 Oct 1773.

2 Sainsbury, *Disaffected Patriots*, p. 28.

3 *The Letters of Junius*, ed. John Cannon (Oxford, 1978), pp. 481–82.

4 Roberts, *Splendid Isolation*, pp. 8 & 11–14. Roberts, 'Macartney in Russia', pp. 38–39.

5 'n'a . . . rien fait de plus horrible que ce que font aujourd'hui les membres de l'Opposition. Ils déchirent impitoyablement le sein de cette patrie qui leur a donné la naissance, sans autre motif que celui d'assouvir la soif qu'ils ont de l'autorité. Je ne fais assurément des voeux pour la prospérité de l'Angleterre, mais je rougis pour l'humanité, non qu'il y ait des âmes aussi dénaturées et aussi atroces, mais des âmes assez foibles et assez imbéciles (et c'est le plus grand nombre) pour encenser comme l'effort le plus généreux de la vertu et de la patriotisme ce qui est le comble du crime et de la trahison': Roberts, *Splendid Isolation*, p. 15, quoting Doniol, *Participation de la France*, I, 95.

6 Jeremy Black, 'The British Navy and British Foreign Policy in the first half of the eighteenth century', in J. M. Black & K. W. Schweizer, eds., *Essays in European History*, (Lennoxville, 1985) p. 151.

7 On the Spanish navy at this period see Mühlmann, *Die Reorganisation der Spanischen Kriegsmarine*; J. R. McNeill, *Atlantic Empires of France and Spain: Louisbourg and Havana, 1700–1763*, (Chapel Hill, 1985); and Merino, *La Armada Española*.

8 Patterson, *The Other Armada*, pp. 21–36.

9 Dull, *French Navy and American Independence*, pp. 11–13.

10 *BFP*, pp. 161–63. Patterson, *The Other Armada*, p. 86. Clark & Morgan, *Naval Documents*, I, 403, C. J. Garnier to Vergennes, 20 Feb 1775 [quoted in rather curious English]. Boutaric, *Correspondence secrète*, II, 186.

11 *Calendar of Home Office Papers*, III, No. 883, S to Rochford, 31 Oct 1771. *SP*, I, 379–84 Rochford to S, 5 Nov & 20 Dec 1771, S to Sir G. B. Rodney, 27 Nov & 30 Dec 1771, 20 Apr 1772. Spinney, *Rodney*, pp. 252–55. Davies, 'Faction' pp. 155–57.

12 Nicholas Tracy, 'Parry of a Threat to India, 1768–74', *MM*, LIX (1973) pp. 35–48. *NDAI*, pp. 100–117.

13 *BFP*, p. 164.

14 Williams, 'Sandwich's Naval Administration', pp. 45 & 48. *NDAI*, p. 26.

15 Mackay, *Hawke*, p. 305.

16 *SP*, I, 19–26, North to S, 5 Sep, & S to North, 10 Sep 1772.

17 Beaglehole, *Cook Journals*, III, 1484, S to D. Barrington, 12 Mar 1774, printing NMM: SAN/F/36/11.

18 *CG3*, II, 447–51 Nos. 1193 & 1194, North to George III & George III to North, 9 Feb 1773.

19 *NDAI*, p. 10.

20 *NDAI*, p. 11.

21 PRO: ADM 7/659 f. 11.

22 *SP*, I, 18, S to [A. Hervey], 13 Jun 1771, & I, 26–28, memo by [A. Hervey].

23 *NDAI*, pp. 11 & 37–38.

24 *CG3*, II, 474 No. 1228, George III to North, 20 Apr 1773.

25 Ross J. S. Hoffman, *Edmund Burke,*

New York Agent, (American Philosophical Society Memoirs Vol. 41, Philadelphia, 1956) p. 513, W. Burke to C. O'Hara, 2 Feb 1772.

26 NMM: SAN/V/6, Jun 15.

27 Simmons & Thomas, *American Debates*, V, 397.

28 *SP*, IV, 309, memo by Sir H. Palliser, 1782.

29 NMM: SAN/F/7/96, J. Gambier to Navy Board, [Oct 1775].

30 NMM: SAN/V/11, p. 6.

31 NMM: SAN/V/11 pp. 20 & 22.

32 *CG3*, II, 282 No. 978, S to George III, 20 Sep 1771. See also Nos 1303, 1305, 1378, 1418, 1420, 1490, 1570, & 1700 as examples of many showing the king's study of naval technology.

33 NMM: SAN/F/45c/20, George III to S, 24 Aug 1773.

34 *CG3*, III, 305 No. 1788, memorandum by Sandwich [misdated by Fortescue to 1775].

35 NMM: SAN/F/45c/12, George III to S, 19 Jun 1773.

36 *CG3*, II, 494 No. 1263, S to George III, 7 Jun 1773. *BFP*, p. 190.

37 *CG3*, II, 502 & 506–7 Nos. 1272 & 1279, S to George III, 12 & 14 Jun 1773. NMM: SAN/F/4/43, A. Hervey to S, 29 May [1773].

38 *CG3*, II, 511–12 No. 1283, S to George III, 18 Jun 1773. NMM: SAN/F/4/7, H. Palliser to S, [Jun 1773]. Hattendorf, *Naval Documents*, No. 254, memo by Palliser. [George Marsh] 'An Account of the Preparations made for and the Entertainment of the King at Portsmouth in June 1773 . . .' [ed. D. Crofton] *Colburn's United Service Magazine*, 1887 Pt. I pp. 433–49 & 517–30, at pp. 441–46 & 523–29. Marsh was a member of the Navy Board.

39 NMM: SAN/F/4/69, Sir H. Palliser to S, 29 Jun 1773. See also NMM: SAN/F/4/74, Sir H. Palliser to S, 30 Jul 1773.

40 PRO: ADM 7/659 ff. 88–90. Bonner-Smith, *Barrington Papers*, I, 436.

41 Simmons & Thomas, *American Debates*, VI, 473.

42 PRO: ADM 7/659 ff. 114–15.

43 *SP*, I, 18, S to [A. Hervey], 13 Jun 1771.

44 NMM: SAN/F/2/35, J. Cawthorne to S, 18 Nov 1771. Other examples are SAN/F/3/54; *SP*, IV, 386–406, J. Balld to S, 28 Apr 1773; T. Wood to S, 8 Apr 1776.

45 Cobbett, *Parliamentary History*, XVIII, 1261.

46 PRO: ADM 7/659 f. 87.

47 Rodger, *Wooden World*, p. 198.

48 Rodger, *Wooden World*, p. 158–59 & 170–71.

49 Clive Emsley, 'The Recruitment of Petty Offenders during the French Wars 1793–1815', *MM*, LXVI (1980) pp. 199–208, at p. 200. BM: Add.MSS 9344 f. 100, S to G. Jackson, 27 Dec 1777. NMM: SAN/F/24/98, Marchmont to S, [ca Sep 1780?]. Cobbett, *Parliamentary History*, XVIII, 1260.

50 *Calendar of Home Office Papers*, III–IV *passim*, under 'Criminal Pardons' especially III Nos. 272, 364, 434, 604, 993 & 1620; there is only one after March 1771. The quotation is from III No. 604, P. Stephens to S. Porten, 23 Mar 1771.

51 PRO: SP 42/51 f. 235, S to Weymouth, 3 Oct 1777.

52 *Ex inf.*, Professor James Cockburn, to whom I am grateful for sharing his researches on the legal system.

53 I avoid entering into the question, much discussed by Australian historians, of whether convict settlement or naval strategy was the primary motive for founding the colony.

54 Baugh, 'Seapower and Science', pp. 1–55.

55 WA: Vol. XXV f. 85, S to Bedford, 14 Apr [1750]. Baugh, 'Seapower and Science', p. 26. *BC*, II, 48–49, Bedford to B. Keene, 24 Apr 1750. Beaglehole, *Cook*, p. 122 attributes the idea to Anson, which is quite possible, but he gives no authority.

56 Beaglehole, *Cook*, pp. 122–23.

57 Beaglehole, *Cook*, pp. 124–27.

58 O'Brian, *Banks*, p. 33

59 Dawson, *Banks Letters*, p. 229, J. Cook to J. Banks, 11 Aug 1771. Beaglehole, *Cook Journals*, I, 637–38.

60 Beaglehole, *Cook Journals*, I, cxiii–cxiv.

61 Davies, *Documents of the American Revolution*, IV, 120, Hillsborough to S, 1 Jul 1772, quoting PRO: CO 5/119 f. 251.

62 Beaglehole, *Cook*, pp. 281 & 285. *SP*, I, 381, Rochford to S, 20 Dec 1771. PRO: SP 42/48 No. 51, S to Rochford, 25 Dec 1771.

63 Beaglehole, *Cook*, pp. 293–97. Beaglehole, *Cook Journals*, II, xxv–xxxi. *CG3*, II, 343–47 No. 1065, J. Banks to S, 30 May 1772.

64 NMM: SAN/V/6, 10 Jun.

65 Beaglehole, *Cook Journals*, II, xxxi n. 1.

66 O'Brian, *Banks*, p. 161.

67 Beaglehole, *Cook Journals*, II, xxv–xxxi & 704–18.

68 Beaglehole, *Cook Journals*, II, 9. NMM: SAN/V/6 2 Jul gives Sandwich's comments.

69 Beaglehole, *Cook Journals*, II, 6.

70 Phipps, *Voyage*. Ann Savours, '"A very interesting point in geography": The 1773 Phipps Expedition towards the Pole', *Arctic*, XXXVII (1984) pp. 402–28.

71 Beaglehole, *Cook*, pp. 447–49. Carter, *Banks*, pp. 125–28.

72 Troide, *Burney Journals*, II, 60–62.

73 Quoted in O'Brian, *Banks*, p. 182.

74 Beaglehole, *Cook*, p. 442, with breezy inaccuracy describes this as 'a yachting trip down Channel', and says that Martha Ray was aboard, which she was not.

75 Beaglehole, *Cook Journals*, II, 958, D. C. Solander to J. Banks, 14 Aug 1775.

76 MC: VI. 8/37, S to J. Banks, 19 Aug 1775.

77 Beaglehole, *Cook*, p. 484. Carter, *Banks*, p. 125.

78 Beaglehole, *Cook Journals*, III, xxx–xxxi.

79 E.g. Beaglehole, *Cook*, p. 275 n. 2.

80 Beaglehole, *Cook*, p. 445.

81 Lonsdale, *Burney*, pp. 111–12.

82 Beaglehole, *Cook*, pp. 290 & 457. *Carteret's Voyage Round the World 1766–1769*, ed. Helen Wallis (Hakluyt Soc. Ser. II Vols. 124–25, Cambridge 1965) II, 464–76.

83 O'Brian, *Banks*, p. 190.

84 Beaglehole, *Cook*, pp. 461–70. Beaglehole, *Cook Journals*, II, xlv, cxlviii–cxlix. Dawson, *Banks Letters*, pp. 335, 339 &c. NMM: SAN/V/12 p. 327, S to D. Barrington, 28 Oct 1775; SAN/F/36/28–32, D. Barrington to S, 7 May–12 Jun 1776.

85 Beaglehole, *Cook Journals*, III, cc n. 1. Dawson, *Banks Letters*, pp. 618–19, S to J. Banks, 23 Sep 1782 & 9 Sep 1784.

86 BM: Eg.MSS 2180 f. 55, S to J. Douglas, 19 Nov 1782.

87 Beaglehole, *Cook Journals*, III, 356 n. 1 & 368 n. 1.

88 Dobrée, *Chesterfield Letters*, III, 882 No. 1129, Chesterfield to S, 13 Mar OS 1746/7.

89 There is extensive correspondence between Cressener, Sandwich and the spy in PRO: SP 81/142 & 144. See also RAW: Cumberland MSS Box 19/46, G. Cressener to S, 29 Nov 1746 NS; WA: unbound MSS of 4th Duke of Bedford, Bedford to Albemarle, 18 Dec 1749 & Albemarle to Bedford, 11 Jan 1750. I have not discovered when this agent ceased reporting.

90 *BFP*, p. 240.

91 Ellis, *Post Office*, pp. 66–67, 70 & 152–53.

92 Mackay, *Hawke Papers*, pp. 290–98.

93 *SP*, I, 424–25, S. Swinton to S, 10 & 12 Mar 1778. NMM: F/13/114, P. Stephens to S, 24 Apr 1778.

94 Breen, 'Yorktown Campaign' p. 38.

95 The *Compagnie des Indes* had in fact just been abolished, but Lorient remained the centre of the French India trade and the obvious place to

pick up intelligence about French activities in the East.

96 NMM: SAN/F/33a/7, J. Walker to S & J. Purling, 1 Aug 1771.

97 There are numerous examples of his reports, almost all anonymous, in *Calendar of Home Office Papers*, (eg IV Nos. 779 & 799); PRO: SP 42/48–49 & 51; SP 78/69 & 301–3. The last I have noted was received in March 1778 (*SP*, I, 350).

98 *SP*, II, 278. PRO: PRO 30/20/26/3 p. 8, G. Jackson to Sir G. B. Rodney, 10 Dec 1779.

99 Ozanam & Antoine, *Correspondance Secrète*, I, 196 & 317, Nos. 101 & 167, de Broglie to Louis XV, 16 Dec 1763 & 21 Feb 1765.

100 Scott, 'Bourbon Naval Reconstruction', p. 32. *BFP*, p. 75. Patterson, *The Other Armada*, pp. 33–36 & 54–56. Clark & Morgan, *Naval Documents*, I, 404–5, 439 & II, 699, Sartine to Vergennes, 20 Feb 1775; Garnier to Vergennes, 20 Mar 1775; Guines to Vergennes, 1 Sep 1775. P. Coquelle, 'Les projets de descente en Angleterre', *Revue d'Histoire Diplomatique*, XV (1901) pp. 433–52 & 591–624; XVI (1902) pp. 134–57, at XVI, 134–35.

101 J. Merino, M. Acerra, & J. Meyer, 'Europäische Kriegsmarinen im 17 und 18 Jahrhundert: ein Überblick', *Wirtschaftskräfte und Wirtschaftswege V, Festschrift für Hermann Kellenbenz*, ed. Jürgen Schneider (*Beiträge zur Wirtschaftsgeschichte*, 8, Stuttgart, 1981), pp. 267–82, at p. 270.

102 *BFP*, p. 214.

103 Steuart, *Walpole's Last Journals*, II, 369. Morris, *Peacemakers*, pp. 132–33.

104 Morris, *Peacemakers*, pp. 139–40. Knight, *Portsmouth Dockyard Papers*, xxix n. 53.

105 Morris, *Peacemakers*, discusses the letter p. 121 & reproduces it facing p. 206 without noticing this point. The hand itself seems to be disguised, but the unique Dutch letter 'ÿ', and such usages as 'under-writter' (transcribed by Morris 'underwritten'), evidently for 'onderschrijver', are unmistakable.

106 F. P. Renaut, *Le Traitre de l'Amirauté ou le mot de l'affaire Montagu Fox, 1780–1782*, (Paris, 1937). Morris, *Peacemakers*, pp. 112–31 is the best account, but more is needed.

CHAPTER XIII

1 Villiers, *Marine Royale, Corsaires et Trafic*, pp. 498–99.

2 Paul D. Nelson, 'British Conduct of the American Revolutionary War: A Review of Interpretations', *Journal of American History*, LXV (1978) pp. 623–53, at p. 623.

3 John Shy, 'The American Revolution: The Military Conflict considered as a Revolutionary War', in *Essays in the American Revolution*, ed. Stephen G. Kurtz & James H. Hutson (Chapel Hill, 1973) pp. 121–56.

4 Bernard Bailyn, *The Ideological Origins of the American Revolution*, (Cambridge, Mass., 1967).

5 Thomas, 'George III and the American Revolution'. Opinion on the king's actions in the 1780s is more evenly divided.

6 Namier, 'George III: A Study of Personality', p. 42.

7 *CG3*, III, 256.

8 James T. Boulton, 'Arbitrary Power: An Eighteenth-Century Obsession', *Studies in Burke and his Times* IX (1968) pp. 905–26.

9 Namier, 'George III: A Study of Personality', p. 44.

10 Langford, 'Old Whigs, Old Tories, and the American Revolution'. Christie & Labaree, *Empire or Independence*, pp. 274–81. Tucker & Hendrickson, *Fall of the First British Empire*, pp. 379–410. Greene, 'The Seven Years' War and the American Revolution', at pp. 87–91. Christie, 'British Politics and the American Revolution', pp. 205–13. Pocock, 'The Revolution against Parliament'.

Van Alstyne, 'Parliamentary Supremacy versus Independence'. Derry, *English Politics*, p. 23.

11 Norris, *Shelburne and Reform*, pp. 93–94. Christie, 'British Politics and the American Revolution'. Van Alstyne, 'Parliamentary Supremacy versus Independence', pp. 206–10.

12 Paul Langford, 'London in the American Revolution', in Stevenson, *London in the Age of Reform*, pp. 55–78. Sainsbury, *Disaffected Patriots*. Colin Bonwick, *English Radicals and the American Revolution*, (Chapel Hill, N.C., 1977).

13 Donoughue, *British Politics and the American Revolution*, pp. 288–89.

14 MPS: Box 52, W. Eden to Stormont, 23 Jan 1778.

15 Norris, *Shelburne and Reform*, p. 93. Mackesy, *War for America*, p. 8.

16 J. H. Plumb, 'British Attitudes to the American Revolution', in *In the Light of History*, (London, 1972) pp. 70–87.

17 *SP*, I, 29, S to Rochford, 15 Nov 1772.

18 Simmons & Thomas, *American Debates*, VI, 229 & 364 (said in 1775).

19 Donoughue, *British Politics and the American Revolution*, pp. 70–71 & 253–54. B. D. Bargar, *Lord Dartmouth and the American Revolution*, (Columbia S.C., 1965), pp. 76 & 132–33.

20 Thomas, *Townshend Duties Crisis*, p. 13.

21 Simmons & Thomas, *American Debates*, II, 338; IV, 420; V, 329–36. Labaree, *Franklin Papers*, XXI, 581.

22 Cobbett, *Parliamentary History*, XVIII, 446. Greene, 'The Seven Years' War and the American Revolution', p. 94. Robson, *American Revolution*, p. 127.

23 Donoughue, *British Politics and the American Revolution*, pp. 280–82. Thomas, *Townshend Duties Crisis*, p. 13. Robert E. Toohey, *Liberty and Empire. British Radical Solutions to the American Problem, 1774–1776*, (Lexington, Kentucky, 1978), p. 112.

24 E. N. Williams, *The Eighteenth-Century Constitution 1688–1815: Documents and Commentary*, (Cambridge, 1960) p. 120.

25 Thomas, 'George III and the American Revolution', p. 17.

26 Ian R. Christie, 'The Cabinet in the Reign of George III, to 1790', in *Myth and Reality*, pp. 55–108. Christie, 'George III and the Historians', pp. 216–18. Pares, *George III and the Politicians*, pp. 153–54.

27 Rose, *Marchmont*, I, 219.

28 Stephen B. Baxter, 'The Conduct of the Seven Years War', in *England's Rise to Greatness, 1660–1763*, ed. Stephen B. Baxter (Berkeley, 1983) pp. 323–48. Middleton, *Bells of Victory*.

29 Brooke, *Chatham Administration*, p. 35.

30 Mackesy, *War for America*, p. xv.

31 Russell, *Memorials of Fox*, II, 38.

32 *SP*, I, 240, J. Robinson to S, 18 Aug 1777.

33 BM: Add.MSS 70990 f. 32, S to North, 14 Sep 1779.

34 MPS: Box 52, W. Eden to Stormont, 25 Oct 1779. I owe this reference to the kindness of Dr H. M. Scott.

35 Quoted by Larrabee, *Decision at the Chesapeake*, p. 23.

36 *CG3*, IV, 215–16 No. 2446, North to George III, 10 Nov 1778.

37 Mackesy, *War for America*, p. 246.

38 NMM: SAN/F/46/93, George III to S, 17 Oct 1779.

39 Margaret M. Spector, *The American Department of the British Government, 1768–1782*, (New York, 1940), p. 27.

40 Thomson, *Secretaries of State*, pp. 85–86.

41 PRO: SP 44/224–32, CO 5/259–60, HO 29/1–7, HO 28/1–13 & 15–53.

42 'Instructions to Captain Cook for his three Voyages', in *The Naval Miscellany Vol. III*, ed. W. G. Perrin (NRS Vol. 63, 1928).

43 Mackesy, *Coward of Minden*.

44 Valentine, *Germain*, pp. 116, 147, 377, 396.

45 Mackesy, *Coward of Minden*, pp. 254–58.
46 Eric Robson, 'The Expedition to the Southern Colonies, 1775–76', *EHR*, LXVI (1951) pp. 535–60, gives examples.
47 *HMC 55 Various Collections*, VI, 180 Lord G. Germain to W. Knox, 1 Nov 1781.
48 Trevor Williams, 'The Cabinet in the Eighteenth Century', *History*, N.S. XXII (1937) pp. 240–52, at p. 245.
49 NUL: NeC 147, H. Pelham to Newcastle, 6 Sep 1748.
50 *SP*, I, 289 n. 1.
51 Mackesy, *War for America*, p. 13.
52 Cobbett, *Parliamentary History*, XIX, 829–30.
53 Simmons & Thomas, *American Debates*, VI, 47–48.
54 Cobbett, *Parliamentary History*, XX, 89.
55 MPS: *passim, ex inf.* Dr H. M. Scott.
56 MPS: Box 13, George III to Stormont, 25 Dec 1779.
57 Cobbett, *Parliamentary History*, XIX, 1296.
58 Cobbett, *Parliamentary History*, XX, 449. Breen, 'Yorktown Campaign', p. 343.
59 Baugh, 'Politics of British Naval Failure', pp. 222–23. G. S. Graham, 'Considerations on the War of American Independence', p. 23. Ritcheson, *British Politics and the American Revolution*, p. 171.
60 Baugh, 'Politics of British Naval Failure' p. 10. Orlando W. Stephenson, 'The Supply of Gunpowder in 1776', *AHR*, XXX (1925) pp. 271–81. R. W. Van Alstyne, 'Great Britain, the War for Independence, and the "Gathering Storm" in Europe, 1775–78', *HLQ*, XXVII (1964) pp. 311–46, at p. 315.
61 Yerxa, 'Graves'.
62 Graham, 'Considerations on the War of American Independence', p. 22.
63 Neil R. Stout, 'Manning the Royal Navy in North America, 1763–75', *AN*, XXIII (1963) pp. 174–85, at p. 185.
64 Miller, *Sir Joseph Yorke*, pp. 41 & 49–50. F. C. van Oosten, 'Some Notes Concerning the Dutch West Indies during the Revolutionary War', *AN*, XXXVI (1976) pp. 155–69. J. Franklin Jameson, 'St Eustatius in the American Revolution', *AHR*, VIII (1903) pp. 683–708. Carrington, *British West Indies*, pp. 128–61. John J. McCusker jr., 'The American Invasion of Nassau in the Bahamas', *AN*, XXV (1965) pp. 189–217, at p. 196.
65 Syrett, *Royal Navy in American Waters*, pp. 20–23 & 30–31. Jamieson, 'War in the Leeward Islands', pp. 107–18.
66 *SP*, I, 64–65.
67 Syrett, *Royal Navy in American Waters*, pp. 1–10.
68 *Calendar of Home Office Papers*, IV No. 1097, Anon, 21 Aug 1775. The 'lower tier' is the main battery of a two-decker.
69 Yerxa, 'Graves', p. 383.
70 Baugh, 'Politics of British Naval Failure', pp. 225–27. *SP*, I, 74 n. 1, S to S. Graves, 18 Sep 1777.
71 *SP*, I, 66–74 print S's correspondence with and about Graves.
72 *HMC 15 Abergavenny*, p. 11, S to J. Robinson, 10 Sep 1775.
73 PRO: PRO 30/29/1/15 f. 725, S to Gower, 24 Sep 1775.
74 *SP*, I, 42–43.
75 NMM: SAN/F/7, correspondence between S and Palliser, Dec 1775-Jan 1776.
76 NMM: RUSI/NM/211, S to C. Douglas, 16 Jan 1776.
77 NMM: SAN/F/7/101, C. Douglas to S, 7 Feb 1776.
78 Mahan, *Major Operations*, p. 11.
79 W. H. Whiteley, 'The British Navy and the Siege of Quebec, 1775–76', *Canadian Historical Review*, LXI (1980) pp. 3–27. *SP*, I, 81–86.
80 NMM: SAN/V/10.
81 NMM: SAN/F/7/99, W. Eden to S, 5 Feb [1776].
82 NMM: SAN/V/10.
83 NMM: SAN/V/10a/15. Williams,

'Sandwich's Naval Administration', p. 68, and Syrett, *Shipping and the American War*, p. 249, give 128,427 tons in July 1776.

84 *SP*, I, 88, Sir H. Palliser to S, 29 Dec 1775.

85 Syrett, *Shipping and the American War*, p. 128.

86 Transport services are dealt with by Syrett, *Shipping and the American War*; Bowler, *Logistics*; & Usher, 'Civil Administration', pp. 263–364.

87 Leland J. Bellot, *William Knox: The Life & Thought of an Eighteenth-Century Imperialist*, (Austin, Texas, 1977), p. 151.

88 David Syrett, 'Lord George Germain and the Protection of Military Storeships 1775–78', *MM*, LX (1974) pp. 395–405.

89 David Syrett, 'Lord George Germain and the Navy Board in Conflict: the *Adamant*, and *Arwin Galley*, Dispute, 1777', *BIHR*, XXXVIII (1965) pp. 163–71.

90 M. K. Barritt, 'The Navy and the Clyde in the American War, 1777–83', *MM*, LV (1969) pp. 33–42, gives a notable example at p. 40. There are numerous others in Syrett, *Shipping and the American War*

91 NMM: MID/7/1/4, undated memorandum by Middleton.

92 Baker, *Government and Contractors*, pp. 241–48. Usher, 'Civil Administration' pp. 263, 276–82 & 295–301.

93 *SP*, I, 119–20 & 125–26, S to M. Shuldham, 13 Feb, & M. Shuldham to S, 22 May 1776. Davies, 'Faction', pp. 21–24.

94 David Syrett, 'The Methodology of British Amphibious Operations during the Seven Years' and American Wars', *MM*, LVIII (1972) pp. 269–80. William L. Calderhead, 'British Naval Failure at Long Island: A Lost Opportunity in the American Revolution', *New York History*, LVII (1976) pp. 321–38.

95 Gruber, *Howe Brothers*. T. S. Anderson, *The Command of the Howe Brothers during the American Revolution*, (New York, 1936).

96 Ira D. Gruber, 'Richard Lord Howe: Admiral as Peacemaker', in Bilias, *George Washington's Opponents*, pp. 233–59.

97 Baugh, 'Politics of British Naval Failure', p. 37.

98 BM: Add.MSS 70990 ff. 92–93, North to Howe, 28 Oct 1777. Hattendorf, *Naval Documents*, No. 228, Howe to Admiralty 10 Dec 1777.

99 Baugh, 'Politics of British Naval Failure', pp. 228–36. Davies, *Documents of the American Revolution*, XIV, 269–70, Howe to P. Stephens, 10 Dec 1777.

100 BM: Add.MSS 70990 f. 27, S to J. Robinson, 17 Aug 1777.

101 Baugh, 'Politics of British Naval Failure', pp. 228–36. Syrett, *Royal Navy in American Waters*, pp. 70–72.

102 H. W. Moomaw, 'The Denouement of General Howe's Campaign of 1777', *EHR*, LXXIX (1964) pp. 498–512.

103 Willcox, 'Too Many Cooks'. Syrett, *Royal Navy in American Waters*, pp. 72–77.

104 Baugh, 'Why did Britain lose command of the Sea?', pp. 153–56.

105 *NDAI*, pp. 122–24.

106 *NDAI*, p. 122.

107 Knight, 'Royal Dockyards', p. 396.

108 PRO: SP 42/49 f. 113, [J. Walker] to S, 13 Sep 1775.

109 Clark & Morgan, *Naval Documents*, I, 433, Vergennes to Garnier, 9 Mar 1775; III, 425, Guines to Vergennes, 15 Dec 1775. *BFP*, p. 208.

110 Patterson, *The Other Armada*, p. 40.

111 *NDAI*, p. 121. *BFP*, p. 209.

112 *SP*, I, 90, Sir H. Palliser to S, 1 Jan 1776.

113 *NDAI*, pp. 129–30. *BFP*, pp. 235–36.

114 PRO: SP 42/49 f. 235, [J. Walker] to S, 25 Jun 1776.

115 *SP*, I, 213–14, S to North 21 Jul 1776. The intelligence referred to must have been that from Walker

dated 15th July, in PRO: SP 42/49 f. 243.

116 *SP*, I, 215–16, S to North, 21 Jul 1776.

117 *NDAI*, p. 134.

118 *FNAI*, pp. 33–35. Murphy, *Vergennes*, p. 256.

119 *FNAI*, pp. 53–56. *NDAI*, p. 136. PRO: SP 42/29 f. 279, [J. Walker] to S, 1 Oct 1776. *BFP*, p. 239.

120 *NDAI*, pp. 136–38.

121 *NDAI*, p. 143. *CG3*, III, 429 No. 1974, J. Robinson to George III, 14 Mar 1777. NMM: SAN/F/10/57, Memo in G. Jackson's hand, 14 Mar 1777. *BFP*, p. 240. Mackesy, *War for America*, p. 172.

122 *FNAI*, p. 84.

123 *FNAI*, p. 84. *BFP*, pp. 253–55.

124 *NDAI*, pp. 148–49.

125 *CG3*, III, 470 No. 2049, North to George III, 22 Aug 1777.

126 PRO: SP 42/51 f. 269, [J. Walker] to S, 1 Nov 1777.

127 NMM: SAN/V/10.

128 Baugh, 'Politics of British Naval Failure', p. 243.

129 R. J. B. Knight, 'The Royal Navy's Recovery after the early phase of the American Revolutionary War' (unpublished paper; I am grateful to Dr Knight for permission to consult it).

130 William J. Morgan, 'American Privateering in America's War for Independence, 1775–83', *AN*, XXXVI (1976) pp. 79–87. Wickwire, 'Naval Warfare', p. 186. Syrett, *Royal Navy in American Waters*, pp. 63, 67 & 88. Cobbett, *Parliamentary History*, XIX, 963.

131 Carrington, *British West Indies*, pp. 68–85.

132 Baugh, 'Politics of British Naval Failure', pp. 47–48. Scott, *British Foreign Policy*, p. 259. Ritcheson, *British Politics and the American Revolution*, pp. 233–57.

133 *SP*, I, 327–35.

134 *FNAI*, pp. 97–98. Baugh, 'Politics of British Naval Failure', p. 239. *NDAI*, pp. 152–53.

135 PRO: SP 42/52 f. 158, Weymouth to Admiralty Board, 21 Mar 1778.

136 *SP*, I, 359–70.

CHAPTER XIV

1 Brown, *The American Secretary*, pp. 154–55. *FNAI*, pp. 116–20.

2 Murphy, *Vergennes*, p. 263. *FNAI*, pp. 97–98.

3 NMM: SAN/F/14/115, A. Keppel to S, 14 Jun 1778.

4 Tunstall, *Naval Warfare*, deals with signalling in detail.

5 'Il est de principe de guerre qu'on doit risquer beaucoup pour défendre ses propres positions, et très peu pour attaquer celles des enemis': Castex, *Les Idées Militaires*, p. 43.

6 BM: Add.MSS 9344 f. 36, J. Jervis to G. Jackson, 31 Jul 1778.

7 Vergé-Franceschi, *Marine et Education*, pp. 353–55. *FNAI*, pp. 19 & 61. James, *British Navy in Adversity*, pp. 79–80. Castex, *Les Idées Militaires*, pp. 121–34.

8 Vergé-Franceschi, *Marine et Education*, pp. 353–55.

9 Langford, *Rockingham Administration*, pp. 271–72. Davies, 'Faction' p. 69. Keppel can be observed as a leader of his party in, e.g., *BC*, III, 366 & 382; Bateson, *Newcastle's Narrative*, pp. 86, 97, 120 & 141; For his views see Smith, *Grenville Papers*, IV, 186.

10 *A New Form of Worship for the 27th of July*, [London, 1782?]

11 Keppel, *Keppel*, I, 378–79.

12 Olson, *Radical Duke*.

13 Keppel, *Keppel*, II, 3–4, Richmond to A. Keppel, 19 Nov 1776.

14 NUL: PwF 6098, A. Keppel to Portland, 18 Feb 1777.

15 *WC*, XXIV, 262 n. 10, quoting *London Chronicle*, 19–21 Nov 1776 xl, 494.

16 *CG3*, IV, 62 No. 2227, George III to North, 16 Mar 1778.

17 W. B. Pemberton, *Lord North*, (London, 1938), p. 293.

18 *SP*, II, 202–5. Broomfield, 'Sand-

19 Van Alstyne, 'Parliamentary Supremacy versus Independence', p. 232.

20 NMM: SAN/F/12/58, A. Keppel to S, 27 Jan 1778.

21 NMM: SAN/V/13 pp. 110, 122, 127 & 170, S to Bristol, 17 Mar, 29 Apr, 3 May & 9 Jul 1778; SAN/F/13/26, 38 & 136, SAN/F/15/21, Bristol to S, 17 & 21 Mar, 30 Apr & 9 Jul 1778.

22 There are many examples in NMM: SAN/F/14; cf. Rodger, *Wooden World*, p. 342.

23 *CG3*, IV, 120 No. 2312, A. Keppel to George III, (Apr 1778?).

24 Keppel, *Keppel*, II, 13.

25 Clark & Morgan, *Naval Documents*, VII, 720.

26 *SP*, II, 15–127 prints some of it, but there is much more in NMM.

27 *Wentworth Woodhouse Manuscripts, Handlist and Index*, (List & Index Society Special Series Vol. 19, 1984) p. 168 No. R1–1771, A. Keppel to Rockingham, 22 Mar 1778; cf. Keppel, *Keppel*, II, 19.

28 NMM: SAN/F/13/92, 'Thoughts' [by Keppel] with S's answers, 15 Apr 1778; printed *SP*, II, 24–27.

29 NMM: SAN/F/15/7, A. Keppel to S, 4 Jul 1778. Mackesy, *War for America*, pp. 202–7.

30 Mainly by Sir Julian Corbett; see his *Principles of Maritime Strategy*.

31 *SP*, II, 369–73 summarizes Keppel's orders.

32 *SP*, II, 98–104. Broomfield, 'Keppel-Palliser Affair', pp. 198–99. Cobbett, *Parliamentary History*, XX, 447. Syrett, 'Home Waters or America?', pp. 374–75. Mackesy, *War for America*, pp. 207–8.

33 Balderstone & Syrett, *Lost War*, pp. 169–70, E. Bowater to Denbigh, 16 Aug 1778.

34 Tunstall, *Naval Warfare*, pp. 137–41. John Creswell, *British Admirals of the Eighteenth Century: Tactics in Battle*, (London, 1972) pp. 120–31.

35 [John Almon] *Memoirs of a Late Eminent Bookseller*, (London, 1790),

pp. 105–6. Werkmeister, *London Daily Press*, p. 117.

36 Mackay, *Hawke*, p. 345.

37 Williams, 'Sandwich's Naval Administration', pp. 450, 456 & 475–76. Knight, 'Royal Dockyards', pp. 344–45.

38 Knight, 'New England Forests'. Williams, 'Sandwich's Naval Administration', pp. 315–28. NMM: SAN/F/15/105, Memo on masts by Middleton, [Aug–Sep 1779?].

39 *SP*, II, 128, A. Keppel to S, 29 Jul 1778.

40 Chevalier, *Marine Française*, pp. 91–92 & 99–101.

41 MC: VI.11/37, S to Mulgrave, 2 Aug 1778.

42 *SP*, II, 127–75 prints Keppel's correspondence with S in this period.

43 Steuart, *Walpole's Last Journals*, II, 223.

44 NMM: SAN/F/12/59, A. Keppel to Sir H. Palliser, 27 Jan [1778]; SAN/F/16/78, A. Keppel to S, 28 Oct 1778. SP II, 110–11, Sir H. Palliser to S, 6 Jul 1778. Broomfield, 'Keppel-Palliser Affair', p. 199.

45 Hannay, *Hood Letters*, p. 2, Sir S. Hood to G. Jackson, 4 Aug 1778 (the original is Add.MSS 34712 f. 1). Broomfield, 'Keppel-Palliser Affair', p. 200.

46 Broomfield, 'Keppel-Palliser Affair' p. 200.

47 Davies, 'Faction', p. 86.

48 Steuart, *Walpole's Last Journals*, II, 197.

49 Steuart, *Walpole's Last Journals*, II, 221–48 offers a fine selection.

50 SP II, 191. *The Names of the Roman Catholics, Nonjurors and others who refus'd to take the Oaths to his late majesty King George . . .*, [ed. James Cosin] (London, 1745), pp. 138–39.

51 Broomfield, 'Keppel-Palliser Affair', p. 201. Davies, 'Faction' p. 87.

52 Broomfield, 'Keppel-Palliser Affair', p. 201. Davies, 'Faction' p. 87.

53 Cobbett, *Parliamentary History*, XIX, 1301–2.
54 Herbert, *Herbert Papers 1734–1780*, p. 367, Lady Pembroke to Herbert, 30 Dec [1779].
55 NMM: SAN/F/16/91 & SAN/F/17/43, printed in *SP*, II, 342 & 211.
56 The charges are printed by Beatson, *Naval and Military Memoirs*, VI, 136–37, and summarized in SP II, 193.
57 Herbert, *Herbert Papers*, p. 141, T. Eyre to Herbert, 1 Jan 1779.
58 Rodger, *Wooden World*, p. 260.
59 Printed by Beatson, *Naval and Military Memoirs*, VI, 137–39.
60 Davies, 'Faction', p. 79. Hunt, *Palliser*, pp. 13–18.
61 *SP*, II, 210.
62 Steuart, *Walpole's Last Journals*, II, 224–26. Broomfield, 'Keppel–Palliser Affair', pp. 202–3. MC: VI.11/49, S to Mulgrave, [11 Dec 1778]. Davies, 'Faction', pp. 95–97. *SP*, II, 274–76 prints S's arguments.
63 *CG3*, IV, 255 No. 2498, G. Jackson to P. Stephens, 8 Jan 1779. Copeland, *Burke Correspondence*, IV, 37–38, E. Burke to Miss F. Pelham, 12 Jan 1779. Steuart, *Walpole's Last Journals*, II, 234–37. SP II, 224–25, Sir H. Palliser to S, ca 5 Feb 1779.
64 Olson, *Radical Duke*, p. 73.
65 *SP*, II, 195, quoting *An Authentic and Impartial copy of the Trial of the Honourable Augustus Keppel*, (Portsmouth, 1779).
66 Steuart, *Walpole's Last Journals*, II, 248.
67 Laughton, *Barham Papers*, I, 267, Sir C. Douglas to C. Middleton, 5 May 1779. The verdict is printed by Beatson, *Naval and Military Memoirs*, VI, 141.
68 *CG3*, IV, 284 No. 2551, George III to North, 19 Feb 1779.
69 *CG3*, IV, 277–78 No. 2540, George III to North, 13 Feb 1779.
70 NMM: SAN/F/27/94, Sir H. Palliser to S, 21 Jun 1781.
71 General accounts of the Keppel–Palliser affair include: *SP*, II, 191–33; Broomfield, 'Keppel–Palliser Affair'; O'Gorman, *Rise of Party in England*, pp. 382–85; Mackesy, *War for America*, pp. 240–42. The printed accounts of the trials, official and unofficial, are listed in *SP*, II, xi–xiv.
72 Mackesy, *War for America*, p. 354.
73 NMM: AGC/7/17, A. Keppel to J. Campbell, 28 Mar 1779.
74 *CG3*, IV, 289–91 No. 2560, A. Keppel to George III, 25 Feb 1779.
75 Broomfield, 'Keppel–Palliser Affair', p. 206. NMM: SAN/F/18/124, Thurlow to S, endorsed Mar 1779.
76 Herbert, *Herbert Papers 1734–1780*, p. 149, Lady Pembroke to Herbert, 18 Feb 1779.
77 O'Gorman, *Rise of Party in England*, p. 386. Broomfield, 'Keppel–Palliser Affair', p. 206.
78 Earl of Malmesbury, ed., *Letters of the First Earl of Malmesbury*, (London, 1870, 2 vols) I, 400.
79 NMM: COR/57, J. Cornwallis to W. Cornwallis, 3 Oct 1779.
80 George, *English Political Caricature*, pp. 161–62.
81 Charles Wesley, *The American War under the Conduct of Sir William Howe*, ed. Donald Baker (London, 1975), p. 23.
82 George, *English Political Caricature*, Pl. 61.
83 *SP*, II, 198. Davies, 'Faction', p. 118. Wraxall, *Memoirs*, II, 268.
84 *SP*, II, 255–81.
85 *CG3*, IV, 240 No. 2486, North to George III, 31 Dec 1778. Usher, 'Civil Administration', p. 3. Davies, 'Faction', pp. 47–51.
86 *CG3*, IV, 293 No. 2565, George III to North, 1 Mar 1779.
87 *CG3*, IV, 325 No. 2611, George III to North, 6 Apr 1779.
88 NMM: SAN/F/22/43, J. Robinson to S, 26 Nov 1779.
89 NMM: SAN/F/41/124, J. Robinson to S, 17 Oct 1779.
90 MC: VI.11/88, S to Mulgrave, 9 Nov 1779.
91 H. Butterfield, *George III, Lord North*

and the People, 1779–80, (London, 1949), pp. 126–27.

92 CG3, V, 96–97 No. 3099, George III to North, 3 Jul 1780; also BM: Eg.MSS 2232 ff. 34–35.

93 Baugh, 'Politics of British Naval Failure', p. 246.

94 NMM: SAN/F/4/5, 'Whisper' to S, 25 Jan 1773. Broomfield, 'Lord Sandwich at the Admiralty Board'.

95 NMM: COR/57 J. Leveson Gower to W. Cornwallis, 27 Feb 1776.

96 CG3, III, 328 No. 1808, S to George III, 10 Jan 1776.

97 WRO: CR2017/C268/39, S to Denbigh, 6 Oct 1775.

98 BM: Add.MSS 20733 f. 12, [J. Blankett] to J. Almon, [Jul 1779]. Werkmeister, London Daily Press, p. 117. Bullocke, Tomlinson Papers, pp. 59, 62–64 & 73.

99 Davies, 'Faction' p. 131. Mackesy, War for America, p. 353.

100 Willcox, Portrait of a General, p. 437 n. 4.

101 CG3, IV, 225–27 No. 2460, List of Keppel's officers (in Sandwich's hand) Nov 1778. It does not seem to be composed by S, for the opinions (e.g. of his friend Walsingham) do not always agree with his. Sir S. Hood would be a likely author.

102 SP, II, 228, Sir S. Hood to S, 10 Feb 1779.

103 CG3, IV, 309 No. 2588, S to George III, 23 Mar 1779.

104 NMM: SAN/F/18/97, R. B. Walsingham to S, [Apr–May 1779].

105 CG3, IV, 422 No. 2763, S to George III, 5 Sep 1779.

106 CG3, IV, 429 No. 2767, S to George III, 7 Sep 1779.

107 SP, IV, 298.

108 FNAI, p. 126.

109 BM: Add.MSS 61863 f. 81, S to North, 21 May 1779.

110 FNAI, pp. 126–45. BFP, pp. 262 & 273.

111 Patterson, The Other Armada, pp. 59–70 & 160–68. G. Lacour-Gayet, 'La Campagne Navale de la

Manche en 1779', Revue Maritime, CL (1901) pp. 1629–73.

112 William Roberts, Memoirs of the Life and Correspondence of Mrs Hannah More, (London, 1834, 4 vols) I, 159.

113 SP, II, 201, J. Robinson to S, [8 Dec 1775]. Gruber, Howe Brothers, pp. 65–67.

114 NMM: SAN/F/6/17, J. Robinson to S, [ca 15 Dec 1775].

115 Davies, 'Faction', pp. 17–42. Gruber, Howe Brothers, pp. 212–13.

116 Davies, 'Faction' pp. 51–60.

117 There is some doubt about his date of birth. He is sometimes confused with his father, Vice-Admiral Sir Charles, who died in 1744.

118 NMM: SAN/F/19/107, Hardy's orders of 29 May 1779.

119 SP, III, 5.

120 Phillips, 'Evangelical Administrator', pp. 126–28.

121 SP, III, 33, Mulgrave to S, 2 Jul 1779.

122 MC: VI.11/68, S to Mulgrave, 8 Jul 1779.

123 SP, III, 51, George III to S, 28 Jul 1779.

124 MC: VI.11/70, S to Mulgrave, 29 Jul 1779.

125 CG3, IV, 396 No. 2717, George III to North, 18 Jul 1779.

126 SP, III, 5–8.

127 MC: VI.11/73, S to Mulgrave, 15 Aug 1779.

128 CG3, IV, 419 No. 2759, S to George III, 4 Sep 1779.

129 Patterson, Other Armada, pp. 160–215 is the standard account of this campaign.

130 Mackesy, War for America, pp. 283–84, puts the argument most cogently.

131 Phillips, 'Evangelical Administrator', pp. 126–28.

132 Kempenfelt's letters to Middleton are in Laughton, Barham Papers, I, 288–365.

133 'The Channel Fleet in 1779: Letters of Benjamin Thompson to Lord George Germain', in The Naval Miscellany Vol. III, ed. W. G.

Perrin (NRS Vol. 63, 1928) pp. 123–54.

134 NMM: SAN/F/46/52, George III to S, 16 Jul 1779.

135 NMM: SAN/F/20/47, R. B. Walsingham to S, 12 Aug 1779.

136 NMM: SAN/F/21/65, P. Osborn to S, 9 Oct 1779.

137 Corbett, *Maritime Strategy*, pp. 257–58.

138 *CG3*, IV, 422 No. 2763, S to George III, 5 Sep 1779.

139 MC: VI.11/69, Mulgrave to S, 11 Jul 1779.

140 Laughton, *Barham Papers*, I, 298, R. Kempenfelt to C. Middleton 19 Sep 1779.

141 Herbert, *Herbert Papers 1734–1780*, p. 287.

142 MC: VI.11/81, Mulgrave to S, 17 Oct 1779.

143 Mackesy, *War for America*, pp. 283–84, 287–88 & 296.

144 MC: VI.11/68, S to Mulgrave, 8 Jul 1779.

145 Rodger, *Wooden World*, p. 305.

146 *CG3*, IV, 419–20 No. 2759, S to George III, 4 Sep 1779.

147 Mackesy, *War for America*, pp. 287–88.

148 *SP*, III, 26–29. Mackesy, *War for America*, pp. 283–84.

CHAPTER XV

1 See the works of G. S. Brown, Mackesy & Valentine in the bibliography.

2 Mackesy, *War for America*.

3 Ryan, 'Blockade of Brest'.

4 A. N. Ryan, 'An ambassador afloat: Vice-Admiral Sir James Saumarez and the Swedish Court, 1808–12', in Black & Woodfine, *Use of Naval Power*, pp. 237–58, at p. 237.

5 Spencer, *Sandwich Diplomatic Correspondence*, p. 9, quoting Basil Williams, *The Life of William Pitt, Earl of Chatham*, (London, 1913, 2 vols) II, p. 274. Cf. Kitchener's remark in 1915, 'one makes war, not as one would like to, but as one must', quoted by Michael Howard, *The Continental Commitment*, (London, 1972) p. 126.

6 Mackesy, *War for America*, pp. 373–75. Harlow, *Second British Empire*, I, 108–11.

7 Which deserves to be studied; see NMM: SAN/F/27/116 & F/28/1, Mulgrave to S, 30 Jun & 3 Jul 1781; MC: VI.2/345 & 353, S to Mulgrave, 4 & 7 Jul 1781; *CG3*, V, 249–52 Nos. 3362 & 3367, S to George III, 24 Jun & 7 Jul 1781.

8 This is the central thesis of Middleton, *Bells of Victory*.

9 By R. J. B. Knight in an unpublished paper, '"Some further degree of merit": the Fall and Rise of the Reputation of Lord Sandwich', referring to *SP*, IV, 297. See also Baugh, 'Politics of British Naval Failure', pp. 227–28, for S's defence of naval policy 1775–77.

10 Cobbett, *Parliamentary History*, XXII, 991. Mackesy, *War for America*, p. xv.

11 Mackesy, *War for America*, pp. 308–9.

12 E. G. Willcox, *Portrait of a General*, pp. 214–18; Willcox's opinions have been generally followed.

13 *CG3*, IV, 434–35 No. 2774, George III to S, 13 Sep 1779.

14 Jamieson, 'War in the Leeward Islands', p. 193.

15 Corbett, *Maritime Strategy*.

16 Wickwire, 'Naval Warfare', p. 194.

17 Richmond, *Navy in the War of 1739–48*, III, 21–23.

18 NMM: SAN/V/53 p. 108, Newcastle to S, 31 Jan 1746/7.

19 Mackesy, *War for America*, p. 309.

20 Syrett, 'Home Waters or America?' is the best and most recent treatment. Others are: Brown, 'Anglo-French Naval Crisis'; Willcox, 'British Strategy in America; Brown, *American Secretary*, pp. 149–72. See also *SP*, II, 22–92.

21 Not then attached to the mainland.

22 Jamieson, 'War in the Leeward Islands', pp. 57–198. 'Barrington Letters' pp. 385–88.

23 PRO: ADM 2/1334 f. 62, Instructions to Howe, 22 Mar 1778. *SP*, I, 365 is a draft of these.

24 *SP*, I, 359–70.

25 *SP*, I, 360.

26 *SP*, I, 327–39. Syrett, *Navy in American Waters*, pp. 94–95.

27 Ritcheson, *British Politics and the American Revolution*, p. 257.

28 Bonner-Smith, *Barrington Papers*, II, xxvi-xxxi, 277–79, 335, 345–50. The collation of S's private letter-book (NMM: SAN/V/13) implies that the letter of 5 Aug was really written on or about that date.

29 BM: Add.MSS 70990 f. 31, S to North, 14 Sep 1779.

30 Bonner-Smith, *Barrington Papers*, II, 316, Barrington to S, 17 Sep 1779.

31 Bonner-Smith, *Barrington Papers*, II, 314–18 & 338–41. Laughton, *Barham Papers*, I, 366.

32 MC: VI.11/103, S to Mulgrave, 21 May 1780.

33 George Grenville, quoted by Brian Tunstall, *William Pitt, Earl of Chatham*, (London, 1938) p. 123.

34 Mackay, *Hawke*, p. 228. *SP*, III, 275.

35 'Boscawen's Letters to his Wife, 1755–1756', ed. Peter K. Kemp, in *The Naval Miscellany Vol. IV*, ed. Christopher Lloyd (NRS Vol. 92, 1952) pp. 163–256, at p. 232.

36 Earl of Rosse's MSS: Letter Book H2 ff. 185–86, Hawke to S. Barrington, Jun 1780.

37 Callender, 'With the Grand Fleet'.

38 *CG3*, V, 110–11 Nos. 3123 & 3125, S to George III, 28 & 30 Aug 1780.

39 Mackesy, *War for America*, pp. 358–59. Callender, 'With the Grand Fleet', pp. 298–99.

40 *SP*, IV, 31, Mulgrave to S, 19 Feb 1781.

41 *SP*, IV, 65, Mulgrave to S, 11 Sep 1781.

42 BM: Add.MSS 70990 f. 27, S to J. Robinson, 17 Aug 1777.

43 *SP*, I, 239, J. Robinson to S, 18 Aug 1777.

44 *SP*, I, 240, J. Robinson to S, 18 Aug 1777.

45 Almon, *Anecdotes*, III, 274–78.

46 *CG3*, IV, 320 No. 2602, S to George III, 4 Apr 1779. *HMC 15 Abergavenny*, pp. 20, 24 & 36. W. F. Elofson, 'The Rockingham Whigs in Transition: The East India Company Issue 1772–1773', *EHR*, CIV (1989) pp. 947–74. Broomfield, 'Lord Sandwich at the Admiralty', pp. 8–9. Davies, 'Faction', pp. 12–13. Fabel, *Bombast and Broadsides*, pp. 130–33. Sutherland, *East India Company*.

47 MPS: Bundle 640: S to Stormont, 26 Dec 1780.

48 Notably by Willcox, 'Arbuthnot, Gambier, and Graves'; 'The British Road to Yorktown', p. 3; *Portrait of a General*, p. 285. Other scholars have followed Willcox.

49 NMM: SAN/F/46/31, George III to S, 7 May 1779.

50 *SP*, III, 128–29 for his initiative in going to the defence of Jersey in May; III, 134–35 for the evacuation of Rhode Island to concentrate against d'Estaing.

51 Willcox, *Portrait of a General*, pp. 123–25.

52 *SP*, III, 237. Syrett, *Royal Navy in North America*, pp. 135–40 gives a good brief account of the expedition.

53 Syrett, *Royal Navy in American Waters*, pp. 167–70. Fraser, 'The Memoranda of William Green', XVII, 128–30.

54 Fraser, 'Memoranda of William Green', XVII, 93. Bowler, *Logistics*, p. 137 says that Clinton's supply situation prevented the army from moving in any case.

55 *Rodney Letter-Books*, I, 44, Sir G. B. Rodney to M. Arbuthnot, 19 Oct 1781. Cf. Spinney, *Rodney*, p. 346, 'His Commission gave him virtually a free hand in the western hemisphere'. Breen, 'Divided Command', does not address this point.

56 PRO: ADM 2/1336 ff. 82–86, orders of 8 Dec 1779. See also PRO: ADM 2/108 pp. 99–111.

57 PRO: ADM 2/1335 ff. 4–6, Orders

of 3 May 1778. Barrington's copy, printed in Bonner-Smith, *Barrington Papers*, II, 6–13 is dated 2nd.

58 *CG3*, V, 121 No. 3136, Cabinet Minute, 14 Sep 1780. PRO: ADM 2/1336 f. 58, orders to M. Arbuthnot, 24 Jun 1779; ADM 2/1337 ff. 60, 62 & 86, orders to Sir P. Parker & Sir G. B. Rodney, 16 Mar 1780, & to M. Arbuthnot, 23 Apr 1780.

59 PRO: ADM 2/1338 f. 4, orders of 2 May 1780. See also PRO: ADM 2/106 pp. 440–48, orders of 5 Apr 1779.

60 PRO: ADM 2/1337 ff. 68–70, orders of 16 Mar 1780.

61 PRO: ADM 2/1334 ff. 54–57, Orders of 21 Mar 1778.

62 PRO: CO 5/263 ff. 15–16, Lord G. Germain to Admiralty, 29 Apr 1778; ADM 2/1335 ff. 11–12, orders of 3 May 1778. Byron's orders are summarized in *SP*, II, 374–76; his order of 18 Jan 1779 to Barrington is printed by Bonner-Smith, *Barrington Papers*, II, 206–8.

63 Davies, 'Faction' p. 216, quoting PRO: PRO 30/20/12, M. Arbuthnot to Sir G. B. Rodney, 2 Nov 1780.

64 Lloyd, 'Rodney' p. 339 is wrong in implying that it was 'normal practice' to go north.

65 Mrs Aubrey Le Blond, *Charlotte Sophie, Countess Bentinck: Her Life and Times, 1715–1800*, (London, 1912, 2 vols) II, 270–72, Sir G. B. Rodney to W. Keene, 1st Oct 1780. BM: Add.MSS 9344 ff. 47–49, Sir G. B. Rodney to G. Jackson, 12 Oct 1780. NMM: SAN/F/25/16, Sir G. B. Rodney to S, 10 Oct 1780. *Rodney Letter-Books*, I, 10–71. Breen, 'Divided Command', pp. 193–94.

66 Breen, 'Yorktown Campaign', pp. 87–90. Davies, 'Faction' pp. 212–21.

67 This was what Hood did in October 1781 when he proposed to Digby to borrow most of his ships of the line for the Leeward Islands: NMM: MID/1/93/5, Sir S. Hood to R. Digby, 31 Oct 1781.

68 *Rodney Letters Books*, I, 71. Syrett, *Navy in American Waters*, pp. 154–56. Willcox, 'Rhode Island' pp. 314–16.

69 *HMC 49 Stopford-Sackville*, II, 190, M. Arbuthnot to Lord G. Germain, 19 Dec 1780.

70 NMM: JCK/1 p. 233, M. Arbuthnot to G. Jackson, 4 Oct 1780.

71 *HMC 49 Stopford-Sackville*, II, 195. Willcox, *Portrait of a General*, pp. 272–73. Willcox, 'Rhode Island', pp. 316.

72 *SP*, IV, 164–65, S to Sir G. B. Rodney, 7 Jul 1781.

73 *SP*, IV, 345. The original paper is NMM: SAN/F/30/39.

74 MC: VI.2/368, Admiralty Office 'Precis of Instructions to Arbuthnot'.

75 MC: VI.2/368, Admiralty Office 'Precis of Instructions to Arbuthnot'.

76 PRO: ADM 2/1228 f. 66, Admiralty to Sir G. B. Rodney, 25 Sep 1780. There is no corresponding order from Germain in PRO: CO 5/263.

77 PRO: CO 5/263 f. 46, Lord G. Germain to Admiralty, 3 Dec 1779; ADM 2/1336 f. 73, orders to H. Parker, 3 Dec 1779.

78 PRO: CO 5/263 ff. 15–16, Lord G. Germain to Admiralty, 29 Apr 1778. These are Byron's primary orders.

79 NMM: HOO/1/65, G. Jackson to [Sir S. Hood], 12 Jan 1782.

80 Jamieson, 'War in the Leeward Islands', p. 28. Pares, *War and Trade in the West Indies*, pp. 276–77.

81 Baugh, 'Hood'.

82 *Two Letters from W. Graves Esq; respecting the Conduct of Rear Admiral Thomas Graves . . .* , [London, 1782], pp. 5–11.

83 This is Thomas Graves, much later Admiral Lord Graves (1725–1802); he is often confused with his first cousin Vice-Admiral Samuel Graves (1713–87), who had commanded at Boston in 1775–76, or with Samuel's nephew the future Admiral Sir Thomas Graves (1747–1841).

84 Breen, 'Yorktown Campaign', pp. 104–8.

85 John Jervis, quoted by Breen, 'York-town Campaign', p. 377.

86 Breen, 'Yorktown Campaign', pp. 282–303.

87 Jamieson, 'War in the Leeward Islands', p. 208. Davies, 'Faction', pp. 202–3. *HMC 49 Stopford-Sackville*, II, 173, Sir G. B. Rodney to Lord G. Germain, 2 Aug 1780.

88 The siege of Yorktown did not begin until 29th September, three weeks after the naval battle.

89 Willcox, 'Arbuthnot, Gambier, and Graves', gives the older interpret-ation of Graves, and has been gener-ally followed.

90 Osinga, *Frankrijk, Vergennes en de Amerikanse Onafhankelijkheid*, pp. 8–16, 73–80, 137–51. Baugh, 'Why did Britain lose Command of the Sea?', p. 161. *FNAI*, pp. 279–80, 297–304 & 333–35 clearly shows the critical French situation. Dull's *A Diplomatic History of the American Revolution*, (New Haven & London, 1985) takes the orthodox view of Vergennes as faithful to the cause of Ameri-can independence (eg p. 119); I find Osinga's argument more per-suasive.

91 *FNAI*, pp. 242–48.

92 *SP*, IV, 342–46 & 351–55.

93 *SP*, II, 352.

94 Jamieson, 'War in the Leeward Islands', p. 322.

95 The Yorktown campaign as a whole is best described by Breen, 'York-town Campaign' (summarised in Breen, 'Graves and Hood'); *FNAI*, pp. 242–48; Willcox, 'The British Road to Yorktown'; and Syrett, *Royal Navy in American Waters*, pp. 177–217. See also *SP*, IV, 141–44, 181–93; Sulivan, 'Graves and Hood'; Hale, 'Naval Side of York-town'; Tunstall, *Naval Warfare*, pp. 172–76.

96 Baugh, 'Why did Britain lose com-mand of the Sea?' *NDAI*, p. 154.

97 *FNAI*, pp. 109 & 279.

98 *FNAI*, pp. 197–99.

99 Wraxall, *Memoirs*, II, 320–21.

100 Gérard de la Mardière, 'Le Conseil de Guerre de Lorient (1783–1784)', *Chronique d'Histoire Maritime*, 19 (1989) pp. 16–36.

101 For the campaigns of Bernardo de Gálvez see: Carmen de Reparaz, *Yo Solo: Bernardo de Gálvez y la toma de Panzacola en 1781*, (Barcelona, 1986) and J. W. Caughey, *Bernardo de Gálvez in Louisiana, 1776–1783*, (Berkeley, 1934; U. C. L. A. Publi-cations in Social Sciences Vol. 4). Juan Manuel Zapatero, *La Guerra del Caribe en el siglo XVIII*, (San Juan, P. R., 1964) is less useful for this war.

102 *FNAI*, pp. 249 & 272.

103 Miller, *Sir Joseph Yorke*, pp. 77–87, 91–100. Syrett, *Neutral Rights*. H. M. Scott, 'Sir Joseph Yorke, Dutch Politics and the Origins of the Fourth Anglo-Dutch War', *HJ*, XXXI (1988) pp. 571–89. *BFP*, pp. 305–9.

104 *HMC No. 55 Various Collections*, VI, 271, note by W. Knox. The Lord President was Lord Bathurst, and the Lord Chancellor, Lord Thurlow.

105 J. H. Owen, 'Operations of the Western Squadron, 1781–82', *Naval Review*, XV (1927) pp. 33–53. *SP*, IV, 80–82. Mackesy, *War for America*, pp. 448–49.

106 Usually on the basis of an uncritical reading of Middleton (eg Laughton, *Barham Papers*, II, 5), who of course had only himself in mind.

107 This is very clear from Mulgrave's papers, which have not hitherto been much used by historians.

108 MC: VI.11/150, S to Mulgrave, 24 May 1782.

109 MC: VI.11/114, Mulgrave to S, 21 Sep 1780.

110 Williams, 'Sandwich's Naval Administration', p. 438.

111 Lavery, *Arming and Fitting*, pp. 62–63.

112 PRO: ADM 7/662 f. 21. Knight, 'Copper Sheathing', pp. 299–300.

113 Lavery, *Arming and Fitting*, p. 63

gives the technical details of the seals.

114 Knight, *Portsmouth Dockyard Papers*, pp. 159–65.

115 NMM: SAN/F/31/39, S to North, [rough draft, 9 or 10 Dec 1782].

116 NMM: MID/1/140/3, P. Patton to C. Middleton, 2 Jul 1779.

117 Knight, 'Royal Dockyards', p. 343.

118 Calculated from Williams, 'Sandwich's Naval Administration', p. 446

119 Knight, *Portsmouth Dockyard Papers*, p. lvi.

120 Laughton, *Barham Papers*, III, 16.

121 *SP*, IV, 80–82, 'Admiral Kempenfelt's ideas about the mode of carrying on the war', 13 Jan 1782.

122 *HMC 49 Stopford-Sackville*, II, 153, Sir G. B. Rodney to Lord G. Germain, 27 Jan 1780.

123 *HMC 24 Rutland*, III, 38, Lord R. Manners to Rutland, 27 Sep 1781.

124 *HMC 24 Rutland*, III, 50, Lord R. Manners to Rutland, 10 Mar 1782.

125 Knight, 'Copper Sheathing', pp. 304–5. Williams, 'Sandwich's Naval Administration', p. 447.

126 Hattendorf, *Naval Documents*, No. 293, Navy Board to Admiralty, 5 Nov 1783.

127 Lavery, *Arming and Fitting*, p. 65. Webb, 'Rebuilding and Repair of the Fleet. For French coppering see *FNAI*, p. 176 n. ; Etienne Taillemite, *L'Histoire ignorée de la marine française*, (Paris, 1988) p. 192; Martine Acerra & Jean Meyer, *Marines et Révolution*, (Rennes, 1988), pp. 64–66 & 79; Villiers, *Marine Royale, Corsaires et Trafic*, pp. 558–59.

128 Knight, 'Royal Dockyards', p. 348.

129 NMM: SAN/F/16/105, T. Lloyd to S, 21 Nov 1778.

130 Rodger, *Wooden World*, pp. 137–45.

131 *SP*, IV, 413–22. Lavery, *Ship of the Line*, I, 116 & II, 151. F. L. Robertson, *The Evolution of Naval Armament*, (London, 1921) pp. 125–34. Peter Padfield, *Guns at Sea*, (London, 1973) pp. 105–8. Phillips,

'Evangelical Administrator', pp. 109–11. Hattendorf, *Naval Documents*, Nos. 291 & 292.

CHAPTER XVI

1 *CG3*, V, 321–22 No. 3481, S to George III, 23 Dec 1781. Cf. *HMC 15 Abergavenny*, p. 47, S to J. Robinson, 13 Jan 1782.

2 MC: VI.11/146, S to Mulgrave, 7 Jan 1782.

3 Christie *The End of North's Ministry*, pp. 268–69.

4 *WC*, XXV, 238, H. Walpole to H. Mann, 17 Jan 1782.

5 NMM: HOO/1/65, G. Jackson to [Sir S. Hood], 12 Jan 1782.

6 Christie *The End of North's Ministry*, pp. 306–12, quoting (p. 312) Col E. Smith MP.

7 Laprade, *Robinson Papers*, p. 41, S to J. Robinson, 15 Mar 1782.

8 Christie *The End of North's Ministry*, pp. 363–69.

9 Hostilities did not end in India until June 1783.

10 *HMC 15 Abergavenny*, p. 53, S to North, 26 Mar 1782.

11 NMM: SAN/F/42/59a, Sir J. Marriott to S, 25 Nov [endorsed 1783; *recte*, 1782?]. Christie *The End of North's Ministry*, pp. 200–6.

12 Cannon, *Fox–North Coalition*, pp. 55 & 72 n. 4.

13 Christie, 'Opposition in the Parliament of 1784', pp. 64–65.

14 SRB: HA 513/4/3, Grafton's Diary, 26 Apr 1782.

15 SRB: HA 513/4/3, Grafton's Diary, 28 Jun 1782.

16 MC: VI.11/156, S to Mulgrave, 23 Aug 1782.

17 Norris, *Shelburne and Reform*, pp. 95–96. C. R. Ritcheson, 'The Earl of Shelburne and Peace with America, 1782–83: Vision and Reality', *IHR*, V (1983) pp. 322–45.

18 Phillips, 'Evangelical Administrator', pp. 299–300.

19 Cannon, *Fox–North Coalition*, pp. 10 & 26.

20 Cannon, *Fox–North Coalition*,

p. 43, quoting Wraxall. *CG3*, VI, 173 & 184, Nos. 4012 4021, George III to Shelburne, 6 & 11 Dec 1782.

21 McCahill, *Order and Equipoise*, p. 184. Cannon, *Fox–North Coalition*, p. 55.

22 NMM: SAN/F/42/64, S to Hinchingbrooke, 16 Feb 1783.

23 Christie, 'Opposition in the Parliament of 1784' pp. 50–55 & 60–61.

24 NMM: SAN/F/42/74 & 77, S to North, 4 & [11?] Apr 1783; F/42/92, S to Orford, 28 Apr 1783 [foul draft]. *HMC 15 Abergavenny*, p. 60, S to J. Robinson, 21 Apr 1783. Cannon, *Fox–North Coalition*, pp. 82–84.

25 MC: VI.11/164, S to Mulgrave, 2 May 1783.

26 Cannon, *Fox–North Coalition*, pp. 106–45.

27 Cannon, *Fox–North Coalition*, pp. 145–228.

28 Cannon, *Fox–North Coalition*, p. 210 n. 3.

29 Aspinall, *Later Correspondence of George III*, I, 16, George III to W. Pitt, 30 Dec 1783. MC: VI.11/166, Mulgrave to S, 25 Dec 1783; 11/167, S to Mulgrave, 26 Dec 1783.

30 McCahill, *Order and Equipoise*, p. 187.

31 Cannon, *Fox–North Coalition*, p. 156.

32 Christie, 'Opposition in the Parliament of 1784', p. 70. Jesse, *George Selwyn*, I, 193. Manufactured lavatory paper was not known in the eighteenth century.

33 *FNAI*, pp. 249, 265–66 & 272. Mackesy, *War for America*, p. 506. Jamieson, 'War in the Leeward Islands', pp. 33 & 301–3.

34 *CG3*, VI, 99 No. 3877, Shelburne to George III, 11 Aug 1782; VI, 106 No. 3887, George III to Shelburne, 21 Aug 1782. Davies, 'Faction' p. 274.

35 Corbett, *Maritime Strategy*, pp. 145–51.

36 Syrett, *Shipping and the American War*, pp. 234–36.

37 *CG3*, VI, 33 & 100 Nos. 3759 & 3878, George III to Shelburne, 18 May & 12 Aug 1782.

38 SRB: HA 513/4/4, Grafton's Diary, 14 [or 15–16?] Jul 1782.

39 Davies, 'Faction' p. 278.

40 Keppel, *Keppel*, II, 391–92, Keppel to J. Jervis, 24 May 1782.

41 Davies, 'Faction' pp. 270–72.

42 SRB: HA 513/4/3, Grafton's Diary, 18 May 1782. Davies, 'Faction' p. 281.

43 MC: VI.11/150, S to Mulgrave, 24 May 1782.

44 George, *English Political Caricature*, p. 166.

45 Christie *The End of North's Ministry*, pp. 177 & 217. Broomfield, 'Lord Sandwich at the Admiralty Board', p. 8.

46 NMM: SAN/V/13 p. 90, S to H. Pigot, 19 Jan 1778. Wraxall, *Memoirs*, II, 185. There is nothing in S's papers to support Pigot's later claim that he was offered a command on unacceptable political conditions.

47 Wraxall, *Memoirs*, II, 329–30.

48 Jamieson, 'War in the Leeward Islands', pp. 72, 91 & 308–21.

49 G. M. Ditchfield, 'The House of Lords and Parliamentary Reform in the Seventeen-Eighties', in Jones & Jones, *Peers, Politics and Power*, pp. 327–45 (originally *BIHR*, LIV (1981) pp. 207–25), at pp. 333 & 340–45.

50 NMM: SAN/F/49/153.

51 I. Macalpine & R. Hunter, *George III and the Mad Business*, (London, 1969).

52 HRO: HINCH/11/217, G. K. Elphinstone to S, 9 Jun 1789.

53 Aspinall, *Later Correspondence of George III*, I, xxxix–xli. Aspinall, *Prince of Wales Correspondence*, I, 413 & 415 Nos. 354 & 357, S to J. W. Payne, [10?] & 13 Dec 1788. HRO: HINCH/7/38, Portland to S, 14 Dec 1788. Walter Sichel, *Sheridan*, (London, 1909, 2 vols) II, 415–16. Mitchell, *Fox*, pp. 135–36. Derry, *Regency Crisis*, pp. 87–88.

54 Ian R. Christie, 'Charles James Fox',

55 Cobbett, *Parliamentary History*, XXVII, 14.

56 Cobbett, *Parliamentary History*, XXVII, 17–18. Barrow, *Howe*, pp. 180–85.

57 HRO: HINCH/8/109, T. Graves to S, 5 Aug 1787. This is Captain Thomas (later Vice-Admiral Sir Thomas), nephew of Admiral Samuel Graves.

58 Harris, *Naval Atlantis*, I, 2–5.

59 Paul Webb, 'The Naval Aspects of the Nootka Sound Crisis', *MM*, LXI (1975) p. 133–54.

60 Webb, 'Rebuilding and Repair of the Fleet', pp. 195–97.

61 Phillips, 'Evangelical Administrator', pp. 76–99. Ehrman, *Younger Pitt*, pp. 314–16. NMM: MID/1/159/3, G. Rose to Sir C. Middleton, 16 Aug 1788. Barrow, *Howe*, pp. 178–79. Laughton, *Barham Papers*, II, 149–314 prints Middleton's correspondence with Keppel, Howe & Chatham.

62 Duke of Buckingham & Chandos, *Memoirs of the Court and Cabinets of George the Third*, (London, 2nd edn. 1853, 2 vols) I, 385, W. W. Grenville to Buckingham, 16 May 1788.

63 NMM: SAN/F/43a/58, Sir C. Middleton to S, 12 Jan 1789; printed from a draft in Laughton, *Barham Papers*, II, 315–16.

64 NMM: SAN/F/41/119, 'Truth' to S, 4 Aug 1779.

65 J. P. de Castro, *The Gordon Riots*, (London, 1926) p. 79. Sandwich, *Voyage*, p. xxv. *WC*, XXXIII, 184, H. Walpole to Lady Ossory, 7 Jun 1780.

66 Hinchingbrooke Library Borrowing Book, now at Mapperton.

67 *WC*, XXXIII, 468, H. Walpole to Lady Ossory, 20–21 Jun 1785.

68 Birmingham, 1st edn. 1784, 2nd edn. 1787, 2 vols.

69 *WC*, XLII, 127–28 & 140, H. Walpole to S, 1 Jan & 2 Apr 1785. Boldey: MS Eng. Misc. d. 149 f. 247, S to M. Noble, 14 Sep 1784; MS Eng. Misc. d. 150 ff. 50–51, S to M. Noble, 31 Jan & 5 Feb 1785. SM: F/51b/14, M. Noble to S, 5 Mar 1786.

70 SM: F/52/57, G. Coleman to S, 26 Mar 1786.

71 *Ways and Means: Or, a Sale of the L★★★s S★★★l and T★★★l . . .*, (London, 1782), p. 21.

72 SM: F/54b/4, S to Miss N. Gordon, 7 Nov 1788; F/62/62, S to Hinchingbrooke, 4 Sep 1788.

73 SM: F/52/66, W. Arabin to S, 25 Sep [1787].

74 SM: F/52/31, Sir W. Williams-Wynn to S, 28 Oct [1784]. NMM: SAN/F/31/104, J. W. Payne to S, 31 Oct [1790]; F/49/113, Sir G. Cooper to S, 23 Nov 1786.

75 Robert Huish, *Memoirs of George the Fourth*, (London, 1830, 2 vols) I, 239–40.

76 BM Music Library: H.2788.ss. Minute Book of Catch Club.

77 He was actually born in 1685, but the date was not corrected until later.

78 It was apparently not Sandwich's own idea; Burney, *Handel Commemoration*, p. 3 ascribes it to Bates, Fitzwilliam & Williams-Wynn.

79 Mackerness, *Social History of Music*, p. 127.

80 They were influential in the early Gothic Revival in architecture.

81 General description from Weber, 'Handel Commemoration'; & Burney, *Handel Commemoration*.

82 KCC: A. H. Mann MSS 'Cambridge Musicians Vol. I': Mrs H. Bates to Mrs Furey, 7 Jun 1784.

83 Johnstone, 'Handel Commemoration' p. 635, quoting the composer John Marsh.

84 J. A. Woods, 'James Sharp: Common Councilor of London in the Time of Wilkes', in *Statesmen, Scholars and Merchants: Essays in Eighteenth-Century History Presented to Dame Lucy Sutherland*, ed. J. S. Bromley, A. Whiteman & P. G. M. Dickson (Oxford, 1973), pp. 276–88, at p. 282.

85 Ribeiro, *Burney Letters*, p. 425.

86 Lonsdale, *Burney*, pp. 297–314. Ribeiro, *Burney Letters*, pp. 424–27.

87 Burney, *Handel Commemoration*, p. 7.

88 Rees, *Cyclopaedia*, s.v. 'Solo' (written by Burney).

89 Johnstone, 'Handel Commemoration', p. 633.

90 Linda Colley, 'The Apotheosis of George III: Loyalty, Royalty and the British Nation 1760–1820', *Past and Present*, No. 102 (1984) pp. 94–129, at p. 104.

91 Weber, 'Handel Commemoration', pp. 45–46, 51–52 & 62.

92 Johnstone, 'Handel Commemoration', p. 632.

93 Revd. Robert Hall, quoted in Jacob Simon, ed., *Handel: A Celebration of his Life and Times, 1685–1759*, (National Portrait Gallery, 1985), p. 261.

94 Jeremy Gregory, 'Anglicanism and the arts: religion, culture and politics in the eighteenth century', in *Culture, Politics and Society in Britain, 1660–1800*, ed. Jeremy Black & Jeremy Gregory (Manchester, 1991) pp. 82–109, at p. 99.

95 Burney, *Handel Commemoration*, p. 112.

96 Johnstone, 'Handel Commemoration' p. 636, quoting the oboist William Parkes.

97 Troide, *Burney Journals*, I, 259 n. 12. Nicholas Cox, *Bridging the Gap: A History of the Corporation of the Sons of the Clergy over 300 Years 1655–1978*, (Oxford, 1978), pp. 78, 82 & 84.

98 Weber, 'Handel Commemoration' p. 47. Burney, *Handel Commemoration*, p. vii.

99 *CG3*, V, 401 No. 3570, North to George III, 20 Mar 1782.

100 Laprade, *Robinson Papers*, p. 41, S to J. Robinson, 15 & 19 Mar 1782. *HMC 15 Abergavenny*, pp. 52–53, S to J. Robinson, 15 Mar 1782; S to North, 26 Mar 1782. Ditchfield, 'The House of Lords in the Age of the American Revolution', p. 210.

101 *HMC 30 Fortescue (Dropmore)*, II, 237, Buckingham to Grenville, 1 Dec 1791.

102 HRO: HINCH/2/10 & HINCH/2/47.

103 HRO: HINCH/2/51.

104 HRO: HINCH/5/70. PRO: C 38/824, Report by Master Ord in Lewis con Sandwich, C 12/652/16.

105 Rowley MSS: S to O. Rowley, 29 Nov 1783.

106 Rowley MSS: S to O. Rowley, 9 Feb 1791.

107 Rowley MSS: S to O. Rowley, 1 Apr 1785.

108 SM: F/57/109, S to?, 14 Jan 1789.

109 Rowley MSS: S to O. Rowley, 18 Nov 1791.

110 HRO: HINCH/2/61. Rowley, 'Owsley Rowley', No. 7 (1987) pp. 29–32.

111 Rowley MSS: S to O. Rowley, 12 Dec 1790, 19 Oct 1791. Rowley, 'Owsley Rowley' No. 8 (1988) pp. 22–32.

112 HRO: HINCH/2/47–48. SM: F/57/83, Sir T. Dundas to S, 25 Jun 1785.

113 SM: F/57/93, S to Sir E. Hughes, 22 Feb 1788.

114 Rowley MSS: S to O. Rowley, 9 May 1791.

115 PRO: C 38/824.

116 NMM: SAN/F/F45a/21, J. W. Payne to S, 10 Nov 1788.

117 Rowley MSS: S to O. Rowley, 22 Mar & 18 Dec 1791. I cannot prove that this is the same Stephens, but it seems probable.

118 BM: Add.MSS 9344 f. 121, S to G. Jackson, 24 Apr 1786.

119 BM: Add.MSS 70990 f. 35, S to J. Robinson, 5 Mar 1782.

120 NMM: SAN/F/31/100, J. Slade to S, 16 Feb 1790.

121 SM: F/57/97, J. Michie to S, 3 May 1788.

122 PRO: C 38/824.

123 PRO: PRO 30/20/22/3 f. 199, S to Rodney, 22 Apr 1783. SM: F/57/101, Rodney to S, 5 Jun 1788.

124 Cust & Colvin, *Society of Dilettanti*, p. 66.

125 Rowley MSS: S to O. Rowley, 18 Dec 1791.
126 NMM: SAN/F/43a/29, Sir W. Rawlinson to S, 19 Dec 1783.
127 MC: VI.11/168 Mulgrave to S, 25 May 1784; 11/173 S to Mulgrave, 8 Jun 1784.
128 SM: F/57/67, Shuldham to S, 15 Jan 1784. Rowley MSS: S to O. Rowley, 18 Nov 1791.
129 SM: F/57/68, Lady Hughes to S, 27 Jan 1784.
130 SM: F/57/93, S to Sir E. Hughes, 22 Feb 1788.
131 SM: F/57/82, Sir E. Hughes to S, 21 May 1785.
132 SM: F/57/93, S to Sir E. Hughes, 22 Feb 1788.
133 SM: F/57/94–95, Sir E. Hughes to S, 23 & 24 Feb 1788.
134 Rowley MSS: S to O. Rowley, 5 Jul 1791.
135 Namier & Brooke, *House of Commons 1754–90*, III, 156.
136 Rowley MSS: Jan-Mar 1791 *passim*
137 Rowley, 'Ousley Rowley' No. 7 (1987) pp. 29–32 & No. 8 (1988) pp. 22–32.
138 Rowley MSS: S to O. Rowley, 24 Mar 1790.
139 Rowley, 'Ousley Rowley' No. 9 (1990) pp. 35–39.
140 SM: F/62/97, S to Hinchingbrooke, [28? Apr 1792].
141 PRO: C 38/824.
142 PRO: C 12/652/16 & C 38/824, Lewis et al con Sandwich. SRO: D615/P(F)/3, 5th Earl of Sandwich to T. Anson, 10 Aug 1792.

CHAPTER XVII

1 Wraxall, *Memoirs*, I, 400.
2 NMM: SAN/F/2/35, J. Cawthorne to S, 18 Nov 1771.
3 BM: Add.MSS 15957 f. 80, S to Anson, 20 Aug 1748 NS.
4 Henry Roseveare, *The Treasury: The Evolution of a British Institution*, (London, 1969), p. 110.
5 Norris, *Shelburne and Reform*, p. 100.
6 D. B. Horn, 'The Diplomatic Experience of Secretaries of State, 1660–1852', *History*, NS XLI (1956) pp. 88–99. But Suffolk was a man of ability who worked hard to learn his job.
7 Pottle, *Boswell's London Journal*, p. 56.
8 Coxe, *Pelham*, II, 108.
9 KHA: Bentinck MSS, Box 6, S to W. Bentinck, 15 May 1749.
10 Butler, *Reminiscences*, p. 69.
11 C. D. Smith, *The Early Career of Lord North the Prime Minister*, (London, 1979) p. 27.
12 Butler, *Reminiscences*, p. 157.
13 Butler, *Reminiscences*, p. 156.
14 Thomas, *North*, pp. 7–8.
15 *HMC 55 Various Manuscripts*, VI, 38–39.
16 Nichols, *Literary Anecdotes*, IV, 647, quoting Edward Wortley-Montagu.
17 Walpole, *Memoirs of George II*, I, 124. WC, XXV, 276, H. Walpole to H. Mann, 5 May 1782.
18 Walpole, *Memoirs of George III*, IV, 170–71.
19 WC, XXIII, 350, H. Walpole to H. Mann, 18 Nov 1771.
20 Wraxall, *Memoirs*, I, 403.
21 Morriss, *Royal Dockyards*, pp. 196–98.
22 Barrow, *Howe*, p. 194, is quite clear about this, and as Secretary of the Admiralty his opinion carries weight.
23 Knight, 'Royal Dockyards', pp. 215–18.
24 Knight, 'Royal Dockyards', pp. 219–20. Williams, 'Sandwich's Naval Administration', pp. 303–05.
25 Laughton, *Barham Papers*, II, 32–34, J. Greenway to E. Hunt, 2 Mar 1782. Knight, 'Royal Dockyards', pp. 247–50.
26 Knight, 'Royal Dockyards', p. 252.
27 Knight, 'Royal Dockyards', pp. 246 & 253–56.
28 Knight, 'Royal Dockyards', p. 69.
29 Knight, 'Building and Maintenance', pp. 35–50.
30 Webb, 'Ochakov Affair', p. 13.

Webb, 'Rebuilding and Repair of the Fleet', pp. 194–209.

31 Hattendorf, *Naval Documents*, No. 339 p. 572, Melville to Liverpool, 28 Jul 1818.

32 *SP*, II, 179–80, S to North, 15 Oct 1778.

33 Cannon, *Aristocratic Century*, p. 154.

34 *CG3*, V, 401 No. 3570, North to George III, 20 Mar 1782.

Sources

In citing manuscripts I have followed the original spelling and punctuation. Editorial omissions are indicated thus . . . , editorial additions [thus], and all words in italic are emphasized in the original. Quotations in foreign languages have been Englished in the text, and the translations are my own.

The principal manuscript collections I have used in writing this book are the following.

NATIONAL MARITIME MUSEUM
Sandwich Papers

The Sandwich Papers, then all at Mapperton, were sorted and listed in 1976 for the Historical Manuscripts Commission by Sir Edward Warner. This invaluable work made the papers fully accessible, and all users of them are indebted to it. It has to be said, however, that Sir Edward's approach of sorting the unbound papers by subject was unsound in principle, and divided many correspondences which belong together. Moreover he did not always understand what the letters were about, and his list contains a proportion of errors which rivals Fortescue's *Correspondence of George III*. The principal components of this collection are:

SAN/1–6 & SAN/V/3–4; Sandwich's records of applications and recommendations for promotion and employment, 1771–1782.

SAN/V/5–10; Minutes of dockyard visitations, 1771–1776.

SAN/V/11; A private journal of the 1775 visitation, kept by Joseph Banks.

SAN/V/12–13; Private out-letter books, mainly 1763–65 & 1770–1782, on all subjects.

SAN/V/14; A volume of political and private in-letters.

SAN/V/17–68; Volumes of Sandwich's official and private correspondence on his diplomatic missions, 1746–48.

SAN/V/69–109; Volumes of Sandwich's official and private correspondence as Secretary of State, 1763–65.

SAN/V/113; 'Al Koran', the Minute Book of the Divan Society.

SAN/F/1–49; Unbound papers in folders, sorted into naval and other categories.

SAN/F/50; A manuscript draft of Sandwich's *Voyage*.

Admiralty Records

The Museum holds a large collection of public records of the Admiralty, Navy Board and other boards, and several of the dockyards, which for various reasons never reached or were not retained by the Public Record Office. I have mainly used Navy Board reports and correspondence in ADM/B.

Middleton Papers

The papers of Sandwich's colleague and occasional sparring-partner Sir Charles Middleton. Many were printed by Laughton, *Barham Papers*, but he was not much interested in the detail of naval administration.

Other Collections

Those useful for this study include the papers of Sir Samuel Hood, William Cornwallis, George Jackson, Thomas Lewes, and the collection formerly belonging to the Royal United Service Institution.

BRITISH MUSEUM (NOW BRITISH LIBRARY)

In the Department of Manuscripts the most material collections are:

Add.MSS 9344 Jackson Manuscripts
Add.MSS 15955–15957 Anson Papers
Add.MSS 32679–33201 Newcastle Papers.
Add.MSS 34712 T. Astle's Collection
Add.MSS 35349–36278 Hardwicke Papers
Add.MSS 38190–38489 Liverpool Papers
Add.MSS 42085 Grenville Papers
Add.MSS 52362 Minute Book of the Egyptian Society
Add.MSS 57804–57837 Grenville Papers
Add.MSS 61863 North (Sheffield Park) Papers
Add.MSS 69795 Correspondence of Lancelot Brown
Add.MSS 70990 Robinson Papers
Eg.MSS 1721 & 1862 Bentinck Manuscripts
Eg.MSS 2136 Letters to Sir F. Dashwood
Eg.MSS 2180 Letters to J. Douglas
Eg.MSS 3401–3497 Holdernesse Papers
Stowe MSS 259 Phelps Papers

In addition the Music Library holds the Minute Books of the Noblemen and Gentlemen's Catch Club.

PUBLIC RECORD OFFICE

The most relevant records for Sandwich's career come from these record groups:

ADM Records of the Admiralty, Navy Board, and other naval boards.
C Records of the Court of Chancery; Sandwich was involved in a number of suits in Chancery during his lifetime, and the proceedings and evidence are informative.
CO Notionally records of the Colonial Office, as created in 1854, but the records of the Board of Trade and Plantations, most of those of the American Secretary, and some from the other two Secretaries, were transferred to it and disarranged.
HO Records of the Home Office, as created by the 1782 re-division of the two Secretaries' responsibilities. The Home Secretary being charged also with military, naval and colonial affairs, these records continue some of those in SP classes.
PRO 30 'Gifts and Deposits' of records not created by government. They include PRO 30/20, Rodney Papers; PRO 30/29, Leveson-Gower Papers;

PRO 30/50, part of the papers of Bedford's sometime secretary R. N. Aldworth;

SP Records of the Secretaries of State, dealing with domestic, foreign, military and naval affairs

T Records of the Treasury Board.

ROYAL ARCHIVES (WINDSOR CASTLE)

Virtually all the correspondence of George III has been printed by Fortescue and Aspinall, but the military papers of the Duke of Cumberland are important for Sandwich's diplomatic mission on the Continent, 1746–48.

BODLEIAN LIBRARY

In Bodley are deposited the papers of Sir Francis Dashwood, later Lord Despencer. There is also some correspondence of Sandwich's friend Joseph Cradock, and of his protégé the Reverend Mark Noble.

HUNTINGDONSHIRE RECORD OFFICE

The Hinchingbrooke Papers consist in principle of estate papers and those dealing with local politics, but in practice both local and national politics, and estate and financial affairs, were indivisible. The collection also includes transcripts of many letters to or from Sandwich in the Abergavenny MSS, not printed by Laprade or the H.M.C.

SUFFOLK RECORD OFFICE
(Bury St Edmund's)

The manuscripts of the Duke of Grafton touch on Sandwich's career at several significant points.

ESSEX RECORD OFFICE

Here is another part of the scattered papers of R. N. Aldworth, later R. N. Neville, a minor member of the Bedford connection.

STAFFORDSHIRE RECORD OFFICE

The Lichfield Papers include a small but valuable collection of Anson papers.

NOTTINGHAM UNIVERSITY LIBRARY

Here are deposited the Newcastle (Clumber) Manuscripts, which represent primarily the correspondence of Newcastle's brother Henry Pelham. There is also some material in the Portland Manuscripts bearing on Sandwich's last years in politics.

WARWICK COUNTY RECORD OFFICE

The papers of Sandwich's musical friend the Earl of Denbigh contain much of interest, some of it printed or calendered by the H.M.C., or by Balderstone & Syrett.

KING'S COLLEGE CAMBRIDGE

In the Rowe Music Library are the papers of A. H. Mann, former fellow and organist of the College, which include transcripts of correspondence of Joah and Sarah Bates and their family.

PUBLIC RECORD OFFICE OF NORTHERN IRELAND
(Belfast)

There is a small quantity of correspondence between Sandwich and his friend Captain the Hon. Robert Boyle Walsingham.

MAPPERTON
(near Beaminster, Dorset)

The Sandwich Papers were until recently all in the family's hands at Mapperton. The collection has now been divided, with the bulk of the papers deposited in the National Maritime Museum, and only personal correspondence and papers retained by the family. Owing, however, to the deficiencies of the arrangement, the distinction is less than clear.

V/110–111; Autograph fair copy of Sandwich's *Voyage*, corrected for the press by Mr Cooke.

F/51–62 Personal, family, political, estate, financial, musical and other correspondence.

WOBURN ABBEY
(Bedfordshire)

The archives until recently held at the Bedford Estate Office in London have now returned to Woburn. The most important collection for my purposes is the papers of the fourth Duke of Bedford; my references are to these unless otherwise indicated. They are of central importance for Sandwich's political career, and for the work of the Admiralty between 1744 and 1748. A proportion of them was published by Russell, but the bulk is unprinted. There is also a small collection of unbound papers of the fourth Duke, and a large collection of the correspondence of his man of business and political agent Robert Butcher.

MULGRAVE CASTLE
(near Whitby, Yorkshire)

The Marquess of Normanby preserves the correspondence of his ancestor Lord Mulgrave, which is of the first importance for the naval side of the American War.

SAUSMAREZ MANOR
(St Martin's, Guernsey)

At Sausmarez Manor is some interesting correspondence of Captain Philip Saumarez, one of Anson's favourite followers, who was killed in action in 1747.

SCONE PALACE
(near Perth)

The Earl of Mansfield's papers include those of his ancestors Lord Mansfield, and his nephew and later heir in the Mansfield title Lord Stormont. The Stormont collection is particularly important for the conduct of the American War.

ROWLEY MANUSCRIPTS

These letters, in the possession of Mr Peter Rowley, descend from his ancestor Ousley Rowley, Sandwich's solicitor and man of business in the last years of his life, and are extremely informative on his personal and financial affairs.

HUNTINGTON LIBRARY

(San Marino, California)

The collections of the Henry E. Huntington Library include correspondence of Sandwich with Lord Loudon, and of Lady Sandwich with Mrs Elizabeth Montagu; also of Lord Howe with his follower Sir Roger Curtis.

CLEMENTS LIBRARY

(Ann Arbor, Michigan)

The William L. Clements Library holds several collections of the first importance for British history in Sandwich's lifetime, notably the Shelburne Papers, which are full of the naval information collected by Shelburne's informants, and Lord George Germain's papers.

KONINKLIJKE HUISARCHIEF

(The Hague)

The Dutch Royal Archives contain the papers of William IV of Orange, and a large part of those of Count William Bentinck, both of which contain some letters to and from Sandwich.

Bibliography

ACERRA, Martine, MERINO José & MEYER Jean, eds., *Les Marines de Guerre Européennes, XVII–XVIIIe siècles* (Paris, 1985). An important collection of essays.

ADOLPHUS, John, *The History of England from the Accession of King George the Third to the Conclusion of Peace in the Year 1783* (London, 1802, 3 vols). A near-contemporary history.

ALBION, R. G., *Forests and Sea Power: The Timber Problem of the Royal Navy, 1652–1862* (Cambridge, Mass., 1926). A classic work, still valuable though some of its arguments have been disproved.

ALLEN, Robert J., *The Clubs of Augustan London* (Cambridge, Mass., 1933; Harvard Studies in English Vol. VII). A serviceable survey.

ALMON, John, *Correspondence of the Late John Wilkes* (London, 1805, 5 vols). Selected to show Wilkes in the best light.

[ALMON, J., ed.], *The New Foundling Hospital for Wit* (London, 1771). A collection of light verse.

[ALMON, John], *Biographical, Literary, and Political Anecdotes of several of the most eminent Persons of the Present Age* (London, 1797, 3 vols). Some useful anecdotes.

ALTHAM, H. S., & SWANTON, E. W., *A History of Cricket* (London, 5th edn. 1962, 2 vols). Useful general history, thin on the eighteenth century.

ANDRÉ, Louis, & BOURGEOIS, Émile, eds., *Receuil des Instructions données aux Ambassadeurs et Ministres de France: XXIII Hollande III (1730–1788)* (Paris, 1924). Official instructions to French diplomats resident in the Netherlands, including those who dealt with Sandwich at Breda and the Congress of Aix-la-Chapelle.

ARNOLD, Walter, *The Life and Death of the Sublime Society of Beefsteaks* (London, 1871). A history by the club's last secretary.

ASHTON, John, *The History of Gambling in England* (London, 1898). Still has some value.

ASPINALL, A., ed., *The Later Correspondence of George III* (Cambridge, 1962–70, 5 vols). A fundamental source for the king's reign from 1783.

ASPINALL, A., ed., *The Correspondence of George Prince of Wales, 1770–1812* (London, 1963–71, 8 vols). In his last years Sandwich was attached to the Prince.

AYLING, Stanley, *George the Third* (London, 1972). An excellent short biography.

BAKER, Norman, *Government and Contractors: The British Treasury and War Supplies, 1775–1783* (London, 1971). Essential background to the war; bears on Sandwich's department as the Navy and Victualling Boards took over parts of the Treasury's work.

BALDERSTONE, Marion, & SYRETT, David, eds., *The Lost War. Letters from British Officers during the American Revolution* (New York, 1975). Letters to Lord Denbigh from relatives serving at sea and on land, from the Denbigh Manuscripts at Warwick.

BARNES, D. G., 'Henry Pelham and the Duke of Newcastle', *JBS* I (1962) No.1 pp. 62–77. Valuable study of the political relationship of the two brothers.

BARNES, G. R., & OWEN, J. H., eds., *The Private Papers of John, Earl of Sandwich . . . 1771–1782* (NRS Vol. 69, 71, 75 & 78, 1932–38). Publishes many of the most important Sandwich Papers bearing on naval policy and operations during these years.

BARROW, Sir John, *The Life of George Lord Anson* (London, 1839). Contains important correspondence from the Anson Papers now in the British Museum.

BARROW, Sir John, *The Life of Richard Earl Howe* (London, 1838). Inadequate as a biographer, as Secretary of the Admiralty Barrow offers useful reflections on the rôle of a First Lord.

BATESON, Mary, ed., *A Narrative of the Changes in the Ministry, 1765–1767, told by the Duke of Newcastle in a Series of Letters to John White, MP* (Camden N.S. Vol. 59, 1898). Bears on the fate of the Grenville ministry.

BAUDI DI VESME, Carlo, *La Politica Mediterranea Inglese . . . 1741–1748* (Turin, 1952). Useful diplomatic history.

BAUDI DI VESME, C., 'Il potere marittimo e la guerra di successione d'Austria', *Nuova Rivista Storica* XXXVII (1953) pp. 19–43. Helpful reflections on grand strategy.

BAUGH, Daniel A., *British Naval Administration in the Age of Walpole* (Princeton, 1965). A work fundamental to all British naval history in the eighteenth century; bears especially on the 1744 Admiralty Board.

BAUGH, Daniel A., ed., *Naval Administration 1715–50* (NRS Vol. 120, 1977). Documents illustrating the same themes.

BAUGH, Daniel A., 'Why did Britain lose command of the Sea during the War for America?' in Black & Woodfine, *Use of Naval Power*, pp. 149–69. The essential starting-point of any reassessment of the naval war.

BAUGH, Daniel A., 'Seapower and Science: The Motives for Pacific Exploration', in *Background to Discovery: Pacific Exploration from Dampier to Cook* ed. Derek Howse (Berkeley, Cal., 1990). A perceptive survey.

BAUGH, Daniel A., 'The Politics of British Naval Failure, 1775–1777', *AN* LII (1992) pp. 221–46. Examines the reasons for the North ministry's failure to mobilize in time.

BAUGH, Daniel A., 'Sir Samuel Hood: Superior Subordinate', in Bilias, *George Washington's Opponents*, pp. 291–326. The best substitute we have for a biography.

BEAGLEHOLE, J. C., ed., *The Journals of Captain James Cook on his Voyages of Discovery* (Hakluyt Soc. Extra Series, Cambridge, 1955–74, 4 vols: Vol. IV is *The Life of Captain James Cook*). Indispensable for any study of Cook; prints or summarizes many documents.

BEAGLEHOLE, J. C., *The Life of Captain James Cook* (London, 1974; also issued as Vol. IV of the Journals). The standard modern life; a magnificent achievement; but not always reliable in detail.

BEATSON, Robert, *Naval and Military Memoirs of Great Britain from 1727 to 1783* (London, 1804, 6 vols). A good near-contemporary history.

BEER, Adolf, 'Holland und der österreichische Erbfolge-Krieg', *Archiv fur österreichische Geschichte*

XLVI (1871) pp. 297–418. Deals in some detail with Sandwich's negotiations at Breda.

BEER, Adolf, 'Zur Geschichte des Friedens von Aachen im Jahre 1748', *Archiv fur österreichische Geschichte* XLVII (1871) pp. 1–196. An Austrian study of the Peace of Aix-la-Chapelle; valuable as a corrective to anglocentricity.

BILIAS, George A., ed., *George Washington's Opponents: British Generals and Admirals in the American Revolution* (New York, 1969). A very useful collection; some parts are more persuasive than others.

BLACK, Clementina, ed., *The Cumberland Letters: Being the Correspondence of Richard Dennison Cumberland and George Cumberland between the Years 1771 & 1784* (London, 1912). Richard Cumberland was a subordinate and diplomatic agent of Germain's.

BLACK, Jeremy, *Natural and Necessary Enemies: Anglo-French Relations in the Eighteenth Century* (London, 1986). Valuable background to eighteenth-century diplomacy.

BLACK, J. M., *British Foreign Policy in the Age of Walpole* (Edinburgh, 1985). Useful as background to Sandwich's early diplomacy.

BLACK, Jeremy, & WOODFINE, Philip, eds., *The British Navy and the Use of Naval Power in the Eighteenth Century* (Leicester, 1988). An important collection modifying many received opinions.

BLACKEY, R. A., 'The Political Career of George Montagu Dunk, 2nd Earl of Halifax, 1748–1771: A Study of an Eighteenth-Century English Minister' (New York Ph.D., 1978). Halifax was at various times Sandwich's schoolfellow, friend, kinsman by marriage, rival and colleague in government.

BLEACKLEY, Horace, *Life of John Wilkes* (London, 1917). Still the most complete biography.

BLUNT, Reginald, ed., *Mrs Montagu,*

Queen of the blues . . . 1762–1800 (London, 1923, 2 vols). The continuation of Climenson's edition of her letters (q.v.).

BONNER-SMITH, D., ed., *The Barrington Papers* (NRS Vols. 77 & 81, 1937–41). The papers of Admiral Barrington contain some important papers bearing on his relations with Sandwich.

[BOULTON, W. B.], *The History of White's with the Betting Book from 1743 to 1878 and a List of Members from 1736 to 1892* (London, 1892, 2 vols). Useful source for wagers.

BOUTARIC, E., ed., *Correspondence secrète inedite de Louis XV sur la Politique Etrangère avec la Comte de Broglie, Tercier etc . . .* (Paris, 1866, 2 vols). Louis XV's private foreign policy, the 'secret du roi'.

BOWLER, R. A., *Logistics and the Failure of the British Army in America 1775–1783* (Princeton, 1975). An important part of the Navy's responsibility during the American War.

BREEN, Kenneth, 'The Navy in the Yorktown Campaign: The Battle of the Chesapeake 1781' (London M.Phil. thesis, 1971). An interesting and persuasive thesis.

BREEN, Kenneth, 'Graves and Hood at the Chesapeake', *MM* LXVI (1980) pp. 53–65). Summarizes a small part of the thesis.

BREEN, Kenneth, 'Divided Command: the West Indies and North America, 1780–1781', in Black & Woodfine, *The British Navy and the Use of Naval Power* pp. 191–206. Studies the (generally poor) relations between successive admirals in North America and the West Indies.

BREWER, John, *Party Ideology and popular Politics at the Accession of George III* (Cambridge, 1976). An important political study.

BROMLEY, J. S., ed., *The Manning of the Royal Navy: Selected Public Pamphlets 1693–1873* (NRS Vol. 119, 1974). The introduction remains the only overview of naval manning; it asks all the right questions but cannot answer them.

BROOKE, John, *The Chatham Administration 1766–1768* (London, 1956). An important monograph.

[BROOKS'S], *Memorials of Brooks's from the Foundation of the Club 1764 to the Close of the Nineteenth Century* (London, 1907). Useful for the lists of members.

BROOMFIELD, J. H., 'Lord Sandwich at the Admiralty Board: Politics and the British Navy, 1771–1778', *MM* LI (1965) pp. 7–25. A useful introduction.

BROOMFIELD, J. H., 'The Keppel–Palliser Affair, 1778–1779', *MM* XLVII (1961) pp. 195–207. The best short account.

BROWN, Gerald S., *The American Secretary: The Colonial Policy of Lord George Germain, 1775–1778* (Ann Arbor, 1963). Useful study of Germain's work in his department.

BROWN, Gerald S., 'The Anglo-French Naval Crisis, 1778: A Study of Conflict in the North Cabinet', *William and Mary Quarterly* 3rd S. XIII (1956) pp. 3–25. Now somewhat out of date.

[BROWN, John], *An Estimate of the Manners and Principles of the Times* (London, 1757–58, 2 vols). A contemporary moralist's view of society.

BROWN, Peter D., & SCHWEIZER, Karl W., eds., *The Devonshire Diary: William Cavendish, Fourth Duke of Devonshire, Memoranda on State Affairs 1759–1762* (Camden Soc. 4th S. XXVII, 1982). Valuable source for the politics of these years.

BROWNING, Reed, *The Duke of Newcastle* (New Haven & London, 1975). A useful short life.

BUCHET, Christian, *La lutte pour l'éspace caraïbe et la façade atlantique de l'Amerique du Sud (1672–1763)* (Paris, 1991, 2 vols). Ambitious comparative history of war in the West Indies over a century.

BUCKLEY, G. B., *Fresh Light on 18th Century Cricket: A Collection of 1,000 new Cricket Notices from 1697 to 1800 AD* (Birmingham, 1935). Compiled chiefly from local newspapers.

BULLOCKE, J. G., ed., *The Tomlinson Papers* (NRS Vol.74, 1935). Publishes correspondence of some sea officers involved in opposition to Sandwich during the American War.

BURGESS, Gilbert, ed., *The Love Letters of Mr H. and Miss R., 1775–1779* (London, 1895). The disputed letters of Martha Ray.

BURNEY, Charles, *An Account of the Musical performances . . . in Commemoration of Handel* (London, 1785). The 1784 Handel Commemoration, organized by Sandwich.

BUSSEMAKERS, T., ed., *Archives ou Correspondance Inédite de la Maison d'Orange-Nassau* 4th Series (Leiden, 1908–1917, 4 vols plus a Supplement ed. F. J. L. Krämer). Official edition of the correspondence of the Princes of Orange from 1747. There is some unpublished correspondence between Sandwich, Bentinck and Orange in the Dutch Royal Archives.

BUTLER, Charles, *Reminiscences* (London, 4th edn. 1824). The barrister and Roman Catholic apologist had many dealings with Sandwich, for whom he wrote a pamphlet.

BUTTERFIELD, Sir Herbert, *George III, Lord North and the People 1779–80* (London, 1949). Still suggestive, though now outdated.

CALENDAR OF HOME OFFICE PAPERS OF THE REIGN OF GEORGE III ed. Joseph Redington & R. A. Roberts (London, H.M.S.O., 1878–99, 4 vols). Nothing to do with the Home Office (founded 1782), but an invaluable calendar of State Papers, mainly but not only Domestic, for the years 1760–75.

CALLENDER, G. A. R., 'With the Grand Fleet in 1780', *MM* IX (1923) pp. 258–70 & 290–304. A study of Geary's cruise.

CANNON, Garland, ed., *The Letters of Sir William Jones* (Oxford, 1970, 2 vols). Though attached to the opposition, the young scholar and orientalist had various dealings with Sandwich.

CANNON, John, *Aristocratic Century: The Peerage of Eighteenth-Century England* (Cambridge, 1984). An important study.

CANNON, John, *Parliamentary Reform, 1640–1832* (Cambridge, 1973). An excellent survey of the subject.

CANNON, John, *The Fox–North Coalition: Crisis of the Constitution, 1782–84* (Cambridge, 1969). The standard treatment of this critical phase in political history, and Sandwich's career; some of its conclusions are controversial.

CANNON, John, *The Letters of Junius* (Oxford, 1978). The best modern edition.

CARRINGTON, Selwyn H. H., *The British West Indies during the American Revolution* (Dordrecht, 1988, Koninklijk Instituut voor Taal-Land- en Volkenkunde Caribbean Series 8). Valuable for the political, social and economic connections of the islands with the mainland American colonies.

CARTER, Harold B., *Sir Joseph Banks, 1743–1820* (London, 1988). The most recent full-scale biography.

CASTEX, R. V. P., *Les Idées Militaires de la Marine du XVIIIme siècle: De Ruyter à Suffren* (Paris, 1911). A Mahanite polemic; to be taken with a pinch of salt, but full of valuable information.

CHADWICK, F. E., ed., *The Graves Papers and other Documents relating to the Naval Operations of the Yorktown Campaign, July to October 1781* (Naval History Soc. Vol. 7, New York, 1916). Not Graves Papers in the ordinary sense, but his official correspondence with the Admiralty.

CHANCE, J. F., ed., *British Diplomatic Instructions 1689–1789: V, Sweden 1727–1789* (Camden Soc. 3rd S. XXXIX, 1928). Includes instructions written by Sandwich as Secretary of State 1763–65.

CHANCE, J. F., ed., *British Diplomatic Instructions 1689–1789: III, Denmark 1727–1789* (Camden Soc. 3rd S. XXXVI, 1926). Includes instructions written by Sandwich as Secretary of State 1763–65.

CHATTERTON, Georgiana, Lady, ed., *Memorials, Personal and Historical, of Admiral Lord Gambier* (London, 1861, 2 vols). A work of piety, with useful information on the naval evangelicals including Middleton.

CHEVALIER, E., *Histoire de la Marine Française pendant la Guerre de l'Independence Americaine* (Paris, 1877). Antiquated but still useful operational history.

CHILDERS, J. W., ed., *Lord Orford's Voyage round the Fens in 1774* (Doncaster, 1868). Eccentric diaries of a pleasure cruise with Sandwich.

CHRISTIE, Ian R., *The End of North's Ministry 1780–1782* (London, 1958). The standard account, on which I base my account of Sandwich's political career during these years.

CHRISTIE, Ian R., *Myth and Reality in Late-Eighteenth Century British Politics and Other Papers* (London, 1970). A stimulating collection of essays.

CHRISTIE, Ian R., 'British Politics and the American Revolution', *Albion* IX (1977) pp. 205–26. Surveys the attitudes towards America of the various parties.

CHRISTIE, Ian R., 'The Anatomy of the Opposition in the Parliament of 1784', *PH* IX (1990) pp. 50–77. Including Sandwich's party.

CHRISTIE, Ian R., 'Party in Politics in the Age of Lord North's Administration' *PH* VI (1987) pp. 47–68. A survey of current opinion on political parties in this period.

CHRISTIE, Ian R., & LABAREE, Benjamin W., *Empire or Independence*

1760–1776: A British-American Dialogue on the Coming of the American Revolution (Oxford, 1976). A neat exposition of contrasting interpretations.

CLARK, J. C. D., *English Society 1688–1832: Ideology, Social Structure and Political Practice during the Ancien Regime* (Cambridge, 1985). A work of massive erudition and controversial opinions.

CLARK, J. C. D., *The Dynamics of Change: The Crisis of the 1750s and English Party System* (Cambridge, 1982). A highly detailed monograph.

CLARK, J. C. D., ed., *The Memoirs and Speeches of James, 2nd Earl Waldegrave, 1742–1763* (Cambridge, 1988). An important source for the politics of this period.

CLARK, W. B., & MORGAN, W. J., eds., *Naval Documents of the American Revolution* (Washington, 1964ff, 9 vols to date covering 1774–77). An immense collection of documents culled from primary and secondary sources; its editorial standards have markedly improved in recent volumes, but it still shows a strong preference for the most trivial detail over anything to do with policy and strategy.

CLIMENSON, Emily J., ed., *Elizabeth Montagu the Queen of the Blue-Stockings: Her Correspondence from 1720 to 1761* (London, 1906, 2 vols). She was Sandwich's cousin by marriage, and a close friend of his wife's. Blunt (q.v.) edits her letters from 1762.

COBBETT, William, ed., *The Parliamentary History of England* (London, 1806–20, 36 vols). The predecessor of Hansard; the best-known, though not the only, source for Parliamentary debates.

COLE, William, *A Journal of my Journey to Paris in the Year 1765*, ed. F. G. Stokes (London, 1931). Includes information gleaned from Lady Sandwich's friends.

COLLEY, Linda, *In Defiance of Oligarchy: The Tory Party 1714–60* (Cambridge, 1982). Important for the political history of this period.

COLLYER, A. D'A., ed., *The Despatches and Correspondence of John, Second Earl of Buckinghamshire, Ambassador to the Court of Catherine II of Russia 1762–1765* (Camden Soc. 3rd S. II & III, 1900–2). From 1763 the correspondence was with Sandwich.

COMPLETE PEERAGE, The, ed. G. E. C[okayne], V. Gibbs *et al.* (London, 2nd edn. 1910–59, 13 vols). The standard source for the descent, dates of birth, death etc of peers.

CONN, Stetson, *Gibraltar in British Diplomacy in the Eighteenth Century* (New Haven, 1942). Both in 1747 and in 1780 Sandwich argued for sacrificing Gibraltar to gain more valuable concessions elsewhere.

COPELAND, T. W., et al., eds., *The Correspondence of Edmund Burke* (Cambridge & Chicago, 1958–78, 10 vols). Essential for the Rockinghamite opposition during the American War.

COQUELLE, P., *L'Alliance franco-hollandaise contre l'Angleterre, 1735–88* (Paris, 1902). Antique and eccentric diplomatic history, but still occasionally useful.

CORBETT, Julian S., ed., *Fighting Instructions 1530–1816* (NRS Vol. 29, 1905). Fundamental texts for the study of naval tactics.

CORBETT, Julian S., *Signals and Instructions, 1776–1794* (NRS Vol. 35, 1909). Further information, especially about the reforms of Kempenfelt and Howe.

CORBETT, Julian S., *Some Principles of Maritime Strategy* (London, 1911). The classic study of naval strategy.

CORK & ORRERY, Countess of, ed., *The Orrery Papers* (London, 1903, 2 vols). Mentions Sandwich and his grandmother.

COXE, William, *Memoirs of the*

Administration of the Right Honourable Henry Pelham (London, 1829, 2 vols). Still an important work, quoting numerous documents.

CRADOCK, J., *Literary and Miscellaneous Memoirs* (London, 1828, 4 vols). Cradock was a close friend of Sandwich.

CRESWELL, John, *British Admirals of the Eighteenth Century: Tactics in Battle* (London, 1972). A valuable short study.

CREWE, D. G., 'British Naval Administration in the West Indies, 1739–48' (Liverpool Ph.D. thesis, 1978). A very useful study.

CRIMMIN, P. K., 'Admiralty Administration, 1783–1806' (London M.Phil. thesis, 1967). A better thesis than many Ph.D.s, and better written.

CRUICKSHANKS, Eveline, *Political Untouchables: The Tories and the '45* (London, 1979). Bears on Sandwich's early political career.

CUMBERLAND, Richard, *Memoirs* (London, 1807, 2 vols). Unreliable memoirs of Germain's protégé.

CUNAT, Charles, *Histoire du Bailli de Suffren* (Rennes, 1852). Still one of the most detailed lives of the great French admiral, and no more partisan than most.

CUST, Lionel, ed., *Records of the Cust Family. Series III, Sir John Cust, Third Baronet* (London, 1927, privately printed). Includes some Sandwich correspondence.

CUST, Lionel, & COLVIN, Sidney, *History of the Society of Dilettanti* (London, 1898). Sandwich was a prominent early member.

D'AILLY, A. J., *Willem Bentinck van Rhoon en de Diplomatieke Betrekkingen tusschen Engeland en de Nederlandsche Republiek gedurende de laatste Jaren voor den Vrede van Aken in 1748* (Amsterdam, 1898). Publishes some of Sandwich's diplomatic correspondence from the Newcastle papers.

DANN, Uriel, *Hannover und England, 1740–1760: Diplomatie und Selbsterhaltung* (Hildesheim, 1986). Valuable study of Hanover's foreign policy. It has now been published in English as *Hanover and Britain, 1740–1760* (Leicester, 1991).

D'ARBLAY, Frances, *Memoirs of Doctor Burney* (London, 1832, 3 vols). Pious life of the great musical historian by his daughter the novelist.

DASHWOOD, Sir Francis, *The Dashwoods of West Wycombe* (London, 1987). Quotes unpublished evidence bearing on the 'Monks of Medmenham'.

DAVIES, C. C., ed., *The Private Correspondence of Lord Macartney, Governor of Madras (1781–1785)* (Camden Soc. 3rd S. LXXVII, 1950). As a former diplomat in Sandwich's department and colonial governor during the American War, Macartney had and maintained many contacts with Sandwich.

DAVIES, John A., 'An Enquiry into Faction among British Naval Officers during the War of the American Revolution' (Liverpool MA thesis, 1964). A most useful and persuasive study.

DAVIES, K. G., ed., *Documents of the American Revolution 1770–1783 (Colonial Office Series)* (Shannon & Dublin, 1972–82, 21 vols). Prints some and calendars all of the American documents in the Public Record Office, CO group (i.e. from the records of the Secretaries of State and the Board of Trade).

DAWSON, Warren R., ed., *The Banks Letters: A Calendar of the Manuscript Correspondence of Sir Joseph Banks* (London, 1958). Banks was a friend of Sandwich, a neighbour both in London and East Anglia, and a fellow-devotee of exploration.

DERRY, John, *English Politics and the American Revolution* (London, 1976). A valuable monograph.

DERRY, John W., *The Regency Crisis and the Whigs, 1788–89* (Cambridge,

'1963). This was Sandwich's last, lost chance of high office.

DICKINSON, H. T., *Liberty and Property: Political Ideology in Eighteenth-century Britain* (London, 1977). Important essay in the history of ideas.

DITCHFIELD, G. M., 'The House of Lords in the Age of the American Revolution', in Jones, *A Pillar of the Constitution*, pp. 199–239. Useful for Sandwich's later career.

DOBRÉE, Bonamy, ed., *The Letters of Philip Dormer Stanhope 4th Earl of Chesterfield* (London, 1932, 6 vols) [paginated continuously]. Important for Sandwich's early diplomatic career; edited by a literary scholar rather than an historian, it prints only Chesterfield's letters, without the replies.

DONIOL, Henri, *Histoire de la Participation de la France à l'etablissment des Etats-Unis d'Amerique* (Paris, 1885–92, 5 vols). A massive official edition of documents selected to prove France's devotion to the American cause.

DONOUGHUE, Bernard, *British Politics and the American Revolution, The Path to War, 1773–75* (London, 1964). A useful study of the early phase of the American crisis as seen in London.

DUFFY, Michael, 'The Establishment of the Western Squadron as the Linchpin of British Naval Strategy', in *Parameters of British Naval Power 1650–1850*, ed. Michael Duffy (Exeter, 1992) pp. 60–81.

DUFFY, Michael, ed., *The English Satirical Prints, 1600–1832* (Cambridge, 1986, 7 vols; Vol. 3 is Duffy's *The Englishman and the Foreigner*, Vol. 6 is H. T. DICKINSON, *Caricatures and the Constitution*, Vol. 7 is P. D. G. THOMAS, *The American Revolution*). Valuable and entertaining visual evidence.

DULL, Jonathan R., *The French Navy and American Independence: A Study of Arms and Diplomacy, 1774–1787* (Princeton, 1975). An excellent study, relating policy and operations.

DULL, J. R., *A diplomatic History of the American Revolution* (New Haven, 1985). Good summary of the conventional wisdom.

EHRMAN, John, *The Younger Pitt: The Years of Acclaim* (London, 1969). The first volume of an outstanding biography.

ELLIS, Kenneth, *The Post Office in the Eighteenth Century, A Study in Administrative History* (London, 1958). The Post Office was important as a source of patronage and intelligence.

ERSKINE, David, ed., *Augustus Hervey's Journal* (London, 2nd edn. 1954). The vivid and picaresque memoir of Sandwich's friend, colleague and eventual rival.

FABEL, Robin F. A., *Bombast and Broadsides, The Lives of George Johnstone* (Tuscaloosa, 1987). A life of the controversial sea officer and politician.

FERLING, John, ed., *The World Turned Upside Down: The American Victory in the War of Independence*, (New York, 1988; Contributions in Military Studies No.79). Essays on the military and naval aspects of the war as it affected the colonies.

FORTESCUE, Sir John, *The Correspondence of King George III from 1760 to December 1783* (London, 1927–28, 6 vols). Absolutely indispensable to any historian of the period, though notorious for the reckless incompetence of the editor. L. B. Namier, *Additions and Corrections to Sir John Fortescue's Edition* (Manchester, 1937), annotates the first volume; thereafter the reader is advised to navigate with great caution.

FRASER, Henry S., ed., 'The Memoranda of William Green, Secretary to Vice-Admiral Marriott Arbuthnot in the American Revolution', *Rhode Island Historical*

Society Collections XVII (1924)
pp. 54–64, 90–104, 126–40; & XVIII
(1925) pp. 112–28 & 154–60. Vivid
and informative notes, but
self-serving and unreliable.

[GARRICK] *The Private Correspondence
of David Garrick* (London, 1831, 2
vols). The great actor-manager was
a close friend of Sandwich. Little &
Kahrl (q.v.) is a better edition, but
does not include letters to Garrick.

GEORGE, M. D., *English Political
Caricature to 1792; A Study of Opinion
and Propaganda* (Oxford, 1959). A
basic source; see Duffy for further
illustration.

GERRETSON, C., & GEYL, P., eds.,
*Briefwisseling en Aantekeningen van
Willem Bentinck, Heer van Rhoon*
(*Historisch Genootschap* 3rd S. Vols. 62
& 86, The Hague 1934–76). The
correspondence and diaries of
Sandwich's diplomatic colleague.

GEYL, Pieter, *Willem IV en Engeland tot
1748* (The Hague, 1924). Important
for Sandwich's relations with the
Orangists while he was on the
Continent, 1746–48.

GLADSTONE, Lord, *A History of the
Noblemen's and Gentlemen's Catch Club*
(London, 1930, privately printed).
The society which Sandwich founded.

GORE BROWN, R., *Chancellor
Thurlow* (London, 1953). A life of
Sandwich's Cabinet colleague and
opponent.

GRAHAM, G. S., 'Considerations on
the War of American Independence',
BIHR XXII (1949) pp. 22–34.
Interesting reflections.

GREENE, Jack P., 'The Seven Years'
War and the American Revolution:
The Causal Relationship
Reconsidered', *JICH* VIII (1979–80)
No.2 pp. 85–105. Examines whether
the capture of French Canada really
led to the colonial rebellion.

GREIG, J. Y. T., ed., *The Letters of
David Hume* (Oxford, 1932, 2 vols).
There is some mention of Sandwich.

GRUBER, Ira D., *The Howe Brothers
and the American Revolution* (Chapel

Hill, N.C., 1972). A detailed study;
its conclusions have been powerfully
attacked.

GWYN, Julian, ed., *The Royal Navy
and North America: The Warren Papers,
1736–1752* (NRS Vol.118, 1973). The
papers of the admiral who captured
Louisbourg in 1745; they bear on
Sandwich's early career at the
Admiralty.

HAAS, James M., 'The Rise of the
Bedfords, 1741–1757: A Study in the
Politics of the Reign of George II'
(Illinois Ph.D., 1960). An important
study for the first part of Sandwich's
political career.

HAAS, James M., 'The Pursuit of
Political Success in
Eighteenth-Century England:
Sandwich, 1740–71', *BIHR* XLIII
(1970) pp. 56–77. Useful
biographical sketch.

HAAS, James M., 'The Royal
Dockyards: The earliest Visitations
and Reform 1749–1778', *HJ* XIII
(1970) pp. 191–215. Helpful as an
introduction to the subject.

HAAS, James M., 'The Introduction of
Task Work into the Royal Dockyards,
1775', *JBS* VIII (1969) No.2 pp. 44–
68. Useful, but needs to be much
modified by the research of Knight
and others.

HAAS, James M., 'Work and
Authority in the Royal Dockyards
from the Seventeenth Century to
1870', *Proceedings of the American
Philosophical Society* CXXIV (1980)
pp. 423–28. A breathless scramble.

HALE, Richard W., 'New Light on the
Naval Side of Yorktown',
*Proceedings of the Massachusetts
Historical Society* LXXI (1959).
Stimulating but impressionistic
sketch.

HALSBAND, Robert, *The Life of Lady
Mary Wortley Montagu* (Oxford,
1956). She was a cousin of Sandwich.

HALSBAND, Robert, ed., *The
Complete Letters of Lady Mary Wortley
Montagu* (Oxford, 1965–67, 3 vols).
She was a cousin of Sandwich.

HAMILTON, Adrian, *The Infamous Essay on Woman, or John Wilkes seated between Vice and Virtue* (London, 1972). A short account of the 'Essay on Woman' affair, reproducing in facsimile the Essay itself and many other relevant documents.

[HANBURY-WILLIAMS], *The Works of the Right Honourable Sir Chas. Hanbury Williams* (London, 1822, 3 vols). Light verse and other writings by a diplomatic colleague.

HANNAY, David, ed., *Letters written by Sir Samuel Hood . . . 1781–83* (NRS Vol. 3, 1895). An important if partisan source for the conduct of the last years of the American War at sea. There is very little for this period in Hannay's 'Extracts from the Papers of Sir Samuel Hood, 1778–98', in *The Naval Miscellany Vol.I*, ed. J. K. Laughton (NRS Vol. 20, 1901), pp. 221–58.

HARLOW, Vincent Y., *The Founding of the Second British Empire, 1763–1793* (London, 1952–64, 2 vols). An important study, though now outdated or disputed in places.

[HARRIS, Joseph], 'Nauticus Junior', *The Naval Atlantis; or, a Display of the Characters of such Flag Officers as were distinguished during the last War* (London, 1788–89, 2 vols in 1). Eccentric and wildly partisan biographical sketches by Admiral Milbanke's secretary.

HARTMANN, C. H., *The Angry Admiral: The Later Career of Edward Vernon, Admiral of the White* (London, 1953). A brief life.

HATTENDORF, John B., et al., eds., *British Naval Documents 1204–1960* (NRS Vol.131, 1993). A compendium of important materials for naval history, including several which bear on Sandwich's career.

HERBERT, Lord, ed., *The Herbert Papers (1734–1780): Letters and Diaries of Henry, Tenth Earl of Pembroke and his Circle* (London, 1942, 2 vols.; Vol. I was originally published 1939 under the title *Henry, Elizabeth and George*).
Pembroke was an extravagant and credulous opposition politician; his wife and friends more intelligent and observant.

HISTORICAL MANUSCRIPTS COMMISSION:*

No.15, Abergavenny Manuscripts (1887). Prints or abstracts much political correspondence of John Robinson, North's Secretary of the Treasury. More was edited by Laprade (q.v.).

No.27, Beaufort and Other Manuscripts (1891). Some mentions of Sandwich.

No.38, Buckinghamshire and Others (1895). Buckingham was a diplomat in Sandwich's department in 1762–65; his diplomatic correspondence is also edited by Collyer (q.v.).

No.28, Charlemont Manuscripts (1891–94, 2 vols). Correspondence of an Irish peer who had some contacts with Sandwich.

No.20, Dartmouth Manuscripts (1887–96, 3 vols). Lord Dartmouth was American Secretary 1772–75.

No.68, Denbigh Manuscripts (1874–1911, 5 vols). Includes correspondence of Sandwich's musical friend the Earl of Denbigh and his family.

No.30, Fortescue Manuscripts at Dropmore (1892–1927, 10 vols). These mainly concern the later years of George III's reign, but make some mention of Sandwich.

No.67, Polwarth Manuscripts (1911–61, 5 vols). Some references to Sandwich.

No.24, Rutland Manuscripts (1888–1905, 4 vols). Valuable for the naval career of Lord Robert Manners.

No.49, Stopford-Sackville Manuscripts (1904–10, 2 vols). Prints or calendars much (but not all) of Lord George Germain's correspondence during the American War; the

* Cited using the Commission's modern system of number and title; many of these volumes were originally issued as appendices to the Commissioners' Annual Reports.

original collection is now at Ann Arbor.

No.55, Various Collections (1901–14, 8 vols). Includes some papers of Germain's Under-Secretary William Knox.

No.10 Underwood Manuscripts (1885). Some mentions of Sandwich.

HOFFMAN, Ross J. S., *The Marquis: A Study of Lord Rockingham, 1730–1782* (New York, 1973). A life of the opposition leader and twice prime minister.

HORN, D. B., *Great Britain and Europe in the Eighteenth Century* (Oxford, 1967). Useful outline of diplomatic history.

HORN, D. B., *The British Diplomatic Service, 1689–1789* Oxford, 1961). Useful for Sandwich's diplomatic career.

HORN, D. B., *Sir Charles Hanbury-Williams and European Diplomacy (1747–1758)* (London, 1930). The career of a fellow-diplomat and society acquaintance of Sandwich.

HOWSE, Derek, *Neville Maskelyne, the Seaman's Astronomer* (Cambridge, 1989). One of Sandwich's scientific contacts.

HUNT, Robert M., *The Life of Sir Hugh Palliser* (London, 1844). Dogged but undistinguished.

ILCHESTER, [Giles Fox-Strangeways] Lord, *Letters to Henry Fox, Lord Holland* (Roxburghe Club, London, 1915). Invaluable correspondence of a leading politician.

JAMES, W. M., *The British Navy in Adversity* (London, 1926). Still useful for naval operations.

JAMIESON, Alan G., 'War in the Leeward Islands, 1775–1783', (Oxford D.Phil. thesis, 1981). An excellent history, much better than anything published on the subject.

JARRETT, J. D., 'The Myth of Patriotism in Eighteenth-Century British Politics', in J. S. Bromley & E. H. Kossmann, eds., *Britain and*

the Netherlands, V (The Hague, 1975). The ideas of the 'patriot' politicians.

JESSE, J. H., *Memoirs of Celebrated Etonians* (London, 1875, 2 vols). Useful anecdotes.

JESSE, J. H., *George Selwyn and his Contemporaries* (London, 1843–44, 4 vols). Prints interesting correspondence.

JOHNSON, Edward, 'The Bedford Connection: The Fourth Duke of Bedford's Political Influence between 1732 and 1771' (Cambridge Ph.D., 1979). Pedestrian but serviceable.

[JOHNSTONE, Charles], *Chrysal, or the Adventures of a Guinea* (London, 1760; 4th edn. 1765, 4 vols). A famous novel, often quarried for evidence for the activities of the 'Monks of Medmenham'.

JOHNSTONE, H. D., 'A Ringside Seat at the Handel Commem-oration', *Musical Times* CXXV (1984) pp. 632–36. Various eye-witness accounts.

JONES, Clyve, ed., *A Pillar of the Constitution: The House of Lords in British Politics, 1640–1784* (London, 1989).

JONES, Clyve, & JONES, David Lewis, eds., *Peers, Politics and Power: The House of Lords 1603–1911* (London, 1986). Two valuable collections of detailed studies.

JONES, Louis C., *The Clubs of the Georgian Rakes* (New York, 1942). Learned but credulous.

JUCKER, N. S., ed., *The Jenkinson Papers, 1760–66* (London, 1949). Correspondence of a minor politician.

KALSHOVEN, A., *De Diplomatieke Verhouding tusschen Engeland en de Republiek der Vereen. Nederlanden, 1747–1756* (The Hague, 1915). Deals with Sandwich's activities in Holland, 1747–48.

KELCH, R. A., *Newcastle – A Duke without Money* (London, 1974). Newcastle's private fortune and public career contrasted.

KEMP, Betty, *Sir Francis Dashwood, An*

Eighteenth-Century Independent (London, 1967). A short life, robustly sceptical about Medmenham.

KENNEDY, P. M., *The Rise and Fall of British Naval Mastery* (London, 1983). A stimulating, influential and usually convincing survey.

KENT, H. S. K., *War and Trade in Northern Seas: Anglo-Scandinavian Economic Relations in the mid-eighteenth century* (Cambridge, 1973). Important for the Baltic trade in naval stores, and as background to the first Armed Neutrality.

KEPPEL, Thomas, *The Life of Augustus Viscount Keppel* (London, 1842, 2 vols). Dull and superficial, but prints some correspondence.

KNIGHT, R. J. B., 'The Royal Dockyards in England at the time of the War of American Independence' (London Ph.D. thesis, 1972). A most important study of naval administration.

KNIGHT, R. J. B., ed., *Portsmouth Dockyard Papers 1774–1783: The American War* (Portsmouth Record Series Vol. 6, 1987). A most informative calendar, showing in detail how a dockyard worked.

KNIGHT, R. J. B., 'New England Forests and British Seapower: Albion Revisited' *AN* XLVI (1986) pp. 221–29. Disproves one of Albion's arguments.

KNIGHT, R. J. B., 'Sandwich, Middleton and Dockyard Appointments', *MM* LVII (1971) pp. 175–92. Important both for Sandwich's relations with Middleton, and as almost the only published work on Sandwich's handling of patronage.

KNIGHT, R. J. B., 'The Introduction of Copper Sheathing into the Royal Navy, 1779–1786', *MM* LIX (1973) pp. 299–309. One of the most important technical innovations in Sandwich's time.

KNIGHT, R. J. B., 'The Building and Maintenance of the British Fleet during the Anglo-French Wars (1688–1815)', in Acerra, Merino & Meyer, *Les Marines de Guerre Européennes*, pp. 35–50. Puts forward an important argument about the relationship of seapower and dockyard capacity.

LABAREE, Benjamin W., et al., eds., *The Papers of Benjamin Franklin* (New Haven, 1959ff, 27 vols to date). They bear only tangentially on Sandwich's career.

LACOUR GAYET, G., *La Marine Militaire de la France sous la Règne de Louis XVI* (Paris, 1905). An old but still useful operational history.

LANGFORD, Paul, *A Polite and Commercial People: England 1727–1783* (Oxford, 1989). An exciting *tour d'horizon*.

LANGFORD, Paul, *The First Rockingham Administration 1765–1766* (London, 1973). A valuable monograph.

LANGFORD, Paul, *Public Life and the Propertied Englishman 1689–1798* (Oxford, 1991). Important for the uses of property in and out of politics.

LANGFORD, Paul, 'Old Whigs, Old Tories, and the American Revolution', *JICH* VIII (1979–80) No.2 pp. 106–30. Important study in political ideas and language.

LANGFORD, Paul, et al., eds., *The Writings and Speeches of Edmund Burke* (Oxford, 1980ff, 9 vols to date). Important for general political history, less so for Sandwich in particular.

LAPRADE, W. T., ed., *Parliamentary Papers of John Robinson, 1774–1784* (Camden 3rd S. XXXIII, 1922). Edits further Robinson papers.

LARRABEE, Harold A., *Decision at the Chesapeake* (London, 1965). A popular and inaccurate account of the naval campaign.

LAUGHTON, Sir J. K., ed., *Letters and Papers of Charles, Lord Barham, Admiral of the Red Squadron, 1758–1813* (NRS Vols 32, 38 & 39, 1906–

10). Indispensable edition of Middleton's papers, though the editor was extremely partisan and not much interested in administration.

LAVER, James, ed., *Poems of Charles Churchill* (London, 1933, 2 vols). A satirical poet of some gifts, an enemy of Sandwich and an habitué of Medmenham.

LAVERY, Brian, *The Ship of the Line* (London, 1983–84, 2 vols). An essential history of the development of warship design.

LAVERY, Brian, *The Arming and Fitting of English Ships of War, 1600–1815* (London, 1987). A detailed study of warships' guns and equipment.

LAWSON, Philip, *George Grenville, A Political Life* (Oxford, 1984). The prime minister under whom Sandwich served as Secretary of State, 1763–65.

LEGG, L. G. W., ed., *British Diplomatic Instructions; France IV* (Camden Soc, 3rd S. XLIX, 1934). Prints Sandwich's instructions in 1746–49.

LEWIS, Michael, *England's Sea Officers* (London, 1939). Self-indulgent and now almost obsolescent social history.

LEWIS, W. S., et al., eds., *Horace Walpole's Correspondence* (New Haven, Connecticut, 1937–83, 48 vols). A massive work of entertainment, erudition and information for all historians of the eighteenth century. The editing is as reliable as Walpole's malicious gossip is unreliable.

LITTLE, David M., & KAHRL, George M., eds., *The Letters of David Garrick* (London, 1963, 3 vols, paginated as one). A good modern edition, but it omits letters to Garrick.

LLOYD, Christopher, 'Sir George Rodney: Lucky Admiral', in Bilias, *George Washington's Opponents*, pp. 327–54. Has some ideas not to be found in Spinney's life.

LLOYD, C. C., KEEVIL, J., &

COULTER, J. L. S., *Medicine and the Navy, 1200–1900* (Edinburgh, 1957–63, 4 vols; vols 3–4 by Lloyd & Coulter). A massive but somewhat uncritical collection of material.

LODGE, Sir Richard, *Studies in Eighteenth-Century Diplomacy, 1740–1748* (London, 1930). Not the best work of a great diplomatic historian, but the only study of the peace negotiations of 1746–49.

LODGE, Sir Richard, ed., *Private Correspondence of Chesterfield and Newcastle, 1744–46* (Camden 3rd S. XLIV, 1930). Bears on the start of Sandwich's career as a diplomat.

LONSDALE, Roger, *Dr Charles Burney: A Literary Biography* (Oxford, 1965). An excellent life.

LOWE, J. A., ed., *Records of the Portsmouth Division of Marines, 1764–1800* (Portsmouth Record Series Vol. 7, Portsmouth 1990). The best of the very few modern sources for the history of the Marines in this period.

McCAHILL, Michael W., *Order and Equipoise: The Peerage and the House of Lords, 1783–1806* (London, 1978). An excellent study which only just overlaps with Sandwich's life.

McCANN, Timothy J., ed., *The Correspondence of the Dukes of Richmond and Newcastle, 1724–1750* (Sussex Record Soc. Vol.73, 1984). An important source for the internal politics of the ministries in which Sandwich served from 1744.

MACKAY, Ruddock F., *Admiral Hawke* (Oxford, 1965). The standard modern life of the admiral whom Sandwich succeeded as First Lord in 1771.

MACKAY, Ruddock F., ed., *The Hawke Papers. A Selection, 1743–1771* (NRS Vol.129, 1990). A collection of the admiral's papers, disappointing for his time as First Lord.

MACKERNESS, E. D., *A Social History of English Music* (London,

1964). Helpful background to Sandwich's musical life.

MACKESY, Piers, *The War for America, 1775–1783* (London, 1964). Easily the best general history of the war; sympathetic to Germain.

MACKESY, Piers, *The Coward of Minden: The Affair of Lord George Sackville* (London, 1979). The Minden affair and the character of Lord George analysed.

McLEAN, Teresa, *The Men in White Coats: Cricket Umpires Past and Present* (London, 1987). Entertaining social history.

MADARIAGA, Isabel de, *Britain, Russia and the Armed Neutrality of 1780* (London, 1962). A brilliant exposition of the diplomatic background to the American War.

MAHAN, A. T., *The Major Operations of the Navies in the War of American Independence* (London, 1913). Still useful for the detail of operations at sea.

[MANN, A. H.] 'Mr and Mrs Joah Bates', *Musical Times* XLVI (1905) pp. 13–20.

[MANN, A. H.] 'Batesiana', *Musical Times* XLVI (1905) pp. 99–100. These two articles constitute virtually all that is in print about the musician and public servant who rose under Sandwich's protection.

MARILLIER, H. C., *A Bit of Eighteenth Century Romance* (London, 1910, privately printed). Prints extracts of Sandwich's correspondence with Lady Mary Fitzgerald.

MARSHALL, Dorothy, *Eighteenth Century England* (London, 2nd edn. 1973). A rewarding general history, beginning to show its age.

MASSIE, Alistair W., 'Great Britain and the Defence of the Low Countries, 1744–1748' (Oxford D.Phil. thesis, 1987). A valuable thesis, supplying context for Sandwich's early diplomatic activity.

MATCHAM, M. E., *A Forgotten John Russell, being Letters to a man of Business, 1724–1751* (London, 1905). A dockyard officer and distant kinsman of the Duke of Bedford whose letters give a worm's eye view of naval administration in the 1740s.

MERINO NAVARRO, J. P., *La Armada Española en el Siglo XVIII* (Madrid, 1981). An important study of policy and administration.

MIDDLETON, Richard, *The Bells of Victory: The Pitt-Newcastle Ministry and the Conduct of the Seven Years' War, 1757–1762* (Cambridge, 1985). Successfully overturns the old idea of how this war was conducted.

MIDDLETON, Richard, 'Pitt, Anson and the Admiralty, 1756–61', *History* NS LV p. 189. Weighs their respective contributions to the war.

MIDDLETON, Richard, 'The Visitation of the Royal Dockyards, 1749', *MM* LXXVII (1991) pp. 21–30. A useful introduction.

MILLER, Daniel A., *Sir Joseph Yorke and Anglo-Dutch Relations, 1774–1780* (The Hague, 1970). Important for the Dutch entry into the American War.

MIMLER, Manfred, *Der Einfluss kolonialer Interessen in Nordamerika auf die Strategie und Diplomatie Grossbritanniens während des 18. Jahrhunderts* (Hildesheim, 1983). Discusses the rise of colonial or 'blue-water' strategic and economic ideas.

MITCHELL, L. G., *Charles James Fox and the Disintegration of the Whig Party, 1782–1794* (London, 1971). At the end of his career Sandwich was an ally of Fox in opposition. His full biography *Charles James Fox* (Oxford, 1992) appeared too late to be used here.

MORGAN, G. W., 'The Impact of War on the Administration of the Army, Navy and Ordnance in Britain, 1739–1754' (Leicester Ph.D. thesis, 1977). A useful thesis.

MORRIS, Richard B., *The Peacemakers: The Great Powers and American Independence* (New York,

1965). Stimulating but uneven survey of the diplomatic scene.

MORRISON, Clifford, 'The Naval Administration of the Fourth Earl of Sandwich' (Ohio State Ph.D. thesis, 1950). As good as a thesis could be without the use of any manuscripts. The British Library's copy is paginated in random order.

MORRISS, Roger, *The Royal Dockyards during the Revolutionary and Napoleonic Wars* (Leicester, 1983). An important study of the process of reform which Sandwich and Middleton had begun.

MÜHLMANN, Rolf, *Die Reorganisation der Spanischen Kriegsmarine im XVIII Jahrhundert* (Cologne & Vienna, 1975). Useful, but Merino (q.v.) is better.

MUNDY, G. B., *The Life and Correspondence of the late Admiral Lord Rodney* (London, 1830, 2 vols). Useful for its correspondence, which however was freely altered by Mundy to save his father-in-law's character.

MURPHY, Orville T., *Charles Gravier, Comte de Vergennes: French Diplomacy in the Age of Revolution, 1719–1787* (Albany, 1982). A good study of Vergennes's policy.

NAMIER, L. B., *The Structure of Politics at the Accession of George III* (London, 2nd edn. 1957). Still a fundamental study of the politics of the era.

NAMIER, Sir Lewis, *England in the Age of the American Revolution* (London, 2nd edn. 1961). Less persuasive than *The Structure of Politics*, but full of valuable material.

NAMIER, Sir Lewis, 'Monarchy and the Party System', in *Personalities and Powers* (London, 1955) pp. 13–38. A stimulating essay.

NAMIER, Sir Lewis, 'King George III: A Study of Personality', in *Personalities and Powers* pp. 39–58. Not the last word, but well worth reading.

NAMIER, Sir Lewis, & BROOKE,

John, *The History of Parliament: The House of Commons 1754–90* (London, 1964, 3 vols). Biographies of members and their constituencies.

NATAN, Alex, ed., *Silver Renaissance: Essays in Eighteenth-Century English History* (London, 1961). Interesting short essays.

NEESER, R. W., ed., *The Despatches of Molyneux Shuldham, Jan–July 1776* (Naval History Soc. Vol. 3, New York, 1913). Official reports from the North American station.

NEESER, R. W., ed., *Letters and Papers relating to the Cruises of Gustavus Conyngham . . . 1777–1779* (New York, 1915). A rebel privateer operating out of French ports.

[NEW GROVE], *The New Grove Dictionary of Music and Musicians* ed. Stanley Sadie (London, 1980, 20 vols). Important for Sandwich's musical career.

NICHOLS, John, *Literary Anecdotes of the Eighteenth Century* (London, 2nd edn. 1812, 7 vols). Mainly derivative, but contains some original information.

NIEDHART, Gottfried, *Handel und Krieg in der britischen Weltpolitik 1738–1763* (Munich, 1979). A study of grand strategic ideas.

NOBBE, George, *The North Briton: A Study in Political Propaganda* (New York, 1939). Wilkes's journalistic enterprise, studied by a friend.

Nocturnal Revels: Or, the History of King's Place, and other Modern Nunneries . . . by a Monk of the Order of St.Francis (London, 2nd edn. 1779, 2 vols). A guide to London brothels, with an account of Medmenham.

NORRIS, John, *Shelburne and Reform* (London, 1963). A study rather than a full life.

O'BRIAN, Patrick, *Joseph Banks: A Life* (London, 1987). Excellent on the interplay of character, as one would expect from a distinguished novelist.

O'GORMAN, Frank, *Voters, Patrons and Parties. The Unreformed Electoral System of Hanoverian England 1734–*

1832 (Oxford, 1989). The latest survey of eighteenth-century electoral politics.

O'GORMAN, Frank, The Rise of Party in England: The Rockingham Whigs 1760–82 (London, 1975). An important study.

OLSON, Alison, The Radical Duke: Career and Correspondence of Charles Lennox third Duke of Richmond (London, 1961). One of the more extreme members of the Rockingham connection.

OSBORN, Emily F. D., ed., Political and Social Letters of a Lady of the Eighteenth Century (London, 1890). Various glimpses of Sandwich.

OSINGA, Jacob, Frankrijk, Vergennes en de Amerikanse Onafhankelijkheid, 1776–1783 (Amsterdam, [1982]). Advances iconoclastic views of French policy towards America, which deserve to stimulate controversy, but seem instead to have been ignored.

OWEN, John B., The Rise of the Pelhams (London, 1957). Important for Sandwich's early political career.

OWEN, J. B., 'George II Reconsidered', in Statesmen, Scholars and Merchants, eds. A. Whiteman, J. S. Bromley & P. G. M. Dickson (Oxford, 1973). A study of the king's politics, showing that he was his own master.

OWEN, J. B., 'The Survival of Country Attitudes in the Eighteenth-Century House of Commons', in J. S. Bromley & E. H. Kossmann, eds., Britain and the Netherlands, IV (The Hague, 1971). Examines the independent members.

OWEN, J.H., 'Operations of the Western Squadron, 1781–82' Naval Review XV (1927) pp. 33–53. Detailed account of operations and strategy.

OWEN, J. H., 'Howe and d'Estaing in North America' Naval Review XV (1927) pp. 257–83. A good detailed study.

OZANAM, Didier, & ANTOINE, Michel, eds., Correspondance Secrète du Comte de Broglie avec Louis XV (1756–1774) (Paris, Soc. de l'Histoire de France, 1956–61, 2 vols). More of Louis XV's secret diplomacy.

PARES, Richard, 'American versus Continental Warfare, 1739–1763', EHR LI (1936) pp. 429–65. A seminal article on eighteenth-century strategic priorities.

PARES, Richard, King George III and the Politicians (Oxford, 1953). An entertaining summary of the then state of knowledge.

PARES, Richard, Colonial Blockade and Neutral Rights, 1739–1763 (Oxford, 1938).

PARES, Richard, War and Trade in the West Indies, 1739–1763 (Oxford, 1936). Valuable studies of war in the colonial world.

PATTERSON, A. Temple, The Other Armada: The Franco-Spanish Attempt to Invade Britain in 1779 (Manchester, 1960). An excellent account of the 1779 campaign and its background.

PERRIN, W. G., ed., 'The Channel Fleet in 1779: Letters of Benjamin Thompson to Lord George Germain', in The Naval Miscellany Vol.III (NRS Vol. 63, 1928). Writes chiefly about himself, also about his surroundings.

PHILLIPS, I. Lloyd, 'The Evangelical Administrator: Sir Charles Middleton at the Navy Board 1778–1790' (Oxford D.Phil. thesis, 1974). A fine thesis.

PHIPPS, Constantine John, Baron Mulgrave, A Voyage towards the North Pole undertaken by His Majesty's Command, 1773 (London, 1774). Official report of the expedition organized by Sandwich.

PIGGOTT, Sir F. T., & OMOND, G. W. T., Documentary History of the Armed Neutralities, 1780 and 1800 . . . (London, 1919). Diplomatic documents on British relations with the Baltic powers.

POCOCK, J. G. A., '1776: The Revolution against Parliament', in

Three British Revolutions: 1641, 1688, 1776 ed. J. G. A. Pocock (Princeton, 1980) pp. 265–88. A study in political ideas.

POOL, Bernard, *Navy Board Contracts 1660–1832: Contract Administration under the Navy Board* (London, 1966). Prints much useful information.

PORTA, A., *Joan en Gerrit Corver: de politieke macht van Amsterdam (1702–1748)* (Assen, 1975). Argues that a British conspiracy, led by Sandwich, overthrew the Dutch government in 1747.

POTTLE, Frederick A., ed., *Boswell's London Journal, 1762–1763* (London, pb edn. 1982). Includes a meeting with Sandwich.

PRITCHARD, James, *Louis XV's Navy, 1748–1762: A Study of Organization and Administration* (Kingston, Ont., 1987). Useful for assessing French naval strength even in Louis XVI's reign.

PROBY, Granville, 'Burgesses of Huntingdon', *Transactions of the Cambridgeshire and Huntingdonshire Archaeological Society* V (Ely, 1937) pp. 201–44. Useful evidence of Sandwich's management of borough politics.

RANFT, B. McL., ed., *The Vernon Papers* (NRS Vol. 99, 1978). Important both for the admiral's strategic thinking and his wartime activities.

[RAY], *The Case and Memoirs of Miss Martha Reay* . . . (London [1779]. A 'brief life' rushed out at the time of her death.

REA, Robert R., *The English Press in Politics, 1760–1774* (Lincoln, Nebraska, 1963). Useful especially for the political sponsorship of newspapers.

REES, Abraham, ed., *The Cyclopaedia, or Universal Dictionary of Arts, Sciences and Literature* (London, 1819 edn., 45 vols). Many of the musical articles were contributed by Burney.

RENAUT, F. P., *l'espionage naval au xviiie siècle* (Paris, 4 vols: inc. *Le Secret Service de l'Amirauté Britannique au temps de la Guerre d'Amerique, 1776–1783* (1936), and *Le Traitre de l'Amirauté ou le mot de l'affaire Montagu Fox, 1780–1781* (1937)). A series of short studies based only on French archives.

RENAUT, F. P., *Les Provinces Unies et la guerre d'Amerique* (Paris, 1924–32, 5 vols, individually titled). Short studies in diplomatic history. Renaut's works are a triumph of the French publisher's art, not only the titles of the books but even the author's name varying constantly from page to page and book to book.

RIBEIRO, Alvaro, ed., *The Letters of Dr Charles Burney*, Vol. I (Oxford, 1991). Important for Sandwich's musical life.

RICHMOND, H. W., *The Navy in the War of 1739–48* (Cambridge, 1920, 3 vols). A powerful study of policy and strategy as well as operations, all the more impressive considering that most of it was written while the author was commanding a battleship.

RICHMOND, Sir H. W., *The Navy in India, 1763–1783* (London, 1931). Primarily an operational study.

RIDDICK, S., 'Lord Barham and Naval Administration, 1778–1806' (Liverpool M.A. thesis, 1939). Superficial and partisan.

RITCHESON, Charles R., *British Politics and the American Revolution* (Norman, Oklahoma, 1954). A thoughtful study, in advance of its time.

ROBERTS, Michael, *Splendid Isolation, 1763–1780* (Reading, 1970). A brief but telling survey of British diplomacy.

ROBERTS, Michael, *British Diplomacy and Swedish Politics, 1758–1773* (London, 1980). Deals with one of the main preoccupations of Sandwich's period as Secretary of State, 1763–65.

ROBERTS, Michael, 'Macartney in Russia', *EHR* Supplement No.7

(1974). The Russian treaty was another of Sandwich's diplomatic responsibilities.

ROBSON, Eric, *The American Revolution in its Political and Military Aspects, 1763–1783* (London, 1955). Suggestive analysis.

RODGER, N. A. M., 'The Continental Commitment in the Eighteenth Century', in *War, Strategy and International Politics: Essays in Honour of Sir Michael Howard*, ed. Lawrence Freedman, Paul Hayes & Robert O'Neill (Oxford, 1992) pp. 39–55. Examines the strategic issue in rhetoric and reality.

RODGER, N. A. M., *The Wooden World: An Anatomy of the Georgian Navy* (London, 1986). A social study of the mid-eighteenth-century Navy.

RODGER, N. A. M., 'Mobilizing Seapower in the Eighteenth Century', in *Etat, Société et Marine: Mélanges offert à Jean Meyer* ed. Jean-Pierre Poussou, André Zysberg & Martine Acerra (Paris, 1993). Looks at a key element of success in war.

[RODNEY] *Letter-Books and Order-Book of George, Lord Rodney . . . 1780–82* [ed. Dorothy C. Barck] (New York HS, 1932, 2 vols). Prints only official correspondence, but still informative on the conduct of operations.

ROSE, Sir George, ed., *A Selection of the Papers of the Earl of Marchmont* (London, 1831, 3 vols). Helpful on politics in the 1740s.

ROWLEY, Peter, 'Owsley Rowley and the Sandwich Family', *Records of Huntingdonshire* Vol. 2 No.7 (1987) pp. 29–32; No.8 (1988) pp. 22–32; No.9 (1990) pp. 35–39. Based on the Rowley Papers, dealing with Sandwich's finances in his last years.

RUDÉ, George, *Wilkes and Liberty: A Social Study of 1763 to 1774* (Oxford, 1962). A classic study of the Wilkite movement.

RUSSELL, Lord John, ed., *Correspondence of John, Fourth Duke of Bedford* (London, 1842–46, 3 vols). Extracts from the Bedford Papers at Woburn, valuable both for politics and naval administration.

RUSSELL, Lord John, ed., *Memorials and Correspondence of Charles James Fox* (London, 1853–57, 4 vols). Sandwich's colleague in opposition in his last years.

RYAN, A. N., 'The Royal Navy and the Blockade of Brest, 1689–1805: Theory and Practice', in Acerra, Merino & Meyer, *Les Marines de Guerre Européennes*, pp. 175–94. A valuable conspectus.

SAINSBURY, John, *Disaffected Patriots: London Supporters of Revolutionary America 1769–1782* (Kingston, Ontario & Gloucester, 1987). Displays the gulf separating even radical politics in London from the colonial rebels.

SAINTY, J. C., *Admiralty Officials 1660–1870* ('Office-Holders in Modern Britain IV', London, 1975). An essential reference book.

[SANDWICH], *A Voyage performed by the Late Earl of Sandwich round the Mediterranean in the years 1738 and 1739, written by himself* ed. John Cooke (London, 1799). Cooke also supplies a 40-page 'Memoir of the Noble Author's Life'.

[SANDWICH], *The Speech of the Earl of Sandwich . . . 14 May 1779* (London, 1779). Sandwich's defence of his administration of Greenwich Hospital.

SANDWICH, 8th Earl of, *Hinchingbrooke* (London, 1910). Notes on the history of the house.

Sbornik Imperatorskago Russkago Istoricheskago Obshchestva (St Petersburg, 1867–1916). The 'journal' (or rather, record series) of the Imperial Russian Historical Society: Vol. 12 prints (in English and Russian) parts of Sandwich's diplomatic correspondence with Lord Buckingham as British ambassador in St Petersburg.

SCHWEIZER, K. W., ed., *Lord Bute:*

Essays in Re-Interpretation (Leicester, 1988). Essays in rehabilitation.

SCOTT, H. M., *British Foreign Policy in the Age of the American Revolution* (Oxford, 1990). An excellent new survey, linking foreign with domestic policy and paying particular attention to naval affairs.

SCOTT, H. M., 'The Importance of Bourbon Naval Reconstruction to the Strategy of Choiseul after the Seven Years' War', *IHR* I (1979) pp. 20–35. An important study of French policy before the American War.

SEDGWICK, Romney, *The History of Parliament: The House of Commons 1715–54* (London, 1970, 2 vols). Biographies of members and their constituencies.

SEDGWICK, Romney, ed., *Letters of George III to Lord Bute, 1756–1766* (London, 1939). Essential for the politics of the early years of the reign.

SIMMONS, R. C., & THOMAS, P. D. G., eds., *Proceedings and Debates of the British Parliaments Respecting North America 1754–1783* (New York, 1982ff, 6 vols to date). Collected from many printed and manuscript sources.

SMITH, W. J., ed., *The Grenville Papers: being the Correspondence of Richard Grenville Earl Temple, K.G., and the Right Hon: George Grenville, their Friends and Contemporaries* (London, 1852–53, 4 vols). There is much correspondence with and about Sandwich from the period of his connection with Grenville.

SMYTH, G., ed., *Memoirs and Correspondence (Official and Familiar) of Sir Robert Murray Keith* (London, 1849, 2 vols). Little of relevance, though his father was Sandwich's private secretary.

SOSIN, Jack M., 'Louisbourg and the Peace of Aix-la-Chapelle, 1748', *William and Mary Quarterly* 3rd S. XIV (1957) pp. 516–35. Examines one of the issues of the 1748 negotiations.

SPECK, W. A., *Stability and Strife: England 1714–1760* (London, 1977). A useful general history.

SPENCER, Frank, ed., *The Fourth Earl of Sandwich: Diplomatic Correspondence 1763–1765* (Manchester, 1961). Edits both official and private correspondence with informative notes.

SPENCER, Frank, 'Lord Sandwich, Russian Masts and American Independence' *MM* XLIV (1958) pp. 116–27. Unforseen consequences of a clause in the 1766 Anglo-Russian commercial treaty.

SPINNEY, David, *Rodney* (London, 1969). The standard modern life of the admiral; reliable on fact, disputable on interpretation.

STEUART, A. Francis, ed., *The Last Journals of Horace Walpole, during the Reign of George III from 1771–1783* (London, 1910, 2 vols). Further instalments of Walpole's wit and malicious gossip; these last journals are less polished and artificial than the earlier ones.

STEVENS, B. F., *Facsimiles of manuscripts in European Archives relating to America, 1773–1783* (London 1889–98, 25 vols). A valuable collection, but unwieldy and now very scarce.

STEVENSON, John, ed., *London in the Age of Reform* (Oxford, 1977). Essays on metropolitan history.

STOUT, N. R., *The Royal Navy in America, 1760–1775* (Annapolis, 1973). Informative on the 'pre-history' of the colonial rebellion.

STROUD, Dorothy, *Capability Brown* (London, 3rd edn. 1975). This edition incorporates new material on Brown's dealings with Sandwich.

SULIVAN, J. A., 'Graves and Hood', *MM* LXIX (1983) pp. 175–94. Not as convincing as Breen.

SUTHERLAND, Lucy S., *The East India Company in Eighteenth-Century Politics* (Oxford, 1952). The seat of Sandwich's most formidable political power.

SYRETT, David, *The Royal Navy in*

American Waters 1775–1783
(Aldershot, 1989). A fine history.

SYRETT, David, *Shipping and the American War 1775–83: A Study of British Transport Organization* (London, 1970). Logistics was fundamental in this transatlantic war; it was also a point of dispute between Sandwich and Germain.

SYRETT, David, 'Home Waters or America? The Dilemma of British Naval Strategy in 1778', *MM* LXXVII (1991) pp. 365–77. The latest and best discussion of the subject.

SYRETT, David, *Neutral Rights and the War in the Narrow Seas, 1778–82* (Fort Leavenworth, Kansas [1985]). Important for the British declaration of war on the Netherlands in 1780.

TAYLOR, W. S., & PRINGLE, J. H., eds., *The Correspondence of William Pitt, Earl of Chatham* (London, 1838–40, 4 vols). Not very informative on Sandwich.

THOMAS, Peter D. G., *British Politics and the Stamp Act Crisis: The first phase of the American Revolution, 1763–1767* (Oxford, 1975)

THOMAS, Peter D. G., *The Townshend Duties Crisis. The Second Phase of the American Revolution 1767–1773* (Oxford, 1987). Two detailed studies of the early phases of the rebellion.

THOMAS, Peter D. G., *Lord North* (London, 1976). An excellent short life.

THOMAS, Peter D. G., 'George III and the American Revolution', *History* N.S. LXX (1985) pp. 16–31. A good summary of current views.

THOMAS, Peter D. G., *The House of Commons in the Eighteenth Century* (Oxford, 1971). Good general survey.

THOMSON, Mark A., *The Secretaries of State 1681–1782* (Oxford, 1932). The standard general study.

TILLEY, John, *The British Navy and the American Revolution* (Columbia, S.C., 1987). It can be recommended for its excellent maps.

TOYNBEE, Paget, ed., 'Horace Walpole's Journals of Visits to Country Seats &c' *Walpole Society* XVI (1927–28) pp. 9–80. Includes his descriptions of Hinchingbrooke and Medmenham.

TRACY, Nicholas, *Navies, Deterrence and American Independence: Britain and Seapower in the 1760s and 1770s* (Vancouver, 1988). Important for foreign policy and deterrence between the wars.

TRACY, Nicholas, 'The Gunboat Diplomacy of the Government of George Grenville, 1764–1765' *HJ* XVII (1974) pp. 711–31. Naval deterrence shown to be effective.

TROIDE, Lars E., *The Early Journals and Letters of Fanny Burney* (Oxford 1988–90, 2 vols to date). The Burneys stood at the intersection of Sandwich's musical, naval and scientific interests.

TUNSTALL, Brian, *Naval Warfare in the Age of Sail: The Evolution of Fighting Tactics 1650–1815* ed. Nicholas Tracy (London, 1990). A minute analysis of the development of signalling and fleet tactics.

TURBERVILLE, A. S., *The House of Lords in the XVIIIth Century* (Oxford, 1927). Still useful.

USHER, Roland G., 'The Civil Administration of the British Navy during the American Revolution' (Michigan Ph.D., 1943). As good as a thesis on this subject could well be without access to British documents.

USHER, R. G., 'Royal Navy Impressment during the American Revolution', *Mississippi Valley Historical Review* XXXVII (1951) pp. 673–88. Thorough and perceptive little study, based on the Shelburne Papers.

VALENTINE, Alan, *Lord George Germain* (Oxford, 1962). Slapdash and superficial; it is unusual among biographies in being openly hostile to its subject.

VAN ALSTYNE, Richard W., 'Parliamentary Supremacy versus Independence: Notes and Documents', *Huntington Library Quarterly* XXVI (1963) pp. 201–33. Identifies the real issues of the rebellion.

VAUCHER, P., ed, *Instructions données aux ambassadeurs et ministres de la France, XXXV-2, Angleterre III* (Paris, 1965). Includes character sketches of British ministers.

VERGÉ-FRANCESCHI, Michel, *Marine et Education sous l'Ancien Régime* (Paris, 1991). Studies the recruitment, professional education and training of French officers.

Victoria History of the County of Huntingdon, ed. William Page, Granville Proby & S. I. Ladds (London, 1926–36, 3 vols). Learned and detailed local history.

VILLIERS, Patrick, *Marine Royale, Corsaires et Trafic dans l'Atlantique de Louis XIV à Louis XVI* (Dunkirk, [1991]). An ambitious synoptic history which does not always carry conviction.

WALLBANK, M. V., 'Eighteenth Century Public Schools and the Education of the Governing Elite', *History of Education* VIII (1979) pp. 1–19. Stimulating discussion of the importance of the public schools.

WALPOLE, Horace, *Memoirs of King George II*, ed. John Brooke (New Haven & London, 1985, 3 vols). The first of Walpole's well-informed but partial contemporary histories.

WALPOLE, Horace, *Memoirs of the Reign of King George III* ed. G. F. Russell Barker (London, 1894, 4 vols). Walpole's history continued, in an older edition.

WATSON, Eric R., 'John Wilkes and the "Essay on Woman"', *Notes and Queries* 11th S. IX (1914) pp. 121–23, 143–45, 162–64, 183–85, 203–5, 222–23, & 241–42. Sorts out various controverted points.

WEBB, Paul, 'The Navy and British Diplomacy, 1783–1793' (Cambridge M.Litt. thesis, 1971). An important study, dealing largely with naval administration as well as diplomacy.

WEBB, Paul L. C., 'Sea Power in the Ochakov Affair of 1791', *IHR* II (1980) pp. 13–33. The last of the eighteenth-century 'armaments' or peacetime mobilizations.

WEBB, P. L. C., 'The Rebuilding and Repair of the Fleet, 1783–93', *BIHR* L (1977) pp. 194–209. Deals with the long-term results of Sandwich's and Middleton's work.

WEBER, William, *The Rise of the Musical Classics in Eighteenth-Century England* (Oxford, 1992). Deals in detail with the Concerts of Ancient Music.

WEBER, William, 'The 1784 Handel Commemoration as Political Ritual', *JBS* XXVIII (1989) pp. 43–69. Brings out its social as well as musical significance.

WELLENREUTHER, Hermann, *Repräsentation und Grossgrundbesitz in England 1730–1770* (Stuttgart, 1979). A study of Bedford's territorial influence in Bedfordshire and Devon; relevant to Sandwich's practice as an electoral manager.

WERKMEISTER, Lucyle, *The London Daily Press 1772–1792* (Lincoln, Nebraska, 1963). The political influence and management of the press.

WICKWIRE, Mary B., 'Lord Sandwich and the King's Ships, A Study of British Naval Administration, 1771–1782' (Yale Ph.D. thesis, 1961). In spite of two years' effort, I was unable to get sight of a copy of this work.

WICKWIRE, Mary B., 'Naval Warfare and the American Victory', in Ferling, *The World turned Upside Down* pp. 185–98. A useful short survey, sympathetic to Sandwich.

[WILKES], *The Life and Political Writings of John Wilkes, Esq.* (Birmingham, 1769). Consists chiefly of extracts from the *North Briton*.

WILKES, J. W., *A Whig in Power; The Political Career of Henry Pelham* (Northwestern UP, 1964). Useful for his handling of finance.

WILLCOX, William B., *Portrait of a General: Sir Henry Clinton in the War of Independence* (New York, 1964). An excellent study.

WILLCOX, William B., 'Too many cooks: British planning before Saratoga' *JBS* II (1962) p. 56. Analyses the confusion between Germain, Howe and Burgoyne.

WILLCOX, William B., 'Arbuthnot, Gambier, and Graves: "Old Women" of the Navy', in Bilias, *George Washington's Opponents*, pp. 260–90. More insult than analysis.

WILLCOX, William B., 'The British Road to Yorktown: A Study in Divided Command', *AHR* LII (1946) pp. 1–35. Displays clear strategic grasp assisted by hindsight.

WILLCOX, William B., 'British Strategy in America, 1778', *JMH* XIX (1947) pp. 97–121. Another look at the 1778 strategic problem; now largely superseded by Syrett.

WILLCOX, William B., 'Rhode Island in British Strategy, 1780–1781', *JMH* XVII (1945) pp. 304–31. A further exercise in strategic analysis.

WILLIAMS, M. J., 'The Naval Administration of the Fourth Earl of Sandwich' (Oxford D.Phil. 1962). Thorough and valuable, if in parts unsophisticated.

WILLIAMSON, Audrey, *Wilkes, 'A Friend to Liberty'* (London, 1974). A popular history.

WINSTANLEY, D. A., *The University of Cambridge in the Eighteenth Century* (Cambridge, 1922). Includes a detailed account of the High Steward contest.

WINSTANLEY, D. A., *Unreformed Cambridge: A Study of certain Aspects of the University in the Eighteenth Century* (Cambridge, 1935). Deals with university politics.

WRAXALL, Sir N. W., *The Historical and Posthumous Memoirs of Sir Nathaniel William Wraxall*, ed. Henry B. Wheatley (London, 1884, 5 vols). Recollections of a back-bench MP.

WRIGHT, J., ed., *Sir Henry Cavendish's Debates..* (London, 1841–42, 2 vols). Prints Bedford's journal, 1766–71.

YERXA, Donald A., 'Vice-Admiral Samuel Graves and the North American Squadron, 1774–1776' *MM* LXII (1976) pp. 371–85. Brings out his problems very clearly.

YORKE, Philip C., *The Life and Correspondence of Philip Yorke, Earl of Hardwicke, Lord High Chancellor of Great Britain* (Cambridge, 1913, 3 vols). Prints much essential correspondence.

Index